CIMA

STRATEGIC

PAPER F3

FINANCIAL STRATEGY

PRACTICE & REVISION KIT

This Kit is for CIMA's exams in 2013

In this Kit we:

- Discuss the **best strategies** for revising and taking your F3 exam
- Show you how to be well prepared for the **2013 exams**
- Give you **lots of great guidance** on tackling questions
- Demonstrate how you can **build your own exams**
- Provide you with **three** mock exams

FOR EXAMS IN 2013

BPP LEARNING MEDIA

First edition 2010

Fourth edition January 2013

ISBN 9781 4453 6619 7
(Previous ISBN 9781 4453 8092 6)
e-ISBN 9781 4453 9282 0

British Library Cataloguing-in-Publication Data
A catalogue record for this book is available from the British
Library

Published by

BPP Learning Media Ltd
BPP House, Aldine Place
142-144 Uxbridge Road
London W12 8AA

www.bpp.com/learningmedia

Printed in the United Kingdom by Ricoh

Ricoh House
Ullswater Crescent, Coulsdon
CR5 2HR

Your learning materials, published by BPP Learning
Media Ltd, are printed on paper obtained from traceable
sustainable sources.

BPP
LEARNING MEDIA

Contents

Question index

The headings in this checklist/index indicate the main topics of questions, but questions often cover several different topics.

Questions set under the old syllabus's *Management Accounting – Financial Strategy* (FS) exam are included because their style and content are similar to those that appear in the Paper F3 exam.

Part C: Investment decisions and project control

Mock exam 1

Questions 101 – 104

Mock exam 2 (September 2012 resit examination)

Questions 105 – 108

Mock exam 3 (November 2012 examination)

Questions 109 – 112

Planning your question practice

Our guidance from page xvi shows you how to organise your question practice, either by attempting questions from each syllabus area or by **building your own exams** – tackling questions as a series of practice exams.

Topic index

Listed below are the key Paper F3 syllabus topics and the numbers of the questions in this Kit covering those topics.

If you need to concentrate your practice and revision on certain topics or if you want to attempt all available questions that refer to a particular subject you will find this index useful.

Using your BPP Learning Media Practice and Revision Kit

Tackling revision and the exam

You can significantly improve your chances of passing by tackling revision and the exam in the right ways. Our advice is based on feedback from CIMA. We focus on Paper F3; we discuss revising the syllabus, what to do (and what not to do) in the exam, how to approach different types of question and ways of obtaining easy marks.

Selecting questions

We provide signposts to help you plan your revision.

- A full **question index**

- A **topic index**, listing all the questions that cover key topics, so that you can locate the questions that provide practice on these topics, and see the different ways in which they might be examined

- **BPP's question plan**, highlighting the most important questions

- **Build your own exams**, showing you how you can practise questions in a series of exams

Making the most of question practice

We realise that you need more than questions and model answers to get the most from your question practice.

- Our **Top tips** provide essential advice on tackling questions and presenting answers

- We show you how you can pick up **Easy marks** on questions, as picking up all readily available marks can make the difference between passing and failing

- We include **marking guides** to show you what the examiner rewards

- We summarise **Examiner's comments** to show you how students coped with the questions

- We refer to the **BPP 2012 Study Text** for detailed coverage of the topics covered in each question

Attempting mock exams

There are three mock exams that provide practice at coping with the pressures of the exam day. We strongly recommend that you attempt them under exam conditions as they reflect the question styles and syllabus coverage of the exam. To help you get the most out of doing these exams, we provide guidance on how you should have approached the whole exam.

Our other products

BPP Learning Media also offers these products for practising and revising the F3 exam:

Passcards	Summarising what you should know in visual, easy to remember, form
Success CDs	Covering the vital elements of the F3 syllabus in less than 90 minutes and also containing exam hints to help you fine tune your strategy
i-Pass	Providing computer-based testing in a variety of formats, ideal for self-assessment
Interactive Passcards	Allowing you to learn actively with a clear visual format summarising what you must know
Case Study Kit	The compulsory question in each Strategic level exam is based on a common pre-seen case study, issued in April and October each year. The BPP Case Study Kit provides analysis of this pre-seen Case Study and special practice questions based on the themes in the Case Study.

You can purchase these products by visiting www.bpp.com/learningmedia

Revising F3

The F3 exam

This will be a time-pressured exam that combines calculations with discussion. It is very important that you do not concentrate completely on the calculations at the expense of fully understanding the strategic issues involved.

Topics to revise

You need to be comfortable with **all areas of the syllabus** as questions, particularly compulsory Question 1, will often span a number of syllabus areas. Question spotting will absolutely **not work** on this paper. It is better to go into the exam knowing a reasonable amount about most of the syllabus rather than concentrating on a few topics.

Formulation of financial strategy

- How financial objectives of different types of organisation are identified and attained

- The links between investment, financing and dividend decisions

- The constraints on formulating financial strategy

- The techniques of ratio analysis and forecasting. The emphasis in this exam will always be on discussion of techniques you employ and using your calculations to support your analysis

- Recommending alternative financial strategies – probably the most important learning outcome in this paper

Financial management

- The determination of long-term capital structure in the form of debt finance, equity finance and leasing
- How securities markets work
- The role of the treasury function
- Essential techniques such as calculating the cost of capital and using the capital asset pricing model

Investment decisions and project control

- Issues connected with investment appraisal
- Complex calculations and techniques need to be practised

Business valuations and acquisitions

- Methods of calculating the valuations of organisations of different types. The most important use of these techniques is in a merger or acquisition situation and this area will be frequently examined

Question practice

Question practice under timed conditions is essential, so that you can get used to the pressures of answering exam questions in **limited time** and practise not only the key techniques but allocating your time between different requirements in each question. It's particularly important to do questions from both sections of the paper in full to see how the numerical and written elements balance in longer questions.

Passing the F3 exam

Avoiding weaknesses

You will enhance your chances significantly if you ensure you avoid these mistakes:

- Little or no time spent studying the preseen ahead of the exam
- Failure to read the question
- Lack of application of knowledge to scenario
- Failure to pick up scenario details eg size of company, listed or unlisted, attitude to risk, dividend policy
- Confusion of scenario details from different questions
- Time management – spending excessive time on strong areas or too long on areas you struggle with
- Poor English, structure and presentation
- Poor knowledge of basic concepts and calculations (earnings per share, cost of debt)
- An incorrect belief that retained earnings are cash
- Poor knowledge of tax and capital allowance calculations

Using the reading time

We recommend that you spend the first part of the reading time choosing the Section B questions you will do, on the basis of your knowledge of syllabus areas tested and whether you can fulfil **all** the question requirements. We suggest that you should note on the paper any ideas that come to you about these questions.

However don't spend the reading time going through and analysing the Section B question requirements in detail; leave that until the three hours writing time. Instead you should be looking to spend as much of the reading time as possible looking at the Section A scenario, and in particular identifying the significance of the additional information you have been given in the unseen.

Whilst you're reading the paper, remember to keep thinking about strategic issues for every scenario that you read.

Choosing which questions to answer first

Spending most of your reading time on the Section A scenario will mean that you can get underway with planning and writing your answer to the Section A question as soon as the three hours start. It will give you more actual writing time during the one and a half hours you should allocate to it and it's writing time that you'll need.

During the second half of the exam, you can put Section A aside and concentrate on the two Section B questions you've chosen.

However our recommendations are not inflexible. If you really think the Section A question looks a lot harder than the Section B questions you've chosen, then do those first, but **DON'T run over time on them.** You must leave yourself an hour and a half to tackle the Section A question. When you come back to it, having had initial thoughts during the reading time, you should be able to generate more ideas and find the question is not as bad as it looks.

Numerical questions

You are likely to see calculation questions covering:

- Forecasts
- Performance evaluation
- Methods of valuation
- Cost of capital
- CAPM
- Net present value, probably with an international dimension
- Purchasing power parity

Even if you do make a mistake on the numbers, you will gain credit for the correct approach on these questions. A brief narrative explaining your approach to tricky calculations will help the marker.

You can expect to come across some very difficult things in the questions. You must learn to move on and do as much of the questions as possible.

Present your numbers neatly in a table format with key numbers underlined and clear workings.

Discussion questions

As well as the limitations of your calculations, you should expect to discuss their results in the context of the organisation's wider situation and strategy. As well as discussing financing, be prepared also to bring relevant knowledge from other strategic level papers such as the risks affecting performance or how well proposals support the organisation's optimum enterprise strategy. Another important area is implementation of strategy (for example what should happen after an acquisition, how an investment project should be controlled).

Remember that strategies you recommend must be suitable and feasible for the organisation, and acceptable to shareholders, managers and perhaps other stakeholders as well.

One important aspect of time allocation is not to spend excessive time on the calculations at the expense of the discussion parts. You need to be strict with yourself as you won't at this level see a question that purely consists of calculations.

Remember that the marking schemes for discussion questions will be fairly general, and you will gain credit for all relevant points. Good discussion focused on the question scenario, with evaluation of pros and cons supported by examples, will score well.

Gaining the easy marks

Unsurprisingly perhaps for a strategic level paper, it is not possible to say where there will definitely be easy marks. However when you're using techniques such as company valuation methods, you will generally be expected to comment on your calculations, so knowledge of the limitations of each technique will earn you marks.

There may be some discussion parts, such as the benefits and limitations of post-completion audits, which are straightforward provided you revise those areas.

If you get a large investment appraisal with lots of different items, there will be easy marks for slotting the simpler figures into your proforma straightaway, before you concentrate on the figures that need a lot of adjustment such as cost of capital.

In the end the easiest marks may be gained (or avoided being lost) through following certain basic techniques:

- Setting out calculations and proformas clearly

- Clearly labelling the points you make in discussions so that the marker can identify them all rather than getting lost in the detail

- Providing answers in the form requested, particularly using report format if asked for and giving recommendations if required

The exam paper

Format of the paper

		Number of marks
Section A:	1 compulsory question, totalling 50 marks, with all subsections relating to a pre-seen case study and further new unseen case material	50
Section B:	2 out of 3 questions, 25 marks each. These do not relate to the pre-seen case study.	50
		100

Time allowed: 3 hours, plus 20 minutes reading time

CIMA guidance

CIMA has stated that credit will be given for focusing on the right principles and making practical evaluations and recommendations in a variety of different business scenarios, including manufacturing, retailing and financial services.

A likely weakness of answers is excessive focus on details. Plausible alternative answers could be given to many questions, so model answers should not be regarded as all-inclusive.

Breadth of question coverage

Questions in *both* sections of the paper may cover more than one syllabus area.

Knowledge from other syllabuses

Candidates should also use their knowledge from other Strategic level papers. One aim of this paper is to prepare candidates for the TOPCIMA T4 – Part B Case Study.

Past papers

November 2012

Section A

1 Business valuations, IPO

Section B

2 Financial strategy, constraints

3 Forecasting, debt and equity finance

4 Investment appraisal, project specific cost of capital, APV

September 2012 (resit exam)

Section A

1 Working capital management, international investment appraisal

Section B

2 Objectives of for profit and not for profit organisations

3 Lease vs buy, sources of finance

4 Investment appraisal, capital rationing

May 2012

Section A

1   Financial performance, dividend policy, international investment appraisal, risks of overseas investment

Section B

2   M&M theory, business valuation, capital structure

3   Working capital management, creditworthiness

4   Investment appraisal, consideration of other project factors

March 2012 (resit exam)

Section A

1   Cost of equity, business valuations, impact of takeover, defensive tactics

Section B

2   Efficient markets hypothesis, dividend policy, scrip dividends, financial strategies

3   Conversion value, cost of debt, WACC, convertible debt versus equity, treasury department

4   Validity of investment appraisal, real options, use of discount rate

November 2011

Section A

1   Investment decisions (uses of funds), business valuations, competition authorities

Section B

2   Financial objectives, treasury function

3   Rights issues

4   International investment decisions (NPV), post completion audit

September 2011 (resit)

Section A

1   Cash flow forecast, exchange rate movements, dividend policy, sources of finance, liquidity issues

Section B

2   Business valuations, amalgamations and restructuring

3   Cost of capital, NPV, APV

4   MBO, business valuations, venture capital

May 2011

Section A

1   NPV, payback, real options (option to abandon)

Section B

2   Financial management decisions, dividend policy, IPOs

3   NPV, leasing

4   Cost of equity, WACC, business valuations

March 2011 (resit)

Section A

1   Cash flow forecasts, NPV, leasing, real options

Section B

2   Operating cycle, working capital financing, international investment

3   NPV, WACC, financial and non-financial objectives

4   Placings, IPOs, bond issues, efficient market hypothesis

November 2010

Section A

1   Cash flow forecast, cash balances, company valuation, public v private sector financial objectives, implications of selling business

Section B

2   Cost of equity, gross yield, methods of finance

3   NPV and PI, discount rate, foreign investment risk

4   MM models, company valuation, cost of equity, WACC, implications of lowering equity value

September 2010 (resit)

Section A

1   Company valuation techniques and acquisition evaluation

Section B

2   Role of the treasury department

3   NPV, IRR and MIRR

4   Dividend policy and dividend irrelevance theory

May 2010

Section A

1   International investment appraisal (NPV), choice of currency

Section B

2   Financing requirements, WACC, alternative approaches to financing

3   Management buyouts

4   Risk, CAPM, asset and equity betas

Specimen paper

Section A

1   NPV with exchange rates and tax rates; divestments

Section B

2   Lease or buy decision; post completion audit

3   Role of treasury department; company objectives

4   Forecast income statement; cash flow forecast

What the examiner means

The table below has been prepared by CIMA to help you interpret exam questions.

Learning objective	Verbs used	Definition	Examples in the Kit
1 Knowledge			
What you are expected to know	• List	• Make a list of	
	• State	• Express, fully or clearly, the details of/facts of	
	• Define	• Give the exact meaning of	
2 Comprehension			
What you are expected to understand	• Describe	• Communicate the key features of	4
	• Distinguish	• Highlight the differences between	
	• Explain	• Make clear or intelligible/state the meaning or purpose of	77
	• Identify	• Recognise, establish or select after consideration	82
	• Illustrate	• Use an example to describe or explain something	12
3 Application			
How you are expected to apply your knowledge	• Apply	• Put to practical use	
	• Calculate/compute	• Ascertain or reckon mathematically	72
	• Demonstrate	• Prove the certainty or exhibit by practical means	78
	• Prepare	• Make or get ready for use	5
	• Reconcile	• Make or prove consistent/ compatible	
	• Solve	• Find an answer to	
	• Tabulate	• Arrange in a table	
4 Analysis			
How you are expected to analyse the detail of what you have learned	• Analyse	• Examine in detail the structure of	3
	• Categorise	• Place into a defined class or division	
	• Compare and contrast	• Show the similarities and/or differences between	22
	• Construct	• Build up or complete	7
	• Discuss	• Examine in detail by argument	79
	• Interpret	• Translate into intelligible or familiar terms	
	• Prioritise	• Place in order of priority or sequence for action	
	• Produce	• Create or bring into existence	
5 Evaluation			
How you are expected to use your learning to evaluate, make decisions or recommendations	• Advise	• Counsel, inform or notify	76
	• Evaluate	• Appraise or assess the value of	43
	• Recommend	• Propose a course of action	26

Planning your question practice

We have already stressed that question practice should be right at the centre of your revision. Whilst you will spend some time looking at your notes and the Paper F3 Passcards, you should spend the majority of your revision time practising questions.

We recommend two ways in which you can practise questions.

- Use **BPP Learning Media's question plan** to work systematically through the syllabus and attempt key and other questions on a section-by-section basis

- **Build your own exams** – attempt the questions as a series of practice exams

These ways are suggestions and simply following them is no guarantee of success. You or your college may prefer an alternative but equally valid approach.

BPP's question plan

The plan below requires you to devote a **minimum of 50 hours** to revision of Paper F3. Any time you can spend over and above this should only increase your chances of success.

 Review your notes and the chapter summaries in the Paper F3 **Passcards** for each section of the syllabus.

 Answer the key questions for that section. These questions have boxes round the question number in the table below and you should answer them in full. Even if you are short of time you must attempt these questions if you want to pass the exam. You should complete your answers without referring to our solutions.

 Attempt the other questions in that section. For some questions we have suggested that you prepare **answer plans or do the calculations** rather than full solutions. Planning an answer means that you should spend about 40% of the time allowance for the questions brainstorming the question and drawing up a list of points to be included in the answer.

 Attempt Mock exams 1, 2 and 3 under strict exam conditions.

Syllabus section	2012 Passcards chapters	Questions in this Kit	Comments	Done ☑
Objectives and constraints	1, 2	1	Answer in full. This question tests your ability to write a purely discussion answer on an important topic.	☐
		3	Answer in full. This question gives you practice at applying your discussion to a specific organisation, an essential skill in this exam.	☐
		14	Answer in full. This question from September 2010 is a good test of your understanding of dividend policy.	☐
Performance analysis and forecasting	3	6	Answer in full. This question tests the preparation of forecasts thoroughly and also requires you to analyse the performance of the company.	☐
		7	Answer in full. This specimen paper question tests the preparation of forecast income statements and cash flow forecasts. You are also required to evaluate the likelihood that the company will meet its objectives.	☐
Short-term financial strategy	4	10	Answer in full. This question thoroughly tests your knowledge of working capital.	☐
Equity finance	5	22	Worth doing an answer plan to get you thinking about equity issues.	☐
Debt finance	6	23	Answer in full. This question from March 2011 covers both private and public issue of bonds and also your understanding of the EMH.	☐
Leasing	7	29	Answer in full. This September 2010 question focuses on leasing as a source of finance and asks you to compare leasing with outright purchase as a method of funding an investment.	☐
		30	Answer in full. This May 2011 question provides further valuable practice on calculating the cost of different sources of finance, including leasing, and recommending the best option.	☐
Cost of capital and the capital structure decision	8, 9	20	Answer in full. This question provides practice in calculating the cost of debt, which is a common weak area in exams. It also involves consideration of a number of financing options.	☐
		31	Answer in full. This question from May 2010 looks at two alternative financing policies. It provides practice in the calculation of financing requirements and WACC as well as the evaluation of different approaches to financing.	☐

Syllabus section	2012 Passcards chapters	Questions in this Kit	Comments	Done ☑
		32	Answer in full. A question from the May 2010 exam. It provides practice in working with CAPM and requires an evaluation of the usefulness of different costs of capital.	☐
		40	Answer in full. This November 2010 question provides a good test of understanding of MM models and the traditional model, as well as calculating cost of equity and WACC.	☐
	10	42	Answer in full. An unusual calculation on portfolio theory.	☐
Investment appraisal and project control	11-14	48	Answer in full. A question testing not just your investment appraisal skills but also requiring discussion of the use of WACC and risks of foreign investment.	☐
		54	Answer in full. This September 2010 question tests a variety of investment appraisal techniques, including MIRR.	☐
		55	Answer in full. This question from March 2011 focuses on the appropriateness of the WACC of one company as the discount rate for another company's investments.	☐
		65	Answer in full. A wide-ranging question on capital rationing and APV.	☐
Business valuations and acquisitions	15, 16	66	Answer in full. This question provides a good test of acquisitions from the viewpoint of the shareholders in the acquired company.	☐
		67	Answer in full. This question gives a slightly different perspective by looking at valuation from the venture capitalists' viewpoint.	☐
		71	Answer in full. This question gives you practice at using betas to calculate cost of capital which is then used to value the business.	☐
		72	Answer in full. This question requires you to value intellectual capital.	☐
		79	Answer in full. A question from the May 2010 exam that covers MBOs.	☐
		80	Answer in full. A wide-ranging question on business valuations from May 2011 which involves WACC calculations as well as the use of different valuation techniques.	☐

Syllabus section	2012 Passcards chapters	Questions in this Kit	Comments	Done ☑
Scenario questions		88	Answer in full. This question gives you practice at using information from a scenario to answer questions from various areas of the syllabus.	☐
		90	Answer in full. This question gives you further practice at using information from a scenario to answer questions from various areas of the syllabus. Useful preparation for the case study question in the real exam.	☐
Preseen questions		91	Answer in full. This question is the case study question from the specimen paper.	☐
		93	Answer in full. This is the case study question from September 2010.	☐
		94	Answer in full. This is the case study question from November 2010.	☐
		96	Answer in full. This is the case study question from May 2011.	☐
		98	Answer in full. This is the case study question from November 2011.	☐
		99	Answer in full. This is the case study question from March 2012.	☐

Build your own exams

Having revised your notes and the BPP Passcards, you can attempt the questions in the Kit as a series of practice exams, making them up yourself or using the mock exams that we have listed below.

	Pilot paper	May 2010	Sept 2010	Nov 2010	Mar 2011	May 2011	Sept 2011	Nov 2011	Mar 2012	May 2012
Section A										
1	91	92	93	94	95	96	97	98	99	100
Section B										
2	24	31	29	39	57	15	81	4	16	41
3	43	79	54	60	55	30	59	18	33	12
4	7	32	14	40	23	80	68	56	52	53

	Practice exams		
	1	2	3
Section A			
1	73	71	78
Section B			
2	71	17	58
3	10	20	3
4	26	72	27

Whichever practice exams you use, you must attempt **Mock exams 1, 2 and 3** at the end of your revision.

QUESTIONS

2

> **FORMULATION OF FINANCIAL STRATEGY**
>
> Questions 1 to 16 cover formulation of financial strategy, the subject of Part A of the BPP Study Text for Paper F3.

1   HG (FS, 11/05)   45 mins

HG is a privately-owned toy manufacturer based in a country in the European Union, but which is not in the European Common Currency Area (ECCA). It trades internationally both as a supplier and a customer. Although HG is privately owned, it has revenue and assets equivalent in amount to some public listed companies. It has a large number of shareholders, but has no intention of seeking a listing at the present time. In fact, the major shareholders have often expressed a wish to buy out some of the smaller investors.

The entity has a long history of sound, if unspectacular, profitability. The directors and shareholders are reasonably happy with this situation and are averse to adopting strategies that they think might involve a substantial increase in risk, for example, acquisition or setting up manufacturing capability overseas, as some of HG's European competitors have done. As a consequence, HG accepts its growth rate will be relatively low, compared with some of its competitors.

The entity is financed 70% equity and 30% debt (based on book values). The debt is a mixture of secured and unsecured bonds carrying interest rates of between 7% and 8·5% and repayable in 5 to 10 years' time. Inflation in HG's country is near zero and interest rates are low and possibly falling. The Company Treasurer is investigating the opportunities for, and consequences of, refinancing.

HG's main financial objective is simply to increase dividends each year. It has one non-financial objective, which is to treat all stakeholders in the organisation with 'fairness and equality'. The Board has decided to review these objectives. The new Finance Director believes maximisation of shareholder wealth should be the sole objective, but the other directors do not agree and think a range of objectives should be considered, for example profits after tax and return on investment and performance improvement across a number of operational areas.

Required

(a)   Evaluate the appropriateness of HG's current objectives and the Finance Director's suggestion, and discuss the issues that the HG Board should consider when determining the new corporate objectives. Conclude with a recommendation.   **(15 marks)**

(b)   Discuss the factors that the treasury department should consider when determining financing, or re-financing strategies in the context of the economic environment described in the scenario and explain how these might impact on the determination of corporate objectives.   **(10 marks)**

(Total = 25 marks)

2   CCC (FS, 11/06)   45 mins

(a)   CCC is a local government entity. It is financed almost equally by a combination of central government funding and local taxation. The funding from central government is determined largely on a *per capita* (per head of population) basis, adjusted to reflect the scale of deprivation (or special needs) deemed to exist in CCC's region. A small percentage of its finance comes from the private sector, for example from renting out City Hall for private functions.

CCC's main objectives are:

- To make the region economically prosperous and an attractive place to live and work;
- To provide service excellence in health and education for the local community.

DDD is a large, listed entity with widespread commercial and geographical interests. For historic reasons, its headquarters are in CCC's region. This is something of an anomaly as most entities of DDD's size would have their HQ in a capital city, or at least a city much larger than where it is.

DDD has one financial objective: To increase shareholder wealth by an average 10% per annum. It also has a series of non-financial objectives that deal with how the entity treats other stakeholders, including the local communities where it operates.

DDD has total net assets of $1·5 billion and a gearing ratio of 45% (debt to debt plus equity), which is typical for its industry. It is currently considering raising a substantial amount of capital to finance an acquisition.

Required

Discuss the criteria that the two very different entities described above have to consider when setting objectives, recognising the needs of each of their main stakeholder groups. Make some reference in your answer to the consequences of each of them failing to meet its declared objectives. **(13 marks)**

(b)   MS is a private entity in a computer-related industry. It has been trading for six years and is managed by its main shareholders, the original founders of the entity. Most of the employees are also shareholders, having been given shares as bonuses. None of the shareholders has attempted to sell shares in the entity so the problem of placing a value on them has not arisen. Dividends have been paid every year at the rate of 60 cents per share, irrespective of profits. So far, profits have always been sufficient to cover the dividend at least once but never more than twice.

MS is all-equity financed at present although $15 million new finance is likely to be required in the near future to finance expansion. Total net assets as at the last statement of financial position date were $45 million.

Required

Discuss and compare the relationship between dividend policy, investment policy and financing policy in the context of the small entity described above, MS, and DDD, the large listed entity described in part (a). **(12 marks)**

(Total = 25 marks)

3   A and B (FS, 11/08)   45 mins

Entity A

A is a publicly listed entity operating largely in the field of training and education. Its sole financial objective is the maximisation of shareholder wealth. It has a cost of capital of 12% and evaluates all its investments using this as the discount rate. This cost of capital is typical of publicly-listed entities in this sector, although analysts believe there is a range of between 10% and 15%.

Entity B

B is a state-owned educational entity. A substantial proportion of its funding is provided by the government, which requires such entities to operate as commercial entities. All investments are evaluated at a standard discount rate of 7%, a rate determined by the government and applied to investments by all state-owned entities.

Most of B's objectives are qualitative, such as provide a high quality of education to a diverse body of students. It has no financial objective other than to stay within cash funding limits.

Required

(a)   (i)   Discuss how the financial objective of entity A might be achieved and measured. **(5 marks)**

       (ii)   Evaluate how the achievement of this financial objective might also benefit other stakeholders in entity A. **(8 marks)**

(b)   Analyse the differences between the objectives of public and private sector entities that could explain the different discount rates between Entity A and Entity B given in the scenario.

Include in your analysis some discussion of the apparent contradiction between the government requiring state-owned entities to operate as commercial entities yet instructing them to use a discount rate substantially below that typically used by private sector entities. **(12 marks)**

(Total = 25 marks)

4 TTT (11/11)

45 mins

TTT is a public place listed company based in Germany with the euro (EUR) as its functional currency. The company is an energy supply, operating a number of electricity generating facilities and electricity grids both in Germany and other European countries (some of which are outside the eurozone). It has a central treasury function based in Germany.

TTT has defined its three financial objectives as follows:

1   To increase dividends by 10% a year.

2   To keep gearing below 40% (where gearing is calculated as debt/(debt + equity)).

3   To expand b internal growth and/or by horizontal integration via acquisition of companies operating in the same industry sector.

TTT has identified a potential takeover candidate, company WWW, which operates three electricity generating stations in Sweden and has Swedish Krona (SKR) as its functional currency. TTT is considering a cash for WWW of approximately SKR 23,000 million but it has not yet been decided whether this would be financed by debt (at an after tax cost of 5% per annum) per equity. If equity were used then shares would be issued on the open market at the current share price of EUR 2.90 per share.

Extracts from TTT's latest financial statements are as follows:

	EUR million
Long term borrowings	9,500
Share capital (EUR 1 shares)	5,000
Retained reserves	4,000

Last year TTT paid a dividend of 16 cents per share, representing a dividend pay-out ratio of 40%. Earnings have grown by 8% a year on average over the last 5 years and the dividend pay-out ratio has been between 30% and 50% over the period.

WWW has a current market capitalisation of SKR 20,000 million and the current EUR/SKR spot rate is EUR/SKR 9.2000 (that is, EUR 1 = SKR 9.000). WWW has a P/E ratio of 10 and earnings are expected to grow at 6% a year in the future years.

Required

(a)   Advise the directors of TTT on:

(i)   The extent to which the company meets its financial objectives both before and after the proposed acquisition of WWW.

(11 marks)

(ii)   The appropriateness of the stated financial objectives for TTT AND how they could be improved.

(7 marks)

(b)   Describe THEE roles that the central treasury function of TTT might play in the evaluation and/or implementation of the proposed acquisition of WWW.

(7 marks)

(Total = 25 marks)

5 CBA   45 mins

CBA is a manufacturing company in the furniture trade. Its sales have risen sharply over the past six months as a result of an improvement in the economy and a strong housing market. The company is now showing signs of 'overtrading' and the financial manager, Ms Smith, is concerned about its liquidity. The company is one month from its year end. Estimated figures for the full 12 months of the current year and forecasts for next year, on present cash management policies, are shown below.

Statement of consolidated income

	Next year £'000	Current year £'000
Revenues	5,200	4,200
Less: Cost of sales (Note 1)	3,224	2,520
Operating expenses	650	500
Operating profit	1,326	1,180
Interest paid	54	48
Profit before tax	1,272	1,132
Tax payable	305	283
Profit after tax	967	849
Dividends declared	387	339
Current assets and liabilities as at the end of the year		
Inventory/work-in-progress	625	350
Receivables	750	520
Cash	0	25
Trade payables	464	320
Other payables (tax and dividends)	692	622
Overdraft	11	0
Net current assets/(liabilities)	208	(47)
Note. Cost of sales includes depreciation of	225	175

Ms Smith is considering methods of improving the cash position. A number of actions are being discussed.

Debtors

Offer a 2% discount to customers who pay within 10 days of despatch of invoices. It is estimated 50% of customers will take advantage of the new discount scheme. The other 50% will continue to take the current average credit period.

Trade payables and inventory

Reduce the number of suppliers currently being used and negotiate better terms with those that remain by introducing a 'just in time' policy. The aim will be to reduce the end-of-year forecast cost of sales (excluding depreciation) by 5% and inventory/WIP levels by 10%. However, the number of days credit taken by the company will have to fall to 30 days to help persuade suppliers to improve their prices.

Other information

- All trade is on credit. *Official* terms of sale at present require payment within 30 days. Interest is not charged on late payments.
- All purchases are made on credit.
- Operating expenses will be £650,000 with the existing or proposed policies.
- Interest payments would be £45,000 if the new policies are implemented.
- Capital expenditure of £550,000 is planned for next year.

Required

(a) Explain the main uses of overdraft facilities as part of a company's working capital management policy.

(5 marks)

(b) Prepare a cash flow forecast for next year, assuming:

(i) The company does not change its policies
(ii) The company's proposals for managing customers, suppliers and inventory are implemented

In both cases, assume a full twelve-month period, that is the changes will be effective from day 1 of next year.

(14 marks)

(c) As Assistant to Ms Smith, write a short report to her discussing the proposed actions. Include comments on the factors, financial and non-financial, that the company should take into account before implementing the new policies.

(6 marks)

(Total = 25 marks)

6   RJ (FS, 11/05)   45 mins

RJ plc is a supplier of surgical instruments and medical supplies (excluding drugs). Its shares are listed on the UK's Alternative Investment Market and are currently quoted at 458 pence per £1 share. The majority of its customers are public sector organisations in the UK. RJ plc is doing well and now needs additional capital to expand operations.

The forecast financial statements are given below.

Extracts from the Statement of consolidated income for the year ended 31 December 20X5

	£'000
Revenue	30,120
Costs and expenses	22,500
Operating profit	7,620
Finance costs	2,650
Profit before tax	4,970
Tax	1,491

Note. Dividends declared for 20X5 are £1,392,000

Statement of financial position as at 31 December 20X5

	£'000	£'000
Total assets		
Non-current assets		14,425
Current assets		
Inventories	4,510	
Trade receivables	3,700	
Cash	198	
		8,408
		22,833
Equity and liabilities		
Equity		
Share capital	8,350	
Retained earnings	4,750	
		13,100
Non-current liabilities		
(secured bonds, 6% 20X8)		4,000
Current liabilities		
Trade payables	2,850	
Other payables (tax and dividends)	2,883	
		5,733
		22,833

You have obtained the following additional information:

1   Revenue is expected to increase by 10% per annum in each of the financial years ending 31 December 20X6 and 20X7. Costs and expenses, excluding depreciation, are expected to increase by an average of 5% per annum. Finance costs are expected to remain unchanged.

2   RJ plc expects to continue to be liable for tax at the marginal rate of 30%. Assume tax is paid or refunded the year following that in which the liability or repayment arises.

3   The ratios of trade receivables to revenue and trade payables to costs and expenses will remain the same for the next two years. The value of inventories is likely to remain at 20X5 levels.

4   The non-current assets are land and buildings, which are not depreciated in RJ plc's books. Capital (tax) allowances on the buildings may be ignored. All other assets used by the entity (machinery, cars and so on) are either rented or leased on operating leases.

5   Dividends will be increased by 5% each year.

6   RJ plc intends to purchase for cash new machinery to the value of £6,000,000 during 20X6, although an investment appraisal exercise has not been carried out. It will be depreciated straight line over 10 years. RJ plc intends to charge a full year's depreciation in the first year of purchase of its assets. Capital (tax) allowances are available at 25% reducing balance on this expenditure.

RJ plc's main financial objectives for the years 20X6-20X7 are to earn a pre-tax return on the closing book value of equity of 35% per annum and a year-on-year increase in earnings of 10%.

Required

Assume you are a consultant working for RJ plc. Evaluate the implications of the financial information you have obtained. You should:

(a)   Provide forecast statement of consolidated incomes, dividends and retentions for the two years ending 31 December 20X6 and 20X7.   **(6 marks)**

(b)   Provide cash flow forecasts for the years 20X6 and 20X7. Comment briefly on how RJ plc might finance any cash deficit.   **(8 marks)**

Note. This is **not** an investment appraisal exercise; you may ignore the timing of cash flows **within** each year and you should not discount the cash flows. You should also ignore interest payable on any cash deficit.

(c)   Discuss the key aspects and implications of the financial information you have obtained in your answer to parts (a) and (b) of the question, in particular whether RJ plc is likely to meet its stated objectives. Provide whatever calculations you think are appropriate to support your discussion. Up to 4 marks are available for calculations in this section of the question.   **(11 marks)**

(Total = 25 marks)

7   EF (Pilot paper)   45 mins

EF is a distributor for branded beverages throughout the world. It is based in the UK but has offices throughout Europe, South America and the Caribbean. Its shares are listed on the UK's Alternative Investment Market (AIM) and are currently quoted at 180 pence per share.

Extracts from EF's forecast financial statements are given below.

Extracts from the (forecast) income statement for the year ended 31 December 20X9

	£'000
Revenue	45,000
Purchase costs and expenses	38,250
Interest on long term debt	450
Profit before tax	6,300
Income tax expense (at 28%)	1,764
Note: Dividends declared	1,814

EF – Statement of financial position as at 31 December 20X9

	£'000
ASSETS	
Non-current assets	14,731
Current assets	
Inventories	5,250
Trade receivables	13,500
Cash and bank balances	348
	19,098
Total assets	33,829
EQUITY AND LIABILITIES	
Equity	
Share capital (ordinary shares of 25 pence)	4,204
Retained earnings	16,210
Total equity	20,414
Non-current liabilities	
Secured bonds, 9% 2015	5,000
Current liabilities	
Trade payables	8,415
Total liabilities	13,415
Total equity and liabilities	33,829

You have obtained the following additional information:

1   Revenue and purchases & expenses are expected to increase by an average of 4% each year for the financial years ending 31 December 20Y0 and 20Y1.

2   EF expects to continue to be liable for tax at the rate of 28 per cent. Assume tax is paid or refunded the year in which the liability arises.

3   The ratios of trade receivables to sales and trade payables to purchase costs and expenses will remain the same for the next two years. The value of inventories is likely to remain at 20X9 levels for 20Y0 and 20Y1.

4   The non-current assets in the statement of financial position at 31 December 20X9 are land and buildings, which are not depreciated in the company's books. Tax depreciation allowances on the buildings may be ignored. All other assets used by the company are currently procured on operating leases.

5   The company intends to purchase early in 20Y0 a fleet of vehicles (trucks and vans). These vehicles are additional to the vehicles currently operated by EF. The vehicles will be provided to all its UK and overseas bases but will be purchased in the UK. The cost of these vehicles will be £5,000,000. The cost will be depreciated on a straight line basis over 10 years. The company charges a full year's depreciation in the first year of purchase of its assets. Tax depreciation allowances are available at 25% reducing balance on this expenditure. Assume the vehicles have a zero residual value at the end of ten years.

6   Dividends will be increased by 5% each year on the 20X9 base. Assume they are paid in the year they are declared.

EF plans to finance the purchase of the vehicles (identified in note 6) from its cash balances and an overdraft. The entity's agreed overdraft facility is currently £1 million.

The company's main financial objectives are to earn a post-tax return on the closing book value of shareholders' funds of 20% per annum and a year on year increase in earnings of 8%

Assumption regarding overdraft interest

It should be assumed that overdraft interest that might have been incurred during 20X9 is included in expenses (that is, you are not expected to calculate overdraft interest for 20Y0 and 20Y1).

Required

Assume you are a consultant working for EF

(a)   Construct a forecast income statement, including dividends and retentions for the years ended 31 December 20Y0 and 20Y1.   **(6 marks)**

(b)   Construct a cash flow forecast for each of the years 20Y0 and 20Y1. Discuss, briefly, how the company might finance any cash deficit.   **(9 marks)**

(c)   Using your results in (a) and (b) above, evaluate whether EF is likely to meet its stated objectives. As part of your evaluation, discuss whether the assumption regarding overdraft interest is reasonable and explain how a more accurate calculation of overdraft interest could be obtained.   **(10 marks)**

(Total = 25 marks)

---

8   AB and YZ   45 mins

AB and YZ both operate department stores in Europe. They operate in similar markets and are generally considered to be direct competitors. Both companies have had similar earnings records over the past ten years and have similar capital structures. The earnings and dividend record of the two companies over the past six years is as follows:

| | AB | | | YZ | | |
| | EPS | DPS | Average | EPS | DPS | Average |
Year to 31 March	cents	cents	share price	cents	cents	share price
20X1	230	60	2,100	240	96	2,200
20X2	150	60	1,500	160	64	1,700
20X3	100	60	1,000	90	36	1,400
20X4	–125	60	800	–110	0	908
20X5	100	60	1,000	90	36	1,250
20X6	150	60	1,400	145	58	1,700

<u>Note</u>. EPS = Earnings per Share and DPS = Dividends per Share

AB has had 25 million shares in issue for the past six years. YZ currently has 25 million shares in issue. At the beginning of 20X5 YZ had a 1 for 4 rights issue. The EPS and DPS have been adjusted in the above table.

The Chairman of AB is concerned that the share price of YZ is higher than his company's, despite the fact that AB has recently earned more per share than YZ and frequently during the past six years has paid a higher dividend.

Required

(a)   Discuss:

     (i)   The apparent dividend policy followed by each company over the past six years and comment on the possible relationship of these policies to the companies' market values and current share prices; and

     (ii)   Whether there is an optimal dividend policy for AB that might increase shareholder value.

     (12 marks)

(b)   Forecast earnings for AB for the year to 31 March 20X7 are €40 million. At present, it has excess cash of €2.5 million and is considering a share repurchase in addition to maintaining last year's dividend. The Chairman thinks this will have a number of benefits for the company, including a positive effect on the share price.

     Advise the Chairman of AB of

     (i)   How a share repurchase may be arranged

     (ii)   The main reasons for a share repurchase

     (iii)   The potential problems of such an action, compared with a one-off extra dividend payment, and any possible effect on the share price of AB   **(13 marks)**

     (Total = 25 marks)

A report format is not required for this question.

9 MAT (FS, 5/08)
45 mins

MAT is a manufacturer of computer components in a rapidly growing niche market. It is a private entity owned and managed by a small group of people who started the business 10 years ago. Although relatively small, it sells its products world-wide. Customers are invoiced in sterling, although this policy is being reviewed. Raw materials are purchased largely in the UK although some are sourced from overseas and paid for in foreign currencies, typically US$.

As the newly-appointed Financial Manager, you are reviewing MAT's financial records to identify any immediate or longer-term areas of risk that require immediate attention. In particular the entity's forecast appears to be uncomfortably close to its unsecured overdraft limit of £450,000.

Extracts from last year's results and the forecast for the next financial year are as follows.

	Last year £'000	Forecast £'000
Non-current assets	3,775	4,325
Current assets		
Accounts receivable	550	950
Inventory	475	575
Cash and marketable securities	250	100
Total current assets	1,275	1,625
Total assets	5,050	5,950
Total equity	3,750	4,050
Non-current liabilities		
Secured bond repayable in 2 years' time	850	850
Current liabilities		
Accounts payable	450	625
Bank overdraft	0	425
Total current liabilities	450	1,050
Total equity and liabilities	5,050	5,950
Revenue	4,500	5,750
Cost of goods sold	1,750	2,300
Profit before tax	1,050	1,208

Required

Prepare a report to the Finance Director of MAT advising on whether the entity could be classified as 'overtrading' and recommending financial strategies that could be used to address the situation.

Your advice and recommendations should be based on analysis of the forecast financial position, making whatever assumptions are necessary and should include brief reference to any additional information that would be useful to MAT at this time. **(25 marks)**

10 LUG (FS, 11/08)
45 mins

LUG manufactures furniture for major retailers and independent customers in country D, which has the euro (€) as its currency. Until this year it sold its products only in its own country.

LUG finances major changes in its investment in working capital by medium-term loans, which often result in short-term cash surpluses. Short-term cash deficits are financed by overdraft or delayed payments to creditors, usually by agreement.

Assume today is 1 January 20X4.

Selected forecast financial outcomes (country D only) are as follows:

	12 months ended *30 September 20X4* *€000*
Revenue	2,585
Cost of goods sold	1,551
Purchases	1,034

	As at *30 September 20X4* *€000*	
Accounts receivable	350	(54.9 days)
Accounts payable	205	(72.4 days)
Inventory	425	

(Raw material = 45%, WIP = 22%, Finished goods = 33%)

Operating cycle = 105 days

Terms of trade of 90% of sales in country D are 30 days credit. The remaining 10% is paid by cash, debit or credit card. Card payments are considered the equivalent of cash. Sales are spread roughly evenly throughout the year. This pattern is not expected to change.

New customers

On 1 October 20X3, LUG entered into contracts with customers in country E, whose currency is the E$. Forecast figures for the year ended 30 September 20X4 will be affected as follows:

- Sales to country E are likely to be affected by economic and political factors. There is a 60% probability sales will be E$750,000 and a 40% probability they will be E$950,000. All sales will be on credit, invoiced in E$, and the accounts receivable of these customers is expected to be 20% of revenue on average. Sales are spread evenly throughout the year.

- The spot rate E$ to the euro on 1 October 20X3 was 1.43. The E$ is expected to weaken against the euro by 3% gradually through the year.

Total inventory figures are expected to be as follows to accommodate sales in country E:

	As at *30 September 20X4* *€000*
Raw material	245
WIP	120
Finished goods	208

Required

(a) (i) Calculate the revised operating cycle for the year ended 30 September 20X4 to incorporate sales made to customers in country E. Assume a full year's trading and sales spread evenly throughout the year.

(ii) Explain, briefly, the main causes of the increase in the operating cycle over the forecast.

(12 marks)

(b) Discuss the benefits and risks of invoicing overseas customers in their own currency and explain what methods are available to help minimise the risks. **(6 marks)**

(c) Discuss the advantages and disadvantages of financing net current operating assets with medium-term loans compared with short-term financing, in general and as appropriate to LUG. Include in your discussion a diagrammatic explanation of aggressive and conservative working capital financing policies. **(7 marks)**

(Total = 25 marks)

11 MNO (FS, 5/06)   45 mins

It is currently May 20X6.

MNO is a private toy distributor situated in the United States of America (US) with a US customer base and local suppliers. There is a central manufacturing base and several marketing units spread across the US. The marketing units are encouraged to adapt to local market conditions, largely acting independently and free from central control. These units are responsible for all aspects of local sales, including collecting sales revenues, which are paid across to Head Office on a monthly basis. Funding is provided by Head Office as required.

Figures for last year to 31 December 20X5 were as follows:

Revenue	$10 million
Gross profit margin	40% of revenue
Accounts receivable days	minimum 20, maximum 30 days
Accounts payable days	minimum 40, maximum 50 days
Inventories	minimum 50, maximum 80 days
Non-current assets	$8 million

Accounts receivable, accounts payable and inventories can all be assumed to be the same on both 31 December 20X4 and 31 December 20X5, but fluctuate between those dates.

The Financial Controller is carrying out an analysis of MNO's working capital levels, as requested by the Treasurer. He is assuming that the peak period for accounts receivable coincides with the peak period for inventories and the lowest level of accounts payable.

MNO is currently in consultation with a potentially significant new supplier in Asia, who will demand payment in its local currency.

Required

(a)   (i)   Calculate the minimum and maximum working capital levels based on the Financial Controller's assumption regarding the timing of peaks and troughs in working capital variables and discuss the validity of that assumption.   **(6 marks)**

      (ii)   Using the figures calculated in (i) above, calculate and draw a chart to show the short-term and long-term (permanent) financing requirements of MNO under each of the following working capital financing policies:

            –   Moderate policy, where long-term financing matches permanent net current assets;

            –   Aggressive policy, where 30% of permanent net current assets are funded by short-term financing;

            –   Conservative policy, where only 40% of fluctuating net current assets are funded by short-term financing.   **(7 marks)**

(b)   Discuss the advantages and disadvantages of an aggressive financing policy and advise whether or not such a policy would be appropriate for MNO.   **(6 marks)**

(c)   Advise MNO whether a profit or cost centre structure would be more appropriate for its treasury department.   **(6 marks)**

(Total = 25 marks)

12 KK (5/12)   45 mins

Today is 24 May 20X2.

KK is based in Europe and has the euro (EUR) as its functional currency. KK manufactures specialised computer parts for sale throughout Europe and has experienced rapid growth in recent years. Much of this growth has been as a result of launching new products.

Despite rapidly increasing revenues, KK has experienced liquidity pressures as evidenced by a growing overdraft. KK is now dangerously close to breaching its overdraft limit of EUR 9.0 million.

Extracts from management accounting information for KK for the 12 months of trading up to 30 April 20X2 are given below:

Results for 6 months to:	30 April 20X2 EUR million	31 October 20X1 EUR million
Revenue	12.6	9.5
Cost of sales	9.6	7.1
Other costs (all settled as incurred)	2.0	1.5
Balances as at:	**30 April 20X2 EUR million**	**31 October 20X1 EUR million**
Accounts receivable	7.1	4.8
Accounts payable	3.2	2.7
Inventory	5.6	3.9
Overdraft	8.5	6.0
Working capital days as at:	**30 April 20X2 Days**	**31 October 20X1 Days**
Accounts receivable	103	92
Accounts payable	61	69
Inventory	106	100

For the purposes of this question, taxation should be ignored.

Required

(a)   (i)   Calculate what the overdraft requirement would have been on 30 April 20X2 if working capital days for the period had remained at 31 October 20X1 levels.   **(5 marks)**

      (ii)   Explain the particular pressures faced by companies in times of rapid expansion in respect of working capital and profit margins. Illustrate your answer with reference to KK.   **(8 marks)**

      (iii) Recommend strategies that KK should consider in order to reduce the amount of funds tied up in working capital.   **(5 marks)**

(b)   Discuss the key factors that a potential lender is likely to consider when assessing the creditworthiness of a business which is experiencing rapid growth.   **(7 marks)**

                                                                    (Total = 25 marks)

13 CRM (FS, 5/09)

45 mins

It is currently May 20X9.

CRM is a UK-based manufacturer of electronic components. Its shares are listed on the UK's Alternative Investment Market. The founder-directors of the entity still own the majority of shares. A combination of private and institutional investors own the remainder of the shares.

CRM has one wholly-owned subsidiary based in Asia.

CRM has three on-going financial objectives, which are:

- Provide a total return to shareholders of at least 15% per annum
- Provide a dividend yield comparable with the industry average
- Generate a return on net assets of 30% per annum

In addition, it has two specific financial objectives for the year to 31 March 20X9. Based on figures for the year to 31 March 20X8 these are:

- Increase revenue by 15%
- Increase earnings per share by 10%

It has a further financial objective to double revenue in sterling terms in its Asian subsidiary within the three years to 31 March 20Y2.

Extracts from the entity's financial statements for the past two years are shown below. The group figures include those for the subsidiary. Figures are for a full 12 month period ending on 31 March.

Income statement

	Group		Asian Sub.	
	20X8	20X9	20X8	20X9
	£ million	£ million	A$ million	A$ million
Revenue	325	355	295	365
Cost of sales	145	156	135	165
Administrative costs	75	82	80	90
Profit before interest and tax	105	117	80	110
Interest payable	9	9	11	11
Taxation payable	27	31	17	20
Earnings	69	77	52	79
Dividends	21	24	0	0

Balance sheet

	Group		Asian Sub.	
	20X8	20X9	20X8	20X9
Assets	£ million	£ million	A$ million	A$ million
Non-current assets	174	190	137	157
Current assets	167	191	105	121
	341	381	242	278
Equity and liabilities				
Total equity	157	210	85	164
Non-current liabilities				
Secured 9% bond 20Y5	100	100	–	–
Long-term loan from parent	–	–	92	92
Current liabilities	84	71	65	22
	341	381	242	278
Number of shares in issue (million)	125	125	100	100

CRM's share price as at:

31 March 20X8 641·0 pence
31 March 20X9 721·8 pence

The entity's equity beta is not available, but for a similar entity quoted on the main stock exchange it was 1·4 for the whole two year period and is not expected to change. The expected risk free rate is 4% and the return on the AIM is 12%. All figures are post-tax.

Selected industry data:

As at 31 March:	20X8	20X9
Dividend yield:	2·8%	3·0%
P/E ratio	8·2	9·0
Gearing (Book values of long term debt to total long terms funds)	44%	46%
FTSE AIM all share index	849	925

Average exchange rates

	Exchange rate Asian $ to £
12 months to 31 March 20X8	6·3
12 months to 31 March 20X9	6·5

Inflation is forecast to average 5·5% per annum in the Asian country and 3·5% per annum in the UK for the foreseeable future.

Required

Assume you are a newly-recruited financial manager with CRM. You have been asked to prepare a report for discussion at the next Board of Directors meeting that analyses the entity's financial performance over the two year period to assess whether it has attained its financial objectives as stated.

Your report should also provide:

- Recommendations for corrective action by the entity if necessary
- Advice about the appropriateness of the stated objectives

You should carefully select and calculate appropriate ratios and performance measures for your analysis. Calculations should be shown in an appendix using sensible roundings.

(Calculations account for up to 15 marks)

(Total = 25 marks)

14   Blue and Green (9/10)   45 mins

Blue

Blue is a multinational furniture retailer listed on its local stock exchange. It has experienced rapid growth in recent years, partly via acquisitions and partly by generic growth. A substantial proportion of the shareholders are institutional investors but there is also a significant proportion of shares held by private individuals.

Blue follows a conservative dividend policy, paying a relatively low dividend with a small but steady growth in dividend levels. This has led to the accumulation of surplus funds. Mr B, a director of a major institutional shareholder of Blue, has recently requested that surplus funds be returned to shareholders. The Directors of Blue are currently considering this request.

Green

Green is a privately-owned, family-run small furniture retail chain with just 10 shareholders.

Historically, Green's dividend payouts have varied considerably year-on-year. Recent payouts have been between 10% and 50% of profit for the year, largely depending on investment opportunities available. In the current year, the shareholders have not been able to agree on an appropriate level of dividend.

Mr G, one of the shareholders, is planning a major extension on his house and has requested a large dividend payment. However, the other shareholders wish to retain cash within the company for investment in future projects.

Both Blue and Green have the primary financial objective of maximising shareholder value.

Required:

(a)   Discuss the rationale behind both Blue and Green's dividend policies and why a listed company such as Blue can be expected to have a different dividend policy to that of a private company such as Green.

(9 marks)

(b)   Explain Modigliani & Miller's dividend irrelevancy theory and its practical relevance to both Blue and Green in seeking to maximise shareholder value.

(8 marks)

(c)   Advise the Directors of Blue and the Directors of Green on an appropriate response to each of Mr B and Mr G's requests.
(8 marks)

(Total = 25 marks)

A report format is not required for this question

15   HJK (5/11)   45 mins

It is currently May 20Y1.

HJK is a long established, family owned and run, IT consultancy company. The company has experienced rapid growth in recent years.

Recent financial history for HJK:

Year ending 31 December	Profit for the year after interest and tax EUR million	Investment in projects or capital expenditure EUR million	Dividend paid EUR million
20X6	6	-	3
20X7	7	10	2
20X8	10	-	5
20X9	11	15	2
20Y0	16	-	8

In recent years, investment has been funded by cash held generated by the business but HJK now requires additional funds to finance significant expansion. The Directors have considered additional bank finance but their preference is for an initial public offering (IPO), that is, an offer for sale of shares to the public. However, the Directors are concerned about the implications of an IPO on the financial strategy of the company in the areas of dividend, financing and investment.
Required:

(a)   Evaluate the current dividend policy of HJK.   **(6 marks)**

(b)   (i)   Describe the process involved in an IPO.   **(3 marks)**

         (ii)   Advise on the potential risks with an IPO and what action can be taken to minimise such risks.
(4 marks)

(c)   Discuss the concerns of the Directors regarding the possible implications of becoming a listed company on dividend, financing and investment strategies and the interrelationship between them.   **(12 marks)**

(Total = 25 marks)

16 QRR (3/12)   45 mins

Assume today is 1 April 20X2.

QRR is a bank located and listed in India. Today's exchange rate for the Indian Rupee (INR) is GBP/INR 76.9231 (that is, GBP 1 = INR 76.9231).

In recent years, QRR has experienced a fall in profits as a result of the credit crunch which has weakened the capital base of the bank. Although revenue has risen by 6.3% in the past year, operating profits have fallen by 19% and earnings per share by 9%. In the past QRR has paid regular quarterly dividends.

Due to the credit crunch and the downturn in the global economy, the Indian banking regulator (together with banking regulators around the world) is in the process of introducing higher capital and liquidity requirements for all banks, which will be a legal requirement in twelve months' time. Currently, QRR would not satisfy these new capital and liquidity requirements.

The board of QRR has recently met to discuss how best to improve capital and liquidity in order to be able to meet the new requirements. The following two suggestions were made by Board members regarding the next quarterly dividend:

- Director A has suggested that no dividend should be paid.

- Director B has suggested that the normal cash dividend be replaced with a scrip dividend (that is, a bonus issue of shares).

Under the proposed scrip dividend, QRR would issue shareholders with the right to subscribe for ordinary shares at zero cost in the proportion of 1 new bonus share for every 50 shares held. The rights to receive bonus shares would be issued on 15 May 20X2, with the new shares being issued on 31 May 20X2. A shareholder would have to choose between the following actions:

1   Sell the rights in the open market for cash at the latest market price for the rights between the dates 15 May 20X2 and 31 May 20X2.

2   Hold onto the rights until 31 May 20X2 and receive new shares in the proportion 1 share for every 50 held on that date.

QRR has 4,300 million INR 100 (nominal) ordinary shares in issue. The market price for selling the rights is expected to be in the order of INR 7 per existing share under the rights. Assume that a typical shareholder in QRR holds 1,000 ordinary shares of nominal value INR100 each and that today's share price is INR 396.

Required

(a)   Discuss the likely impacts on QRR's share price of an announcement that no dividend will be paid, as suggested by Director A.   **(8 marks)**

(b)   Evaluate which of the following actions would be more beneficial to a typical shareholder if Director B's suggestion is implemented:

    (i)   Accepting the shares offered under the scrip dividend.

    (ii)   Selling the rights under the scrip dividend in the market.

    Your answer should include an estimate of the change in shareholder value in each case based upon today's share price.   **(8 marks)**

(c)   Recommend which, if either, of the strategies suggested by Director A and Director B, QRR should adopt.   **(5 marks)**

(d)   Identify alternative financial strategies (other than changing the dividend policy) that could help improve QRR's liquidity position.   **(4 marks)**

(Total = 25 marks)

FINANCING DECISIONS

Questions 17 to 43 cover financing decisions, the subject of Part B of the BPP Study Text for Paper F3.

---

17   XTA (FS, 5/05)   45 mins

XTA plc is the parent company of a transport and distribution group based in the United Kingdom (UK). The group owns and operates a network of distribution centres and a fleet of trucks (large delivery vehicles) in the UK. It is currently planning to expand into Continental Europe, operating through a new subsidiary company in Germany. The subsidiary will purchase distribution centres in Germany and invest in a new fleet of trucks to be based at those centres. The German subsidiary will be operationally independent of the UK parent.

Alternative proposals have been put forward by Messrs A, B and C, Board members of XTA plc on how best to structure the financing of the new German operation as follows:

Mr A: 'I would feel much more comfortable if we were to borrow in our base currency, sterling, where we already have long-standing banking relationships and a good reputation in the capital markets. Surely it would be much more complicated for us to borrow in euros?'

Mr B: 'I am concerned about the exposure of our consolidated statement of financial position and investor ratios to sterling/euro exchange rate movements. How will we be able to explain large fluctuations to our shareholders? If we were to raise long-term euro borrowings, wouldn't this avoid exchange rate risk altogether? We would also benefit from euro interest rates which have been historically lower than sterling rates.'

Mr C: 'We know from our market research that we will be facing stiff competition in Germany from local distribution companies. This is a high-risk project with a lot of capital at stake and we should finance this new venture by XTA plc raising new equity finance to reflect this high risk.'

Assume that today is Saturday 1 October 20X5. A summary of the latest forecast consolidated statement of financial position for the XTA Group at 31 December 20X5 is given below. It has been prepared BEFORE taking into account the proposed German investment:

	£m
Assets	
Total assets	450
Equity and liabilities	
Equity	250
Long-term borrowings (there were no other non-current liabilities)	150
Current liabilities	50
Total equity and liabilities	450

The proposed investment in Germany is scheduled for the final quarter of 20X5 at a cost of £60 million for the distribution centres and £20 million for the fleet of trucks when translated from euros at today's exchange rate of £/€1.50 (that is, £1 = €1.50). The directors believe that the euro could weaken against sterling to £/€2.00 (that is, £1 = €2.00) by 31 December 20X5, but it can be assumed that this will not occur until after the investment has been made. The subsidiary's statement of financial position at 31 December 20X5 will only contain the new distribution centres and fleet of trucks matched by an equal equity investment by XTA plc and will only become operationally active from 1 January 20X6.

Required

(a)   Write a memorandum to the Board of XTA plc to explain the advantages and disadvantages of using each of the following sources of finance:

(i)   A rights issue versus a placing (assuming UK equity finance is chosen to fund the new German subsidiary)

(ii)   A euro bank loan versus a euro-denominated eurobond (assuming euro borrowings are chosen)

(8 marks)

(b) Evaluate EACH of the alternative proposals of Messrs A, B and C for financing the new German subsidiary and recommend the most appropriate form of financing for the group. Support your discussion of each proposal with:

(i) A summary forecast consolidated statement of financial position for the XTA group at 31 December 20X5 incorporating the new investment; and

(ii) Calculations of gearing using book values using year end exchange rates of both £/€1.50 and £/€2.00.

(17 marks)

(Total = 25 marks)

18 DCD (11/11)   45 mins

DCD is manufacturer of heavy construction equipment. It has manufacturing facilities around the world.

DCD's Ordinary Share Capital has a nominal value of $70 million ($0.50 shares) and the current market price per share is $6.00. The market price per share three months ago was $5.40.

DCD has experienced rapid growth in demand in recent years and expects revenues to continue to grow in future years. The current manufacturing facilites are already operating close to full capacity.

Proposed new manufacturing facility

The Board is planning to build a new manufacturing facility and has already identified a suitable site and prepared a schedule of forecast cash flows arising from the project. It is expected that the proposed new facility would be fully operational within a year of the initial investment and that the project would generate a rate of return on funds invesed of 20%. This is greater than the return on existing funds of 15% due to the greater efficiency of the new manufacturing facility.

Rights issue

The Board has decided to use a rights issue to finance the initial investment of $250 million. The rights issue will be underwritten. The exact costs of underwriting are not known but average underwriting costs in the market are estimated to be 2% of the monies raised. The underwriting costs will be paid out of DCD's existing funds rather than out of the funds raised in the rights issue.

A board meeting has been called to agree the terms of the rights issue. A decision has to be made as to whether the new shares will be issued at a discount of the eighter 25% or 40% on current market price.

• Director A is concerned that a 40% discount will result in share price which would adversely affect the value of shareholder wealth. He is supporting the lower discount of 25% as he feels that the impact would be redunced.

• Director B is recommending a higher discount of 40% as she believes this will improve take up of the rights issue.

• Director C is concerned about the impact of a rights issue on future dividend policy. DCD has traditionally operated a stable dividend policy and she is questioning whether this can be sustained following the proposed rights issue.

Next month after the Board meeting, a press statement will be released in which the project and related rights issue will be made public.

Required

(a) Calculate:

(i) The terms of the rights issue (to the nearest whole number of shares) at a discount of both 25% and 40%.
(3 marks)

(ii) The yield adjusted theoretical ex-rights price per share at a rights discount of both 25% and 40%.
(4 marks)

(b) Demonstrate the likely impact of the proposed project together with the related rights issue on the wealth of a shareholder with 100 ordinary shares. Your answer should consider a rights discounts of both 25% and 40%.
(4 marks)

(c)   Recommend an appropriate, if any, for the rights issue. Your answer should address the concerns raised by each of the Directors A, B and C.

(8 marks)

(d)   Advise the Directors of DCD on factors that are likely to affect the company's share price both before and after next month's planned press statement.

(6 marks)

(Total = 25 marks)

19 EFG (FS, 5/06)   45 mins

EFG is a South American entity specialising in providing information systems solutions to large corporates. It is going through a period of rapid expansion and requires additional funds to finance the long-term working capital needs of the business.

EFG has issued one million $1 ordinary shares, which are listed on the local stock market at a current market price of $15, with typical increases of 10% per annum expected in the next five year period. Dividend payout is kept constant at a level of 10% of post-tax profits. EFG also has $10 million of bank borrowings.

It is estimated that a further $3 million is required to satisfy the funding requirements of the business for the next five-year period beginning 1 July 20X6. Two major institutional shareholders have indicated that they are not prepared to invest further in EFG at the present time and so a rights issue is unlikely to succeed. The directors are therefore considering various forms of debt finance. Three alternative structures are under discussion as shown below:

*   Five-year unsecured bank loan at a fixed interest rate of 7% per annum;
*   Five-year unsecured bond with a coupon of 5% per annum, redeemable at par and issued at a 6% discount to par;
*   A convertible bond, issued at par, with an annual coupon of 45% and a conversion option in five years' time of five shares for each $100 nominal of debt.

There have been lengthy boardroom discussions on the relative merits of each instrument and you, as Finance Director, have been asked to address the following queries:

Sr. A: 'The bank loan would seem to be more expensive than the unsecured bond. Is this actually the case?'

Sr. B: 'Surely the convertible bond would be the cheapest form of borrowing with such a low interest rate?'

Sr. C: 'If we want to increase our equity base, why use a convertible bond, rather than a straight equity issue?'

Required

(a)   Write a response to Sr. A, Sr. B and Sr. C, directors of EFG, discussing the issues raised and advising on the most appropriate financing instrument for EFG. In your answer, include calculations of:

*   Expected conversion value of the convertible bond in five years' time;
*   Yield to maturity (redemption yield) of the five-year unsecured bond.

Ignore tax.

(18 marks)
(including up to 8 marks for calculations)

(b)   Advise a prospective investor in the five-year unsecured bond issued by EFG on what information he should expect to be provided with and what further analysis he should undertake in order to assess the creditworthiness of the proposed investment.

(7 marks)

(Total = 25 marks)

20 DDD   45 mins

DDD, a listed company, runs a chain of 26 garden centres which sell plants, gardening implements and a range of other gardening products. It is listed on an international stock exchange and it has an accounting year end of 30 June.

The company plans to open three new garden SuperCentres in 20X4. Unlike existing stores, they will also sell garden furniture.

Each of the three new stores will cost £6 million to build and each will carry £3.5 million of stocks. The following budgeted summary statement of financial position at 30 June 20X3 (which *excludes* the three new SuperCentres) was presented at a meeting of the board:

	£m
Land and buildings	26
Other non-current assets	13
Inventory	16
Receivables	1
Cash	1
	57
Share capital (£1 shares)	10
Accumulated profits	20
Loans	24
Trade creditors	3
	57

The statement of financial position valuation for land and buildings reflects their current market values.

Chief Executive

'I believe that we should raise new equity to finance the new SuperCentres. Our share price has risen from £4 a year ago to £6 today. I believe that we should take advantage of this high share price and issue shares now in case the share price falls again. Moreover, our dividend yield is only 3% – this is cheap finance at low risk.'

Non-Executive Director

'I am not keen on raising new external finance. We should use our retained profits of £20 million to finance most of the new land, buildings and inventory. To finance the remaining amount, we should sell the least profitable of our existing garden centres. This approach will save all the issue costs and all the uncertainty involved in raising new external finance.'

Finance Director

'I am in favour of raising new debt to finance the expansion. The return on these new SuperCentres is bound to be greater than the cost of debt, so a profit is assured, and thus the risk is minimal.'

There are two alternatives:

Alternative 1: Issue £30 million of 7% corporate bonds. These would be issued on 1 July 20X3 at a 5% discount and would be repayable on 30 June 20X8 at their nominal value. Interest would be payable annually in arrears on 30 June each year.

Alternative 2: Raise a bank loan of £28.5 million on 1 July 20X3. The interest rate would be 5% per annum for the first 3 years and 10% per annum for the following 3 years. The loan would be repayable on 30 June 20X9.

Interest would be payable annually in arrears on 30 June each year. Assume that interest paid can be relieved for tax at a rate of 30%. Assume tax is payable at the end of the year in which the taxable profits arise and sufficient profits exist to set off all interest payments.

Required

(a)   Calculate the after-tax cost of debt for each of the two alternatives.

Briefly discuss any further factors that would need to be considered, other than the cost of debt, before choosing between these two alternatives.   **(11 marks)**

(b)   Write a memorandum to the board, as a member of DDD's treasury department, which discusses the financing options for expansion put forward at the board meeting. In so doing, evaluate the comments of the Directors.   **(14 marks)**

(Total = 25 marks)

---

21   DEF (FS, 11/07)   45 mins

DEF is a telecommunications entity. It provides a variety of services to the major tele-communications operators in Europe and parts of Asia. It has been trading for 10 years and has shown spectacular growth in revenue and profits over the 10-year period, although there has been some volatility year to year. Revenue for the current year is likely to be €550 million and earnings €50 million. These figures make it one of the largest private operators, but it is still much smaller than most of its customers and its nearest publicly-listed direct rival.

DEF has been financed by equity provided by the original shareholders, many of whom still work in the entity, and by loans from banks. There are 50,000 shares currently in issue. The current debt : equity ratio is 80 : 20, using book values. No shares have changed hands over the past 10 years, so there has been no serious attempt to place a value on them. New investments are evaluated using a cost of capital of 10%, which is the average for the industry and also judged by DEF's bankers and other advisors to reflect the average business risk of DEF's operations. The average P/E for the industry is currently 14.

DEF's bankers are now suggesting an initial public offering (IPO) of DEF's shares as most European stock markets have shown strong sustained growth over the past three or four years.

The shareholders are in agreement with the suggestion in principle but have asked you, DEF's Financial Manager, to advise them.

Required

(a)   Discuss the advantages, disadvantages and challenges of pursuing an IPO in DEF's circumstances at the present time. Conclude with a recommendation.

Calculations are not the main purpose of this question, but credit is available for calculating some simple figures to support your discussion.   **(9 marks)**

(b)   Advise on the roles that would be played by the following organisations in DEF's IPO:

- Investment bank
- Stockbroker
- Potential institutional investors in the issue
- DEF's Treasury Department

(9 marks)

(c)   The following methods of issuing shares are being suggested:

- Private placing
- Public offer for sale by either fixed price or tender

Discuss the features, advantages and disadvantages of these methods and conclude with a recommendation of the preferred method of issue for DEF.   **(7 marks)**

A report format is **not** required for this question.   **(Total = 25 marks)**

22 Gregory (FS, 11/09)   45 mins

Gregory, a listed entity based in Europe, provides private medical care through private hospitals. Additional funds are required to fund the construction of a new medical support unit. This was already public knowledge in August 20X9

A rights issue was announced in a press statement on 1 September 20X9. Ordinary shares are to be issued at a discount of 20% on market price and the issue is expected to raise a total sum of €29.3million.

Gregory already has 40million €1 ordinary shares in issue. The share price on 1 September 20X9 before the press statement was released was 458 cents.

Mr X holds 200,000 €1 ordinary shares in Gregory and is wondering whether or not to take up the rights being offered.

Required

(a)   (i)   Calculate the number of ordinary shares to be issued under the rights issue.   **(2 marks)**

       (ii)   Calculate the theoretical ex-rights price.   **(3 marks)**

       (iii)   Calculate the expected trading price for the rights.   **(2 marks)**

       (iv)   Evaluate and discuss the impact of the rights issue on the personal wealth of shareholder Mr X for each of the following three alternative responses to the rights offer:

            •   does not take up the rights
            •   takes up the rights
            •   sells just enough rights to provide the funds needed to purchase the remaining rights
                                                            (10 marks)

George

George, a competitor of Gregory, is also based in Europe and operates in the medical services industry. It has been highly successful in recent years and has accumulated a large amount of surplus cash representing 10% of total equity value. It now wishes to return this surplus cash to shareholders. Gearing is defined as net debt to net debt plus equity where net debt is debt after deduction of surplus cash.

Current market values: € million
       Debt   37
       Surplus cash   7
       Equity   70

The entity is considering the best method to achieve the return of surplus cash to the shareholders, preferably also reducing the cost of capital but not changing the balance of share ownership.

The two main methods being considered are:

     (i)   share repurchase
     (ii)   one-off special dividend

Required

(b)   Compare and contrast the advantages to George of each of the two proposed methods of returning surplus cash to shareholders and recommend which of these methods George should use.   **(8 marks)**

                                                                      (Total = 25 marks)

23 RED (3/11)

45 mins

RED is a family run and owned company based in the United Kingdom which designs and manufactures state-of-the-art vacuum cleaners. It has grown steadily during the eight years since it was founded and the directors consider that the company is now of a suitable size to be listed on the Alternative Investment Market (AIM), which is a market for the shares of smaller companies.

The company is currently in the early stages of development of a new product that it is hoped will be highly successful and will significantly increase the company's share of the vacuum cleaner market. Information about the product's development will be made public at various stages during 20X1. Information may also become public knowledge through other means as more people and organisations become involved in the testing and implementation of production of the new product.

Significant amounts of new funding will be required to finance the final development, production and launch of this product but the existing shareholders are now not able to provide this. Therefore the directors of RED are planning to raise the necessary funds by means of a bond issue followed by an IPO (initial public offering). The bond issue is planned for the middle of 20X1 and the IPO towards the end of the year.

Required:

(a) Compare and contrast the features of a private placing and a public issue for the bonds and advise the directors of RED which method would be most appropriate. **(12 marks)**

(b) (i) Describe the three forms of the efficient market hypothesis and state which form is most likely to apply in practice. **(4 marks)**

(ii) Advise the directors of RED on what steps can be taken to improve the chances of a successful IPO issue and a high share price after the issue. Your answer should include reference to the efficient market hypothesis. **(9 marks)**

(Total = 25 marks)

24 AB (Pilot paper)

45 mins

It is currently November 20X9.

AB is a large retailing organisation with revenue in the last financial year exceeding €1 billion. Its head office is in a country in the euro zone and its shares are listed on a major European stock exchange. Over the last few years AB has opened several new stores in a number of European capital cities, not all of them in the euro zone. AB is planning to allow all of its stores to accept the world's major currencies as cash payment for its goods and this will require a major upgrade of its points of sale (POS) system to handle multiple currencies and increased volumes of transactions AB has already carried out a replacement investment appraisal exercise and has evaluated appropriate systems. It is now in the process of placing an order with a large information technology entity for the supply, installation and maintenance of a new POS system. The acquisition of the system will include the provision of hardware and software. Routine servicing and software upgrading will be arranged separately and does not affect the investment appraisal decision.

AB is considering the following alternative methods of acquiring and financing the new POS system:

Alternative I

• Pay the whole capital cost of €25 million on 1 January 20Y0, funded by bank borrowings. This cost includes the initial installation of the POS system.

• The system will have no resale value outside AB

Alternative 2

• Enter into a finance lease with the system supplier. AB will pay a fixed amount of €7.0 million each year in advance, commencing 1 January 20Y0, for four years.

• At the end of four years, ownership of the system will pass to AB without further payment.

Other information

- AB can borrow for a period of four years at a pre-tax fixed interest rate of 7% a year. The entity's cost of equity is currently 12%.

- AB is liable to corporate tax at a marginal rate of 30% which is settled at the end of the year in which it arises..

- AB accounts for depreciation on a straight-line basis at the end of each year

- Under Alternative 1, tax depreciation allowances on the full capital cost are available in equal instalments over the first four years of operation.

- Under Alternative 2, both the accounting depreciation and the interest element of the finance lease payments are tax deductible.

- Once a decision on the payment method has been made and the new system is installed, AB will commission a post completion audit (PCA).

Required

(a) (i) Calculate which payment method is expected to be cheaper for AB and recommend which should be chosen based solely on the present value of the two alternatives as at 1 January 20Y0.

(10 marks)

(ii) Explain the reasons for your choice of discount factor in the present value calculations.

(3 marks)

(iii) Discuss other factors that AB should consider before deciding on the method of financing the acquisition of the system.

(3 marks)

(b) Advise the Directors of AB on the following:

(i) The main purpose and content of a post completion audit (PCA)

(ii) The limitations of a PCA to AB in the context of the POS system

(9 marks)

(Total = 25 marks)

25 RZ (FS, Pilot paper)   45 mins

RZ is a privately-owned textile manufacturer based in the UK with sales revenue in the last financial year of £68 million and earnings of £4.5 million. The directors of the company have been evaluating a cost saving project, which will require purchasing new machinery from the USA at a capital cost of $1.5 million. The directors expect the new machinery to have a life of at least 5 years and to provide cost savings (including capital allowances) of £240,000 after tax each year. Cash flows beyond 5 years are ignored by RZ in all its investment decisions. The discount rate that the company applies to investment decisions of this nature is its post-tax real cost of capital of 9% per annum.

RZ at present has no debt in its capital structure. The directors, who are the major shareholders, would be prepared to finance the purchase of the new machinery via a rights issue but believe an all-equity capital structure fails to take advantage of the tax benefits of debt. They therefore propose to finance with one of the following methods:

(i) Undated debt, raised in the UK and secured on the company's assets. The current pre-tax rate of interest required by the market on corporate debt of this risk is 7% per annum. Interest payments would be made at the end of each year.

(ii) A finance lease raised in the USA repayable over 5 years. The terms would be 5 annual payments of US$325,000 payable at the *beginning* of each year. The machinery could be bought by RZ from the finance company at the end of the five year lease contract for a nominal amount of $1. Assume the whole amount of each annual payment is tax deductible.

(iii) An operating lease. No cost details are available at present.

Other information

- The company's marginal tax rate is 30%. Tax is payable in the year in which the liability arises.
- Capital allowances are available at 25% reducing balance
- If bought outright, the machinery is estimated to have a residual value in real cash flow terms, at the end of five years, of 10% of the original purchase price.
- The spot rate is £/US$1.58 (that is, £1 = US$1.58).
- Interest rates in the USA and UK are currently 2.5% and 3.5% respectively.

Required

(a)   Discuss the advisability of the investment and the advantages and disadvantages of financing with either (i) undated debt, (ii) a finance lease or (iii) an operating lease compared with new equity raised via a rights issue and comment on whether the choice of method of finance should affect the investment decision.

Provide appropriate and relevant calculations and assumptions to support your discussion.   **(18 marks)**

(b)   Discuss the benefits and potential problems of financing assets in the same currency as their purchase.

(7 marks)

(Total = 25 marks)

26 FLG (FS, 5/05)   45 mins

FLG Inc is an airline operator based in the United States, operating a wide network of both domestic and international flights. It has recently obtained a new licence to operate direct flights to a new European destination which will necessitate the acquisition of four identical secondhand aeroplanes at a total cost of $100 million. The aeroplanes are expected to be in service for five years and each one is expected to have a residual value of $12.5 million at the end of the five years. However, the residual value is highly dependent on the state of the airline industry at the end of the five-year period and there is a risk that the residual value could be much lower if there is a general reduction in air travel at that time.

The company has been offered a lease contract with total lease payments of $15 million per annum for five years, payable in advance, with all maintenance costs being borne by the lessee.

Alternatively, the aeroplanes could be purchased outright and the bank has offered the company a five-year loan with variable interest payments payable semi-annually six months in arrears at a margin of 1% per annum above a reference six-month $ inter-bank rate. The reference six-month $ inter-bank rate is forecast to be at a flat rate of 2.4% for each six-month period, for the duration of the loan.

The company pays tax at 30% and expects to make taxable profits in excess of the lease payments, interest charges and tax depreciation allowances arising over the next five years. Tax depreciation on the purchase of the aeroplanes can be claimed at a rate of 20% at the end of each financial year on a written-down value basis, with a delay of one year between the tax depreciation allowance arising and the deduction from tax paid.

Required

(a)   Calculate:

(i)   The compound annualised post-tax cost of debt

(ii)   The NPV of the lease versus purchase decision at discount rates of both 4% and 5%

(iii) The breakeven post-tax cost of debt at which FLG Inc is indifferent between leasing and purchasing the aeroplanes   **(10 marks)**

(b)   Recommend, with reasons, whether FLG Inc should purchase with a loan or lease the aeroplanes.

Your answer should include appropriate calculations of the sensitivity of the lease versus purchase decision to changes in EACH of the following:

(i)   The reference $ inter-bank rate for the duration of the loan
(ii)   The residual value of the aeroplanes   **(15 marks)**

(Total = 25 marks)

27 LEE (FS, 5/07)   45 mins

LEE is a manufacturing entity located in Newland, a country with the dollar ($) as its currency. LOR is a leasing entity that is also located in Newland.

LEE plans to replace a key piece of machinery and is initially considering the following two approaches:

- Alternative 1 – purchase the machinery, financed by borrowing for a five-year term
- Alternative 2 – lease the machinery from LOR on a five-year operating lease

The machinery and maintenance costs

The machinery has a useful life of approximately 10 years, but LEE is aware that the industry is facing a period of intense competition and the machinery may not be needed in five years' time. It would cost LEE $5,000 to buy the machinery, but LOR has greater purchasing power and could acquire the machinery for $4,000. Maintenance costs are estimated to be $60 in each of years 1 to 3 and $100 in each of years 4 and 5, arising at the *end* of the year.

Alternative 1 – purchase financed by borrowing for a five year term

$ interbank borrowing rates in Newland are currently 5.5% per annum. LEE can borrow at interbank rates plus a margin of 1.7% and expects $ interbank rates to remain constant over the five year period. It has estimated that the machinery could be sold for $2,000 at the end of five years.

Alternative 2 – five year operating lease

Under the operating lease, LOR would be responsible for maintenance costs and would charge LEE lease rentals of $850 annually *in advance* for five years. LOR knows that LEE is keen to lease rather than buy the machine and wants to take advantage of this position by increasing the rentals on the operating lease. However, it does not want to lose LEE's custom and requires advice on how high a lease rental LEE would be likely to accept.

Tax regulations

Newland's tax rules for operating leases give the lessor tax depreciation allowances on the asset and give the lessee full tax relief on the lease payments. Tax depreciation allowances are available to the purchaser of a business asset at 25% per annum on a reducing balance basis. The business tax rate is 30% and tax should be assumed to arise at the end of each year and be paid one year later. Maintenance costs are not an allowable expense.

Alternative 3 – late proposal by production manager

During the evaluation process for Alternatives 1 and 2, the production manager suggested that another lease structure should also be considered, to be referred to as 'Alternative 3'. No figures are available at present to enable a numerical evaluation to be carried out for Alternative 3. The basic structure would be a five-year lease with the option to renew at the end of the five-year term for an additional five-year term at negligible rental. LEE would be responsible for maintenance costs.

Required

(a)   (i)   Use discounted cash flow analysis to evaluate and compare the cost to LEE of each of
            Alternatives 1 and 2.   **(9 marks)**

      (ii) Advise LOR on the highest lease rentals that LEE would be likely to accept under Alternative 2.
                                                                                         (4 marks)

(b)   Discuss both the financial and non-financial factors that might affect LEE's choice between Alternatives 1,
      2 and 3. No further calculations are required in part (b).   **(12 marks)**

                                                                                (Total = 25 marks)

28 BEN (FS, 5/08)

It is currently May 20X8.

BEN is a large, listed entity based in a country in the eurozone. Its principal activity is the manufacture and distribution of electrical consumer goods. Manufacturing operations are located in the home country but goods are sold to wholesalers worldwide, priced in the customer's local currency. The group has experienced rapid growth in recent years and many of its IS/IT systems need upgrading to handle large volumes and increased complexity.

Group treasury is centralised at the head office and its key responsibilities include arranging sufficient long-term and short-term liquidity resources for the group and hedging foreign exchange exposures.

One of the first projects is a replacement treasury management system (TMS) to provide an integrated IS/IT system. The new integrated TMS will record all treasury transactions and provide information for the management and control of the treasury operations. It replaces the current system which consists of a series of spreadsheets for each part of the treasury operations.

BEN is considering the following choice of payment methods for the new integrated TMS.

Method 1

- Pay the whole capital cost of €800,000 on 1 July 20X8, funded by bank borrowings.
- Pay on-going consultation and maintenance costs annually in arrears; these costs will depend on the actual time spent supporting the system each year but are expected to be in the order of €60,000 in the first year and, on average, to increase by 5% a year due to inflation.
- The system is expected to have no resale value after five years although it could still be usable within the entity.

Method 2

- Enter into an operating lease with the supplier paying a fixed amount of €250,000 a year in advance commencing 1 July 20X8, for five years. This fee will include consultation and maintenance.
- At the end of five years there is an option to continue the lease agreement for a further three years, paying for maintenance on a time and materials basis. This has not been costed.

Other information

- BEN can borrow for a period of five years at a gross fixed interest rate of 8% a year.
- The entity is liable to tax at a marginal rate of 25%, payable 12 months after the end of the year in which the liability arises (that is, a time lag of one year). This rate is not expected to change.
- In **Method 1**, tax depreciation on the capital cost is available in equal instalments over the first five years of operation.

Required

(a) Calculate and recommend which payment method is expected to be cheaper for BEN in NPV terms.

(8 marks)

(b) Evaluate the benefits that might result from the introduction of the new TMS. Include in your evaluation some reference to the control factors that need to be considered during the implementation stage.

(8 marks)

(c) Advise the Directors of BEN on the following

- The main purpose of a post-completion audit (PCA)
- What should be covered in a PCA of the TMS project
- The importance and limitations of a PCA to BEN in the context of the TMS project **(9 marks)**

(Total = 25 marks)

29 EM (9/10)   45 mins

It is currently September 20X0.

EM is a manufacturer of high value electronic equipment based in Country A in Asia. It has 285million shares in issue, which are, today, trading at A$15.65. EM is currently all-equity financed. It is proposing to invest in equipment for a new production line that will be introduced in 20X1. The cost of the new equipment is A$360million and payment is due on 01 January 20X1. The equipment is expected to have a useful life of four years and have negligible value at the end of the four years.

The investment appraisal has shown a positive NPV using the company's weighted average cost of capital.

EM is considering three alternative methods of financing the purchase of the equipment.

Alternative1

Purchase outright and fund with bank borrowings at an annual cost of 5.0% (after-tax). Interest payments would be made at the end of each year. Tax depreciation allowances would be available to EM on the cost of the equipment at a rate of 100% in the first year.

Alternative 2

Take out a finance lease with a local finance house. The lease would have a four year term and ownership of the equipment would pass to EM at the end of the lease period without additional payment. Lease rentals would be A$105million per annum, payable at the end of each year. Tax relief would be available on the accounting depreciation plus the interest implicit in the lease rentals.

Alternative 3

Purchase outright and undertake a rights issue at a discount of 15% on today's share price.

Other relevant information

EM pays corporate tax at a marginal rate of 20% and tax is payable one year in arrears.

Required

Assume you work in the Treasury Department of EM.

(a)   Describe the role of the Treasury Department in the management of funding for major investments, making specific reference to the three alternative financing methods under consideration.

(7 marks)

(b)   Advise the Finance Director on the appropriateness of each of the THREE proposed alternative methods of finance and recommend which, if any, should be chosen.

In your answer, include a calculation of whether the outright purchase funded by bank borrowings or the finance lease is expected to be the cheaper source of debt funding.

(18 marks)

(Total = 25 marks)

30 AB (5/11)   45 mins

It is currently May 20X1.

AB is a spin-off company from a major South American university. AB works with large manufacturing companies to find effective ways to reduce carbon emissions. Revenue was $300 million in the year ended 30 June 20X0 and the company is expected to earn its first profit in the year ending 30 June 20X1. Demand for its services is very high in a market which is developing very rapidly. A proposal to invest in specialist equipment has been appraised and shows a positive NPV using the company's weighted average cost of capital.

The specialist equipment will cost $50 million and is estimated to have a useful economic life of five years with no residual value. The equipment will need to be installed on 1 July 20X1.

Three alternative methods of financing the equipment are being considered, each of which would commence on 1 July 20X1. These are as follows:

Alternative 1

- Buy the equipment outright on 1 July 20X1, funded by a five year bank borrowing that has an after-tax cost of debt of 7% per annum.

Alternative 2

- Enter into a finance lease. AB would make a payment of $14.0 million in advance and then five further annual payments of $9.0 million on 1 July each year, starting in 20X2. The interest rate implicit in the finance lease has been calculated to be approximately 8.4% and the implied interest has been calculated as follows:

Year to	30 June 20X2	30 June 20X3	30 June 20X4	30 June 20X5	30 June 20X6
Implied interest at 8.4% ($ million)	3.0	2.5	2.0	1.4	0.7

- Tax relief is available on both the accounting depreciation and the interest element of the finance lease payments.

Alternative 3

- Enter into a lease that is classified as an operating lease for tax purposes. AB would make payments of $16.5 million annually in arrears for three years, with the first payment on 1 July 20X2. It is possible that on termination of the lease a new operating lease would be available for two further years for more advanced equipment at an estimated cost of $15.0 million per annum payable in arrears.

Other information

- AB's accounting policy is to depreciate specialist equipment on a straight line basis over its economic useful life.

- Corporate income tax is charged at 25% on taxable profits and is paid at the end of the year in which the taxable profit arises.

- A tax depreciation allowance is available on a straight line basis over the economic useful life of an asset.

- Due to the nature of the specialist equipment maintenance costs are expected to be fairly high at $2 million a year, payable at the end of each year. These will be the responsibility of AB under the terms of the finance lease and with an outright purchase. However, maintenance costs will be the responsibility of the lessor under the terms of the operating lease.

Required:

(a) Calculate the present value, as at 1 July 20X1, of the cash-flows associated with each of the three alternative financing methods under consideration. **(13 marks)**

(b) Recommend, with reasons, which of the three alternative financing methods should be chosen. **(8 marks)**

(c) Discuss how an immediate change in government policy to improve tax depreciation allowances on equipment used in low carbon emission technology would impact on the decision. No further calculations are required. **(4 marks)**

(Total = 25 marks)

31 PIC (5/10)   45 mins

PIC is a furniture retailing company in a developed country in Asia. It has 15 stores spread around the country. Each store has some freedom to adapt its buying patterns to local market conditions although around 80% of its products must be obtained through central purchasing. Sales receipts are paid to head office on a monthly basis. PIC offers 60-day credit to a few key high-profile and agency customers who account for a substantial proportion of sales by value. However, the majority of customers pay immediately by cash.

The treasurer has observed that working capital levels fluctuate quite substantially from month to month. Based on forecast revenue for next year, the average days and minimum and maximum working capital levels for next year are likely to be as follows:

	Average Days	Minimum A$million	Maximum A$million
Inventories	105	17.26	29.59
Accounts Receivable	15	1.64	3.29
Accounts Payable	60	7.40	14.79

At present PIC follows an aggressive policy for financing net current assets. All fluctuating net current assets and 20% of permanent net current assets are funded by overdraft. PIC currently has an overdraft facility of up to A$20million, secured as a floating charge on the entity's current assets. Interest is charged at 7% (pre-tax) on daily balances. Over the past year PIC has used its maximum overdraft facility. The treasurer thinks this is too risky a policy in present economic conditions and is proposing a more conservative policy where 100% of permanent net current assets and 20% of fluctuating net current assets are financed by medium or long term finance. To achieve this, PIC is proposing to issue a bond, redeemable at par in 5 years' time, with an annual coupon of 8%. Interest would be paid annually at the end of each year. Other similar corporate bonds have a yield to maturity of 9%.

PIC's shares are listed on a secondary market. The market value of the shares is currently A$350 million and its cost of equity is 10%. PIC also has long term debt in issue with a market value of A$100 million at an average pre-tax cost of 8.125%. PIC pays corporate tax at 20%.

Required

(a)

(i) Calculate the short-term and long-term (permanent) financing requirements of PIC under the aggressive policy for financing net current assets that is currently being used and also under the proposed new conservative policy. **(5 marks)**

(ii) Calculate the implied issue price per A$100 nominal of the bond being considered by the treasurer. **(3 marks)**

(iii) Calculate the weighted average cost of capital (WACC) of PIC at present and discuss, briefly, the likely effect on WACC if PIC changes its policy for financing net current assets. **(4 marks)**

(b)

(i) Evaluate PIC's proposal to change from an aggressive to a conservative policy for financing net current assets. **(9 marks)**

(ii) Advise PIC, briefly, on alternative approaches to financing net current assets that it should consider. **(4 marks)**

(Total = 25 marks)

A report format is not required for this question.

32 CIP (5/10)　　　　　　　　　　　　　　　　　　45 mins

CIP is a family-controlled company. The family owns 80% of the shares. The remaining 20% is owned by a number of non-family shareholders, none of whom owns more than 1% of the shares in issue. The Board of Directors has convened a special Board meeting to review two investment opportunities and, at the request of the new Finance Director, decide on an appropriate discount rate, or rates, to use in the evaluation of these investments. Each of the two investments being considered is in a non-listed company and will be financed 60% by equity and 40% by debt.

In the past, CIP has used an estimated post-tax weighted average cost of capital of 12% to calculate the net present value (NPV) of all investments. The Managing Director thinks this rate should continue to be used, adjusted if necessary by plus or minus 1% or 2% to reflect greater or lesser risk than the "average" investment.

The Finance Director disagrees and suggests using the capital asset pricing model (CAPM) to determine a discount rate that reflects the systematic risk of each of the proposed investments based on proxy companies that operate in similar businesses. The Finance Director has obtained the betas and debt ratios of two listed companies (Company A and Company B) that could be used as proxies. These are:

	Equity Beta	Debt Beta	Debt ratio (debt: equity)
Company A (proxy for Investment 1)	1.3	0.3	1:3
Company B (proxy for Investment 2)	0.9	0	1:6

Other information:

- The expected annual post-tax return on the market is 8% and the risk-free rate is 3%.

- Assume the debt that CIP raises to finance the investments is risk-free.

- All three companies (CIP, Company A and Company B) pay corporate tax at 25%.

- CIP has one financial objective, which is to increase earnings each year to enable its dividend payment to increase by 4% per annum.

The Managing Director and the other Board members are confused about the terminology being used in the CAPM calculation and do not understand why they are being asked to consider a different method of calculating discount rates for use in evaluating the proposed investments.

Required

(a) Discuss the meaning of the terms "systematic" and "unsystematic" risk and their relationship to a company's equity beta. Include in your answer an appropriate diagram to demonstrate the difference between the two types of risk. **(6 marks)**

(b) Using the CAPM and the information given in the scenario about CIP and Companies A and B, calculate for each of CIP's proposed investments:

  - An asset beta.
  - An appropriate discount rate to be used in the evaluation of the investment. **(6 marks)**

(c) Evaluate the benefits and limitations of using each of the following in CIP's appraisal of the two investments:

  - CIP's WACC.
  - An adjusted WACC as suggested by the Managing Director.
  - CAPM-derived rates that use proxy (or surrogate) companies' betas. **(6 marks)**

(d) Discuss, briefly, how an asset beta differs from an equity beta and why the former is more appropriate to CIP's investment decision. Include in your discussion some reference to how the use of the CAPM can assist CIP to achieve its financial objective. **(7 marks)**

(Total = 25 marks)

33 CBA (3/12)   45 mins

Assume today is 1 April 20X2.

CBA is a manufacturing company, operating in the United Kingdom (UK), whose shares are listed on the main UK stock exchange. The board needs to raise GBP 250 million to fund a number of planned new investments and is considering issuing either a convertible bond or additional shares.

CBA currently has 280 million GBP 1 ordinary shares in issue and today's share price is GBP 3.60 per share. It also has GBP 195 million (nominal) of undated 6% preference shares. The preference shares each have a nominal value of GBP 1 and are currently quoted at GBP 1.05 per share. CBA currently has no debt.

Financial position prior to new investment or new financing

Earnings per share for the last financial year ended 31 March 20X2 are 45 pence per share and the dividend pay-out ratio has been maintained as close as possible to 50% of earnings. Assume that the dividend for the year ended 31 March 20X2 has just been paid and was based on 50% of estimated earnings for the year.

The proposed convertible bond

The convertible bond would be issued at a 7% discount to its nominal value and carry a coupon rate of 3% per annum. The bond would be convertible into ordinary shares in 4 years' time at the ratio of 23 ordinary shares per GBP 100 nominal of the bond.

Forecast position after issuing the convertible bond and making the new investments

Assuming the new investments are undertaken and financed by convertible debt, CBA expects its earnings to grow by 5% per annum for the foreseeable future and to maintain its dividend pay-out ratio at 50%. The share price is expected to rise by 6% per year over the next four year period.

Other information

- CBA pays corporate income tax at a rate of 30% on taxable profits and tax is payable at the end of the year in which the taxable profit arises.

- CBA has sufficient taxable profits to benefit from any tax relief available.

Required

(a)   Calculate the following values assuming that the proposed convertible bond is issued on 1 April 20X2:

   (i)   The forecast conversion value for the convertible bond in four years' time.   **(2 marks)**

   (ii)   The post-tax cost of debt for the convertible bond based on its yield over the next four years up to and including conversion.   **(5 marks)**

   (iii) CBA's post-tax weighted average cost of capital (WACC). For the purpose of this calculation, assume no change in the market value of the ordinary and preference shares as a result of the convertible bond issue.   **(6 marks)**

(b)   Advise on the benefits and limitations to CBA of issuing a convertible bond rather than new equity.
                                                                                          (7 marks)

(c)   Explain the role of CBA's treasury department in evaluating and implementing the convertible bond issue.
                                                                                          (5 marks)

                                                                                  (Total = 25 marks)

34   Horatio (FS, 11/09)   **45 mins**

Horatio is a manufacturing entity based in the UK. It is considering installing energy efficient equipment at its plant in the UK at a capital cost of £10 million. The new equipment is estimated to have a useful life of nine years. However, it involves the use of new technology that has largely only been tested in laboratory conditions. Therefore the introduction of this equipment carries significant risks.

The project to install this new energy efficient equipment has been evaluated using the entity's WACC but the Finance Director is concerned that this may not be the most appropriate approach in view of the high risks involved.

Three alternative sources of finance for the new equipment are being considered as follows:

Alternative 1
Irredeemable 5.5% preference shares to be issued at a price of £1.20 per £1 share.

Alternative 2
A 9-year bond with an annual coupon of 4%, issued at par and redeemable at £110 per £100 nominal.

Alternative 3
A 5-year bond denominated in US dollars, issued and redeemed at par and expected to be quoted at a low dollar yield to maturity of 2.8% on the issue date. The US dollar is expected to strengthen against the British pound by 2.5% per annum.

Assume business tax of 35% is payable one year after the year in which it is incurred.

Required

(a) (i) Calculate the cost of debt for each of the THREE alternative sources of finance listed above.

Accurate calculations are required for Alternatives 1 and 2 but only an estimate of the equivalent yield in British pounds is required for Alternative 3.   **(10 marks)**

(ii) Discuss the advantages and disadvantages of each alternative source of finance in the context of Horatio and recommend which should be selected.   **(7 marks)**

(b) For TWO of the following THREE methods, explain how each could be used to incorporate risk in NPV calculations and advise to what extent each would be useful to Horatio when evaluating the proposed project:

- decision trees
- risk-adjusted discount rate
- certainty equivalents

(8 marks)

(Total = 25 marks)

35 WZ (FS, 11/05)   45 mins

WZ is a manufacturer of specialist components for the motor trade. It is based in Zafran, a country in the Far East. The entity's capital structure is as follows:

(i) 5 million ordinary shares of Z$1 each, currently quoted at Z$12.5 per share.

(ii) 10 million preference shares of Z$1 each, currently quoted at Z$0.80 per share, paying a dividend of 7% per annum.

(iii) Z$20 million, 8% undated debt, secured on the entity's non-current assets. This debt is currently trading at Z$90 per Z$100 nominal.

To finance expansion, the directors of WZ want to raise Z$5 million for additional working capital. Cash flow from trading, before interest and tax is currently Z$15 million per annum. If the expansion goes ahead, this is expected to rise to Z$17 million. The current rate of tax, which is expected to continue for the foreseeable future, is 30%.

Assume for the purposes of simplicity:

(i) That profit after interest and tax equals cash flow

(ii) The required rate of return on equity will remain at the current rate of 12% per annum irrespective of the type of finance raised

(iii) There are no transaction costs

The directors of WZ are considering three forms of finance:

(i) Equity via a rights issue at 15% discount to current market price

(ii) 9% bonds repayable in 20X9 secured as a floating charge on the entity's current assets

(iii) Factoring the entity's trade receivables. This is likely to provide a one-off release of funds of approximately Z$5 million

Required

(a) Calculate for the current situation and financing alternatives (i) and (ii) the expected

(i) Earnings per share
(ii) Market value of equity, using the capitalisation of earnings at the cost of equity
(iii) Market value of the entity
(iv) Gearing ratios (debt to total value of the entity), using market values
(v) Weighted average cost of capital

State whatever assumptions you consider necessary.   **(12 marks)**

(b) Assume you are a Financial Manager with WZ. Advise directors of WZ of the issues to be considered before deciding on which form of finance to choose, including factoring, and make your own recommendation. **(13 marks)**

(Total = 25 marks)

36 CAP

45 mins

CAP is a listed company that owns and operates a large number of farms throughout the world. A variety of crops are grown.

Financing structure

The following is an extract from the statement of financial position of CAP at 30 September 20X2.

	£m
Ordinary shares of £1 each	200
Reserves	100
9% irredeemable £1 preference shares	50
8% loan stock 20X3	250
	600

The ordinary shares were quoted at £3 per share ex div on 30 September 20X2. The beta of CAP's equity shares is 0.8, the annual yield on treasury bills is 5%, and financial markets expect an average annual return of 15% on the market index.

The market price per preference share was £0.90 ex div on 30 September 20X2.

Loan stock interest is paid annually in arrears and is allowable for tax at a tax rate of 30%. The loan stock was priced at £100.57 ex interest per £100 nominal on 30 September 20X2. Loan stock is redeemable on 30 September 20X3.

Assume that taxation is payable at the end of the year in which taxable profits arise.

A new project

Difficult trading conditions in European farming have caused CAP to decide to convert a number of its farms in Southern Europe into camping sites with effect from the 20X3 holiday season. Providing the necessary facilities for campers will require major investment, and this will be financed by a new issue of loan stock. The returns on the new campsite business are likely to have a very low correlation with those of the existing farming business.

CAPM and arbitrage pricing theory

One of the directors has read a report that arbitrage pricing theory may be more useful for some companies than the capital asset pricing model, and wonders if this is true for CAP.

Required

(a) Using the capital asset pricing model, calculate the required rate of return on equity of CAP at 30 September 20X2. Ignore any impact from the new campsite project. Briefly explain the implications of a Beta of less than 1, such as that for CAP. **(3 marks)**

(b) Calculate the weighted average cost of capital of CAP at 30 September 20X2 (use your calculation in answer to requirement (a) above for the cost of equity). Ignore any impact from the new campsite project. **(10 marks)**

(c) Without further calculations, identify and explain the factors that may change CAP's equity beta during the year ending 30 September 20X3. **(5 marks)**

(d) Explain the limitations of the capital asset pricing model and discuss whether the arbitrage pricing model would be more suitable for CAP. **(7 marks)**

(Total = 25 marks)

37   ABC (FS, 11/07)   45 mins

ABC is an entity based in the UK with diverse international interests. Its shares and debenture stock are quoted on a major international stock exchange.

ABC is evaluating the potential for investment in the production and distribution of films, an area in which it has not previously been involved. This investment will require £600 million to purchase premises, equipment and provide working capital. An alternative approach would be to acquire a small entity in this field, but a preliminary search has revealed none suitable.

Extracts from the most recent (20X7) statement of financial position of ABC are shown below:

	£million
Assets	
Non-current assets	1,920
Current assets	1,880
Equity and liabilities	3,800
Equity	
Share capital (Shares of £1)	300
Retained earnings	1,000
	1,300
Non current liabilities	
8.4% Secured debenture repayable 20Y2	1,100
Current liabilities	1,400
	3,800
Current share price (pence)	800
Debenture price (£100)	105
Equity beta	1.2

ABC proposes to finance the £600 million investment with a combination of debt and equity as follows:

- £260 million in debt paying interest at 8% per annum, secured on the new premises and repayable in 20Y4.
- £340 million in equity via a rights issue. A discount of 15% on the current share price is likely.

A marginally positive NPV of the proposed investment has been calculated using a discount rate of 15%. This is the entity's cost of equity plus a small premium, a rate judged to reflect the risk of this venture. The Chief Executive of ABC thinks this is too marginal and is doubtful whether the investment should go ahead. However, there is some disagreement among the Directors about how this project was evaluated, in particular about the discount rate that has been used.

Director A: Suggests the entity's current WACC is more appropriate.

Director B: Suggests calculating a discount rate using data from XYZ, a quoted entity, the main business of which is film production. Relevant data for this entity is as follows:

- Shares in issue: 400 million currently quoted at 373 pence each
- Debt outstanding: £350 million variable rate bank loan
- Equity beta: 1.6

Other relevant information

- The risk-free rate is estimated at 5% per annum and the return on the market 12% per annum. These rates are not expected to change in the foreseeable future.
- ABC pays corporate tax at 30% and this rate is not expected to change in the foreseeable future.
- Assume both ABC's and XYZ's debt has a beta of zero.
- Issue costs should be ignored.

You are a financial adviser working for ABC's bankers.

Required

(a)   Discuss the appropriateness of the two Directors' suggestions about the discount rate when evaluating the proposed investment and recommend an appropriate rate to use. You should support your discussion and

recommendation with calculations of two separate discount rates – one for each Director's suggestion. Show all your workings. **(18 marks)**

Calculations count for up to 12 marks

(b)   Discuss how ABC's market capitalisation might change during the week the proposed investment becomes public knowledge. **No** calculations are required for this part of the question.   **(7 marks)**

A report format is **not** required for this question.   **(Total = 25 marks)**

38   BZ (FS, 5/09)   45 mins

BZ is a textile wholesaler based in a country in the Euro zone.

Summary financial information is as follows:

- Revenue and earnings last year were €121 million and €23·5 million respectively

- BZ's shares are not listed but they occasionally change hands in private transactions. The shares most recently traded a month ago at €4 per share. There are 39 million shares in issue

- BZ also has €121·5 million of undated debt on its balance sheet. This debt is secured on the entity's assets and carries an interest rate of 8%. The current cost of debt to an entity such as BZ is 9% before tax

- BZ estimates its cost of equity at 11%

- BZ operates an overdraft facility for short-term financing requirements

The entity currently sells its products in the USA via a distributor. However, its sales in this market are increasing to the extent that BZ is considering setting up its own distribution network in the USA. A State in the south of the USA has offered BZ financial support to establish a base there. BZ management thinks this is not the ideal location but an attractive financing package might persuade them otherwise.

The financing package currently on offer from the State in the south of the USA would take the form of a US$50 million loan at a subsidised interest rate of 3.5% per annum. Interest would be payable at the end of each year and the principal repaid at the end of five years.

The current rate of exchange is €/US$1.2 (that is €1 = US$1.2). This rate is not expected to change in the foreseeable future.

The marginal corporate tax rate in both countries is 28%.

Required

(a)   Calculate BZ's current WACC using market values and the cost of equity in the scenario. Assume the current debt ratio remains the same.   **(5 marks)**

(b)   Advise the board of BZ about how to determine an appropriate discount rate to use when evaluating the proposal to establish a subsidiary in the USA.   **(6 marks)**

(c)   Discuss the advantages and disadvantages of using government subsidies in any international investment decision. Include a calculation of the value of the subsidy implied in the US State loan.   **(8 marks)**

(d)   Discuss and recommend to the board of BZ how its US business operations might be financed when the US State loan is repaid.   **(6 marks)**

(Total = 25 marks)

39   GUC (11/10)   45 mins

Today's date is 25 November 20X0.

GUC provides gas utility products and services in South America. Its functional currency is P$. The Board is considering raising additional finance to provide capital for future acquisitions.

Three alternative sources of finance are being considered:

(1)   New equity by means of a rights issue at a 15% discount to current share price.

(2)   A five year bond with a yield of 0.5% below the industry average yield for comparable bonds.

(3)   A convertible bond issued at par with a coupon rate of 3%. The bond would be convertible into ordinary shares in five years' time at the ratio of 11 ordinary shares per P$100 nominal of the bond.

Extracts from the financial statements of GUC for the year ended 30 September 20X0 and other relevant financial information are shown below:

• Revenue	P$4,500 million
• Earnings	P$ 864 million
• Number of equity shares in issue (par value 50 cents)	785 million
• Share price as at 30 September 20X0	P$8.20
• Share price as at 25 November 20X0	P$7.70
• Industry average P/E ratio	8.4
• Gearing ratio (dept: debt + equity, current market values)	34%
• Industry average gearing ratio	45%
• Corporate income tax rate	30%

GUC forecasts that the share price will grow in line with the expected growth in earnings and dividends of 6% per annum. The yield to maturity for bonds without conversion rights, issued by utility companies of similar size to GUC, is currently 6.5%

The shareholder profile is as follows:

Institutions (such as pension funds etc)	72%
Small individual non-employee investors	15%
Employees and directors	13%

Required:

(a)   Calculate:

    (i)   GUC's current cost of equity

    (ii)   The gross yield to maturity of the convertible bond up to and including conversion, assuming the convertible bond is issued on 25 November 20X0.

    State any assumptions made.   **(10 marks)**

(b)   Evaluate the THREE alternative methods of finance being considered by GUC and advise which method might be most appropriate.   **(15 marks)**

                                                                                          (Total = 25 marks)

40   ADS (11/10)   45 mins

ADS operates a number of large department stores based in a developed country in Asia. Its shares are listed on an Asian stock exchange. It has shown year-on-year growth in earnings and dividends every year since it became a listed company in 2000. Some years have shown better growth than others but even in a relatively poor year earnings in real terms have been higher than in the previous year. It is currently all-equity financed. Approximately half of its shareholders are institutional investors; the other half is made up of large holdings by the original founding family members and small investors including many employees of ADS.

The directors of ADS are proposing to raise A$250 million to invest in new, smaller stores. This investment will carry similar risk to ADS's current business. It is proposed that the investment will be financed by an issue of an undated bond carrying 5% interest pre-tax. This rate is deemed to reflect the returns required by the market for the risk and duration of the bond. Some of the directors are reluctant to agree to debt finance as they think it will lower the value of equity and this might be a matter of concern for shareholders. The investment is planned for the end of 2010.

The following information is relevant:

•   Earnings for ADS are forecast to be A$127.1 million in 2011. This forecast assumes that the new stores are already fully operational at the start of 2011. From the year 2012 onwards, earnings are expected to increase at a rate of 4% per annum indefinitely.

•   The corporate income tax rate is 25%. This is not expected to change.

- The cost of equity for ADS as an all-equity financed company is 9%.

- There are 300 million shares in issue, currently quoted at A$8.50.

One of ADS's directors has recently read an article about company valuation and the differences between Modigliani and Miller (MM) models and the 'traditional' view.

Required:

(a) Discuss:

- How the MM models, both with and without corporate taxes, differ from the 'traditional' view of the relationship between gearing and cost of capital. Accompany your discussion with appropriate graphical illustrations.

- The limitations of MM models in 'real world' situations. **(10marks)**

(b)

(i) Calculate the value of ADS's equity using discounted cash flow techniques, assuming that the new stores are financed by equity. **(2 marks)**

(ii) Calculate, assuming that the new stores are financed by the undated bond and using the MM model with corporate taxes, the following:

- The value of ADS's equity;
- The expected cost of equity;
- The weighted average cost of capital (WACC). **(6 marks)**

(c) Explain your results in (b) above and advise the directors whether their concern about lowering the value of equity is valid. **(7 marks)**

(Total = 25 marks)

41 FF (5/12)   45 mins

FF is a company that specialises in the manufacture, supply and installation of fixtures and fittings for offices. It uses F$ as its currency. FF is currently evaluating a project to build a new distribution and sales centre.

The company is currently wholly equity funded and has 30 million shares in issue. The share price is F$11 per share before announcing the proposed project and the ungeared cost of equity is 9%. FF pays corporate income tax at 25%.

The proposed project requires an initial capital investment of F$80 million. The present value of future cash flows following this initial investment is estimated to be of the order of F$110 million, based on a discount rate of 9%. The F$30 million forecast increase in entity value is expected to be fully reflected in the share price immediately the project is announced.

There has been some discussion amongst the directors of FF about how the F$80 million capital investment should be funded. Any new equity would be raised through a rights issue and any borrowings would be at a pre-tax cost of 7%. Both would be required indefinitely. Three alternative financing structures are being considered as follows:

A: F$80 million equity funding.
B: F$80 million borrowings.
C: F$48 million equity plus F$32 million borrowings.

Required

(a) Calculate the following, based on Modigliani and Miller's (MM's) capital theory with tax and assuming the project goes ahead:

(i) The total value of FF (before deducting debt) on a discounted cash flow basis for each of the financing structures A, B and C. **(6 marks)**

(ii) FF's WACC for each of the financing structures A, B and C. **(6 marks)**

Note that MM formulae are provided on the formulae sheet.

(b)   Explain your results in (a) above with reference to MM's capital theory with tax, illustrating your answer by drawing graphs of your results in (a) above. Use the graph paper provided.   **(9 marks)**

(c)   Advise, with reasons, which financing structure FF should adopt.   **(4 marks)**

(Total = 25 marks)

42 DAN (FS, 5/08)   45 mins

You are a financial adviser working for a large financial institution. One of your clients, Dan, has a portfolio currently worth £100,000. He has invested in good quality stocks that are spread over diversified industries with an average beta of 1.2; a risk profile he is happy with. He holds other assets, such as property and bank deposits, worth approximately £150,000 (excluding his own home, on which he has a 75% mortgage).

He has recently inherited £40,000 which he intends to invest in equities. He has done some research himself and is considering investing in the following entities in equal proportions.

Entity A is a large, listed entity in a mature industry. Dan already has 15% of his equity investments in this industry sector.

Entity B is a relatively small entity whose shares have been listed on the UK's Alternative Investment Market for the past three years. Its main area of operations is bio-technology, a sector in which Dan has no investments.

Market data for the share of the two entities are as follows.

Entity	Current share prices (buy price)	Beta	P/E ratio
A	250 pence cum rights	1.1	10
B	500 pence cum dividend	n/a*	20

* Your financial institution estimates a return of 15.8% is required on this stock.

Your transaction charges will be 2.5% of the capital amount.

Financial strategies of the two entities

Entity A is planning a rights issue. The terms will be 1 new share for every 4 held at a cost of 200 pence.

Entity B will allow investors registered at 30 June 20X8 the option of taking a dividend of 45 pence a share or a scrip dividend of 1 share for every 10 shares held.

The policy of Entity B has been to offer scrip dividends as an alternative to cash dividends since its shares were first listed three years ago.

The risk free rate is 5% and the return on the market is 11%. These rates are not expected to change in the foreseeable future.

Required

(a)   Calculate the risk and expected return of Dan's equity investment portfolio if he goes ahead with his proposed investments. Work to a maximum of 2 decimal points in your calculations.   **(5 marks)**

(b)   (i)   Explain the difference between systematic risk (or market risk) and unsystematic risk (or specific risk) and, briefly, the meaning of beta and how it is measured.   **(4 marks)**

        (ii)   Discuss how and to what extent the beta of Entity A and the implied beta of Entity B:

               –   Might affect Dan's investment decision;
               –   Could be of interest to the directors of single entities such as A and B.   **(6 marks)**

(c)   Evaluate the implications for shareholder value of Entity A's and Entity B's proposed financial strategies and advise Dan on how these strategies might affect his investment decision. Include appropriate calculations.   **(10 marks)**

(Total = 25 marks)

43 CD (Pilot paper) 45 mins

CD is a privately-owned entity based in Country X, which is a popular holiday destination. Its principal business is the manufacture and sale of a wide variety of items for the tourist market, mainly souvenirs, gifts and beachwear. CD manufactures approximately 80% of the goods it sells. The remaining 20% is purchased from other countries in a number of different currencies. CD owns and operates 5 retail stores in Country X but also sells its products on a wholesale basis to other local retail outlets.

Although CD is privately owned, it has revenue and assets equivalent in amount to some entities that are listed on smaller stock markets (such as the UK's Alternative Investment Market (AIM)). It is controlled by family shareholders but also has a number of non-family shareholders, such as employees and trade associates. It has no intention of seeking a listing at the present time although some of the family shareholders have often expressed a wish to buy out the smaller investors.

CD has been largely unaffected by the recent world recession and has increased its sales volume and profits each year for the past 5 years. The directors think this is because it provides value for money; providing high quality goods that are competitively priced at the lower end of its market. Future growth is expected to be modest as the directors and shareholders do not wish to adopt strategies that they think might involve substantial increase in risks, for example by moving the manufacturing base to another country where labour rates are lower. Some of the smaller shareholders disagree with this strategy and would prefer higher growth even if it involves greater risk.

The entity is financed 80% by equity and 20% by debt (based on book values). The debt is a mixture of bonds secured on assets and unsecured overdraft. The interest rate on the secured bonds is fixed at 7% and the overdraft rate is currently 8%, which compares to a relatively recent historic rate as high as 13%. The bonds are due to be repaid in five years' time. Inflation in CD's country is near zero at the present time and interest rates are expected to fall.

CD's treasury department is centralised at the head office and its key responsibilities include arranging sufficient long and short term financing for the group and hedging foreign exchange exposures. The Treasurer is investigating the opportunities for and consequences of refinancing.

CD's sole financial objective is to increase dividends each year. It has no non-financial objective. This financial objective and the lack of non-financial objectives are shortly to be subject to review and discussion by the board. The new Finance Director believes maximisation of shareholder wealth should be the sole objective, but the other directors do not agree and think that new objectives should be considered, including target profit after tax and return on investment.

Required

(a)   Discuss the role of the treasury department when determining financing or refinancing strategies in the context of the economic environment described in the scenario and explain how these might impact on the determination of corporate objectives.   **(15 marks)**

(b)   Evaluate the appropriateness of CD's current objective and of the two new objectives being considered. Discuss alternative objectives that might be appropriate for CD and conclude with a recommendation.
                                                                                                            (10 marks)

(Total = 25 marks)

Investment decisions and project control

Questions 44 to 81 cover investment decisions and project control, the subject of Part C of the BPP Study Text for Paper F3.

44   Claudia (FS, 11/09)   45 mins

Claudia is based in Asia and is considering installing a new computer system in order to upgrade the web-based sales system to bring it in line with that of Claudia's main competitors. The cost of $10 million is payable up front but the new system will take a full year to implement. Increased pre-tax operating earnings of $770,000 a year are expected from year 2 onwards indefinitely to reflect increased operational efficiencies and increased revenue from web-based sales.

Claudia is currently funded by ordinary shares and an irredeemable bond as follows:

	Nominal value	Market value
20 million ordinary shares	$1 each	$2.50 each
5.4% irredeemable bond	$33 million	trading at par

Additional debt finance of $10 million will be taken out (also at 5.4%) if the project is approved.

Additional information:

- Cost of equity is 6.2%

- The project is not expected to have any impact on either the current cost of equity or the cost of debt.

- The share price is expected to react very quickly on announcement of the project to reflect the anticipated NPV of the project.

- Business tax is payable and refundable at 35% in the year in which it is incurred.

- No tax depreciation allowances can be claimed

- Assume earnings equal net cash inflow

- Cash flows arise at the end of a year

Required

(a)   Calculate the current WACC of Claudia (before taking the project into account).   **(3 marks)**

(b)   Evaluate the project using the current WACC calculated in part (a).   **(4 marks)**

(c)   Calculate the post-project WACC for Claudia after adjusting for the NPV of the project and the increased debt, and discuss your results. Discuss and advise whether the pre-project WACC was an appropriate discount rate for Claudia to use in this scenario.   **(6 marks)**

(d)   Discuss the key factors that Claudia should take into account in respect of this project when:
      (i)   assessing customer requirements
      (ii)   drawing up an implementation plan

                                                                                  (12 marks)

                                                                          (Total = 25 marks)

45 Dominique (FS, 11/09)   45 mins

It is currently September 20W9.

Dominique is a multinational group. The head office and parent entity are based in Country D which uses currency D$. The group runs a chain of supermarkets both in Country D and in neighbouring countries. Dominique sources its supplies from its home country D, neighbouring countries and also from some more distant countries.

Dominique is funded by a mix of equity and long-term borrowings. The borrowings are largely floating rate bonds denominated in D$.

<u>Proposed new project</u>
The proposed new project is to open a number of new supermarkets in Country T, a neighbouring country, which uses currency T$.   Market research has already been undertaken at a cost of D$ 0.3 million. If the proposed project is approved additional logistics planning will be commissioned at a cost of D$ 0.38 million payable at the start of 20X0.

Other forecast project cash flows:

Initial investment on 1 January 20X0	T$ million	150
Residual value at the end of 20X4	T$ million	40
Net operating cash inflows		
20X0	T$ million	45
20X1 and 20X2	growing at 20% a year from 20X0 levels	
20X3 and 20X4	growing at 6% a year from 20X2 levels	

Additional information:

- On 1 January 20X0, the spot rate for converting D$ to T$ is expected to be D$1 = T$ 2.1145. Dominique has received two conflicting exchange rate forecasts for the D$/T$ during the life of the project as follows:

  Forecast A   A stable exchange rate of D$1 = T$2.1145
  Forecast B   A devaluation of the T$ against the D$ of 5.4% a year

- Business tax is 20% in Country T, payable in the year in which it is incurred.

- Tax depreciation allowances are available in Country T at 20% a year on a reducing balance basis

- All net cash flows in Country T are to be remitted to Country D at the end of each year

- An additional 5% tax is payable in Country D based on remitted net cash flows net of D$ costs but no tax is payable or refundable on the initial investment and residual value capital flows.

The project is to be evaluated, in D$, at a discount rate of 12% over a five year period.

Required

(a) Calculate and discuss the D$ NPV of the project cash flows as at 1 January 20X0 using each of the two different exchange rate scenarios, Forecast A and Forecast B. Briefly advise Dominique whether or not it should proceed with the project.   **(18 marks)**

(b) Discuss the likely impact of changes in exchange rates and tax rates on the performance of the Dominique group as a whole and how this is likely to influence the financial strategy of the group. No further calculations are required.   **(7 marks)**

(Total = 25 marks)

46 CTC (FS, 5/05)

45 mins

CTC Technology College (CTC) is a non-profit making institution located in Ireland, where the national currency is the euro. The college is funded by a combination of student fees and government grants.

The number of students enrolled on the part-time Information Technology course at CTC has fallen over recent years due to competition from other colleges and the wide range of different courses available. The number of students enrolling on the current course, ITS (IT Skills) has stabilised at around 150 students per annum and there are currently 20 computers surplus to requirements which CTC plans to sell for an estimated €100 each; the current book value of each computer is €200. However, this sale will not occur if the college goes ahead with its plan to replace the current ITS course with an updated course, as it is expected that a new course would result in a significant increase in student numbers.

CTC realises that the financial viability of switching courses is highly dependent on the number of students that the college can attract onto the new course and has commissioned some market research, at a cost of €10,000, into the best course content and likely increase in student numbers. The results of this research indicate that an ITC (IT Competence) course would be the most popular and lead to a significant increase in student enrolments at the college. It is also estimated that there could be an additional benefit to the college of average net revenues of €20 per additional student over and above 150 as a result of those students being attracted to the college and taking other courses at the college at the same time as the ITC course.

The new ITC course would be run by existing staff currently working on the ITS course at a cost of €50,000 per annum. If, however, the numbers of students on ITC were to rise above 200 per annum, an additional part-time member of staff would be needed at a cost of €10,000 per annum, payable in advance. If ITC is adopted, several computers would need to be upgraded at a total one-off cost of €15,000.

Other relevant data is as follows:

	ITS	ITC
	€	€
Fee for the course (per student, payable in advance)	350	360
Directly attributable course costs (per annum, payable in arrears)	1,000	2,000
Books and consumables per student, payable in advance	50	60
Apportionment of college overheads (excluding staff costs) (per annum, charged at the end of the year)	20,000	25,000
Staff training and course development (initial set-up cost)	0	30,000

The planning horizon for the college is four years and projects are evaluated using a discount rate of 8% and on the basis of a zero terminal value at the end of the four-year period. Each course is of one year duration and student enrolments should be assumed to remain constant throughout the four-year period, with ITS attracting 150 students each year.

Taxation and inflation should be ignored.

Required

(a) Evaluate the number of student enrolments required on the ITC course in order for it to be financially beneficial, on a net present value of cash flow basis, for the college to replace the ITS course with the ITC course. **(15 marks)**

(b) Advise the governing body of the college on the following issues:

(i) How to monitor and control the costs and revenues of the project from the decision to introduce the new course to the start date of the course. **(5 marks)**

(ii) Options available if only 150 students enrol on the new ITC course by the enrolment deadline two weeks before the beginning of the course by which time all other course preparations will have been completed. **(5 marks)**

(Total = 25 marks)

47 KH   45 mins

KH is a large food and drink manufacturer and retailer based in the United States of America. To date, the company has operated only in the US but is planning to expand into South America by acquiring a group of stores similar to those operated in the US. Projected cash flows in the US and South America for the first three years of the project, in real terms, are estimated as follows.

	Year 0	Year 1	Year 2	Year 3
Cash flows in the USA:				
In US$'000	–10,000	–300	–400	–500
Cash flows in the South American country:				
In SA currency'000	–1,000,000	+250,000	+350,000	+450,000

US$ cash flows are mainly incremental administration costs associated with the project. SA currency cash flows are cash receipts from sales less all related cash costs and expenses.

The exchange rate for the South American country's currency is extremely volatile. Inflation is currently 40% a year. Inflation in the US is 4% a year. Best estimates by KH's treasurer suggest these rates are likely to continue for the foreseeable future. The current exchange rate is US$/SA currency 30 (that is US$1 = SA currency 30).

The following information is relevant

- KH evaluates all investments using nominal cash flows and a nominal discount rate.
- SA currency cash flows are converted into US$ and discounted at a risk-adjusted US rate.
- All cash flows for this project will be discounted at 20%, a nominal rate judged to reflect its high risk.
- For the purposes of evaluation, assume the year 3 nominal cash flows will continue to be earned each year indefinitely.

<u>Note</u>. Ignore taxation

Required

Assume that you are the financial manager of KH. Prepare a report to the finance director that evaluates the proposed investment. Include in your report the following.

(a) Calculation of the net present value of the proposed investment and a recommendation as to whether the company should proceed with the investment, supported by your reasons for the recommendation.

(12 marks)

(b) Discussion of the main political risks that might be faced by the company and provision of advice on management strategies that could be implemented to counter those risks. **(13 marks)**

(Total = 25 marks)

48 DAC   45 mins

DAC is a manufacturer of expensive, built-to-order motor cars. The company has been trading for 25 years and has seen year-on-year growth of sales and profits. Whereas most of the large, mass-production motor manufacturers have experienced over-capacity and falling profit margins in recent years, DAC has a waiting list of six months for a new car. All cars are manufactured in the UK, but there are sales outlets throughout Europe and the Far East. The chief executive of the company, who is still the major shareholder, is considering extending the distributor network into the USA where there is a rising demand. At present, American customers have to order direct from the UK.

A detailed assessment of the costs and likely incremental revenues of opening distributorships into major US cities has been carried out. The initial cost of the investment is US$4.5 million. The cash flows, all positive and net of all taxes, are summarised below.

Year	1	2	3	4
Cash flow (US$ million)	1.75	1.95	2.50	3.50

The following information is available.

- The expected inflation rate in the USA is 2 per cent a year.
- Real interest rates in the UK and USA are the same. They are expected to remain the same for the foreseeable future.
- The current spot rate is £/US$ 1.6 (that is, £1 = US$1.6).
- The risk-free rate of interest in the USA is 4 per cent per annum and in Britain 5 per cent per annum. These rates are not expected to change in the foreseeable future.
- The company's post-tax WACC is 14 per cent per annum, which it uses to evaluate all investment decisions.
- The company is financed by £10 million shareholders' funds (book values) and £2 million long-term debt which is due to be retired in two years' time.

The company can finance part of the investment from cash flow but, as it is also expanding operations in the UK, the chief executive would prefer external finance if this is available on acceptable terms. He has noted that borrowing rates in the euro-debt market appear very favourable at the present time. At 3 per cent they are below the rates in both the UK and the USA.

Required

(a) Calculate the *sterling* net present value of the project using both of the following methods:

    (i) By discounting annual cash flows in sterling.

    (ii) By discounting annual cash flows in US$. **(10 marks)**

(b) Discuss:

    (i) The use of WACC as a discount rate in an international investment decision, in general terms and as it applies to DAC.

    (ii) The main risks to be faced by a company such as DAC when it moves into a new international market, and how it might manage those risks.

    (iii) The main methods of financing overseas operations and the factors that the company should consider before making a decision about borrowing in euro debt. **(15 marks)**

(Total = 25 marks)

49 CD (FS, 11/06)   45 mins

CD is a furniture manufacturer based in the UK. It manufactures a limited range of furniture products to a very high quality and sells to a small number of retail outlets worldwide.

At a recent meeting with one of its major customers it became clear that the market is changing and the final consumer of CD's products is now more interested in variety and choice rather than exclusivity and exceptional quality.

CD is therefore reviewing two mutually exclusive alternatives to apply to a selection of its products:

Alternative 1

To continue to manufacture, but expand its product range and reduce its quality. The net present value (NPV), internal rate of return (IRR) and modified internal rate of return (MIRR) for this alternative have already been calculated as follows:

NPV = £1.45 million using a nominal discount rate of 9%
IRR = 10.5%
MIRR = Approximately 13.2%

Alternative 2

To import furniture carcasses in 'flat packs' from the USA. The imports would be in a variety of types of wood and unvarnished. CD would buy in bulk from its US suppliers, assemble and varnish the furniture and re-sell, mainly to existing customers. An initial investigation into potential sources of supply and costs of transportation has already been carried out by a consultancy entity at a cost of £75,000.

CD's Finance Director has provided estimates of net sterling and US$ cash flows for this alternative. These net cash flows, in **real** terms, are shown below.

Year	0	1	2	3
US$m	(25.00)	2.60	3.80	4.10
£m	0	3.70	4.20	4.60

The following information is relevant:

- CD evaluates all its investments using nominal sterling cash flows and a nominal discount rate. All non-UK customers are invoiced in US$. US$ nominal cash flows are converted to sterling at the forward rate and discounted at the UK nominal rate.

- For the purposes of evaluation, assume the entity has a three year time horizon for investment appraisals.

- Based on recent economic forecasts, inflation rates in the US are expected to be constant at 4% per annum. UK inflation rates are expected to be 3% per annum. The current exchange rate is £/US$1.6 (that is, £1 = US$1·6).

<u>Note</u>. Ignore taxation.

Required

Assume that you are the Financial Manager of CD.

(a)   Calculate the net present value (NPV), internal rate of return (IRR) and (approximate) modified internal rate of return (MIRR) of alternative 2.   **(12 marks)**

(b)   Briefly discuss the appropriateness and possible advantages of providing MIRRs for the evaluation of the two alternatives.   **(4 marks)**

(c)   Evaluate the two alternatives and recommend which alternative the entity should choose. Include in your answer some discussion about what other criteria could or should be considered before a final decision is taken.   **(9 marks)**

A report format is **not** required for this question.   **(Total = 25 marks)**

50   UVW (FS, 11/07)   45 mins

UVW is a manufacturer of specialist components for the motor trade. Most of the entity's business is 'to order'; very little is manufactured for inventory. The components are sold to customers worldwide but, to date, have been manufactured solely in the UK. The Directors of UVW are reviewing the opportunity to establish a manufacturing base in Asia. There would be some loss of productivity, especially in the first year of operations, but the long-term cost savings would outweigh this.

Two senior managers from the UK will be sent to the Asian country to establish the overseas operation and remain there for the first 12 months. The cost of their salaries, travel and accommodation while in Asia is budgeted at £250,000 for the year.

This cost is included in the figures below.

Capital equipment purchased in UK for the Asian project:	£2 million
Premises and equipment purchased in Asia:	Asian $100 million

Operating cash flows are (Year):	One	Two	Three
Costs of Asian operation (Asian $million)	–70.0	–65.0	–60.0
Comparable costs of UK operation (£million)	–1.5	–4.5	–4.75

Other information available:

- Assume all cash flows are after tax and that operating cash flows occur at the end of each year.

- The year three cost advantage in sterling is assumed to maintain from year four until year eight. UVW does not evaluate investments beyond eight years.

- The current spot rate is £/Asian$20 (that is, £1 = Asian $20).

- A feasibility study has been carried out in the Asian country at a cost of Asian $1.2 million.

- Expected inflation rate in the Asian country is 8% per annum. In the UK, it is 4% per annum. The risk free rate in the UK is 3%.
- UVW uses a discount rate of 10% for all its investment decisions.

The entity's Finance Manager does not think 10% adequately reflects the risk of this project. He believes the cost advantage of the Asian operation could fall short of the evaluated DCFs by as much as 20% in year one; 25% in year two, and 30% from year three onwards. His rough calculations suggest that, using his estimates, the project shows a substantial negative NPV.

Required

(a) (i) Calculate the sterling NPV of the project both with, and without, adjusting for certainty equivalents. **(12 marks)**

(ii) Discuss briefly other internal factors the entity should consider before deciding whether the project should proceed. You are NOT required to discuss external economic factors or hedging techniques. Include comments on the use of certainty equivalents and why the Finance Manager's 'rough calculations' might have been wrong. **(6 marks)**

(b) Advise the Directors of UVW whether or not the management of working capital should be carried out in the Asian country compared with maintaining a centralised function in the UK. **(7 marks)**

A report format is **not** required for this question. **(Total = 25 marks)**

51 CM (FS, 5/08) | 45 mins

CM Limited (CM) is a private entity that supplies and distributes equipment to the oil industry in the UK. It is evaluating two potential investments. **Investment 1** would expand its operations in the UK, **Investment 2** would establish a base in Asia that would allow it to market and sell its products to entities in a wider geographical area. The currency in the Asian country is the $.

CM does not wish to undertake both investments at the present time. **Investment 1** would require less capital expenditure than **Investment 2**, but its operating costs would be higher. Profit forecasts for the two investments are as follows.

	Year 1 £'000s	Year 2 £'000s	Year 3 £'000s
Investment 1			
Revenue	375	450	575
Production costs (excluding depreciation)	131	158	201
Depreciation	267	267	266
Profit/(loss) before tax	(23)	25	108
Investment 2	A$000s	A$000s	A$000s
Revenue	1,300	1,450	1,650
Production costs (excluding depreciation)	260	290	330
Depreciation	967	967	966
Profit/(loss) before tax	73	193	354

Additional information

1   The capital expenditure required for **Investment 1** is £1.1 million with an expected residual value at the end of Year 3 of £300,000. The capital cost of **Investment 2** will be A$2.9 million with no residual value.

2   CM depreciates the estimated net cost of its assets (initial cost less estimated residual value) straight line over the life of the investment.

3   Tax depreciation is available on the equipment purchased for **Investment 1** at 40% per annum on the reducing balance basis. Capital expenditure or **Investment 2** can be written off for tax purposes in the year in which it is purchased.

4   Corporate tax rate in the UK is 25%. There are tax concessions in the Asian country. The net effect is that CM would pay tax on profits generated in the Asian country at 10%. No additional tax would be payable in the UK. Tax would be refunded or paid on both investments at the end of the year in which the liability arises.

5   **Investment 1** would be financed by internal funds. **Investment 2** would be financed by a combination of internal funds and loans raised overseas.

6   Assume revenue and production costs excluding depreciation equal cash flows.

7   The cash flow forecasts are in nominal terms. The entity's real cost of capital is 8% and inflation is expected to be 2.75% per annum constant in the UK.

8   CM evaluates all its investments over a three-year time horizon.

9   Cash flows are assumed to occur at the end of each year except the initial capital cost which is incurred in Year 0.

10 Operating cash flows for **Investment 2** are in A$. The current exchange rate is £/A$2 (that is, £1 = A$2). Sterling is expected to weaken against the A$ by 4.5% per annum over the next three years.

11 CM's expected accounting return on investment is 15%, calculated as average profits after tax as a percentage of average investment over the life of the assets.

Required

(a)   For each of the two investments, calculate

    (i)   The average annual accounting return on investment using average profit after tax and average investment over the life of the assets.   **(9 marks)**

    (ii) The NPV using an appropriate discount rate calculated from the information given in the scenario.   **(9 marks)**

    (<u>Note</u>. You should round the calculated discount rate to the nearest whole number).

(b)   Recommend, with reasons, which, if either, of the investments should be undertaken. Discuss any non-financial factors that might influence the choice of investment.   **(7 marks)**

(Total = 25 marks)

52   RST (3/12)   45 mins

Assume today is 1 April 20X2.

RST is a privately owned specialist equipment supply and support company based in Sydney, Australia with a strong local customer base. RST made a profit of 20 million Australian dollars (AUD) in the last financial year and relies heavily on debt finance.

The company is considering setting up an operation in Perth, Australia, a five hour plane journey from Sydney. It would be the first time that RST has operated outside Sydney. Perth is currently experiencing rapid growth due to the development of the mining industry which has created new opportunities for supplying specialist equipment.

The new operation in Perth would supply specialised mining equipment to the local mines and also provide maintenance support. RST would lease office space in Perth for a five year period and hire new local sales people and technicians. A significant proportion of the lease premium will need to be paid on the first day of the lease period. In all, it is anticipated that the new operation will require an initial investment of AUD 25 million.

If successful, this new operation would increase the size of RST significantly and also provide an opportunity for establishing a permanent operation in Perth. However, it involves a considerable amount of risk and uncertainty, largely because of the new location. In addition, the new operation will be targeted at the mining industry which is a new type of industry sector for RST. As a result, the business risk of this new operation in Perth will be different from that of the current operations in Sydney.

RST's finance department has produced information on likely future cash flows for the Perth operation on the basis of three possible out-turn scenarios. Net present value (NPV) calculations have been undertaken based on an appropriate WACC for RST. The cost of equity used in the WACC was based on the beta of a proxy company located in Perth that operates in a similar industry sector. The results are given below:

Out-turn scenario	Probability of occurrence	NPV (AUD million)
Best case	30%	54
Average case	50%	30
Worst case	20%	-48

This gives an overall expected NPV of AUD 21.6 million. The finance manager is happy with this level of return and is prepared to recommend the new operation on the basis of its expected NPV.

There have been some lengthy discussions amongst Board members on the results of the NPV evaluation and on how best to finance the new operation if it goes ahead.

Director S supports the idea of debt finance because the NPV calculations could then be re-performed at the lower cost of debt, making the new operation even more attractive. However, she has some concerns about the risks involved in increasing gearing any further. Director S has also pointed out that the USD has a lower interest rate than the AUD and has therefore suggested that RST use USD denominated debt rather than AUD denominated debt.

Required

(a) Advise the board of RST on the validity of:

    (i) The appraisal approach adopted (including the use of CAPM and NPV). **(4 marks)**

    (ii) The conclusion reached by the finance manager that RST should proceed with the investment in Perth. **(4 marks)**

(b) Explain, using examples from the scenario, what "real options" are AND what impact they might have on an investment decision. **(9 marks)**

(c) Evaluate the comments made by Director S. **(8 marks)**

(Total = 25 marks)

53 PP (5/12)   45 mins

PP is a large architectural partnership based in the USA. Its client base ranges from large corporations to an extensive range of smaller companies and individuals.

Much of PP's marketing and client liaison efforts to date have focussed on the larger corporations because there tends to be repeat business from such clients. However, a recent client survey has revealed that 75% of new business results from referrals from satisfied smaller clients. PP is therefore keen to improve its marketing efforts within the smaller client market. Improvements in the information technology (IT) systems currently used by PP are considered to be essential to such a development, to enable increased visibility of the company and its achievements across the whole client base and help promote new business.

PP's current annual revenue is USD 10 million.

Proposed IT project for a new Customer Relationship Management (CRM) system

PP is considering introducing a new Customer Relationship Management (CRM) system to help maintain more regular and better targeted communication with both current and potential new clients. The project is to be appraised over a four year time horizon.

An initial investment of USD 600,000 is required on 1 July 20X2, with no residual value at the end of the four year period. It is estimated that there would be on-going system maintenance costs of USD 50,000 a year but no other annual incremental costs attributable to the project. In terms of savings, it is planned that staff numbers would be reduced by one person at an annual saving of salary costs of USD 80,000 and also a saving of other costs of USD 20,000 per annum. However, redundancy pay and costs involved with redundancy arrangements would be approximately USD 200,000, payable on 1 July 20X2. Unless stated otherwise, all costs and revenue should be assumed to be paid or received at the end of the year in which they arise.

The partners of the practice are unsure how much new business would be generated by the new CRM system. The number of different unknown variables involved has made it very difficult to arrive at a firm answer. However, it is anticipated that any new business generated as a result of the CRM system would give rise to an increase in net cash inflows in each year that is equivalent to 52% of the annual cash inflow generated by new

business. Assume that the additional net cash inflow generated by new business is the same in each of years 1 to 4.

PP evaluates IT projects using a conventional discounted cash flow approach based on costs and benefits that can be quantified with a degree of confidence. The partnership's cost of capital of 12% is to be used as the discount rate.

For the purposes of this question, taxation should be ignored.

Required

(a) (i) Calculate the net present value (NPV) of the proposed IT project as at 1 July 20X2, ignoring the additional cash flows that might arise from new business. **(5 marks)**

(ii) Calculate the additional annual cash inflow from new business that is required in order to achieve a breakeven result. Use your answer from part (a)(i) as the starting point for your calculation. **(6 marks)**

(b) (i) Discuss the appropriateness of using a conventional discounted cash flow approach to appraise an IT project. **(6 marks)**

(ii) Advise what other financial and strategic factors should be considered when deciding whether to proceed with this project. **(8 marks)**

(Total = 25 marks)

---

54 MR (9/10)   45 mins

It is currently September 20X0.

MR is a large retail chain of retail stores operating in the USA. It sells top-of the-range, expensive clothes to a wealthy clientele throughout the country. Currently, MR only operates in the USA. Its current market capitalisation is US$760million and the current market value of debt is US$350million.

At last month's management meeting the marketing director explained that sales volume had increased slightly in the previous year, largely due to heavy discounting in most of its stores. The finance director expressed concern that such a strategy might damage the image of the company and reduce profits over the longer term.

An alternative strategy to increase sales volume has recently been proposed by the marketing department. This would involve introducing a new range of clothing specifically aimed at the middle-income market. The new range of clothing would be expected to be attractive to consumers in Canada and Europe, giving the possibility of opening stores in Canada and possibly Europe in the longer term.

Assume you are a financial manager with MR and have been asked to evaluate the marketing department's proposal to introduce a new range of clothing. An initial investigation into the potential markets has been undertaken by a firm of consultants at a cost of US$100,000 but this amount has not yet been paid. It is intended to settle the amount due in three months' time. With the help of a small multi-department team of staff you have estimated the following cash flows for the proposed project:

- The initial investment required would be US$46million, payable on 01 January 20X1. This comprises US$30million for non-current assets and US$16million for net current assets (working capital).

- For accounting purposes, non-current assets are depreciated on a straight line basis over three years after allowing for a residual value of 10%. Tax depreciation allowances can be assumed to be the same as accounting depreciation.

- The value of net current assets at the end of the evaluation period can be assumed to be the same as at the start of the period.

- Net operating cash flows (before taxation) are forecast to be US$14million in 20X1, US$17million in 2012 and US$22million in 20X3 and should be assumed to arise at the end of each year.

The following information is also relevant:

- The proposed project is to be evaluated over a three-year time horizon.

- MR usually evaluates its investments using a after-tax discount rate of 8%. The proposed project is considered to be riskier than average and so a risk-adjusted rate of 9% will be used for this project.

- Corporate tax is payable at 25% in the same year in which the liability arises.

- MR would need to borrow 50% of the initial investment cost .

- Ignore inflation.

MR's primary financial objectives are:

1. To earn a return on shareholders' funds (based on market values) of 11% per annum on average over a three- year period.

2. To keep its gearing ratio, (debt to debt plus equity based on market values), at below 35%.

Required

(a) (i)   Calculate the net present value (NPV), internal rate of return (IRR) and (approximate) modified internal rate of return (MIRR) as at 01 January 20X1 for the proposed project. **(13 marks)**

     (ii) Discuss the advantages and limitations of MIRR in comparison with NPV and IRR. **(6 marks)**

(b) Evaluate the likely impact of the project on MR's ability to meet its financial objectives assuming the project goes ahead. **(6 marks)**

(Total = 25 marks)

A report format is not required for this question

55   GOH (3/11)   45 mins

It is currently March 20X1.

GOH is a local government organisation in Gohland, a country that has the G$ as its currency.

GOH is currently evaluating a proposed investment involving the construction and operation of a new health centre in the local region. Some fees will be collected from users of the centre but the majority of services will be provided free of charge.

The Gohland Government sets down strict guidelines to be used by all local government organisations in their appraisal of projects. In relation to investment projects of this nature the guidelines are that:

- A discount rate of 4% should be used as this is the rate specified by the government for use in evaluating such projects.

- Projects of this nature should be evaluated over a 15 year time horizon.

- Discounted cash flow analysis should take into account both the capital investment and the opportunity cost of the land that is required by the project.

- All costs, income and other benefits of the project should be identified and included in the appraisal. These should include the estimated value of benefits to society in terms of health impacts and also any environment and social impacts.

Financial figures for the proposed project

The capital cost of the investment (buildings and equipment) is estimated at G$950 million and would be payable on 1 April 20X1.

The health centre is to be built on a portion of land already owned by GOH. A developer has expressed an interest in buying the land at a price of G$250 million. This is considered a reasonable market value by GOH's Estates Department.

The residual value of the land, buildings and equipment at the end of 15 years is difficult to forecast but the Estates Department thinks at that time the land will be worth approximately G$600 million and the buildings and equipment G$150 million.

Net future benefits (income and other benefits net of costs) for the new regional health centre for use in the NPV analysis are forecast to be as follows:

Year ending 31 March	20X2	20X3	20X4	20X5 to 20Y6
G$ million	90	110	120	130 per year

GOH's financial director has just joined GOH from a private-sector company and has proposed that instead of using a discount rate of 4% a more commercial discount rate should be used based upon a private sector organisation.

He has identified a private health care company, JKL, which operates a number of health centres in Gohland, to be used as a proxy company for calculating a comparable private sector discount rate for GOH. JKL is currently funded as follows:

Equity: 24.5 million shares quoted on the local market at G$13.00. JKL's cost of equity is estimated at 9%.

Debt: G$100 million of long dated bonds issued at par and paying a coupon rate of 5.5%. The debt is currently trading at G$95 per G$100 nominal.

Additional information:

- The corporate income tax rate is 30% in Gohland.
- Net future benefits should be assumed to occur at the end of the year.

Required:

(a) (i) Calculate the weighted average cost of capital of JKL. **(4 marks)**

    (ii) Advise on the appropriateness of using the WACC of JKL as the discount rate in GOH's project appraisal, including reference to the differences in the financial and non-financial objectives between the public sector and private sector. **(8 marks)**

(b) (i) Calculate the project NPV following Gohland government's guidelines. **(5 marks)**

    (ii) Advise GOH on other issues that need to be taken into account before deciding whether or not to proceed with the proposed project. **(8 marks)**

(Total = 25 marks)

56 CMec (11/11)   45 mins

Assume today is 1 January 20X2

CMec is a major retail chain that specialises in household products and is based in the UK. It has retail stores throughout the UK which sell a wide range of household products with will-known brand names. It also sells under its own brand label. These goods are produced and packaged by leading manufacturers in the UK on behalf of CMec as CMec does not have its own manufacturing facility.

Proposed investment

The board is considering expanding CMec's operations into a country in Asia, Country A, which has the A$ as its currency. The expansion would be achieved by acquiring a number of stores from a supermarket chain operating in Country A. This is the first time that CMec has invested in a foreign country.

The cost of purchasing the stores is A$425 million, payable on 1 January 20X2. The cost of re-branding and fitting-out the stores has been estimated at A$170 million. For the purposes of evaluation these costs can be assumed to be paid on 1 January 20X2. After three years, the stores are expected to be worth A450 million.

The new stores will require an investment in working capital of A$150 million at the start of the first year and the working capital requirement is expected to grow by 10% a year for the foreseeable future but is expected to be fully recoverable at the end of the project.

The net operating cash flows for the new stores for the first three years of operation are expected to be:

Year to 31 December:	20X2	20X3	20X4
Operating cash flows			
Arising in Country A (A$ million)	200	250	350
Arising in the UK (GBP million)	(14)	(14)	(14)

Due to risky nature of the project, CMec has decided to evaluate the project on the basis that the new stores will only be operational for three years and the stores are sold at the end of the project.

The following additional information applies:

- CMec operates an accounting year that runs from 1 January to 31 December.

- GBP/A$ spot is expected to be GBP/A$ 1.3000 on 1 January 20X2 (that is, GBP 1 = A$1.3000).

- The risk free rate of interest is 7.5% in Country A and 2.0% in the UK.

- CMec uses a GBP discount rate of 10.0% to evaluate UK investments.

- Cash flows, other than the initial investment and refit costs can be assumed to occur at the end of the year to which they relate.

- All funds are remitted to the UK at the end of each year.

For the purposes of this question, taxation can be ignored.

Required

(a)   Calculate, showing full workings, the GBP net present value (NPV) of the proposed investment as at 1 January 20X2 based on a three year period, by:

   (i)   Discounting GBP cash flows at CMec's GBP discount rate.
   (ii)   Discounting A$ cash flows at a corresponding A$ discount rate.   **(10 marks)**

(b)   Explain why you would expect the NPVs in (a)(i) and (a)(ii) above to be the same.   **(3 marks)**

(c)   Advise how the project evaluation could be adapted to take into account the additional risks involved in foreign investments.   **(6 marks)**

(d)   Discuss to what extent a post completion audit report prepared by CMec for a previously completed UK project might be useful when planning the implementation of this proposed investment in a foreign country.   **(6 marks)**

(Total = 25 marks)

---

57   TM (3/11)   45 mins

Today's date is 4 March 20X1.

TM is a privately owned company which manufactures children's toys and is based in a country in Asia which has the A$ as its currency. In the financial year to 31 December 20X1 (assuming that there are no policy changes) it is expected that approximately 70% of TM's revenue will be from sales to companies in its home market. The other 30% of revenue will be from sales to companies in a foreign country which has the euro (EUR) as its currency. Export sales are currently priced in A$.

Approximately 10% of TM's home customers are cash buyers, the other 90% are on credit. Export sales are all on credit. Some customers in both the home and export markets regularly exceed their agreed credit period. TM makes no charge for this but refuses repeat orders if customers regularly make late payments beyond their agreed credit period.

In order to increase export sales, TM is planning to make the following policy changes with effect from 1 April 20X1:

1   Relax its credit terms in its export market by offering 90 days credit, an increase of 30 days on its normal terms in this market.

2   Invoice in euro rather than A$, converting the A$ price list to produce a euro price list at the current exchange rate of A$/EUR 0.4000 (A$1 = EUR 0.4000). This euro price list will then be used for pricing export sales for the remainder of the year.

It is expected that these policy changes will result in an increase in export sales of one-third between the first and second quarters of 20X1.

Provisional forecast results for TM (including both home and export sales) for the first two quarters of 20X1, after taking into account the planned policy changes and using the exchange of A$/EUR 0.4000, are shown below:

	First quarter 20X1 (1 January to 31 March) A$ thousands	Second quarter 20X1 (1 April to 30 June) A$ thousands
Revenue	5,750	6,325
Cost of goods sold	3,163	3,529
Purchases	2,150	2,350

	Balances at 31 March 20X1 A$ thousands	Balances at 30 June 20X1 A$ thousands
Accounts receivable	5,000	7,000
Accounts payable	1,800	2,600
Inventory		
Raw materials	1,500	1,700
Work in Progress	740	860
Finished goods	420	500

Additional relevant information is given below:

- All purchases were, and will continue to be, sourced in the home country and paid for in A$.
- Net current assets are currently financed by an overdraft. This policy is under review.

There is concern that the value of the euro against the A$ may fall to A$/EUR 0.4600 at the beginning of the second quarter of 20X1. However, other exchange rate forecasters predict that the exchange rate will remain unchanged. If the exchange rate were to change, the directors do not expect to be able to increase TM's euro prices to reflect the devaluation of the euro in view of the current poor economic environment in Europe.

Required:

(a)   Evaluate the likely impact of the movement in exchange rates from A$/EUR 0.4000 to A$/EUR 0.4600 on 1 April 20X1 on the results for the second quarter of 20X1, assuming that the exchange rate remains unchanged for the remainder of the quarter.   **(6 marks)**

(b)   (i)   Calculate the operating cycle of TM for:

- The first quarter of 20X1.

- The second quarter of 20X1 using an exchange rate of A$/EUR 0.4000 as proposed in the policy change.

- The second quarter of 20X1 using an exchange rate of A$/EUR 0.4600 throughout the second quarter.   **(9 marks)**

(ii)   Briefly discuss whether the changes in any of the component parts of the cycle give cause for concern.   **(3 marks)**

(c)   Advise the directors of TM on an appropriate financing structure for net current assets and explain the benefits and potential problems of using euro denominated finance.   **(7 marks)**

(Total = 25 marks)

58 FBQ
45 mins

FBQ is a profitable, listed manufacturing company which is considering a project to update its production facilities. This would involve the purchase of a computer controlled machine with a production capacity of 70,000 units. The machine would cost $900,000 and have a useful life of four years, after which it would be sold for $200,000 and replaced with a more up-to-date model.

Demand in the first year for the machine's output would be 35,000 units and this demand is expected to grow by 25% per annum in each subsequent year of production.

The following information concerning current costs and selling price is available:

	$/unit	Annual inflation %
Selling price	50	3
Variable production cost	16	4
Fixed production overhead cost	25	5

Fixed production overhead is based on expected first-year demand.

FBQ depreciates assets on a straight-line basis over their useful economic life. Writing down allowances on machinery can be claimed on a 25% reducing balance basis and FBQ pays tax on profits at an annual rate of 30% in the year in which the liability arises.

The project will raise FBQ's debt capacity by $600,000 for the duration of the project at an interest rate of 4%. The costs of raising this loan are estimated at $15,000 (net of tax).

The risk-free rate of return is 4%, the return from the market as a whole is 10% and the equity beta of FBQ is 1.35. FBQ's ratio of the market value of debt to the market value of equity is currently 1:2 and the cost of debt is 4%.

Required

(a) Advise FBQ on whether or not to proceed with the project based on a calculation of its adjusted present value (APV).   **(17 marks)**

(b) Discuss the main factors that will influence FBQ's choice of finance between debt or equity and long-term or short-term debt.   **(8 marks)**

(Total = 25 marks)

59 CIP (9/11)
45 mins

Assume today is 1 October 20X1.

CIP is a manufacturing company based in an Eastern European country, which has the euro as its currency. The CIP board is evaluating a potential project which involves the launch of a new product that has a limited life of six years and which will require an initial investment in specialised machinery.

Project cash flows:

The specialised machinery will cost EUR 6.5 million and will be installed and paid for on 1 January 20X2. The Management Accountant has forecast that the net after tax cash flows associated with the new product will be as follows:

Year to 31 December	20X2	20X3	20X4	20X5 - X7
Net after tax cash flows (EUR '000)	750	950	1,400	2,100

The project will have no residual value as the specialised machinery cannot be used elsewhere or sold at the end of the project. The net after tax cash flows can be assumed to arise at the end of the year to which they relate.

Financing the project

The proposed investment is in a development region of the country and the local government is offering subsidised borrowing for 40% of the initial capital investment at an annual interest rate of 1% to encourage investment.

A further 20% of the capital required will be raised by bank borrowing, at an annual interest rate of 6%, which is the same as CIP's pre-tax cost of debt.

The duration of the borrowings will match the duration of the investment with the full amount of the borrowings repayable at the end of the six year term. The corporate income tax rate is 30% and tax is payable or recoverable at the end of the year to which it relates. There are sufficient taxable profits within CIP to benefit in full from the tax relief available on interest payments.

CIP has sufficient cash to fund the remaining 40% of the capital expenditure.

Other information:

- CIPs current market debt: equity ratio is 1:3.

- CIP's current WACC (weighted average cost of capital), which it typically uses for investment appraisal, is 10%. The proposed project is in a market which is expected to be riskier than its normal operations and therefore some of the board of CIP are unsure whether 10% is an appropriate rate at which to appraise the investment. The Management Accountant has suggested that either a risk adjusted WACC should be used as a discount rate (based upon a cost of equity reflecting the business risk of the project and CIP's existing gearing) in an NPV (net present value) evaluation or, alternatively, an APV (adjusted present value) approach should be adopted. He has identified PPP as a company that operates exclusively in the market of the proposed project. PPP's equity beta is 1.95 and it has a current market debt:equity ratio of 1:4. The post-tax risk free rate of return and market rate of return are expected to be 4% and 9% respectively for the foreseeable future.

- Administrative costs of arranging the two borrowings are expected to be 1% of the amounts raised.

Required:

(a) Calculate, as at 1 January 20X2:

    (i)   The NPV of the project at CIP's existing WACC of 10%. **(2 marks)**

    (ii)   The NPV of the project at a risk adjusted WACC using PPP as a proxy company in respect of business risk. **(5 marks)**

    (iii)   The APV of the project. **(8 marks)**

(b) Evaluate the potential financial benefits of the project. Your answer should include discussion on the appropriateness of each of the methods used in part (a) to appraise the project. **(8 marks)**

(c) Advise the directors of CIP whether they should proceed with the project. **(2 marks)**

(Total = 25 marks)

60 PEI (11/10)   45 mins

It is currently November 20X0.

PEI is a privately-owned college of higher education in the UK. It competes directly with other private and government-funded schools and colleges. The college directors are considering two investment opportunities that would allow the college to expand in the UK (known as Projects A and B) and a third opportunity to set up a satellite training centre in a foreign country (known as Project C). Ideally, it would invest in all three projects but the company has only GBP 25 million of cash available (where GBP is British Pounds). PEI currently has borrowings of GBP 50 million and does not wish to increase indebtedness at the present time. PEI's shares are not listed.

The initial capital investment required (on 1 January 20X1) and likely net operating cash inflows arising from the investments in each project are as follows.

	Initial Investment GBP million	Net Operating Cash inflows (after tax)
Project A	15.50	GBP 1.75 million each year from year 1 indefinitely.
Project B	10.20	GBP 1.15 million in year 1, and GBP 3.10 million a year in years 2 to 7.
Project C	9.50	A$ 9.30 million each year for years 1 to 5.

Notes:

1   The projects are not divisible.

2   Project B has a residual value of GBP 2.5 million. The other projects are expected to have no residual value.

3   Projects A and B are to be discounted at 8%. The Finance Director considers that a GBP discount rate of 9% is more appropriate for Project C as it carries slightly greater risk.

4   The GBP/A$ exchange rate is expected to be GBP/A$ 2.00 on 1 January 20X1 (that is, GBP 1 = A$ 2.00). The A$ is expected to weaken against GBP by 1.5% per annum for the duration of the project.

5   Assume cash flows, other than the initial investment, occur at the end of each year.

Required:

(a)

    (i)   Calculate the NPV and PI of each of the THREE projects based on the GBP cash flows.

          (8 marks)

    (ii)   Evaluate your results and advise PEI which project or combination of projects to accept.

          (7 marks)

(b)   Explain the alternative method of evaluating Project C using an A$ discount rate, illustrating your answer with a calculation of an appropriate A$ discount rate.   **(4 marks)**

(c)   Discuss the key financial factors, other than the NPV decision, that should be considered before investing in a project located in a foreign country rather than the home country.   **(6 marks)**

          (Total = 25 marks)

61 REM   45 mins

REM is a family-owned business. The family owns 80% of the shares. The remaining 20% is owned by four non-family shareholders. The board of directors is considering the purchase of two second-hand (that is, previously used) freight planes to deliver its goods within its key markets in the USA. The managing director, an ex-pilot and one of the non-family shareholders, commissioned an evaluation from the company's accountants and was advised that the company would save money and be more efficient if it performed these delivery operations itself instead of 'outsourcing' them to established courier and postal services. The accountants built into their evaluation an assumption that the company would be able to sell spare capacity on the planes to other companies in the locality.

The managing director has decided that the accountants' recommendation will be conducted as a 'trial' for 5 years when its success or otherwise will be evaluated. The net, post-tax operating cash flows of this investment are estimated as:

Year 0   –$12.50 million (the initial capital investment)
Years 1 to 4 $3.15 million each year
Year 5 $5.85 million

Year 5 includes an estimate of the residual value of the planes.

The company normally uses an estimated post-tax weighted average cost of capital of 12% to evaluate investments. However, this investment is different from its usual business operations and the finance director suggests using the capital asset pricing model (CAPM) when determining a discount rate. REM, being unlisted, does not have a published beta so the finance director has obtained a beta of 1.3 for a courier company that is listed. This company has a debt ratio (debt to equity) of 1:2, compared with REM whose debt ratio is 1:5.

Other information:

•   The expected annual post-tax return on the market is 9% and the risk-free is 5%.
•   Assume both companies' debt is virtually risk-free.
•   Both companies pay tax at 30%.

Required

(a) Using the CAPM, calculate:

    (i)   An asset beta for REM

    (ii)   An equity beta for REM

    (iii) An appropriate discount rate to be used in the evaluation of this project

    (iv) The NPV of the project using the discount rate calculated in (iii); and comment briefly on your choice of discount rate in part (iii). **(11 marks)**

(b) Evaluate the benefits and limitations of using a proxy company's beta to determine the rate to be used by REM in the circumstances here, and recommend alternative methods of adjusting for risk in the valuation that could be considered by the company. **(9 marks)**

(c) Advise the managing director on the benefits of a post-completion audit. **(5 marks)**

A report format is not required in answering this question. **(Total = 25 marks)**

62 GHI (FS, 5/06)   45 mins

GHI is a mobile phone manufacturer based in France with a wide customer base in France and Germany, with all costs and revenues based in euro (€). GHI is considering expanding into the UK market and has begun investigating how to break into this market and is designing a new phone specifically for it. A small project committee has been formed to plan and control the project.

After careful investigation, the following project cash flows have been identified:

Year	£million
0	(10)
1	5
2	5
3	4
4	3
5	3

The project is to be funded by a loan of €16 million at an annual interest rate of 5% and repayable at the end of five years. Loan issue costs amount to 2% and are tax deductible.

GHI has a debt : equity ratio of 40 : 60 based on market values, a pre-tax cost of debt of 5.0% and a cost of equity of 10.7%.

Tax on entity profits in France can be assumed to be at a rate of 35%, payable in the year in which it arises. UK tax at 25% is deductible in full against French tax in the same time period under the terms of the double tax treaty between the UK and France. The initial investment of £10 million will not qualify for any tax relief.

Assume the current spot rate is £/€1.60 (that is, £1 = €1.60) and sterling (£) is expected to weaken against the euro by 3% per annum (so that in year 1 it is worth only 97% of its value in euro (€) in year 0).

Required

(a) Advise GHI on whether or not to proceed with the project based on a calculation of its adjusted present value (APV) and describe the limitations of an APV approach in this context. **(15 marks)**

(b) Explain the function of the project committee of GHI in the following stages of the project:

    (i)   Determining customer requirements and an appropriate product design for the UK market; and **(5 marks)**

    (ii)   Controlling the implementation stage of the project. **(5 marks)**

(Total = 25 marks)

63 QE
45 mins

QE is a medium-sized food manufacturing company. It has recently sold a subsidiary that traded in what the company considered to be non-core business. The sale raised £1.4 million in cash.

The company's long-term debt to equity ratio is relatively high compared with other companies in the industry and the directors have ruled out further borrowing at the present time. In fact, one of the directors thinks the cash raised from the sale of the subsidiary should be used to repay some of the company's outstanding debt.

This is not a view shared by the other directors who are evaluating three small but potentially profitable acquisition opportunities. The directors believe that the shareholders of all three target companies would not be opposed to a bid at this time, especially to a cash offer. However, to acquire all of them would require £2.3 million. The share price is standing at an all-time high – a level considered unsustainable by the directors based on the company's projected earnings. The directors therefore intend to limit their expenditure to the £1.4 million cash raised by the sale of the subsidiary.

Expected after-tax cash flows

Company	Year 1	Year 2	Year 3	Acquisition price
	£'000	£'000	£'000	£'000
AB	(100)	750	1,100	(1,100)
CD	125	275	380	(550)
EF	200	325	450	(650)

Note. The cash flows are in real terms, ie they do not include inflation. QE plc's shareholders currently require a real return of 12% on their investment in the company. The company uses this rate to evaluate all its investment decisions, including acquisitions.

Required

Assume you are a financial manager with QE. Write a report to the directors evaluating the potential acquisitions. You should include the following information in your report.

(a) The expected net present value and profitability indexes of the three projects. Based solely on these calculations, discuss which company(ies) should be chosen for acquisition and discuss the use of 12% as a discount rate in the circumstances here. **(10 marks)**

(b) Recommendation of uses for any cash that is left over after the acquisitions have been made. **(4 marks)**

(c) Discussion of the directors' decisions

   (i)   To invest rather than repay debt, and

   (ii) To limit their investment for the current year to cash purchases rather than raise new capital in the form of debt or equity **(6 marks)**

(d) Discussion of the advantages and disadvantages of growth by acquisition as compared with growth by internal (or organic) investment. **(5 marks)**

(Total = 25 marks)

64 RST (FS, 5/06)
45 mins

RST is a publicly-owned and funded health organisation based in the Far East. It is reviewing a number of interesting possibilities for new development projects in the area and has narrowed down the choice to the five projects detailed below. RST is aware that government budget restrictions may be tighter in a year's time and so does not want to commit to a capital budget of more than $30 million in year 1. In addition, any project cash inflows in year 1 may be used to fund capital expenditure in that year. There is sufficient capital budget remaining in year 0 to enable all projects to be undertaken. Under government funding rules, any unused capital in year 0 cannot be carried over to year 1 and no interest may be earned on unused capital. No borrowings are permitted.

RST assesses capital projects at a hurdle rate of 15% based on the equity beta of health-based companies in the private sector.

Project	Cash outflows Year 0 $ million	Cash outflows Year 1 $ million	Cash inflows $ million	
A	9	16	4	from year 1 in perpetuity
B	10	10	4	from year 2 in perpetuity
C	10	12	5	in years 1 to 10
D	8	5	6	in years 3 to 7
E	9	8	2 }	in years 1 to 5
			5 }	in years 6 to 15

Notes

- The projects are not divisible
- Each project can only be undertaken once
- Ignore tax

Required

(a)   Advise RST on the best combination of projects based on an evaluation of each project on the basis of both:

(i)   NPV of cashflows;

(ii)   A profitability index for use in this capital rationing analysis.   **(15 marks)**

(b)   Discuss

(i)   Whether or not capital rationing techniques based on NPV analysis are appropriate for a publicly-owned entity such as RST.   **(5 marks)**

(ii)   As a publicly-owned entity, what other factors RST should consider and what other analysis it should undertake before making a final decision on which project(s) to accept.   **(5 marks)**

(Total = 25 marks)

65   HIJ (FS, 11/07, amended)   45 mins

HIJ is a private transport and distribution entity. It is considering three investment opportunities, which are not mutually exclusive. HIJ is currently all equity financed, it has no cash reserves, but could borrow a maximum of $30 million at the present time at a gross interest rate of 10%. Borrowing above this amount might be possible, but at a much higher rate of interest.

The initial capital investment required, the NPV and the duration of each project is as follows:

	Initial investment $million	NPV $million (after tax)	Duration Years
Project A	15.4	2.75	6
Project B	19.0	3.60	7
Project C	12.8	3.25	Indefinite

Notes

1   The projects are not divisible and cannot be postponed.

2   The discount rate considered appropriate for all three investments is the current cost of equity, which is 12%.

3   HIJ pays corporate tax at 30%.

4   Assume cash flows, other than the initial investment, occur evenly throughout the duration of the investments.

Required

(a) (i) Calculate the profitability index and equivalent annual annuities for all three projects; explain the usefulness of these methods of evaluation in the circumstances here; and recommend which project(s) should be undertaken. **(10 marks)**

(ii) Explain the differences between 'hard' and 'soft' capital rationing and which type is evident in the scenario here. Discuss, briefly, the advisability of the directors of HIJ limiting their capital expenditure in this way. **(5 marks)**

(iii) You later discover that the discount rate used was nominal, but the cash flows have been calculated in real terms.

Explain, briefly, how the calculation for NPV should be adjusted and what effect the changes might have and on your recommendation. You are **not** required to do any calculations for this section of the question. **(4 marks)**

(b) Assume that Project B, and B only, could attract Government support as follows:

(i) A non-repayable grant of $3.5 million payable as soon as the project commenced; plus

(ii) Subsidised bank lending of 50% of the initial investment (after the government grant), secured on the non-current assets that would be acquired for this project.
The capital amount of the debt would be repayable in eight years' time. Interest (before tax) is at the rate of 8% per annum and will be paid in equal instalments annually at the end of each year.

Discuss, with supporting calculations, whether this new information would change your recommendation using an APV approach incorporating the NPV in the scenario as the 'base case'. **(6 marks)**

A report format is **not** required for this question. **(Total = 25 marks)**

66 BA
45 mins

BA is a firm of recruitment and selection consultants. It has been trading for 10 years and obtained a stock market listing 4 years ago. It has pursued a policy of aggressive growth and specialises in providing services to companies in high-technology and high-growth sectors. It is all-equity financed by ordinary share capital of $50 million in shares of $0.20 nominal (or par) value. The company's results to the end of June 20X2 have just been announced. Profits before tax were $126.6 million. The chairman's statement included a forecast that earnings might be expected to rise by 4%, which is a lower annual rate than in recent years. This is blamed on economic factors that have had a particularly adverse effect on high-technology companies.

YZ is in the same business but has been established much longer. It services more traditional business sectors and its earnings record has been erratic. Press comment has frequently blamed this on poor management and the company's shares have been out of favour with the stock market for some time. Its current earnings growth forecast is also 4% for the foreseeable future. YZ has an issued ordinary share capital of $180 million in $1 shares. Pre-tax profits for the year to 30 June 20X2 were $112.5 million.

BA has recently approached the shareholders of YZ with a bid of 5 new shares in BA for every 6 YZ shares. There is a cash alternative of 345 cents per share.

Following the announcement of the bid, the market price of BA shares fell 10% while the price of YZ shares rose 14%. The P/E ratio and dividend yield for BA, YZ and two other listed companies in the same industry *immediately prior* to the bid announcement are shown below. All share prices are in cents.

High	20X2 Low	Company	P/E	Dividend yield %
425	325	BA	11	2.4
350	285	YZ	7	3.1
187	122	CD	9	5.2
230	159	WX	16	2.4

Both BA and YZ pay tax at 30%.

BA's post-tax cost of equity capital is estimated at 13% per annum and YZ's at 11% per annum.

Assume you are a shareholder in YZ. You have a large, but not controlling, shareholding and are a qualified management accountant. You bought the shares some years ago and have been very disappointed with their

performance. Two years ago you formed a 'protest group' with fellow shareholders with the principal aim of replacing members of the board. You call a meeting of this group to discuss the bid.

Required

In preparation for your meeting, write a briefing note for your group to discuss. Your note should:

(a) Evaluate whether the proposed share-for-share offer is likely to be beneficial to shareholders in *both* BA and YZ. You should use the information and merger terms available, plus appropriate assumptions, to forecast post-merger values. As a benchmark, you should then value the two companies using the constant growth form of the dividend valuation model. **(13 marks)**

(b) Discuss the factors to consider when deciding whether to accept or reject the bid and the relative benefits/disadvantages of accepting shares or cash. **(8 marks)**

(c) Advise your shareholder group on what its members should do with their investment in YZ, based on your calculations/considerations. **(4 marks)**

(Total = 25 marks)

67 PDQ
45 mins

PDQ is a software company and Internet provider that was established in the dot-com boom of the late twentieth century.

The three founding shareholders, who are still directors and managers of the company, own 30% of PDQ. Employees, friends and relatives of the founders own a further 15%. The majority 55% shareholding is owned by a venture capital company that bought a stake in PDQ four years ago for £12 million. The venture capital company now wishes to dispose of the holding. The 45% minority shareholders and non-shareholding employees are considering a management buyout.

PDQ has sustained losses for the past three years but believes it is now moving into profit. Because of these losses, no liability to tax will arise in 20X4 but the company will begin to pay tax at 30% per annum from 20X5. It has not declared or paid a dividend since the company was formed. A summary of forecast key financial information for the current year and for 20X4 is as follows:

Statement of consolidated income for the year ended:	31 December 20X4 £ million	31 December 20X3 £ million
Revenues	15.25	14.52
Direct costs and expenses	12.50	16.97
Profit/(loss) before tax	2.75	(2.45)

Statement of financial position at:	31 December 20X4 £ million	£ million	31 December 20X3 £ million	£ million
Non-current assets (NBV)		0.50		0.50
Current assets				
Inventory	1.25		1.25	
Receivables	4.25		3.25	
Cash and marketable securities	0.50		0.00	
		6.00		4.50
		6.50		5.00
Ordinary share capital (Ordinary shares of £1)		0.25		0.25
Total reserves		3.45		0.70
Equity shareholders' funds		3.70		0.95
Current liabilities				
Trade payables	2.80		3.20	
Bank overdraft	0.00		0.85	
		2.80		4.05
		6.50		5.00

The directors expect growth of 20% each year for the three years 20X5 to 20X7 inclusive, falling to 5% each year after that. The average P/E ratio for established listed companies in the industry is currently 28.4 but there is a wide range of between 7.5 and 51.5. The average post-tax cost of equity capital for the industry, according to a recent survey, is 15%.

Required

Assume today is 31 December 20X3.

Advise the founders/employees on the following.

(a)   The price they might have to offer the venture capitalist to succeed with a management buyout. You should include in your discussion the various methods of share valuation that might be suitable in the circumstances. Make and state whatever assumptions you feel are necessary and appropriate.

(18 marks)

(b)   The advantages and disadvantages of pursuing a management buyout at the present time compared with the possibility of a sale of the venture capitalist's shareholding to another investor.   **(7 marks)**

<u>Note</u>. A report format is NOT required in answering this question.   **(Total = 25 marks)**

68 YY (9/11)   45 mins

Assume today is 1 October 20X1.

YY Group is a manufacturer of consumer electronic appliances and its shares are listed on a major stock exchange. The functional currency of the YY group is the $.

The Board of YY is considering the disposal of a wholly-owned subsidiary, TS, that manufactures telecommunications equipment. The CEO of YY thinks this subsidiary is not central to the group's main financial objective and strategic direction and utilises valuable resources that could be more profitably employed in its core businesses. TS, while profitable, has consistently reported lower growth rates than the group as a whole and therefore the CEO is recommending the disposal of the subsidiary.

The Finance Director of YY is not convinced of the need for disposal. He has correctly noted that this subsidiary continues to make a contribution to profits. He thinks that unless an opportunity can be identified that requires this level of investment and can better aid the achievement of the group's objective, YY should not sell TS. His estimate is that TS is worth just under $1 billion ($1,000 million).

The senior managers of TS have indicated they are interested in pursuing a management buyout (MBO). The Board of YY is willing to consider this but some Board members, who agree with the divestment of TS in principle, think a trade sale would be a better alternative.

A meeting of the management team of TS has been called by Mr A, the Managing Director of TS, to discuss a range of issues that need to be considered if they are to launch an MBO. The following views have been expressed by various members of the management team of TS.

<u>Mr A - Managing Director of TS</u>

"I am convinced that we, the management team, can add value to TS. We need to identify how and why, under our own control, we can achieve greater returns from the business than under YY's control. We also need to be able to convince the Board of YY that selling the business to us by means of an MBO is more attractive for them than a trade sale."

<u>Ms B - Financial Manager of TS</u>

"Financing will be a major problem if the Finance Director of YY is correct in his valuation. The TS management team and employees would be able to raise no more than 20% of this value. I have therefore had informal discussions with a venture capital organisation. It is very interested and has money available. However, before starting formal negotiations, I would like to know more about the advantages and disadvantages of venture capital financing in our situation and also whether there are any realistic alternatives."

<u>Mr C - Marketing Manager of TS</u>

"Ms B has explained to me that the $1 billion ($1,000 million) valuation produced by the Finance Director of YY is based on YY's P/E ratio. I have three questions:

1   How is the $1 billion ($1,000 million) calculated? This seems excessive as the net asset value is substantially less than this.

2   Is the net asset value the one we should be focussing on?

3   Are there any other, more appropriate, valuations or methods of valuation?"

Summary financial data

	YY Group (including TS)	TS
Earnings in the financial year ended 31 August 20X1 ($ million)	1,260	75
Book value of net assets as at 31 August 20X1 ($ million)	8,050	735
(Net assets are stated after deducting borrowings.)		
Shares in issue on 31 August (unchanged at 1 October 20X1)	525 million	25 million
Share price on 31 August 20X1 ($)	31.20	n/a
Share price on 1 October 20X1 ($)	31.50	n/a

The P/E ratios of companies in the telecommunications industry in the region generally range from 8 to 25. The average P/E ratio is 15.

Assume you are an independent advisor retained and paid by the management team of TS to advise on the proposed MBO.

Required:

Prepare briefing notes for a forthcoming meeting with the management team of TS in which you evaluate the concerns raised in respect of the proposed MBO by the following people:

(a)   Mr A - Managing Director of TS   **(7 marks)**

(b)   Ms B - Financial Manager of TS   **(7 marks)**

(c)   Mr C - Marketing Manager of TS   **(11 marks)**

Up to 4 marks are available for calculations in part (c).

(Total = 25 marks)

69   PCO (FS, Pilot paper)   45 mins

PCO plc operates in oil and related industries. Its shares are quoted on the London International Stock Exchange. In its retailing operations the company has concentrated on providing high quality service and facilities at its service stations rather than competing solely on the price of petrol. Approximately 75% of its revenue and 60% of its profits are from petrol, the remainder coming from other services (car wash and retail sales from its convenience stores which are available at each service station).

The company has been highly profitable in the past as a result of astute buying of petroleum products on the open market. The company does not enter into supplier agreements with the major oil companies except on very short-term deals. However, profit margins are now under increasing pressure as a result of intensifying competition and the cost of complying with environmental legislation.

The managing director of the company is assessing a possible acquisition that would help the company increase the percentage of its non-petroleum revenue and profits. OT plc specialises in oil distribution from the depots owned by the major oil companies to their retail outlets. Its shares have been quoted on the UK Alternative Investment Market for the past 2 years. It operates a fleet of oil tankers, some owned and some leased. PCO plc has used its services in the past and knows it has an up to date and well-managed fleet. However, a bid for OT plc would almost certainly be hostile and, as the directors and their families own 40% of the shares, a successful bid is far from assured.

Extracts from PCO plc's Statement of financial position at 31 December 20X3

	£m
Assets Employed	
Cash and marketable securities	105.00
Accounts receivable and inventories	95.00
Less current liabilities	(75.00)
Working capital	125.00
Property, plant and equipment	160.00
Less long term liabilities	(80.00)
Secured loan stock 7% repayable 20X9	205.00

Shareholders' equity

Share capital (Authorised £50 million)	
Issued	40.00
Accumulated profits	165.00
Net Assets Employed	<u>205.00</u>

PCO plc's financial advisors have produced estimates of the expected NPV and the first full year post-acquisition earnings of PCO plc and OT plc:

	Estimated post-acquisition earnings in first full year following acquisition	Estimated NPV of combined organisation
PCO plc plus OT plc	£70 million	£720 million

Summary financial statistics

	PCO plc	OT plc
Last year end	31 December 20X3	31 December 20X3
Shares in issue (millions)	40	24
Earnings per share (pence)	106	92
Dividend per share (pence)	32	21
Share price (pence)	967	1,020
Book value of non-current assets and current assets less current liabilities (£ million)	285	145
Debt ratio (outstanding debt as % of total market value)	17.0	14.0
Forecast growth rate %(constant, annualised)	5	9
Beta co-efficient	0.9	1.2

Required

(a)   Calculate, for PCO plc and OT plc *before* the acquisition:

    (i)   The current market value and P/E ratio.

    (ii)   The cost of equity using the CAPM, assuming the return on the market is 8% and the return on the risk free asset is 4%.

    (iii)   The prospective share price and market value using the dividend valuation model.   **(6 marks)**

(b)   Discuss and advise on the following issues:

    (i)   The price to be offered to the target company's shareholders. You should recommend a range of terms within which PCO plc should be prepared to negotiate.

    (ii)   The most appropriate form of funding the bid and the financial effects (assume cash or share exchange are the options).

    (iii)   The business implications (effect on existing operation, growth prospects, risk and so on).

           (19 marks)

Marks are split roughly equally between sections of part (b) of the question.   **(Total = 25 marks)**

70   BiOs (FS, Pilot paper)   45 mins

BiOs Limited (BiOs) is an unquoted company that provides consultancy services to the biotechnology industry. It has been trading for 4 years. It has an excellent reputation for providing innovative and technologically advanced solutions to clients' problems. The company employs 18 consultants plus a number of self employed contract staff and is planning to recruit additional consultants to handle a large new contract. The company 'outsources' most administrative and accounting functions. A problem is recruiting well qualified experienced consultants and BiOs has had to turn down work in the past because of lack of appropriate staff.

The company's two owners/directors have been approached by the marketing department of an investment bank and asked if they have considered using venture capital financing to expand the business. No detailed proposal has been made but the bank has implied that a venture capital company would require a substantial percentage of the equity in return for a large injection of capital. The venture capitalist would want to exit from the investment in 4-5 years' time.

The company is all-equity financed and neither of the directors is wholly convinced that such a large injection of capital is appropriate for the company at the present time.

Financial information

Revenue in year to 31 December 20X3	£3,600,000
Shares in issue (ordinary £1 shares)	100,000
Earnings per share	756p
Dividend per share	0
Net asset value	£395,000 (Note 1)

Note. The net assets of BiOs are the net book values of purchased and/or leased buildings, equipment and vehicles plus net working capital. The book valuations are considered to reflect current realisable values.

Forecast

- Sales revenue for the year to 31 December 20X4 – £4,250,000. This is heavily dependent on whether or not the company obtains the new contract.

- Operating costs, inclusive of depreciation, are expected to average 50% of revenue in the year to 31 December 20X4.

- Tax is expected to be payable at 30%.

- Assume book depreciation equals capital allowances for tax purposes. Also assume, for simplicity, that profit after tax equals cash flow.

Growth in earnings in the years to 31 December 20X5 and 20X6 is expected to be 30% per annum, falling to 10% per annum after that. This assumes that no new long-term capital is raised. If the firm is to grow at a faster rate then new financing will be needed.

This is a niche market and there are relatively few listed companies doing precisely what BiOs does. However, if the definition of the industry is broadened the following figures are relevant:

P/E Ratios

Industry Average:	18
Range (individual companies)	12 to 90

Cost of Equity

Industry average	12%
Individual companies	Not available

BiOs does not know what its cost of equity is.

Required

(a) Calculate a range of values for the company that could be used in negotiation with a venture capitalist, using whatever information is currently available and relevant. Make and state whatever assumptions you think are necessary. Explain, briefly, the relevance of each method to a company such as BiOs.

(15 marks)

(b) Discuss the advantages and disadvantages of using either venture capital financing to assist with expansion or alternatively a flotation on the stock market in 2-3 years' time. Include in your discussion likely exit routes for the venture capital company.

(10 marks)

(Total = 25 marks)

71 FS (FS, 11/05)   45 mins

It is currently November 20X5.

FS provides industrial and commercial cleaning services to organisations throughout a country in the European Union. Its shares have been listed for 15 years and, until two years ago, the entity followed a policy of aggressive growth, mainly by acquisition.

However, in the last two years, there have been few suitable takeover opportunities and, as a consequence, growth has slowed. The market has downgraded FS's shares and they are currently trading at €3·57, the lowest price for five years. The market as a whole has declined in value, but not to the same extent as FS's shares. FS's bank has recently informed FS's directors of a possible takeover opportunity of another of its clients, MT. This is a large private entity in the same industry as FS. MT's directors have indicated to the bank that if the price is right they may be prepared to sell the entity. MT's directors have made their financial forecasts and other strategic documentation available to the bank on a strictly confidential basis, requesting that this information only be released to a serious potential bidder. After much discussion between the bank and the two companies, MT agrees that FS should have the information.

MT's results for the past three years and the directors' estimates for the current year are as follows:

Year to 30 June	Revenue €million	Earnings €million
20X3	925	55.5
20X4	1,020	62.7
20X5	1,150	71.5
20X6 (forecast)	1,350	88.9

For 20X7 onwards, growth in earnings and dividends is likely to fall to 4% per annum, according to MT's directors. MT has paid a dividend of 50% of its earnings for the past 10 years.

Summary statement of financial positions as at 30 June 20X5 for both FS and MT are as follows:

	FS €million	MT € million
Total assets		
Non-current assets	1,944	1,040
Current assets*	796	375
	2,740	1,415
Equity and liabilities		
Equity		
Share capital (shares of €1)	420	
(shares of 50 cents)		220
Retained earnings	1,080	680
	1,500	900
Non-current liabilities		
Secured bonds, 6% 20X9	750	
Unsecured bonds, 7% 20X9		300
Current liabilities	490	215
	1,240	515
	2,740	1,415
* Includes cash of	250	65

FS's revenues and earnings for the year ended 30 June 20X5 were €2,250 million and €128·5 million respectively.

After thoroughly examining the information on MT, financial managers in FS have identified a number of savings and potential synergies that would arise if the takeover were to go ahead. These synergies are estimated to have a net present value of €200 million. However, the FS directors believe MT's forecast earnings are over-optimistic and think earnings growth for 20X6 onwards is likely to be in the range 2% to 4%. The bank advisers disagree, but they are in a delicate situation trying to balance the interests of two clients.

FS's cost of equity is 8·5%. MT has not provided information on its cost of capital, but the two entity's asset betas are likely to be the same. FS's equity beta is quoted as 1·1. The expected risk free rate of return is 3% and

the expected return on the market is 8%. Assume that the debt beta for both companies is 0·2 and that FS's debt is trading at par.

Ignore tax in your calculations.

Required

Assume you are a Financial Manager with FS. Advise the directors of FS on:

(a) The appropriate cost of capital to be used when valuing MT. Accompany your comments with a calculation of the cost of equity for MT. **(6 marks)**

(b) A bidding strategy; that is the initial price to be offered and the maximum FS should be prepared to offer for the shares in MT. Use whatever methods of valuation you think appropriate and accompany each with brief comments on their suitability in the circumstances here. In calculations of value that require a discount rate, use the cost of equity you have calculated in (i) above. Your answer should consider the interests of both groups of shareholders. **(13 marks)**

(c) The most appropriate form of consideration to use in the circumstances. Assume the choice is either a share exchange or cash. Your answer should consider the interests of both groups of shareholders. **(6 marks)**

(Total = 25 marks)

72 AB (FS, 11/06)   45 mins

It is currently November 20X6.

AB is a telecommunications consultancy based in Europe that trades globally. It was established 15 years ago. The four founding shareholders own 25% of the issued share capital each and are also executive directors of the entity. The shareholders are considering a flotation of AB on a European stock exchange and have started discussing the process and a value for the entity with financial advisers. The four founding shareholders, and many of the entity's employees, are technical experts in their field, but have little idea how entities such as theirs are valued.

Assume you are one of AB's financial advisors. You have been asked to estimate a value for the entity and explain your calculations and approach to the directors. You have obtained the following information.

Summary financial data for the past three years and forecast revenue and costs for the next two years is as follows:

Statement of consolidated income for the years ended 31 March

	Actual			Forecast	
	20X4	20X5	20X6	20X7	20X8
	€ million	€ million	€ million	€ million	€ million
Revenue	125.0	137.5	149.9	172.0	198.0
Less: Cash operating costs	37.5	41.3	45.0	52.0	59.0
Depreciation	20.0	22.0	48.0	48.0	48.0
Pre-tax earnings	67.5	74.2	56.9	72.0	91.0
Taxation	20.3	22.3	17.1	22.0	27.0

Statement of financial position at 31 March

	20X4	20X5	20X6
	€ million	€ million	€ million
Assets			
Non-current assets			
Property, plant and equipment	150	175	201
Current assets	48	54	62
	198	229	263

	20X4 € million	20X5 € million	20X6 € million
Equity and liabilities			
Equity			
Share capital (Shares of €1)	30	30	30
Retained earnings	148	179	203
	178	209	233
Current liabilities	20	20	30
	198	229	263

Note. The book valuations of non-current assets are considered to reflect current realisable values.

Other information/assumptions

- Growth in after tax cash flows for 20X9 and beyond (assume indefinitely) is expected to be 3% per annum. Cash operating costs can be assumed to remain at the same percentage of revenue as in previous years. Depreciation will fluctuate but, for purposes of evaluation, assume the 20X8 charge will continue indefinitely. Tax has been payable at 30% per annum for the last three years. This rate is expected to continue for the foreseeable future and tax will be payable in the year in which the liability arises.

- The average P/E ratio for telecommunication entities' shares quoted on European stock exchanges has been 12·5 over the past 12 months. However, there is a wide variation around this average and AB might be able to command a rating up to 30% higher than this.

- An estimated cost of equity capital for the industry is 10% after tax.

- The average pre-tax return on total assets for the industry over the past 3 years has been 15%.

Required

(a) Calculate a range of values for AB, in total and per share, using methods of valuation that you consider appropriate. Where relevant, include an estimate of value for intellectual capital. **(12 marks)**

(b) Discuss the methods of valuation you have used, explaining the relevance of each method to an entity such as AB. Conclude with a recommendation of an approximate flotation value for AB, in total and per share. **(13 marks)**

A report format is **not** required for this question. **(Total = 25 marks)**

73 VCI (FS, 11/06) — 45 mins

It is currently November 20X6.

VCI is a venture capital investor that specialises in providing finance to small but established businesses. At present, its expected average pre-tax return on equity investment is a nominal 30% per annum over a five-year investment period.

YZ is a typical client of VCI. It is a 100% family owned transport and distribution business whose shares are unlisted. The company sustained a series of losses a few years ago, but the recruitment of some professional managers and an aggressive marketing policy returned the company to profitability. Its most recent accounts show revenue of $105 million and profit before interest and tax of $28·83 million. Other relevant information is as follows:

- For the last three years dividends have been paid at 40% of earnings and the directors have no plans to change this payout ratio.

- Taxation has averaged 28% per annum over the past few years and this rate is likely to continue.

- The directors are forecasting growth in earnings and dividends for the foreseeable future of 6% per annum.

- YZ's accountants estimated the entity's cost of equity capital at 10% some years ago. The data they worked with was incomplete and now out of date. The current cost could be as high as 15%.

Extracts from its most recent statement of financial position **at 31 March 20X6** are shown below.

	$ million
Assets	
Non-current assets	
Property, plant and equipment	35.50
Current assets	4.50
	40.00
Equity and liabilities	
Equity	
Share capital (Nominal value of 10 cents)	2.25
Retained earnings	18.00
	20.25
Non-current liabilities	
7% Secured bond repayable in ten years' time	15.00
Current liabilities	4.75
	19.75
	40.00

<u>Note</u>. The entity's vehicles are mainly financed by operating leases.

YZ has now reached a stage in its development that requires additional capital of $25 million. The directors, and major shareholders, are considering a number of alternative forms of finance. One of the alternatives they are considering is venture capital funding and they have approached VCI. In preliminary discussions, VCI has suggested it might be able to finance the necessary $25 million by purchasing a percentage of YZ's equity. This will, of course, involve YZ issuing new equity.

Required

(a) Assume you work for VCI and have been asked to evaluate the potential investment.

    (i) Using YZ's forecast of growth and its estimates of cost of capital, calculate the number of new shares that YZ will have to issue to VCI in return for its investment and the percentage of the entity VCI will then own. Comment briefly on your result. **(9 marks)**

    (ii) Evaluate exit strategies that might be available to VCI in five years' time and their likely acceptability to YZ. **(6 marks)**

    <u>Note</u>. Use sensible roundings in your calculations.

(b) Discuss the advantages and disadvantages to an established business such as YZ of using a venture capital entity to provide finance for expansion as compared with long term debt. Advise YZ about which type of finance it should choose, based on the information available so far. **(10 marks)**

A report format is **not** required for this question. **(Total = 25 marks)**

74 GG (FS, 5/07)   45 mins

GG, a large engineering and project management group, has announced plans to sell its wholly owned telecommunications subsidiary, BB, so that it can concentrate on its core business of major infrastructure developments.

HH, an entity with diverse business interests, has expressed an interest in making a bid for BB, but the directors of HH are aware that there are likely to be several other interested parties.

News of the possible sale has been well received in the financial markets and GG has seen its share price rise by 15% in the last two months. HH expects to be able to use its good reputation and strong market presence to enhance the prospects of BB by improving BB's annual earnings by 10% from the date of acquisition.

<u>Financial information as at today, 23 May 20X7, ignoring any potential synergistic benefits arising from the possible acquisition of BB by HH:</u>

- Profit after tax for BB for the year ended 30 April 20X7 is estimated as $1 million
- BB's profit after tax has increased by 7% each year in recent years and this trend is expected to continue
- The gearing level of BB can be assumed to be the same as for GG

- The business tax rate is 30%
- Estimated post-tax return on the market is 8% and the risk free rate is 3% and these rates are not expected to change in the foreseeable future
- Assume a debt beta of zero

	HH	GG	Proxy entity for BB in the same industry
Number of ordinary shares in issue	8 million	4 million	–
Current share price	613 cents	800 cents	–
P/E ratios today	11	14	13
Dividend payout	40%	50%	50%
Equity beta	1.1	1.4	1.4
Gearing (debt:equity at market values)	1:2	1:2.5	1:4
Forecast earnings growth	5%	6%	–

Required

(a) Calculate an appropriate cost of equity for BB based on the data provided for the proxy entity. **(3 marks)**

(b) (i) Calculate a range of values for BB both before and after any potential synergistic benefits to HH of the acquisition. **(8 marks)**

(ii) Discuss your results in (b) (i) and advise the directors of HH on a suitable initial cash offer for BB. **(7 marks)**

(c) Advise the directors of GG on both the potential benefits and potential drawbacks arising from the divestment of its subsidiary, BB. **(7 marks)**

(Total = 25 marks)

75 Q & Z (FS, 5/07)   45 mins

Country Y

Country Y is a large industrialised country with strong motor vehicle and construction industries. The glass industry supplies glass to these industries as well as to specialist users of glass such as contact lens manufacturers. There are five major glass manufacturing entities, each with market coverage in Country Y of between 5% and 40%.

Entity Q

Entity Q is a quoted entity and a major player in the glass industry. It has a market share in Country Y of approximately 35%. It is an old, well-established entity with a number of factories used to manufacture glass both locally and abroad. It has a stable, but unexciting, growth rate of 3% per annum and is facing increasing competition from new glass manufacturing entities setting up in its key markets. However, Q's high earnings levels of earlier years have resulted in relatively low levels of debt.

The head office building of Q is in the far north of Country Y in a remote geographical area. It is a considerable distance from the capital city and major centres of population in the south of the country. The building is much larger than the entity requires and several floors are unoccupied.

The management team of Q is highly experienced; the majority of the senior managers have worked for Q for the whole of their working lives.

The computer systems of Q were written especially for the entity, but are in need of replacement in favour of something more flexible and adaptable to changing circumstances.

Entity Z

Entity Z, with a market share in Country Y of 10%, is a comparatively new and small, but fast growing unquoted family-owned entity. It specialises in certain niche markets for high security and extra heat resistant glass. The patents for this specialist glass were developed by the founder owner who now acts as Managing Director. The development of the business has largely been funded by high levels of borrowings at rates of interest well above standard market rates. In addition, the directors have often been required to provide personal guarantees against personal assets.

The management team of Z works in the capital city of Country Y, which is in the more prosperous southern part of the country. Z has a manufacturing base on the outskirts of the capital city.

The management team of Z is enthusiastic to grow the business, but is continually frustrated by a lack of financial and human resources and marketing network that would enable Z to expand into international markets. Also, on a personal level, many of the senior managers own a substantial number of shares in Z and are keen to realise some of their capital gains and become financially more secure.

The computer systems of Z consist of a basic accounting package and an internal network of PCs. Spreadsheet packages are widely used for budgeting and other financial reporting.

Takeover bid

The directors of Q have approached the directors of Z with a view to making a takeover bid for Z. A condition of the bid would be the retention of the current management team of Z, who have vital knowledge of the specialist manufacturing techniques required to manufacture the product range of Z. The directors of Z have been initially quite positive about the bid.

Both parties are concerned that the deal may be referred to Country Y's Competition Directorate, which regulates the country's competition policy, for approval and that conditions may be imposed that could make the takeover less attractive.

Required

(a)   Explain the role of competition authorities such as Country Y's Competition Directorate.   **(6 marks)**

(b)   Advise the directors of Q and Z on the potential problems of merging the management structure and systems of the two entities and how these could be minimised.   **(9 marks)**

(c)   Discuss whether the choice of capital structure for the new combined entity is likely to affect the overall value of the entity. Include references to Modigliani and Miller's (MM's) theory of capital structure in your answer.   **(10 marks)**

(Total = 25 marks)

76   SB (FS, 11/08)   45 mins

SB plc (SB) is an unquoted entity that provides technical advisory services and human resources to the oil exploration industry. It is based in the UK, but operates worldwide. It has been trading for 15 years. The four founding directors work full time in the business. Other employees are a combination of full time technical consultants and managers, and experts retained for specific contracts. Recruiting and retaining qualified consultants is a challenge and SB has to offer very competitive remuneration packages.

The market for the type of services that SB offers is growing. The large multinational oil entities are currently looking at exploration possibilities in the Caribbean. This will open up substantial new opportunities for SB which will require additional funding. However, the concessions for operating in this region are still under discussion with the various Caribbean governments and the oil multinationals have not yet started formal bidding.

In recent years, SB has been informally approached by some of its competitors and also its major customers to sell out. The directors have so far rejected these approaches but are now re-considering the possibilities. An alternative also being considered is an Initial Public Offering (IPO), that is, a stock market flotation.

Assume today is 1 January 20X4.

Current financial information

- Revenue in the year to 31 December 20X3 was £40,250,000 and earnings (profit after tax) were £20,188,000. There are five million shares in issue owned equally by the four directors. No dividends have been paid in any year to date.

- Net book value of buildings, equipment and vehicles plus net working capital is £22,595,000. The book valuations are considered to reflect current realisable values.

- SB is currently all equity financed.

Forecast financial information

- Sales revenue for the year to 31 December 20X4 is expected to be £52,250,000.
- Growth in revenue in the years to 31 December 20X5 and 20X6 is expected to be 20% per annum.
- Operating costs, inclusive of depreciation, are expected in the future to average 60% of revenue each year.
- Assume that book depreciation equals tax depreciation and that profit after tax equals cash flow.
- The marginal rate of tax is expected to remain at 28% per annum, payable in the year in which the liability arises.
- Assume from 20X7 onwards that the 20X6 pre-discounted cash flow will grow at 6% per annum indefinitely. This assumes that no new long-term capital is raised. If the entity is to grow at a faster rate then new financing will be needed.

Industry statistics

The average P/E ratio for the industry, using a very broad definition, is 12 with a range of 9 to 25. The average cost of capital for the industry is 12%. Cost of capital figures by individual entity are not available.

Required

(a) Assume you are a financial advisor to SB

(i) Calculate a range of values, in total and per share, for SB.

(ii) Advise the directors of SB on the relevance and limitations of each method of valuation to an entity such as theirs, and in the circumstances of the two alternative disposal strategies being considered.

(iii) Recommend a suitable valuation figure that could be used for a trade sale or an IPO.

Use whatever methods of valuation you think appropriate and can be estimated with the information available. **(18 marks)**

Note. Calculations in part (i) count for up to 10 marks.

(b) Advise the directors of SB on the advantages and disadvantages of a trade sale compared with a stock market flotation at the present time, and recommend a course of action. **(7 marks)**

(Total = 25 marks)

77 RV (FS, 5/09)   45 mins

RV is a private entity based in the UK and operating in a service industry. It has been trading for five years. All the directors and most of the employees are shareholders. None of them has attempted to sell shares in the entity so the problem of placing a value on them has not arisen. It has one external shareholder, which is a venture capital trust. This trust owns 15% of the share capital.

Revenue and profit before tax last year (20X8) were £109 million and £10 million respectively. RV pays corporate tax at 30%. The book value of total net assets as at the last balance sheet date was £25 million.

The entity is currently all-equity financed. The ordinary share capital of the entity is £4 million in shares of 20 pence par value. Dividends have been paid each year since 20X4 at a fixed payout ratio of 25% of earnings. In the current year (20X9) earnings are likely to be slightly lower than in 20X8 by approximately 5%. However, RV's directors have decided to pay a dividend of the same amount per share as in 20X8.

The directors are evaluating investment opportunities that would require all the entity's free cash flow for 20X9 plus long term borrowings of £20 million carrying an interest rate of 8% before tax. If the entity does not borrow to invest, growth in earnings and dividends will be zero for the foreseeable future. If it does borrow and invest, then growth in earnings and dividends are expected to be an average of 6% per annum from 20Y0 onwards.

RV's cost of equity is currently 12%. This is expected to rise to 13% if borrowing takes place.

Required

(a) (i) Calculate, in total and per share, a value for equity under each of the following two bases:

- Using the dividend valuation model and assuming **no** new investment

- Using Modigliani and Miller's theory of capital structure/gearing and assuming the entity borrows and invests **(8 marks)**

(ii) Discuss the limitations of the two methods of valuation you have just used and advise RV on a more appropriate method. **(7 marks)**

(b) Assuming some of the employees, who between them own 5% of the share capital, wish to sell their shares:

- Advise RV's directors whether either of the values you have calculated in part (a) would be an appropriate valuation for these small shareholdings as compared with a valuation for the whole entity. Include some discussion about how dividend policy might affect the valuation of an entity such as RV.

- Explain how and to whom the shares might be sold. **(10 marks)**

(Up to 14 marks are available for calculations)
(Total = 25 marks)

78 LP (FS, 5/09)   45 mins

LP's shares are listed on the London Stock Exchange. The directors of LP have made an offer for 100% of the shares in MQ. MQ's directors have rejected the bid. If the bid eventually succeeds, the new combined entity will become the largest in its industry in the UK.

Relevant information is as follows:

	LP	MQ
Share price as at today (20 May 20X9)	305 pence	680 pence
Share price one month ago	310 pence	610 pence
Shares in issue	480 million	130 million
Earnings per share for the year to 31 March 20X9	95 pence	120 pence
Debt outstanding as at 31 March 20X9 (book value)	£350 million	£105 million

- 30% of LP's debt is repayable in 20Y2; 30% of MQ's in 20Y3

- LP's cost of equity is 10%

- LP has cash available of £330 million. MQ's cash balances at the last balance sheet date (31 December 20X8) were £25 million

Terms of the bid

LP's directors made an opening bid one week ago of 2 LP shares for 1 MQ share. The entity's advisers have told the directors that, in order to succeed, they must consider a cash alternative to the proposed share exchange. If a cash alternative is offered and the bid eventually succeeds, 40% of shareholders are expected to accept the share exchange, and 60% the cash alternative.

Required

Assume you are a financial manager with LP.

(a) Discuss and advise the directors on the likely success of the bid based on the current offer and current market data. Recommend, if necessary, revised terms for the share exchange. **(9 marks)**

(b)   (i)   Discuss the advantages and disadvantages of offering a cash alternative to a share exchange. You should include the following calculations in your answer:

- The amount of cash that would be needed based on your recommendation of revised terms in part (a) above

- The impact of the proposed finance on the combined entity's gearing (debt to debt plus equity)   **(11 marks)**

(ii)   Recommend how the cash alternative might be financed.   **(5 marks)**

(Total = 25 marks)

79 XK (5/10)   45 mins

It is currently May 20X0.

XK is a multinational manufacturer of household electrical goods. Its headquarters and main manufacturing base are in the USA. Each manufacturing operation is usually established as a separate wholly-owned subsidiary. The larger electrical appliances tend to carry higher margins and there is a general move away from manufacturing smaller appliances.

Extracts from XK Group's latest statement of financial position at 30 April 20X0:

	US$ millions
ASSETS	
Non-current assets	2,250
Current assets	700
Total assets	2,950
EQUITY AND LIABILITIES	
Equity	
Share capital (Common shares of US$1)	375
Retained earnings	1,150
Total equity	1,525
Non-current liabilities	
Secured 7.5% bonds repayable 20Y0	1,000
Current liabilities	425
Total liabilities	1,425
Total equity and liabilities	2,950

Notes:

- XK's bonds are secured on its non-current assets.

- The current liabilities include overdraft of US$150 million. The conditions of the overdraft require XK to maintain a current ratio of at least 1.5 : 1.

- Group earnings for the year to 30 April 20X0 were US$510 million.

- XK pays corporate tax at 25% per annum.

- XK's share price has risen 5% over the past 3 months to its present level of US$8.75. The stock market price index has fallen by 3% in the same period.

The XK Board is discussing the divestment of one of its US subsidiaries, Company Y, which manufactures smaller appliances. Historically, the subsidiary company, Y, has accounted for 6% of group earnings. XK's accountants, with some input from the subsidiary's management team, have determined a net present value (NPV) to be placed on Company Y of US$325million. The Executive Directors of Y believe they can transform the business if they have the freedom to respond to market challenges and are considering a management buy out (MBO).

Financing the MBO:

The financing of the MBO will be by a combination of funding from the Executive Directors of Y, an investment bank and a Venture Capitalist.

The Executive Directors of Y expect to be able to raise US$5million between themselves as equity.

The investment bank will lend a maximum of 90% of the non-current assets of the business secured on those non-current assets, which are valued in the accounts at US$220 million. The interest rate will be 6% and the principal will be repayable in 5 years' time. This rate compares with current prime, or base, rate of 2% and commercial bank secured lending rates of between 3% and 4%.

The venture capitalist will supply the balance of the funding required. The venture capitalist expects a return on its investment averaging 25% per annum (on a compound basis) by 31 March 20X5 and requires all earnings to be retained in the business for 5 years. Some of the MBO team are not happy with this requirement.

Required

(a) Evaluate the interests of the various stakeholder groups in both XK and its subsidiary Company Y, and how these might be affected by the divestment. **(7 marks)**

(b) Discuss the economic and market factors that might impact on the negotiations between XK and the various financiers of the divestment (the Executive Directors of Y, the investment bank and the venture capitalist). **(7 marks)**

(c) Evaluate the advantages and disadvantages of the proposed buyout structure, and recommend alternative financing structures for the buyout.

Up to 5 marks are available for calculations **(11 marks)**

(Total = 25 marks)

80 WW (5/11)   45 mins

Today's date is 26 May 20X1.

WW is a publishing company that is listed in an Asian country, Country A, which uses the A$ as its currency. WW operates as three separate divisions according to type of publication as follows:

- Public Division – magazines and journals that are widely available in retail stores for purchase by the general public.

- Specialist Division - specialist magazines for particular industry sectors which are only available for delivery by post.

- In-house Division – company in-house journals for circulation to its own staff members.

WW has been disappointed with the recent performance of the Specialist Division and is considering selling that division. WW manages the company's debt centrally and measures the performance of the divisions on the basis of EBIT (earnings before interest and tax).

XX, a book publishing company, has expressed an interest in purchasing the Specialist Division. XX is also located in Country A and is confident that it has the expertise required to improve the performance of the Specialist Division. XX would purchase the net assets employed in the division (that is, non-current assets plus working capital). All borrowings would remain with WW.

There has been some discussion amongst the Directors of XX as to the most appropriate method to use to value the Specialist Division.

Director A has suggested that an asset-based valuation should be used.

Director B has proposed that the valuation should be based on the future operating cash flows of the division, adjusted for tax and discounted by XX's existing weighted average cost of capital (WACC).

Director C has suggested that the WACC used in the valuation should be derived from a proxy company. He has identified YY as a possible proxy for the Specialist Division. YY's sole activity is publishing specialist magazines in a similar market to the Specialist Division.

Director D has suggested that the earnings valuation model should be used based on an estimated cost of equity for the Specialist Division.

Financial data for WW's Specialist Division

The management of WW have provided XX with the following financial data for the Specialist Division:

- The net assets employed in the division had a book value of A\$ 15.0 million and an estimated replacement value of A\$ 20.0 million on 31 March 20X1.

- Operating cash flows adjusted for tax were A\$ 2.5 million in the year ended 31 March 20X1.

- Operating cash flows are forecast to grow by only 1% per annum in perpetuity if the division remains within WW.

Financial data for XX and YY

	XX	YY
Equity beta	1.5	0.8
Gearing ratio (debt/(debt plus equity))	40%	25%
Pre tax cost of debt	6%	7%
Market capitalisation	A\$ 150 million	A\$ 30 million

Additional relevant information for all companies WW, XX and YY:

- Corporate income tax rate is 30%.
- Risk free rate is 5%.
- The premium over the risk free rate by the market is 6%.
- Debt betas are zero.

Required:

(a) Calculate:

   (i) XX's existing cost of equity. **(1 mark)**

   (ii) XX's existing weighted average cost of capital (WACC). **(2 marks)**

   (iii) A suitable WACC for the Specialist Division based on proxy YY, adjusted for XX's gearing. **(5 marks)**

(b) (i) Calculate a range of values for the Specialist Division based on the different methods suggested by Directors A, B and C (but not Director D). **(5 marks)**

   (ii) Discuss the validity of the methods suggested by each of the four Directors A, B, C and D. **(8 marks)**

   (iii) Advise XX on an appropriate price for the purchase of the Specialist Division. **(4 marks)**

(Total = 25 marks)

81 MMM (9/11)   45 mins

MMM is a recruitment agency. It has seen rapid growth in recent years and obtained a stock market listing 3 years ago. However, recent profits have been disappointing, largely as a result of poor economic conditions leading to limited employment opportunities.

MMM is planning a takeover bid for JJJ, a rival recruitment agency in a specialist, growing market that has not been affected to such an extent by the poor economic conditions. JJJ has an advanced information technology and information system which was developed in-house and which MMM would acquire the rights to use. MMM plans to adopt JJJ's information technology and information system following the acquisition and this is expected to be a major contributor to the overall estimated synergistic benefits of the acquisition, which are estimated to be in the order of $8 million.

MMM has 30 million shares in issue and a current share price of $6.90 before any public announcement of the planned takeover. MMM is forecasting growth in earnings of 6% a year for the foreseeable future.

JJJ has 5 million shares in issue and a current share price of $12.84. It is forecasting growth in earnings of 9% a year for the foreseeable future.

The directors of MMM are considering 2 alternative bid offers:

Bid offer A - Share based bid of 2 MMM shares for each JJJ share.
Bid offer B - Cash offer of $13.50 per JJJ share.

Required

(a)   Assuming synergistic benefits are realised, evaluate bid offer A and bid offer B from the viewpoint of:

(i)   MMM's existing shareholders.

(ii)   JJJ's shareholders.

Up to 7 marks are available for calculations   **(11 marks)**

(b)   Advise the directors of MMM on:

(i)   The potential impact on the shareholders of both MMM and JJJ of not successfully realising the potential synergistic benefits after the takeover.

Up to 5 marks are available for calculations   **(8 marks)**

(ii)   The steps that could be taken to minimise the risk of failing to realise the potential synergistic benefits arising from the adoption of JJJ's information technology and information system.

(6 marks)

(Total = 25 marks)

82 Groots (FS, 5/05) 90 mins

Scenario

It is now 25 May 20X5.

Business background – The Groots Group

The Groots Group (Groots) is a retailer of clothing for women and children. The group started as a single store in France in the early 1900s. The business grew by acquisition of new premises and, occasionally, by buying out small competitors. Expansion outside France started fifty years ago and the group now has stores in most European cities. The parent company obtained a listing thirty-five years ago, although at that time the founding family still owned the majority of the shares. It is no longer controlled by the family although the grandson of the founder is a board member and owns 2% of the share capital. The company's other directors and senior managers own a further 8% between them.

The style of clothing sold in the Group's stores has changed over the years and its main theme now might be described as 'ethnic'. Most of its goods are manufactured outside Europe, predominantly in India and other parts of Asia.

Corporate objectives

Groots has two financial objectives and one non-financial objective. These are:

- To increase earnings and dividends per share year on year by 5% per annum
- To maintain an optimal debt/equity ratio within the range 25-30%
- To adhere to ethical trading policies and recognise the interests of its various stakeholder groups in all our business activities

Proposed acquisition

The directors of Groots believe they have exhausted possibilities for further expansion in Europe unless they are to diversify into different products such as men's clothing or household goods. They have, therefore, been reviewing opportunities for investment further afield for the past year. They have identified a small group of clothing stores trading in the East Caribbean and parts of South America, Cocomos Limited (Cocomos).

Cocomos is a listed company whose shares trade on an East Caribbean Stock Exchange. It has 18 stores as outlets for its products. Twelve of them are operated by the company itself and six are operated by franchisees. The clothing is at the expensive end of the market and aimed mainly at tourists.

Cocomos has followed a policy of buying locally-made clothing from within the Caribbean, Cuba or Puerto Rico, mainly from small co-operative-type manufacturers. The advantage of this policy is that the cost base is low, allowing for a substantial mark-up to retail. The disadvantage is that the quality is variable. If the acquisition proceeds, Groots would aim to review the product sources to improve the quality and expand the range. One alternative would be to supply the stores from sources in India, which already supply some of the European stores.

The directors of Cocomos and their families own 51% of the shares. A further 15% of the shares are owned by a local pension fund. The remaining 34% are owned by a number of wealthy individual investors, including a few who live most of the time in Europe or Canada.

Cocomos' directors are believed to be interested in opening discussions about a bid from Groots, but the franchisees are likely to be hostile. Although the franchisees are not shareholders, they will use the 'stealing our national assets' argument to agitate the press, local politicians and, ultimately, the local population.

On the basis of published accounts, industry information and discussions with Cocomos' directors, the Groots' directors have forecast the following post-tax cash flows for Cocomos:

| | Year | | | |
	1	2	3	4
Net cash flows (C$millions)	31.5	37.5	41.5	47.2

Post-tax cash flows beyond year 4 are estimated to grow at 2% per annum.

The cash flows are in real terms; that is they do not include inflation. Groots evaluates all its domestic investment decisions at a nominal, post-tax discount rate of 10%. Cocomos' directors estimate their company's cost of capital as 12%. However, Groots' directors think this rate of 12% does not adequately reflect the risk of Cocomos' cash flows.

Summary of financial statements of bidder and target companies

	Groots Group €m	Cocomos Ltd Caribbean $
Statement of consolidated income for the year ended 31 March 20X5		
Revenue	1,051.5	215.8
Operating profit	241.5	63.6
Finance costs (including overdraft interest)	48.0	15.0
Profit before tax	193.5	48.6
Taxation	46.9	11.5
Statement of financial position as at 31 March 20X5		
Assets		
Non-current assets		
Property, plant and equipment	895.0	245.0
Current assets		
Trade receivables and inventories	275.0	88.0
Cash and cash equivalents	45.0	12.0
Total assets	1,215.0	345.0
Equity and liabilities		
Equity		
Share capital (Nominal value of €1 and C$1 respectively)	245.0	55.0
Retained earnings	290.0	100.0
Total equity	535.0	155.0
Non-current liabilities		
Secured loan stock 7% repayable 20X9	475.0	
Secured loan stock 10% repayable 20X8		135.0
Current liabilities		
Trade and other payables	205.0	55.0
Total liabilities	680.0	190.0
Total equity and liabilities	1,215.0	345.0

Other financial information

	€	C$
Share price today	6.85	6.95
Shares last traded on	19 May 20X5	31 January 20X5
High-Low share prices in past 12 months	9.25–6.25	7.50–5.50
Debt value (market) per €100	105.50	N/A
Debt last traded on	30 December 20X4	N/A

Notes

Exchange rate C$/€, interest and inflation rates

The spot exchange rate is C$/€0.30 (that is, C$1 = €0.30). Forecast economic data relevant to the Caribbean, the US and the European Common Currency Area (ECCA) are as follows:

	ECCA %	Caribbean %
Risk-free interest rate per annum	3.5	6.5
Inflation rate per annum	2.5	4.5

You should assume the theory of interest rate parity applies when forecasting exchange rates.

Taxation

Both companies will pay tax at an average of 25% from next year for the foreseeable future. Assume a double taxation treaty is in existence between France and the Caribbean country.

Debt agreement

There is a clause in Cocomos' debt agreement that says the whole of the C$135 million debt is repayable immediately in the event of a successful takeover bid.

Required

(a) (i) Calculate the maximum price that Groots would be prepared to pay for Cocomos based on the present value in euros of the forecast cash flows. Using appropriate discount rates, you should calculate present value using *both* the recognised methods of evaluating international investments.
(7 marks)

(ii) Comment briefly on why, in theory, these two methods should give the same answer and why, in practice, the answers might be different.
(3 marks)

(iii) Calculate the number of shares Groots might need to issue if it offers its own shares in exchange for Cocomos using the higher of the values for the company you have calculated in (i). Comment briefly on your calculations and/or assumptions.
(4 marks)

(b) Assume you are a financial manager with Groots. Write a report to the directors of Groots which should include the following:

(i) A recommendation of the maximum price to be offered to Cocomos. You should base your recommendation on the figures you calculated in part (a) and *other* suitable methods of company valuation.

(ii) Identify and discuss alternative methods of financing the acquisition and make a recommendation of the most appropriate method in the situation here.

(iii) An analysis of strategies for enhancing the value of the combined company following the acquisition.

(iv) Advice on the benefits and limitations of a post-completion audit and review in the context of the acquisition.

Use additional calculations to support your arguments, wherever relevant and appropriate, for which up to 10 marks are available. Marks are distributed roughly equally between sections of the report.
(36 marks)

(Total = 50 marks)

83 GAS (FS, 11/05)   90 mins

Scenario

It is now May 20X5.

Description of the business

GAS plc is an international energy entity with a head office in the UK. Through its principal operating subsidiaries based in the UK and elsewhere in Europe, it generates electricity and supplies gas and electricity via energy supply networks across Europe.

GAS plc's strategy is to generate future growth through investment in new power stations, energy supply networks and gas storage assets. Its current focus for new investment is Bustan, a large Asian country that is in urgent need of major improvements in its electricity generation and supply systems to support the recent rapid increase in industrial production.

Group profile

On 31 December 20X4, GAS plc had 1,200 million 50 pence ordinary shares in issue and a share price of 335 pence ex-dividend. Shareholders expect a return on equity of 9·4%. Dividends for GAS plc for the year ended 31 December 20X4 were 14 pence a share, maintaining the 5% annual increase in dividends that has been

achieved in recent years. For simplicity, dividends should be assumed to be declared and paid on 31 December each year.

Investment project

The new investment in Bustan has been at the planning stage since the beginning of 20X4 when the government of Bustan first invited proposals for a large construction project from interested parties.

The project was evaluated over a 10-year period beginning January 20X5 and the project net operating cashflows in B$, the local currency of Bustan, were estimated to be as follows:

Year	B$ million
1	20
2	150
3	250
4–10	300

All cash flows should be assumed to arise on 31 December of each year. It should also be assumed that annual cash flows, less tax, are paid across to the UK on the final day of each year.

The cost of the initial investment in plant and other equipment at the beginning of January 20X5 was B$700 million and this is subject to depreciation charged in the subsidiary accounts on a straight line basis at 5% per annum. An additional B$50 million was required to finance working capital at the beginning of January 20X5.

Tax

Bustan charges entity tax at a preferential rate of 20% for the first 10 years of such investment projects, rather than the normal rate of 40%. In Bustan, tax depreciation allowances are calculated on the same basis as accounting depreciation allowances. The tax rate in the UK is 30%, but a double tax treaty allows taxes charged in Bustan to be deducted from UK taxes charged in the same period. Assume that Bustan taxes are payable in the year in which they are incurred and that UK taxes are payable one year in arrears.

Exchange rates

At 31 December 20X4, the spot exchange rate was £/B$0.7778 (that is, £1 = B$0.7778). The B$ is expected to weaken against the British pound (sterling) in line with the differential in long term interest rates between the two countries over the life of the project. Long term interest rates are expected to remain stable at 4·8% per annum in the UK and 10% per annum in Bustan for the foreseeable future.

Financing the project

The total initial investment of B$750 million was funded by GAS plc at the beginning of 20X5. The B$700 million investment in plant and equipment was funded by a rights issue and the B$50 million working capital requirement out of surplus cash.

GAS plc evaluated the project on the basis of a realisable residual value of B$350 million for the plant and equipment and that 80% of the investment in working capital would be realised at the end of the project. Both these amounts are to be repaid in full to the UK without any taxes payable in either Bustan or the UK.

Press statements

In June 20X4, GAS plc issued a press statement announcing its intention to submit a proposal for the project. On the same day, it announced its plans to use a 1 for 4 rights issue to fund the B$700 million capital investment in the event of the proposal being accepted. GAS plc's proposal was accepted on 1 January 20X5 and a press release issued to announce the acceptance of the proposal and GAS plc's intention to proceed with the project without delay. The press statement also announced GAS plc's intention to temporarily reduce dividend growth rates during the development stage of the project. Revised dividend plans are as follows:

20X5-20X7 Dividend per share to be frozen at December 20X4 levels

20X8 onwards 7% per annum growth

Investment criteria

Criterion 1

GAS plc requires overseas projects to generate an accounting rate of return in the overseas country, which is Bustan in this instance, of at least 25% per annum. Accounting rate of return is defined as:

$$\frac{\text{average annual accounting profit before interest and taxes}}{\text{average annual (written down) investment}}$$

Criterion 2

GAS plc also assesses investment projects based on the net present value of the cashflows and applies a risk-adjusted sterling discount rate of 10·5% to overseas projects of this nature.

Required

(a) Show, by calculation, that the proposed investment project in Bustan met the two minimum investment criteria set by GAS plc. **(18 marks)**

(b) Discuss the major risk issues that should have been considered by GAS plc when evaluating the project **(7 marks)**

(c) The board of GAS plc has been concerned about the unusually volatile movements in the entity's share price in 20X4 and 20X5 and has asked you, an external management consultant, to draft a report to the board of GAS plc that critically addresses the issues detailed below. Assume a semi-strong efficient market applies.

   (i) Explain the possible reasons for the unusually volatile movements in GAS plc's share price in the twelve months up to and including 1 January 20X5. No calculations are required. **(6 marks)**

   (ii) Advise what would have been a fair market price for GAS plc's shares in January 20X5 following the announcement of the acceptance of the proposal and after adjusting for the proposed rights issue. As part of your answer, calculate GAS plc's share price on each of the bases listed below and discuss the relevance of each result in determining a fair market price for the entity's shares:

   - The theoretical ex-rights price *before* adjusting for the project cashflows
   - The theoretical ex-rights price *after* adjusting for the project cashflows
   - Directors' dividend forecast issued in January 20X5 **(14 marks)**

   (iii) Advise on how and to what extent directors are able to influence their entity's share price. **(5 marks)**

Within the overall mark allocation, up to 4 marks are available for structure and presentation.

(Total = 50 marks)

84 PM (FS, 5/06)   90 mins

Scenario

It is now May 20X6

Background

PM Industries plc (PM) is a UK-based entity with shares trading on a UK Stock Exchange. It is a long established business with widespread commercial and industrial interests worldwide. It had a modest growth and profitability record until four years ago when a new Chief Executive Officer (CEO) was appointed from the United States of America (US). This new CEO has transformed the business by divesting poor performing, or non-core, subsidiaries or business units and focusing on volume growth in the remaining units. Some of this growth has been internally generated and some has come about because of financially sound acquisitions. A particular area of strength is in non-drug pharmaceutical materials such as packaging. PM now controls the largest share of this market in the UK and Europe.

Financial objectives

PM's current financial objectives are:

- To increase EPS by 5% per annum;
- To maintain a gearing ratio (market values of long-term debt to equity) below 30%;
- To maintain a P/E ratio above the industry average.

Proposed merger

The senior management of PM is currently negotiating a merger with NQ Inc (NQ), a US-based entity with shares trading on a US Stock Exchange. NQ is an entity of similar size to PM, in terms of revenue and assets, with a similar spread of commercial and industrial interests, especially pharmaceutical materials, which is why PM originally became attracted to NQ.

NQ has had a less impressive track record of growth than PM over the last two years because of some poor performing business units. As a result, PM's market capitalisation is substantially higher than NQ's. Although this will, in reality, be an acquisition, PM's CEO refers to it as a 'merger' in negotiations to avoid irritating the NQ Board, which is very sensitive to the issue.

NQ holds some software licences to products that the CEO of PM thinks are not being marketed as well as they could be. He believes he could sell these licences to a large software entity in the UK for around £100 million. He does not see the commercial logic in retaining them, as information technology is not a core business. The value of these licences is included in NQ's statement of financial position at $US125 million.

Both entities believe a merger between them makes commercial and financial sense, as long as terms can be agreed. The CEO of PM thinks his entity will have the upper hand in negotiations because of the share price performance of PM over the last 12 months and his own reputation in the City. He also believes he can boost the entity's share value if he can convince the market his entity's growth rating can be applied to NQ's earnings.

Summary of relevant financial data

Extracts from the Statement of consolidated incomes for the year ended 31 March 20X6

	PM £ million	NQ $ million
Revenue	1,560	2,500
Operating profit	546	750
Earnings available for ordinary shareholders	273	300

Extracts from the Statement of financial positions as at 31 March 20X6

	PM £ million	NQ $ million
Total net assets	2,000	2,100
Total equity	850	1,550
Total long term debt	1,150	550

Other data

Number of shares in issue

Ordinary shares of 10 pence	950,000,000	
Common stock of $1		850,000,000
Share price as at today (24 May 20X6)	456 pence	450 cents
High/low share price over last 12 months	475 pence/326 pence	520 cents/280 cents
Industry average P/E ratio	14	13
Debt traded within last week at	£105	Par

Five-year revenue and earnings record

	PM (£m)		NQ (US$m)	
Year ended 31 March	Revenue	Earnings	Revenue	Earnings
20X2	1,050	225	1,850	250
20X3	1,125	231	1,950	265
20X4	1,250	245	2,150	280
20X5	1,400	258	2,336	290
20X6	1,560	273	2,500	300

The two entities' revenue and operating profits are generated in the following five geographical areas, with average figures over the past five years as follows:

Percentage of total:	PM		NQ	
	Revenue	Profits	Revenue	Profits
UK	30	28	20	17
US	22	23	75	76
Mainland Europe	20	17	5	7
Asia (mainly Japan)	18	20	0	0
Rest of World	10	12	0	0

Economic data

PM's bankers have provided forecast interest and inflation rates in the two main areas of operation for the next 12 months as follows:

	Interest rates Current forecast %	Inflation rate Current forecast %
UK	4.5	2.0
US	2.5	1.5

Terms of the merger

PM intends to open the negotiations by suggesting terms of 1 PM share for 2 NQ stock units. The Finance Director of PM, plus the entity's professional advisors, have forecast the following data, post-merger, for PM. They believe this is a 'conservative' estimate as it excludes their estimate of value of the software licences. The current spot exchange rate is £/US$1.85 (that is, £1 = US$1.85).

Market capitalisation	£6,905 million
EPS	31.65 pence

A cash offer as an alternative to a share exchange is unlikely, although the CEO of PM has not ruled it out should the bid turn hostile. However, this would require substantial borrowing by PM, even if only 50% of NQ's shareholders opt for cash.

Except for the potential profit on the sale of the licences, no savings or synergies from the merger have as yet been identified.

Required

Assume you are one of the financial advisors working for PM.

(a) (i) Explain, with supporting calculations, how the Finance Director and advisors of PM have arrived at their estimates of post-merger values. **(10 marks)**

(ii) Calculate and comment briefly on the likely impact on the share price and market capitalisation for each of PM and NQ when the bid terms are announced. Make appropriate assumptions based on the information given in the scenario. **(4 marks)**

(iii) If NQ rejects the terms offered, calculate

- the maximum total amount and price per share to be paid for the entity; and

- the resulting share exchange terms PM should be prepared to agree without reducing PM's shareholder wealth. **(6 marks)**

(Total for part (a) = 20 marks)

(b) Write a report to the Board of PM that evaluates and discusses the following issues:

(i) How the merger might contribute to the achievement of PM's financial objectives, assuming the merger goes ahead on the terms you have calculated in (a) (iii). If you have not managed to calculate terms, make sensible assumptions; **(12 marks)**

(ii) External economic forces that might help and/or hinder the achievement of the merger's financial objectives. Comment also on the policies the merged entity could consider to help reduce adverse effects of such economic forces; **(8 marks)**

(iii) Potential post-merger value enhancing strategies that could increase shareholder wealth. **(10 marks)**

(Total for part (b) = 30 marks)

Up to 4 marks are available for structure and presentation. **(Total = 50 marks)**

85   SHINE (FS, 11/06)   90 mins

Scenario

It is now June 20X6.

Business background

SHINE is a publicly owned multinational group based in Germany with its main business centred on the production and distribution of gas and electricity to industrial and domestic consumers. It has recently begun investing in research and development in relation to renewable energy, exploiting solar, wave or wind energy to generate electricity.

Corporate objectives

Developing renewable energy sources is an important non-financial objective for the SHINE Group in order to protect and enhance the group's reputation. Renewable energy projects have been given a high profile in recent investor communications and television advertising campaigns.

Wind farm investment project

The latest renewable energy project under consideration is the development of a wind farm in the USA. This would involve the construction of 65 wind powered electricity generators which would be owned and operated by a new, local subsidiary entity and electricity that is generated by the farm would be sold to the local electricity grid. A suitable site, subject to planning permission, has been located.

Forecast operating cash flows for the project are as follows:

	Year(s)	US$ million
Initial investment (including working capital)	0	200
Residual value	4	50
Pre-tax operating net cash inflows	1 to 4	70

Other relevant data and assumptions:

- The initial investment is expected to be made on 30 November 20X6 and cash flows will arise at any point in the year.

- However, in any net present value (NPV) exercise, all cash flows should be assumed to arise on 31 December of each year.

- The local tax rate in the USA for this industry is set at a preferential rate of 10% to encourage environmentally-friendly projects rather than the normal rate of 25%.

- Tax is payable in the year in which it arises.

- No tax depreciation allowances are available.

- No additional tax is payable in Germany under the terms of the double tax treaties with the USA.

- Net cash flows are to be paid to the German parent entity as dividends at the end of each year.

Uncertainties affecting the outcome of the project

There is some uncertainty over the US tax rate over the period of the project, with extensive discussion at local government level about raising the tax rate to 25% with immediate effect. A vote will be taken in the next six months to decide whether to retain the preferential 10% tax rate, or to increase it to 25%. Once the vote has been taken and a decision made, the tax rate will not be open for debate again for at least four years.

Economic forecasters expect the value of the euro to either stay constant against the value of the US dollar for the next four years or to strengthen by 7% per annum. Assume that there is an equal probability of each of these two different exchange rate forecasts.

There is also significant risk to the project from strong objections to the wind farm scheme from local farmers in the USA who are concerned about the impact of acid water run-off from boring holes for the 65 windmills. In addition, there are a number of executive holiday homes nearby whose owners are objecting to the visual impact of the windmills.

Investment criteria

The SHINE Group evaluates foreign projects of this nature based on a euro cost of capital of 12% which reflects the risk profile of the proposed investment.

Extracts from the forecast financial statements for the SHINE Group at 31 December 20X6, the end of the current financial year:

	€ million	€ million
Assets		
Total assets		28,000
Equity and liabilities		
Equity		
Share capital (3,000 million €1 ords)	3,000	
Retained earnings	8,300	
		11,300
Non-current liabilities		
Floating rate borrowings		4,000
Current liabilities		12,700
		28,000

Alternative financing methods

The SHINE Group aims to maintain the group gearing ratio (debt as a proportion of debt plus equity) below 40% based on book values.

The following alternative methods are being considered by the SHINE parent entity for financing the new investment:

- Long-term borrowings denominated in euro.
- Long-term borrowings denominated in US dollars.

Required

(a) Calculate the NPV of the cash flows for the proposed investment for **each** of the following four possible scenarios:

    (i)   Constant exchange rate and a tax rate of 10%.

    (ii)   Constant exchange rate and a tax rate of 25%.

    (iii)   The euro to strengthen against the US dollar by 7% a year and a tax rate of 10%.

    (iv)   The euro to strengthen against the US dollar by 7% a year and a tax rate of 25%.

    In each case, assume that the exchange rate at year 0 is US$1.10 = €1.00. **(12 marks)**

(b) Prepare the forecast statement of financial position of the SHINE Group on 31 December 20X6, incorporating the project under each of the two alternative financing structures and each of the following two exchange rate scenarios A and B:

Date	Exchange rates under scenario A	Exchange rates under scenario B
30 November 20X6 (date of the initial investment and arrangement of financing)	€1.00 = US$1.10	€1.00 = US$1.10
31 December 20X6 (financial reporting/statement of financial position date)	€1.00 = US$1.10 (no change)	€1.00 = US$1.40

Assume that no other project cash flows occur until 20X7. **(8 marks)**

(c) Write a report addressed to the Directors of the SHINE Group in which you, as Finance Director, address the following issues relating to the evaluation and implementation of the proposed wind farm project:

    (i)   Discuss the internal and external constraints affecting the investment decision and advise the SHINE Group how to proceed. In your answer, include reference to your calculations in part (a) above. **(9 marks)**

    (ii)   Discuss the comparative advantages of each of the two proposed alternative financing structures and advise the SHINE group which one to adopt. In your answer include reference to your results in part (b) above, and further analysis and discussion of the impact of each proposed financial structure on the group's statement of financial position. **(9 marks)**

      (iii)   Discuss the differing roles and responsibilities of the treasury department and finance department in evaluating and implementing the US project and the interaction of the two departments throughout the process. **(8 marks)**

Marks available for structure and presentation. **(4 marks)**

(Total = 50 marks)

86 Sandyfoot (FS, 5/07)   90 mins

Background

Sandyfoot College of Higher Education (Sandyfoot) is a long-established, privately-owned college in an English-speaking country – Esco. It competes effectively with public sector universities, but on a narrower range of subjects. It operates using commercial principles although it is established as an educational trust in order to be exempt from Esco taxation. The new Chief Executive believes the college should be more aggressive in its expansion strategy in order to meet its long-term objectives of offering the same range of courses as its main public sector rivals and developing its student market internationally. He has commissioned and received a study of a potential investment overseas, but many of his senior managers and teaching staff would prefer expansion at home first. The college does not have the resources, financial or non-financial, to expand on both fronts at the same time.

Investment opportunities

Details about the two alternatives are as follows:

Alternative 1 – 'New Build' in the home country – Esco

In the present facilities there is little scope for increasing student numbers or the range of courses offered. Suitable development land for expansion has been identified a few miles away. Sandyfoot has already opened discussions with the seller of the land and the local authority has been approached about outline planning permission. The land is in an area being considered by the Esco government as a development area. If this is approved there will be some financial assistance available to a purchaser such as Sandyfoot. However, a decision is not expected for at least six months.

A disadvantage of this investment is the travelling that staff would be required to do between sites, as the proposed new site is not large enough to accommodate all operations, old and new. A major advantage is that it increases the catchment area for part-time students. An estimate of the additional fees from these students has been included in the figures given below. There has been a lot of interest in the land that is for sale and Sandyfoot has paid a nonrefundable deposit of Esco $50,000 pending the outcome of its investment evaluation. The seller requires a decision within six months.

Alternative 2 – 'New Build' in a Middle Eastern Country – Midco

Sandyfoot already attracts a number of full-time students from Midco and teaching staff have taught short courses there. The government of Midco is very keen to attract inward investment although it generally insists on some involvement in the investment and puts certain restrictions in contracts. For example, the government would insist on approving all courses to be taught before they could be marketed. A suitable site is available for Sandyfoot on the basis of a long-term leasehold, with an option to acquire the freehold at an unspecified price in 15 years' time. There will be break clauses in the contract at five-year intervals whereby either party can terminate the agreement. Should Sandyfoot wish to withdraw, the entity will not be entitled to any refund of the lease premium.

Teaching would be done by a combination of local (Midco) tutors and tutors from Esco on two or three year contracts to work in Midco.

A disadvantage would be the introduction of foreign exchange risk into the college's finances. To require fee payments in Esco $ would be a negative factor to many students. The US$ is widely used in Midco, so Sandyfoot has decided to request fee payments in US$. All payments in Midco, with the exception of the capital costs, can also be made in US$.

Cash flows for both alternatives

Capital costs

	Alternative 1 Esco $'000	Alternative 2 Midco $'000
Freehold capital cost of land	6,000	
Purchase of 15 year lease		20,000
Building costs	3,000	10,000
Equipment costs	1,000	5,000

Freehold land is not depreciated. Buildings and equipment for Alternative 1 will be depreciated straight line over 20 years. The total capital costs of Alternative 2 will be written off over the period of the lease. Refurbishment of buildings and replacement of equipment will be needed within the life of both investments, but these costs have not as yet been identified and have been excluded from the evaluation.

Operating cash flows

	Alternative 1 Esco			Alternative 2 US		
	Year 1 $'000	Year 2 $'000	Year 3 $'000	Year 1 $'000	Year 2 $'000	Year 3 $'000
Fees	1,750	2,250	2,700	4,650	5,350	6,450

Other information

1   In Alternative 1, fees and costs are expected to increase by 3% per annum from year 4 indefinitely. This is approximately the expected rate of inflation in Esco.

2   Current spot rates are Esco $/Midco $6.5 (that is, Esco $1 = Midco $6.50) and Esco $/US$1.8 (that is, Esco $1 = US $1.8). Risk-free interest rates are currently 4% in Esco and 5% in the US. These rates are likely to be maintained until year 3.

3   In Midco, there is no official interest rate and no forecast of inflation. The Sandyfoot directors therefore assume, for convenience, that in Alternative 2 the fees receivable in year 3 in Esco $ terms will remain constant, in nominal terms, until year 15.

4   Cash operating costs are assumed to be 60% of fees received each year in both alternatives.

5   Assume all capital costs are incurred in year 0 and all operating cash flows are received or incurred at the end of each year.

6   A survey of the land in Esco has been undertaken at a cost of Esco $10,000. A report on the Midco investment has been undertaken at a cost of Esco $20,000.

7   If Alternative 1 is chosen, there will be an opportunity cost to the investment of lecturers' 'lost' time in travelling between sites. This is estimated at 1% of fees each year.

8   If the investment in Midco goes ahead, fees on existing programmes in Esco are likely to fall by Esco $250,000 per annum for the duration of the investment.

9   Sandyfoot has not made an investment on this scale before, but for the investment in Esco (Alternative 1) the directors believe, with justification, that 12% would be an adequate return to reflect the risks involved. A premium on the Esco rate of +4% is considered appropriate for the investment in Midco (Alternative 2).

Method of funding

Sandyfoot has accumulated cash reserves of Esco $3 million. The remaining capital costs will be funded by long-term borrowings.

If Alternative 1 is chosen, it will be funded by a 20 year commercial mortgage secured on the land and buildings. Interest will be fixed at 9% per annum, payable annually. Sandyfoot currently has no other long-term borrowings.

If Alternative 2 is chosen, it will be funded by one of the following methods:

(a)   A 15-year commercial loan taken out in Esco $ at 10% per annum interest, capital repayable at the end of the term;

(b)   A 15-year interest-free, non-repayable Midco $ government loan, but for the duration of the loan the Midco government would take a 'dividend' each year equivalent to 20% of the *profits* earned in Midco;

(c)   A euro-denominated Eurobond. Borrowing rates in this market appear very favourable at the present time and are below the rates for both Esco\$ bonds and US\$ bonds. This option has not been investigated further at present.

Required

(a)   Calculate the net present value (NPV) in Esco \$ for the two alternative investments, using the cash flows and discount rates given in the scenario.   **(17 marks)**

(b)   Assume you are the Financial Manager for Sandyfoot. Prepare a report to the Chief Executive evaluating the investment decision and its funding. Your report should include the following sections:

    (i)   An evaluation of the two investments, including discussion of the key risk factors Sandyfoot should consider, the choice of discount rates used in the evaluation, and the real option features that are implied in the two investments. Discuss how these option features might impact on the investment decision being made.   **(14 marks)**

    (ii)   A discussion of the advantages and disadvantages of the three methods of funding outlined in the scenario for Alternative 2. Use appropriate calculations, where possible, to support your arguments.   **(11 marks)**

    (iii)   Recommendations about the choice of investment alternative and, if relevant, the method of funding.   **(5 marks)**

Additional marks for structure and presentation.   **(3 marks)**

(Total = 50 marks)

---

87   PT (FS, 11/07)   90 mins

It is now November 20X7.

The PT group is based in Germany and operates mail, express courier and air and ocean freight services worldwide. Its customers and operations are largely centred in Europe, but the group also operates in North America and Asia/Pacific. Currently, the largest growth area is in China, which is experiencing rapid economic development in all areas and requires increased use of express mail and freight services to support that growth.

The key financial objectives of the PT group are as follows:

- To increase group earnings by an average of 10% per annum over the next three years;
- To increase earnings per share to above 110 cents within three years;
- To maintain a gearing ratio (long-term borrowings/long-term borrowings plus equity) of less than 40%.

Based on current information available about the PT group in its present form:

- Group earnings are expected to increase by a compound average of 9.4% per annum over the next three years;
- Earnings per share are expected to rise to 91 cents within three years;
- Gearing is expected to remain below 40%.

The PT group also has publicised the following strategic objectives:

- Modernise its IT and distribution network in order to improve customer service;
- Increase its worldwide coverage, particularly in rapidly growing economies of the world such as China.

The Directors of PT group are considering making an acquisition on 31 December 20X7 which would help to improve its growth prospects. The Directors have been approached by the Directors of ITPT, a courier service based in Italy, who consider it to be in the best interests of the ITPT shareholders for ITPT to merge with a larger entity to take advantage of the increasing globalisation of the courier market.

ITPT

ITPT operates a courier service across Italy and neighbouring European countries in the eurozone. ITPT has an excellent reputation in terms of reliability and speed of delivery as well as for its efficient and friendly customer service. It is supported by an efficient, modern IT and distribution operation.

Competitive pricing has also helped promote the rapid growth of the business, with earnings increasing by an average of 12% per annum in recent years. However, such a high level of growth is not considered to be sustainable indefinitely.

Proposed opening bid price and alternative bid structures

An opening bid of €2,500 million has been proposed by the Directors of the PT group on the basis of estimated synergistic savings of the order of €60 million per annum from merging the distribution networks of the two entities.

The bid is to be structured as either:

- A cash offer of €2,500 million; or
- A share-for-share offer worth €2,500 million at the PT group's current share price.

Mr A, a Director of the PT group, has suggested that all, or part, of the cost of the cash offer could be financed by the PT group by a reduction in dividend payments.

Financial information for the individual entities, before taking into account the proposed acquisition
Summary forecast statement of financial position at 31 December 20X7

	PT group €million	ITPT €million
ASSETS		
Non-current assets		
Property, plant and equipment (book values)	8,626	1,021
Intangible assets	7,270	0
Current assets		
Inventories	226	42
Receivables	5,867	815
Cash and cash equivalents	635	72
	22,624	1,950
EQUITY AND LIABILITIES		
Equity		
Issued capital (€1 ordinary shares)	1,012	300
Reserves	7,970	477
Non-current liabilities		
Long-term borrowings (floating rate)	2,180	675
Provisions	5,478	0
Current liabilities	5,948	498
	22,624	1,950

Other key financial data at 31 December 20X7		
Share price	€4.80	€7.80
Earnings per share *	69.5 cents	78.0 cents
Dividend per share	29.0 cents	34.0 cents
Cost of equity	15%	13%
Current interest rate on borrowings	10%	10%
Tax rate	20%	20%
Forecast earnings for the years ended	€million	€million
31 December 20X8	766.9	262.1
31 December 20X9	839.2	293.5
31 December 20Y0	921.1	328.8

* (100 cents = €1)

Additional information for ITPT:

- Annual growth in earnings is expected to fall to 5% per annum from 20Y1 onwards.
- A consistent dividend payout ratio will be maintained.
- Property, plant and equipment current replacement value is estimated as €1,500 million.
- Average return on net tangible assets over the last three years was 20%.
- Average year end net tangible assets over the last three years was €1,300 million.
- Courier industry average return on net tangible assets in the last three years was 12%.
- Courier industry average cost of capital is 15%.

Note. Net tangible assets are at book values.

Required

(a) Calculate a range of values at 31 December 20X7 for:

    (i)   The intangible assets of ITPT; and

    (ii)   The total value of ITPT;

    and briefly interpret the significance of each result. **(15 marks)**

(b) As an external consultant engaged by the Directors of the PT group to advise on the proposed acquisition of ITPT, write a report which covers the following issues:

    (i)   Advise whether the proposed bid price of €2,500 million appears to be appropriate. **(4 marks)**

    (ii)   Evaluate whether the acquisition of ITPT would help the PT group to meet its stated financial objectives for each of the two alternative bid structures. **(12 marks)**

    (iii) Advise how best to structure and finance the bid offer, including a discussion of Mr A's suggestion that part, or all, of the cost of a cash offer could be financed by a reduction in dividend payments, rather than borrowings (**no** additional calculations are required in part (iii)) **(8 marks)**

    (iv) Discuss the broader strategic implications of the proposed acquisition of ITPT and recommend whether or not to proceed. **(7 marks)**

Additional marks for structure and presentation **(4 marks)**

(Total = 50 marks)

88 Ancona (FS, 5/08)   90 mins

It is now May 20X8.

Background and organisational structure

Ancona International is an international advertising agency. Its shares are listed on the London Stock Exchange. Its revenue has doubled on average every four years over the past 16 years, which is satisfactory but unspectacular by industry standards. Its growth has come largely from focusing on providing high quality services and advertising products to existing clientele; its 'churn' rate (the rate at which an entity replaces old customers with new ones) is low and it enjoys considerable customer loyalty. The majority of new business comes from referrals by existing customers. Ancona International usually does not bid for highly competitive, large contracts which involve very high investment costs and which, generally have only modest chances of success.

The entity has its headquarters in the UK. Operations in other countries are established as wholly-owned subsidiaries. Because of its international interests Ancona International prepares its consolidated accounts in US$.

Proposals

The new vice president of the USA subsidiary, Ancona USA is Mr de Z. He does not agree with the entity's policy of growth through existing business and 'word of mouth'. He wants to be able to tender for major advertising contracts with leading USA entities. These tenders are typically fiercely competitive and require substantial management time and effort to prepare.

The Chief Executive Officer (CEO) of Ancona International thinks such a move would change the risk profile of the entity, although he recognises the merit of Mr de Z's proposal. After much discussion between the main board and the management of Ancona USA a proposal has been made to allow Mr de Z and his fellow managers and other employees to take over the USA business. This proposal would require shareholder approval, but Ancona International's CEO is confident he would get the support of most of, if not all, the institutional investors who account for 80% of the entity's shareholders.

Financial information

Statement of financial positions at 31 March 20X8 for Ancona International and its wholly-owned US subsidiary are shown below.

All figures are in US$ millions

	Ancona International (Group consolidated accounts)	Ancona USA
Non-current assets	3,975	340
Current assets	550	95
Total assets	4,525	435
Equity		
Common shares of US$1	350	5
Retained earnings	1,750	170
Total equity	2,100	175
Non current liabilities		
Secured 8% bonds repayable 20Z5	2,050	
Undated borrowings from parent at variable rate		200
Current liabilities	375	60
Total liabilities	2,425	260
Total equity and liabilities	4,525	435

Notes

- Ancona International's bonds are secured on its non-current assets.
- Figures for Ancona International include those for Ancona USA.

After-tax earnings for Ancona International for the year ended 31 March 20X8 were US$680 million. This included earnings from the US operation of US$102 million. Ancona International's share price is currently US$18. Its debt is trading at par.

If Mr de Z's proposal goes ahead, a new entity will be established to acquire the USA interests of Ancona International to be named Zola Agencies Inc.

Forecast net cash flows for Ancona USA as part of Ancona International and as a separate entity for the next five years have been prepared by the Finance Department at Ancona International and are shown below.

All figures are in US$ millions

	Ancona USA (USA operation based on current policies)			Zola Agencies (USA operation as a separate entity)		
31 March	20X9	20Y0	20Y1-Y3	20X9	20Y0	20Y1-Y3
After-tax net cash flows (assume = earnings)	118	131	210	138	172	250

Notes

- These forecasts are in **nominal** terms
- The 20Y1-20Y3 cash flows are assumed to remain constant in **nominal** terms each year
- Cash flow beyond 20Y3 are considered too uncertain and have been ignored

Other financial information

- Ancona International's weighted average after-tax cost of capital is 12% **nominal** compared with an industry average of 13%. The entity with policies and risk profile most similar to those proposed for Zola Agencies is financed 100% equity and has a quoted equity beta of 2.5.
- The risk free rate in the USA is currently 5% and the return on the market 9%. These rates are not expected to change in the foreseeable future.
- Corporate taxes are payable at 30% in the year in which the liability arises.

Assume that the directors and management of Ancona International and the proposed Zola Agencies have access to the same forecasts.

Financing the deal

Information about two financing alternatives is shown below.

Alternative 1: Introduce a private equity investor

An investor has been identified, PE Capital. This entity will provide up to 95% of the capital required. It expects a return on its investment averaging 30% per annum compound by 31 March 20Y3.

Its most likely exit route will be by initial public offering (IPO). PE Capital has two conditions; a director of PE sits on the board of Zola Agencies and all earnings are to be retained in the business for five years. Mr De Z and his colleagues are able to fund 5% of the equity required.

Alternative 2: Obtain a consortium of funding of equity plus debt

DW bank, an investment bank based in Europe, has expressed interest in providing debt finance of up to 75% of the capital requirement. This will be a complex structure combining secured and unsecured borrowing and equity warrants, as follows.

$US250 million in euro debt secured on Zola Agencies current and non-current assets. The interest rate will be 10% and the principal repayable in five years' time. The balance of debt required will be by unsecured borrowings at a variable rate, which currently would be 11%, with equity warrants attached. The terms and conditions of the warrants have not yet been agreed.

Mr de Z and his colleagues will provide 5% of the total funding required as equity as in **Alternative 1**. They believe they can raise the additional 20% from a consortium of private investors, mainly friends and business associates, who would require a regular dividend of at least 20% of earnings.

Required

(a)   (i)   Calculate the present value of the forecast cash flows for Ancona USA, both as part of Ancona International and as a separate entity (Zola Agencies), based on the information in the scenario and using discount rates that you consider appropriate. Assume in your calculations:

- Finance for a separate US entity will be all-equity
- You are conducting the valuation on 1 April 20X8
- Cash flows occur on 31 March each year.   **(5 marks)**

(ii)   Discuss briefly your choice of discount rates and explain any reasons why they might not be accurate. Support your explanation with additional calculations where necessary   **(4 marks)**

(b)   Assume you are an independent financial adviser retained by Ancona International to advise on the sale of its USA operations. Write a report to the directors of Ancona International that:

(i)   Evaluates the interests of the various stakeholder groups in both Ancona International and Ancona USA and how they might be affected by the sale of the USA operations.   **(7 marks)**

(ii)   Evaluates the economic and market factors that might impact on the negotiations between Ancona International and Mr de Z.   **(7 marks)**

(iii) Recommends, with reasons, an appropriate valuation for the Ancona USA operations. You should provide a range of values on which to base your discussion including the values calculated in part (a).   **(8 marks)**

(c)   Ancona International and Mr de Z eventually agreed a purchase value of US$650 million and 50 million shares are issued by Zola Agencies.

(i)   Calculate:

- The value that would need to be placed on Zola Agencies at 31 March 20Y3 if financing is a **Alternative 1**, and PE Capital is to receive its required return;

- The impact on earnings and earnings per share for the years ending 31 March 20X9 and 20Y3 under **Alternative 2**.   **(7 marks)**

(ii)   Evaluate the advantages and disadvantages of the two alternative methods of finance being considered by Mr de Z and recommend the most appropriate source in the circumstances. Provide additional calculations where necessary.   **(9 marks)**

Additional marks for structure and presentation for all this question.   **(3 marks)**

(Total = 50 marks)

89 KEN (FS, 11/08)　　　　　　　　　　　　　　　90 mins

KEN is a property development company located in country A whose currency is A$. KEN specialises in the construction of domestic housing in country A and is listed on the local stock exchange.

KEN has been highly successful in recent years and has built a strong reputation based on high build quality and meeting deadlines.

However, in recent months house prices have fallen and interest rates have risen, making it harder to sell houses, even at significantly lower prices.

Domestic housing construction project

One of KEN's current projects is the construction of 300 houses. This project has been planned in three distinct phases, each in a self-contained plot of land. Good progress has been made with the development since work began in 20X1.

The position at 1 January 20X4 is expected to be as follows:

Phase 1

- 80 houses
- Construction completed and all houses sold and occupied

Phase 2

- 100 houses
- 30 houses were sold in 20X3
- Remaining 70 houses in this Phase to be actively marketed in 20X4

Phase 3

- 120 houses
- Planning approval obtained but no construction work or marketing begun at 1 January 20X4

Forecast figures for 20X4 – 20X6			
	20X4	20X5	20X6
House sales (number of houses)			
Phase 2	70	–	–
Phase 3	–	80	40
Cost of running the sales office (A$)			
Salaries and other staff costs	100,000	140,000	80,000
Other	30,000	30,000	30,000

Other financial information on the domestic housing project:

The forecast average selling price per house BEFORE the recent fall in house prices was as follows:

- Phase 2: A$350,000
- Phase 3: A$400,000

However, due to the recent fall in house prices in country A, the forecast average selling prices listed above are considered to be overstated by 20% on unsold houses at 1 January 20X4.

- A 10% deposit is received on agreeing a house sale and the selling price is agreed at this stage. The remaining 90% is due on completion a year later.
- Construction costs are, on average, 60% of the forecast selling price. 70% of the construction costs are incurred in the year in which the sale is agreed and 30% are incurred in the following year. These costs already take into account government estimates of inflation and are not expected to be affected by the recent fall in house prices. Construction costs should therefore be calculated on the forecast selling prices before the recent fall in house prices.
- All sales office costs forecast for 20X4 relate to Phase 2 and forecast costs for 20X5 and 20X6 relate to Phase 3.
- Business tax is 30% on profits and capital gains, payable one year in arrears.
- All cash flows should be assumed to arise at the end of the year.

Strategic choices for KEN

The fall in house prices has created potential liquidity problems for KEN and KEN is considering what its strategic response should be at this time.

The following strategies are being considered:

Strategy 1: Abandon Phase 3 and sell the land
Strategy 2: Merge with another property development entity

Strategy 1: Abandon Phase 3 of the domestic housing project

If KEN were to abandon Phase 3 of the project, the land would be sold and the sales office staff would be made redundant. All this would be expected to take place at the end of 20X4. Phase 2 of the project would continue as planned since KEN is already committed to completing this phase of the project.

The land for Phase 3 was purchased in 20X1 at a cost A$2·5 million without planning permission. Planning permission was obtained in 20X1 at a cost of A$100,000 and the land could be sold in 20X4, with planning permission, for A$4·4 million.

It is estimated that it would cost A$60,000 to make the sales office staff redundant at the end of 20X4. Normal running costs and salaries would be paid up to the end of 20X4, at which point the sales office would be closed.

Strategy 2: Merger

KEN has also been approached by another property development entity located in country A that is interested in merging the businesses. Discussions are still at a very early stage but KEN is interested in investigating this possibility further.

Investment appraisal

KEN uses DCF to evaluate investments at an after-tax nominal discount rate of 12%.

Required

(a)   For Phase 2 of the project, calculate the fall in after-tax sales receipts in each of the years 20X4 and 20X5 as a result of the fall in house prices. Ignore the time value of money.   **(4 marks)**

(b)   Discuss the industry, economic and market factors that affect KEN's business cash flows and liquidity and funding issues.   **(6 marks)**

(c)   Explain the role of the treasury function in

(i)   liquidity management, and
(ii)   funding management.   **(6 marks)**

(d)   Assume you are the Finance Director of KEN and write a report to the Board of Directors of KEN on the strategic choices facing KEN at this time.

Your report should address the following issues:

Strategy 1:

(i)   Calculate the net present value of the Phase 3 cash flows AFTER the fall in house prices and compare this with the net present value of the cash flows associated with selling the land.

(17 marks)

(ii)   Advise whether or not to proceed with Strategy 1. As part of your answer discuss what other real options are available to KEN, and what other factors should be taken into account.   **(7 marks)**

Strategy 2:

(iii)   Identify and explain the possible reasons why KEN might consider a merger at this time and the potential problems with such a merger.   **(7 marks)**

Additional marks for structure and presentation in part (d).   **(3 marks)**

(Total = 50 marks)

90 T Industries (FS, 11/09)   90 mins

It is now November 20W9.

Background information

T Industries provides a variety of goods and services to the construction industry. Its main areas of operation include building construction, repairs and renovations, consultancy and design planning services. Its main market is in the UK but it also operates in countries in the Euro zone. Its shares are quoted on a recognised Stock Exchange.

The entity has been highly profitable in the past but revenue and profit margins have suffered in the past year as a consequence of the economic downturn and increased costs of complying with ever changing building regulations in the countries in which it operates. However, the poor economic situation has provided opportunities. Some of T Industries' competitors have ceased trading and it has picked up some of their business. Also, its long term debt is repayable in nine months' time and falling interest rates mean it should be able to re-finance at more favourable terms.

Financial objectives

T Industries has two financial objectives:

1   To increase EPS year on year

2   To improve shareholder value, as measured by growth in dividends and increase in share price, by an average of 8% per annum over a rolling 5 year period.

These objectives have been achieved each year over the past 9 years but the directors believe they now need to be reviewed.

Acquisition opportunity

A specific opportunity is the acquisition of L Products, an entity in a related but not identical business whose shares are listed on the UK's Alternative Investment Market (AIM). Its share price has fallen 40% over the past 5 months and it has recently announced it will not pay a dividend in the coming financial year. This acquisition would broaden T Industries' business base and provide access to technical expertise that is a scarce resource. However, it is likely to be a hostile bid at the initial approach and T Industries' directors are aware other entities might be viewing L Products as a potential takeover target.

T Industries' financial advisors have produced estimates of the expected future growth in earnings. The forecast growth rates are based on publicly available information and assume both entities continue to operate independently and that dividend policy, capital structure and risk characteristics remain unchanged.

| | Annual percentage growth rates in earnings. | |
	T Industries	L Products
Financial year to 30 June 20X0	0	- 5
Financial year to 20X1	+3	+ 10
Years 20X2 onwards	+4	+2.5

Even if the bid succeeds, T Industries' directors believe it would be difficult to improve on the forecast earnings in either entity in 20X0 or 20X1 but from 20X2 onwards they are confident that they will be able to obtain growth in L Products' earnings equivalent to their own projected growth rate of 4%. They also believe that by re-financing the combined debt of the group and by lowering its overall business risk they can obtain a group cost of equity of 10% from 20X2 onwards.

Extracts from both entities' Balance Sheets as at 30 June 20W9

	T Industries £millions	L Products £millions
Assets		
Non-current assets (NBV)		
Land and buildings	435	125
Plant and equipment	250	87
	685	212
Current assets:		
Inventory and accounts receivable	120	95
Cash and cash equivalents	25	0
	145	95
	830	307
Equity and liabilities		
Equity		
Issued share capital (nominal value £1)*	120	
Issued share capital (nominal value 25 pence)*		15
Retained earnings	210	55
Total equity	330	70
Non Current Liabilities	450	220
Current liabilities	50	17
	830	307

*All Authorised Share Capital is in issue.

Other financial information

Earnings for year to 30 June 20W9 (£m)	65.0	22.5
Dividends declared for year to 30 June 20W9 (£m)	26.0	11.4
Share price as at 30 June 20W9 (pence)	885	620
Share price as at today, 25 November 20W9, (pence):	670	375
Beta co-efficient	1.17	n/a

No beta is available for L Products. The beta of a larger, quoted entity in a similar line of business is 1.4. This entity has a debt ratio (debt:debt + equity) of 40%. Assume a debt beta of 0.2. Assume both entities' debt is quoted at par.

Required

(a) Calculate for T Industries and for L Products as independent entities:
   (i) The P/E ratio and current market capitalisation **(3 marks)**
   (ii) The cost of equity using the CAPM **(6 marks)**
   (iii) Estimated value using the discounted cash flow method **(5 marks)**

   Notes
   • The expected return on the market is 9% and the expected return on the risk-free asset is 3%.
   • Assume earnings equal net cash flows.
   • Ignore taxation in your calculations.
   • Use sensible roundings throughout your answer.

(b) Calculate the increase in value generated by combining the two businesses assuming the acquisition goes ahead and:

   • The present value of the two entities' cash flows up to and including 20X1 is as you have calculated in part (a)iii

   • The present value of the combined group cash flows from 20X2 onwards is as explained in the scenario (growth in earnings of 4% and a cost of equity of 10%). **(5 marks)**

(c) Assume you are T Industries' Finance Director. Write a report for review by the entity's Board which includes the following:

(i) Discussion and advice on the range of values within which T Industries should be prepared to negotiate. Include in your discussion brief comments on how share prices are determined and how the stock market might assess the value of the two entities. Conclude your discussion here with a recommendation of an opening bid for L Products expressed as a **price per share**. **(12 marks)**

(ii) Discussion and recommendation on the most appropriate method of financing the bid, taking into account the possible effect on risk and earnings and other key factors. Assume that the two alternative methods under consideration are a share exchange or the issue of new debt. Include any calculations you consider appropriate to support your discussion.

(8 marks)

(iii) Discussion and evaluation of the implications of the proposed acquisition for the achievement of T Industries' current financial objectives in the context of the current economic environment of low and falling interest and inflation rates. Include in your discussion an evaluation of how financing and dividend policies could be adapted to assist in the achievement of T's objectives. **(8 marks)**

Note: If you have been unable to complete the calculations for parts (a) and (b) of the question, make sensible assumptions in your answer for part (c).

Structure and presentation **(3 marks)**

(Total = 50 marks)

91 Power Utilities (Pilot Paper)   90 mins

Pre-seen Case Study

Background

Power Utilities (PU) is located in a democratic Asian country. Just over 12 months ago, the former nationalised Electricity Generating Corporation (EGC) was privatised and became PU. EGC was established as a nationalised industry many years ago. Its home government at that time had determined that the provision of the utility services of electricity generation production should be managed by boards that were accountable directly to Government. In theory, nationalised industries should be run efficiently, on behalf of the public, without the need to provide any form of risk related return to the funding providers. In other words, EGC, along with other nationalised industries was a non-profit making organisation. This, the Government claimed at the time, would enable prices charged to the final consumer to be kept low.

Privatisation of EGC

The Prime Minister first announced three years ago that the Government intended to pursue the privatisation of the nationalised industries within the country. The first priority was to be the privatisation of the power generating utilities and EGC was selected as the first nationalised industry to be privatised. The main purpose of this strategy was to encourage public subscription for share capital. In addition, the Government's intention was that PU should take a full and active part in commercial activities such as raising capital and earning higher revenue by increasing its share of the power generation and supply market by achieving growth either organically or through making acquisitions. This, of course, also meant that PU was exposed to commercial pressures itself, including satisfying the requirements of shareholders and becoming a potential target for take-over. The major shareholder, with a 51% share, would be the Government. However, the Minister of Energy has recently stated that the Government intends to reduce its shareholding in PU over time after the privatisation takes place.

Industry structure

PU operates 12 coal-fired power stations across the country and transmits electricity through an integrated national grid system which it manages and controls. It is organised into three regions, Northern, Eastern and Western. Each region generates electricity which is sold to 10 private sector electricity distribution companies which are PU's customers.

The three PU regions transmit the electricity they generate into the national grid system. A shortage of electricity generation in one region can be made up by taking from the national grid. This is particularly important when there is a national emergency, such as exceptional weather conditions.

The nationalised utility industries, including the former EGC, were set up in a monopolistic position. As such, no other providers of these particular services were permitted to enter the market within the country. Therefore, when EGC was privatised and became PU it remained the sole generator of electricity in the country. The electricity generating facilities, in the form of the 12 coal-fired power stations, were all built over 15 years ago and some date back to before EGC came into being.

The 10 private sector distribution companies are the suppliers of electricity to final users including households and industry within the country, and are not under the management or control of PU. They are completely independent companies owned by shareholders.

The 10 private sector distribution companies serve a variety of users of electricity. Some, such as AB, mainly serve domestic users whereas others, such as DP, only supply electricity to a few industrial clients. In fact, DP has a limited portfolio of industrial customers and 3 major clients, an industrial conglomerate, a local administrative authority and a supermarket chain. DP finds these clients costly to service.

Structure of PU

The structure of PU is that it has a Board of Directors headed by an independent Chairman and a separate Managing Director. The Chairman of PU was nominated by the Government at the time the announcement that

BPP
LEARNING MEDIA

EGC was to be privatised was made. His background is that he is a former Chairman of an industrial conglomerate within the country. There was no previous Chairman of EGC which was managed by a Management Board, headed by the Managing Director. The former EGC Managing Director retired on privatisation and a new Managing Director was appointed.

The structure of PU comprises a hierarchy of many levels of management authority. In addition to the Chairman and Managing Director, the Board consists of the Directors of each of the Northern, Eastern and Western regions, a Technical Director, the Company Secretary and the Finance Director. All of these except the Chairman are the Executive Directors of PU. The Government also appointed seven Non Executive Directors to PU's Board. With the exception of the Company Secretary and Finance Director, all the Executive Directors are qualified electrical engineers. The Chairman and Managing Director of PU have worked hard to overcome some of the inertia which was an attitude that some staff had developed within the former EGC. PU is now operating efficiently as a private sector company. There have been many staff changes at a middle management level within the organisation.

Within the structure of PU's headquarters, there are five support functions; engineering, finance (which includes PU's Internal Audit department), corporate treasury, human resource management (HRM) and administration, each with its own chief officers, apart from HRM. Two Senior HRM Officers and Chief Administrative Officer report to the Company Secretary. The Chief Accountant and Corporate Treasurer each report to the Finance Director. These functions, except Internal Audit, are replicated in each region, each with its own regional officers and support staff. Internal Audit is an organisation wide function and is based at PU headquarters.

Regional Directors of EGC

The Regional Directors all studied in the field of electrical engineering at the country's leading university and have worked together for a long time. Although they did not all attend the university at the same time, they have a strong belief in the quality of their education. After graduation from university, each of the Regional Directors started work at EGC in a junior capacity and then subsequently gained professional electrical engineering qualifications. They believe that the experience of working up through the ranks of EGC has enabled them to have a clear understanding of EGC's culture and the technical aspects of the industry as a whole. Each of the Regional Managers has recognised the changed environment that PU now operates within, compared with the former EGC, and they are now working hard to help PU achieve success as a private sector electricity generator. The Regional Directors are well regarded by both the Chairman and Managing Director, both in terms of their technical skill and managerial competence.

Governance of EGC

Previously, the Managing Director of the Management Board of EGC reported to senior civil servants in the Ministry of Energy. There were no shareholders and ownership of the Corporation rested entirely with the Government. That has now changed. The Government holds 51% of the shares in PU and the Board of Directors is responsible to the shareholders but, inevitably, the Chairman has close links directly with the Minister of Energy, who represents the major shareholder.

The Board meetings are held regularly, normally weekly, and are properly conducted with full minutes being taken. In addition, there is a Remuneration Committee, an Audit Committee and an Appointments Committee, all in accordance with best practice. The model which has been used is the Combined Code on Corporate Governance which applies to companies which have full listing status on the London Stock Exchange. Although PU is not listed on the London Stock Exchange, the principles of the Combined Code were considered by the Government to be appropriate to be applied with regard to the corporate governance of the company.

Currently, PU does not have an effective Executive Information System and this has recently been raised at a Board meeting by one of the non-executive directors because he believes this inhibits the function of the Board and consequently is disadvantageous to the governance of PU.

Remuneration of Executive Directors

In order to provide a financial incentive, the Remuneration Committee of PU has agreed that the Executive Directors be entitled to performance related pay, based on a bonus scheme, in addition to their fixed salary and health benefits.

Capital market

PU exists in a country which has a well developed capital market relating both to equity and loan stock funding. There are well established international institutions which are able to provide funds and corporate entities are

free to issue their own loan stock in accordance with internationally recognised principles. PU is listed on the country's main stock exchange.

Strategic opportunity

The Board of PU is considering the possibility of vertical integration into electricity supply and has begun preliminary discussion with DP's Chairman with a view to making an offer for DP. PU's Board is attracted by DP's strong reputation for customer service but is aware, through press comment, that DP has received an increase in complaints regarding its service to customers over the last year. When the former EGC was a nationalised business, breakdowns were categorised by the Government as "urgent", when there was a danger to life, and "non-urgent" which was all others. Both the former EGC and DP had a very high success rate in meeting the government's requirements that a service engineer should attend the urgent break-down within 60 minutes. DP's record over this last year in attending urgent breakdowns has deteriorated seriously and if PU takes DP over, this situation would need to improve.

Energy consumption within the country and Government drive for increased efficiency and concern for the environment

Energy consumption has doubled in the country over the last 10 years. As PU continues to use coal-fired power stations, it now consumes most of the coal mined within the country.

The Minister of Energy has indicated to the Chairman of PU that the Government wishes to encourage more efficient methods of energy production. This includes the need to reduce production costs. The Government has limited resources for capital investment in energy production and wishes to be sure that future energy production facilities are more efficient and effective than at present.

The Minister of Energy has also expressed the Government's wish to see a reduction in harmful emissions from the country's power stations. (The term harmful emissions in this context, refers to pollution coming out of electricity generating power stations which damage the environment.)

One of PU's non-executive directors is aware that another Asian country is a market leader in coal gasification which is a fuel technology that could be used to replace coal for power generation. In the coal gasification process, coal is mixed with oxygen and water vapour under pressure, normally underground, and then pumped to the surface where the gas can be used in power stations. The process significantly reduces carbon dioxide emissions although it is not widely used at present and not on any significant commercial scale.

Another alternative to coal fired power stations being actively considered by PU's Board is the construction of a dam to generate hydro-electric power. The Board is mindful of the likely adverse response of the public living and working in the area where the dam would be built.

In response to the Government's wishes, PU has established environmental objectives relating to improved efficiency in energy production and reducing harmful emissions such as greenhouse gases. PU has also established an ethical code. Included within the code are sections relating to recycling and reduction in harmful emissions as well as to terms and conditions of employment.

Introduction of commercial accounting practices at EGC

The first financial statements have been produced for PU for 20X8. Extracts from the Statement of Financial Position from this are shown in Appendix A. Within these financial statements, some of EGC's loans were "notionally" converted by the Government into ordinary shares. Interest is payable on the Government loans as shown in the statement of financial position. Reserves is a sum which was vested in EGC when it was first nationalised. This represents the initial capital stock valued on a historical cost basis from the former electricity generating organisations which became consolidated into EGC when it was first nationalised.

Being previously a nationalised industry and effectively this being the first "commercially based" financial statements, there are no retained earnings brought forward into 20X8.

EXTRACTS FROM THE PRO FORMA FINANCIAL STATEMENTS OF
THE ELECTRICITY GENERATING CORPORATION

Statement of financial position as at 31 December 20X8

	P$m
ASSETS	
Non-current assets	15,837
Current assets	
Inventories	1,529
Receivables	2,679
Cash and Cash equivalents	133
	4,341
Total assets	20,178
EQUITY AND LIABILITIES	
Equity	
Share capital	5,525
Reserves	1,231
Total equity	6,756
Non-current liabilities	
Government loans	9,560
Current liabilities	
Payables	3,862
Total liabilities	13,422
Total equity and liabilities	20,178

Unseen material for Case Study

Background

Assume today is 20 May 20X9.

Power Utilities (PU) is located in an Asian country. It is planning to diversify its business activities by moving away from total reliance on coal fired power stations and building a hydroelectric power station to produce electricity using natural resources. A dam would need to be constructed to create a reservoir of water above the dam. Electricity would be generated by releasing water from the upper reservoir through the dam. Modern hydroelectric power stations can be very responsive to consumer demand and it is expected that the power station would be able to generate up to 100 megawatts of electricity within 60 seconds of the need arising.

Hydroelectric power stations do not directly produce harmful emissions such as carbon dioxide. However, some carbon dioxide will be produced during the construction phase. There is also a potential source of harmful greenhouse gases in the form of methane gas from decaying plant matter in flooded areas.

Public opinion on the project has been very mixed and there is a significant risk of opposition to the project from local people. Their housing and farming businesses will be seriously affected by the proposed development which will require flooding of local land to construct the dam.

Corporate objectives

Corporate objectives in line with a recent government drive include:

- Improved efficiency of energy production
- Reduction in harmful emissions such as greenhouse gases

Financial objectives include maintaining group gearing (debt:debt plus equity) below 40% based on market values.

Hydroelectric power station project

Initial research has shown that a major river in the south of the country may be suitable for use in this project.

Extensive engineering and environmental studies have already begun to assess the viability of the project. These are expected to cost US$15,000,000 in total, payable in three equal instalments at the end of the calendar years 20X8, 20X9 and 20Y0. The payment for 20X8 has already been made. PU is committed to pay the 20X9 instalment but a clause in the contract would enable it to cancel the payment due in 20Y0 if it decides to withdraw from the project and future viability studies before the end of 20X9.

Construction costs will be payable in US$. Other project costs and all project revenue will be in PU's functional currency, P$.

Construction and operating cash flows for the project are as follows:

	Year(s)	US$m	P$m
Construction costs	3 and 4	60 payment each year	–
Pre-tax net operating cash flows	5 to 24	–	150 receipt each year

Additional information:

- Time 0 is 1 January 20Y0

- Cash flows should be assumed to arise at the end of each year

- Business tax is 30% and is payable a year in arrears; also note that the government has announced plans to reduce the tax rate to 10% from 1 January 20Y4 on "clean" energy schemes such as this one (and would therefore only affect the tax position of the operating cash flows); however, this still needs to be approved by parliament and there is a risk that approval will not be obtained

- Tax depreciation allowances of 100% can be claimed on construction costs but no tax relief is available on the cost of the engineering and environmental studies

- The assets of the project have no residual value

- Exchange rate as at today, 20 May 20X9, is US$/P$6.3958 (that is, US$1 = P$6.3958). Some economic forecasters expect this exchange rate to remain constant over the period of the project but other forecasts predict that the US$ will strengthen against the P$ by 5% each year

- PU normally uses a cost of capital net of tax of 10% to assess investments of this type.

Financial information for PU

Extracts from the latest available financial statements for PU are provided in the pre-seen material. The ordinary share capital consists of P$1 shares and the current share price on 20 May 20X9 is P$2.80. The long term government borrowings shown in the statement of financial position are floating rate loans and the amount borrowed is unchanged since 31 December 20X8.

Financing the project

Two alternative financing schemes are being considered which would each raise the equivalent of US$130 million on 1 January 20Y2. These are:

1   A five-year P$ loan at a fixed interest rate of 5% per annum

2   A subsidised loan denominated in US$ from an international organisation that promotes "clean energy" schemes. There would not be any interest payments but US$145 million would be repayable at the end of the five year term.

Required

(a)   Calculate the NPV of the project as at 1 January 20Y0 for each of the two different exchange rate forecasts and the two tax rates.   **(14 marks)**

(b)   Write a report to the Directors of PU in which you, as Finance Director, address each of the following issues:

   (i)   Explain your results in part (a) and explain and evaluate other relevant factors that need to be taken into account when deciding whether or not to undertake the project. Conclude by advising PU how to proceed.   **(15 marks)**

   (ii)   Explain and evaluate the costs and risks arising from the use of foreign currency borrowings as proposed by financing scheme (ii) and advise PU on the most appropriate financing structure for the project. Up to 7 marks are available for calculations.   **(11 marks)**

(c)   In the event, the Board of Directors of PU decided to go ahead with the project and it has now been operational for six years. The Board has, however, now decided to dispose of the hydroelectric power station. To assist with these plans, a new entity, PP, has been formed and the plant and its operations have been transferred to PP.

   Required

   Discuss why PU might wish to dispose of the hydroelectric power station and advise the Directors of PU on alternative methods for achieving the divestment.   **(10 marks)**

   (Total = 50 marks)

92   Aybe (1) (5/10)   90 mins

Pre-seen Case Study

The following pre-seen material is applicable to both Q92 and Q93.

Background

Aybe, located in Country C, was formed by the merger of two companies in 2001. It is a listed company which manufactures, markets and distributes a large range of components throughout Europe and the United States of America. Aybe employs approximately 700 people at its three factories in Eastern Europe and supplies products to over 0.5 million customers in 20 countries. Aybe holds stocks of about 100,000 different electronic components.

Aybe is regarded within its industry as being a well-established business. Company Ay had operated successfully for nearly 17 years before its merger with Company Be. Company Ay can therefore trace its history back for 25 years which is a long time in the fast moving electronic component business.

The company is organised into three divisions, the Domestic Electronic Components division (DEC), the Industrial Electronic Components division (IEC) and the Specialist Components division (SC). The Domestic and Industrial Electronic Components divisions supply standard electronic components for domestic and industrial use whereas the Specialist Components division supplies components which are often unique and made to specific customer requirements. Each of the three divisions has its own factory in Country C.

Composition of the Board of Directors

The Board of Directors has three executive directors, the Company Secretary and five non-executive directors. The Chairman is one of the five independent non-executive directors. The executive directors are the Chief Executive, Finance Director and Director of Operations. There is also an Audit Committee, a Remuneration Committee and a Nominations Committee. All three committees are made up entirely of the non-executive directors.

Organisational structure

Aybe is organised along traditional functional/unitary lines. The Board considers continuity to be a very important value. The present structure was established by Company Ay in 1990 and continued after the merger with

Company Be. Many of Aybe's competitors have carried out structural reorganisations since then. In 2008, Aybe commissioned a review of its organisational structure from a human resource consultancy. The consultants suggested alternative structures which they thought Aybe could employ to its advantage. However, Aybe's Board felt that continuity was more important and no change to the organisational structure took place.

Product and service delivery

Customers are increasingly seeking assistance from their component suppliers with the design of their products and the associated manufacturing and assembly processes. Aybe's Board views this as a growth area. The Board has recognised that Aybe needs to develop web-based services and tools which can be accessed by customers. The traditional method of listing the company's range of components in a catalogue is becoming less effective because customers are increasingly seeking specially designed custom made components as the electronics industry becomes more sophisticated.

Financial data

Aybe's historical financial record, denominated in C's currency of C$, over the last five years is shown below.

	Year ended 31 December:				
	2009	2008	2007	2006	2005
	C$m	C$m	C$m	C$m	C$m
Revenue	620	600	475	433	360
Operating profit	41	39	35	20	13
Profit for the year	23	21	16	9	5
Earnings per share (C$)	0.128	0.117	0.089	0.050	0.028
Dividend per share (C$)	0.064	0.058	0	0	0

Extracts from the 2009 financial statements are given at Appendix A. There are currently 180 million ordinary shares in issue with a nominal value of C$0.10 each. The share price at 31 December 2009 was C$0.64. No dividend was paid in the three years 2005 to 2007 due to losses sustained in the first few years after the merger in 2001.

Aybe's bank has imposed an overdraft limit of C$10 million and two covenants: (i) that its interest cover must not fall below 5 and (ii) its ratio of non-current liabilities to equity must not increase beyond 0.75:1. Aybe's Finance Director is comfortable with this overdraft limit and the two covenants.

The ordinary shareholding of Aybe is broken down as follows:

Percentage of ordinary shares held at 31 December 2009

Institutional investors	55
Executive Directors and Company Secretary	10
Employees	5
Individual investors	30

The Executive Directors, Company Secretary and other senior managers are entitled to take part in an Executive Share Option Scheme offered by Aybe.

Performance Review

Aybe's three divisions have been profitable throughout the last five years. The revenue and operating profit of the three divisions of Aybe for 2009 were as follows:

	DEC Division	IEC Division	SC Division
	C$m	C$m	C$m
Revenue	212	284	124
Operating profit	14	16	11

Financial objectives of Aybe

The Board has generally taken a cautious approach to providing strategic direction for the company. Most board members feel that this has been appropriate because the company was unprofitable for the three year period after the merger and needed to be turned around. Also, most board members think a cautious approach has been justified given the constrained economic circumstances which have affected Aybe's markets since 2008. While shareholders have been disappointed with Aybe's performance over the last five years, they have remained loyal and supported the Board in its attempts to move the company into profit. The institutional shareholders however are now looking for increased growth and profitability.

The Board has set the following financial objectives which it considers reflect the caution for which Aybe is well known:

(i)   Dividend payout to remain at 50% of profit for the year;

(ii)   No further equity shares to be issued over the next five years in order to avoid diluting earnings per share.

Capital budget overspends

Aybe has an internal audit department. The Chief Internal Auditor, who leads this department, reports directly to the Finance Director. Investigation by the Internal Audit department has revealed that managers with responsibility for capital expenditure have often paid little attention to expenditure authorisation levels approved by the Board. They have justified overspending on the grounds that the original budgets were inadequate and in order not to jeopardise the capital projects, the overspends were necessary.

An example of this was the building of an extension to the main factory at the DEC division that was completed in 2009 at a final cost of nearly C$3 million which was almost 50% over budget. The capital budget for the extension was set at the outset and the capital investment appraisal showed a positive net present value. It subsequently became apparent that the site clearance costs and on-going construction expenditure were under-estimated. These estimates were provided by a qualified quantity surveyor who was a contractor to Aybe. The estimates supplied by the quantity surveyor were accurately included in Aybe's capital investment appraisal system which was performed on a spreadsheet. However, no regular checks were carried out to compare the phased budgeted expenditure with actual costs incurred. It came as a surprise to the Board when the Finance Director finally produced the capital expenditure project report which showed the cost of the extension was nearly 50% overspent.

Strategic development

Aybe applies a traditional rational model in carrying out its strategic planning process. This encompasses an annual exercise to review the previous plan, creation of a revenue and capital budget for the next five years and instruction to managers within Aybe to maintain their expenditure within the budget limits approved by the Board.

Debates have taken place within the Board regarding the strategic direction in which Aybe should move. Most board members are generally satisfied that Aybe has been turned around over the last five years and were pleased that the company increased its profit in 2009 even though the global economy slowed down. Aybe benefited from a number of long-term contractual arrangements with customers throughout 2009 which were agreed in previous years. However, many of these are not being renewed due to the current economic climate.

The Board stated in its annual report, published in March 2010, that the overall strategic aim of the company is to:

"Achieve growth and increase shareholder returns by continuing to produce and distribute high quality electronic components and develop our international presence through expansion into new overseas markets."

Aybe's Chief Executive said in the annual report that the strategic aim is clear and straightforward. He said "Aybe will strive to maintain its share of the electronic development, operational, maintenance and repair markets in which it is engaged. This is despite the global economic difficulties which Aybe, along with its competitors, has faced since 2008. Aybe will continue to apply the highest ethical standards in its business activities."

In order to facilitate the achievement of the strategic aim, Aybe's Board has established the following strategic goals:

1   Enhance the provision of products and services which are demanded by customers;
2   Invest in engineering and web-based support for customers;
3   Maintain the search for environmentally friendly products;
4   Pursue options for expansion into new overseas markets.

The Board has also stated that Aybe is a responsible corporate organisation and recognises the social and environmental effects of its operational activities.

Concern over the rate of growth

Aybe's recently appointed Director of Operations and one of its Non-Executive Directors have privately expressed their concern to the Chief Executive at what they perceive to be the very slow growth of the company. While they accept that shareholder expectations should not be raised too high, they feel that the Board is not providing sufficient impetus to move the company forward. They fear that the results for 2010 will be worse than for 2009. They think that Aybe should be much more ambitious and fear that the institutional shareholders in particular, will not remain patient if Aybe does not create stronger earnings growth than has previously been achieved.

Development approaches

The Board has discussed different ways of expanding overseas in order to meet the overall strategic aim. It has, in the past, been reluctant to move from the current approach of exporting components. However the Director of Operations has now begun preparing a plan for the IEC division to open up a trading company in Asia. The DEC division is also establishing a subsidiary in Africa.

APPENDIX A

Extracts of Aybe's Income Statement and Statement of Financial Position

Income statement for the year ended 31 December 2009

	2009 C$million
Revenue	620
Operating costs	(579)
Finance costs	(4)
Profit before tax	37
Income tax expense	(14)
Profit for the year	23

Statement of financial position as at 31 December 2009

	2009 C$million
Assets	
Non-current assets	111
Current assets	
Inventories	40
Trade and other receivables	81
Cash and cash equivalents	3
Total current assets	124
Total assets	235
Equity and liabilities	
Equity	
Share capital	18
Share premium	9
Other reserves	8
Retained earnings	75
Total equity	110
Non-current liabilities	
Bank loan (8% interest, repayable 2015)	40
Current liabilities	
Trade and other payables	73
Current tax payable	8
Bank overdraft	4
Total current liabilities	85
Total liabilities	125
Total equity and liabilities	235

Unseen material for Case Study

<u>Background</u>

Today's date is 27 May 2010.

The Specialist Components division (SC) of Aybe has recently been successful in researching and developing a new state-of-the-art range of products with the help of a research faculty in the USA. These are now ready to be produced. They will be sold in Europe and the USA.

In order to manufacture the new products, major investment is required. Aybe is considering two alternative ways forward:

- Project 1:   The complete refit of SC's factory located in the home country, Country C.

- Project 2:   Build a factory in the USA in a designated development area where a government grant would be available towards the cost of construction.

The new products will be priced in US$ for all worldwide sales. Each project is to be evaluated over a 5 year time period, referred to internally as the 'planning horizon'. The period commences 1 January 2011.

Note: Only one project will be undertaken.

<u>Project 1 – Factory refit in Country C</u>

The current factory would need to be refitted to accommodate the new product range but would then continue producing the current products alongside the new product range. It is estimated that the disruption to production of the current products would result in a loss of up to three or four months operating profit, that is, approximately C$4million (pre-tax cash loss) in 2011. Specialist consultants from the USA may also be needed to oversee the development and manage the manufacturing process but no figures are available for these costs at this time.

Other information:

- The cost of the factory refit is estimated to be C$35million, payable in 2011. The residual value is estimated to be C$4million at the end of 5 years.

- Pre-tax operating cash flows from the new product line begin in 2012 and annual cash flows are forecast to be:

    – Cash inflows: US$160million a year
    – Cash outflows: C$30million a year.

- Tax relief on the cost of the factory refit is available at a rate of 50% in the first year and then at 25% on a reducing balance basis in subsequent years; balancing charges are charged on any residual values.

- The corporate tax rate in Country C for the period of the project is 25% and the tax is paid in the period in which it arises.

- This project is to be evaluated at an after-tax discount rate of 8%.

<u>Project 2 – New factory in the USA</u>

A possible site for a new factory has been identified in the USA. A significant amount of interest has been expressed in the site by other potential developers. As a precautionary measure, therefore, on 1 May 2010 Aybe paid a fee of US$200,000 for the option of purchasing the full ownership rights of the land at any time up to 1 January 2011 at an agreed price of US$20million. It was considered that eight months would allow sufficient time for Aybe to apply for the necessary planning permission to construct the manufacturing facility on the site and also to carry out a more detailed financial assessment of the proposed investment.

If a new factory were to be built in the USA, Aybe would be eligible for a grant of US$15million in each of the first three years of the project, with the first of the three payments being made at the end of 2012. The grant is a revenue grant towards employee and other operating costs and is not repayable as long as certain conditions are met. Corporate tax is payable on the grant at the standard rate.

The new USA operation would be set up as a separate legal entity which would be a subsidiary company of Aybe.

Other information:

- Assume the land is purchased on 1 January 2011.

- The development cost (excluding land) is estimated as US$120million, with half this sum payable at the end of 2011 and the other half at the end of 2012.

- The residual value of the project at the end of 2015 is estimated as US$40million, including US$20million for the land.

- Net pre-tax operating cash inflows from the new product line begin in 2012 and are forecast to be US$50million per annum (excluding the grant).

- Tax relief on the development cost is at a rate of 100% in the first year and balancing charges are applied to any residual value. No tax relief is available on the purchase of the land.

- For simplicity and for the purposes of this question, assume that the relevant corporate tax rate in the USA is 30% and that tax is paid in the period in which it arises.

- Assume that no further tax is due or refundable in Country C in respect of this project.

- This project is to be evaluated at a higher after-tax discount rate of 11% to reflect the increased risk of a foreign project.

Additional financial information applicable to both projects

- The C$/US$ exchange rate is expected to be C$/US$4.000 on 31 December 2010 (that is, C$1=US$4.000) and the US$ can be assumed to strengthen against C$ by 5% a year in 2011 and subsequent years.

- All cash flows arise at the end of the year, unless otherwise stated.

- Assume cash flows are nominal cash flows, that is, they include assumptions on inflation.

Required

Assume you are an external consultant engaged by Aybe to evaluate the proposed projects.

Write a report, suitable for presentation to the Directors of Aybe, in which you:

(a)   Calculate the Net Present Value (NPV) of each of Project 1 and Project 2 as at 1 January 2011 for the 5 year planning horizon. State any assumptions made.   **(17 marks)**

(b)   Evaluate how other relevant factors such as changes to the planning horizon might affect the choice of project and advise Aybe how to proceed.

Up to 6 marks are available for calculations.   **(14 marks)**

(c)   Advise on the choice of currency if long term borrowings should be required to finance the new USA subsidiary in Project 2.   **(5 marks)**

(d)   Advise the Directors on how to achieve efficient management and control of the implementation of the proposed projects. Your answer should include discussion of the different issues arising for each project.   **(11 marks)**

Additional marks available for structure and presentation.   **(3 marks)**

(Total = 50 marks)

93 Aybe (2) (9/10)   90 mins

Refer to Q92 for pre-seen material

Unseen material for Case Study

Background

Today's date is 04 September 2010.

The Specialist Components division (SC) of Aybe has been considering various alternative opportunities for expansion and has recently identified NN, a company operating in Europe, as a possible acquisition candidate. NN manufactures a relatively new product line that can be tailored to meet the specific needs of individual customers. This business model has, so far, proved to be highly successful. In many respects, it is considered to be a good 'fit' with SC's business and it is considered that many of SC's customers may be interested in NN's products. At present SC has an average year-on-year growth in profit after tax of 3% whereas NN's profit after tax is forecast to grow at a rate of 8% a year for the next 3 years and then at a steady rate of 3% in subsequent years.

Should the acquisition go ahead, SC expects to achieve synergistic benefits that will result in an increase in NN's current estimate for a year-on year growth in profits from 8% a year to a growth rate of 14% a year in each of the next 3 years. Growth would then revert to a steady state of 3% a year for year 4 onwards. The additional growth would be largely achieved by improved access to non-European markets for NN's products. However, there are also expected to be exceptional one-off up-front costs arising from the integration of the two businesses in euro (EUR) of approximately EUR2.5million (that have no impact on the underlying operating profit).

NN

NN is privately owned. It has been trading for five years and has seen rapid growth in its reported profits. However, the cash flows are lagging behind the growth in profits. NN has four founding Directors, each of whom owns 20% of the company. The other 20% of the share capital is owned by a variety of small investors. The Directors are looking for ways to realise their investment and have expressed an interest in selling the company to Aybe. They have the backing of the minority shareholders. The Directors would be prepared to work for the SC division of Aybe if sufficiently attractive terms of employment were offered.

Extracts from the latest annual financial statements for NN are as follows:

Income statement for NN for the year ended 31 December 2009

	EURmillion
Revenue	40
Operating costs	(20)
Finance costs	(4)
Profit before tax	16
Income tax expense	(6)
Profit For The Year	10

Statement of financial position for NN as at 31 December 2009

Assets	EURmillion
Non-current assets	72
Inventories and receivables	15
Cash and cash equivalents	3
Total assets	90
Equity And Liabilities	
Share capital	5
Retained earnings	30
Non-current liabilities	45
(bank borrowings at floating rate)	
Current liabilities	10
Total equity and liabilities	90

Latest estimates for the year ending 31 December 2010 show profit for the year of EUR11million.

Being a privately-owned company, there is no share price available for NN. However, a 5% parcel of shares was sold by private arrangement for EUR3million six months ago.

A similar sized company to NN in the same market, QQ, has been identified for use as a proxy company for the purpose of valuing NN. QQ has a P/E ratio of 9, an equity beta of 1.7 and the same gearing as NN. QQ is, however, a somewhat more mature company than NN and has largely passed the early days of extraordinary returns and high risk. It is therefore considered appropriate to increase QQ's cost of equity by a factor of 15% in order to arrive at an appropriate cost of equity for NN. (For example, a discount rate of 10% for QQ would be increased to 11.5% for NN). Debt beta can be assumed to be zero, the risk-free market rate is 2% and the market premium above the risk free rate is 6%.

Pricing the bid

The Finance Director of Aybe, Director A, has suggested that an initial offer of EUR75million should be made for the acquisition of NN for transfer of ownership on 01 January 2011. The acquisition would be funded by either issuing bonds or arranging bank borrowings. It is not yet clear whether the debt would be denominated in C$ or in EUR. The present bank borrowings of NN are subject to a bank covenant that would require the borrowings to be repaid as part of any acquisition agreement. In addition, Aybe's current borrowings are subject to the following two bank covenants: (i) interest cover must not fall below 5 and (ii) the ratio of non-current liabilities to equity must not increase beyond 0.75:1 (based on market values of equity).

Additional information:

- The spot exchange rate is expected to be C$/EUR3.000 (C$1 = EUR3.000) on 01 January 2011 and the euro is expected to weaken against the C$ at approximately 3% a year thereafter.

- Corporate tax is payable by both Aybe and NN at 30% for the year 2010 onwards and there is a double tax treaty in place under which no additional tax would be payable by Aybe on profits generated by NN.

- On 01 January 2011, Aybe's share price and non-current liabilities are forecast to be C$0.70 and C$45million respectively. The number of shares in issue is expected to remain unchanged at 180million shares.

Required

(a) (i) Calculate a range of values for NN as at 01 January 2011 using:

- The price achieved in the recent sale of a 5% parcel of shares.
- P/E basis.
- Discounted cash flow basis, ignoring potential synergistic benefits and integration costs.

(11 marks)

(ii) Explain briefly the suitability of each method used in part (a)(i).

(6 marks)

(b) Assume you are an external consultant engaged by Aybe to evaluate the proposed acquisition of NN. Write a report, suitable for presentation to the Directors of Aybe, in which you:

(i) Evaluate the proposed initial offer price of EUR75million from the viewpoint of both the shareholders of NN and the shareholders of Aybe, concluding with advice on an appropriate adjusted offer price. **(11 marks)**

(ii) Discuss the potential problems and issues that could arise from the integration of NN into the SC Division of Aybe. **(7 marks)**

(iii) Advise on issues that affect the choice of debt finance (bonds or bank borrowings, C$ or EUR), including their potential impact on Aybe's bank covenants.

(12 marks)

Additional marks available for structure and presentation. **(3 marks)**

(Total = 50 marks)

94 DEF (1) (11/10)   90 mins

Pre-seen case study

> The following pre-seen material is applicable to both Q94 and Q95.

<u>Overview</u>

DEF Airport is situated in country D within Europe but which is outside the Eurozone. The local currency is D$. It is located near to the town of DEF. It began life in the 1930s as a flying club and was extended in 1947, providing scheduled services within central Europe. A group of four local state governments, which are all in easy reach of the airport (hereafter referred to as the LSGs), took over the running of the airport in 1961. The four LSGs are named North (NLSG), South (SLSG), East (ELSG) and West (WLSG). These names place their geographical location in relation to the airport. In the early 1970s flights from the airport to European holiday destinations commenced with charter flights operated by holiday companies. In 1986, the first transatlantic flight was established and the airport terminal building was extended in 1987.

By 1989 the airport was handling 500,000 passengers per year which is forecast to increase to 3.5 million for both incoming and outgoing passengers in the current financial year to 30 June 2011. The airport mainly serves holidaymakers flying to destinations within Europe and only 5% of the passengers who use the airport are business travellers.

DEF Airport was converted into a company in 1990 and the four LSGs became the shareholders, each with an equal share. The company is not listed on a stock exchange. The airport has undertaken extensive development since 2000, with improvements to its single terminal building. The improvements have mainly been to improve the airport's catering facilities and to increase the number of check-in desks. There has also been investment in the aircraft maintenance facilities offered to the airlines operating out of the airport.

<u>Governance</u>

The Board of Directors has four Executive directors: the Chief Executive, the Director of Facilities Management, the Finance Director and the Commercial Director. In addition there is a Company Secretary and a Non-Executive Chairman. In accordance with DEF Airport's Articles of Association, the Non-Executive Chairman is drawn from one of the four LSGs. The Non-Executive Chairman is the sole representative of all four LSGs. The Chairmanship changes every two years with each of the four LSGs taking turns to nominate the Chair.

The four LSGs have indicated that they may wish to sell their shareholdings in the airport in the near future. If any LSG wishes to sell its shares in the airport it must first offer them to the other three LSGs. Any shares that are not purchased by the other LSGs may then be sold on the open market. A local investment bank (IVB) has written to the Chairman expressing an interest in investing in the airport in return for a shareholding together with a seat on the Board.

<u>Mission statement</u>

The Board of Directors drew up a mission statement in 2008. It states "At DEF Airport we aim to outperform all other regional airports in Europe by ensuring that we offer our customers a range of services that are of the highest quality, provided by the best people and conform to the highest ethical standards. We aim to be a good corporate citizen in everything we do."

<u>DEF Airport development plan</u>

The Board of Directors produced a development plan in 2009. The Board of Directors consulted with businesses in the area and followed central government airport planning guidelines. It was assumed that the views of other local stakeholders would be represented by the four LSGs which would feed comments to the Board through the Chairman.

The plan relates to the development of DEF Airport and its forecast passenger growth for the next two decades. The Board proposed that future development of the airport will be phased and gradual in order to avoid unexpected consequences for the local communities and industry.

Strategic objectives

The following strategic objectives have been established in the development plan:

1   Create a planning framework which enables DEF Airport to meet the demands of the forecast passenger numbers;

2   Reduce to a minimum the visual and audible impacts of the operation of the airport on the local environment;

3   Ensure that the airport is financially secure;

4   Improve land based access to the airport;

5   Minimise the pollution effects of the operation of the airport.

6   Maintain / increase employment opportunities for people living close to the airport.

By the year ending 30 June 2015, DEF Airport is expected to support about 3,000 local jobs and have a throughput of 5 million passengers per year, an increase of 1.5 million from the 3.5 million passengers forecast for the current financial year ending 30 June 2011. In order to accommodate the forecast increased number of passengers and attain the development objectives, it will be necessary for the airport to extend its operational area to the east of the land it currently occupies.

Financial objectives

Extracts from DEF Airport's forecast income statement for the year ending 30 June 2011 and forecast statement of financial position as at that date are presented in the Appendix. The four LSGs have made it clear to the Board of Directors that the airport must at least achieve financial self-sufficiency. The financial objectives of the airport are to ensure that:

1   The airport does not run at a loss;

2   All creditors are paid on time;

3   Gearing levels must not exceed 20% (where gearing is defined as debt to debt plus equity) and any long-term borrowings are financed from sources approved by the four LSGs.

Corporate Social Responsibility

A key feature of DEF Airport's development plan is to develop "Sustainable Aviation" initiatives in order to reduce the effects of flying on the environment. One effect on the environment is that the airport is subject to specific planning restrictions affecting flights between the hours of 11 p.m. (2300 hours) and 7 a.m. (0700 hours) to reduce aircraft noise. Flights are permitted between these times, but must be specially authorised. Typically, flights between these times would be as a result of an emergency landing request.

A leading international consultancy, QEG, which specialises in auditing the corporate social responsibility (CSR) issues of commercial enterprises, has offered to provide a CSR audit to DEF Airport free of charge. QEG is based in the USA and hopes to expand by offering its services to European enterprises.

DEF Airport's competitors

TUV Airport is located about 100 kilometres away from DEF Airport and serves a highly populated industrial city. The Board of Directors of DEF Airport considers TUV Airport to be its main competitor. There are another three competing airports within 80 kilometres of DEF Airport. TUV Airport purchased one of these three competitor airports and subsequently reduced services from it in order to reduce the competitive threat to itself.

Airlines

Airlines are keen to negotiate the most cost effective deal they can with airports. DEF Airport applies a set of standard charges to airlines but is aware that some of its competitor airports have offered inducements to airlines in order to attract DEF's business.

Airlines across the world are facing rising fuel and staff costs as well as strong competition from within the industry. There has been an overall increase in customer demand for air travel in recent years and low-priced airlines have emerged and are threatening the well-established, traditional airlines. Consequently, the traditional airlines have begun to cut the number of destinations to which they fly.

There are several low-priced airlines that serve DEF Airport's competitors, but only one, S, also operates out of DEF Airport. S is exploring ways in which it might increase its flights to and from DEF Airport.

DEF's Board of Directors has been approached by a North American airline that wishes to operate services from DEF Airport. This airline specialises in flights for business and first class passengers. However, this airline insists that it would pay DEF Airport in US$. This is contrary to the airport's policy of accepting payment only in D$, which is the local currency.

Analysis of revenue by business segment

The forecast split of total revenue of D$23.4 million by business segment for the current financial year ending 30 June 2011 is:

	%
Aviation income	48
Retail concessions at the airport	20
Car Parking	15
Other income	17

(Other income includes income from property rentals, and other fees and charges.)

DEF Airport offers discounts for prompt payment.

Aviation income

In addition to the standard charges, which are set out below, there is a range of surcharges which are levied on airlines for such items as "noisy aircraft" (charged when aircraft exceed the Government limits for acceptable noise levels), recovery of costs and expenses arising from cleaning or making safe any spillages from aircraft and extraordinary policing of flights (for example, arrests made as a result of anti-social behaviour on aircraft).

Standard charges made by DEF Airport to the airlines:

Charges per aircraft
Landing charges – large aircraft: D$300
Landing charges – medium aircraft: D$170

Parking charges for the first two hours are included in the landing charge. Thereafter, a charge of D$200 per hour is imposed for each large aircraft and D$250 per hour for each medium aircraft. The parking charge is lower for large aircraft because they take at least two hours to clean and refuel, so they almost always have to pay for an hour's parking, and also because there is less demand for the parking areas used for large aircraft. Medium aircraft tend to take off again within one hour of landing. Approximately 10% of medium sized aircraft landings result in the airline incurring parking charges for one hour. This is normally either because their scheduled departure time requires them to park or because of delays imposed by air traffic restrictions, technical malfunctions or problems with passengers.

Charges per passenger
Passenger Load:

Flights to European destinations:	D$1.60 per departing passenger
Flights outside Europe:	D$4.00 per departing passenger
Passenger security	D$1.20 per passenger arriving or departing

Retail concessions

DEF Airport provides the facilities for a range of shops, bureau de change (dealing in foreign exchange currency transactions for passengers), bars and cafes for the budget conscious passenger.

DEF Airport has a monopoly in the provision of retail concessions and therefore faces no competition.

Car parking

Car parking is an important source of DEF Airport's revenue. The airport has extended its own car parking facilities for customers over recent years. Car parks occupy a large area of what was green belt land (that is land which was not previously built on) around its perimeter. The land was acquired by the airport specifically for the purpose of car parking. A free passenger bus service is provided to take passengers to and from the car parks into the airport terminal building.

Competitors have established alternative car parking facilities off-site and provide bus services to and from the airport's terminal. The parking charges made by the competitors are lower than those levied by the airport.

Competitor car park operators offer additional services to passengers, such as car maintenance and valeting, which are undertaken while the car is left in their care.

DEF Airport does not have a hotel on its premises. There is a hotel within walking distance of the airport which offers special rates for passengers to stay the night before their flight and then to park their cars at the hotel for the duration of their trip.

Other income

This heading contains a mixture of revenue streams. The Commercial Director reported that some have good growth prospects. Property rental income is likely to decline though as there has been much building development around the airport perimeter.

DEF Airport security

Passengers and their baggage are required to go through rigorous security checks. There is a fast track service provided which can be accessed by all passengers at an extra charge. This is intended to speed up the security process. However, on some occasions this leads to passengers on the normal route becoming frustrated because they are required to wait in lengthy queues to pass through the security checks. Airport security staff are required by law to search all departing passengers and their baggage for suspicious or dangerous items. On the very rare occasions that they discover anything they report their concerns to the police. There are always several police officers on patrol at the airport at any given time and so the police can respond to any report very quickly.

In addition to passenger and baggage screening, DEF Airport security staff are responsible for the security of parked aircraft and airport property. They do this primarily by monitoring all arriving and departing vehicles and their drivers and by monitoring the many closed circuit television cameras that cover the airport.

The airport has had a good record with regard to the prevention of theft from passenger baggage. This is frequently a serious matter at other airports, but DEF Airport has received very few complaints that baggage has been tampered with. DEF Airport's Head of Security regards the security of baggage as very low risk because of this low level of complaints.

The Head of Security at DEF Airport was appointed to his current role in 1990, when the airport was very much smaller than it is today. He was a police sergeant before he joined the airport staff. Immediately before his appointment he was responsible for the front desk of DEF town's main police station, a job that involved managing the day-to-day activities of the other police officers on duty. He was happy to accept the post of Head of Security because the police service was starting to make far greater use of computers. He had always relied on a comprehensive paper-based system for documenting and filing reports.

The Head of Security is directly responsible for all security matters at DEF Airport. In practice, he has to delegate most of the actual supervision of staff to shift managers and team leaders because he cannot be expected to be on duty for 24 hours per day or to manage the security arrangements in great detail while administering the security department. The overall responsibilities of the Head of Security have not been reviewed since his appointment.

Strategic options

The Board of Directors is now actively considering its strategic options which could be implemented in the future in order to meet the strategic objectives which were set out in the airport's development plan.

APPENDIX 1

Extracts of DEF Airport's forecast income statement for the year ending 30 June 2011 and statement of financial position as at 30 June 2011

Forecast income statement for the year ending 30 June 2011

	Note	D$000
Revenue		23,400
Operating costs	1	(25,450)
Net operating loss		(2,050)
Interest income		70
Finance costs		(1,590)
Corporate income tax expense		(130)
LOSS FOR THE YEAR		(3,700)

Forecast statement of financial position as at 30 June 2011

	D$000
ASSETS	
Non-current assets	150,000
Current assets	
Inventories	400
Trade and other receivables	9,250
Cash and cash equivalents	3,030
Total current assets	12,680
Total assets	162,680
EQUITY AND LIABILITIES	
Equity	
Share capital (Note 2)	17,700
Share premium	530
Revaluation reserve	89,100
Retained earnings	23,200
Total equity	130,530
Non-current liabilities	
Long term borrowings (Note 3)	22,700
Current liabilities	
Trade and other payables	9,450
Total liabilities	32,150
Total equity and liabilities	162,680

Notes:

1   Operating costs include depreciation of D$5.0 million.

2   There are 17.7 million ordinary shares of D$1 each in issue.

3   The long-term borrowings comprise a D$6.3 million loan for capital expenditure which is repayable on 1 July 2015 and D$16.4 million owed to the 4 LSGs. This has no fixed repayment schedule and is not expected to be repaid in the next year.

Unseen case material

<u>Background</u>

Today's date is 25 November 2010.

The Directors of DEF Airport have recently received information that TUV Airport, a competitor airport located approximately 100 kilometres from DEF, is interested in acquiring the company.

TUV Airport is privately owned and has the overall financial objective of maximising shareholder wealth. Its strategic objectives support this financial objective by focussing on opportunities for growth, both internally and by expansion through acquisition.

The Directors of DEF Airport have informed the four LSGs about the potential takeover bid and the Directors and the LSGs have been discussing the implications of the sale of their shares to TUV Airport. On the one hand, the potential takeover bid appears quite attractive because running the airport has proved to be very challenging in recent months due to a global economic downturn. On the other hand, the LSGs are reluctant to give up direct control over local air transport and the interest income received on funds which the LSGs advanced to DEF.

The most likely date for the proposed takeover is considered to be 1 July 2011.

DEF Airport's forecast financial statements for the year ending 30 June 2011 are set out in the pre-seen material on page 7. Financial and strategic objectives can be found on page 3.

<u>Financial information for DEF Airport</u>

Forecast revenue for the year ending 30 June 2011 can further be analysed by business segment as follows:

	%	D$ million
Aviation income	48	11.23
Retail concessions	20	4.68
Car parking	15	3.51
Other income	17	3.98
TOTAL	100	23.40

Forecast total operating costs for the year ending 30 June 2011 are D$25.45 million.

<u>Years ending 30 June 2012 and 30 June 2013</u>

- The total number of passengers is estimated to be 3.5 million in the year ending 30 June 2011 and to grow by 5% in the year ending 30 June 2012 and then by 8% in the year ending 30 June 2013.

- Aviation income should be assumed to be directly related to the number of passengers. The average aviation income per passenger in the year ending 30 June 2011 is forecast to be D$3.21 and this is expected to increase at a rate of 4% a year in each of the years ending 30 June 2012 and 30 June 2013.

- Car parking income should be assumed to be directly related to the number of passengers. The average car parking income per passenger is forecast to be D$1.00 in the year ending 30 June 2011 and this is expected to increase at a rate of 10% a year in each of the years ending 30 June 2012 and 30 June 2013.

- Retail concessions and other income are expected to increase by 7% a year in each of the years ending 30 June 2012 and 30 June 2013 and are not dependent on passenger numbers.

- Operating costs excluding depreciation are expected to increase by 4% a year in each of the years ending 30 June 2012 and 30 June 2013. Operating costs are not dependent on passenger numbers.

- Depreciation is expected to remain constant at D$5 million in each of the years ending 30 June 2012 and 30 June 2013. No capital expenditure or disposals of non-current assets are planned for either of these two financial years.

- Working capital is expected to remain constant.

- The interest rate payable on borrowings is 7%. No repayments of long-term borrowings are due in each of the years ending 30 June 2012 and 30 June 2013. Interest of 4% is received on cash and cash equivalents. Interest should be calculated on the opening balances of borrowings and cash and cash equivalents in each year.

- Corporate income tax is charged at at 30% on taxable profits and is paid at the end of the year in which the taxable profit arises. No tax refunds are available on losses for tax purposes as these are carried forward to be offset against future taxable profits.

- Tax depreciation allowances are available on a reducing balance basis at a rate of 25% per annum. On 1 July 2011, the opening balance of non-current assets that quality for tax depreciation allowances can be assumed to be D$3 million.

- Operating cash flows can be assumed to equate to operating profit or loss after adjusting for the non-cash items specified above.

<u>Year ending 30 June 2014 onwards</u>

For the financial years ending 30 June 2014 to 30 June 2016, assume annual profits after tax of D$6 million, D$8 million and D$9 million respectively and that these are equivalent to cash flows.

For the year ending 30 June 2017 onwards, assume annual profits after tax (that is, cash) grow by 5% a year in perpetuity.

<u>Valuation of DEF Airport</u>

The Directors of DEF Airport consider 11% to be an appropriate after tax discount rate to use in discounting future cash flows. All cash flows should be assumed to arise at the end of the year.

In the event of the acquisition going ahead, TUV Airport is expected to be able to benefit from a one-off synergistic benefit of D$3 million (after tax) in the year ending 30 June 2012. It pays corporate income tax at a rate of 30% and expects to be able to obtain tax relief on any future losses for tax purposes arising from DEF Airport by offsetting against taxable profits elsewhere in the group in the same year.

Required:

(a)   Construct, for each of the financial years ending 30 June 2012 and 30 June 2013:

- A forecast of the net cash flow for the year;

- A statement of opening and closing balances for cash and cash equivalents and long term borrowings.   **(13 marks)**

(b)   Assume you are an external consultant engaged by the Board to prepare a report on the factors that need to be considered should a takeover bid be received from TUV Airport.

Write a report addressed to the Board in which you:

(i)   Calculate a range of values for DEF Airport as at 1 July 2011. Discuss your results and advise on an appropriate valuation for use in negotiations with TUV Airport.

(Up to 7 marks are available for calculations)   **(14 marks)**

(ii)   Explain the main differences in the financial objectives of public and private sector organisations, illustrating your answer by reference to the stated financial objectives of both DEF Airport and TUV Airport.   **(8 marks)**

(iii)   Discuss the strategic implications of the proposed sale of the business for the LSGs and also for each of the other major stakeholder groups. Advise the LSGs whether or not to negotiate a sale of the business to TUV Airport.   **(12 marks)**

Additional marks available for structure and presentation: **(3 marks)**

(Total = 50 marks)

95 DEF (2) (3/11)   90 mins

Refer to Q94 for pre-seen material

Unseen case material

Background

Today's date is 4 March 2011.

The directors of DEF Airport are considering the future development and management of the company's on-site car parking business. DEF operates on-site car parking facilities close to the airport terminal buildings. Other operators offer off-site car parking some distance away. DEF has been facing increasing levels of competition from these off-site operators due primarily to their lower parking charges and additional services such as car maintenance and valeting.

Currently, on-site car parks are operating at approximately 80% of maximum occupancy and if nothing is done, this is set to decline further. In order to attempt to reverse this, the directors are considering an investment of D\$ 4 million to improve services and provide a more regular, faster link to the terminal buildings. It is felt that because off-site facilities are some distance from the Airport that this will prove enough of an incentive to attract more passengers to park their cars at the Airport. However, there is also an urgent need to refurbish the terminal buildings and funds are not available for both investments.

The LSGs are under considerable financial pressure and are not able to invest additional funds in the business. Therefore any investment in the on-site car parks or terminal buildings would need to be financed by borrowings.

Financial information relating to DEF Airport

Extracts from DEF Airport's forecast financial statements for the year ending 30 June 2011 are set out in the pre-seen material on page 7. Financial and strategic objectives can be found on page 3.

Financial information relating to DEF's car parks

DEF car parking revenue in any year is directly linked both to the number of cars using the on-site car parking facilities managed by DEF and the average fee charged per car.

For the year ending 30 June 2011

In the year ending 30 June 2011, the total number of cars using either on-site car parking facilities provided by DEF or off-site facilities provided by competitors is forecast to be 1,400,000. DEF is expected to have a 50% share of this market (based on the number of cars) providing on-site car parking for 700,000 cars at an average fee of D\$ 5 per car.

Operating costs for the car parking business in the year are forecast to be D\$ 2.7 million (which includes a depreciation charge of D\$ 0.2 million).

For the year ending 30 June 2012 and onwards assuming no investment

Forecast data for the year ending 30 June 2012 and onwards indicate:

- The total number of cars requiring either on-site or off-site parking is expected to increase by 6% in each of the years ending 30 June 2012 and 30 June 2013 and then to remain constant into the foreseeable future.

- DEF Airport's share of the total car parking market, is expected to fall to:

    - 40% (of cars using both on-site and off-site airport parking) in the year ending 30 June 2012;
    - 35% in the year ending 30 June 2013 onwards into the foreseeable future.

- In the year ending 30 June 2012, operating costs (before charging depreciation) are expected to be D\$ 2.6 million and then increase by 4% a year in subsequent years.

- DEF only expects to be able to increase its average car parking fee at a rate of 3% a year for the foreseeable future from a base level of D\$ 5 in the year ending 30 June 2011.

For the year ending 30 June 2012 onwards assuming the investment is made

The initial investment of D\$ 4.0 million would be payable by DEF on 1 July 2011. This initial investment would be eligible for a 100% tax depreciation allowance, which would be claimed at the end of that financial year. It

would also be subject to accounting depreciation on a straight line basis over ten years and can be assumed to have no residual value after ten years.

Relevant data assuming the investment goes ahead:

- The total number of cars requiring either on-site or off-site car parking facilities would not be affected by the investment

- DEF's share of the market would be constant at 50% of all cars using car parking facilities.

- Annual operating costs would increase to D$ 3.1 million (before charging depreciation) in the year ending 30 June 2012 and increase by 4% a year in subsequent years.

- DEF expects to be able to increase average car parking fees by 4% a year.

Additional information

- Cash flows can be assumed to equal profits (after adjusting for depreciation where appropriate) and to arise at the end of each year.

- Corporate income tax is charged at 30% on taxable profits and is paid at the end of the financial year in which the taxable profit arises.

- Assume that DEF will have sufficient taxable profits in future years to cover tax depreciation allowances.

- DEF's existing WACC of 12% is considered to be an appropriate nominal discount rate to use for investment appraisal and valuation purposes.

Alternative schemes for the operation of the on-site car parking facilities assuming DEF proceeds with its proposed investment to up-grade those facilities

Two alternative schemes are being considered, following on from the investment:

Scheme A: DEF would retain control of the on-site car parks.

Scheme B: DEF would lease both the land and the upgraded facilities used in the car park business to ABC, a third party operator, for a 10 year period from 1 July 2011. ABC would take over responsibility for operating the on-site car parking business for 10 years and all operating costs and revenues would be paid and retained by ABC. Ownership of the land would be retained by DEF. A lease payment would be paid by ABC to DEF at the end of each of the next 10 years.

Required:

(a) Evaluate the importance of the car parking business to DEF as a whole with reference to the forecast results for the year ended 30 June 2011 only. **(6 marks)**

(b) Calculate the present value on 1 July 2011 of the net cash flows of DEF's car parking business over a 10 year time period assuming:

    (i) no investment in upgrading the on-site car parking facilities is made;

    (ii) the proposed investment to upgrade on-site car parking facilities is made. **(15 marks)**

Assume you are the Financial Controller of DEF. Write a report addressed to the Board of Directors regarding the proposed investment and subsequent operation of the on-site car parks as detailed below.

(c) Advise the directors whether to proceed with the proposed investment to upgrade the on-site car parking facilities. **(5 marks)**

(d) Assuming the proposed investment in on-site car parking facilities goes ahead:

    (i) Recommend an appropriate annual lease payment to be made by ABC under Scheme B (based on a calculation of the payment at which Schemes A and B are equally attractive to DEF from a financial perspective over a 10 year period). **(6 marks)**

    (ii) Advise the directors of DEF whether to choose Scheme A or Scheme B. As part of your answer you should:

        - Compare and contrast Schemes A and B with reference to DEF's financial and strategic objectives.

        - Discuss any real options attaching to each scheme. **(14 marks)**

Additional marks available for structure and presentation in parts (a) to (d): **(4 marks)**

(Total = 50 marks)

96   F plc (1) (5/11)   90 mins

Pre-seen case study

The following pre-seen material is applicable to both Q96 and Q97.

<u>Introduction</u>

F plc is a food manufacturer based in the United Kingdom. It generates its revenue from three divisions named the Meals, Snacks and Desserts divisions. Each division specialises in the production of different types of food and operates from its own factory located on three different sites in England. F plc's head office is located in a remote part of England and is about equidistant from each of the company's three divisions.

Currently, F plc has a total employment establishment of about 10,000 full-time equivalent employees, about 97% of whom are employed in its three divisions. It is constantly running with about 700 full-time vacancies, mostly in the Desserts Division. This vacancy factor in the Desserts Division impedes its productivity.

The company was founded over 150 years ago by an entrepreneurial farmer who saw the opportunity to expand his farming business by vertically integrating into food production. Instead of selling his crops on the open market, he established a mill and produced flour. From this, it was a natural progression to diversify into producing other crops which were then processed into different ingredients for food products.

The company grew steadily and it became clear at the beginning of the 20th Century that increased production facilities were needed. It was at this point that the company built its first factory which at the time was a state of the art manufacturing facility. As demand continued to grow during the 20th Century, the company required additional manufacturing facilities and made a public offering of shares in 1960 to finance this expansion. The public offer was successful and F Limited was established. The original family's holding in the company fell to 25% at this point. Although a second factory was opened with the capital that had been raised, F Limited continued to manage the company on a centralised basis.

The next phase of development came in the late 1980's when F Limited became F plc. After this, F plc had a successful rights issue which raised sufficient capital to enable a third factory to be built. It was at this point that the divisionalised and de-centralised structure was established. Prior to this, the company managed its factories directly from its head office. The family shareholding fell to 20% at this point, with one family member holding 10% of the shares and family trusts holding the other 10%.

The environment in which F plc trades is dynamic, particularly with regard to the growth of legislation relating to food hygiene and production methods. F plc now exports many of its products as well as obtaining ingredients from foreign producers, which means that F plc must observe legislative requirements and food standard protocols in different countries.

<u>Mission statement</u>

F plc's mission statement, which was set in the year 2000, is as follows:

"F plc is committed to continually seek ways to increase its return to investors by expanding its share of both its domestic and overseas markets. It will achieve this by sourcing high quality ingredients, using efficient processes and maintaining the highest standards of hygiene in its production methods and paying fair prices for the goods and services it uses."

<u>Strategic aims</u>

The strategic aims are set in order to enable F plc to meet the obligations contained in its mission statement. F plc aims to:

(i)   increase profitability of each of its divisions through increased market share in both domestic and overseas markets

(ii)   source high quality ingredients to enhance product attractiveness

(iii)   ensure that its factories adhere to the highest standards of food hygiene which guarantee the quality of its products

(iv)   strive to be at the forefront in food manufacturing techniques by being innovative and increasing efficiency of production with least waste.

Corporate Social Responsibility

F plc takes Corporate Social Responsibility (CSR) seriously. The post of Environmental Effects Manager was created two years ago and a qualified environmental scientist was appointed to it. The Environmental Effects Manager reports directly to the Director of Operations. The role of the Environmental Effects Manager is to develop initiatives to reduce environmental impacts, capture data on the environmental effects of divisional and head office operations and report to the Board of Directors on the progress towards the achievement of F plc's CSR targets. An extract from F plc's internal CSR report for 2010 is shown in Appendix 1. F plc does not publish its CSR report externally.

Last year, F plc received criticism in the national press in England and in other countries for exploiting some of its suppliers in Africa by paying low prices for ingredients. This resulted in an extensive public relations campaign by F plc to counter these accusations. It established a programme to channel funds to support farmers in Africa via payments made through African government agencies. The programme, which is managed through F plc's head office, received initial financing from F plc itself and is now widening its remit to draw funding from other sources including public funding from the European Union.

The Board of Directors

The Board of Directors comprises five executive and five non-executive members all of whom are British. No member of the Board is from an ethnic minority.

The Chairman is a senior non-executive director and a retired Chief Executive of a major quoted retail clothing company based in England. He received a knighthood two years ago for services to industry.

The Chief Executive is 52 years old and was Director of Operations at F plc before taking up his current post three years ago.

The Finance Director is 49 years old and a qualified CIMA accountant. He has experience in a variety of manufacturing and retail organisations.

The Director of Operations is 65 years old and is a member of the original family which founded the business. He has been employed by F plc for all of his working life. He took up his current post three years ago following the promotion of the previous post holder to the role of Chief Executive.

The Marketing Director is 43 years old and has held various positions in sales and marketing for different organisations before being appointed to the Board. He came to the attention of the Chief Executive when he was instrumental in a successful initiative to market a new shopping complex in the city in which F plc's head office is based. At the time, the Marketing Director was the Chief Marketing Officer for the local government authority in the area.

The Director of Human Resources, the only female member of the Board, is 38 years old and holds a recognised HR professional qualification. Last year she was presented with a national award which recognised her achievements in the development of human resource management practices.

In addition there are four other non-executive directors on the Board. Two of them previously worked in senior positions alongside the Chairman when he was Chief Executive of the retail clothing company. One of them was the clothing company's finance director, but is now retired and the other was its marketing director but is now the sales and marketing director for a pharmaceutical company. One of the other non-executive directors is a practising lawyer and the other is a sports personality of national renown and a personal friend of the Chairman.

The Divisional General Managers, responsible for each of the three divisions, are not members of F plc's board. The Divisions are organised along traditional functional lines. Each division is managed by a Divisional Board which is headed by a Divisional General Manager. Each Divisional Board comprises the posts of Divisional Operations Manager, Divisional Accountant, Divisional Marketing Manager and Divisional Human Resources Manager. Each division undertakes its own marketing and human resource management. The divisional accountants are responsible for the management accounting functions within their divisions. Each member of the divisional boards is directly accountable to the Divisional General Manager but have professional accountability to the relevant functional F plc executive board members.

Financial position and borrowing facilities

Extracts from F plc's financial statements for the year ended 31 December 2010 are shown in Appendix 2.

F plc's long term borrowings are made up of a £160 million bank loan for capital expenditure and a £74 million revolving credit facility (RCF).

The bank loan is secured on F plc's assets and is repayable on 1 January 2018.

The RCF allows F plc to borrow, make repayments and then re-borrow over the term of the agreement. This provides F plc with flexibility because it can continue to obtain loans as long as it remains at or below £80 million, being the total amount agreed for this facility. The RCF expires on 31 December 2013.

Planning process

The planning process employed by F plc is one which can be described as adhering to classical rational principles. This has been the method of planning used for many years and culminates in the production of a five year forecast. The annual budget cycle feeds in to the strategic plan which is then updated on an annual basis. All F plc's revenue is derived through the operations of the three divisions. The only income generated by F plc's head office is from investments. The five year forecast for sales revenue and net operating profit for each division and F plc in total, after deduction of head office operating costs, is shown in Appendix 3. This shows that F plc is seeking to increase its sales revenue and net operating profit over the five year plan period.

Competition within the industry

F plc is one of the largest food production companies in England. It had an overall share of about 6% of its home market in 2010. Its nearest competitors held 5% and 7% market share respectively in 2010. The products in the industry have varying product life cycles. Competition is intense and there is a high failure rate for new products. Usually, new products require significant marketing support particularly if a new brand is being established.

Organisational culture within each division

Different cultures have emerged within each division.

Meals Division:

In the Meals Division, each function operates with little direct interference from the Divisional Board members. The approach is to allow each function to operate with as little control as possible being exercised by the Divisional Board.

Snacks Division:

In the Snacks Division, the emphasis of the Divisional Board is on product research and development and marketing. The Snacks Divisional Board expects its divisional marketing staff to undertake market research into customer tastes and preferences and then for products which satisfy these to be developed by its divisional research staff.

Desserts Division:

In the Desserts Division, the finance function is the dominant force. The finance functions in the other two divisions exert less influence over operations than is the case in the Desserts Division. It is not unusual for the Divisional Accountant in the Desserts Division to have confrontational meetings with managers of other functions. Such confrontation is particularly evident in the monthly meetings between the Divisional Accountant and the Divisional Marketing staff. It is clear that within the Desserts Division, the Divisional General Manager, a food technologist by profession, and the Divisional Accountant, formerly an auditor with a local government authority, maintain strict control over the operation of the division.

Further details relating to the three divisions are as follows:

Meals Division

The Meals division is located in the South of England. It specialises in manufacturing frozen meals, which are designed to be easy for consumers to quickly heat up and serve. The meals are sold to supermarkets and other retail outlets. Some are manufactured under F plc's own brand and others are manufactured under supermarkets' own labels. The division is also increasing its sales to welfare organisations which support elderly and infirm people. These organisations purchase simple frozen meals in bulk which they then heat up to provide a hot meal each day to those people in their care. In 2010, the Meals Division earned 14% of its revenue from outside the United Kingdom.

One of the Meals Division's most profitable products is a steak pie that is flavoured with special gravy that was developed by one of F plc's founding family members in the early part of the 20th

Two of the Meals Division's products are currently subject to investigation by the Food Standards Authority of a European country. Please see Appendix 1 under the heading "Food labelling" for more information on this.

Century. F plc's competitors cannot copy this gravy because the ingredients have to be combined in a very precise manner and then cooked in a particular way. The recipe for this gravy is known only to F plc's Director of Operations and the manager of the pie factory.

Snacks Division

The Snacks Division, located in the East of England, mainly manufactures confectionery such as packet savouries and chocolate bars. Its main customers are supermarkets and retail shops. It has a growing market in continental Europe and in 2010 the division earned 19% of its revenue from non-United Kingdom sales. Many of its products are F plc's own brands, although, similarly with the Meals Division, it supplies products to supermarkets under their own label.

The Snacks Division successfully launched a new premium brand of chocolate bars in the UK in 2010.

Desserts Division

The Desserts Division is located in the North of England where road, rail and air links are not well developed. This has resulted in high transportation costs for goods into and out of the factory. Originally, this location was chosen because the lease terms for the factory were very competitive but in recent times the local taxes placed on the factory have become expensive. There is some limited room for expansion on the site the factory occupies but the local government authority has repeatedly rejected the expansion plans when the Division has sought the necessary planning permission to put its plans into action. This has caused the Divisional Board to consider whether it should move its entire operation to another part of England where its expansion plans may be more easily accomplished.

The Division has experienced technical and managerial staff shortages. The workforce of the Division has an establishment of 4,700 full-time equivalent employees. Despite there being a ready supply of manual labour for production work, the Desserts division runs with an average of 385 full-time vacancies at any one time.

The Division's products range from cold desserts, particularly ice cream, which can be eaten directly from the packaging, to those which require some preparation by the final purchaser before the product can be consumed. The Divisional Marketing Department has been investigating the possibility of negotiating 'Freezer deals' by which the Desserts Division would supply ice cream freezers to independent retailers which sell the Division's ice cream products. An independent retailer is a shop or outlet that is not part of a larger chain. This is in order to investigate the possibility of increasing the Division's share of the ice cream market sold by independent retailers.

The Division's sales increase in the periods which lead up to national and international festive periods such as Christmas and Chinese New Year. The Division is constantly researching new markets in an effort to increase its foreign earnings. Revenue from outside the United Kingdom in 2010 represented 23% of the Division's total revenue.

Inventory control and IT systems

There have been a number of problems across all three divisions in respect of inventory control. Poor inventory control has led to high levels of wastage and obsolete inventory being carried. This has been particularly problematic in respect of perishable ingredients. In the case of the Desserts Division, the Divisional Accountant has estimated that 5% of the Division's potential revenue has been lost as a result of not being able to satisfy customer orders on time, due to poor inventory control.

F plc operates a standard information management system across all the Divisions and at Head Office. The Information Technology in use has been unreliable due to technical malfunctions since the information management system was installed in 2001. Monthly management accounts, provided by each division to head office are often late, sometimes not being made available for up to three weeks into the subsequent month.

Internal audit

Until now, F plc's Internal Audit function, which is based at Head Office, has tended to concentrate its efforts on reviewing activities in the Meals and Snacks divisions as they each produce lower revenues and net operating profits in absolute terms compared with the Desserts division. The Internal Audit function's approach of applying a "light touch" to the Desserts Division is also in recognition of the influence exerted by the Divisional Finance function over the Division's operational activities.

Strategic development

The Board of Directors is now midway through its strategic planning cycle and is considering how the company should move forward. There is a proposal to build and operate a factory in West Africa to reduce air kilometres being flown in supplying the Meals Division with fresh vegetables. It is intended that the African factory will freeze the vegetables and then transport them to the Meals Division's factory in England by refrigerated ship.

APPENDIX 1

Extracts from F plc's internal Corporate Social Responsibility report for the year ended 31 December 2010.

This report was produced by the Environmental Effects Manager and presented to the Board of F plc in February 2011.

Fair trading

In accordance with its mission statement, F plc is committed to paying a fair price for the ingredients it uses in its products, particularly to farmers in the less developed economies of the world.

Waste reduction and recycling

F plc set a target for the financial year 2010 that waste of ingredients should be cut by 2%, measured by weight, from the 2009 levels. The actual ingredient waste was 2.5% lower in 2010 than in 2009 as measured by weight.

A target was also set for F plc to recycle 90% of its used packaging in the year 2010. It was recorded that 85% of packaging in 2010 was actually recycled.

Food labelling

Legal requirements demand accuracy in food labelling, in respect of ingredients, product description and cooking instructions in many countries. F plc employs a Compliance Manager to ensure that relevant labelling laws in each country, with which the company trades, are adhered to. A target is set for F plc to justify 100% of its claims in food labelling. Two products manufactured in the Meals Division are currently undergoing investigations by the Food Standards Authority of a European country following allegations that the labelling is inaccurate.

(Update: Eight elderly people were admitted to hospital in February 2011 with suspected food poisoning after eating one of the packaged meal products which is under investigation by the Food Standards Authority.)

Transportation

Following adverse press coverage relating to the high number of kilometres travelled when importing and exporting goods from and to overseas countries, F plc introduced a target that its use of air travel should be reduced by 10% in 2010 compared with the amount used in 2009. F plc fell short of its target by only reducing air kilometres travelled by 3% in 2010 compared with 2009. Road kilometres travelled increased by 5% in 2010 compared with 2009.

Efficiency of energy usage in production

In an effort to reduce carbon emissions from the three divisions and head office, a target was set that by 2015, F plc will become carbon neutral in terms of its usage of energy. Energy usage in 2010 was at the same level as 2009. It has been proposed that energy efficient lighting should replace the current energy inefficient lighting at all three factories and at head office in 2011 and smart meters should be installed in all of F plc's premises to keep the waste of electricity to a minimum.

APPENDIX 2

Extracts from F plc's income statement and statement of financial position

Income statement for the year ended 31 December 2010

	£ million (GBP million)
Revenue	986
Operating costs	(938)
Net operating profit	48
Interest income	1
Finance costs	(16)
Corporate income tax	(10)
PROFIT FOR THE YEAR	23

Statement of financial position as at 31 December 2010

	Notes	£ million (GBP million)
ASSETS		
Non-current assets		465
Current assets		
Inventories		90
Trade and other receivables		112
Cash and cash equivalents		20
Total current assets		222
Total assets		687
EQUITY AND LIABILITIES		
Equity		
Share capital	1	140
Share premium		40
Retained earnings		61
Total equity		241
Non-current liabilities		
Long term borrowings	2	234
Current liabilities		
Trade and other payables		212
Total liabilities		446
Total equity and liabilities		687

Notes:

1   There are 560 million ordinary shares of £0.25 each in issue.

2   The long term borrowings comprise £160 million loan for capital expenditure which is repayable on 1 January 2018 and a £74 million revolving credit facility which expires on 31 December 2013.

APPENDIX 3

Five year forecast of sales revenue and net operating profit for each division and F plc in total and operating costs for head office

All figures are shown in £ million (GBP million)

	2010 (Actual)	2011	2012	2013	2014	2015
Meals Division						
Sales revenue	266	287	310	335	362	391
Net operating profit	31	34	40	47	54	63
Snacks Division						
Sales revenue	176	194	213	234	258	283
Net operating profit	44	48	53	58	64	71
Desserts Division						
Sales revenue	544	571	600	630	661	694
Net operating profit	72	80	90	101	112	125
Head office						
Operating costs	(99)	(107)	(112)	(118)	(124)	(130)
F plc total						
Sales revenue	986	1,052	1,123	1,199	1,281	1,368
Net operating profit	48	55	71	88	106	129

Unseen case material

Background

Today's date is 26 May 2011.

In 2010, the Snacks Division successfully launched a new premium brand of chocolate bars, MATT SNACKS, in the UK. The Divisional Board of the Snacks Division is now considering plans put forward by the Divisional Marketing Manager to launch the full range of MATT SNACKS in France, priced in euro (EUR). The launch is planned for 1 January 2012.

It is well known within the industry that it can be very difficult for a foreign company to break into the French market for chocolate snacks because there is significant loyalty towards local French brands and imported Swiss and Belgian brands. Initial market research based on free tasting sessions has met with an encouraging response but there is still some uncertainty over the success of the launch. However, the greatest danger to the success of MATT SNACKS in France is considered to be the risk that a UK competitor might launch a similar range of products in the same market.

Financial data for the project

To date, British Pounds (GBP) 0.5 million has been spent on initial market research for the products in the French market.

If the project is approved, an additional GBP 2.0 million will be required for detailed market research and packaging design. The cost of the launch itself includes an expensive radio and television advertising campaign in France and is expected to be of the order of GBP 1.0 million. Both of these costs are tax deductible. In addition, EUR 8.4 million will be spent on a distribution centre in France. All of these one-off costs are payable on 1 January 2012.

Estimates of net operating cash flows for the project vary considerably according to assumptions made regarding consumer and competitor reaction to the launch of MATT SNACKS in France. Forecast cash flow figures for the sales revenue and associated costs for the project for the year ending 31 December 2012 have been estimated based on two possible outcomes, known as Scenario A and Scenario B. The forecasts are:

Forecast operating cash flow figures for the year ending 31 December 2012

Scenario A:	Sales revenue	EUR 10.0 million
	Costs	EUR 1.0 million plus GBP 2.0 million
Scenario B:	Sales revenue	EUR 5.5 million
	Costs	EUR 1.0 million plus GBP 1.5 million

All operating cash flows shown above are expected to grow by 5% per annum in subsequent years for the duration of the project.

It can be assumed that if Scenario A occurs in 2012, it will also occur in all subsequent years. The same is true for Scenario B. It is estimated that there is a 70% probability of occurrence of Scenario A and a 30% probability of Scenario B.

Other relevant financial information:

- The Snacks Division evaluates projects of this nature at a risk-adjusted after-tax discount rate of 15% over a 4 year period.

- The proposed new distribution centre to be built in France is expected to have a residual value of EUR 5.2 million after 4 years.

- Corporate income tax is charged at 35% on taxable profits and is paid at the end of the year in which the taxable profit arises. Tax depreciation allowances are available on all capital expenditure associated with the project at a rate of 100%. Balancing charges will arise on any residual value. There are sufficient profits elsewhere in the group to be able to take advantage of these tax benefits or any taxable losses that occur.

- Operating cash flows should be assumed to arise at the end of the year to which they relate.

- The exchange rate is expected to be GBP/EUR 1.2000 (GBP 1 = EUR 1.2000) on 1 January 2012 and British Pounds are expected to strengthen against the euro by 2% a year in each of the next 4 years.

- The project could be abandoned on 1 January 2013 and the distribution centre sold for an estimated EUR 7.0 million. If the project were abandoned on 1 January 2013, no further cash inflows or outflows would arise from then onwards and there would be no penalties for pulling out of the market.

Required:

Assume that you are the Management Accountant of the Snacks Division and have been asked to write a Report addressed to the Divisional Board of the Snacks Division of F plc that will assist it in deciding whether or not to proceed with the proposed product launch. In your report you are required to:

(a) Ignoring the abandonment option:

(i) Calculate the NPV for the project as at 1 January 2012 for Scenarios A and B individually as well as the overall total expected NPV. **(13 marks)**

(ii) Calculate the payback period for the project for each of Scenarios A and B. **(4 marks)**

(iii) Interpret your results from (a)(i) and (a)(ii). **(6 marks)**

(b) Evaluate whether or not the project should be abandoned on 1 January 2013 if Scenario B occurs. **(8 marks)**

(c) Advise how real options and other strategic financial issues might influence the initial investment decision. **(12 marks)**

(d) Recommend, with reasons, whether or not to proceed with the proposed product launch on 1 January 2012. **(4 marks)**

Additional marks available for structure and presentation: **(3 marks)**

(Total = 50 marks)

97 F plc (2) (9/11)   90 mins

Refer to Q96 for pre-seen material

Unseen case material

Assume today is 1 October 2011.

Background

F plc made a small profit in the year ended 31 December 2010 of GBP 23 million. In the years prior to that, however, F plc had struggled to make positive returns as a result of a downturn in the general economic environment and also a lack of investment by the company. The directors now believe that the general economic environment has improved sufficiently for them to begin implementing a number of large projects to increase profitability and growth. Each of the three divisions is planning a major launch of new product ranges in the next two or three years.

There was no increase in dividends between 2009 and 2010 but the directors plan to increase the annual dividend by 8% a year starting in 2011 to reflect increased confidence in future performance. It is felt that this will also enhance the share price which has lost value over the last few years. This proposed new dividend policy has already been publicised in the market.

The expansion plans have been supported by the market. Although F plc's share price had lost a considerable proportion of its value over recent years during a tough trading period, there was a marked increase in the share price in the two days before the announcement of the major expansion plans. The share price has now stabilised at about 60 pence per share.

F plc operates within the United Kingdom but also exports to various countries within the eurozone (countries in Europe with the euro as their currency) and therefore receives a significant proportion of its revenue in euro.

Directors' concerns

The directors have expressed concern about the risk of movements in the value of the euro (EUR) against British pounds (GBP) affecting their ability to meet the financial and strategic plans of the company.

In particular, the directors are concerned about the impact that a weakening of the euro would have on F plc's performance, share price and ability to support a growing dividend.

The current GBP/EUR spot rate is 1.3000 (GBP 1 = EUR 1.3000), but is considered to be likely to change over the next few years, with the euro weakening against the British pound.

There has also been some discussion on whether the current funding provisions are adequate to support the planned expansion. The directors note that as at 31 December 2010, the company had already drawn down GBP 74 million under the revolving credit facility (RCF) of the maximum allowed of GBP 80 million and that the RCF will need to be replaced or negotiated before it expires on 31 December 2013.

The Finance Director has been asked to prepare a report for his fellow directors which would include a three year cash flow forecast based on each of two different exchange rate assumptions.

Financial data for F plc

The current borrowing facilities are described in the pre-seen material on page 4 and the latest financial statements for F plc are included in the pre-seen material on page 8.

The five year forecast of sales revenue and net operating profit shown on page 9 of the pre-seen material is now out of date and a revised cash flow forecast is required that takes account of possible exchange rate movements and other new information.

The Management Accountant has made a start on a revised cash flow forecast for a three year period by compiling a forecast of operating cash flows including cash flows arising from new projects. This is provided below.

Operating cash flows	2011	2012	2013
EUR cash inflows	EUR 280m	EUR 370m	EUR 440m
Net GBP cash outflows	GBP (148m)	GBP (218m)	GBP (241m)

Additional relevant information:

• The above cash forecast does not yet include the up-front investments which have been estimated to be GBP 30 million in 2012 and GBP 20 million in 2013 after taking account of the tax relief available on tax depreciation allowances.

• F plc pays interest of 7% on all borrowings and receives interest at 3% on cash and cash equivalents, calculated on opening balances.

• F plc has a policy of maintaining a cash and cash equivalents balance of GBP 20 million as a buffer and therefore the net cash inflow or outflow each year should be adjusted through borrowings.

• For the purposes of the cash flow forecast, it should be assumed that, if necessary, additional borrowings can be obtained at an interest rate of 7%.

• Dividends paid in the year ended 31 December 2010 amounted to GBP 16 million. Assume that dividends paid increase by 8% a year in subsequent years.

• Corporate income tax is charged at 35% on taxable profits and is paid at the end of the year in which the taxable profit arises.

• All cash flows should be assumed to arise at the end of the year.

• It should be assumed that EUR cash inflows are converted into GBP on receipt.

Required

Assume you are the Finance Director of F plc and have been asked to write a report for presentation at the next Board meeting. In the report you should:

(a) Prepare cash flow forecasts in GBP for the three year period 1 January 2011 to 31 December 2013, under each of the following exchange rate assumptions:

(i) A constant exchange rate of GBP/EUR 1.3000.

(ii) A weakening of the euro against British pounds of 6% a year from a base position of GBP/EUR 1.3000 at the end of 2010. **(16 marks)**

(b) Using your results in part (a) above and considering the three year period from 1 January 2011 to 31 December 2013:

(i) Evaluate the possible impact of exchange rate movements on F plc's:

• Annual and cumulative cash flow.
• Share price. **(9 marks)**

(ii) Advise whether the proposed dividend policy is likely to be sustainable AND what alternative dividend policies should be considered. **(7 marks)**

(iii) Advise on the additional financing requirements of F plc, including appropriate sources of finance. **(8 marks)**

(c) Advise on the overall impact of possible exchange rate movements and liquidity constraints on the financial and strategic decisions of F plc, including the planned product launches. **(6 marks)**

Additional marks available for structure and presentation: **(4 marks)**

(Total = 50 marks)

98   M plc (1) (11/11)   90 mins

Pre-seen case study

The following pre-seen material is applicable to both Q98 and Q99.

Introduction

M plc is a long established publisher of newspapers and provider of web media. It is based in London and has had a full listing on the London Stock Exchange since 1983. The company has three operating divisions which are managed from the United Kingdom (UK). These are the Newspapers Division, the Web Division and the Advertising Division.

Newspapers Division

The Newspapers Division publishes three daily newspapers and one Sunday newspaper in the UK. The Division has three offices and two printing sites. Between them the three offices edit the three daily newspapers and the Sunday newspaper. The Newspaper Division has two subsidiary publishing companies, FR and N. FR is based in France within the Eurozone and N in an Eastern European country which is outside the Eurozone. Printing for all the Division's publications, except those produced by FR and N, is undertaken at the two printing sites. FR and N have their own printing sites.

Web Division

The Web Division maintains and develops 200 websites which it owns. Some of these websites are much more popular in terms of the number of "hits" they receive than others. Web material is an increasing part of M plc's business. In the last ten years, the Web Division has developed an online version of all the newspapers produced by the Newspapers Division.

Advertising Division

The sale of advertising space is undertaken for the whole of M plc by the Advertising Division. Therefore, advertisements which appear in the print media and on the web pages produced by the Newspapers Division (including that produced by FR and N) and the Web Division respectively are all handled by the Advertising Division.

Group Headquarters

In addition to the three operating divisions, M plc also has a head office, based in the UK, which is the group's corporate headquarters where the Board of Directors is located. The main role of M plc's headquarters is to develop and administer its policies and procedures as well as to deal with its group corporate affairs.

Mission statement

M plc established a simple mission statement in 2005. This drove the initiative to acquire FR in 2008 and remains a driving force for the company. M plc's mission is "to be the best news media organisation in Europe, providing quality reporting and information on European and world-wide events".

Strategic objectives

Four main strategic objectives were established in 2005 by M plc's Board of Directors. These are to:

1   Meet the needs of readers for reliable and well informed news.

2   Expand the geographical spread of M plc's output to reach as many potential newspaper and website readers as possible.

3   Publish some newspapers which help meet the needs of native English speakers who live in countries which do not have English as their first language.

4   Increase advertising income so that the group moves towards offering as many news titles as possible free of charge to the public.

Financial objectives

In meeting these strategic objectives, M plc has developed the following financial objectives:

(i)   To ensure that revenue and operating profit grow by an average of 4% per year.

(ii) To achieve steady growth in dividend per share.

(iii) To maintain gearing below 40%, where gearing is calculated as debt/(debt plus equity) based on the market value of equity and the book value of debt.

Forecast revenue and operating profit

M plc's forecast revenue and net operating profit for the year ending 31 March 2012 are £280 million and £73 million respectively.

Extracts from M plc's forecast income statement for the year ending 31 March 2012 and forecast statement of financial position as at 31 March 2012 are shown in the appendix.

Comparative divisional performance and headquarters financial information

The following information is provided showing the revenue generated, the operating profit achieved and the capital employed for each division and the operating costs incurred and capital employed in M plc's headquarters. This information covers the last two years and also gives a forecast for the year ending 31 March 2012. All M plc's revenue is earned by the three divisions.

Newspapers Division	*Year ended 31.3.2010 £million*	*Year ended 31.3.2011 £million*	*Forecast for year ending 31.3.2012 £million*
Revenue external	91	94	94
Revenue internal transfers	90	91	96
Net operating profit	45	46	48
Non-current assets	420	490	548
Net current assets	4	8	(10)

Web Division	*Year ended 31.3.2010 £million*	*Year ended 31.3.2011 £million*	*Forecast for year ending 31.3.2012 £million*
Revenue internal transfers	55	60	66
Net operating profit	10	13	16
Non-current assets	37	40	43
Net current assets	1	1	(2)

Advertising Division	*Year ended 31.3.2010 £million*	*Year ended 31.3.2011 £million*	*Forecast for year ending 31.3.2012 £million*
Revenue external	162	180	186
Internal transfers	(145)	(151)	(162)
Net operating profit	10	18	19
Non-current assets	3	6	7
Net current assets	1	1	(2)

Headquarters	*Year ended 31.3.2010 £million*	*Year ended 31.3.2011 £million*	*Forecast for year ending 31.3.2012 £million*
Operating costs	8	9	10
Non-current assets	37	39	43
Net current assets	1	1	(1)

Notes:

1   The Advertising Division remits advertising revenue to both the Newspapers and Web Divisions after deducting its own commission.

2   The Web Division's entire revenue is generated from advertising.

3   The revenues and operating profits shown for the Newspapers Division include those earned by FR and N. The converted revenue and operating profit from N are forecast to be £20 million and £4 million respectively for the year ending 31 March 2012. FR is forecast to make a small operating profit in the year ending 31 March 2012. The Board of M plc is disappointed with the profit FR has achieved.

Additional information on each of M plc's divisions

Newspapers Division

FR is wholly owned and was acquired in 2008. Its financial statements are translated into British pounds and consolidated into M plc's group accounts and included within the Newspaper Division's results for internal reporting purposes.

Shortly after it was acquired by M plc, FR launched a pan-European weekly newspaper. This newspaper, which is written in English, is produced in France and then distributed throughout Europe. M plc's board thought that this newspaper would become very popular because it provides a snapshot of the week's news, focused particularly on European issues but viewed from a British perspective. Sales have, however, been disappointing.

N, which publishes local newspapers in its home Eastern European country, is also treated as part of the Newspapers Division. M plc acquired 80% of its equity in 2010. At that time, M plc's board thought that Eastern Europe was a growing market for newspapers. The subsidiary has proved to be profitable mainly because local production costs are lower than those in the UK relative to the selling prices.

The Newspapers Division's journalists incur a high level of expenses in order to carry out their duties. The overall level of expenses claimed by the journalists has been ignored by M plc in previous years because it has been viewed as a necessary cost of running the business. However, these expenses have risen significantly in recent years and have attracted the attention of M plc's internal audit department.

There has been significant capital investment in the Newspapers Division since 2009/10. The printing press facilities at each of the two printing sites have been modernised. These modernisations have improved the quality of output and have enabled improved levels of efficiency to be achieved in order to meet the increasing workloads demanded in the last two years. Surveys carried out before and after the modernisation have indicated higher levels of customer satisfaction with the improved quality of printing.

The increased mechanisation and efficiency has reduced costs and led to a reduction in the number of employees required to operate the printing presses. This has led to some dis-satisfaction among the divisional staff. Staff in the other divisions have been unaffected by the discontent in the Newspapers Division. Staff turnover has been relatively static across the three divisions, with the exception of the department which operates the printing presses in the Newspapers Division where some redundancies have occurred due to fewer staff being required since the modernisation.

Web Division

The web versions of the newspapers are shorter versions of the printed ones. There is currently no charge for access to the web versions of the newspapers. Revenues are generated from sales by the Advertising Division of advertising space on the web pages. Some of the websites permit unsolicited comments from the public to be posted on them and they have proved to be very popular. The Web Division is undertaking a review of all its costs, particularly those relating to energy, employees and website development.

The Web Division's management accounting is not sophisticated: for example, although it reports monthly on the Division's revenue and profitability, it cannot disaggregate costs so as to produce monthly results for each of the 200 websites. The Division is at a similar disadvantage as regards strategic management accounting as it lacks information about the websites' market share and growth rates. This has not mattered in the past as M plc was content that the Web Division has always been profitable. However, one of M plc's directors, the Business Development Director (see below under The Board of Directors and group shareholding) thinks that the Web Division could increase its profitability considerably and wants to undertake a review of its 200 websites.

Advertising Division

The Advertising Division remits advertising revenue to both the Newspapers and Web Divisions after deducting its own commission. In addition, the Advertising Division offers an advertising service to corporate clients. Such services include television and radio advertising and poster campaigns on bill boards. Advertisements are also placed in newspapers and magazines which are not produced by M plc, if the client so wishes. An increasing element of the work undertaken by the Advertising Division is in providing pop-up advertisements on websites.

Planning process

Each division carries out its own planning process. The Newspapers Division operates a rational model and prepares annual plans which it presents to M plc's board for approval. The Web Division takes advantage of opportunities as they arise and is operating in a growth market, unlike the other two divisions. Its planning approach might best be described as one of logical incrementalism. Increased capital expenditure in 2010/11 helped the Advertising Division to achieve an 11% increase in revenue in that year. The Divisional Managers of both the Web Division and the Advertising Division are keen to develop their businesses and are considering growth options including converting their businesses into outsource service providers to M plc.

The Board of Directors and group shareholding

M plc's Board of Directors comprises six executive directors and six non-executive directors, one of whom is the Non-executive Chairman. The executive directors are the Chief Executive, and the Directors of Strategy, Corporate Affairs, Finance, Human Resources and Business Development. The Business Development Director did not work for M plc in 2005 and so had no part in drafting the strategic objectives. She thinks that objective number four has become out- dated as it does not reflect current day practice. The Business Development Director has a great deal of experience working with subscription-based websites and this was one of the main reasons M plc recruited her in March 2011. Her previous experience also incorporated the management of product portfolios including product development and portfolio rationalisation.

There are divisional managing directors for each of the three divisions who are not board members but report directly to the Chief Executive.

One of M plc's non-executive directors was appointed at the insistence of the bank which holds 10% of M plc's shares. Another was appointed by a private charity which owns a further 10% of the shares in M plc. The charity represents the interests of print workers and provides long-term care to retired print workers and their dependents. Two other non-executive directors were appointed by a financial institution which owns 20% of the shares in M plc. The remaining 60% of shares are held by private investors. The board members between them hold 5% of the shares in issue. None of the other private investors holds more than 70,000 of the total 140 million shares in issue.

It has become clear that there is some tension between the board members. Four of the non- executive directors, those appointed by the bank, the charity and the financial institution, have had disagreements with the other board members. They are dissatisfied with the rate of growth and profitability of the company and wish to see more positive action to secure M plc's financial objectives.

Some board members feel that the newspapers market is declining because fewer people can make time to read printed publications. Some of the non-executive directors think that many people are more likely to watch a television news channel than read a newspaper.

Editorial policy

M plc's board applies a policy of editorial freedom provided that the published material is within the law and is accurate. The editors of each of the publications printed in the UK and France and of the websites have complete autonomy over what is published. They are also responsible for adhering to regulatory constraints and voluntary industry codes of practice relating to articles and photographs which might be considered offensive by some readers.

There is less scrutiny of the accuracy of the reporting in N's home country than in other countries. The Eastern European country in which N is situated has become politically unstable in the last two years. Much of this unrest is fuelled by the public distaste for the perceived blatant corruption and bribery which is endemic within the country's Government and business community. It is well known that journalists have accepted bribes to present only the Government's version of events, rather than a balanced view. There is

also widespread plagiarism of published material by the country's newspapers and copyright laws are simply ignored.

Corporate Social Responsibility

A policy is in place throughout M plc in order to eliminate bribery and corruption among staff especially those who have front line responsibility for obtaining business. This policy was established 15 years ago. All new employees are made aware of the policy and other staff policies and procedures during their induction. The Director of Human Resources has confidence in the procedures applied by his staff at induction and is proud that no action has ever been brought against an employee of M plc for breach of the bribery and corruption policy.

M plc is trying to reduce its carbon footprint and is in the process of developing policies to limit its energy consumption, reduce the mileage travelled by its staff and source environmentally friendly supplies of paper for its printing presses. The Newspapers Division purchases the paper it uses for printing newspapers from a supplier in a Scandinavian country. This paper is purchased because it provides a satisfactory level of quality at a relatively cheap price. The Scandinavian country from which the paper is sourced is not the same country in which N is situated.

Strategic Development

The Board of Directors is now reviewing M plc's competitive position. The Board of Directors is under pressure from the non-executive directors appointed by the bank, the charity and the financial institution (which between them own 40% of the shares in M plc), to devise a strategic plan before June 2012 which is aimed at achieving M plc's stated financial objectives.

APPENDIX 1

Extracts from M plc's forecast group income statement and forecast statement of financial position

Forecast income statement for the group for the year ending 31 March 2012

	Notes	£ million (GBP million)
Revenue		280
Operating costs		(207)
Net operating profit		73
Interest income		1
Finance costs		(11)
Corporate income tax	1	(19)
FORECAST PROFIT FOR THE YEAR		44

Forecast statement of the group financial position as at 31 March 2012

	Notes	£ million (GBP million)
ASSETS		
Non-current assets		641
Current assets		
Inventories		2
Trade and other receivables		27
Cash and cash equivalents		2
Total current assets		31
Total assets		672
EQUITY AND LIABILITIES		
Equity		
Share capital	2	140
Share premium		35
Retained earnings		185
Non-controlling interest		16
Total equity		376
Non-current liabilities		
Long term borrowings	3	250
Current liabilities		
Trade and other payables		46
Total liabilities		296
Total equity and liabilities		672

Notes:

1   The corporate income tax rate can be assumed to be 30%.

2   There are 140 million £1 shares currently in issue.

3   The long-term borrowings include £83 million of loan capital which is due for repayment on 1 April 2013 and the remainder is due for repayment on 1 April 2019.

End of Pre-seen Material

Unseen case material

Background

Assume today is 1 December 2011.

The results from M plc's French subsidiary, FR, have been disappointing.

FR was originally acquired at the beginning of 2008 in order to provide M plc with printing capacity in Europe from which to launch a new English language pan European newspaper. FR already printed regional French newspapers but had spare printing capacity that M plc was able to use. After acquisition, FR continued to produce the regional French newspapers and launched the pan European newspaper in the middle of 2008. However, since M plc took over the business there has been a fall in circulation of the regional French newspapers and the pan European newspaper has not been as well received as had been expected.

The Board of M plc has decided that, whilst it believes that a pan European weekly newspaper in English is still a viable concept, it would like to sell FR as a going concern. The most serious interest in FR is from PP which is a large competitor in the newspaper business, based in France and listed on the French Stock Exchange. PP already prints and distributes a European edition of a US newspaper across Europe and so has proven experience in this market and an established distribution network. However, PP is already quite a dominant force in the newspaper industry in France and there is some concern that the proposed takeover of FR by PP might be referred to the competition authorities in France.

The proposed sale of FR would involve the settlement of its intra-group borrowings. The sale price would therefore consist of two parts:

1.	EUR 25 million to settle FR's intra-group debt.
2.	A second payment to acquire M plc's shares in FR.

FR has no external debt and the purchaser would therefore acquire the net assets of FR on a going concern basis with no debt attached.

The Board of M plc hopes to raise a significant amount of funds from the sale of FR, possibly as much as EUR 75 million (which includes the EUR 25 million required to settle FR's intra-group debt)

Discussion at a recent M plc board meeting regarding possible uses of the funds generated by the sale of FR

The following possible uses of the sale proceeds were identified at a recent board meeting:

*	Reinvesting the funds in a new project.
*	Repaying debt.
*	Rewarding shareholders with a one-off dividend payment.

Financial data for M plc

Extracts from the forecast financial statements for the M plc group for the year ending 31 March 2012 can be found on page 7 of the pre-seen material. The strategic and financial objectives for M plc are on pages 2 and 3 of the pre-seen material.

On 1 December 2011, M plc's share price is GBP 3.50 per share.

Financial data for FR

Book values of FR's assets and debt as at 30 November 2011:

	EUR million	
Non-current assets	50	with a market value of EUR 56 million
Net current assets	2	
Long term liabilities	(25)	which consist of intra-group debt only
	27	

FR's results for the 12 months to 30 November 2011:

	EUR million	
Operating profit	6.7	after charging depreciation of EUR 0.5 million
Finance charge	(1.4)	
Tax	(1.3)	
Earnings	4.0	

The management of FR has established that there needs to be an investment in working capital and non-current assets of EUR 1.8 million per annum in order to maintain the current level of operations. M plc forecasts that FR's free cash flow will grow by just 2% a year for the foreseeable future.

M plc considers that PP has a similar level of business risk to FR and approximately the same level of gearing as M plc and therefore plans to use PP as a proxy when valuing FR using a discounted cash flow (DCF) approach.

Financial data for PP

PP is funded as follows:

	Nominal value	Today's market value
Ordinary EUR 1 shares	EUR 50.0 million	EUR 5.80 per share
8% irredeemable EUR 1 preference shares	EUR 20.0 million	EUR 1.35 per share
6% Bond maturing in 3 years' time at par	EUR 120.0 million	EUR 103.0 per EUR 100.0

Other information:

- PP has a published equity beta of 1.5 and a P/E ratio of 13.

- M plc estimates that PP could achieve economies of scale of approximately EUR 0.7 million a year after tax by merging with FR. Note that this figure is not expected to grow from year to year but is expected to remain at EUR 0.7 million a year for the foreseeable future.

Financial data common to all three companies:

- For both the UK and France, assume a risk free interest rate of 3% and a market premium of 5%.

- Assume a debt beta of zero.

- Corporate income tax is charged at 30% on all taxable profits and is paid at the end of the year in which the taxable profit arises in both the UK and France.

- The spot rate on 1 December 2011 is EUR/GBP 0.8900 (that is, EUR 1 = GBP 0.8900) and is expected to remain unchanged for the foreseeable future.

Required:

Assume you are an adviser to M plc and have been asked to write a report in which you:

(a)   Evaluate the THREE possible uses of the funds generated by the sale of FR that were identified during the recent M plc board meeting.   **(10 marks)**

(Up to 5 marks are available for calculations.)

(b)   (i)   Calculate, as at 1 December 2011, a range of euro denominated values for FR, both with and without synergistic benefits arising from the acquisition. Your answer should include a discounted free cash flow valuation using PP's weighted average cost of capital (WACC).   **(18 marks)**

(ii)   Discuss the appropriateness of each of the valuation approaches used in your answer to part (b)(i).   **(8 marks)**

(iii)   Advise on an appropriate minimum and maximum cash price for the sale of FR.   **(5 marks)**

(c)   Evaluate the risks that arise from investigations by competition authorities into planned takeovers. Include reference to the proposed sale of FR.   **(6 marks)**

Additional marks available for structure and presentation: **(3 marks)**

(Total = 50 marks)

99   M plc (2) (3/12)   90 mins

Refer to Q98 for pre-seen material

Background

Today is 1 April 2012.

The Board of M plc is considering the acquisition of a company that specialises in producing pre-recorded news reports and programmes which are sold to television networks for them to broadcast. Television news has been identified as an area of growth in the media industry and has a different business cycle to that of M plc. That is, at times of increased demand for television news, newspaper sales tend to decline and vice versa.

Synergistic benefits might also arise from a move into television news since M plc's worldwide network of journalists could feed news items into both the newspapers and television news programmes.

The Board of M plc has identified GG as a possible takeover target. GG is a company based in the USA that specialises in producing news programmes and recorded video clips for sale to television networks that broadcast in the English language.

Planned bid offer for GG

Initial plans are for the bid offer to be in the form of a share exchange due to the scale of the takeover.

The Board of M plc believes that there is likely to be a negative response from the Board of GG to a bid offer but cannot yet assess how the shareholders of GG will react. No official announcement has been made to the market concerning the potential takeover. However, in recent weeks there has been significant movement in the share prices of both GG and M plc, which is considered to be largely due to the leaking of information on the proposed bid into the public domain. There has been a 10% increase in GG's share price and a 5% decrease in M plc's share price during this period.

Financial information for M plc and GG

The latest available version of M plc's financial statements as at 31 March 2012 can be found in the pre-seen on page 7. Strategic and financial can be found on pages 2 and 3 of the pre-seen.

Additional financial information as at 1 April 2012:

	M plc	GG
Corporate income tax rate	30%	30%
Published equity beta	1.8	2.5
Last year's earnings	GBP 44 million	USD 30 million
Shares in issue	140 million	40 million
	GBP 1 ordinary shares	USD 1 common stock (equivalent to ordinary shares)
Share price	GBP 3.77 per share	USD 7.50 per share
Forecast earnings growth in perpetuity	4% pa	8% pa
Risk free rate	1.1%	3.0%
Market premium	4.0%	4.0%

Additional relevant information:

- GG's free cash flow can be assumed to be approximately 60% of its annual earnings and arise at the end of a year. Free cash flow is defined as cash flow from operations after deducting interest, tax and ongoing capital expenditure.

- GG has approximately the same gearing ratio as M plc.

- It is believed that GG's lenders would accept the change of ownership of GG's business and would reassign GG's borrowings to M plc.

- The GBP/USD spot rate is currently 1.6300 (that is GBP 1 = USD 1.6300). GBP is expected to appreciate against USD by 2% a year in each of the next 3 years. It is not considered to be possible to predict currency movements beyond 3 years and so the spot exchange rate should be assumed to remain constant after 1 April 2015 for the purposes of any evaluation.

Required:

Assume you are the Financial Director of M plc and have been asked to prepare a briefing paper for the Board of M plc regarding the proposed takeover bid for GG in which you:

(a)   (i)   Calculate the current cost of equity for:

  •   M plc.
  •   GG.
  •   M plc adjusted for the business risk of GG.   **(3 marks)**

      (ii)   Explain the reasons for the differences in your three cost of equity results in part (a) (i) above.
                                                                                 (4 marks)

(b)   (i)   Calculate a range of values for GG as at 1 April 2012. Note that only one discounted cash flow
            calculation is required.   **(8 marks)**

      (ii)   Advise on:

  •   The validity of your results in (b)(i) above as the basis for an initial bid offer for GG.
  •   An appropriate initial offer value for GG and appropriate share exchange terms. **(10 marks)**

(c)   Advise whether M plc should proceed with the bid offer for GG. Your answer should take into account:

  •   The potential impact of the takeover on the attainment of M plc's financial objectives.
  •   Other relevant factors affecting the decision.

      (Up to 4 marks are available for calculations)   **(14 marks)**

(d)   Explain:

  •   The actions GG could take to fight the takeover bid.
  •   The actions M plc could take to help ensure a positive response to the bid offer. **(7 marks)**

Additional marks available for structure and presentation: **(4 marks)**

                                                                    (Total = 50 marks)

100 B Supermarkets (1) (5/12)   90 mins

Pre-seen case study

Introduction

B Supermarkets (B) was founded as a grocery retailer in a European country in 1963. Its sales consist mainly of food and household items including clothing. B now owns or franchises over 15,000 stores world-wide in 36 countries. The company has stores in Europe (in both eurozone and non-eurozone countries), Asia and North America. B's head office is located in a eurozone country. B has become one of the world's largest chains of stores.

B's Board thinks that there are opportunities to take advantage of the rapid economic growth of some Asian countries and the associated increases in demand for food and consumer goods.

Structure

The B Group is structured into a holding company, B, and three subsidiary companies which are located in each of the regions of the world in which it operates (Europe, Asia and North America). The subsidiary companies, referred to as "Regions" within B, are respectively B-Europe, B-Asia and B-North America.

Store operations, sales mix and staffing

B operates four types of store: supermarkets, hypermarkets, discount stores and convenience stores. For the purpose of this case study, the definition of each of these types of store is as follows:

A *supermarket* is a self-service store which sells a wide variety of food and household goods such as washing and cleaning materials, cooking utensils and other items which are easily carried by customers out of the store.

A *hypermarket* is a superstore or very large store which sells the same type of products as a supermarket but in addition it sells a wide range of other items such as consumer durable white goods, for example refrigerators, freezers, washing machines and furniture. Hypermarkets are often located on out-of-town sites.

A *discount store* is a retail store that sells a variety of goods such as electrical appliances and electronic equipment. Discount stores in general usually sell branded products and pursue a high-volume, low priced strategy and aim their marketing at customers who seek goods at prices which are usually less than can be found in a hypermarket.

A *convenience store* is a small shop or store in an urban area that sells goods which are purchased regularly by customers. These would typically include groceries, toiletries, alcoholic beverages, soft drinks and confectionery. They are convenient for shoppers as they are located in or near residential areas and are often open for long hours. Customers are willing to pay premium prices for the convenience of having the store close by.

B sells food products and clothing in its supermarkets and hypermarkets at a higher price than many of its competitors because the Board thinks that its customers are prepared to pay higher prices for better quality food products. B also sells good quality consumer durable products in its supermarkets and hypermarkets but it is forced to sell these at competitive prices as there is strong competition for the sale of such goods. B's discount stores sell good quality electrical products usually at lower prices than those charged in its supermarkets and hypermarkets, B only sells electronic equipment in its discount stores. Customers have a greater range from which to choose in the discount stores as compared with supermarkets and hypermarkets because the discount stores specialise in the goods which they sell. B's convenience stores do not have the availability of space to carry a wide range of products and they charge a higher price for the same brand and type of goods which it sells in its supermarkets.

Although B owns most of its stores, it has granted franchises for the operation of some stores which carry its name.

Nearly 0.5 million full-time equivalent staff are employed world-wide in the Group. B tries when possible to recruit local staff to fill job vacancies within its stores.

Value statement and mission

In recognition of the strong competitive and dynamic markets in which it operates, B's Board has established an overall value statement as follows: "We aim to satisfy our customers wherever we trade. We intend to employ different generic competitive strategies depending on the market segment in which our stores trade."

The Board has also produced the following mission statement:

"B practises sustainable investment within a healthy ethical and thoughtful culture and strives to achieve customer satisfaction by giving a courteous and efficient service, selling high quality goods at a reasonable price, sourcing goods from local suppliers where possible and causing the least damage possible to the natural environment. By this, we aim to satisfy the expectations of our shareholders by achieving consistent growth in our share price and also to enhance our reputation for being an environmentally responsible company."

Strategic objectives

The following objectives have been derived from the mission statement:

1   Build shareholder value through consistent growth in the company's share price.

2   Increase customer satisfaction ratings to 95% as measured by customer feedback surveys.

3   Increase commitment to local suppliers by working towards achieving 40% of our supplies from sources which are local to where B stores trade.

4   Reduce carbon emissions calculated by internationally agreed measures by at least 1% per year until B becomes totally carbon neutral.

5   Maximise returns to shareholders by employing different generic competitive strategies depending on the market segment in which B stores trade.

Financial objectives

The Board has set the following financial objectives:

1   Achieve consistent growth in earnings per share of 7% each year.

2   Maintain a dividend pay-out ratio of 50% each year.

3   Gearing levels as measured by long-term debt divided by long-term debt plus equity should not exceed 40% based on book value.

Governance

The main board comprises the Non-executive Chairman, the Chief Executive and nine Executive directors. These cover the functions of finance, human resources, corporate affairs (including legal and public relations), marketing, planning and procurement. There is also one executive director for each of the three regions, being the Regional Managing Directors of B-Europe, B-Asia and B-North America. There are also nine non-executive main board members in addition to the Chairman.

The main Board of Directors has separate committees responsible for audit, remuneration, appointments, corporate governance and risk assessment and control. The Risk Assessment and Control Committee's tasks were formerly included within the Audit Committee's role. It was agreed by the Board in 2009 that these tasks should be separated out in order not to overload the Audit Committee which has responsibilities to review the probity of the company. B's expansion has been very rapid in some countries. The expansion has been so rapid that B has not been able to carry out any internal audit activities in some of these countries to date. The regional boards do not have a committee structure.

Each of the Regional Managing Directors chairs his or her own Regional Board. All of the Regional Boards have their own directors for finance, human resources, corporate affairs, marketing, planning and procurement but their structure is different for the directors who have responsibility for the stores. In B-Asia, one regional director is responsible for the hypermarkets and supermarkets and another is responsible for discount stores and convenience stores. In B-North America, one regional director is responsible for the hypermarkets and supermarkets and another is responsible for discount stores (B does not have any convenience stores in North America). In B-Europe there is one regional director responsible for supermarkets and hypermarkets, one for discount stores and one for convenience stores. In all regions the regional directors have line accountability to their respective regional managing director and professional accountability to the relevant main board director. There are no non-executive directors on the regional boards. Appendix 1 shows the main board and regional board structures.

Treasury

Each of B's three regions has a regional treasury department managed by a regional treasurer who has direct accountability to the respective Regional Director of Finance and professional accountability to the Group Treasurer. The Group Treasurer manages the central corporate treasury department which is located in B's head

office. The Group Treasurer, who is not a main board member, reports to the Director of Finance on the main board.

Shareholding, year-end share prices and dividends paid for the last five years

B is listed on a major European stock exchange within the eurozone and it wholly owns its subsidiaries. There are five major shareholders of B, including employees taken as a group, which between them hold 25% of the 1,350 million total shares in issue. The major shareholders comprise two long term investment trusts which each owns 4%, a hedge fund owns 5%, employees own 5% and the founding family trust owns 7% of the shares. The remaining 75% of shares are owned by the general public.

The year-end share prices and the dividends paid for the last five years were as follows:

	200	2008	2009	2010	2011
	€	€	€	€	€
Share price at 31 December	47.38	25.45	28.68	29.44	31.37
Net Dividend per share	1.54	1.54	1.54	1.62	1.65

Planning and management control

B has a very structured planning process. Each regional board produces a five year strategic plan for its region relating to specific objectives set for it by the main board and submits this to the main board for approval. The main board then produces a consolidated strategic plan for the whole company. This is reviewed on a three yearly cycle and results in a revised and updated group five year plan being produced every three years.

B's management control system, which operates throughout its regions and at head office, is well known in the industry to be bureaucratic and authoritarian. Strict financial authority levels for development purposes are imposed from the main Board. There is tension between the main Board and the regional boards. The regional board members feel that they are not able to manage effectively despite being located much closer to their own regional markets than the members of the main Board. The main Board members, on the other hand, think that they need to exercise tight control because they are remote from the markets. This often stifles planning initiatives within each region. This tension is also felt lower down the organisation as the regional board members exercise strict financial and management control over operational managers in their regions in order to ensure that the main Board directives are carried out.

Competitive overview

B operates in highly competitive markets for all the products it sells. The characteristics of each of the markets in which it operates are different. For example, there are different planning restrictions applying within each region. In some countries, B is required to operate each of its stores in a partnership arrangement with local enterprises, whereas no such restriction exists within other countries in which it trades. B needs to be aware of different customer tastes and preferences which differ from country to country. The following table provides a break-down of B's stores in each region.

	B Europe	B Asia	B North America
Supermarkets and hypermarkets	3,456	619	512
Discount stores	5,168	380	780
Convenience stores	4,586	35	

B is one of the largest retailing companies in the world and faces different levels of competition in each region. B's overall market share in terms of retail sales for all supermarkets, hypermarkets, discount stores and convenience stores in each of its regions is as follows:

	Market share
Europe	20%
Asia	1%
North America	1.5%

The following table shows the sales revenue and net operating profit earned by B in each of its regions for the year ended 31 December 2011:

	B Europe € million	B Asia € million	B North America € million
Revenue	89,899	10,105	9,708
Net Operating Profit	4,795	743	673

B is constantly seeking other areas of the world into which it can expand, especially within Asia where it perceives many countries have an increasing population and strengthening economies.

Corporate Social Responsibility (CSR)

B is meeting its CSR obligations by establishing environmental targets for carbon emissions (greenhouse gas emissions), careful monitoring of its supply chain, undertaking sustainable investments and investing in its human capital.

Environmental targets for carbon emissions:

B's main board is keen to demonstrate the company's concern for the environment by pursuing continuous improvement in the reduction of its carbon emissions and by developing ways of increasing sustainability in its trading practices. A number of environmental indicators have been established to provide transparency in B's overall performance in respect of sustainability. These published measures were verified by B's statutory auditor and are calculated on a like-for-like basis for the stores in operation over the period measured.

In the year ended 31 December 2011, B reduced its consumption of kilowatt hours (kWh) per square metre of sales area as compared with the year ended 31 December 2008 by 9%. The target reduction for that period was 5%. In the same period it reduced the number of free disposable plastic bags provided to customers per square metre of sales area, by 51% against a target of 60%. Its overall greenhouse gas emissions (measured by kilogrammes of carbon dioxide per square metre of sales area) reduced by 1% in 2011 which was exactly on target.

B provides funding for the development of local amenity projects in all of the countries where B stores operate. (An amenity project is one which provides benefit to the local population, such as providing a park, community gardens or a swimming pool.)

Distribution and sourcing:

Distribution from suppliers across such a wide geographical area is an issue for B. While supplies are sourced from the country in which a store is located as much as possible, there is nevertheless still a requirement for transportation across long distances either by road or air. Approximately 20% of the physical quantity of goods sold across the group as a whole is sourced locally, that is within the country in which the goods are sold. These tend to be perishable items such as fruit and vegetables. The remaining 80% of goods are sourced from large international manufacturers and distributors. These tend to be large items such as electrical or electronic equipment which are bought under contracts which are set up by the regional procurement departments. B, due to its size and scope of operations, is able to place orders for goods made to its own specification and packaged as under its own brand label. Some contracts are agreed between manufacturers and the Group Procurement Director for the supply of goods to the whole of the B group world-wide.

B's inventory is rarely transported by rail except within Europe. This has resulted in lower average reductions in carbon emissions per square metre of sales area by stores operated by B-Asia and B-North America than for those stores operated by B-Europe. This is because the carbon emission statistics take into account the transportation of goods into B's stores.

Sustainable investments:

B aspires to become carbon neutral over the long term. The Board aims to reduce its carbon emissions by investing in state of the art technology in its new store developments and by carrying out modifications to existing stores.

Human Resources:

B prides itself on the training it provides to its staff. The training of store staff is carried out in store by specialist teams which operate in each country where B trades. In this way, B believes that training is consistent across all of its stores. In some countries, the training is considered to be at a sufficiently high level to be recognised by

national training bodies. The average number of training hours per employee in the year ended 31 December 2011 was 17 compared with 13 hours in the year ended 31 December 2010. In 2011, B employed 45% more staff with declared disabilities compared with 2010.

Information systems and inventory management

In order to operate efficiently, B's Board has recognised that it must have up-to-date information systems including electronic point of sale (EPOS) systems. An EPOS system uses computers or specialised terminals that can be combined with other hardware such as bar-code readers to accurately capture the sale and adjust the inventory levels within the store. EPOS systems installation is on-going. B has installed EPOS systems in its stores in some countries but not in all its stores world-wide.

B's information systems are not perfect as stock-outs do occur from time-to-time, especially in the European stores. This can be damaging to sales revenue when stock-outs occur during peak sales periods such as the days leading up to a public holiday. In Asia and North America in particular, B's information technology systems sometimes provide misleading information. This has led to doubts in the minds of some head office staff about just how robust are B's inventory control systems.

As is normal in chain store groups, there is a certain degree of loss through theft by staff and customers. Another way that loss is suffered is through goods which have gone past their "sell-by" date and mainly relates to perishable food items which are wasted as they cannot be sold to the public. In most countries, such food items which cannot be sold to the public may be sold to local farmers for animal feed.

Regulatory issues

B's subsidiaries in Asia and North America have sometimes experienced governmental regulatory difficulties in some countries which have hindered the installation of improved information systems. To overcome some of these regulatory restrictions, B-Asia and B-North America have, on occasions, resorted to paying inducements to government officials in order for the regulations to be relaxed.

APPENDIX 1

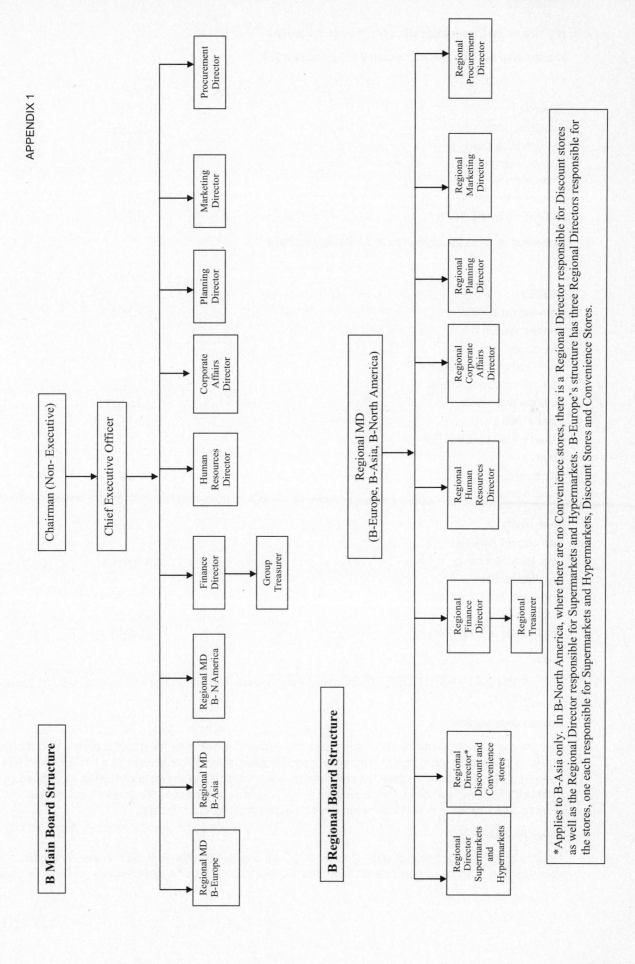

B Main Board Structure

Chairman (Non- Executive)

Chief Executive Officer

Regional MD B-Europe

Regional MD B-Asia

Regional MD B- N America

Finance Director

Group Treasurer

Human Resources Director

Corporate Affairs Director

Planning Director

Marketing Director

Procurement Director

B Regional Board Structure

Regional MD (B-Europe, B-Asia, B-North America)

Regional Director Supermarkets and Hypermarkets

Regional Director* Discount and Convenience stores

Regional Finance Director

Regional Treasurer

Regional Human Resources Director

Regional Corporate Affairs Director

Regional Planning Director

Regional Marketing Director

Regional Procurement Director

*Applies to B-Asia only. In B-North America, where there are no Convenience stores, there is a Regional Director responsible for Discount stores as well as the Regional Director responsible for Supermarkets and Hypermarkets. B-Europe's structure has three Regional Directors responsible for the stores, one each responsible for Supermarkets and Hypermarkets, Discount Stores and Convenience Stores.

BPP
LEARNING MEDIA

B's income statement and statement of financial position.

Income statement for the year ended 31 December 2011

	Notes	€ million
Revenue		109,712
Operating costs		(103,501)
Net operating profit		6,211
Interest income		165
Finance costs		(852)
Corporate income tax		(1,933)
PROFIT FOR THE YEAR		3,591

Statement of financial position as at 31 December 2011

		€ million
ASSETS		
Non-current assets		57,502
Current assets		
Inventories		7,670
Trade and other receivables		1,521
Cash and cash equivalents		3,847
Total current assets		13,038
Total assets		70,540
EQUITY AND LIABILITIES		
Equity		
Share capital	1	2,025
Share premium		3,040
Retained earnings		18,954
Total equity		24,019
Non-current liabilities		
Long term borrowings		15,744
Current liabilities		
Trade and other payables		30,777
Total liabilities		46,521
Total equity and liabilities		70,540

Notes:

1   There are 1,350 million €1.50 shares currently in issue. The share price at 31 December 2011 was €31.37.

Unseen case material

The directors of B are aware that B's results have been slow to recover after the global economic downturn of 2008. In the medium term, growth prospects for the European business continue to be poor. The group has publicised plans for continued growth and the directors are therefore looking for opportunities for expansion outside of Europe. In particular, they are exploring the possibility of expanding B's presence in the rapidly growing Asian market in order to counterbalance poor growth prospects in Europe.

Financial data for B

Extracts from the group financial statements for 2011 are provided on page 8 of the Pre-seen. Financial objectives can be found on page 3 and share price and dividend data for the last five years are listed on page 4.

Additional data is provided below:

Year	2007	2008	2009	2010	2011
Number of shares in issue throughout the year (million)	1,284	1,284	1,350	1,350	1,350
Earnings for the year (€ million)	3,945	2,818	3,097	3,366	3,591

Expansion strategy into Country A in Asia

One possibility being considered by the directors of B is to establish a presence in Country A, a country in Asia which uses the A$ as its currency. B has no existing operations in Country A.

In the past, small, family-owned local businesses dominated retail food sales in Country A, with consumers typically shopping on a daily basis. In recent years, however, shopping patterns have moved away from daily shopping and new supermarkets have been successfully opened across the country. These supermarkets operate in much the same way as supermarkets in other countries, selling a combination of both food and household items.

The directors of B have been considering the best strategy for starting to operate in Country A and have concluded that the lowest risk route would be to acquire a small chain of existing supermarkets. These supermarkets would then be rebranded. If the rebranding exercise proved to be successful and produced a profitable return for B within an experimental period of three years, B would consider either purchasing or building additional supermarkets or other types of store in Country A. The potential for growth is considered to be huge in such a large and rapidly developing market and there is a possibility that it could lead to an increase in B's Asian revenue stream to more than four times current levels.

To satisfy this strategy, a company called Alpha Supermarkets has been identified as a potential acquisition target. Alpha Supermarkets operates a small chain of supermarkets in Country A.

Financial data concerning the proposed acquisition and rebranding of Alpha Supermarkets

Alpha Supermarkets is owned and managed as a private family business and comprises 15 small supermarkets in a single region of Country A.

The directors of B are aware that an offer was made recently to the family shareholders of Alpha Supermarkets to buy the whole business for A$960 million. This offer was not accepted but is, nonetheless, considered to represent the fair value of the Alpha Supermarket business in its current form. The main shareholders of Alpha Supermarkets have indicated that they would be prepared to consider an offer from B at a 20% premium above this previous takeover offer price.

The directors of B realise that significant investment would be required to rebrand the Alpha supermarkets after acquisition, including renewing store fittings and changing the types of food and household goods sold.

The following table provides estimated incremental capital and operating cash flows for the first three years of operation for a typical Alpha supermarket following acquisition by B. Estimated financial results of the rebranding exercise for a single supermarket are:

Item	Incremental cash flows A$ million	Timing
Initial capital investment	35	Year 0
Additional operating revenue in year 1, increasing by 12% a year in years 2 and 3	30	
Additional operating costs in year 1, increasing by 8% a year in years 2 and 3	13	
Reinvestment of operating cash flows (OCF)	3	Year 1 and Year 2
Residual value of B's capital investments, including reinvested OCF	30	Year 3

Additional information:

- Country A has a 32% corporate income tax rate.

- Both the initial capital investment and subsequent reinvestment of funds in the business attract immediate 100% tax depreciation allowances. Balancing charges apply to the residual value.

- No additional tax or refunds of tax are due on funds remitted to B.

- The €/A$ spot rate at Year 0 can be assumed to be €/A$7.5000 (that is, €1 = A$ 7.5000).

- B considers that an A$ post-tax discount rate of 15% is an appropriate rate to use when evaluating an investment of this nature.

- All cash flows should be assumed to arise at the end of the year unless stated otherwise and tax should be assumed to be settled at the end of the year in which it arises. However, any tax refunds due will be carried forward and set off against the next tax liability in a future year.

Required:

(a) For each of the years 2007 to 2011 inclusive:

(i) Calculate, in respect of B:

- Earnings per share
- P/E ratio
- Dividend payout ratio **(8 marks)**

(ii) Evaluate B's financial performance. Your answer should include reference to the attainment of Financial objective 1.

Up to 3 marks are available for relevant additional calculations. **(9 marks)**

(iii) Explain the possible rationale behind B's dividend pay-out history. **(6 marks)**

(b) Assuming you are the Financial Director of B, write a briefing paper for the Board of B regarding the proposed acquisition of Alpha Supermarkets in which you:

(i) Calculate the expected financial benefit to B of the rebranding exercise on a discounted cash flows basis over a three year time period. **(10 marks)**

(ii) Evaluate the potential risks and opportunities arising from the proposed acquisition AND advise whether to proceed. **(14 marks)**

Additional marks available for structure and presentation: **(3 marks)**

(Total = 50 marks)

ANSWERS

1 HG

> **Text references.** Chapter 1 covers objectives of organisations and financial management decisions.
>
> **Top tips**. (a) requires detailed analysis of stakeholders but also a realisation that the primary objective must be maximisation of shareholder wealth. Hopefully you discussed the lack of a strategic plan. It is possible to use other frameworks in (b), such as grouping the decisions under what is acceptable, suitable and feasible; our answer focuses on the key decisions that have to be made. You must make sure that your discussion is applied to the specific circumstances of HG as far as possible.
>
> **Easy marks.** Splitting the requirements up into each sub-requirement should ensure that you address all areas of the question (see bold headings in the solution below).
>
> **Examiner's comments.** The main areas of weakness were providing vague and insubstantial discussion and not concluding with valid recommendations.

(a)   Evaluation of objectives

HG has two main objectives at present:

- To treat all stakeholders with fairness and equity
- To increase dividends each year

Fairness and equity

It is important for objectives to recognise that there will always be a number of **stakeholder groups** interested in a company's operations, including shareholders, loan creditors, directors and managers, other employees, customers, suppliers, government (including tax authorities), and the communities in which the company is based.

The primary stakeholders are the **shareholders,** who are the owners of the company. They appoint **directors as agents** to run the company on their behalf. In a private company like HG the directors will almost invariably also be shareholders. Thus private sector companies **must have a primary objective** that is related to the needs of shareholders.

Some of the stakeholder groups (eg loan creditors and the national and local tax authorities) have **clear legal rights** to payments by the company, and the concept of 'equity and fairness' will not really apply. For the most part these are stakeholders whose sole need is for the law to be satisfied, that is they expect to be paid on time, and any negotiations start from this premise.

For the other stakeholders, the concept of fairness and equity is a good general approach to adopt. Even those who assert that a company's **sole objective** should be to benefit shareholders will agree that this is best done by considering the needs of other stakeholder groups. For example:

(1)   **Customers** should **not be cheated** on the quality of goods (or they will buy elsewhere). This may explain HG's aversion to overseas investments which may bring the risk of a drop in quality.

(2)   **Suppliers** should **not be made to wait unduly** for payment (or they will increase their prices).

(3)   **Directors and key managers** should be given **fair rewards** for their successes (or they will lose motivation, divert benefits to themselves or leave the company); however they should not be allowed to take the same rewards if they are unsuccessful.

(4)   **Other employees** should **not only be paid fair market rates** but also encouraged to participate in company plans.

(5)   **The local community** should **not be subjected** to **unnecessary noise or pollution**, and can provide powerful good publicity for the company. It may be important to HG to maintain a strong profile as a **local** employer, which again may explain their reluctance to invest overseas.

However, the objectives of HG could be improved by **clearly identifying** the **key stakeholder groups** and by identifying a **measurable objective** for the most important of them. For example, if customers are important, the number of complaints would be a useful measure.

Increasing dividends each year

Although it correctly focuses on shareholders, the objective of increasing dividends each year is unsatisfactory as a primary objective for HG. This is because the pattern of dividends may need to be

varied to take advantage of **investment opportunities**. In some years it may be wise to restrict dividends in order to reinvest in the company for growth.

Maximisation of shareholder wealth

The limitations of the dividend objective are recognised by the finance director who suggests that 'maximisation of shareholder wealth' should be the **sole objective**. However, this will be **difficult to measure for an unlisted company** like HG which does not have a share price. A value could be calculated using techniques such as **shareholder value analysis**.

Other objectives

The other directors propose a range of financial and operational 'objectives'. Profit based measures (profits after tax and return on investment) are **not suitable** as the main objectives of the business. They are easy to **manipulate**, are **historic** and may encourage **excessive risk-taking**. These financial and operational measures are probably best described as **targets,** designed to help achieve the main objective of shareholder wealth creation. Thus a target return on investment is a way of trying to increase shareholder wealth. In setting these financial targets, however, it is vital to recognise the **relationship between risk and return** and to put boundaries on risks taken in pursuit of the targets.

Recommendations

HG's existing objectives are reasonable but are too vague and unquantified to be of any use. The company's main objective should be to **pay shareholders a minimum rate of return** consistent with the **risk** they are prepared to accept. The company should investigate attitudes to risk among its main shareholders.

The main objective should be presented in conjunction with statements that that the company will **fulfil its legal obligations** and will **treat other specific stakeholders with equity and fairness.**

The main objective should then be accompanied by a set of **financial and non-financial targets**, ie a balanced scorecard, based on the **strategic plan**.

HG needs to be careful that its attitude to overseas investment does not **conflict** with its commitment to its shareholders.

(b)   ## Financing or refinancing strategies

The treasury department should develop a **financing strategy** based on its ongoing business and investment plans, and the cash requirements forecasts that come out of these plans. There are a number of **general issues** that the financing strategy should consider:

(1)   Treasury should **evaluate the project plans** in conjunction with the **gearing ratio** and decide whether it is **worthwhile taking out more debt or redeeming it with surplus cash** instead of paying dividends. Some investments will provide **good security** for borrowing and may allow gearing to be increased without taking undue financial risk. Other investments are **less certain** in the development stage and are **better financed with equity.** The directors may also wish to consider **ownership** implications, the tax shield effects of debt, and the **interest commitment** made if debt is taken out.

(2)   Treasury should review the **mix** of short and long term debt, in order to manage financing risk at the minimum interest cost. In general **long term debt** will be **more secure** but **more expensive** because the lender does not have the option to withdraw it so soon. The policy should consider **financing assets out of funds** from the **same type of duration**. For example non-current assets and the permanent part of working capital can be financed from equity and longer term loans, whereas fluctuating working capital should be financed from overdraft or other short term funds.

The economic environment

In the context of HG's stated economic environment of low and falling rates of interest, HG should look to **increase its use of debt finance**. The use of **variable rate** borrowing would be beneficial as interest rates are forecast to fall.

The low inflation and low growth environment suggests that opportunities for growth may be limited. HG should therefore consider whether to **return more funds to shareholders**. This could be achieved through a **higher dividend** or a **share buyback**. Debt finance is **cheaper** than equity as it is of lower risk to investors and attracts tax relief. HG may be under-geared and could therefore increase its value to shareholders by increasing debt and using the funds to finance share buybacks.

Impact on the determination of corporate objectives

Financing strategies will be reflected in the company's overall strategic plan. It could be suggested that HG should increase its commitment to return funds to shareholders and to finance this by the increased use of debt finance.

2 CCC

Text references. Objectives are covered in Chapter 1 and financial strategies in Chapter 4.

Top tips. It is essential to plan a discussion question such as this and continually check you are applying your comments to the specific entities in the scenarios. You must make a comment for each stakeholder discussed about the consequences of failing to meet their needs.

Easy marks. There are easy marks available for sensible use of your general knowledge.

Examiner's comments. The main weaknesses were failing to address the scenario and writing at length on irrelevant issues.

(a)   Objective setting criteria

Stakeholders are groups that have an **interest in the activities of an organisation**. It is important for any organisation to understand the needs of its **key stakeholders** and to set objectives that meet their needs.

CCC

Central government provides the council with most of its funding which makes it a **very powerful stakeholder**.

Central government is likely to scrutinise the **value for money** being achieved by the council. Failure to achieve **economy** in the acquisition of goods and services, or **efficient** use of resources to **effectively** meet the needs of the community, may mean that the spending of poorly performing councils could be **capped**.

Another key stakeholder group is formed by the members of the local community: individuals, groups, businesses and other organisations that use the council's services. The council's job is to set a budget that **prioritises** competing claims for services between these customers, and then to deliver **effectively** the services for which it has budgeted.

The consequences for the council of failing to deliver adequate services is that the customers will start to **express dissatisfaction**, often by starting lobby groups and contacting the media (local newspapers, radio and television), and will get their chance to vote the councillors out of office at the next local election. Hence the importance of the key objective to **provide service excellence** – especially in health and education, to which the public are politically very sensitive.

The **employees** of local government will also be an important stakeholder group. They require **adequate compensation** for their work, usually lower than in equivalent private sector jobs. Their salary scales are usually outside of the control of the individual local authority and they may not be rewarded by **financial bonuses**, but are more likely to be **motivated** by teamwork, good working conditions and a sense of doing a good job. The consequences of failing to meet the objective of good working conditions is that good employees will leave, resulting in poorer service delivery and ultimate dissatisfaction from customers and taxpayers.

Conclusion

CCC local government exists to **provide services** for its community. Its outputs cannot usually be expressed in financial terms. Value for money objectives need to be **quantified** as far as possible to ensure the needs of its key stakeholder groups are being met.

DDD

Unlike governments, private sector businesses likes DDD produce goods and services with a monetary (sales) value which can be directly compared with the cost of production and delivery. Hence businesses have '**profit making**' as their primary objective, and this is ultimately measured by valuing the **wealth of their owners**, the shareholders. DDD's primary objective is to increase shareholder wealth by an average of 10%

per annum. If the directors fail to achieve satisfactory returns for shareholders, the share price will fall and the directors may be removed from office or the company will find itself subject to a **takeover bid** which will force a change in management.

The vast majority of shareholders of a large listed company have no executive power, having appointed **directors** to run the business on their behalf. Because these directors have enormous decision making powers, it is usually beneficial to **reward** them in ways that are related to furtherance of shareholders' objectives, such as share options or other forms of bonus schemes. The consequences of failing to reward directors in appropriate ways is that they can **pursue their own objectives** which may be more concerned with prestige than equity value.

Clearly the directors cannot create shareholder wealth by focusing solely on shareholders. They must match the company's products to **customers**. Hence **market intelligence** and **customer care** become major non-financial objectives for most companies. The consequences of failing to look after customers are that sales, profits and share price will fall rapidly.

The company must also work with its **suppliers** of goods and services to ensure that these are procured when and where required and at the right price. CCC is less likely to state an objective relating to suppliers than to customers, but the failure to treat suppliers fairly (eg by delaying payments) may have **adverse consequences** for delivery schedules and input prices.

As regards **lenders**, DDD is planning to raise a significant amount of funding in the near future. Lenders will be concerned that the company may struggle to repay this debt. It is important that DDD's strategic plan does not expose the company to excessive levels of financial or business **risk**. Failure to recognise the needs of lenders could result in difficulties in raising the necessary finance or a higher rate of interest being charged.

DDD is certain to state **non-financial objectives** concerning its **employees**, usually concerned with fair remuneration rates, good working conditions, opportunities, and consultation over matters that affect employees. A company with the size and geographical spread of DDD, that may outsource substantial parts of its production to suppliers, must also be particularly sensitive to **working conditions** at those suppliers. Even if they are legally not responsible for those conditions, bad publicity can result from being associated with them if, for example, child labour is being used.

Finally, the company will probably state objectives relating to working with the **local community** to improve prosperity. DDD's links with the local community in CCC's region are significant due to the location of its Head Office in a relatively small city. Since it makes a significant impact on the local environment, DDD must be careful to minimise pollution (eg waste, smoke, noise) or will risk lawsuits and significant adverse publicity. On the positive side, the company may decide to support local community activities and charitable events, including providing donations to educational and health facilities.

Conclusion

DDD has a clear obligation to meet the needs of its shareholders, but will also need to consider the needs of its customers and other providers of finance, especially if it completes the planned acquisition.

(b)   MS and DDD are at **different stages in their lifecycles**. MS is a young company whereas DDD is more mature. They would therefore be expected to have a different approach to the formulation of financial strategy.

MS dividend investment and financing policy

The shareholders of MS obtain cash returns from their investment entirely through dividends, which have been **constant and predictable** over the company's six year life. For the founding shareholders the dividends now probably form a substantial part of their annual rewards from the company, while other employees are likely to regard their dividends as annual bonuses.

The value of the company's shares has undoubtedly increased over the last few years, but no shareholders have yet attempted to realise these gains by selling their shares, even though this might in theory represent a more **tax efficient** way of receiving returns. The practical difficulties of selling effectively lower the sales price and act as a deterrent. Thus the danger of continuing with the current policy is that MS may not have adequate funds to finance its **investment plans** and may need to use excessive debt finance.

For a specialised private company like MS, **investment** usually means **expansion** of the existing business by direct capital investment in assets and working capital. Opportunities for acquiring other businesses will occur, but the size of these acquisitions will be limited by the need to **finance** in cash. This means that the current dividend policy is questionable unless the no debt finance policy is changed.

MS wishes to finance a $15 million expansion of its business, equivalent to one third of its existing assets. Restricting the dividend payout would not raise enough for this project and, as argued above, would reduce the only cash return that the shareholders receive on their investment. To reduce the dividend substantially would require agreement between the company directors/shareholders and careful explanation to employees that a sacrifice now would pay off in the longer run.

A rights issue of new shares to existing shareholders in existing proportions would be difficult to get agreement on, but the shareholders may give permission for new shares to be purchased by just those who wish to subscribe. This may raise sufficient cash but, equally, it may also change the **relative ownership** of the company.

As the company is all-equity financed, borrowing $15 million would be feasible, bringing the gearing to approximately 25%, which is below the level where the directors need be concerned about excess **financial risk**. The relatively cheap interest and issue costs of debt, combined with the tax relief on interest paid, make **borrowing** a good source of finance for MS's expansion. Although the company really needs a long term loan at a fixed interest rate, for private companies the most feasible borrowing sources are banks, which usually offer medium term loans at floating rate, and this is the route the company will probably take.

Conclusion

The current relationships between investment, financing and dividend policy do not appear to be ideal for MS. As a young company looking to invest substantially, MS will probably need to reconsider its dividend policy and financing structure.

DDD dividend, investment and financing policy

Because shares in listed companies can easily be sold, the shareholders of DDD will be less concerned than those of MS if dividends are restricted in order to finance investments. They can easily make up the cash shortfall by selling their shares to make **capital gains**. Nevertheless, dividend policy is regarded as important in listed companies because it is part of the way that the directors give **information** to investors and manage market expectations. They will usually aim for a **smooth** stream of dividends reflecting underlying **long term growth trends**.

DDD will have a wider range of investment opportunities because its activities are diversified and is less likely to be constrained by its dividend policy because its shares are listed. In particular, **growth by acquisition** of other businesses is much easier because the company can offer its shares as purchase consideration.

DDD needs a **substantial** amount of capital to finance an acquisition. Again, restriction of the company's dividend will not by itself provide sufficient cash, and may send the wrong signal to the market about performance prospects. In this case an issue of **new shares** in DDD to the target company's shareholders is very suitable. No cash need be involved and there is no increased risk from borrowing. A decision would need to be made about whether the target company would have any representation of the board of DDD.

DDD could also consider **borrowing** in order to acquire the target company for cash, but this may increase gearing to beyond the desired level. A further alternative would be to offer a **mix of equity and cash**, borrowing to raise the cash portion of the purchase consideration.

Conclusion

DDD is a more mature company than MS. It has more stable cash flows so can more confidently consider using debt finance and possibly also a rights issue to finance its investment plans.

3 A and B

> **Text references.** Objectives are covered in Chapter 1.
>
> **Top tips.** Do not choose an optional question until you have **read all the requirements**. Here, Part (b) is potentially difficult and is worth 12 marks. Do an answer plan for each section before you start to write and then use your plan as headers in your answer. This will help you to focus on the specific requirements of the question.
>
> **Easy marks.** There are some easy marks available for basic explanations of objectives.
>
> **Examiner's comments.** This question was generally quite poorly answered with many candidates demonstrating a relatively weak understanding of the particular problems faced by the public sector when setting financial strategy.

(a) (i) <u>Achievement of maximisation of shareholder wealth objective</u>

The usual assumption in financial management for the private sector is that the primary financial objective of the company is to maximise shareholders' wealth. The wealth of the shareholders in a company comes from the **dividends** received and the **market value** of the shares

If a company's shares are traded on a stock market, as is the case here, the wealth of shareholders is increased when the share price goes up. The price of a company's shares will go up when the company makes decisions that increase future cash flows which it pays out as **dividends** or **re-invests** in the business to achieve future profit growth and dividend growth. However, to increase the share price the company should avoid excessive **business risks** and **financial risks** which worry shareholders.

It is usually assumed that if a company invests in projects with a positive net present value, shareholder wealth will be increased.

Achievement of shareholder wealth maximisation will require sound financial performance, so management should set **targets** for factors which they can influence directly, such as **profits** and **dividend growth**. A financial objective might be expressed as the aim of increasing profits, earnings per share and dividend per share. **Non financial targets** are also important, for example high exam pass rates and high levels of customer satisfaction; targets should be set in these areas too.

<u>Measurement of the financial objective</u>

The measurement of shareholder wealth can be made in the form of **total shareholder return.** This measure looks at the return on the opening share price which a company provides either by increasing the share price and/or by paying dividends.

(ii) <u>Benefit to other stakeholders</u>

Stakeholders are individuals or groups who are affected by the activities of the firm. They can be classified as **internal** (employees and managers), **connected** (shareholders, customers and suppliers) and **external** (local communities, pressure groups, government).

<u>Internal stakeholders</u>

Employees and managers will usually want to **maximise the rewards** paid to them in salaries and benefits, influenced by the particular skills and the rewards available in alternative employment. Most employees will also want continuity of employment. A successful entity will enable these stakeholders to achieve this. Participation in a **profit-sharing scheme** or in a share options scheme should help tie them into the company.

However, an entity which is aiming to maximise profits by **minimising costs** may make employees work harder and award below inflation wage rises. In a **service business** such as Entity A, this approach would be unwise because of the impact that it would have on the morale of skilled staff and therefore it is unlikely to be followed.

<u>Connected stakeholders</u>

Suppliers will generally be profit-maximising firms themselves and have the objective of being paid the full amount due by the date agreed. On the other hand, they usually wish to ensure that they

continue their **trading relationship** with the firm and may sometimes be prepared to accept later payment to avoid jeopardising that relationship. Suppliers are likely to gain from higher trading levels with Entity A.

Customers will be attracted to a successful entity as in order to be profitable, the entity will have to be competitive and provide what customers want. A profit maximising entity with **market power** may however have the power to increase prices. Customers are likely to benefit from Entity A's success unless Entity A is exploiting them with higher prices.

External stakeholders

Governments earn taxation from profits so will benefit from successful profit-maximising entities. If Entity A is contributing to an increase in the skill levels of the economy, this is likely to benefit the government too since employment levels will be higher and unemployment benefits lower.

Professional and regulatory bodies will be interested in ensuring that Entity A provides **quality** training. Quality may conflict with profit maximisation unless it is an essential part of the offering to customers. For example, class sizes may be increased which may result in a fall in the quality of tuition provided.

(b)   ### Differences between the objectives of public and private sector entities

Private sector entities usually have **shareholder wealth maximisation** as their main objective. Their survival depends on being able to offer a satisfactory return to their owners.

Objectives of **public sector** entities will be based on achieving **good value for money** from the funds that they receive from the government. This means that they tend to have **multiple objectives** so that even if they can all be clearly identified, it is impossible to say which is the overriding objective.

For entity B possible objectives include:

*   Economy – the acquisition of suitable inputs at lowest cost (for example cost / lecturer)
*   Efficiency – maximising the use of these inputs (for example students / lecturer)
*   Effectiveness – achieving goals (for example high pass rates)

Discount rates

The **discount rate** is used to identify projects which will generate a positive NPV and reflects the **required compensation** for the providers of finance.

A higher discount rate will reflect the additional **risk** involved in a project. Entity A with its cost of capital of 12% could have to:

*   **Take risks** (for example exploring web based training)

*   **Adjust pricing** (possibly charging higher prices to generate the required returns)

*   **Focus on the most profitable areas of the market** (for example high income students, or students with financial support from their employers).

By only requiring a 7% return for entity B, the government is encouraging entity B to behave in a way that the government prefers ie **limited risk taking** with public funds, **lower prices** (so more people will be able to afford the training and inflation will be lower).

The 7% cost of capital also reflects the ability of the government to **raise lower cost finance** because of its perceived low risk of default.

The use of a lower discount rate for Entity B will be more likely to make its potential investments appear viable. This will then **encourage investment** which would otherwise not take place in the private sector. For example, the provision of training for qualifications that it would not be profitable for Entity A to offer.

Conclusion

The requirement to operate as a **commercial entity** implies that Entity B should be capable of earning a **commercial return.** However given the **multiple objectives** that Entity B will be expected to achieve, it would not be reasonable for a 12% return to be required.

4 TTT

Text references. Financial objectives are covered in Chapter 1. The treasury function is dealt with in Chapter 10.

Top tips. There is quite a lot to do in this question, particularly in part (a)(i). Make sure you consider the objectives both before AND after the proposed acquisition. You are being tested partly on the conflicts between financial objectives so make it clear that you understand these. For example, dividend growth and expansion objectives contradict each other.

Part (a)(ii) is almost in two parts – don't spend too long on discussing the appropriateness of the objectives at the moment, you must ensure you advise on how to improve these objectives based on the scenario you are given.

It would be easy to just list three roles of the treasury function in part (b), however you are asked to describe these roles in the context of the proposed acquisition. Ensure your answer is appropriate to this particular scenario – don't just give a generic answer.

Easy marks. Part (b) should offer some fairly straightforward marks when talking about the specific roles of the treasury function. Remember to answer the question though!

Examiner's comments. The main weakness in part (a)(i) was the evaluation of the impact of the acquisition from increasing dividends per share by 10% a year. Candidates tended to concentrate on calculating different levels of gearing and the assessment of impact on growth. Where book values of equity were used in calculations, many students did not include retained earnings. The question was vague on whether market or book values should be used to calculate gearing and either method received credit.

In part (b) candidates often discussed the general roles of the treasury department rather than the specific question set.

(a)   (i)   <u>The extent to which TTT meets its financial objectives</u>

Dividend growth of 10% per annum

The effect of the acquisition on earnings per share and dividend growth will depend on whether the acquisition is financed by debt or equity. If financed by debt, interest costs will increase by €125m [(SKR23,000m/9.2000) x 5%] which will reduce earnings attributable to shareholders. However earnings are expected to increase by 8% per annum which, compounded with expected growth in WWW's earnings of 6%, will reduce the effect of the additional finance costs.

If the acquisition is financed by equity there will be an additional 862m shares in issue [(SKR23,000m/9.2000)/2.90] – an increase of 17%. Trying to sustain a stable dividend payout with such an increase in shares will be a challenge never mind trying to grow dividends by 10% per annum.

If TTT wishes to increase dividends by 10% this will mean a dividend of 17.6 cents per share. If dividend payout ratio remains at 40%, this would mean earnings per share of 44 cents. Total earnings for 5,862m shares would have to be €2,579.28m – an increase of €579.28m (current earnings = 44 cents x 5,000m shares = €2,000m) or 29%.

Given that average growth in earnings is 8% it is extremely unlikely, even with the growth prospects of WWW, that earnings will grow by this amount. As a result the dividend growth objective is unlikely to be achieved.

Keep gearing below 40%

Current gearing (based on book values) = 9,500/(9,500 + 5,000 + 4,000) = 51.4%

Based on market values = 9,500/(9,500 + (5,000 x €2.90)) = 39.6%

The company is fulfilling its gearing objective if gearing is based on market values.

If the acquisition goes ahead:

If debt is used to finance the acquisition, a total loan of SKR23,000m/9.2000 = €2,500m

Gearing (book values) = (9,500 + 2,500)/(9,500 + 2,500 + 5,000 + 4,000) = 57.1%

Gearing (market values)

= (9,500 + 2,500)/(9,500 + 2,500 + (5,000 x €2.90))

= 45.3%

The gearing objective is not fulfilled on either basis.

If **equity** is used to finance the acquisition:

Number of shares to be issued at a current price of €2.90 = 862m

Gearing (book value) = 9,500/(9,500 + 2,500 + 9,000) = 45.2%

Gearing (market value) = 9,500/(9,500 + [(5,000 + 862) x 2.90]) = 35.8%

The gearing objective based on market value will be fulfilled if the acquisition is financed by equity. Based on book values again the objective is not met.

Expansion by internal growth and/or by horizontal integration

Current EPS = Current dividend/dividend payout ratio = 16/0.4 = 40 cents per share

Current P/E ratio = 2.90/0.4 = 7.25

Earnings have been growing at an average rate of 8% per annum which suggests that the objective of expansion by internal growth is being fulfilled.

TTT is pursuing its objective of expansion by horizontal integration by targeting WWW as a potential takeover candidate.

WWW has a P/E ratio of 10 which is higher than TTT's current P/E ratio of 7.25 and WWW's earnings are expected to grow at a rate of 6% per annum. If this growth in earnings continues – along with TTT's expected growth – the combined company should have sufficient earnings to fund expansion projects.

(ii) <u>Appropriateness of the stated financial objectives</u>

Dividend growth of 10%

A policy of dividend growth is quite awkward as it is difficult to generate the correct signal. TTT has an objective of expansion - trying to increase its dividend conflicts with this objective as money is being given back to shareholders that could be retained within the business to fund investment projects.

A policy of increasing dividends could send the signal that the company has fewer profitable investment opportunities available and is therefore returning the money to its shareholders. Although earnings are increasing by an average of 8%, the target dividend growth of 10% means that there is **no gain in retained earnings**.

The policy of trying to increase dividends when the number of shares will potentially increase by almost 30% will put a huge strain on earnings and is probably **not appropriate** given the company's other objectives.

Such an objective might be improved by having a target of dividend maintenance or a much smaller (but sustainable) growth rate of say 2%. The shareholders will still be receiving a dividend but more earnings will be retained for investment purposes.

To keep gearing below 40%

Current gearing based on market values is 39.6%. This will climb to just over 45% if the acquisition is financed by debt but will fall to 35.8% if financed by equity.

This objective does not give the company much scope for **financing investment via debt**, which limits TTT's growth potential (and thus conflicts with the third objective).

Earnings are increasing at an average rate of 8% (before considering growth potential if the target company is acquired) therefore the company should be able to sustain increased finance costs – particularly if dividend growth targets are reduced.

It would be worthwhile finding out what the industry average gearing ratio is – that will give the company an idea of whether its gearing targets are too ambitious.

Depending on the industry average – and as the company is expanding - the objective could be improved by **increasing the target gearing ratio** to a level that will allow the company to fund future projects using debt (cheaper option than equity).

Expand by internal growth and/or by horizontal integration

The expansion objective appears to be reasonable given average earnings growth. TTT does not have to just focus on horizontal acquisitions however – it could consider vertical acquisitions whereby it not only supplies the energy but could also be responsible for customer equipment, billing and paying services and distribution lines.

Whilst expansion is desirable, TTT should guard against trying to expand **just for the sake of fulfilling its objective**. There is a danger of acquiring companies that do not fit well with TTT's structure or investing in projects that will ultimately be unprofitable.

The previous objectives conflict somewhat with the objective as funds are being paid out as dividends (rather than being retained for expansion purposes) and the restrictive gearing target will limit the profitable investment opportunities that can be pursued.

Suggestions have been made above on how the first two objectives can be brought more into line with the expansion expectations. However this will depend which objective TTT views as being the most important. If **dividends** are viewed as being the number one priority then TTT may have to revise its expansion plans as money cannot be retained within the business AND paid out to shareholders.

At the moment the objectives are **not compatible**. TTT should revisit what it considers to be most important and revise its other objectives accordingly.

(b)   <u>Three roles of the treasury function in the evaluation/implementation of acquisition of WWW</u>

Any three from:

Capital markets and funding

One important role of the treasury function could be **evaluating the various sources of finance** available to determine which should be used. Whilst debt is cheaper than equity, the treasury function will have to consider the impact of using debt on the strategic objective of maintaining gearing below 40%.

Treasury staff will also be instrumental in building relationships with lenders and investors, as well as liaising with credit rating agencies and credit analysts.

Integration of WWW's treasury system into that of TTT

One of the main reasons acquisitions fail is because little or no attention is paid to the **integration of key systems and personnel**. The treasury function will be able to play a significant role in the integration of such systems, particularly those related to cash management, working capital management and liquidity management.

Corporate financial management

This involves monitoring the company's business strategy and financial strategy and ensuring the two are in harmony with each other. The treasury function can therefore **evaluate the proposed acquisition** of WWW and determine whether this investment will fit in with the future strategy of TTT. It can also consider the most appropriate capital structure to be put in place to fund this investment (ensuring that this fits with the financial strategy of the company).

Risk management

Investing in a new country involves numerous risks, including foreign currency risk. WWW's costs and revenues will be in Swedish Krona therefore there is exposure to translation risk when the results are consolidated at the end of the year. There may also be **transaction risk** if TTT enters into contracts with WWW and the exchange rate moves.

The treasury function may be required to construct hedging packages to minimise such risk and look at the most efficient methods available. As TTT is already exposed to currency risk (as it operates in

countries outside the eurozone) the function should already be skilled in the implementation of hedging techniques and have knowledge of which techniques are most suitable for the business.

Cash and liquidity management

Cash is the lifeblood of an organisation and any proposed expansion of a business will involve **careful cash and liquidity management**. The treasury function may get involved in forecasting the cash required not only to purchase WWW but also to run it on a day-to-day basis. These requirements can then be integrated into existing cash requirements. This will allow the treasury function to determine how best to manage group-wide cash flows, short-term loans and cash balances to ensure there are no liquidity problems.

5 CBA

Text references. The preparation of forecasts is revised in Chapter 3 and working capital management is covered in Chapter 4.

Top tips. Changes in working capital management and the effect on cash flow are significant areas in the syllabus. (a) emphasises the key points for and against overdraft finance (flexibility v frequent re-negotiation), and also touches on strategic aspects of working capital finance that are important in this paper.

In (b) a clear layout is essential. It is not essential to follow IAS 7.

As (c) offers only 6 marks for a report, you do not have time to develop any of the points in too great a depth. Your answer should have referred to the calculations in (b).

Easy marks. (a) is a straightforward lead in to this question.

(a) Uses of overdrafts

The overdraft is a **key source of finance** for **working capital** because of its flexibility: the finance **varies automatically** up to the **agreed limit**, enabling the company to handle **peaks and troughs** in cash flows without incurring excess interest charges with the company's cash flow. The potential disadvantage for an expanding company is that the **overdraft limit** may have to be **frequently renegotiated**. There is also a tendency for expanding companies to ignore the need to underpin their growth with **longer term finance.**

Need for other funds

When considering alternatives to the bank overdraft, it is essential to consider the need for **longer term funds** (loans or equity funds) to finance the **permanent element** of working capital. Although such funds may be more expensive than short term finance, they provide a longer term stability for planning.

(b) Cash flow forecasts

(i) No change in policies

		£'000
Operating profit		1,326
Add depreciation		225
Less: increase in inventory		(275)
increase in receivables		(230)
Add: increase in trade payables		144
Net cash flow from operating activities		1,190
Finance payments		
Interest	54	
Dividends	339	
		(393)
Tax paid		(283)
Acquisition of non-current assets		(550)
Reduction in cash/increase in borrowings (25 + 11)		(36)

(ii) Proposals are implemented

	£'000	£'000
Original operating profit		1,326
Add reduction in cost of sales (W3)		150
Less 2% sales discount (W1)		(52)
Revised operating profit		1,424
Add depreciation		225
Less increase in inventory (W4)		(213)
Add decrease in receivables (W2)		74
Less decrease in trade payables (W5)		(86)
Net cash flow from operating activities		1,424
Finance payments		
Interest	45	
Dividends	339	
		(384)
Tax paid		(283)
Acquisition of fixed assets		(550)
Increase in cash		207

Workings

1 2% discount on 50% of sales = (£'000) 2% × 50% × 5,200 = 52.

2 Revised receivables will be (£'000): 750/2 + (2,600 × 10/365) = 446. Annual decrease in receivables = 520 − 446 = 74.

3 Cost of sales (excluding depreciation) is reduced by (£'000): 5% × (3,224 − 225) = 150 reduction to 2,849.

4 Inventory is reduced to (£'000): 90% × 625 = 563. Annual increase in inventory = 563 − 350 = 213.

5 Trade payables fall to (£'000): 2,849 × 30/365 = 234. Annual decrease in trade payables= 320 − 234 = 86.

(c)
To:	Ms Smith, Financial Manager
From:	Assistant
Date:	21 November 20X0
Subject:	Evaluation of working capital management proposals

Receivables

Although customers are supposed to pay within 30 days, they are currently taking **45 days** and are predicted to take 53 days next year. The discount scheme offered to customers who pay within 10 days is predicted to reduce the average payment period to (10 +53)/2 days = 31.5 days. The **discount cost**, estimated at £52,000, will be partially paid for by interest savings on the reduction in average receivables of from £625,000 to £446,000. There is also the possibility of bad debt savings, which have not been quantified. A rough cost of this scheme is 17% per annum (see below) which is fairly expensive, and before implementing it, we should consider **tightening up** on our **credit control** procedures to speed up payments. This must be done with care and tact, in order to preserve customers' goodwill.

Trade payables and inventory

Our original plans showed an **increase in credit** from suppliers from 50 to 56 days. The revised proposals will require us to pay in 30 days, but enable a 5% reduction in cost of sales through reduced prices and other purchasing costs. On the basis of our assumptions for the 'just in time' policy, the projected financial effects are extremely good. Cost of sales is reduced by £150,000 and there are interest savings on inventory reductions of £62,500, and although these are offset by interest costs on the cash requirement to reduce trade payables from £464,000 to £234,000, the overall effect is beneficial. However, our predictions may be optimistic as suppliers are likely to **require higher prices** to deliver 'just in time'. Also, this system will increase our dependence on fewer suppliers and will greatly increase the likelihood of production breakdowns due to lack of stock unless we implement higher quality processes.

Profitability and cash flow

Overall, on the basis of our projections, the scheme will improve profitability before tax by £'000 (150 – 52 + 9) = £107,000, a factor of 8%, and cash flow will be improved by £36,000 + £207,000 = £243,000 although there will be an impact on tax payable the following year. Despite some of the reservations above, the proposals are worth implementing.

Workings

	Next year	*Current year*
Average receivables payment period: receivables/sales × 365	53 days	45 days

Approximate cost of discount is 2% for (53 – 10) = 43 days, that is 2% × 365/43 per year = 17% per year.

	Next year	*Current year*
Cost of purchased goods (cost of sales less dep'n): £'000	2,999	2,345
Average credit from suppliers:		
trade payables/cost of purchased goods × 365	56 days	50 days

6 RJ

Text references. Forecasting and performance measures are revised in Chapter 3.

Top tips. Tax is complicated in part (a) by the difference between depreciation and tax allowances but this is only worth 2 marks. You need a working for payables and receivables although a full statement of financial position is not required. Note (b) is quite similar to a question in the May 2005 exam; the fact that the finance is only needed short-term is significant.

Easy marks. You would get some marks for the more straightforward figures such as revenue and cost forecasts in part (a).

Examiner's comments. Part (a) was generally well answered except for the impact of capital allowances in the taxation calculation. In Part (b), the presentation of figures could have been improved.

(a)   Forecast statements of consolidated income

Year	*20X5*	*20X6*	*20X7*	
	£'000	£'000	£'000	
Revenue	30,120	33,132	36,445	Up 10%
Cash based costs and expenses	(22,500)	(23,625)	(24,806)	Up 5%
Depreciation	–	(600)	(600)	10% straight line on £6m
Operating profit	7,620	8,907	11,039	
Finance costs	(2,650)	(2,650)	(2,650)	Unchanged
Profit before tax	4,970	6,257	8,389	
Tax	(1,491)	(1,607)	(2,359)	W1
Profit after tax	3,479	4,650	6,030	
Dividend	(1,392)	(1,462)	(1,535)	Up 5% Paid following year
Retained profit for the year	2,087	3,188	4,495	
Retained earnings b/f		4,750	7,938	
Retained earnings c/f		7,938	12,433	

Working 1: Tax payable

	20X6	*20X7*
	£'000	£'000
Plant value at start of year	6,000	4,500
Tax allowance (25% reducing balance)	(1,500)	(1,125)
Profit before tax	6,257	8,389
Add back depreciation	600	600
Less tax allowance	(1,500)	(1,125)
Taxable profit	5,357	7,864

(b)   <u>Cash flow forecasts</u>

Year ended	20X6 £'000	20X7 £'000	
Cash from sales (33,132 + 3700 − 4070) (W2)	32,762	36,038	Up 10%
Cash on costs and expenses			
(23,625 + 2,850 − 2,993)	(23,482)		Up 5%
		(24,656)	
Cash from operations	9,280	11,382	
Finance costs	(2,650)	(2,650)	Constant
Dividend paid	(1,392)	(1,462)	Previous year's div.
Tax paid	(1,491)	(1,607)	Previous year's tax
Purchase of plant and machinery	(6,000)	–	
Net cash flow	(2,253)	5,663	
Balance brought forward	198	(2,055)	
Balance carried forward	(2,055)	3,608	

<u>Working 2: Trade receivables and payables</u>

	20X5 £'000	20X6 £'000	20X7 £'000
Trade receivables			
(grow by 10% pa)	3,700	4,070	4,477
Trade payables (grow by 5% pa)	2,850	2,993	3,143

Alternative (generating the cash flow from the statement of financial position forecast)

<u>Statement of financial position extract</u>

	20X5 £'000	20X6 £'000	20X7 £'000	
Non-current assets	14,425	19,825	19,225	Depreciation @ £600 pa
Inventories	4,510	4,510	4,510	
Trade receivables	3,700	4,070	4,477	10% increase pa
Trade payables	2,850	2,993	3,143	5% increase pa
Other payables	2,883	3,069	3,894	Tax plus dividends
<u>Cash flow</u>				
Retained profit for the year	2,087	3,188	4,495	
Change in assets				
Non-current assets		(5,400)	600	
Inventories		0	0	
Trade receivables		(370)	(407)	
Change in liabilities				
Trade payables		143	150	
Other payables		186	825	
Cash flow for the year		(2,253)	5,663	
Balance brought forward		198	(2,055)	
Balance carried forward		(2,055)	3,608	

<u>Financing of cash deficit</u>

The cash deficit in 20X6 could be financed by **increasing the company's overdraft;** by **taking out a medium term loan;** by **reducing the dividend** (would only finance part of the deficit); or by using a **source of short term finance** based on its **receivables** (factoring or invoice discounting). The deficit is not large enough and does not last long enough to consider a longer term source of funds such as a share issue or long term loan. The situation may be complicated if there are **restrictive covenants** in the company's borrowing based on **liquidity and/or gearing levels,** in which case equity funds would be needed unless the company can renegotiate terms with its bankers.

Reducing the dividend would require **careful explanation to shareholders** and most quoted companies would probably opt to increase borrowings rather than reduce the dividend when the profitability trend is firmly upwards.

(c)   <u>Key aspects of the company's performance</u>

<u>Pre-tax return</u>

The company's stated targets are concerned with profitability and growth. On the basis of above forecasts, the pre-tax return on closing book value of equity is forecast to stay consistently above the target of 35% pa and to show steady growth:

20X5: 4,970 / (8,350 + 4,750) = 37.9%
20X6: 6,257 / (8,350 + 7,938) = 38.4%
20X7: 8,389 / (8,350 + 12,433) = 40.4%

<u>Growth in equity earnings</u>

At the same time, the forecast annual growth in equity earnings (profit after tax) is much higher than the company's target.

20X6: 4,650 / 3,479 – 1 = 33.7%
20X7: 6,030 / 4,650 – 1 = 29.7%

These results are excellent, especially as an **increase in sales** (or reduction in cost) specifically from the investment in plant has not been **factored** into the forecasts.

<u>Liquidity position</u>

However, the results cannot be looked at in isolation of the company's liquidity position. The investment and rapid growth will cause a significant drop in the cash resources during 20X6, though this is predicted to turn round in 20X7.

The liquidity ratios will change as follows:

	20X5	20X6	20X7
	£'000	£'000	£'000
Inventories	4,510	4,510	4,510
Trade receivables	3,700	4,070	4,477
Cash	198		3,608
	8,408	8,580	12,595
Current liabilities			
Trade payables	2,850	2,993	3,143
Other payables: Tax and dividends	2,883	3,069	3,894
Overdraft		2,055	
	5,733	8,117	7,037
Current ratio (current assets/ current liabilities)	1.47	1.06	1.79
Quick ratio (current assets – inventory/current liabilities)	0.68	0.50	1.15

Although the liquidity position is only bad for one year, the company will need to increase its overdraft facility with its bankers, or use one of the other sources of funds mentioned in part (b) above.

The 6% bonds will need to be **redeemed in 20X8** and there will probably be enough cash by then to do this, although an alternative would be to refinance with more long term debt at that stage.

7   EF

Text references. Forecasting is covered in Chapter 3.

Top tips. Don't forget in part (a) that tax is charged on profit **before** accounting depreciation less capital allowances, otherwise tax relief is effectively given twice for depreciation. Part (b) should cause few problems but don't forget the discussion on how to finance the cash deficit.

In part (c) you will have to calculate the ratios and then comment on whether the company has fulfilled its objectives. If you are unsure how to calculate a particular ratio, make an assumption, state the ratio you are using and carry on from there. You will still get marks for technique and comments on your results which is much better than leaving a blank space that will gain no marks.

Easy marks. You should be able to pick up some easy marks in parts (a) and (b), particularly in the calculation of cash receipts and payments in part (b).

(a)   <u>Forecast income statement</u>

31 December

	20Y0		20Y1	
	£'000	£'000	£'000	£'000
Revenue (4% increase pa)		46,800		48,672
Purchase costs and expenses	(39,780)		(41,371)	
Depreciation	(500)		(500)	
		(40,280)		(41,871)
Profit before interest and tax		6,520		6,801
Interest on long-term debt		(450)		(450)
Profit before tax		6,070		6,351
Tax (W1)		(1,490)		(1,656)
Profit after tax		4,580		4,695
Dividends declared and paid		(1,905)		(2,000)
Retained earnings		2,675		2,695

<u>Working</u>

	£'000
20Y0	
Cost	5,000
Capital allowance (25%)	(1,250)
Tax written down value	3,750
20Y1	
Capital allowance (25% of tax written down value)	(938)
Tax written down value	2,812

Tax is calculated on profit before depreciation less capital allowances:

	20Y0	20Y1
	£'000	£'000
Profit before tax	6,070	6,351
Add: depreciation	500	500
Less: capital allowances	(1,250)	(938)
Taxable profit	5,320	5,913
Tax at 28%	1,490	1,656

(b)   <u>Cash flow forecast</u>

31 December

	20Y0		20Y1	
	£'000	£'000	£'000	£'000
Sales receipts (W1)		46,260		48,110
Purchases and expenses (W2)	39,443		41,021	
Tax	1,490		1,656	
Vehicles	5,000		–	
Interest	450		450	
Dividends	1,905		2,000	
Total cash payments		(48,288)		(45,127)
Net cash flow for the year		(2,028)		2,983
Cash/(deficit) brought forward		348		(1,680)
Cash/(deficit) carried forward		(1,680)		1,303

Workings

(1) Sales cash receipts

	20Y0 £'000	20Y1 £'000
Sales revenue	46,800	48,672
Add: opening trade receivables	13,500	14,040
Less: closing trade receivables		
[(13,500/45,000) × sales revenue]	(14,040)	(14,602)
Sales cash receipts	46,260	48,110

(2) Purchases and expenses cash payments

	20Y0 £'000	20Y1 £'000
Purchases and expenses	39,780	41,371
Add: opening trade payables	8,415	8,752
Less: closing trade payables		
[(8,415/38,250) x purchases]	(8,752)	(9,102)
Purchases and expenses cash payments	39,443	41,021

How the company might finance a cash deficit

At the end of 20Y0 there is a cash deficit of £1,680,000, due mainly to the purchase of the fleet of vehicles for £5,000,000. It is not clear when the vehicles were actually purchased. If they were purchased in the early part of the year, financing for the cash deficit would be needed much sooner than the end of the year.

The company has an overdraft facility of £1 million. Given that the cash deficit is due to the purchase of non-current assets, it is unlikely to be a problem to have the facility extended. Whilst it could be argued that non-current assets should be funded by **long-term finance**, the amount required is **small** in comparison to the size of the company. This suggests that **short-term finance** in the form of an overdraft would be sufficient. In addition, the financing is only needed for a short period of time (the company has a cash surplus by the end of 20Y1) therefore long-term finance is not really needed.

Other forms of short-term finance that might be considered are **short-term leasing** and obtaining **more credit from suppliers**.

One way of reducing the cash deficit (and thus reducing the need for financing) is to **close the gap** between the length of credit granted to customers and the length of credit taken from suppliers. At the moment, trade payables are 22% (£8,415/£38,250) of purchases and expenses, whilst trade receivables are 30% (£13,500/£45,000) of revenue. This suggests that customers are taking longer to pay EF than EF is taking to pay its suppliers. If EF can tighten its credit control policy it might close the gap between the receipt and payment of cash. This will **reduce** the cash deficit and thus the need for a sizeable overdraft.

(c) EF's stated objectives are to:

(i) Earn a post-tax return on closing book value of shareholders' funds of 20% per annum
(ii) Have a year-on-year increase in earnings of 8%

	20X9 £'000	20Y0 £'000	20Y1 £'000
Shareholders' funds:			
Share capital	4,204	4,204	4,204
Retained earnings	16,210	18,885	21,580
Total shareholders' funds	20,414	23,089	25,784
Profit after interest and tax but before dividends	4,536	4,580	4,695
Return on closing BV of shareholders' funds	**22.2%**	**19.8%**	**18.2%**
Earnings per share	27.0p	27.2p	27.9p
% increase in EPS	–	**0.7%**	**2.6%**

Return on shareholders' funds

EF managed to exceed its target of a 20% return in 20X9. However the ratio falls below 20% in 20Y0 and declines still further in 20Y1. Retained earnings are not growing at a sufficient rate to sustain a return in excess of 20%.

Increase in earnings

The increase in earnings falls considerably short of the 8% target. However growth in earnings is increasing, which should instil confidence that the target is not unattainable. Growth is restricted by the considerable increase in depreciation charges in 20Y0 (due to the purchase of the vehicles). It will be worthwhile to examine costs as they are increasing at the same rate as sales revenue. Are there ways in which costs could be reduced, perhaps by changing suppliers or taking advantage of discounts? Are all costs necessary or could they be restricted or eliminated?

Increase in dividends

EF has the objective of increasing dividends at a rate of 5% per annum. By doing this, growth in retained earnings (based on forecasts) is being restricted to below that required to sustain a return in excess of 20%. However if target growth for dividends is 5% and target growth for earnings is 8%, EF will be building up retained earnings for potential future investments. If profitable investments are likely to be available, this strategy makes sense. However if there are limited profitable investments, such a strategy will result in a build-up of funds that should eventually be given back to the shareholders (perhaps by a review of dividend payouts).

Assumption regarding overdraft interest

This is a **key assumption**, the removal of which could have a significant effect on earnings. Given that EPS is increasing at such a slow rate, the inclusion of overdraft interest could result in **zero growth** or indeed a decline in EPS.

EF should take a more **realistic approach** to overdraft interest. It should try to determine the **rate** at which such interest will be paid (and indeed received in the case of positive cash balances) to obtain a more accurate view of the cost (or income) and its likely effect on earnings. By estimating the **timing** of significant items of expenditure such as tax or purchase of vehicles, EF can then calculate a more accurate figure for interest. This figure will not only affect earnings, it will also affect cash flow.

8   AB and YZ

Text references. Dividend policy is discussed in Chapter 4.

Top tips. On inspection you can see that AB is paying out the same dividend, and you may have been able to see that YZ's payout ratio is also constant; a quick calculation would show you in any event. The other information and the hints given in the question about share price should have helped you realize that you needed to calculate the price-earnings ratio. You don't have time to say very much about other factors that may affect market value but these certainly should be briefly mentioned.

(a) (ii) discusses the main points of the Modigliani and Miller theory; when planning you should have noted these and then thought how each might relate to the two companies.

(b) is a good summary of the main issues on a share repurchase. The question requirements helpfully detail the principal points.

Easy marks. Whether you choose a question in the exam will depend on how well you know share repurchases. You could score close to full marks on (b) if you know share repurchases well, but would probably avoid the question if you weren't confident.

Examiner's comments. Discussions on the actual dividend policy in (a) tended to be rather better than discussions of the optimal dividend policy. Some candidates were confused when answering (b) between share repurchases and reprivatisations.

(a)   (i)   <u>Dividend policies followed by AB and YZ</u>

<u>Payout and price earnings ratio</u>

	AB		YZ	
	Payout % DPS/EPS	P/E	Payout % DPS/EPS	P/E
20X1	26	9.1	40	9.2
20X2	40	10.0	40	10.6
20X3	60	10.0	40	15.6
20X4	–	–	–	–
20X5	60	10.0	40	13.9
20X6	40	9.3	40	11.7

<u>AB's dividend policy</u>

Over the past six years, AB and YZ have had virtually identical earnings per share (after adjusting for YZ's rights issue), but have had **different dividend policies.** AB has paid **constant dividends per share**, maintaining its dividend during the period of falling profits from 20X1 to 20X4, but not increasing them when profits recovered in 20X5 and 20X6. This has resulted in an overall average dividend payout ratio over the six year period of 60% of earnings.

<u>YZ's dividend policy</u>

By contrast YZ has maintained a **consistent dividend payout ratio of 40%** of equity earnings each year, the only exception being in 20X4 when losses were made and no dividend was paid.

Both companies operate in the same industry and have **similar capital structures** and, as stated above, virtually identical earnings records. However, throughout the six year period YZ has had a **consistently higher share price** (and hence lower cost of capital) than AB. On average, YZ's share price has been **17% higher**. This seems to provide evidence that the constant payout ratio policy of YZ has been superior to the constant dividend policy of AB. This may also be confirmed by events in 20X4, when YZ made a loss, failed to pay a dividend and its share price declined by 35%, whereas AB's share price only fell by 20%.

<u>Other factors</u>

The share price will **not only** be **determined** by dividend policy. If the market is well informed about investment policy, it may value YZ higher, because AB has, by paying a constant dividend, reduced the amount of funds invested and therefore limited future earnings. The market may also feel generally that YZ's overall strategy is superior, for example that the rights issue was a good decision despite being launched just after YZ had made a loss.

(ii)   <u>Is there an optimal dividend policy?</u>

<u>Modigliani and Miller's theory</u>

Modigliani and Miller's theory of **dividend irrelevance** suggests that the value of the two companies' shares should be identical, because share value depends on the present value of future cash surpluses generated, not on the manner in which they are distributed. This theory has been criticized because of its unrealistic assumptions:

- Perfect capital markets, with no transaction costs
- Investor indifference between dividends and capital gains
- Full information about future investments

In theory companies either have positive NPV investments that they should **finance** by **retained earnings,** thus paying zero dividends, or they have no investments, in which case all earnings should be paid as dividends. In practice they do not do this.

<u>Signalling</u>

The traditional view that dividends act as a signal to shareholders has led to **widespread adoption** by companies of policies of constant dividends or constant growth in dividends. Under such policies, dividends are **never reduced** unless it is really unavoidable. Yet although AB has followed such a policy, it has led to a lower share price than that of YZ, thus offering some evidence against the effectiveness of this strategy.

Agency theory

Agency theory predicts that payment of dividends helps to **reduce the agency conflict** between shareholders and managers. This might work in several ways. In general, the **higher the dividend, the lower the agency costs** (favouring AB over YZ), but it may be that in paying a dividend which is a fixed percentage of profits, YZ's managers are demonstrating that they are aware that profits belong to the shareholders. This may result in **lower agency costs for YZ** than for AB, and hence a lower cost of capital and higher share price.

To maximize share values, AB's directors should ensure that they always **keep shareholders informed** about company plans and results. Their current policy of constant dividends could be regarded as an attempt to hide operations from shareholders.

Taxation

Tax regimes where **dividends** are **taxed at a higher effective rate** than **capital gains** tend to make high dividend pay-outs disadvantageous.

Conclusion

In summary, there is no simple solution to an optimal dividend policy. Some shareholders are likely to prefer dividends, some eventual capital appreciation.

(b)   Share repurchase

(i)   How a share repurchase may be arranged

Special resolution

If permitted by its articles, AB may pass a special resolution to **authorise the company** to **buy back some of its shares**, but it cannot do so if this would leave only redeemable shares in issue. The terms of the special resolution will depend on whether it is a 'market purchase' (that is, an open market purchase made on the stock exchange), a tender offer to all shareholders or an individual arrangement with certain shareholders.

Treatment of shares purchased

Generally, when a company purchases its own shares, the **shares are cancelled** on their return to the company. However, a listed company may be able to hold the shares 'in treasury' for resale or **transfer to an employees' shares scheme** at a later date.

(ii)   Main reasons for a share repurchase

Use of surplus cash

AB will have more cash than is needed for its investments and must therefore choose **what to do with its surplus cash.** The cash could be used to **increase the dividend**. However, companies like AB, which maintain a steady dividend policy, usually take the view that when a dividend is increased this will lead the shareholders to expect a similar increase in future years.

If AB is not sure that this increase can be maintained, it will **keep the dividend constant** and use one of a number of alternative actions including **purchasing own shares** or **repaying debt.** Repayment of debt is the most common approach used by companies like AB, but if this is not feasible (eg because of high termination costs) they may choose to repurchase shares. The repurchase of shares will signal a 'one-off special payment' to shareholders rather than trigger expectations of a permanent increase in dividend.

Reduction of future total dividends

If the company is maintaining levels of dividend per share, then **fewer shares** will mean **smaller total dividends.**

Enhancement of earnings per share

Fewer shares will mean an **enhancement of earnings per share,** perhaps resulting in an increased market price per share.

Control

By buying out problem shareholders, those **currently in control of the company** can improve their position. One consequence may be that **AB** becomes **less vulnerable** to a hostile takeover bid.

Tax position of shareholders

Shareholders may be better off tax-wise than if they **receive a higher dividend.** A share repurchase may lead to a capital gains tax liability; however a special dividend will attract a (possibly higher) income tax liability.

Effect on cost of capital

Repurchase of shares will **increase the company's gearing,** possibly ensuring that the company is nearer an optimal gearing level, thus lowering the cost of capital.

(iii)   Potential problems

Lack of new ideas

Purchase of own shares may be interpreted as a sign that the company has **no new ideas** for **future investment strategy.** This may cause the share price to fall. Other shareholders may, of course, be thankful that the management is not gambling shareholder funds in areas it knows little about. They may consider that they can diversify more effectively than AB.

Costs

Compared with making a one-off extra dividend payment, purchase of shares requires **more time and transaction costs** to arrange. It may require more cash than the company has available.

Shareholder consent

Shareholders will have to pass a **special resolution** and it may be difficult to obtain their consent. Determining the right price may be difficult.

Agency theory

Agency theory would explain a preference for dividends by saying:

(1)   Shareholders need a **commitment by company management** that they will distribute free cash flow and not invest it in unprofitable activities

(2)   In this regard **dividends are perceived as a stronger commitment** than the repurchase of shares.

Gearing

If the equity base is reduced and gearing is increased, then **shareholders' financial risk** may be **increased.**

Effect on share price

In theory in a **perfect market** shareholders should be **indifferent** between a repurchase of own shares and a dividend.

However in practice the **market's reaction** may be **difficult to predict,** depending on how the market views an **increase in earnings per share,** versus the market believing that a **repurchase** demonstrates a **lack of future opportunities** and hence **limited prospects of future increases in earnings per share**. If the cash is not reinvested for growth the share price will fall and/or the company may be subject to a takeover bid.

9 MAT

> **Text references**. Performance analysis is covered in Chapter 3 and working capital management in Chapter 4.
>
> **Top tips**. The difficulty in a question like this is knowing where to start. The word 'overtrading' should make you think of liquidity ratios and some quick initial calculations will help you to understand what is going on. Planning your answer before you begin to write is essential here.
>
> **Easy marks**. The question asks for a report format which provides a few easy marks. Put your calculations in an appendix and do this first.
>
> **Examiner's comments**. This question drew heavily on knowledge gained from earlier papers. A common error was failure to provide an operating cycle figure. Analysis of possible causes and consequences of the changes was required in the discussion.

Appendix – Summary of calculations

Increase in revenue	$\dfrac{5,750-4,500}{4,500} \times 100 = 27.8\%$	
Increase in cost of goods sold	$\dfrac{2,300-1,750}{1,750} \times 100 = 31.4\%$	
Increase in profit before tax	$\dfrac{1,208-1,050}{1,050} \times 100 = 15.0\%$	
Increase in non-current assets	$\dfrac{4,325-3,775}{3,775} \times 100 = 14.6\%$	
Increase in current assets	$\dfrac{1,625-1,275}{1,275} \times 100 = 27.5\%$	

	Last year	Forecast
Current ratio	$\dfrac{1,275}{450} = 2.83$	$\dfrac{1,625}{1,050} = 1.55$
Quick ratio	$\dfrac{1,275-475}{450} = 1.78$	$\dfrac{1,625-575}{1,050} = 1.00$
Sales/net current assets	$\dfrac{4,500}{1,275-450} = 5.5$ times	$\dfrac{5,750}{1,625-1,050} = 10.0$ times
Receivables collection period	$\dfrac{550}{4,500} \times 365 = 44.6$ days	$\dfrac{950}{5,750} \times 365 = 60.3$ days

	Last year	Forecast
Inventory days	$\dfrac{475}{1,750} \times 365 = 99.1$ days	$\dfrac{575}{2,300} \times 365 = 91.3$ days
Payables payment period	$\dfrac{450}{1,750} \times 365 = 93.9$ days	$\dfrac{625}{2,300} \times 365 = 99.2$ days
Cash operating cycle	$99.1 - 93.9 + 44.6 = 49.8$ days	$91.3 - 99.2 + 60.3 = 52.4$ days
Debt/equity	$\dfrac{850}{3,750} \times 100\% = 22.7\%$	$\dfrac{850}{4,050} \times 100\% = 21.0\%$
Revenue/non-current assets	$\dfrac{4,500}{3,775} = 1.19$ times	$\dfrac{5,750}{4,325} = 1.33$ times

REPORT

To: Finance Director of MAT
From:
Date:
Re: Re: Overtrading and financial strategies

Introduction

This report will analyse the last year's results and forecast information for MAT and advise whether the entity is overtrading. It will also recommend financial strategies that could be used to address the situation.

What is overtrading

Overtrading happens when a business tries to **do too much to quickly** with too **little long-term capital** so that it is trying to support too large a volume of trade with the capital resources at its disposal.

Symptoms

(a)   There is a **rapid increase in turnover**.

(b)   There is a **rapid increase in the volume of current assets** and possibly also non-current assets. Inventory turnover and accounts receivable turnover might slow down.

(c)   There is only a **small increase in proprietors' capital** (perhaps through retained profits). Most of the increase in assets is financed by credit, especially **trade accounts payable** and a **bank overdraft**.

(d)   The **proportion of total assets** financed by proprietors' capital falls and the proportion financed by credit rises.

Is MAT overtrading?

The calculations presented in the Appendix indicate signs of overtrading.

(a)   **Turnover** is expected to increase by 27.8% which is **rapid growth** as is to be expected in a rapidly growing niche market. However, cost of sales is up by 31.4%. Sales to net current assets is expected to increase from 5.5 times to 10 times.

(b)   **Current assets** are forecast to grow by 27.5% compared to growth in non-current assets of only 14.6%. **Accounts receivable collection period** is forecast to increase by 35% (60.3 – 44.6/44.6). However, **inventory days** are expected to fall slightly. The overall **cash operating cycle** would be expected to increase if the entity was overtrading but the increase is only 5% (52.4 – 49.8/49.8).

(c)   **Equity** is expected to increase by only 18% (5,950 – 5,050/5,050) but the **accounts payable period** is increasing and an **overdraft** of £425,000 is forecast.

(d)   The **gearing ratio** is actually expected to fall rather than rise but it does look as though the purchase of non-current assets is being financed with an **overdraft** rather than long-term debt.

In conclusion, MAT is demonstrating some signs of overtrading but the evidence is not conclusive.

Recommended financial strategies

Overtrading can result in **business failure** due to **liquidity problems**. The deterioration in current and quick ratios does not indicate impending financial distress but action should be take to improve the situation.

(a)   **Better control** could be applied to accounts receivable. The danger is that sales could be damaged by more stringent credit control.

(b)   MAT could take even **more credit from suppliers** but this risks retaliatory action as a long credit period is already taken.

(c)   **New capital** could be injected into the business by the owners. The size of the business probably means that it is too small to consider a flotation so this does make it difficult to raise equity finance.

(d)   New **long-term debt finance** could be raised, especially as re-financing will be required in two years' time.

(e)   MAT could **abandon plans** to purchase more **non-current assets** until the business has had time to consolidate its position and build up its capital base with retained profits.

Additional information

(a)   More specific information on the **inventory** would be useful, especially as the entity is a manufacturer so needs to hold raw material and work-in-progress inventory.

(b)   An annual forecast does not provide sufficient information on monthly or seasonal peaks and troughs. A more **detailed cash flow analysis** would be useful.

(c)   More information on **accounts receivable balances** and **policies** would help to improve credit control.

(d)   Detailed information on the **planned purchase of non-current assets** would enable an informed decision to be made on whether to purchase.

10 LUG

Text references. The cash operating cycle is covered in Chapter 3 and working capital financing in Chapter 4.

Top tips. If you get stuck on the ratio calculations in part (a) (i), you can use the sample ratios given in the question to check your approach. However, there is a lot to do in the time available so don't waste too much time here. You do not need the answer to part (a) to do the rest of the question.

Easy marks. Even if you find the calculations challenging in part (a), there are plenty of marks available for straightforward discussions in parts (b) and (c).

Examiner's comments. Many candidates struggled with the basic concepts in this question. There were problems with the calculations in part (a) and a failure to relate answers in parts (b) and (c) to LUG's situation.

(a)   (i)   <u>Country E</u>

<u>Revenue</u>

Expected sales in E\$ = (E\$750,000 × 0.6) + (E\$950,000 × 0.4) = E\$830,000

Average exchange rate during the year = 1.43 × 1.015 = 1.45

Expected sales in € = E\$830,000/1.45 = €572,414

Accounts receivable = 20% × €572,414 = €114,483

<u>Revised financial outcomes</u>

		Country D €'000		Country E €'000	Total €'000
Credit sales	90% of revenue	2,327		572	2,899
Receivables		350		114	464
Inventory					
Raw material	45% × 425	191		54	245
WIP	22% × 425	94		26	120
Finished goods	33% × 425	140		68	208
Total		425		148	573
Cost of goods sold		1,551	1,551/2,585 × 572	343	1,894
Purchases		1,034	1,034/2,585 × 572	229	1,263
Accounts payable		205	205/1,034 × 229	45	250

<u>Revised operating cycle</u>

		Days
Receivables	464/2,899 × 365	58.4
Payables	250/1,263 × 365	(72.3)
Inventory		
Raw material	245/1,263 × 365	70.8
WIP	120/1,894 × 365	23.1
Finished goods	208/1,894 × 365	40.1
Operating cycle		120.1

(ii) <u>Causes of the increase</u>

     <u>Original operating cycle</u>

		Days
Receivables		54.9
Payables		(72.4)
Inventory		
Raw material	$191/1{,}034 \times 365$	67.4
WIP	$94/1{,}551 \times 365$	22.1
Finished goods	$140/1{,}551 \times 365$	<u>33.0</u>
Operating cycle		<u><u>105.0</u></u>

     <u>Accounts receivable</u>

All of the sales to Country E are on credit with customers expected to take much **longer to pay** ($114/572 \times 365 = 73$ days) than in Country D. This may be due to the difficulties with **credit management** in a foreign country.

<u>Inventory</u>

All of the types of inventory are held for **longer** in Country E than in Country D. This is presumably in order to provide **safety inventory** in a country where sales are likely to be affected by economic and political factors. Raw material inventory is in excess of purchases so LUG must have exported raw materials ready for production to start.

(b) <u>Benefits of invoicing overseas customers in their own currency</u>

The main benefit is **competitive advantage.** Customers are less likely to buy goods from an overseas entity if they have to worry about exchange rate movements.

The entity may find that there has been a **beneficial movement** in the exchange rate by the time the invoice is paid and it now receives more money in its home currency than it expected.

<u>Risks</u>

The risk involved is **transaction risk.** This arises when the prices of exports are fixed in foreign currency terms and there is movement in the exchange rate between the date when the price is agreed and the date when the cash is received in settlement. The risk is that the entity will receive less money in its home currency than it expected.

If a large proportion of cash flow is generated overseas, this can make **cash flow management** very difficult.

<u>Methods to minimise the risks</u>

If an exporter is able to quote and invoice an overseas buyer in **its own currency**, then the **foreign exchange risk** is in effect **transferred** to the overseas buyer. The customer must **accept** the exchange risk, since there will be a period of time elapsing between agreeing a contract and paying for the goods (unless payment is made with the order). Who bears the risk may depend on bargaining strength.

The entity could take out a **forward exchange contract** which specifies in advance the rate at which a specified quantity of currency will be sold.

Money market hedging involves borrowing an appropriate amount in the foreign currency today, converting it immediately to the home currency, placing the funds on deposit and repaying the foreign currency loan when the cash is received from the customer.

Foreign currency derivatives can also be used to hedge foreign currency risk.

(c) <u>Financing net current operating assets</u>

Short-term finance is usually **cheaper** than medium-term finance (under a normal yield curve).

The diagram below illustrates three alternative types of policy A, B and C. The dotted lines A, B and C are the cut-off levels between short-term and long-term financing for each of the policies A, B and C respectively: assets above the relevant dotted line are financed by short-term funding while assets below the dotted line are financed by medium or long-term funding.

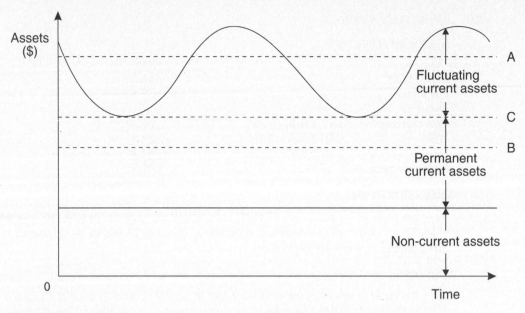

Conservative approach

Policy A can be characterised as a **conservative approach** to financing working capital. All non-current assets and permanent current assets, as well as part of the fluctuating current assets, are financed by medium or long-term funding. There is only a need to call upon short-term financing at times when fluctuations in current assets push total assets above the level of dotted line A. At times when fluctuating current assets are low and total assets fall below line A, there will be **surplus cash** which the company will be able to invest in marketable securities.

Aggressive approach

Policy B is a more **aggressive approach** to financing working capital. Not only are fluctuating current assets all financed out of short-term sources, but so are some of the permanent current assets. This policy represents an **increased risk of liquidity and cash flow problems**, although **potential returns** will be increased if short-term financing can be obtained more cheaply than medium or long-term finance. It enables **greater flexibility** in financing.

Moderate approach

Policy C is a **moderate approach** which attempts to achieve a **balance** between risk and return. This seems to be the policy adopted by LUG. It finances major changes in working capital with medium-term loans but also uses an overdraft and delayed payments for short-term funding.

11 MNO

Text references. Working capital management is covered in Chapter 4 and treasury departments are discussed in Chapter 10.

Top tips. In part (a) make sure you base your calculations for accounts payables and inventories on **cost of sales** and recognise that maximum accounts payable coincides with minimum working capital. Do not forget to discuss the validity of the Financial Controller's assumptions.

Easy marks. Parts (b) and (c) are a straightforward discussion of textbook knowledge but you must make sure you **apply** your discussion to MNO.

Examiner's comments. This question was avoided by the majority of candidates even though it was a standard working capital and financing question. Many candidates ignored the financing aspects and the main weakness was the inability to provide the calculations required.

(a) (i) <u>Workings</u>

	Minimum ($m)	*Maximum ($m)*
Accounts receivable	20/365 × 10 = 0.55	30/365 × 10 = 0.82
Accounts payable (Cost of sales 60% × 10 = 6)	40/365 × 6 = 0.66	50/365 × 6 = 0.82
Inventories	50/365 × 6 = 0.82	80/365 × 6 = 1.32

<u>Maximum level of working capital</u> = peak accounts receivable + peak inventories – lowest accounts payable

= 0.82 + 1.32 – 0.66 = $1.48m

<u>Minimum level of working capital</u> = lowest accounts receivable + lowest inventories – peak accounts payable

= 0.55 + 0.82 – 0.82 = $0.55m

The Financial Controller has assumed that the peak period for accounts receivable coincides with the peak period for inventories and the lowest level of accounts payable. However, if sales have been **particularly high** resulting in accounts receivable peaking, it is likely that inventories will be lower. If inventories are high it is likely that there has been increased spending on purchases and accounts payable will be higher.

Working capital levels will be affected by many factors and monitoring the fluctuations over a year in order to identify any **relationships** and **cyclical patterns** would produce a more **accurate** forecast.

(ii) Permanent net current assets = $0.55m
Fluctuating net current assets = $(1.48 – 0.55) = $0.93m
Non-current assets = $8m

	Moderate ($m)	*Aggressive ($m)*	*Conservative ($m)*
Short-term financing	0.93	(30% × 0.55) + 0.93 = 1.09	40% × 0.93 = 0.37
Long-term financing	0.55 + 8 = 8.55	(70% × 0.55) + 8 = 8.39	(60% × 0.93) + 8 + 0.55 = 9.11

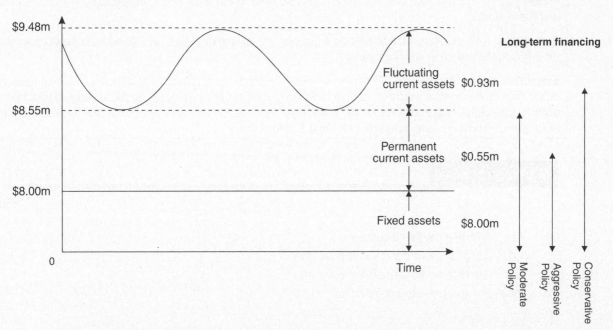

(b) The **advantages** of an aggressive financing policy are that it carries the greatest returns. It aims to reduce the financing costs, as short-term financing is cheaper than long-term, and increase profitability by cutting inventories, speeding up collections from customers and delaying payments to suppliers. It also enables greater flexibility in financing.

However, there is an increased risk of **illiquidity** and managers will need to spend a significant amount of time managing and renewing short-term sources of finance. Short-term finance may not always be easily available.

MNO is likely to have **large fluctuations** in its levels of working capital requirements and would therefore find the **flexibility** of an aggressive financing policy beneficial.

(c) The treasury department is usually run as a **cost centre** if its main focus is to keep costs within budgeted spending targets. In a cost centre, managers have an incentive only to keep the costs of the department within budgeted spending targets. The cost centre approach implies that the treasury is there to perform a **service** of a certain standard to other departments in the enterprise. The treasury is treated much like any other service department.

It may be run as a **profit centre** if there is a high level of foreign exchange transactions, or the business wishes to make speculative profits. Treating the treasury department as a profit centre recognises the fact that treasury activities such as **speculation** may earn revenues for the company, and may as a result make treasury staff more **motivated**. It also means that treasury departments have to operate with a greater degree of commercial awareness, in for example the management of working capital, by reducing interest and bank spreads. The profit can also be made by charging individual business units a **market rate for services** with a lover cost of provision.

In MNO, the treasury department is unlikely to be run as a profit centre as it is a relatively **small entity** so finance savings will be limited. There are currently no foreign exchange dealings, and, although this is due to change, there will be no opportunity to make a profit by netting cash flows as there will be only payments in the Asian currency. MNO **is de-centralised** which makes it harder to impose central finance policies although Head Office does provide funds as required.

In conclusion, a cost centre structure is probably the most appropriate for the treasury department of MNO.

12 KK

Text references. Working capital management is considered in Chapter 4.

Top tips. In part (a) (i) it is important to recognise that the figures given are for six months not a full year and therefore the working capital calculations should be done over a six month period ie 182.5 days.

For part (a) (ii) consider each area separately and also think about other potential effects such as those on staff and the overdraft.

Easy marks. You should be able to pick up a number of easy marks in part (a) (iii) when suggesting ways to have less funds tied up in working capital.

Examiner's comments. Part (a) (iii) had a number of common errors: Discussing different financing methods rather than how to reduce the funds tied up in working capital, failing to recognise the associated effects of some actions, for example suggesting KK should reduce the credit period and not mentioning that this could impact on sales. Some candidates even suggested KK should reduce sales.

Marking scheme

			Marks
(a)	(i)	Working capital calculations	5
	(ii)	Up to 2 marks per relevant point max	8
	(iii)	Up to 2 marks per relevant point max	5
(b)		Up to 2 marks per relevant point max	7
			25

(a) (i) If working capital days at 31 October 20X1 were unchanged for six months, the following balances would be expected on 30 April 20X2.

It is assumed the number of days in 6 months is 182.5 days.

Accounts receivable

Existing days × Revenue / Number of days = 92 days × €12.6m / 182.5 = €6.4m

Accounts payable

Existing days × Cost of sales / Number of days = 69 days × €9.6m / 182.5 = €3.6m

Inventory

Existing days × Cost of sales / Number of days = 100 days × €9.6m / 182.5 = €5.3m

The total investment in working capital at 30 April 20X2 would have been
€6.4m + €5.3m – €3.6m = €8.1m
compared to €7.1m + €5.6m – €3.2m = €9.5m

This represents a difference of €1.4 million and would have led to an to overdraft at 30 April 20X2 of €7.1 million instead of €8.1 million.

(ii)   During rapid expansion, many businesses face pressure on the elements of working capital and also on profit margins. These are considered below.

Inventory

KK's inventory has increased by €1.7 million to €5.6 million in the six month period from 31 October 20X1 to 30 April 20X2. **Without an increase** in inventory days, the inventory level would still have increased to €5.3 million.

Inventory management systems are put under more pressure as the number of different products manufactured increases. KK is introducing **new products** and so a significant investment in inventories will be required in order to support the increase in sales.

Accounts receivable

KK's accounts receivable balance has increased by €2.3 million to €7.1 million in the six month period from 31 October 20X1 to 30 April 20X2. **Without an increase** in accounts receivable days, the accounts receivable level would still have increased to €6.4 million.

With the product range expanding, KK will attract additional business from new and existing customers. Where business comes from existing customers, although the total level of receivables will increase the receivables days would be expected to remain the same. Where new customers are taken on, however, there may be **additional risk** of either late or non-payment. This is especially the case if credit checks are inadequate or not made at all prior to accepting orders.

Accounts payable

Expansion will impact accounts payable. The accounts payable balance has increased by €0.5 million to €3.2 million in the six month period from 31 October 20X1 to 30 April 20X2. The precise impact on working capital depends on the credit terms.

It was expected that the accounts payable balance would be €3.6 million, due to increased cost of sales and assuming accounts payable days remain unchanged. However, KK's accounts payable days have fallen from 69 days to 61 days. This suggests that either some suppliers are being paid earlier, or new suppliers have been used who have **shorter credit terms** than the current suppliers.

Profit margins

Profit margins can suffer where expansion is as a result of reducing selling prices to increase sales volume. For KK though expansion is from the launch of new products. Sometimes when new products are launched they are sold at a **premium** and profit margins are actually increased. Alternatively the new products may be in a **highly competitive market** and margins may be lower than existing products. From the financial information given, the gross profit margin for the six months to 31 October 20X1 was ((9.5 – 7.1)/9.5) = 25.3%. The gross profit margin for the six months to 30 April 20X2 was ((12.6 – 9.6)/12.6) = 23.8% so the new business appears to have a lower profit margin than the existing business.

Impact on employees

Expansion can also create pressure on employees. If there is a significant increase in customers, then **extra staff** are likely to be needed in credit control or there will be issues in controlling the

level of receivables. Even if extra staff have been recruited they will need to be trained, which will take time and so there may still be short-term effects on working capital.

Overdraft

In part (a) (i) it was shown that if working capital days had remained the same then the overdraft would have only grown by €1.1 million, not €2.5 million. Combined with increased profits and a worsening working capital cycle an increasing overdraft is a typical symptom of overtrading.

(iii)   The following are areas that KK could consider to reduce the amount of funds tied up in working capital. In all areas good working capital management is required to achieve this.

A JIT inventory system could be set up to reduce inventory holding costs. This will need close co-operation with suppliers to ensure **stockouts do not occur**.

A debt factor could be used to ensure liquidity regarding accounts receivable. Alternatively an early settlement discount could be offered to customers, although this would **reduce profit margins**.

KK could negotiate an increase in credit terms from suppliers, taking care not to damage the relationship with the supplier.

(b)   When assessing the creditworthiness of a rapidly growing business, a potential lender will consider a number of issues. It will mainly be concerned with the **future prospects** of the company. As a result it will want to study any budgets or cash forecasts showing the expected growth and the impact on profitability and cash flow. Detailed, well documented and sensible projections will mean that a lender is more likely to offer credit. The lender may also be worried about reducing sales margins to increase sales volume and may agree limits for profit margins. The lender will also consider the nature of the new business and how **sustainable** it is as well as the state of the economy and the position of the expanding company within the market.

Other factors that the lenders will want to consider include:

(i)   The quality of management, looking at both their past successes and the quality of their forecasts.

(ii)   The purpose of the additional borrowing. If it represents short-term financing then it is important to match it to short-term investment, typically for supporting fluctuating working capital. A lender is less likely to advance short-term funds for long-term investments.

(iii)   The existing capital structure and any existing debt. In particular the lender would want to assess the repayment terms and any restrictive covenants to ensure repayment is not due in the near future and that covenants would not be breached.

(iv)   Short-term liquidity measures, such as the current or quick ratios to establish the current position of the company.

(v)   Reports from third party credit agencies could be sought.

13   CRM

> **Text references.** Objectives are covered in Chapter 1 and performance analysis in Chapter 3. Forecasting exchange rates is in Chapter 12.
>
> **Top tips.** Show your workings and calculations clearly in an appendix and don't forget to use a proper report format. The six objectives mentioned in the exam scenario should provide the headings in your report and give a clear structure. Make sure that you apply your comments to the specific circumstances of a company listed on the alternative investment market.
>
> **Easy marks.** There are plenty of marks available for straightforward ratio calculations.

Appendix – Summary of calculations

Exchange rates

31/3/X8   6.30

31/3/X9   6.50

31/3/Y0 $6.50 \times 1.055/1.035 = 6.63$

31/3/Y1 $6.63 \times 1.055/1.035 = 6.76$

31/3/Y2 $6.76 \times 1.055/1.035 = 6.89$

Translated balance sheet figures for Asian Sub

	20X8	20X9
	£m	£m
Revenue	46.8	56.2
PBIT	12.7	16.9
Earnings	8.3	12.2
Net assets	$(242 - 65)/6.3 = 28.1$	39.4

Key ratios

	CRM	Asian Sub
Increase in revenue	$(355 - 325)/325 \times 100 = 9.2\%$	$(365 - 295)/295 \times 100 = 23.7\%$
Increase in earnings	$(77 - 69)/69 \times 100 = 11.6\%$	$(79 - 52)/52 \times 100 = 51.9\%$

	20X8	20X9	20X8	20X9
Return on net assets (PAT/Net Assets)	$69/(341 - 184) \times 100 = 43.9\%$	$77/(381 - 171) \times 100 = 36.7\%$	$52/(242 - 65 - 92) \times 100 = 61.2\%$	$79/(278 - 22 - 92) \times 100 = 48.2\%$

	CRM		Industry data	
	20X8	20X9	20X8	20X9
Dividend yield	$21/125 \div 6.41 \times 100 = 2.62\%$	$24/125 \div 7.218 \times 100 = 2.66\%$	2.8%	3.0%
Gearing	$100/257 \times 100 = 38.9\%$	$100/310 \times 100 = 32.3\%$	44.0%	46.0%
EPS	$69/125 = 0.552$	$77/125 = 0.616$		
P/E ratio	$6.41/0.552 = 11.6$	$7.218/0.616 = 11.7$	8.2	9.0

Return to shareholders = (capital gain + dividend per share)/original share price
$$= ((7.218 - 6.41) + (24/125))/6.41 \times 100$$
$$= 15.6\%$$

Expected return using CAPM $= R_f + (R_m - R_f) \beta$
$$= 4 + ((12 - 4) \times 1.4)$$
$$= 15.2\%$$

Using a 25% higher beta value $= 4 + ((12 - 4) \times (1.4 \times 1.25)) = 18\%$

REPORT

To: Board of Directors
From: Financial Manager
Date:
Re: Analysis of financial performance and attainment of financial objectives

Introduction

This report will analyse CRM's performance over the period from 31st March 20X8 to 31st March 20X9 to assess whether it has attained its financial objectives. It will also provide recommendations for corrective action by CRM if necessary and advice about the appropriateness of stated objectives.

Provide a total return to shareholders of at least 15% per annum

Total shareholder return comprises **capital gain** plus **dividend per share** and during this period, it was 15.6%. This **exceeds the target,** but it would be useful to determine how a target of 15% was arrived at. If the **capital asset pricing model** was used to calculate the expected return, the **beta** used in the calculation may have been **too low**.

The only beta available is one for a similar entity quoted on the main stock exchange. Share prices on the main market are likely to be **less volatile** than on the alternative listed market and the **risk** associated with CRM's shares is likely to be **higher**. This would **increase** the expected shareholder return. If the beta is increased by, for example 25%, the expected return becomes 18%.

Provide a dividend yield comparable with the industry average

The dividend yield is slightly **higher** in 20X9 than in 20X8 but is still **below** the industry average. A lower dividend yield indicates that a company **retains** a larger proportion of profits to reinvest. This is to be expected in AIM shares whose investors tend to **prefer capital gains**.

Investors tend to want a **stable** dividend policy where dividends adjust only gradually to changes in earnings. This is more important than a comparison with an industry average which will contain a very broad range of companies.

Generate a return on assets of 30% per annum

Return on assets for CRM is **above** the 30% target in both years but has **fallen** from 43.9% to 36.7%. Both assets and earnings have increased but earnings have not increased as much as assets.

The return on assets for the Asian subsidiary is higher than the group's overall return but again it fell from 20X8 to 20X9.

Increase revenue by 15% for the year to 31st March 20X9

Revenue increased by only 9.2% for CRM overall which is below the target. This would have been even lower without the much greater 23.7% increase in revenue achieved by the Asian subsidiary.

Increase earnings per share by 10% for the year to 31st March 20X9

Earnings increased by 11.6% for the group overall which meets the target. Much of this growth was as a result of the 51.9% increase in earnings achieved by the Asian subsidiary.

Double revenue in sterling terms in Asian Sub within the three years to 31st March 20Y2

The Asian subsidiary's revenue was £46.8m in 20X8 and £56.2m in 20X9. This is a **growth rate** of about 20% (56.2/46.8 -1). In order to achieve the target, revenue will have to grow by 26% per annum ($^{3}\sqrt{(112.4/56.2)}$ − 1). This may be very difficult to achieve.

Inflation is forecast to average 5.5% in the Asian country which is higher than in the UK. This is likely to lead to a depreciation in the A$ of approximately 2% per annum (1.055/1.035 − 1) which would lower the £ revenues even further.

Advice about the appropriateness of the stated objectives

The objective concerning **dividend yield** compared to an industry average is not an appropriate objective for CRM. Shareholders will be more concerned with their **total return** which also includes the capital gain arising from an increase in the share price.

The **target shareholder return** of 15% should also be reviewed as CRM's shareholders may require a greater return as compensation for the risk of investing in an AIM listed company.

Recommendations for corrective action

CRM has met two of its objectives but only if the results from the Asian subsidiary are included. Any **downturn** in the Asian economy could have a serious impact on CRM's ability to hit its targets. **Diversification** into alternative markets could be a way to achieve the required growth.

Gearing is relatively **low** compared to the industry average and has fallen in 20X9. CRM could consider raising **debt finance** in order to reduce the cost of capital and fund expansion.

14 Blue and Green

Text references. Dividend policy is covered in Chapter 4.

Top tips. This is quite a straightforward question on dividend policy and tests your understanding of why different types of organisations can have different attitudes towards dividend payouts. However with such a question it is easy to get carried away with writing everything you know about dividend policy. Keep your answer focused on the two organisations in the scenario and watch out for 'requirements within requirements'. For example, part (a) asks you for the rationale behind the two dividend policies but also asks you to discuss why a public company is likely to have a different policy to a private company.

Whilst part (b) simply asks you to explain the MM theory, you are also expected to provide a critique of why it is unlikely to be relevant in practice. Remember to answer both elements of the requirement – the second element tests your ability to apply theories to practical scenarios.

Easy marks. If you are familiar with dividend policy, there are numerous easy marks to be picked up throughout this question.

Examiner's comments. There was a wide range of marks on this question. Candidates with good knowledge of the subject scored well but there was a number of very poor answers. Common errors included:

– inability to explain why a private company might be expected to have a different dividend policy from a publicly quoted company

– lack of knowledge of the basic premise of MM's theory of dividend irrelevance

– inappropriate responses to Mr B and Mr G

Marking scheme

			Marks
(a)	Blue's dividend policy – up to 2 marks per relevant point discussed		
	Green's dividend policy – up to 2 marks per relevant point discussed		
			Max 9
(b)	Explanation of MM's dividend irrelevance theory	Max 5	
	Relevance to Blue	Max 2	
	Relevance to Green	Max 2	
			Max 8
(c)	Mr B – appropriateness of returning cash to shareholders, how it might be done – up to 2 marks per valid point	Max 4	
	Mr G – how he can fulfil his cash requirements – up to 2 points per valid point	Max 4	
			Max 8
		Total	25

(a)   Blue's dividend policy

As a multinational limited company, Blue will be aware of the **signalling effect** of dividends, hence its policy of a steady growth in dividend levels. Its shareholders will not have access to information regarding underlying project cash flows therefore its directors – who do have access to such information – can use dividends as a signal about the strength of these cash flows. A stable growth in dividends signals a stable company and the prospect of steady future returns to shareholders. This is important for the market as it does react favourably to instability.

A substantial proportion of Blue's shareholders is made up of institutional investors. Historically such investors prefer a small steady dividend which may have affected Blue's choice of dividend policy. The smaller shareholders may have been attracted to Blue for its stable dividend policy. This is known as the **clientele effect**.

However the build-up of surplus cash should indicate to the Board of Directors that the dividend policy should be reviewed. There is obviously insufficient profitable investment opportunities to support such a prudent dividend policy therefore it may be time to return some of the surplus cash to the shareholders.

Green's dividend policy

Green is a private family-run company with only 10 shareholders. As it is not listed on the Stock Exchange, Green does not face the pressures and expectations of the stock market. It is likely that the majority (if not all) of the shareholders are involved in the running of the business and therefore have access to information relating to business performance and prospects. There is therefore no need to worry about the signalling effect of dividends.

Green only distributes dividends when there are no profitable investment opportunities available (the residual theory of dividends). Until recently, shareholders have agreed with this policy, which implies they are confident that the funds will be invested at a higher rate within the business than they would have been able to achieve on their own.

Reasons for differences in dividend policies

The dividend policies of the two businesses should be expected to differ. **Blue** is concerned with **maintaining its share price**, which can be helped by maintaining a steady dividend payout rate. **Green** has no share price to protect and is more concerned with keeping the small number of **shareholders happy** (whilst at the same time maximising their value).

(b)   Modigliani and Miller's dividend irrelevance theory

Modigliani and Miller (MM) proposed that in a tax-free world, shareholders are **indifferent** between dividends and capital gains and value of the company is determined solely by the 'earning power' of its assets and investments.

MM argued that if a company decides to pay a dividend – meaning that there will be a shortfall in the funds available for profitable investments – this shortfall will be made up by obtaining additional funds from external sources. As a result of obtaining external finance rather than using retained earnings:

Loss of value in existing shares = Amount of dividend paid

The assumptions behind this theory are as follows.

(i)   A perfect market exists, meaning that no one investor has the power to influence market price significantly, and there are no transactions costs. As a result, an investor can increase income by selling shares, making the dividend payout ratio irrelevant.

(ii)   Investors are indifferent between income in the form of dividends and capital gains in the form of increased share price.

(iii)   Debt and equity are priced correctly by the market, making the availability of internal funds for investment irrelevant. Companies can obtain external funds to make up the shortfall in retained earnings caused by payment of dividends.

MM's theory implies that no one dividend policy is better for maximising shareholder value. This means that Blue and Green are free to choose whichever policy they prefer in order to pursue their objective of maximising the wealth of their shareholders.

Application of MM theory in reality

Unfortunately the assumptions that make the MM theory hold do not exist in reality. Shareholders will place some value on the ability to predict future dividends – that is, there is value to be gained from a stable dividend policy. There also tends to be a preference for either capital gains or income, particularly from a taxation point of view. Also, due to the existence of transactions costs in the sale of shares, investors may prefer to receive dividends rather than sell shares in order to obtain cash.

The MM theory does not allow for the fact that investors may buy shares in a certain company because of its dividend policy. Investors in Blue may rely on dividend payouts as a source of income and are therefore not indifferent to dividend payments or selling shares. They may also have been attracted by the low risk strategy that Blue takes towards dividend payouts.

There is no real market for Green's shares so the MM theory does not hold here. It would be extremely difficult for Green's shareholders to sell their shares to create an income stream therefore they are highly unlikely to be indifferent between dividends and selling shares.

(c) <u>Appropriate response to Blue directors</u>

It is important that Blue's directors and Green's directors act in the best interests of the shareholders, therefore they should find out the shareholders' preferences with regard to dividend payout.

An increase in the general level of dividends is one way of reducing Blue's surplus cash level. However other ways in which surplus cash could be reduced include the payment of a **one-off special dividend** or a **share repurchase**.

Special dividend

A one-off special dividend would be paid to all shareholders and may be particularly suitable for Blue. As well as solving the problem of surplus cash, it would also signal a high level of confidence in the company which would help to increase the share price.

A one-off special dividend would be unsuitable for Green as only one of the shareholders wishes to have a high dividend payout.

Share repurchase

A share repurchase gives individual shareholders the opportunity to take advantage of the company's offer to buy back their shares. It is a more flexible arrangement than one-off dividends (where shareholders do not have the choice to accept or reject the payment) and it likely to be the best alternative for Blue. Such a scheme will also lower the cost of future dividend payouts as there are less shares in issue on which dividends must be paid.

A share repurchase – if it can be arranged – is likely to be the best solution for Green's dividend dilemma. 90% of the shareholders are in favour of keeping the dividend policy as it is, therefore if they can be persuaded to buy some or all of Mr G's shares, Mr G will realise the cash he wants.

15 HJK

Text references. The three main financial management decisions – dividend, financing and investment – are covered in Chapter 1. Dividend policy is covered in Chapter 4. IPOs are dealt with in Chapter 5.

Top tips. The requirement in part (a) might have left you wondering what was actually required in your answer! You should look at the payout ratio for each year first and try to establish a pattern. Once you've got some figures you can start to evaluate any apparent policy that HJK employs. Remember that 'evaluation' does not just mean stating what is happening – you have to express an opinion on how suitable (or not) the current policy is.

Parts (b) and (c) are fairly generic, although be careful to relate your answer in part (c) to HJK's current approach to dividend policy.

Easy marks. Part (b) is quite straightforward and generic and you should be able to pick up quite a few marks in part (c) if you are familiar with the three main financial management decisions for a listed company.

Examiner's comments. This question was poorly attempted. Many candidates demonstrated weak knowledge of dividend policy and IPOs and/or were unable to apply their knowledge to the question scenario.

(a) <u>Evaluation of current dividend policy of HJK</u>

Year	Profit after interest and tax €m	Capital expenditure/investment in projects €m	Dividend paid €m	Payout ratio (as % of profit)
20X6	6	Nil	3	50%
20X7	7	10	2	29%
20X8	10	Nil	5	50%
20X9	11	15	2	18%
20Y0	16	Nil	8	50%

Given the figures above the current dividend policy appears to be as follows.

No investment takes place

When no investment or capital expenditure takes place, HJK pays out 50% of its profits after interest and tax as dividends.

Major investment or capital expenditure takes place

When major investment or capital expenditure takes place, HJK appears to pay out €2m regardless of the level of profit or the size of the investment.

Comments of current dividend policy

The current dividend policy appears to be quite **unstable** and does not give the shareholders a predictable level of income. Given that HJK is a private company, this is not surprising. Private companies' payout policies tend to be influenced by the needs of the company and the expectations of individual shareholders.

Shareholders are guaranteed a minimum payout of €2m but the maximum payout over the five year period has been €8m. The shareholders are apparently amenable to the policy of reinvesting all surplus cash above €2m in the business (assuming there are profitable investment opportunities available). Reinvesting in such profitable projects will **increase shareholders' wealth** and also reduces the need to depend on debt finance. This has the effect of keeping gearing ratios at a minimum, thus **reducing risk** and therefore the cost of capital.

(b) (i) The IPO process

An **Initial Public Offering** (IPO) is an invitation to the public to apply for shares in a company based on information contained in a prospectus. When a company goes public for the first time, a large issue usually takes the form of an IPO.

The shares will be issued by an **issuing house** (usually an investment bank although can sometimes be a firm of stockbrokers) which firstly acquires the shares. The issuing house will publish an invitation to the public to apply for shares, either at a fixed price (the **offer price**) or on a tender basis. When an offer for sale is made by tender, a **minimum price** is set and the public will be invited to tender for shares at prices equal to or above the minimum price. Shares are allotted at the highest price where all the shares will be taken up. This is known as the **striking price**.

(ii) Potential risks and actions to alleviate these risks

Not all shares will be taken up

This is the major risk of an IPO and can result in the IPO not raising sufficient funds for the company. If a minimum price was set, this price might have been considered too high by potential investors. Alternatively the economic outlook for the company may have deteriorated, discouraging investment, perhaps due to a general downturn in the industry or to adverse publicity.

The main action that can be taken to alleviate this risk is to have underwriters. This means that a third party will buy any outstanding shares. However this form of insurance can be very expensive and may also result in an immediate fall in the share price after the issue.

Oversubscription of shares

Whilst this may not seem to be a risk, it may mean that the price was set at too low a level and investors saw a bargain possibility. Although the company will not be short of funds – it is assumed that selling the entire pot of shares at the agreed price would raise the necessary funds – the company's reputation may be damaged.

The main way of avoiding such a problem would be to set a minimum price with a tender offer.

(c) Implications of a listing on dividend, financing and investment strategies

Dividend strategy

It was mentioned in part (a) that HJK's dividend payout policy seemed to be unstable. This instability is not acceptable for publicly listed companies – the market does not react well to unpredictability. Public

companies try to aim for a constant dividend payout ratio or a payout ratio that increases at a constant rate in line with growth in profits.

Dividend policy also acts as a signal to the markets regarding how the company views itself and its position. If dividend payout increases significantly, this may indicate to the market that there are fewer profitable investment opportunities available and the company is returning its excess cash to the shareholders. A privately owned company does not have this issue as its shareholders are usually very well informed about what is happening within the company. Signalling issues are another reason for **maintaining a stable dividend payout policy**.

The signalling effects of dividends can have an impact on the quoted share price. As the market prefers stable payouts, any unpredictable dividend behaviour may reduce confidence in the company and thus have an adverse effect on the share price.

The number of shareholders in a public company will be significantly greater than that of a private company. It is often the case that most shareholders will have similar expectations of dividend payout as they will have chosen to invest in a company that meets their expectations. **Large institutional investors** such as pension funds have a preference for stable payouts to allow them to plan their future cash flows.

As HJK's current dividend policy is unstable and unpredictable, the company will have to change its policy if it is to perform well on the Stock Exchange. Any changes in policy should be notified to the market as far in advance as possible.

Financing strategy

Listed companies have access to a much wider range of finance resources, both debt and equity. HJK's listing on the Stock Exchange will enable it to build up a credit reputation which will make it easier to raise future finance and at a more favourable rate. Once the IPO has allowed HJK to enter the Stock Exchange, further equity finance can be raised via much cheaper means, such as rights issues.

Investment strategy

HJK will have a much greater number of shareholders when it becomes a listed company and its every move will be **analysed by the market**. It is therefore essential that HJK makes the correct investment decisions that will maximise the wealth of its shareholders, otherwise its share price will be adversely affected. The effects of any potential investments on future performance should be notified to the market as soon as possible. The market does not like surprises and any unexpected results will be punished.

HJK will have access to additional sources of finance (see above) which should allow it to invest in more profitable projects in the future.

Interrelationship between dividend, financing and investment strategies

As with all listed companies, HJK's dividend, financing and investment strategies will be closely interrelated. Decisions will have to be taken regarding whether funds should be kept in the company for reinvestment purposes or paid out as dividends. Funds that are paid out as dividends are obviously not available for reinvestment, which means that HJK will either have to reduce the number of projects it invests in or increase its dependence on finance (either debt or equity).

If HJK reduces its possible investment activity, this means it will not be **maximising shareholder wealth** which could have a downward effect on share price. If greater dependence is placed on finance, this may increase gearing levels and thus perceived company risk. As a result, HJK may have to increase its cost of capital as debt becomes more expensive and equity holders expect higher returns from their investments.

For listed companies, there is a close link between the three strategies which has to be managed carefully to ensure that the companies perform to their maximum potential.

16 QRR

Text references. Dividend policy is covered in Chapter 4 and the efficient markets hypothesis in Chapter 5.

Top tips. Ensure that you cover both the efficient markets hypothesis and the reaction of the market to the news in part (a).

For part (b) you should have noted in the question that the typical shareholder holds 1,000 shares so base your calculations on this.

In part (c) make sure you consider the relative advantages and disadvantages of both options to QRR before making a recommendation.

Easy marks. You should be able to pick up a number of easy marks in part (b) when calculating shareholder wealth and also identifying alternative strategies in part (d).

Examiner's comments. Some candidates struggled on this question as a result of not understanding that a scrip issue is simply a transfer of capital and has no overall effect on the value of the organisation.

(a)   The effect of an announcement of no dividend to be paid will depend on the speed of the reaction and also how the market views the announcement.

Speed of reaction

The speed of the reaction will depend on the efficiency level, of which there are three types given by the **efficient markets hypothesis**.

If the market is **weak form efficient,** then any reaction from the market will be slow. The share price reacts slowly to new information released, as it only reflects past information.

In a **semi-strong form efficient** market the reaction will be instant because the share price reflects all publicly known information. As soon as the announcement is made the information will be public.

In a **strong form efficient** market the market will have already reacted to the zero dividend as all information is already reflected in the share price. As a result the public announcement will have no effect on the share price.

Markets are generally thought to be semi-strong form efficient and so it is expected that the market reaction to the announcement will be instant.

Reaction of the market

There are a number of factors that will influence whether the share price will go up or down, or perhaps remain unchanged.

Modigliani and Miller theorised that dividends simply transfer cash from being cash held by the company that the shareholders own to cash in the shareholders' own pockets. As a result the theoretical value of the company does not change and the **dividend policy** is **irrelevant** to the value of the company and therefore also to the share price. The theory, however, is based on perfect capital markets, which do not exist in real life.

In many markets, dividends are taken as a **signal of the prospects** of a company. Investors prefer dividends to be stable or increasing. Therefore a policy of paying regular dividends is adopted by many companies. As QRR has been paying regular quarterly dividends, the announcement that there will not be a dividend for a quarter may be taken as a sign of poor performance and investors may sell shares, causing the **share price to fall**.

However, the market will be aware of the **poor economic conditions** and the incoming capital and liquidity requirements. This should therefore be built into any expectations for dividends and as such a lower or zero dividend may already be **expected**. This would mean a much lower fall in the share price (or maybe no fall at all) as investors support the decision taken by management.

(b) (i) <u>Shareholder who accepts the shares</u>

A typical shareholder has 1,000 shares and therefore is entitled to 20 new shares (1,000/50 = 20)

However the total value of the company is unchanged, therefore the total value of the shares will also be unchanged.

1,000 shares at a share price of INR 396 is a total value of INR 396,000.

The revised share price is therefore expected to be

INR 396,000 / 1,020 = INR 388.24

(ii) <u>Shareholder who sells the rights</u>

The market price for selling the rights is INR 7 per existing share.

The typical shareholder will therefore receive INR 7,000 by selling the rights.

The value of 1,000 shares at the revised price is

1,000 × 388.24 = INR 388,240

Shareholder wealth will therefore be INR 395,240

The shareholder is marginally worse off by selling the rights. There may be a perception of increased value by selling the rights, but this does not take into account the corresponding fall in the share price.

Note: Arbitrage will mean that any difference between two options will be closed out, so that the shareholder would be largely indifferent between the options.

(c) Shareholders should be **indifferent** between a zero dividend and a scrip dividend and the value of QRR should be the same regardless of the choice made. However, the Board needs to understand fully how the market will react before making a choice.

For the reasons discussed in part (a), the market may already be expecting a change in the dividend policy due to the environment. In this case the market may react better to Director B's suggestion of a scrip dividend as investors will feel that they are getting something.

However, more sophisticated investors will realise that the scrip dividend will **not add any value** to their investment.

The scrip dividend does suffer from a number of **disadvantages** compared to a zero dividend. A scrip issue will mean QRR incurs the costs of issuing shares which a zero dividend would avoid. There will also be **more shares** in issue, which may increase the pressure for dividends in the future and the same level of dividend per share will become **more expensive** for QRR. A scrip dividend also **moves funds** from distributable to non-distributable reserves by increasing share capital. This means there are fewer reserves available for distribution as dividends at a later date.

Despite these disadvantages, scrip dividends have been used by a number of companies in order to give the impression that they are giving a payout to investors. Assuming that the administration costs are not significant, it is **recommended** that the scrip dividend option is chosen.

(d) <u>Alternative strategies to improve liquidity</u>

(i) Reduce the **cost base**. This may involve making staff redundant.

(ii) **Sell assets**. This could involve selling off under-used branches of the bank.

(iii) **Issue equity**. This may be through a new issue or a rights issue. Whether this would be successful depends upon the current market conditions. As noted earlier the increased number of shares may mean higher dividend payments in the future if QRR wants to maintain the same dividend per share.

(iv) **Issue debt.** The debt issue may be more successful than an equity issue, but will depend on the risk appetite of the investors.

17 XTA

(a)   Memorandum

To: Board of directors of XTA plc
From: Management Accountant
Date: 13 December 20X5

Rights issues versus placings

Rights issue

In a **rights issue,** existing shareholders are given the right to **subscribe to new shares** in the company at a given issue price. They can either action these rights or sell them to other parties. A **placing** can only be made if existing shareholders pass an **ordinary resolution** to allow it, but it opens the issue up to a wider potential shareholder base. In a placing a bank, or other agent acting on behalf of the company, arranges for a limited number of its clients or other contacts to subscribe for the new shares being issued by the company.

Advantages of rights issue vs placing

(i)   Existing shareholders need not fear that their **holdings** will be **diluted.**

(ii)   The **issue price** is **relatively unimportant** because shareholders who subscribe will end up with the same proportional shareholding and those who do not can sell their rights to make cash equivalent to any loss of value in their shareholding. With a placing, the **issue price** is **important:** if the price is too low, existing shareholders will lose out.

Disadvantages of rights issue vs placing

(i)   The number of potential subscribers to a rights issue is **limited** to the current shareholder base.

(ii)   A rights issue may be **more time-consuming, costly** and **complicated to arrange** than a placing. A placing is the **cheapest way** of issuing new equity shares because the costs of advertising, publicity and printing are much less than for rights issues or other forms of public issue.

Euro bank loan versus euro denominated eurobond

Euro bank loan

A **euro bank loan** is arranged directly from a bank and the **terms** (including the nature and pattern of interest payments and repayment of the principal) can be **tailored** to the exact needs of the borrower. Euro eurobonds are **loan certificates**, denominated in euros, issued by the company direct to lenders, who might be banks or large corporates. Issuing eurobonds can only be done if the company wishes to raise large amounts. They can be issued to **raise long term debt** (up to 20 years).

Advantages of Euro bank loans vs Eurobonds

(i)   Bank loans can be more **quickly arranged.**

(ii)   **Issue costs** are **not high.**

(iii)   Bank loans can be arranged on **flexible terms;** Eurobonds are **less versatile** in **interest and repayment schedules** than bank loans.

(iv)   **Syndicated credit arrangements** mean that there is **access to a wider pool** of **funds.**

(v)   Bank loans are **not dependent** on a good **credit rating**.

Disadvantages of Euro bank loans vs Eurobonds

(i)   The **amount of funds** banks are **prepared to advance** is limited and may be insufficient for larger investments.

(ii)   Bank loans **cannot be obtained for long maturities**: 5 years would be a long term.

(iii)   Eurobonds may be available at **lower costs of finance**.

(b)   New investment

The new investment costs £80 million, which at today's exchange rate, is €120 million.

There appear to be two possible scenarios for the pound/euro exchange rate, either it remains at £/€1.50 or strengthens to £/€2.00. For the sake of completeness we also need to consider what happens if the **pound weakens,** say to £/€1.20. The company has current long term gearing of debt/(debt + equity) = 150/400, ie 37.5%.

Mr A's proposal: Borrowing in sterling

Mr A is may be **incorrect** in saying that **borrowing in sterling** is **easier** than borrowing in euros Long-standing banking relationships should enable the company to borrow easily in euros in today's global markets.

However the sterling loan offers **no protection** against **currency risk.** As seen from the statement of financial position below the company is risking a **translation loss** of €20 million if the pound strengthens to £/€2.00. Although it would make an equivalent translation gain if the pound weakens, the company's embarrassment at a significant currency loss may weigh heavier than the advantage of a currency gain.

	€m	£m £/€1.50	£m £/€2	£m £/€1.20
UK assets		450	450	450
German assets	120	80	60	100
		530	510	550
Equity: original value		250	250	250
Equity: translation gain / (loss)		–	(20)	20
Long term £ borrowings		230	230	230
Current liabilities		50	50	50
		530	510	550

Under this method of financing we get the disadvantage of **no currency hedge,** and **gearing** is **highest** when the **euro weakens,** at 230/460 = 50%.

Mr B's proposal: Euro borrowings

Mr B is correct in thinking that the euro loan will help the company **avoid currency risk,** as seen from the statement of financial positions below. There is **no translation risk** because if the euro weakens, the declining value of the foreign assets is offset by the declining value of the euro loan.

The same consideration applies to **economic risk.** If the euro weakens, the declining stream of income from Germany will be offset by the reduced interest payments on the euro loan.

However, with Mr B's proposal **gearing** may still be a problem. Debt/(debt + equity) is highest if the **euro strengthens,** when it moves to 250/500 = 50%.

	€m	£/€1.50	£m £/€2	£/€1.20
UK assets		as above		
German assets				
Equity: original value		250	250	250
Equity: translation gain / (loss)		–	–	–
Long term £ borrowings		150	150	150
Long term € borrowings	120	80	60	100
Current liabilities		50	50	50
		530	510	550

Mr B is wrong in his last two statements. Borrowing in euros will not eliminate all currency risk. There can still be **short term transaction losses** which can create embarrassing losses if not properly hedged. Many aspects of **economic risk cannot be eliminated** by the matching investment-borrowing strategy.

Also the fact that **euro interest rates** have been **lower in the past** is **no guarantee** that they will **remain low.** And even if an interest rate remains low, **interest rate parity** will predict that the currency will strengthen and hence the repayment cost will be high.

Mr C's proposal: UK equity funding

Mr C is correct that equity funding is better if a project bears **high risk** because in the event of cash flow difficulties, **dividends** do not need to be paid, whereas interest does.

However, equity capital, like a sterling loan, **does not provide any hedge** against exchange rate risk and is thus inferior to the euro loan in this respect.

	£/€1.50	£m £/€2	£/€1.20
UK assets	as above		
Equity: original value	250	250	250
New equity finance	80	80	80
Equity: translation gain / (loss)	–	(20)	20
Long term £ borrowings	150	150	150
Current liabilities	50	50	50
	530	510	550

Gearing under this form of finance remains **relatively low,** rising to a maximum of 150/460 = 33% if currency losses are made.

Summary of gearing movements under the three forms of finance

In the figures below, gearing is measured by long term debt / (long term debt + equity). The starting value before investing in the project was 37.5%.

Currency movement	£/€1.50	£/€2	£/€1.20
A: Borrowing in sterling	48%	50%	46%
B: Borrowing in euros	48%	46%	50%
C: Equity funds	31%	33%	30%

Recommendation

The most appropriate form of finance would be **euro borrowings, raised by the German subsidiary** to the extent that it is possible. The parent company will need to give a **guarantee** if the assets of the German subsidiary are insufficient as security for the loan.

If borrowing restrictions prevent the full amount being raised as a euro loan, the balance should be raised using **equity funds** (a rights issue).

18 DCD

Text references. Rights issues are dealt with in Chapter 5.

Top tips. Make sure you use the correct formula for calculating the yield-adjusted TERP. It is not the formula that is given in the formula sheet.

In part (b) the option of 'if any' discount rate should be recommended is irrelevant – a rights issue will normally be set at a discount otherwise investors would just buy the shares at the prevailing market price in the market.

Your answer to part (d) should focus on the information given in the question rather than just a generic list of potential factors.

Easy marks. Calculating the terms of the rights issue offers some straightforward marks and if you can remember the formula for yield-adjusted TERP you should be able to pick up some marks in (a)(ii).

Examiner's comments. In part (a) many candidates did not calculate a yield-adjusted TERP. Those who attempted it often used an incorrect basis for the adjustment in returns.

In part (c), discussions of the directors' views were often confused and even contradicted or made no reference to the calculations attempted in part (b).

Part (d) was left unanswered by a number of candidates.

(a) (i) <u>Terms of the rights issue</u>

25% discount:

Rights price = 75% of $6.00 = $4.50

Number of shares required to raise $250m = 55.6m

Terms of the rights issue = 140m/55.6m = 1 rights issue share for every 2.5 shares (or 2 for 5)

The terms are thus: 'a 2 for 5 rights issue at $4.50 per share'

40% discount:

Rights price = 60% of $6.00 = $3.60

Number of shares required to raise $250m = 69.4m

Terms of the rights issue = 140m/69.4m = 1 rights issue share for every 2 shares

The terms are thus: 'a 1 for 2 rights issue at $3.60 per share'

(ii) <u>Yield adjusted TERP</u>

25% discount:

$$\text{Yield-adjusted TERP} = \left[\frac{\text{Cum rights price} \times N}{(N+1)}\right] + \left[\frac{\text{Issue price}}{(N+1)} \times \frac{\text{Yield on new funds}}{\text{Yield on existing funds}}\right]$$

Yield-adjusted TERP = [(6 x 2.5)/(2.5 + 1)] + [(4.5/[2.5 + 1]) x (0.2/0.15)]

Yield-adjusted TERP = $6

40% discount:

Yield-adjusted TERP = [(6 x 2)/(2 + 1)] + [(3.6/[2 + 1]) x (0.2/0.15)] = $5.60

(b) <u>Likely impact of proposed project and related rights issue</u>

Current shareholding = 100 shares

25% discount:

Number of shares that can be purchased under rights issue with 100 existing shares = 100/2.5 = 40

Shareholder's wealth = 140 shares x TERP ($6) = $840

Current wealth = 100 x $6 = $600

$$\text{Value of a right} = \frac{\text{Theoretical ex-rights price} - \text{Issue price}}{N}$$

Value of a right = (6.00 – 4.50) = $1.50

If the shareholder purchased the rights and then sold them, he would make a gain of 40 x $1.50 = $60

40% discount:

Number of shares that can be purchased under rights issue with 100 existing shares = 100/2 = 50

Shareholder's wealth = 150 shares x TERP ($5.60) = $840

Current wealth = 100 x $6 = $600

Value of a right = (5.60 – 3.60) = $2

If the shareholder purchased the rights and then sold them, he would make a gain of 50 x $2 = $100

However there is also a capital loss of $0.40 on the existing shares = $0.40 × 100 = $40.

The overall gain is therefore $100 – $40 = $60 so shareholder wealth is unaffected by this

(c) Appropriate discount for the rights issue

We will consider the concerns raised by each of the Directors.

Director A

Director A is concerned that a 40% discount will have an adverse effect on shareholder wealth and therefore would prefer the lower discount of 25%.

From the calculations above, it can be shown that the choice of discount rate **makes no difference to shareholder wealth** based on the theoretical ex-rights prices.

The 40% discount rate may prove more popular as far as take-up is concerned which means that more shares will enter the market. This will probably mean a fall in share price as there are more shares in issue and these were issued at a discount.

The choice of discount rate **should be irrelevant** to shareholder wealth, but it will depend on the market's reaction to the issue as the **actual and theoretical ex-rights prices are not necessarily the same**.

Director B

Director B recommends the higher discount of 40% as she believes this will improve take-up of the rights issue.

Whilst this is possibly the case it must be borne in mind that a lower price will mean more shares having to be issued in order to raise the required capital (69.4m rather than 55.6m). This will result in a dilution in earnings per share which shareholders may not be happy with.

The advantage of a higher discount is that **underwriting costs are likely to be lower** as there is more likelihood that shareholders will take up their rights. This means that less funds will have to be paid out of existing funds to cover these costs.

Director C

Director C is concerned about the impact of the rights issue on dividend policy.

A 25% discount will result in 55.6m new shares whilst a 40% discount will result in 69.4m new shares (assuming the rights issue is fully taken up).

No information has been given about the dividend payout therefore we have to look at the company's predicted future performance to determine whether the dividend policy is likely to be sustainable.

It is predicted that DCD will continue to increase its revenues in future years due to increased demand which therefore suggests that **earnings attributable to shareholders will also increase**. If dividends were, for example, 10 cents per share, DCD would have to find an additional $5.56m per annum if the 25% discount rights issue was fully taken up ($6.94m per annum for a fully subscribed 40% discount issue). It will be for the directors to decide whether they think this annual increase is sustainable.

Recommendation

Rights issues are normally made at a discount otherwise the shareholders will be unlikely to buy (as they can purchase shares at the current market price on the stock market). It is therefore recommended that a 25% discount is offered. This will encourage shareholders to take up the offer but will not result in so many new shares being issued (thus protecting the EPS). Fewer new shares means less strain on the sustainability of the current dividend policy.

In addition the Yield-Adjusted TERP at a 25% discount is the same as the current share price therefore there will be no adverse effect on shareholder value.

(d)   Factors that are likely to affect share price before and after the planned press statement

Before the press statement

Prior to the press statement being made, DCD's share price is likely to be affected by its rapid growth in demand and expectations that revenue will continue to grow in the foreseeable future. Its share price has risen by 11% in the last three months based on similar performance and it may be **reasonable to expect that this will continue**.

The increase in share price could be due to a number of different factors, such as general economic conditions, confidence in the industry or speculation about future investments.

However there is the issue of the current manufacturing facilities operating at close to full capacity. As the market is unaware that investment in new facilities is planned, there may be a feeling that DCD **cannot sustain its rapid growth** which could have a downward effect on the share price.

After the press statement

When a rights issue is announced the share price generally falls. This is due to uncertainties in the market about the consequences of the issue for future profits, earnings and dividends.

However the announcement that investment in new manufacturing facilities is being made may have a positive effect on share price as the market will see this as an indication that past growth trends can continue. The announcement of higher expected returns due to greater efficiency of the new facilities is also likely to have a positive effect on share price.

The extent to which the share price will be affected in the 12 months following the announcement of the rights issue will depend on the efficiency of the market, the degree to which the market supports the rights issue and the extent to which the market agrees with the company's evaluation of project benefits. Markets are generally assumed to be **semi-strong** therefore will react immediately to information when it is made public.

If the rights issue is made at a 40% discount this may signal to the market that DCD is not confident of raising sufficient interest at a lower discount rate. The market could see this as a panic measure and pass this sentiment onto investors, which could cause the share price to fall.

19   EFG

Text references. Debt finance is covered in Chapter 6.

Top tips. Set out your calculations clearly and make sure you recommend the most appropriate financing instrument in part (a).

Easy marks. The calculations are quite straightforward if you are well prepared and the discussion in part (b) requires general financial knowledge and common sense.

Examiner's comments. This was the least popular question on the paper but those who attempted it tended to score well on the calculations.

(a) Workings

Conversion value of convertible bond

Current market price = $15
Share price in 5 years = $15 × $(1.1)^5$ = $24.16
Conversion value = 5 shares for each $100 nominal @ $24.16 = $120.80
Capital gain = $(24.16 – 15) = $9.16
Yield = $(120.8/100)^{1/5}$ – 1 = 3.85%

Yield to maturity of five-year unsecured bond

Year	Cash flow $	Discount factor 5%	Present value $	Discount factor 7%	Present value $
0	(94)	1.000	(94.00)	1.000	(94.00)
1–5	5	4.329	21.64	4.100	20.50
5	100	0.784	78.40	0.713	71.30
		NPV	6.04	NPV	(2.20)

$$\text{Yield to maturity} = 5\% + \left(\frac{6.04}{(6.04 + 2.20)}\right) \times 2\% = 6.47\%$$

Response to Sr A

The bank loan is indeed more expensive than the unsecured bond, but not by as much as might have been expected. The true cost of the bond is given by its **yield to maturity**, which is 6.47%, compared to the 7% annual interest rate of the bank loan. The yield to maturity allows for the **time value** of money and is effectively the internal rate of return of the cash flows. However, the bond may have **issue costs** which need to be accounted for.

Response to Sr B

The coupon rate on the convertible bond is 4.5% and does look to be the cheapest form of borrowing. However, the predicted share price increase of 10% per annum would create a $9.16 **capital gain** on each bond after 5 years. This is equivalent to an additional yield of 3.85% per annum and makes the bond significantly **more expensive** than the alternative structures. Furthermore, the shares created on conversion will be entitled to dividends, increasing further the cost of capital.

Response to Sr C

A straight equity issue is **unlikely to succeed** due to the influence of major institutional shareholders, and so would generate less funds and incur heavy underwriting costs. The convertible bond will be more attractive to investors as they can make the decision whether or not to convert after reviewing the entity's performance over the next 5 years. EFG benefits from **lower finance costs** for 5 years.

In conclusion, the convertible bond is the most appropriate type of finance structure for a **rapidly growing** entity such as EFG. It will benefit from lower finance costs for 5 years and can hopefully increase its equity base at the end of this period.

(b) An unsecured bond is **riskier** than a secured loan as it does not carry a charge on assets. The investor will therefore benefit from a higher rate of interest to compensate for the increased risk but will need to obtain information on the following.

- Purpose of the loan – does the business plan seem reasonable? Are the revenues and costs forecast realistic?
- Amount of finance needed – is this high relative to the financial resources of the borrower?
- Repayment terms – is this in instalments or a lump sum at the end of the bond?
- Time period – the longer the term of the bond, the higher the risk.

Further analysis to be undertaken will include:

- Ratio analysis of gearing, liquidity, interest cover, dividend cover
- Free cash flow
- Risk analysis of the business and the markets it operates in
- The credit rating of the company

20 DDD

Text references. Debt finance is covered in Chapter 6. The capital structure decision is discussed in Chapter 9.

Top tips. Do **NOT** assume in (a) that the cost of debt is 7% for Alternative 1, and a weighted average of 5% and 10% for Alternative 2. You need to do an internal rate of return calculation for both. 7% is a reasonable starting point for the calculation in Alternative 1, and you can use the same two test rates in Alternative 2 as the answers are unlikely to be very far apart. Don't forget the tax! You would probably say that by inspection the IRR for Alternative 1 is close to 6% and for Alternative 2 it is close to 5%. This would mean you would avoid the interpolation calculations and save time.

Easy marks. The IRR calculation hopefully provided you remembered to use it because the debt is **redeemable**.

Examiner's comments. Although (a) was answered quite well, some answers were plainly unrealistic, for example costs of debt over 50%. Other candidates:

- Treated the debt as irredeemable
- Ignored tax
- Failed to calculate the cost of debt as a percentage return
- Took a mean average of the two instruments

Answers to (b) were poor, with discussions not being adequately focused on the circumstances of the question. Candidates failed to question the use of retained profits when there was an obvious lack of cash in the statement of financial position. Other points that were not adequately considered included:

- The size of the project in relation to existing operations
- The need for additional finance
- The effect on gearing
- Risk
- The efficient market hypothesis
- Dividend yield
- How to adjust the returns on capital

(a) <u>Alternative 1</u>

Year		Cash flow £'000	Discount factor 7%	PV £'000	Discount factor 5%	PV £'000
0	Bond issue (£30m×0.95)	(28,500)	1.000	(28,500)	1.000	(28,500)
1–5	Interest (£30m × 7% × 70%)	1,470	4.100	6,027	4.329	6,364
5	Repayment	30,000	0.713	21,390	0.784	23,520
				(1,083)		1,384

Using the IRR Formula : Cost of capital $= a + \left[\dfrac{NPV_a}{NPV_a - NPV_b} \times (b-a) \right]$

Cost of capital $= 5 + \dfrac{(1,384(7-5))}{1,384 - (-1,083)}$

$= 6.12\%$

<u>Alternative 2</u>

Year		Cash flow £'000	Discount factor 7%	PV £'000	Discount factor 5%	PV £'000
0	Loan	(28,500)	1.000	(28,500)	1.000	(28,500)
1-3	Interest (£28.5 m × 5% × 70%)	998	2.624	2,619	2.723	2,718
4-6	Interest (£28.5 m × 10% × 70%)	1,995	2.143*	4,275	2.353*	4,694
6	Repayment	28,500	0.666	18,981	0.746	21,261
				(2,625)		173

* Cumulative discount factor years 4 – 6 =

Cumulative discount factor years 1–6 – Cumulative discount factor years 1–3

For 7%, 4.767 − 2.624 = 2.143

For 5%, 5.076 − 2.723 = 2.353

$$\text{Cost of capital} = 5 + \frac{(173(7-5))}{173+2,625}$$

$$= 5.12\%$$

The bank loan has the lower cost of debt.

<u>Other factors to be considered</u>

<u>Arrangement costs</u>

DDD will incur **issue costs** if it issues the bonds, whereas the arrangement fees for the bank loan should be much smaller.

<u>Cash flow during the loan period</u>

The bank loan requires a **lower rate of interest** during the **first three years** of the loan, and **higher interest** subsequently. This pattern of payments may match better with the income from the new garden centres, lower in the first few years and higher subsequently as their customer base builds up.

<u>Repayment of loan capital</u>

DDD will need **sufficient funds** for repayment of the capital at the end of the period of the loans. The extra year it has to raise funds to repay the bank loan may be significant.

<u>Renewal</u>

DDD's directors should consider whether there is a **possibility of renewal** of either or both loans, and if so what the terms are likely to be.

<u>Security</u>

Security is likely to be required both on the **bonds** and on the **bank loan**. The directors should take into account the nature of the security demanded, and whether any **onerous restrictions** will be placed on DDD's ability to operate as a result of giving the security.

(b) To: Board
From: Treasury department
Date: 22 May 20X3
Subject: Financing of new garden centres

<u>Introduction</u>

The purpose of this memo is to discuss the various **financing options** that have been put forward to fund the **very significant expenditure** of £28.5 million on the planned new centres. The expenditure is almost equal to current net assets. It is assumed that the finance required is £28.5 million, In practice additional finance may be needed to fund further fittings and equipment purchases, but it is assumed that existing sources such as current cash balances or extension of trade credit can be used to finance these.

(i)   <u>Chief Executive's comments</u>

<u>Gearing</u>

Assuming the market value of debt in the statement of financial position is equal to its book value, the company's current gearing on market values can be calculated as $\dfrac{\text{Loans}}{\text{Loans} + \text{Share capital}}$

ie $\dfrac{24}{(10 \times 6) + 24} = 29\%$

Assuming £28.5 million is raised from a share issue, gearing would fall to:

$$\frac{24}{(10 \times 6) + 24 + 28.5} = 21\%$$

The fall in gearing would mean that DDD's **financial risk** would fall. This may be desirable because currently the security provided, land and buildings, is only just greater than long-term loans (£26.5 million versus £24 million). A decrease in financial risk might also be weighed against a **possible increase in overall business risk**, because the investment involves some diversification into new products.

Level of share price

The chief executive's comments appear to imply that share prices may go up or down at any time, that the market is not very rational. If however the stock market is efficient, share prices will be influenced by available information about a company's **future prospects**. Hence if the market believed that the expansion would lead to greater profits, shares would not lose their value for that reason.

Dividend yield

Dividend yield is the dividend expressed as a % of the share's market price, representing the shareholder's rate of return. However the dividend yield is measured using **current dividends**, not the future dividends that will be important for this project. Also the dividend yield does not reflect the **total reward** that may be demanded by shareholders, since they may also require a **capital gain**. In addition for shareholders **equity finance** is not necessarily **low risk**; it would carry a higher risk than providing **debt finance**.

(ii)   Non-executive director's comments

Issue costs and uncertainty

The director is right in stating that use of internal sources will **avoid issue costs**. He is also correct in raising the issue of **uncertainty**; however as DDD is an established, listed company whose share price has recently risen significantly, it should be possible to raise the external finance required on reasonable terms.

Use of retained profits

However the director has misunderstood the nature of retained profits. Retained profits **do not reflect cash balances** that can be drawn on for capital expenditure; they reflect the amount of equity capital tied up in the whole business, not just cash. The business only has £1 million, not £20 million, surplus cash.

Sale of least profitable garden centres

Certainly a sale of garden centres would raise some cash. However a sale of the least profitable centres is **unlikely to raise much cash**, because of their poor current performance. Sale will also involve **transaction costs**. Sale of a number of centres might mean that overall the company has **less long-term assets** to secure debt.

(iii)   Finance director's comments

Gearing

If more debt is issued, gearing would rise from 29% to:

$$\frac{24+28.5}{(10\times6)+24+28.5}=47\%$$

This will mean **increased financial risk**, along with the possible **increase in business risk**. The security that the company provides compared with the debt it has will also not improve.

Return on investment

There appears to be a confusion in the finance director's remarks between the **investment** decision and the **financing** decision. To establish whether it is worthwhile to open the new garden centres, DDD should **appraise** the future returns using a **weighted average cost of capital (WACC)** based on the different costs of all the sources of finance the company uses. WACC should be calculated using a **revised cost of equity** that takes account of the increases in business and financial risk. The **cost of other forms of debt** may also rise because of the increased risks.

Cost of debt

The cost of debt capital should be compared with the costs of other sources of finance (equity shares). In addition (as illustrated in (a)) there is no single cost that applies to all types of debt. **Different forms of debt** themselves have **different costs**.

21 DEF

Text references. Equity finance is covered in Chapter 5.

Top tips. This is a purely discussion question and you will need to have plenty of knowledge to be able to write sufficiently detailed answers. Make sure you answer the specific requirement of each part of the question and don't go off on a random waffle!

Easy marks. Use of your general financial knowledge and common sense will earn you some marks.

Examiner's comments. Common errors included not discussing challenges; not making a recommendation; not relating the answer to DEF.

(a)   Pursuing an IPO

An initial public offer (IPO) is a means of selling the shares of a company to the public at large. It entails the acquisition by **an issuing house** of a large block of shares of a company with a view to offering them for sale to the public and investing institutions.

The value of DEF can be estimated using the average P/E for the industry of 14, at **€700 million** (14 × €50m) and using discounted cash flow at **€500 million** (€50m/0.1). No attempt has been made recently to value the current shares but this does amount to a significant amount of money that would be raised by the IPO.

Advantages

Realisation of investment

The **current shareholders** of DEF will be able to realise their investment and will become instantly much wealthier individuals on paper. They could then sell their shares to obtain funds for other projects or investments. European stock markets are currently buoyant so this is an opportunity to maximise the value of their holdings.

Prestige

A publicly listed company enjoys **greater prestige** and an enhanced public image. This could help DEF to compete in the highly competitive telecommunications industry where any competitive advantage is vital.

Finance opportunities

A public listing will provide **access to a wider pool of finance** for fund investments and it would be easier to **seek growth through acquisition** of other companies. DEF is currently much smaller than most of its customers and direct rival and may need to grow in order to survive.

Disadvantages

Formality

There will be significantly greater **public regulation, accountability** and **scrutiny.** The legal requirements DEF faces will be greater and the company will also be subject to the rules of the stock exchange on which its shares are listed. This will be costly in terms of administrative systems and auditing required.

Cost

There are also **additional costs** associated with making share issues, including brokerage commissions and underwriting fees. The planning of an IPO is a lengthy procedure which **diverts management effort**.

Investor requirements

A **wider circle of investors** with more exacting requirements will hold shares and may be more interested in short-term gain rather than the long-term future of the company. A public listing also makes DEF much

more **susceptible to a takeover**, particularly as it is so much smaller than most of its customers and its direct rival.

Challenges

Share price

The hardest aspect of organising an IPO is **deciding on the share price** and this could prove particularly challenging for DEF.

Gearing

Gearing is currently high at 80% using book values and this increases the **financial risk** of the company for prospective investors. This could mean that the value of the company is less than anticipated.

Profit volatility

Revenue and profits have been **volatile** and this again will impact on the perceived risk of the company from an investor's point of view.

Future stock market trends

There is no guarantee that the stock market will continue to be buoyant and the IPO could be hit if there was a sudden downturn.

Recommendation

It is recommended that DEF goes ahead with the IPO as market conditions and the performance of the company are currently favourable to obtaining the best possible price.

(b)   Investment bank

The investment bank acts as the **issuing house** and acquires the shares, either as a direct allotment from the company or by purchase from the existing members. It also acts as the **sponsor** of the issue and provides assurance to the regulatory authorities that all obligations have been met.

The investment bank will be responsible for the issuing of the **prospectus.** A **prospectus** is a legal document used to describe the securities being offered. It provides investors with material information such as a description of the company's business, financial statements and biographies of officers and directors.

The investment bank will usually also act as the **underwriter** of the issue. This means it takes on the risk of distributing the securities. Should it not be able to find enough investors, then it may end up holding some securities itself.

Stockbroker

The role of the stockbroker overlaps with that of the investment bank and they may well **work in tandem**.

The stockbroker usually advises on the **pricing** and **timing** of the issue taking into consideration the **market conditions.** The stockbroker is responsible for **selling the shares to institutional clients.** This can involve making presentations and other marketing strategies.

The broker will also decide on the **allocation of shares** if the issue is over-subscribed.

Potential institutional investors

Institutional investors are institutions which have **large amounts of funds** which they want to invest in shares or other assets which offer satisfactory returns and security, for example, pension funds, insurance companies and unit trusts. It is likely that the vast majority of the shares will be sold to these institutions.

An **analyst** within an institutional investment organisation will review the IPO and decide if the investor wants to participate. The order for shares will then be passed through the broker.

DEF's Treasury Department

Two of the roles of the Treasury Department are **funding management** and **corporate finance.** Initially this involves deciding **how much finance is needed** and how much of this should be in the form of **equity**.

The Treasury Department will then be responsible for obtaining the stock exchange listing and will **liaise** with the investment bank and stockbrokers. It will also need to ensure that there is **full disclosure of relevant information**.

Employees of the Treasury Department will be expected to be informed experts in corporate finance, and responsible for ensuring that the IPO is a success as far as DEF is concerned.

(c)   Private placing

A placing is an arrangement where the shares are not offered to the public, but instead, the issuing house arranges for most of the issue to be bought by a small number of investors, usually institutional investors. This method has become increasingly popular but placing permission may not be granted by the stock exchange authorities if the issue is too large.

The **advantage** is that a placing is **cheaper** and **quicker to arrange** than an IPO as it involves less marketing and administration. It is also likely to involve **less disclosure of information.**

The **disadvantage** is that most of the shares will be placed with a **relatively small number of institutional shareholders** and most of the shares are unlikely to be available for trading after the flotation. This means that it is these institutional shareholders who will have **control of the company** and they may not have the same objectives as the existing management. The **price obtained** may also be less than a public offer for sale.

Public offer for sale

Fixed price

As stated above, the stockbroker will decide on a **fixed price** for the shares based on current market conditions. The danger is that **market conditions will change** and either, the shares will not all be taken up if the price is too high or, a higher price could have been obtained. The former situation would be less of a problem for DEF as the underwriter will take up any unallocated shares at the original fixed price.

Tender

Potential investors are invited to **name the price** that they are willing to pay. DEF would name a **reserve price** as a minimum below which the shares cannot be sold. The investor therefore knows the lowest selling price. The price at which the shares are issued is the **highest price** that will dispose of all the shares.

The pricing of shares of companies that have not previously had a quotation is very difficult and the **advantage** of a tender offer is that it leaves the fixing of the price to the public which may be more beneficial for DEF.

The **disadvantage** of this type of issue is that is more expensive due to the extra costs of administration and marketing.

Recommendation

It is recommended that DEF use the method of a **public offer for sale at a fixed price**. This will avoid giving too much control to a limited number of institutional investors.

22   Gregory

> **Text references.** Rights issues are covered in Chapter 5. Share repurchases are covered in Chapter 4.
>
> **Top tips.** Remember to include the payment from underwriters in the 'do not take up rights' calculation. You are given the TERP formula in the exam so your calculations in (a)(ii) should be made easier. In part (b) don't be tempted to give a generic answer when discussing the relative advantages of share repurchases and special dividends – George does have specific requirements re cost of capital and balance of share ownership so make sure your answer relates to the specific scenario.
>
> **Easy marks.** There are easy marks to be gained in part (a) (particularly (i) and (ii)).

(a)   (i)   Number of ordinary shares to be issued under rights issue

Discounted price = 80% of 458p = 366.4p

Number of shares to be issued = £29.3m/366.4p = 8 million

(ii)   Theoretic ex-rights price (TERP)

$$\text{TERP} = \frac{1}{N+1}\left[(N \times \text{cum rights price}) + \text{issue price}\right]$$

Cum rights price = 458c

Issue price = 366.4c

Number of shares required to 'buy' one new share (N) = 40m/8m = 5

TERP = [1/(5 + 1)] x [(5 x 458c) + 366.4c] = 442.7c

(iii) Expected trading price for the rights

= TERP – discounted issue price

= 442.7c – 366.4c

= 76.3c

(iv) Impact on personal wealth of shareholder Mr X

Mr X has the chance to take up 40,000 (200,000/5) discounted shares

Does not take up the rights

> **Tutorial note**: Assume that the underwriters will pay Mr X the expected trading price of the rights – that is 76.3p per share.

Value of shareholding

	€
Current shareholding at TERP (200,000 x 442.7c)	885,400
Add payment from underwriters (40,000 x 76.3c)	30,520
Total	915,920

Takes up the rights

Value of shareholding

	€
Total shares at TERP (240,000 x 442.7c)	1,062,480
Less cost of purchase (40,000 x 366.4c)	(146,560)
Total	915,920

Sells sufficient rights to pay for remaining rights

Trading price of rights = 76.3c

Number of rights to be purchased = (76.3/442.7) x 40,000 = 6,894

> **Alternative method**
>
> Sell X rights
>
> 76.3X = 366.4 x (40,000 – X)
>
> 76.3X = 14,656,000 – 366.4X
>
> 442.7X = 14,656,000
>
> X = 33,104
>
> This means that Mr X would purchase 6,894 shares

Value of shareholding

	€
(200,000 + 6,894) x 442.7	915,920

Discussion of impact on personal wealth of Mr X

The theoretical results for each scenario are the same. In practice they are likely to be slightly different, due to the following factors.

Price received from underwriters

The price received from underwriters was assumed to be the same as the expected trading price (77 cents). However in practice this may be slightly lower than the expected trading price as the payment from the underwriters is made from a residual pool of funds. This pool may not be sufficient to cover the

full 77 cents per share, particularly if the rights issue failed and the underwriters were left with numerous unsold rights.

Price of rights in the market

The actual market price of the rights will be driven by market forces. The price obtained by Mr X will depend on how the market forces move in response to the rights issue and how popular the rights issue proves to be.

(b)   <u>Share repurchase v one-off special dividend</u>

Current level of gearing

	€m
Debt (37 – 7)	30.0
Equity	70.0
Total debt + equity	100.0
Gearing (30/100)	30%

If the surplus cash is used to repurchase shares or pay a special dividend:

Revised level of gearing

	€m
Debt	37.0
Equity (70 – 7)	63.0
Total debt + equity	100.0
Gearing (30/100)	37%

Insufficient information is available to determine whether the change in gearing would affect George's cost of capital. If George is not approaching his maximum debt capacity and the revised level of gearing (37%) is still on the downward slope of the WACC curve, then cost of capital is likely to fall.

Advantages of share repurchase

(i)   It leads to an increase in earnings per share by reducing the number of shares in issue. This should lead to an increase in the share price and George should be able to pay a higher dividend per share in the future.

(ii)   If George does not wish to pay a higher dividend to remaining shareholders, he will not need as much cash to pay the current dividend rate to these shareholders.

(iii)   George has managed to increase his level of gearing without having to increase his total long-term funding.

(iv)   The money that George's shareholders receive from the share repurchase will be taxed at the capital gains tax rate, which may be lower than the income tax rate.

(v)   A share repurchase scheme will reduce the possibility of a takeover as there is less cash on the balance sheet.

<u>Advantages of one-off special dividend over share repurchase</u>

(i)   Payment of a special dividend is easier to arrange than a share repurchase.

(ii)   There is no change in the balance of ownership for existing shareholders (assuming that they had the choice of whether to sell their shares in a share repurchase scheme).

(iii)   Like the share repurchase scheme, the payment of a special dividend will reduce the possibility of a takeover as the surplus cash on the balance sheet has been used up.

<u>Conclusion</u>

If George still wants the balance of share ownership to remain unchanged, the use of a special dividend to reduce surplus cash is preferable. However the final decision will depend on the consideration of the above factors and shareholder preferences.

23 RED

> **Text references**. Placings and IPOs are covered in Chapter 5 whilst bond issues are dealt with in Chapter 6. Efficient market hypothesis and its three forms are covered in Chapter 5.
>
> **Top tips**. It is very tempting in this question to simply write everything you know about private placings and public issues but forget to relate your answer to the scenario. As with all F3 exam questions, you are expected to apply your knowledge to particular situations and this is no exception. Don't forget to provide advice based on your comparison of the two methods and bear in mind that the question relates to bond issue rather than share issue.
>
> Part (b)(i) has a descriptive requirement but don't write too much – remember it is only worth 4 marks.
>
> You might find yourself struggling with (b)(ii). Use some common sense in this part of the question – just ask yourself what would normally contribute to higher share prices (good financial performance for one thing) and consider what you would have to do to increase the likelihood of persuading investors to take up a share offer. If you don't get too bogged down with technicalities it sometimes makes answering such questions less daunting.
>
> **Easy marks**. You should be able to pick up easy marks in part (b)(i) as you should be familiar with the different forms of market efficiency. If you are familiar with private placings and IPOs, part (a) should also give some easy marks.
>
> **Examiner's comments**. There was a lack of in-depth knowledge of the process involved in a public and private placement of bonds and issues affecting the success of an IPO. Many candidates also struggled with the impact of the efficient market hypothesis.

(a)   Features of a private placing and a public issue of bonds

Private placing

If a private placing of bonds is made, this means that the bonds are not offered to the public. The bonds will instead be 'placed' with (generally) institutional investors such as pension funds and insurance companies by an issuing house (normally a stockbroker). A private placing of bonds is cheaper than a public issue and also quicker. There is likely to be less risk attached to a private placing as the stockbroker will not go ahead with the placing unless there is a high degree of certainty that the institutional investors will subscribe to the issue.

Public issue

A public issue of bonds will involve the issuing house acquiring the bonds and offering them for sale to the public, either at a fixed price or on a tender basis. The issuing house will publish an invitation to the public to apply for the bonds and may have to use underwriters if it is uncertain that the offer will be successful.

If the offer is over-subscribed it will be scaled down on a basis that will have been determined before the offer was made public.

Advantages of a private placing for RED

(i)   **Cost**. As mentioned above, a private placing is likely to be much cheaper than a public issue. There are no underwriting costs and no expensive 'roadshows' that will be necessary with a public issue.

(ii)   **Speed**. A private placing is much quicker than a public issue as there are fewer investors involved and interest will have been established prior to the placing being made.

(iii)   **Availability of interested parties**. RED is a family company that may not be sufficiently well known to generate enough interest for a public issue to be successful. A private placing has the advantage of targeting a small number of large investors rather than trying to raise interest from a large number of smaller investors.

Advantages of a public issue

(i)   The only real advantage of a relatively expensive and slow public issue would be added exposure to the markets prior to the IPO. If RED held roadshows to support the public offering, these will raise awareness of the company and hopefully heighten the possibility of a successful IPO.

Recommendation to the directors of RED

Given the above evaluation, a private placing appears to be more suitable for RED. This approach is likely to be more successful for an unlisted company that has limited or no market exposure. It will help to raise the company's profile prior to the planned IPO.

(b)   (i)   The three forms of efficient market hypothesis

Weak form efficiency

Under the **weak form hypothesis** of market efficiency, share prices reflect all available information about past changes in the share price. As new information will arrive unexpectedly any changes in share prices will occur in a random fashion. Using technical analysis to predict the share price will not give anyone an advantage as the information on which the analysis is based is already reflected in the share price.

Semi-strong form efficiency

If the market displays **semi-strong form efficiency**, current share prices will reflect:

(1) all relevant information about past price movements and their implications, and

(2) all knowledge which is publicly available

This means that individual investors cannot 'beat the market' by reading newspapers or annual reports as the information contained in these will already be reflected in the share price.

Strong form efficiency

If a market displays a **strong form of efficiency**, this means that share prices will reflect **all** information whether publicly available or not. This includes information

(1) from past price changes

(2) from public knowledge or anticipation

(3) from specialists' or experts' insider knowledge

This form of the theory is difficult to test as the use of insider knowledge to influence share prices ('insider trading') is illegal in many countries.

The form that is most likely to apply in practice is the **semi-strong form**.

(ii)   Steps to improve the chances of a successful IPO issue

Carefully timed communication

It is important to plan the **timing of information** to potential investors. If the timing is wrong then the issuing house may not get the interest it was expecting (perhaps due to prevailing market conditions) which will jeopardise the success of the IPO.

Choice of issue price

The issue price should be slightly below the perceived market value. If it is set too high, there will be **insufficient interest** from potential investors. If the issue is under-priced then current shareholders will suffer.

Underwriting

Underwriting may be put in place to remove the risk of the issue being under-subscribed. The underwriters will buy the outstanding shares at the issue price. However this service is **expensive**.

Timing with respect to new product development

The greater the perception that the new product will be successful, the more likely it is that the IPO will also be successful. It is therefore important to time the issue at a point where the new product is sufficiently developed, patents obtained etc.

Well-planned and well-chosen communication

Prospective investors are there to be impressed. It is therefore important that communication is well-planned. Equally as important is choosing the correct information to communicate to them – information that conveys the required message but is **not so detailed as to distract them** from the main issues.

Steps to ensure a high share price

Once the issue has been made it is important to grow the share price. This can be done be ensuring RED delivers a positive financial performance and publicising this performance. By doing so, the market can react appropriately to the information being released. If the semi-strong form of market efficiency is in evidence then this positive information will be reflected in the share price.

24 AB

> **Text references.** Lease or buy decisions are covered in Chapter 7. Post-completion audits are dealt with in Chapter 14.
>
> **Top tips.** You will have to determine an interest rate in the Alternative 2 calculations in part (a). Don't be tempted to pick the cost of borrowing given in the question or the cost of capital that is also given in the question. Base your calculations on the annual lease payments and the total cost of the capital equipment to find the annuity factor related to the interest rate. You can then use the annuity tables to find the appropriate interest rate.
>
> **Easy marks.** You should be able to pick up a number of easy marks in part (c) on post-completion audits.

(a)   (i)   Alternative 1

This alternative involves paying the whole capital cost up front. We have been told that the pre-tax cost of borrowing is 7%.

Capital allowances

Annual capital allowance = 25% of cost = 25% of €25m = €6.25m

Tax saving on capital allowances = 30% of €6.25m = €1.875m

NPV calculation

	Year 0	Years 1–4
	€m	€m
Cost	(25)	0
Capital allowance	0	1.875
Cum. discount factor (5%) (W1)	1.000	3.546
Discounted cash flow	(25)	6.649

NPV = € (18.351)m

Working

Cost of capital = post-tax cost of borrowing = 7% x (1 – 0.3) = 4.9% (say 5%)

> **Tutorial note** Remember to use the post-tax cost of borrowing as the discount rate as you will have already taken capital allowances into consideration – that is, you will be discounting the post-tax cash flows.

Alternative 2

Calculation of interest rate

Using sum of digits method:

Sum of digits = 1 + 2 + 3 + 4 = 10   (the lease has a four year term)

Total lease payments = 4 x €7m = €28m

Implicit interest = €28m - €25m = €3m

Year	1	2	3	4
Proportion of interest	4/10	3/10	2/10	1/10
Implicit interest	1.2	0.9	0.6	0.3

Alternative approach

Using the actuarial method:

Annual interest cost = €7m

Total future capital cost (excluding amount paid in advance) = €25m – €7m = €18m

Divide future capital cost by annual interest cost to find annuity factor of interest rate = 2.571

This is the three year annuity (one year's interest has been paid in advance) of the interest rate. Looking at the annuity table, this is closest to the three year annuity for 8%. We can therefore assume that this is the interest rate.

Tutorial note. We exclude the amount paid in advance from the capital cost as we are trying to find the annuity factor. Remember that annuity factors are the sum of discount factors from **Year 1** onwards therefore any cash movements in Year 0 should be ignored.

Annual interest

Interest will be charged on the reducing balance of the total capital cost.

	Year 1 €m	Year 2 €m	Year 3 €m
Capital cost balance	18.00	12.44	6.44
Interest (8%)	1.44	1.00	0.52
Lease payment	(7.00)	(7.00)	(7.00)
Balance	12.44	6.44	(0.04)

The final balance is approximately zero – difference due to rounding.

Tax relief

	Year 1 €m	Year 2 €m	Year 3 €m	Year 4 €m
Annual interest	1.20	0.90	0.60	0.30
Accounting depreciation (€25/4)	6.25	6.25	6.25	6.25
Total available for tax relief	7.45	7.15	6.85	6.55
Tax relief at 30%	2.24	2.15	2.06	1.97

NPV calculation

Tutorial note We are still using the after-tax cost of borrowing as the discount rate as leasing can be seen as a direct alternative to borrowing the full amount and paying up front.

	Year 0 €m	Year 1 €m	Year 2 €m	Year 3 €m	Year 4 €m
Lease payments	(7.00)	(7.00)	(7.00)	(7.00)	
Tax relief		2.24	2.15	2.06	1.97
Net cash flow	(7.00)	(4.76)	(4.85)	(4.94)	1.97
Dis. factor (5%)	1.000	0.952	0.907	0.864	0.823
DCF	(7.00)	(4.53)	(4.40)	(4.27)	1.62

NPV = €(18.58)m

Conclusion

As the NPV of purchasing the POS system is slightly lower than the NPV of leasing, AB should purchase the system outright.

(ii)   Reasons for choice of discount factor

A discount factor of 5% (approximately) was chosen for **Alternative 1** as this reflects the after-tax cost of borrowing. The cash flows are being discounted after taking tax relief into account.

The same discount rate is used for **Alternative 2**. This is because the discount rate should represent the **opportunity cost** of finance. As leasing is considered to be a direct alternative to paying for the system outright this is the correct discount rate to use.

The **cost of capital** given in the question (12%) should not be used as this does not represent the opportunity cost of finance. Instead it represents the cost of capital to the **entity** – the discount rate that would have been used to evaluate whether to undertake the overall POS project.

(iii)   Other factors to consider

If AB is considering paying for the system outright, by borrowing the entire €25m, management should consider the potential effect on its **capital structure**. If its gearing levels increase significantly, this could have an effect on its **perceived risk** and thus the returns that investors might require from the company.

The difference in NPVs between leasing and buying is quite insignificant compared with the size of the investment (€0.2m compared with €25m). AB should consider whether it is worth saving a relatively insignificant amount to borrow a sum that may have a considerable effect on its gearing levels.

Tax relief plays a major part in the outcomes of the individual lease and buy NPVs. AB should consider the likelihood of the tax rate remaining at 30% and the potential impact on the decision should the rate change.

No information is given on the **schedule of repayment of debt** if Alternative 1 was chosen. This could have an effect on the method of financing. One advantage of the leasing option is the constant payment schedule.

(b)   Post-completion audit

A post-completion audit compares the **actual** cash flows (inwards and outwards) of a project after it has reached the end of its life with the **estimated** cash inflows and outflows that were used in the original investment appraisal process. It is similar to carrying out variance analysis and the manager responsible for the project should be required to explain any **significant variations** from the estimated figures. It is used to aid the **control** process and lessons learned from the post-completion audit of a project can be fed into the next investment appraisal process.

An essential feature of a post-completion audit is the **proper completion of an investment proposal**, which should have clearly identified objectives that are ideally measurable. If AB has not done this in advance then a post-completion audit is of limited value as there will be nothing to compare the actual results to.

As far as AB is concerned, the **main benefits** that management should be looking for from a post-completion audit include the following:

(i) The chance to **evaluate** whoever was in overall charge of the project – were their cash flow estimates accurate or significantly different from reality? Have they performed well? How efficient have they been in the management of the project?

(ii) An opportunity to **identify** any problems in the forecasting techniques used. This information can be used to improve these techniques for the appraisal of future investments.

(iii) An opportunity to **investigate** any significant deviations from estimates and the reasons for these deviations. The determination of potential causes can be useful when estimating future cash flows.

The **main limitations** of a post-completion audit to AB include the following:

(i) Project managers may feel post-completion audits will be used to apportion '**blame**' rather than for 'learning' purposes. They may try to claim credit for favourable results over which they had no influence whilst blaming external factors for adverse results that they could have prevented.

(ii) Post-completion audits can be **expensive** to undertake and as such may not be carried out. AB may regard the POS project as one that is unlikely to repeated very often and fail to see any benefits from carrying out such an expensive process.

(iii) It may be difficult to **identify** and **quantify** the specific potential benefits of the POS project. If this is the case then a post-completion audit will not be possible as there will be no figures with which to compare actual results.

25 RZ

> **Text references.** Leasing is covered in Chapter 7 and debt finance in Chapter 6.
>
> **Top tips.** It's important to use the correct discount rate when evaluating a lease or buy decision. When evaluating whether to obtain the asset at all, cash flows should be discounted using the investment cost of capital (generally the WACC). The different financing options are then evaluated using the financing cost of capital, the after-tax cost of debt.
>
> You need to read the question carefully to identify the relevant costs that you will need to take into account when considering whether to take out the loan or lease. These are (i) The purchase price (ii) The lease payments (net of tax) (iii) The trade-in value (only available if you buy) (iv) The capital allowances.
>
> The reason why the tax shield is discussed in detail is that you are asked to compare using debt finance with using equity finance.
>
> **Easy marks.** The general advantages and disadvantages of debt and lease finance are basic core knowledge.

(a) <u>Acquisition decision</u>

If the investment is financed with equity funds, the project can be appraised by finding its net present value at a discount rate of 9% per annum, the post-tax cost of existing capital, which is all equity.

	$'000	Ex. Rate	£'000	9% factors	PV £'000
Machine capital cost	1,500	1.580	(949.37)	1.000	(949.37)
After tax annual cost savings 5 yrs including capital allowances			240.00	3.890	933.60
Residual value year 5			94.94	0.650	61.71
NPV					45.94

The residual value at the end of year 5 is estimated as 10% of the original purchase price. We assume that the balancing allowance on sale is included in the capital allowances.

On the basis of these figures, the machinery is marginally worthwhile if financed by equity funds, having a net present value of **£45,940**. This ignores the value of the tax shelter.

Financing decision

(i)   Underlined debt

Discount differential cash flows at after-tax cost of debt:

	0 £'000	1 £'000	2 £'000	3 £'000	4 £'000	5 £'000
Machine cost (W1)	(949.37)					
Trade-in value						94.94
Tax credits (W2)		71.20	53.40	40.05	30.04	61.63
Cash flows	949.37	71.20	53.40	40.05	30.04	156.57
Discount factors 5%	1.000	0.952	0.907	0.864	0.823	0.784
Discounted cash flows	(949.37)	67.78	48.43	34.60	24.72	122.75

Net cash flows = £(651,090)

Workings

1   Machine capital cost in £ = $\dfrac{\$1,500,000}{1.58}$ = £949,370

2   Capital allowances

Year	Written down value	25% writing down allowance	30% tax saving
0	949.37		
1	712.03	237.34	71.20
2	534.02	178.01	53.40
3	400.51	133.51	40.05
4	300.38	100.13	30.04
5*	94.94	205.44	61.63

* The 'writing down allowance' in the last year is a balancing allowance to arrive at the residual value of £94,940.

Conclusion

The main advantages of using debt are:

- The **present value of buying** is **lower than that of leasing**
- Because RZ is equity-financed, it will **benefit** from the tax shield

The main disadvantage is that gearing will increase.

Advantages of debt

Tax shield

Debt interest is an allowable expense against corporate taxation, which RZ pays at the rate of 30% of taxable profits. 7% perpetual debt on £949,370 will require interest payments of 7% × £949,370 per year, and will allow tax savings of 7% × £949,370 × 30% per year in perpetuity.

Tax shield in perpetuity

The present value of these tax savings (known as the tax shield) can be found by discounting at the cost of debt, 7% (because the tax savings have the same risk level as the interest payments, ie they are virtually certain).

For a perpetuity, this simply means dividing by 7%:
The PV is 7% × £949,370 × 30%/7% = £949,370 × 30% = £284,811.

(Note. This is the Modigliani-Miller formula for the tax shield on perpetual debt: TBc.)

Provided the company can earn taxable profits to perpetuity, this tax shield will be reflected in an increased company value. However, it is not fair to attribute all of this increased value to the new cost saving project. How much is attributable depends on the extent to which the new project assets enable the company **to borrow**.

Tax shield for borrowing

Assuming the new equipment represents a replacement of a major part of the company's assets, a better assumption might be that all the tax relief for the duration of the project (5 years) is attributable to the project.

The present value of tax savings for 5 years is found as follows:

Annual tax savings = 7% × £949,370 × 30% = £19,937
PV of 5 years' savings at 7% = 4.100 × £19,937 = £81,742

Thus borrowing can be argued to increase the project's base case net present value to an adjusted present value of £45,940 + £81,742 = **£127,682**

Other advantages of debt

(1)   Debt will **not change** the **pattern of ownership** of the company or earnings per share.
(2)   The cost of debt is **lower** than that of equity.

Disadvantages of debt

(1)   Because of the gearing effect, **equity earnings** become **more volatile** in response to changes in operating cash flows.

(2)   In an extreme case of low earnings the company may be forced into **bankruptcy** by its loan creditor. This latter is unlikely, however, given the current earnings level of £4.5 million and expected interest cost of only £66,000 per year.

(ii)   Finance lease

A 5 year finance lease on an asset with a useful life of 5 years, and with a right to buy for $1 at the end, is **effectively equivalent to a 5 year loan** enabling RZ to buy the asset. It can there be appraised by comparison with a loan. The after tax cash flows associated with the lease can be appraised by discounting at the after tax cost of borrowing, 5%.

Year	0	1	2	3	4	5
Annual lease payment $'000	(325.00)	(325.00)	(325.00)	(325.00)	(325.00)	
	£'000	£'000	£'000	£'000	£'000	£'000
Converted to £'000 (W1)	(205.70)	(207.71)	(209.73)	(211.78)	(213.84)	
Tax savings 30%		61.71	62.31	62.92	63.53	64.15
	(205.70)	(146.00)	(147.42)	(148.86)	(150.31)	64.15
5% factors	1	0.952	0.907	0.864	0.823	0.784
PV	(205.70)	(138.99)	(133.71)	(128.62)	(123.71)	50.29

The net present value of the finance lease is £(680,440) compared with borrowing of £(651,090) showing that borrowing is cheaper.

Working

Exchange rates

Using the formula for interest rate parity:

$$\text{Future spot rate £/\$} = \text{Spot rate £/\$} \times \frac{(1 + \text{US interest rate})}{(1 + \text{UK interest rate})}$$

the year 1 exchange rate = 1.58 × (1.025)/(1.035)= 1.5647. Subsequent exchange rates will be calculated in a similar way, using the previous year's exchange rate as the spot rate.

Year	0	1	2	3	4	5
Exchange rate	1.5800	1.5647	1.5496	1.5346	1.5198	1.5051

Other factors

Advantages of finance lease

(1) The lease may be **easier to organise** than a loan, particularly if the machinery vendor assists in organising it as an incentive to buy the machinery.

(2) The **lease** is paid off **within five years**.

Disadvantages of finance lease

(1) The lease is **riskier** than a **sterling loan**, because it is denominated in a foreign currency. A higher discount rate may need to be used because of this.

(2) RZ will **not be able** to **claim capital allowances** or take advantage of the trade-in value.

(iii) Operating lease

With an operating lease the lessee (RZ) does **not receive** the **rights and benefits** of ownership of the asset. It is akin to a rental agreement.

Advantages of operating lease

(1) There would normally be **break points** in the contract that allowed the lessee to terminate the contract if the asset is no longer required.

(2) **Disclosure** in financial accounts is **less onerous**. However this is unlikely to concern the shareholders of a private company.

(3) Unlike the other methods, the lessor will be responsible for **servicing and maintaining the lease**.

Disadvantages of operating lease

The **main disadvantage** is the cost, which is likely to be **more expensive** than the other forms of finance discussed.

(b) Benefits and problems of financing assets in the same currency as their purchase

If an asset **generates income** in a foreign currency, it is advantageous to **finance its acquisition** in the same currency. In this way, if the foreign currency depreciates, the loss in income is offset by **lower financing costs**.

Existence of long-term currency risk

However, if, as in the case of RZ, the asset is **purchased** and **financed** in a foreign currency but used to **generate** *home* **currency income** or savings, there is a **long term currency risk** over the period of the finance. For example if RZ negotiates a dollar lease and the dollar then strengthens by 10%, the costs of acquiring the asset will rise by 10% whereas the benefits of owning it in the UK will be unchanged. This factor significantly reduces the attractiveness of RZ's dollar lease.

Of course, if the dollar weakened, the company would make **exchange gains** on its finance. On balance, however, investors are **risk averse** and tend to fear exchange losses more than they welcome the chance of exchange gains.

Significance of interest rate parity

A loan raised in a foreign currency often **carries a lower interest rate** than a **home currency loan**. This is true in the example, where US interest rates are lower than sterling rates. However, the principle of interest rate parity suggests that the **foreign currency** will **strengthen** to compensate for this, resulting in an **increased home currency value** of loan or lease repayments.

26   FLG

> **Text references.** Leasing is covered in Chapter 7.
>
> **Top tips.** Presenting the NPV of leasing versus buying as one calculation in part (b) makes sensitivity analysis easier.
>
> **Easy marks.** 6 marks were available in (a) for the NPV calculations, and you could have obtained these even if you got the cost of debt calculation wrong. However some of the other calculations were unusual, and this would have been a question to avoid if you weren't sure what to do.
>
> **Examiner's comments.** Most candidates answered (a) (i) incorrectly. In (ii) many answers wrongly **excluded** the tax on lease payments and **included** interest and loan principal cash flows. Residual value was either omitted from capital allowance computations or calculated as for a single plane. Many answers to (b) did little more than repeat the question, and lacked quantitative and qualitative analysis.

(a)   (i)   <u>Compound annualised post-tax cost of debt</u>

The **6 month reference rate** is 2.4% for a 6 month period. This is a compound annualised pre-tax cost of $1.024^2 - 1 = 4.86\%$. The company's rate is 1% pa above this, which is 5.86% per annum.

The after tax cost will therefore be 5.86% (1 – 0.3) = 4.10%.

(ii)   <u>NPV of lease versus purchase decision at 4% and 5%</u>

The PV of the **lease payments** after tax relief, at 4% and 5%, is shown below. The lease is assumed to be an operating lease because the lessor retains the risk of loss on the residual value of the aircraft.

	Year	$m	4% factors	PV $m	5% factors	PV $m
Lease payments	0–4	(15.0)	4.630	(69.45)	4.546	(68.19)
Tax relief	1–5	4.5	4.452	20.03	4.329	19.48
				(49.42)		(48.71)

The planes cost $100m and their **residual value** is estimated as 4 × $12.5m = $50m. If they are bought, the tax savings from capital allowances will be as computed below. It is assumed that a balancing charge is made in year 5 because the assets are depreciated below their residual value.

Year	Value at start of year $m	20% writing down allowance $m	30% tax saved $m
1	100.0	20.0	6.0
2	80.0	16.0	4.8
3	64.0	12.8	3.8
4	51.2	10.2	3.1
5	41.0	(9.0)	(2.7)
		50.0	15.0

The **PV of purchasing the planes** can then be estimated at 4% and 5%.

Year	$m	4% factor	PV $m	5% factor	PV $m
0 Purchase	(100)	1.000	(100)	1.000	(100)
5 Residual value	50	0.822	41.10	0.784	39.20
2 Tax	6.0	0.925	5.55	0.907	5.44
3 "	4.8	0.889	4.27	0.864	4.15
4 "	3.8	0.855	3.25	0.823	3.13
5 "	3.1	0.822	2.55	0.784	2.43
6 "	(2.7)	0.790	(2.13)	0.746	(2.01)
			(45.41)		(47.66)

Thus the **additional present value** of cost expected if the planes are leased rather than purchased is expected to be:

At 4% cost of borrowing: 49.42m - 45.41m = $4.01m.

At 5% cost of borrowing: 48.71m - 47.66m = $1.05m.

(iii)   The **breakeven post tax cost of debt** at which there is no difference between the cost of leasing and the cost of purchasing will be just higher than 5% and can be estimated by extrapolating these results.

Break-even cost of borrowing = 5% + [1.05 / (4.01 – 1.05)] × 1% = **5.35%**.

(b)   Purchase or lease

On the basis of the above figures, if the company's post tax borrowing rate is 4.1%, **purchasing is cheaper than leasing**, but this needs to be investigated further by looking at the sensitivity of the decision to some key variables.

Sensitivity to the reference 6-month $ inter-bank rate

Leasing is more expensive unless FLG's post tax cost of debt rises to 5.35% pa. This is a pre-tax rate of 5.35% / 0.7 = 7.643% pa.

This implies a 6-month rate of $1.07643^{0.5} - 1 = 3.75\%$ per 6 month period.

Taking off FLG's risk premium of 0.5% gives a maximum reference 6-month $ inter-bank rate of **3.25%**, compared with the present figure of 2.4%.

Thus if interest rates rise more than 85 basis points (0.85% increase), leasing will be cheaper.

NPV of benefits of leasing

Year	0	1	2	3	4	5	6
	$m	$m	$m	$m	$m	$m	$m
Lease payments	(15.0)	(15.0)	(15.0)	(15.0)	(15.0)		
Tax relief		4.5	4.5	4.5	4.5	4.5	
Purchase cost saved	100.0						
Residual value lost						(50.0)	
Tax allowances lost			(6.0)	(4.8)	(3.8)	(3.1)	2.7
Net cash flow	85.0	(10.5)	(16.5)	(15.3)	(14.3)	(48.6)	2.7
Discount factor 4.1% (W1)	1.0	0.961	0.923	0.886	0.852	0.818	0.786
PV	85.0	(10.1)	(15.2)	(13.6)	(12.2)	(39.8)	2.1
NPV	(3.8)						

Workings

(1)   Discount factors: Year 1 $\dfrac{1}{1.041} = 0.961$

Year 2 $\dfrac{1}{(1.041)^2} = 0.923$

Year 3 $\dfrac{1}{(1.041)^3} = 0.886$

Year 4 etc

The PV of the residual value of the aeroplanes $= \dfrac{\$50m}{1.041^5} = \$40.9\,m$

The sensitivity of the calculation to changes in the residual value $= \dfrac{3.8}{40.9} = 9.3\%$

Thus although purchasing is expected to be cheaper, it carries **interest rate risk** and the risk of a fall in the planes' residual value. Neither of these variables need to move far before the lease is a better option.

Other factors

Other factors affecting the decision include:

(i)   It is assumed that the **planes** are **identical** whether leased or purchased.

(ii)   It is assumed that there will be **no restrictions** put on fittings, conversions or upgrades to the aircraft if they are leased (eg refitting of passenger seats).

(iii) It may be **more difficult to break the lease early** than to sell the planes if business suffers a downturn. On the other hand if the planes are kept for the full 5 years, leasing avoids the risk of a drop in residual value.

(iv) Purchasing becomes a **progressively better option** the longer the planes can be kept in service beyond 5 years.

Recommendation

In expected value terms, leasing is only **slightly more expensive** than purchasing. Assuming the planes will be replaced after 5 years, no earlier and no later, leasing is likely to be the **better choice of finance**, as it avoids the significant risk attached to residual value. If the period of use is uncertain, then purchasing may still be a better option.

27 LEE

> **Text references.** Lease or buy decisions are covered in Chapter 7 and sensitivity analysis in Chapter 11.
>
> **Top tips.** In part (a) (i) schedule the cash flows for both the purchase option and the lease option.
>
> There are various ways of calculating the highest lease rental in part (a) (ii) but we have chosen the quickest and easiest method. You could also have used interpolation to calculate the breakeven lease rental or an algebraic approach.
>
> Part (b) will need some thought and planning. Detailed discussion is needed for 12 marks.
>
> **Easy marks.** If you have practised lease or buy calculations the calculations in part (a) should be very straightforward.
>
> **Examiner's comments.** There were a number of errors in the tax calculations for part (a) and a tendency to list text book factors in part (b) without applying knowledge to the particular business position and risk exposures of LEE.

(a)   (i)   Tax depreciation allowances

Year	Value at start of year $	25% depreciation $	30% tax allowance $
1	5,000.00	1,250.00	375.00
2	3,750.00	937.50	281.25
3	2,812.50	703.13	210.94
4	2,109.37	527.34	158.20
5	1,582.03	Balance 417.97	(125.39)

Residual value (2,000.00)

The **discount rate** to be used in the NPV calculations is the after-tax cost of borrowing
= $(5.5\% + 1.7\%) \times 70\% = 5\%$

NPV of purchase

Year	0 $	1 $	2 $	3 $	4 $	5 $	6 $
Purchase cost	(5,000.00)						
Tax allowances			375.00	281.25	210.94	158.20	(125.39)
Sale proceeds						2,000.00	
Maintenance costs		(60.00)	(60.00)	(60.00)	(100.00)	(100.00)	
Net cash flow	(5,000.00)	(60.00)	315.00	221.25	110.94	2,058.20	(125.39)
Discount factor 5%	1	0.952	0.907	0.864	0.823	0.784	0.746
PV	(5,000.00)	(57.12)	285.71	191.16	91.30	1,613.63	(93.54)
NPV	(2,968.86)						

NPV of lease payments

Year	0	1	2	3	4	5	6
	$	$	$	$	$	$	$
Lease payment	(850.00)	(850.00)	(850.00)	(850.00)	(850.00)		
Tax saved			255.00	255.00	255.00	255.00	255.00
Net cash flow	(850.00)	(850.00)	(595.00)	(595.00)	(595.00)	255.00	255.00
Discount factor 5%	1	0.952	0.907	0.864	0.823	0.784	0.746
PV	(850.00)	(809.20)	(539.67)	(514.08)	(489.69)	199.92	190.23
NPV	(2,812.49)						

Alternative solution

Year	Lease Rentals	Tax deductions on rentals 30%	Discount factor 5%	NPV
	$	$		
0-4	(850.00)	–	4.546	(3,864.10)
2-6	–	255.00	4.124 (W1)	1,051.62
				2,812.48

Working
6 year cumulative present value factor 5%	5.076
1 Year cumulative present value factor 5%	(0.952)
	4.124

The net benefit of leasing is $156.37 therefore LEE should **lease** rather than purchase the machinery.

(ii)   The net present value of lease payments can increase by $156.37 before the net present value of the lease benefits is equal to zero.

The **sensitivity** of the net present value of the benefits of leasing to the value of the lease payments is:

$$\frac{156.37}{2,812.48} = 5.56\%$$

The lease payments can therefore increase to $850 + 5.56% = $897 before the NPV of the lease costs is equal to the NPV of the purchase costs. The **highest lease rental** that LEE would be likely to accept is therefore $897.

(b)   **Alternative 1** is a **purchase** financed by borrowing for a five year term, **Alternative 2** is a five year **operating lease** and **Alternative 3** is a **finance lease** for a five year term with an option to renew for an additional five year term at negligible rental.

Financial factors affecting LEE's choice

(1)   Cash flow
Leasing is attractive if the lessee **does not have enough cash** to pay for the asset and would have **difficulty obtaining a bank loan** to buy it. If LEE is suffering cash-flow difficulties, lease payments may offer a smoother cash flow.

(2)   Cost of finance
Alternative 3 is a finance lease and, although no figures are available, these are **cheaper** than bank loans and surveys suggest this is a major reason why leases are used. The logic is that the lessor is prepared to **lend at a lower cost** because he possesses greater security ie the ownership of the asset.

(3)   Maintenance costs
With an operating lease, the lessor is responsible for maintenance and servicing and the costs are therefore known in terms of timing and extent. This **reduction in uncertainty** may be attractive to LEE, especially if cash-flow is an issue.

(4) Taxation

In the financial analysis in part (a) (i), operating lease payments are tax deductible but the tax allowable depreciation from purchase of the asset is lost. A finance lease may be taxed differently to an operating lease and this may make Alternative 3 less attractive.

(5) Gearing capacity

Alternatives 1 and 3 would both have to be shown on LEE's statement of financial position whereas Alternative 2, the operating lease, would be **off statement of financial position** and would therefore not affect LEE's gearing ratio.

Non-financial factors affecting LEE's choice

(1) Risk of obsolescence

An operating lease may provide greater **flexibility** to replace or upgrade the machinery should it become obsolete during the period of the lease. However, this does depend on the terms of the lease agreement and it may be that the purchase option offers greater flexibility if the leases are for a fixed minimum term of five years.

(2) Maintenance

Lee may prefer to be responsible for servicing and maintenance of the asset to ensure a **business critical asset** is not out of action for a damaging period of time. This would make the purchase or finance lease options more attractive than the operating lease.

(3) Useful life and residual value

The useful life and residual value of the machinery are both **uncertain** and changes may impact on the choice of alternatives. For example, a longer time period for the machine to be used would make the purchase and finance lease options more attractive. If the residual value of the machinery in five years' time is less than expected, it makes the purchase option even less attractive.

28 BEN

> **Text references**. The lease versus buy decision is covered in Chapter 7.
>
> **Top tips**. Part (a) is a straightforward calculation that you should be able to do quite quickly if you have practised this technique. We have assumed that the purchase and lease payments are at the start of Year 1 and therefore the tax benefit is received in Year 2.
>
> You should use your knowledge from P3 *Performance Strategy* and E3 *Enterprise Strategy* to help you in your answer to parts (b) and (c). Planning your answers will ensure you answer the specific questions.
>
> **Easy marks**. Part (a) has 8 marks for a very straightforward lease v buy calculation.
>
> **Examiner's comments**. This question was very popular and was generally done very well. Most candidates attempting it gained very high marks.

(a) The **discount** rate to be used is the after-tax cost of borrowing which is 8% × (1 − 0.25) = **6%**

Method 1

Year	0	1	2	3	4	5	6
	€	€	€	€	€	€	€
Purchase cost	(800,000)						
Tax depreciation			40,000	40,000	40,000	40,000	40,000
Service costs		(60,000)	(63,000)	(66,150)	(69,458)	(72,931)	
Tax relief @ 25%			15,000	15,750	16,538	17,364	18,233
Net costs	(800,000)	(60,000)	(8,000)	(10,400)	(12,920)	(15,567)	58,233
Discount factor @ 6%	1.000	0.943	0.890	0.840	0.792	0.747	0.705
Present value	(800,000)	(56,580)	(7,120)	(8,736)	(10,233)	(11,629)	41,054
Total	**(853,244)**						

Method 2

Year	0	1	2	3	4	5	6
	€	€	€	€	€	€	€
Annual lease payment	(250,000)	(250,000)	(250,000)	(250,000)	(250,000)		
Tax relief @ 25%			62,500	62,500	62,500	62,500	62,500
Net costs	(250,000)	(250,000)	(187,500)	(187,500)	(187,500)	62,500	62,500
Discount factor @ 6%	1.000	0.943	0.890	0.840	0.792	0.747	0.705
Present value	(250,000)	(235,750)	(166,875)	(157,500)	(148,500)	46,688	44,063
Total	**(867,874)**						

Recommendation

BEN should choose **Method 1** as it is less expensive.

(b) Benefits

(i) The main benefit is that the new system will be **integrated** rather than a collection of different spreadsheets. This will enable direct comparisons to be made and generally improve the **quality** of **management information**.

(ii) It is often the case that much time is spent **converting** and **interpreting** information from different spreadsheets and this time will be saved. **Accuracy** should also be improved.

(iii) The new system should be **more secure** than a series of spreadsheets, with in-built protection and back-up procedures.

(iv) **Costs should be reduced** as a result of improved efficiency and saving of labour time. The management information generated should improve the efficiency of **treasury management** which will also save costs and possibly generate income. **Maintenance costs** of the new system should also be lower.

(v) The benefits accruing from a new system do depend on the **quality of the system**. A **bespoke** system is more likely to fit the specific needs of the entity but will be more expensive.

Control factors

(i) The **requirements of the system** need to be carefully thought out and clearly expressed. Systems are only effective if they are fit for purpose.

(ii) BEN should ensure that the system is **sufficiently flexible** to adapt to change in the business.

(iii) The system itself needs to **aid control** in the business. It should be able to **identify variances** from expected performance to allow managers to take **corrective action**.

(c) Purpose of a post-completion audit (PCA)

A PCA is an objective, independent **assessment** of the **success** of a capital project in relation to plan. It covers the whole life of the project and provides **feedback** to managers to aid the implementation and control of **future projects**.

What should be covered?

(i) The **actual cash flows** should be measured and compared with the estimates contained in the original capital expenditure appraisal. The manager responsible for the project should be asked to explain any significant variances.

(ii) The **objectives** of the project should have been clearly defined and **measurable** so that **achievement** of objectives can be determined.

Importance of a PCA to BEN

(i) The **threat** of a PCA ensures that managers will pay attention to benefits and costs throughout the implementation of the project. Original estimates may also be **more realistic**.

(ii) A PCA might **identify weaknesses** in the forecasting and estimating techniques used to evaluate projects, and so should help to improve the **quality of forecasting** for future investment decisions.

Limitations

(i) PCAs are **costly** and **time consuming**.

(ii) There are many **uncontrollable** factors in long-term investments. Resulting variances may therefore be meaningless.

(iii)   It may not be possible to **identify separately** the costs and benefits of a project.

(iv)   Applied punitively, PCAs may lead managers to become **over cautious** and unnecessarily **risk averse**.

(v)   The **strategic effects** of a project may take years to materialise and it may never be possible to identify or quantify them effectively.

29   EM

Text references. The treasury function is covered in Chapter 10. Leasing is covered in Chapter 7.

Top tips. As with all F3 questions, make sure you relate your answer to the scenario. Part (a) specifically asks you to make reference to the three financing alternatives so don't just write all you know about the treasury function. Part (b) contains the bulk of the marks but you are given no indication of how these marks are broken down. However you are told to include calculations regarding the debt and leasing options so this should give you a starting point.

If you struggled with determining the implicit interest rate for the leasing calculations, make an assumption about the figure (stating the figure you are using) and carry on with the calculations. Whilst you won't gain the marks for calculating the implicit interest rate, you will gain marks for the remainder of your calculations and the recommendations based on the figures you produce.

To save yourself time when comparing the three alternatives, remember that debt finance and leasing are treated in a similar manner in the financial statements, therefore you can compare both of these to the rights issue at the same time. When making comparisons, don't forget to consider the duration of the project in question versus the duration of the different alternatives.

Easy marks. There are some easy marks to be gained in part (a) when discussing treasury functions and in part (b) when calculating the NPV of debt financing.

Examiner's comments. This question was more successfully answered than previous exam questions on treasury functions but knowledge of finance issues in part (b) was generally poor. The appraisal of the finance lease versus buy/borrow was disappointing and, as this was a major focus in this question, had a large impact on marks achieved.

Common errors included:

–   including debt interest cash flows in the DCF calculations
–   including loan repayment cash flows each year in the DCF calculations
–   inability to calculate implied interest in the lease evaluation
–   including implied interest rather than the tax relief in the DCF calculations
–   using the incorrect discount rate
–   a misconception that introducing debt somehow reduces risk

Marking scheme

			Marks
(a)	1 – 2 marks per point covered on each of the three financing methods		Max 7
(b)	Bank borrowings calculations:		
	Capital allowances and tax relief	2.0	
	Initial investment	0.5	
	Discounting and NPV calculations	1.0	
	Finance lease calculations		
	Tax relief on accounting depreciation	1.5	
	Calculation of implied interest and related tax relief	3.0	
	Lease payments	1.0	
	Discounting using correct discount rate (5%)	1.0	
	Discussion of key points – 2 marks per relevant point	Max <u>8.0</u>	
			<u>18</u>
	Total		<u>25</u>

(a)   <u>Role of the treasury function</u>

The main functions of the treasury function are:

- **Liquidity** management
- **Funding** management
- **Currency** management
- **Corporate finance**

This particular scenario deals with the issue of **funding management** – that is, considering various ways of funding a particular project and recommending the most efficient means of finance. Members of the treasury department require detailed knowledge of the sources of funding available, what each source will cost and whether any collateral is required to secure funding.

The treasury function is involved at all levels of decision-making – **operational, tactical and strategic**. Amongst the **strategic** decisions that treasury will be involved in are

- Determining the optimal capital structure of the organisation

- Dividend payment and retention policies – including the level of dividend to be paid

- Raising share capital – including new issues and rights issues

- Obtaining information on the various available sources of finance and the proportion of funds to be raised from each source

- Assessing alternative sources of finance and making recommendations on which sources to use in different scenarios

EM's treasury function will be involved in many of the above activities as they are faced with various alternative sources of finance for the purchase of new production equipment. They will asked to advise on the advantages and disadvantages of each of the alternative funding sources, taking such factors as current capital structure and taxation into consideration.

From a **tactical** viewpoint, the treasury function will have to consider the risks associated with each source of finance and, depending on which source is chosen, take steps to manage this risk. For example, the choice of alternative 1 (bank borrowings) will leave EM exposed to any movements in interest rates and tax rates and the treasury function may have to consider ways of hedging against such movements.

Operational activities for each alternative might include the following.

Alternative 1 – liaise with the bank and negotiate favourable interest rates on the borrowings. Any issues regarding security may also be discussed.

Alternative 2 – liaise with finance houses to negotiate the best possible lease price.

Alternative 3 – liaise with financial advisers and underwriters to ensure a successful rights issue.

(b)   <u>Appropriateness of each of the three proposed alternatives</u>

Alternative 1

Year	0	1	2
	A$m	A$m	A$m
Initial investment	(360.0)		
Tax relief (A$360m x 20%)			72.0
Discount factor (5%)	1.000	0.952	0.907
Present value	(360.0)	0.0	65.3

Net present value = A$(294.7)m

Alternative 2

Workings

(i)   <u>Accounting depreciation</u>

Accounting depreciation = A$360m/4 = A$90m per annum

(ii)   Implicit interest

Using the sum of digits method:

Sum of digits (1 + 2 + 3 + 4) = 10   (lease has a four year term)

Total lease payments = 4 x A$105m = A$420m

Implicit interest = A$420m – A$360m = A$60m

Year	1	2	3	4
Proportion of interest	4/10	3/10	2/10	1/10
Implicit interest	24	18	12	6

Alternative approach

Using the actuarial method:

4 year Annuity factor for the lease

= cost of equipment/annual lease payment = A$360m/A$105m = 3.429

Using the annuity tables – 4 year annuity factor of 3.429 lies between the annuity factors for 6% (3.465) and 7% (3.387)

By interpolation the interest rate = 6 + (3.465 – 3.429)/(3.465 – 3.387) = 6.46%

We can now calculate the interest element of the payments using an implicit interest rate of 6.46%. (Implicit interest is calculated on the outstanding capital balance at the beginning of each year).

Opening balance A$m	Interest at 6.46% A$m	Total repayment A$m	Closing balance A$m
360.0	23.3	(105.0)	278.3
278.3	18.0	(105.0)	191.3
191.3	12.4	(105.0)	98.7
98.7	6.4	(105.0)	0.1

NPV of leasing

	0 A$m	1 A$m	2 A$m	3 A$m	4 A$m	5 A$m
Acc. depreciation		90.0	90.0	90.0	90.0	
Implicit interest		24.0	18.0	12.0	6.0	
Total available for tax relief		113.0	108.0	102.0	96.0	
Tax relief at 20%			22.6	21.6	20.4	19.2
Lease payment		(105.0)	(105.0)	(105.0)	(105.0)	
Net cash flow		(105.0)	(82.4)	(83.4)	(84.6)	19.2
Discount factor (5%)	1.000	0.952	0.907	0.864	0.823	0.784
Present value	0.0	(100.0)	(74.7)	(72.1)	(69.6)	15.1

Net present value = A$(301.3)m

Lease or buy decision

The choice between alternatives 1 and 2 amounts to a lease or buy decision. The decision is made mainly, but not exclusively, on financial grounds. The cost of buying the equipment using debt finance is A$294.7m whilst the cost of leasing the equipment using a finance lease is A$301.3m. There is only a marginal difference between the two alternatives.

Factors that may need to be considered before making a final decision include the following.

(i)   **Effect on cash flows** – if EM is suffering cash flow difficulties, lease payments may offer a smoother cash flow pattern than one large lump sum. Debt also has to be repaid at some time in

the future and funding has to be found for the repayment of the lump sum. This does not happen with finance leases.

(ii) **Introduction of debt** – EM is currently financed entirely by equity therefore the introduction of debt financing will allow the company to take advantage of tax relief on interest and reduce WACC. Leasing and debt financing will both be treated as debt in the financial statements therefore gearing will remain the same with either option.

(iii) **Ease of arrangement** – a finance lease may be easier to arrange than a bank loan. Arrangement costs of a lease are generally lower than either debt or equity which may also have a bearing on the final decision (these costs are not accounted for in the calculations above).

(iv) **No recalculation of investment decision NPV** – the NPV of the project is already positive and this will only increase if the lower cost debt is used as the means of finance.

Advantages of debt/lease over rights issue

(i) Debt/lease options match financing to the length of the project. Equity is a long-term (more or less permanent) source of finance which is not appropriate for the project being considered.

(ii) Interest payments on debt and lease payments are tax deductible.

(iii) Cost of debt tends to be lower than cost of equity as debt holders receive priority in terms of being paid. If a higher cost of equity was used in the NPV calculations, it may render the project infeasible.

(iv) A rights issue is expensive to arrange and administer. It also carries the risk of failure if the rights are not taken up by the shareholders. Debt finance and leases are likely to be less expensive and less risky.

(v) There is no dilution of share ownership if debt finance or leasing is used.

Disadvantages of debt/lease over rights issue

(i) Debt gives rise to the problem of how to repay or refinance the capital at the end of the loan term. There is no such problem with equity.

(ii) There are no legal obligations to pay dividends to shareholders but interest payments must be met. If EH encounters liquidity problems, it may be unable to meet its interest obligations and be at risk of bankruptcy. There does not appear to be any immediate risk given the size of the company and the fact that EH has no medium or long-term debt at present.

Recommendation

Given the analysis above, it would appear that a **finance lease** is the most appropriate method of financing the investment. Whilst it may be slightly more expensive in terms of NPV, there are less administrative costs attached to arranging a lease compared with debt finance. A rights issue would be inappropriate as the duration of such financing would be inappropriate for a medium-term project. It is also expensive and carries considerable risks.

30 AB

Text references. NPV is covered in Chapter 11. Leases are covered in Chapter 7.

Top tips. In part (a) remember that there are no maintenance payments with the operating lease as these costs are met by the lessor.

Don't forget to make a recommendation in part (b) after considering each of the alternatives.

Easy marks. There are some straightforward marks to be picked up in part (a) when carrying out the NPV calculations on each of the three alternatives.

Examiner's comments. Candidates regularly struggle with leasing questions and this was no exception. Candidates failed to understand how to apply tax relief in the different scenarios and the use of an incorrect discount rate, or rates, was also a common error.

(a)   Alternative 1 – buy equipment outright

	Workings	Year 0 $m	Years 1 - 5 $m
Purchase cost		(50)	
Maintenance (after tax relief)	$2m x (1 – 0.25)		(1.5)
Writing down allowance	(50/5) x 0.25		2.5
Net cash flow		(50)	1.0
Discount factor (7%)		1.000	4.100
Discounted cash flow		(50)	4.100

Net present value = $(45.9)m

Alternative 2 – finance lease

	0 $m	1 $m	2 $m	3 $m	4 $m	5 $m
Lease payments	(14)	(9.0)	(9.0)	(9.0)	(9.0)	(9.0)
Tax shield on depreciation and interest (W1)		3.25	3.13	3.0	2.85	2.68
Maintenance [$2m x (1 – 0.25)		(1.5)	(1.5)	(1.5)	(1.5)	(1.5)
Net cash flow	(14)	(7.25)	(7.37)	(7.5)	(7.65)	(7.82)
Discount factor (7%)	1.000	0.935	0.873	0.816	0.763	0.713
DCF	(14)	(6.78)	(6.43)	(6.12)	(5.84)	(5.58)

NPV = $(44.75)m

Working (1)

	0 $m	1 $m	2 $m	3 $m	4 $m	5 $m
Depreciation ($50m/5)		10.0	10.0	10.0	10.0	10.0
Interest (given in question)		3.0	2.5	2.0	1.4	0.7
Total attracting tax relief		13.0	12.5	12.0	11.4	10.7
Tax relief at 25%		3.25	3.13	3.0	2.85	2.68

Alternative 3 – operating lease

	0 $m	1 $m	2 $m	3 $m	4 $m	5 $m
Lease payments		(16.5)	(16.5)	(16.5)	(15.0)	(15.0)
Tax relief (25%)		4.13	4.13	4.13	3.75	3.75
Net cash flow		(12.37)	(12.37)	(12.37)	(11.25)	(11.25)
Discount factor (7%)		0.935	0.873	0.816	0.763	0.713
DCF		(11.57)	(10.80)	(10.09)	(8.58)	(8.02)

NPV = $(49.06)m

(b)   Recommendation

Cost

Of the three alternatives, the finance lease (alternative 2) is the least expensive. If the decision was based on cost alone, alternative 2 should be recommended. There are considerable cash flow advantages from leasing rather than purchasing – for example, there is no huge cash outflow in Year 0.

Risk

The operating lease, whilst the **most expensive** of the three alternatives, carries the **least risk** as responsibility for maintenance and obsolescence lies with the lessor. The estimated cost of the second operating lease may be rather high due to advances in technology being likely to reduce the cost of the new equipment.

Another advantage of the operating lease is that it allows the use of more advanced technology after three years, whilst the finance lease forces AB to use the original equipment for five years. Note that the present value of the initial operating lease is $32.46m ($11.57m + $10.8m + $10.09m), whilst the cost of the finance lease is $44.75m. If the machine was only needed for three years (unlikely but possible) then the operating lease would be cheaper.

Gearing

Operating leases **do not have to be disclosed** in the statement of financial position of the lessee therefore this may improve the gearing of the company.

Conclusion

The preferred financing option may depend on the directors' attitude towards the risk of obsolescence of the equipment. The finance lease is the least expensive, however it does lock the company into using the equipment for five years. Whilst the operating lease is the most expensive, it does give the company the opportunity of using more advanced equipment after three years.

(c)   Change in government policy to improve tax depreciation allowances

If the tax depreciation rules changed to allow a 100% first year allowance, this would benefit the 'purchase' option due to the earlier cash flow benefit of tax relief (assuming of course that the company can take full advantage of this tax relief). The company forecasts that it will make its first profit in 20X1 – if this profit is sufficient to take advantage of the tax relief, the benefit will be at the company's marginal rate of tax.

Timing is important with capital allowances. If the deal is signed prior to the new rules taking effect then the company may be unable to take advantage of the greater benefits (apart from when the new operating lease is entered into in three years' time).

The impact on finance and operating leases is less certain. The benefit will likely fall to the lessor (who will purchase the equipment) rather than the lessee. Whether AB will benefit in the form of reduced lease payments will depend on the **lessor**.

31 PIC

Text references. Debt finance is covered in Chapter 6. WACC is covered in Chapter 8.

Top tips. Be careful when calculating maximum and minimum working capital in part (a). Minimum working capital will involve deducting *maximum* accounts payable and vice versa for maximum working capital.

In part (b)(i) be aware that you are required to *evaluate* the proposed change in policy so you should be looking for pros and cons as well as any other issues that PIC might have to consider. In (b)(ii) make sure you suggest *appropriate* approaches rather than just a general list of alternative sources of finance. You will not gain any marks for making infeasible suggestions.

Easy marks. If you are familiar with the formula you should gain some easy marks in (a)(ii) when calculating the implied issue price.

Examiner's comments. Parts (a)(i) and (a)(ii) were very poorly attempted, if attempted at all. In (a)(i) the majority of candidates failed to appreciate that creditors represented negative working capital and the most common error in (a)(ii) was to use the annuity factor for 8% rather than 9%. Part (a)(iii) was generally well attempted – if candidates ignored the overdraft they were not penalised for doing so. Many candidates misinterpreted (b)(i) as an evaluation of the level of working capital needed and made too few points about the financing of net current assets. Answers to (b)(ii) were often inappropriate (for example, recommending a rights issue).

Marking scheme

				Marks
(a)	(i)	Working capital requirements	2.0	
		Aggressive policy	1.5	
		Conservative policy	1.5	
				5
	(ii)	Use of correct discount rate	1.0	
		Use of correct formula	1.0	
		Correct implied issue price	1.0	
				3
	(iii)	WACC calculation	2.0	
		Comments – 1 mark per relevant point	Max 2.0	
				4
(b)	(i)	Advantages of current policy – 1 mark per relevant point	Max 2.0	
		Disadvantages of current policy – 1 mark per relevant point	Max 2.0	
		Features of new proposal	1.0	
		Other relevant factors to support evaluation	Max 4.0	
				9
	(ii)	Up to 1.5 marks per relevant method	Max	4
			Total	25

(a)   (i)   <u>Working capital requirements</u>

Minimum payable = Minimum inventories + minimum accounts receivable – maximum accounts

= A\$17.26m + A\$1.64m – A\$14.79m

= A\$4.11m

Maximum payable = Maximum inventories + maximum accounts receivable – minimum accounts

= A\$29.59m + A\$3.29m – A\$7.40m

= A\$25.48m

The fluctuating portion of working capital is the difference between the minimum and maximum requirements – that is A\$21.37m. The permanent requirement is A\$4.11m.

<u>Long and short-term financing requirements</u>

	Aggressive policy A\$m	Conservative policy A\$m
Short-term financing	21.37 + (20% of 4.11) = 22.19	80% of 21.37 = 17.10
Long-term financing	80% of 4.11 = 3.29	4.11 + (20% of 21.37) = 8.38
Total financing	25.48	25.48

(ii)   <u>Implied issue price of bond</u>

Use the yield to maturity of 9% as the discount rate. Face value of bond is A\$100 therefore annual interest is A\$8 (8% of A\$100).

Value of debt

= (Interest earnings x Annuity factor$_{t=5, 9\%}$) + (Redemption value x Discounted cash flow factor)

= (A\$8 x 3.89) + (A\$100 x 0.650)

= A\$96.12 per A\$100 nominal

(iii)   <u>Weighted average cost of capital (WACC)</u>

$$WACC = k_e(\frac{V_E}{V_E + V_D}) + k_d(\frac{V_D}{V_E + V_D})$$

Type of finance	Market value A\$m	Proportion of total %	Rate of return %	Weighted return %
Overdraft	20.0	4.3	(7 x 0.8) = 5.6	0.24
Long-term debt	100.0	21.3	(8.125 x 0.8)= 6.5	1.38
Equity	<u>350.0</u>	<u>74.4</u>	10.0	<u>7.44</u>
Total	470.0	100.0		9.06

The current WACC is 9.06%. If PIC switched from an aggressive to a conservative policy for funding net current assets, this would result in a relative shift from short-term to long-term finance. This might mean a change in the cost of overdraft finance and also in the cost of equity. However the effect on the overall WACC is likely to be insignificant as the difference in cost of the two policies is small. Net current assets' financing does not tend to attract a lot of attention from the markets unless the amount involved is significant thus the effect on cost of capital is likely to be minimal.

(b)   (i)   <u>Proposal to change from aggressive to conservative policy for financing net current assets</u>

One of the main advantages of the current **aggressive policy** is that it makes full use of **cheaper** short-term overdraft financing. As a result this policy should provide a higher return than the conservative policy.

In addition, there is **more flexibility** to be had from the aggressive policy which will be of benefit given the high degree of fluctuation in net current assets. Overdrafts are generally easier to arrange than long-term finance, a degree of liquidity that would be advantageous in the event of a sudden upward fluctuation in net current assets.

However PIC should be aware of the administration time it takes for its management to rearrange overdraft facilities. The cost of the resource may outweigh the benefits of the short-term finance.

There is a risk of the aggressive policy being **less liquid** due to the overdraft facility required. Unless the bank is willing to extend the facility where necessary, PIC may find itself short of funding for the short-term portion of net current assets.

PIC should also consider several other factors when making the final decision on its financing policy.

It is currently making use of suppliers' credit to finance fluctuating working capital (average of 60 days' credit is taken as opposed to the 15 days given to customers). This is not unusual but it may be costly. PIC may be giving up the chance for **early payment discounts** in order to use suppliers' credit as a means of finance.

The **conservative policy** suggests using more medium and long-term funds to finance fluctuating (as well as permanent) net current assets. Such funding (particularly in relatively small amounts) can be expensive to issue and PIC should consider whether this cost will outweigh the benefits of using longer-term debt.

PIC's current overdraft limit is A\$20m but it is likely that A\$22m will be needed to finance short-term net current assets if the aggressive policy is continued. There is a chance that PIC's overdraft facility will not be extended and if it is the overdraft cost could increase.

Whilst PIC currently observes fluctuations in working capital on a monthly basis, weekly or even daily observations would not be excessive in the case of a large retailing organisation. This would give PIC a better understanding of the fluctuations involved and the type of financing policy that might be most appropriate.

(ii)   <u>Alternative approaches to financing net current assets</u>

So far, PIC has suggested either an aggressive policy or a conservative policy. The company could consider something between the two extremes where short-term funding would be used to finance fluctuating net current assets and longer-term funding matched to the permanent portion as well as non-current assets.

A **factoring service** could be considered to deal with receivables. PIC could hand over the responsibility of collecting these debts to a factoring company and receive in return a percentage of the debt up front. PIC could also take advantage of available credit checking facilities before taking on new customers.

PIC could also consider **invoice discounting** whereby a copy of the customer's invoice is sent to a lender who will then calculate available funds. PIC would then be able to borrow up to 90% of the invoice value up front (and would therefore not have to wait until the customer pays in order to benefit from the majority of the debt). When the customer finally pays, PIC would receive the remainder of the debt (less the service fee).

32 CIP

Text references. Risk, CAPM and WACC are covered in Chapter 8. Geared and ungeared (asset) betas are covered in Chapter 9.

Top tips. Remember to keep referring to the scenario when discussing points. Don't be tempted to give completely generic answers that could be lifted straight from a text!

Easy marks. You should know what systematic and unsystematic risk are so there are some easy marks available in part (a). The calculations in part (b) are not overly difficult and you are given the formulae already, so you should be able to pick up several marks there.

Examiner's comments. Candidates tended to perform well on this question although the most common errors were confusing systematic and unsystematic risk (and also asset beta and equity beta) and providing poor attempts at the diagram. Many candidates provided a diagram of the security market line.

Marking scheme

			Marks
(a)	Systematic risk	2	
	Unsystematic risk	2	
	Diagram	2	6
(b)	Beta calculations	3	
	Calculation of cost of equity via CAPM	1	
	Calculation of discount rates	2	
			6
(c)	WACC	Up to 2	
	Adjusted WACC	1	
	CAPM-derived rates	Up to 3	
			Max 6
(d)	Asset beta v equity beta – 1 mark per valid point	Max 4	
	CAPM assistance – 1 mark per valid point	Max 3	
			7
		Total	25

(a) **Systematic and unsystematic risk**

Systematic risk (or market risk) is risk that cannot be diversified away. This is due to the fact that some investments are simply more risky than others. By holding such investments you have to accept the risk attached to them but you will expect to earn a higher return than that on a risk-free security.

Risk that can be diversified away is known as unsystematic risk. Such risk can be reduced or eliminated by holding a well-diversified portfolio where investments that perform well and those that perform badly will tend to cancel each other out. Average return should be more or less as expected.

Total risk is the sum of systematic and unsystematic risk and can be measured by standard deviation. Systematic risk is measured using equity beta.

Beta is the measure of the systematic risk of a security relative to the market portfolio. For example, if a share rose or fell at twice the rate of the market, it would have a beta of 2. A beta of less than 1 denotes less than average risk, whilst a beta of more than 1 denotes greater than average risk. A beta of exactly 1 indicates average risk.

Beta is determined by plotting the share's movements against movements in the market and using regression analysis to calculate the slope of the line. The slope is the beta factor.

The following graph illustrates the difference between systematic and unsystematic risk. Note how unsystematic risk falls as the number of investments increases but systematic risk is not being diversified away.

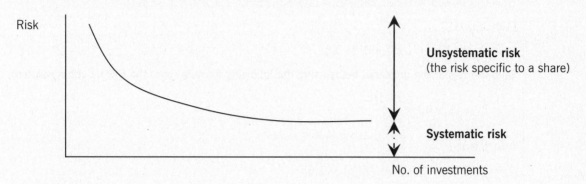

(b)   <u>Beta and discount rate calculations</u>

<u>Approach 1</u>

Step 1 – degear the proxy companies' betas using the following formula

$$\beta_u = \beta_g \frac{V_E}{V_E + V_D(1-t)} + \beta_d \frac{V_D(1-t)}{V_E + V_D(1-t)}$$

Company A

ß$_u$ = 1.3 x [3/(3 + 1 x 0.75)] + 0.3 x [(1 x 0.75)/(3 + 1 x 0.75)] = 1.10

Company B

ß$_u$ = 0.9 x [6/(6 + 1 x 0.75)] = 0.8

Step 2 – use the ungeared beta to calculate the ungeared k$_{eu}$

Investment 1

k$_{eu}$ = 3 + (8 – 3) x 1.1 = 8.5%

Investment 2

k$_{eu}$ = 3 + (8 – 3) x 0.8 = 7%

Step 3 – Use the ungeared k$_{eu}$ to calculate the WACC using the MM formula

k$_{adj}$ = k$_{eu}$(1 – tL)

Investment 1

k$_{adj}$ = 8.5 x (1 – [0.25 x 0.4]) = 7.65%

Investment 2

k$_{adj}$ = 7 x (1 – [0.25 x 0.4]) = 6.3%

Alternative approach

Approach 2

Step 1 – degear the proxy companies' betas using the following formula:

$$\beta_u = \beta_g \frac{V_E}{V_E + V_D(1-t)} + \beta_d \frac{V_D(1-t)}{V_E + V_D(1-t)}$$

Company A

$\beta_u = 1.3 \times [3/(3 + 1 \times 0.75)] + 0.3 \times [(1 \times 0.75)/(3 + 1 \times 0.75)] = 1.10$

Company B

$\beta_u = 0.9 \times [6/(6 + 1 \times 0.75)] = 0.8$

Step 2 – regear the ungeared betas using the following formula (note the CIP's debt is risk-free)

$$\beta_g = \beta_u + (\beta_u - \beta_d)\frac{V_D(1-t)}{V_E}$$

Investment 1

$\beta_g = 1.10 + 1.10 [(2 \times 0.75)/3] = 1.65$

Investment 2

$\beta_g = 0.8 + 0.8 [(2 \times 0.75)/3] = 1.2$

Step 3 – use the betas and the CAPM to calculate the discount rates

The CAPM formula is as follows.

$k_e = R_f + (R_m - R_f) \beta$

Investment 1

$k_e = 3 + (8 - 3) \times 1.65 = 11.25\%$

Investment 2

$k_e = 3 + (8 - 3) \times 1.2 = 9\%$

Using WACC

It is possible to calculate WACC for each of the two investments if we assume that the cost of the debt is 3% (risk-free rate).

Investment 1

WACC = (0.6 x 11.25%) + (0.4 x 3% x 0.75) = 7.65%

Investment 2

WACC = (0.6 x 9%) + (0.4 x 3% x 0.75) = 6.3%

(c) Benefits and limitations of using WACC

The main benefit of using WACC is that it tends to be understood by non-financial staff. In addition it is assumed that it reflects the company's long-term capital structure.

However there are several limitations. The investments being proposed may have **different business risk** to CIP's existing business risk therefore the return required by investors may differ from existing WACC. In addition, the funds required may **change CIP's capital structure** and hence its perceived financial risk. Again this may have an impact on the return required by investors.

Benefits and limitations of using adjusted WACC

There are no theoretical foundations for using an adjusted WACC in the manner suggested by the Managing Director. The adjustments appear to be random and not based on any financial knowledge – there is nothing to suggest that the proposed adjustments would be sufficient to compensate for 'greater' or 'less' risk.

The main benefit – as with basic WACC above – is that the concept is easily understood by non-financial staff.

<u>Benefits and limitations of using CAPM-derived rates</u>

The main benefit of CAPM is that it is a theoretically acceptable way of determining discount rates.

There are several limitations however. **Beta can change over time** and is also subject to errors in statistical analysis. CAPM assumes that beta will continue to stay the same over time which is unrealistic.

The use of proxy companies' information assumes very similar business risk and activities – however no two companies are exactly the same. Whilst activities may be similar, business risk may be quite different.

CAPM assumes that unsystematic risk can be diversified away and investors will therefore not be looking for a premium for this risk. However CIP is a small company which **may not be sufficiently diversified** to have eliminated unsystematic risk therefore CAPM will underestimate the return required.

The CAPM is a single-period model but CIP is using the discount rate calculated for five-year investments. The risk of the investments could change over time, meaning that the NPV calculations using the original rate will be invalid.

(d)   An **asset beta** is an **ungeared** beta – that is, it reflects the business risk of a company assuming it has no debt.

An **equity beta** is the **published** beta – it is the beta that is attached to the company's shares and assumes the company has some level of gearing.

Using an asset beta is more appropriate for CIP as it incorporates the business risk of Companies A and B but removes the effect of the capital structures of these proxy companies. The equity beta for the investments is obtained by regearing the asset (ungeared) betas. This introduces the actual capital structure of the investments. This geared beta is then incorporated into the CAPM which gives a cost of capital that reflects both the business risk of the investment and its capital structure.

CIP currently has a WACC of 12%. CAPM can be used to determine whether this rate is still appropriate for all investments. The calculations in part (b) suggest that 12% is too high for the investments being considered. Had 12% been used, these investments may have been rejected, resulting in a lost opportunity to increase earnings (CIP's financial objective). However CAPM might also show that the current rate is too low. This means that CIP is not offering sufficient returns to shareholders to compensate for any unsystematic risk that might be present. The long-term result could be the demise of the business, not just inability to pay dividends.

Whilst the usefulness of CAPM to CIP is apparent, the Board should not ignore the limitations of the model that were mentioned in part (c).

33   CBA

(a)   (i)   Premium on conversion

Share price now:	£3.60
Predicted share price in four years: ($£3.60 \times 1.06^4$)	£4.54
Conversion value (23 shares at predicted value)	£104.42

(ii)

		Cash flow	DF@7%	PV	DF@5%	PV
0	Loan capital (7% discount)	(93.00)	1.000	(93.00)	1.000	(93.00)
1 – 4	Annual interest (3 × 0.7)	2.10	3.387	7.11	3.546	7.45
4	Capital redemption	104.42	0.763	79.67	0.823	85.94
				(6.22)		0.39

The post tax cost of debt using interpolation is

$0.05 + [0.39/(0.39 + 6.22)] (0.07 - 0.05) = 0.0512 = 5.12\%$

Note: The interpolation result will depend on the discount rates used. Given that the result using 5% above was close to zero, it would be acceptable to use 5% as K_d.

(iii)   Calculation of WACC

	Market value £m		Cost of capital	MV Cost of capital £m
Ordinary shares	280m × 3.60	1,008	11.56%	116.52
Preference shares	195m × 1.05	205	5.71%	11.71
Debt		250	5.12%	12.80
		1,463		141.03

WACC = 141.03/1,463 = 9.64%

Workings

$K_p = (0.06 / 1.05) = 0.0571 = 5.71\%$

Dividend $= (0.45 \times 0.5) = 0.225$

Dividend in one year $= 0.225 \times 1.05 = 0.23625$

$K_e = 0.23625/3.60 + 0.05 = 0.1156 = 11.56\%$

(b)   Benefits of convertible debt over equity

Debt is normally **cheaper than equity** for the company because the interest payments carry tax relief whereas dividends do not. As debt is also less risky for the providers of finance, therefore the rate of return required by debt holders will be lower than for equity holders.

Issue costs will be lower for convertible debt than a new issue of equity. It will also be quicker to obtain than equity, although not as quick as straight debt.

Earnings are **not diluted** when the debt is issued, but debt interest must be paid before equity dividends are paid. Dilution would occur when the debt is converted, but the finance raised should be used to increase earnings, which should allow all shareholders to be paid without reducing earnings per share.

Since there is no existing debt, CBA is **not taking advantage** of the tax relief available on interest payments. Gearing is low at 17% (205/(1,008 + 205)) and the introduction of convertible debt at a lower cost of capital is likely to reduce the overall WACC. This is because the return required by equity holders is unlikely to rise unless they perceive the risk of CBA to be increased by the new debt.

Disadvantages of convertible debt of equity

Interest payments are **mandatory**. Failure to make these payments may result in CBA being put into insolvency proceedings. This risk is common to all forms of debt.

At high levels of gearing, the risk may be **unacceptable** to equity holders, which would mean an increase in the cost of equity and therefore WACC. This does not seem to be the case in this instance as gearing is currently 17% and would increase to 31% ((250 + 205)/1,463) if the debt was issued. The gearing should also **decrease** in four years' time when conversion takes place.

Recommendation

In the absence of information about the **industry average** gearing level and the general risk of CBA, it is difficult to make a full recommendation. However, the gearing level appears low and an issue of convertible debt seems unlikely to increase the cost of equity significantly. There is **no evidence** that investors would react adversely to the issue of convertible debt, therefore this is the more attractive option to CBA.

(c) The treasury department will be involved in several different areas of the convertible bond issue.

It will be responsible for **determining the conversion ratio** and also the interest rate on the debt.

It will also be responsible for managing the **relationship** with the issuer of the debt, which is likely to be an investment bank.

It will **calculate the costs of capital** and ensure that the debt issue will not adversely affect the value of CBA. It will also carry out forecasts to ensure interest payments can be met and that dividend payouts can be maintained to both ordinary and preference shareholders.

In addition to the above, it will also need to prepare all the relevant paperwork and a timetable for the issue.

34 Horatio

Text references. Equity finance is covered in Chapter 5 and debt finance in Chapter 6. Risk-adjusted discount rates decision trees and certainty equivalents are covered in Chapter 11.

Top tips. Note that you are only required to calculate an estimate of the equivalent yield in part (a)(i). Don't waste time trying to obtain an accurate answer.

Remember in part (b) that you are required to offer advice as to the usefulness of each method to Horatio. Try to think of how the merits of each method could be applied to Horatio's proposed project.

Easy marks. There are some straightforward calculations in part (a) which should allow you to pick up some marks quickly.

(a) (i) *Alternative 1*

Cost of preference shares = 5.50/1.20 = 4.583%

Alternative 2

Cost of bond – calculate Yield to Maturity (IRR of the bond)

<u>Using annual coupon of 4%</u>

Time	0	1 - 9	2 - 10	9
	£m	£m	£m	£m
Initial investment	10.00			
Interest		(0.40)		
Tax relief (0.4 x 0.35)			0.14	
Redemption of bond				(11.00)
Discount factor (4%)	1.000	7.435	7.149[(*)]	0.703
DCF	10.00	(2.974)	1.00	(7.73)

NPV = £0.296m

(*) Annuity factor = 10 year 4% annuity factor – year 1 4% discount factor

$$= 8.111 - 0.962$$

$$= 7.149$$

<u>Try 3%</u>

Time	0	1 - 9	2 - 10	9
	£m	£m	£m	£m
Initial investment	10.00			
Interest		(0.40)		
Tax relief (0.4 x 0.35)			0.14	
Redemption of bond				(11.00)
Discount factor (3%)	1.000	7.786	7.559	0.766
DCF	10.00	(3.114)	1.058	(8.426)

NPV = £(0.482)m

Using the IRR formula to calculate Yield to Maturity (YTM):

$$IRR \approx a + \left(\left(\frac{NPV_a}{NPV_a - NPV_b}\right)(b - a)\right)\%$$

$$YTM = 3 + \frac{0.482}{(0.482 + 0.296)} \times (4 - 3) = 3.620\%$$

Alternative 3

Estimated sterling yield to maturity = (1.028 x 1.025) – 1 = 5.37%

After-tax yield to maturity = 5.37 x (1 - 0.35) = 3.49%

> **Tutorial note**. This is only an estimate (as required by the question). A more accurate answer could be determined using the full yield to maturity calculation.

(ii) <u>Advantages and disadvantages of the alternative sources of finance</u>

Alternative 1

Preference shares have the advantage that they have **no finite life** – that is, there is no specified maturity date. This is beneficial if the length of time the funds are needed for varies from expected – there will be no need to arrange alternative financing as would be the case for funding with a specified maturity date. However this can also be a disadvantage if the funds are only required for a relatively short period - Horatio is required to keep servicing preference shareholders long after the need for funding has finished.

There are two main problems with preference shares. Firstly, it is expensive to raise preference share capital and secondly preference dividends are **not tax-deductible**. It is therefore more expensive to compensate preference shareholders than debt holders.

Alternatives 2 and 3

Both of these alternatives involve the issue of **redeemable debt**. Alternative 2 is redeemable shortly before the end of the project whilst alternative 3 is redeemable approximately half-way through the project's life. It is unclear how long the funds will be required for as the payback period has not been

given therefore the appropriateness of the redemption periods cannot be determined. However both have the advantage of being redeemable, unlike the preference shares in alternative 1.

Alternative 3 is denominated in US$ which adds the problem of **foreign exchange risk**. Any unexpected appreciation of sterling against the US$ may result in the bond being insufficient to cover the cost of the project. However if the US$ strengthens against sterling as expected, there is the danger of servicing a loan that is actually too large.

The foreign currency loan (alternative 3) is marginally less expensive than the home currency debt. However, given the foreign currency exposure mentioned above, it may be worthwhile investigating the cost of hedging against the risk in order to fix the future exchange rate.

<u>Recommendation</u>

The recommended source of funding will depend on the **length of time** for which funding is required.

If funding is required for the **full term** of the project, **alternative 2** is the recommended source. It is cheaper than alternative 1 and matches both currency and maturity.

If funding is only required for **5 years**, **alternative 3** may be the preferred source if currency rates can be hedged in a cost-efficient manner.

(b)   <u>Methods of adjusting for risk</u>

> **Tutorial note**. You are only required to provide explanations for two out of the three methods. Details of all three methods are given here to ensure full coverage of the methods.
>
> **Decision trees** were covered in detail in Paper P1.

Decision trees

Decision trees are used to model a finite number of outcomes where more than one variable that affects the final outcome is unknown or uncertain. The value of some of the variables may depend on the value of other variables.

Probabilities are attached to each outcome and expected values (probabilities x payoff) can then be determined.

This method of incorporating risk may be useful to Horatio if there is a risk of the project failing completely (perhaps as a result of new technology not being sufficiently tested).

Risk-adjusted discount rate

These rates reflect that fact that, the greater the risk, the higher the returns investors require on their investments. Risk-adjusted discount rates can be used for particular risk classes of investments to reflect relative risks. For example, a high discount rate can be used so that a cash flow that occurs in the relatively distant future will have less effect on the decision.

In Horatio's case, a high discount rate might be applied in the early years of the project to reflect the greater risk of using new technology (as it is more likely that something will go wrong towards the beginning of the project). A lower discount rate can be applied to later years as the technology becomes established.

Certainty equivalents

The certainty equivalent approach involves converting expected cash flows from the project to equivalent riskless amounts. The greater the risk of an expected cash flow, the lower will be its certainty equivalent value (receipts) or the higher will be the certainty equivalent value (payments). One of the main issues with this approach is the degree of subjectivity involved in establishing the certainty equivalents.

This technique is likely to be of limited use to Horatio. The technology is new therefore there will be little or no information to use in the determination of certainty equivalents. The high degree of subjectivity will be such that the results will be very unreliable.

35 WZ

(a) Alternative 1

For Alternative 1, the **rights issue** price will be 85% of **current market price** Z$12.50 = Z$10.625 per share. Number of shares issued = 5 m / 10.625 = 0.471 million.

	Current situation Z$m	Alternative 1 Z$m	Alternative 2 Z$m
Earnings before interest	15.00	17.00	17.00
Interest on 8% debt	(1.60)	(1.60)	(1.60)
Interest on Z$5m 9% bonds	–	–	(0.45)
Profit before tax	13.40	15.40	14.95
Tax @ 30%	(4.02)	(4.62)	(4.49)
Profit after tax	9.38	10.78	10.46
Preference dividend	(0.70)	(0.70)	(0.70)
Equity earnings	8.68	10.08	9.76
No. of shares (million)	5.00	5.471	5.00

		Current situation	Alternative 1	Alternative 2
(i)	**Earnings per share (Z$)**	**1.74**	**1.84**	**1.95**
	Market value per share (Z$) (eps / 12%)	14.50	15.33	16.25
(ii)	**Total market value of equity (Z$m)**	**72.50**	**83.87**	**81.25**
	Value of preference shares (10m × Z$0.8)	8.00	8.00	8.00
	Value of 8% debt (Z$20m × 0.9)	18.00	18.00	18.00
	Value of 9% bonds			5.00
(iii)	**Market value of the entity**	**98.5**	**109.87**	**112.25**
(iv)	**Gearing (debt / total value)**	**18.3%**	**16.4%**	**20.5%**

(v) Weighted average cost of capital

The after tax cost of the 8% debt is 8/90 (1 – 0.3) = 6.22% pa.
The cost of the preference shares is 7/80 = 8.75% pa.

Current situation

	MV Z$m	Cost %	MV × Cost/98.5
Equity	72.50	12.00	8.83
Preference shares	8.00	8.75	0.71
8% unsecured debt	18.00	6.22	1.14
	98.50		10.68

WACC = 10.68%.

Alternative 1

	MV Z$m	Cost %	MV × Cost/109.87
Equity	83.87	12.00	9.16
Preference shares	8.00	8.75	0.64
8% unsecured debt	18.00	6.22	1.02
	109.87		10.82

WACC = 10.82%.

Alternative 2

	MV Z$m	Cost %	MV × Cost/112.25
Market value of equity	81.25	12.00	8.69
Preference shares	8.00	8.75	0.62
8% unsecured debt	18.00	6.22	1.00
9% bonds	5.00	6.30	0.28
	112.25		10.59

WACC = 10.59%.

The above calculations ignore issue costs.

(b) Issues to be considered

Period of finance

The **injection of working capital** is needed to **underpin general expansion**. This implies it is a **permanent increase** and should be financed from **permanent** or **long term funds.** In this respect, the best is **equity capital,** followed by the **10-year bond.** Factoring should not really be used as a source of permanent funds. It is best held in reserve for short term funding needs.

Cost of the funds

From the calculations above, the 10 year bond (Alternative 2) is **cheaper than equity** (Alternative 1). The bond **lowers WACC** whereas the equity issue **raises it.** Although these calculations ignore the fact that as **gearing increases** the **cost of equity** will rise to compensate for increased financial risk, the **over-riding effect** will still be that debt attracts **tax savings** on interest whereas **equity dividends** are **not tax allowable.** Furthermore the debt will probably have **lower issue costs** than the equity. Rates of interest for factoring the receivables can be very competitive and might be cheaper than the bond issue.

Gearing and liquidity

The equity issue **reduces gearing** whereas the **debt issue increases** it. In terms of economic substance, factoring debtors would also increase gearing, as it is a form of borrowing. The gearing of the company is not unduly high, so this consideration would probably be outweighed by the cheaper cost of debt funds than equity.

The only source of funds to affect liquidity would be the **factoring**. Insufficient information is available to test the result, but the effect of using short term sources of funds to finance long term needs will usually strain liquidity.

Flexibility of funding

It is possible that the **debt** can be **'drawn down'** as needed, though this is **more difficult** for **bonds** than for a bank loan. The equity is a one-time issue. Factoring is very flexible, automatically varying with the size of the receivables ledger.

Ease of raising the funds

Factoring is easy to arrange. The ease of raising funds through bonds and share issues depends on the **state of the market,** but if bonds are difficult there is always the alternative of a **bank loan,** though this might have to be at floating rate interest. Share issues require a prospectus and a lot more administrative time than loan issues.

Recommendation

Because the gearing of the company is not unduly high, and a relatively permanent source of funds is needed, the **loan** is **recommended.** This is likely to reduce the overall cost of capital.

36 CAP

Text references. The capital asset pricing model is discussed in Chapter 9.

Top tips. In (a) you should give a brief definition of the beta factor and what it measures. This will help you to explain the implications of a beta factor of less than one. Preference shares do not count as equity and should be ignored at this stage of the calculations.

In (b) there are a number of valid approaches that can be used to find the cost of the loan stock. The most usual of these, using the internal rate of return, is described in the suggested solution. Using 5% as we have means you only need to calculate one rate. It is equally correct to use a higher and lower rate, say 7% and 4%, and then to use interpolation to find the discount rate at which the NPV approaches zero.

Another possible approach is to calculate the net cash flow at the end of year 1 (£105.60) and divide this into the initial cash flow (£100.57). The result is 0.952. You can then look at the discount tables, where you will see that this is the 5% discount factor for year 1.

In (c) you may find it helpful to think in terms of financial factors and factors affecting the level of business risk when structuring your answer.

Easy marks. Limitations of CAPM should always represent straightforward marks.

Examiner's comments. A number of candidates failed to complete the calculation correctly; a common mistake was using 0.8 as a to the power of function. Candidates also failed to explain the link between risk and returns, and what a beta of 0.8 meant in relation to the market as a whole.

Many candidates did (b) well but poorer candidates made various basic mistakes.

Answers to (c) were generally poor, and were insufficiently focused on correlation and systematic risk. Few candidates discussed the significance of gearing levels.

(a) The cost of equity can be found using the following formula:

$$k_e = R_f + (R_m - R_f)\beta$$

where k_e is the cost of equity capital – expected equity return
R_f is the risk-free rate of return
R_m is the return from the market as a whole
β is the beta factor of the individual security

Here: R_f = 5% (annual yield on treasury bills)
R_m = 15%
β = 0.8
k_e = 5% + (15% – 5%)0.8
= 13%

The required rate of return on equity of CAP at 30 September 2002 is therefore 13%.

Beta factor levels

The beta factor is a measure of **systematic risk**, that is, the element of risk that cannot be avoided by **diversification**. The beta factor measures the **variability in returns** for a given security in relation to the variation in returns for the market as a whole.

A beta factor of 1.0 means that if the market goes up by x%, all other things being equal, one would expect the return on the security to go up by x% as well. A beta factor of less than 1.0 means that the return on the security is likely to be less variable than the return on the market as a whole. A beta value of 0.8 means that if the market returns go up by 5%, the return on the security would only be expected to go up by 4% (5% × 0.8). Similarly, if the market returns fall by 5%, the return on the security would only be expected to fall by 4%.

(b) Weighted average cost of capital

The weighted average cost of capital (WACC) is the **average cost** of the **company's finance** weighted according to the proportion each element bears to the total pool of capital. Weighting is usually based on market values, current yields and costs after tax. Where market values can be used, as in this case, reserves can be ignored.

Equity

The cost of equity has already been calculated at 13%.

The market value of equity (V_E) is the number of shares in issue multiplied by the market price (ex div):

V_E = 200m × £3
    = £600m

Preference shares

Preference shares are irredeemable. The interest on preference shares is not tax deductible. The cost of the preference shares (k_{pref}) is therefore:

k_{pref} = d/P_0

where: d = annual dividend in perpetuity
P_0 = current ex div price
k_{pref} = 9%/0.90
    = 10%

The market value of the preference shares (V_P) is the number of shares in issue multiplied by the market price (ex div):

V_P = 50m × £0.90
    = £45m

Loan stock

The loan stock pays interest of 8%, which is allowable against tax. Tax is paid at the end of the year in which taxable profits arise, in other words, at the same time as the interest payment at the end of year 1.

Since the net cost of the interest is 5.6% (8% × 0.7), and the current market price of the stock is just above par, we will try an initial rate of return of 5%.

Year		Cash flow £	5% disc factors	Present value £
0	Market value	(100.57)	1.000	(100.57)
1	Interest	8.00	0.952	7.62
1	Tax saved	(2.40)	0.952	(2.28)
1	Redemption	100.00	0.952	95.20
	Net present value			(0.03)

This net present value is virtually zero, and therefore the effective cost of the loan stock is 5%.

The market value of the loan stock (V_D) is the number of units in issue multiplied by the market price:

V_D = 250m × £100.57/100.00
    = £251.4m

WACC

Total market value = 600.0 + 45.0 + 251.4 = 896.4

$$\text{WACC} = k_e \left[\frac{V_E}{V_E + V_P + V_D} \right] + k_{pref} \left[\frac{V_P}{V_E + V_P + V_D} \right] + k_d \left[\frac{V_D}{V_E + V_P + V_D} \right]$$

$$= 13 \left[\frac{600.0}{896.4} \right] + 10 \left[\frac{45}{896.4} \right] + 5 \left[\frac{251.4}{896.4} \right] = 10.6\%$$

Alternative working			
	MV £'000	Cost %	Weighted average (MV × cost/896.4)
Equity	600.0	13	8.70
Preference shares	45.0	10	0.50
Loan stock	251.4	5	1.40
	896.4		10.60

(c) **Factors affecting equity beta**

CAP's equity beta will be affected by factors that change the perceived **volatility in returns** to the ordinary shareholders.

Rise in gearing

Following the new issue of loan stock, the **gearing will rise**. This in turn is likely to affect the **volatility** of the returns to equity in relation to the market index. As a consequence, the beta may rise.

Effect of diversification

Since the returns on the campsite business are likely to have a very **low correlation** with those of the existing farming business, the effect of the new investment will be to **smooth out the earnings pattern**. This will reduce the volatility of the returns to equity. However the beta value will be affected by how the **campsite returns vary** in relation to **returns on the market portfolio**, and they may **vary more or less** than the **returns from the farming activities**. The equity beta will be the weighted average of the betas of the two sorts of activity.

Refinancing

As well as raising new debt, the company also has to redeem its existing debt in 20X3. If it replaces existing debt with similar debt, there will be little or no effect on the beta. However, if the debt is **replaced by equity** and gearing reduced, volatility of returns on equity and hence the **beta factor** are likely to fall.

Investor perceptions

This is a major diversification by CAP, and investors may perceive this to be a **risky strategy**. As a consequence in the short-term, the beta could rise to reflect this. Investors may feel that CAP's managers **lack the skills required** to manage campsites, as managing camping sites is a very different job from farming. As a consequence this will increase the risk of the new investment, and hence the equity beta may rise. There are also **start-up costs** associated with the new investments. These may depress the profits in the first year of trading, which in turn may cause investors to perceive the new business to be riskier than it really is. The effect of this will be to cause a short-term rise in the beta value.

(d) **Limitations of CAPM**

Diversification

Under the CAPM, the return required from a security is **related** to its **systematic risk** rather than its total risk. Only the risks that **cannot** be **eliminated** by diversification are **relevant**. The assumption is that investors will hold a **fully diversified portfolio** and therefore deal with the unsystematic risk themselves. However, in practice, markets are **not totally efficient** and investors do not all hold fully diversified portfolios. This means that total risk is relevant to investment decisions, and that therefore the relevance of the CAPM may be limited.

Excess return

In practice, it is difficult to determine the excess return ($R_m - R_f$). **Expected rather than historical returns** should be used, although historical returns are used in practice.

Risk-free rate

It is similarly difficult to **determine the risk-free rate**. A risk-free investment might be a government security; however, interest rates vary with the term of the debt.

Risk aversion

Shareholders are risk averse, and therefore **demand higher returns** in compensation for increased levels of risk.

Beta factors

Beta factors based on historical data may be a **poor basis** for future **decision making**, since evidence suggests that beta values fluctuate over time.

Unusual circumstances

The CAPM is unable to forecast accurately returns for companies with low price/earnings ratios, and to take account of seasonal 'month-of-the-year' effects and 'day-of-the-week' effects that appear to influence returns on shares.

Arbitrage pricing theory

Arbitrage pricing theory may be more suitable for a company like CAP, since it is based on the assumption that returns are determined by a number of **independent factors**, to which a particular risk premium is attached. These could include the various economic factors that have impacted on the conditions CAP has been facing.

If arbitrage pricing theory is used, there will be no need to identify the market portfolio. However CAP will then face the problem of identifying what **factors are relevant**, and what their **risk premiums** are.

37 ABC

Text references. Cost of capital is covered in Chapter 8 and the efficient market hypothesis in Chapter 5.

Top tips. Use clear workings and a logical approach to the calculations in part (a). They should be straightforward if you have done enough practice but make sure you do not spend too long on them.

Part (b) requires a detailed discussion applied to the specific circumstances of this company. Don't just write a list of bulletin points or everything you know about the efficient market hypothesis.

Easy marks. There are plenty of marks available for some straightforward calculations.

Examiner's comments. The main weaknesses in part (a) were in the calculations of WACC using Director B's suggestion. The efficient market hypothesis needs to be discussed in part (b) but not **only** the EMH.

(a)   Director A: current WACC

Cost of debt

Year		Cash flow £	Discount factor 3%	PV £	Discount factor 5%	PV £
0	Debenture price	(105.00)	1.000	(105.00)	1.000	(105.00)
1-5	Interest (8.4 × (1 – 0.3))	5.88	4.580	26.93	4.329	25.45
5	Repayment	100.00	0.863	86.30	0.784	78.40
				8.23		(1.15)

Calculate the cost of debt using an IRR calculation.

$$IRR = a\% + \left[\frac{NPV_a}{NPV_a - NPV_b} \times (b - a) \right]\%$$

Cost of debt = 3 + [8.23/(8.23 + 1.15)] x (5 – 3)

= 4.75%

Cost of equity

$k_e = R_f + (R_m - R_f)\beta$

$R_f = 5\%$

$R_m = 12\%$

$\beta = 1.2$

$k_e = 5\% + (12\% - 5\%)1.2$
    $= 13.4\%$

Weighted average cost of capital

$V_E = 300 \times 8 = £2,400m$

$V_D = 1,100 \times 1.05 = £1,155m$

$$WACC = k_e\left[\frac{V_E}{V_E + V_D}\right] + k_d\left[\frac{V_D}{V_E + V_D}\right]$$

$$= 13.4\% \times \frac{2,400}{3,555} + 4.75\% \times \frac{1,155}{3,555}$$

$$= 9.05\% + 1.54\% = 10.59\%$$

Director B: project specific cost of capital

Ungear XYZ beta

$$\beta_u = \beta_g\left[\frac{V_E}{V_E + V_D[1-t]}\right] + \beta_d\left[\frac{V_D[1-t]}{V_E + V_D[1-t]}\right]$$

For XYZ:

$V_E = 400 \times 3.73 = £1,492m$
$V_D = £350m$

$\beta_u = 1.6 \times (1,492/(1,492 + (350 \times 0.7))$
$= 1.374$

Re-gearing

$V_E = £340$
$V_D = £260$

$$\beta_g = \beta_u + [\beta_u - \beta_d]\frac{V_D[1-t]}{V_E}$$

$\beta_g = 1.374 + 1.374 \times [(260 \times 0.7)/340]$

$= 2.109$

Cost of equity

$k_e = R_f + (R_m - R_f)\beta$
$= 5\% + (12\% - 5\%)2.109$
$= 19.8\%$

Cost of debt

$k_d = 8\% (1 - 30\%)$
$= 5.6\%$

Weighted average cost of capital

$$WACC = k_e\left[\frac{V_E}{V_E + V_D}\right] + k_d(1-t)\left[\frac{V_D}{V_E + V_D}\right]$$

$$= \left[19.8\% \times \frac{340}{600}\right] + \left[5.6\% \times \frac{260}{600}\right]$$

$$= 11.22\% + 2.43\%$$

$$= 13.65\%$$

Alternative approach

Using the adjusted cost of capital (MM formula)

$k_{adj} = k_{eu}[1 - tL]$

$k_{eu} = R_f + (R_m - R_f)\,\beta_u$

$\phantom{k_{eu}} = 5 + (1.374 \times (12 - 5))$

$\phantom{k_{eu}} = 14.62\%$

$k_{adj} = 14.62 \times \left[1 - \left(30\% \times \dfrac{260}{340 + 260}\right)\right]$

$\phantom{k_{adj}} = 12.72\%$

Appropriateness of the discount rates

The project specific cost of capital is **higher** than the current WACC and this reflects the additional **business and financial risk** of the new investment.

Business risk

The new investment is in the film industry in which ABC has not previously been involved and which is notoriously fickle. The business risk is therefore **higher** than that of ABC's existing operations and the **return required by investors** is likely to go up. The current WACC will not incorporate this additional business risk.

The equity beta of XYZ is higher than that of ABC, and when this beta is re-geared to reflect ABC's gearing ratio, it is **considerably higher**. This presumably reflects the additional risk of the industry in which ABC operates. However, a number of factors contribute to the beta value, not all of which will apply to ABC.

Financial risk

The finance that is raised to fund a new investment might substantially **change the capital structure** and the perceived financial risk of investing in the company. For this investment the proportion of debt is 43% (260/600 × 100%) whereas it was previously 32% (1,155/3,555 × 100%). The financial risk has therefore increased and it could therefore be argued that the current WACC is not an acceptable discount rate.

Recommendation

The current WACC does not reflect the additional business risk that arises from undertaking an investment in a new, risky sector.

15% is **too high** a rate to use as it is based only on the relatively high cost of equity and ignores the amount of debt that will be used to finance the investment. It is therefore recommended that a **project specific cost of capital** is used.

(b) Market capitalisation

The market capitalisation is the market value of the company's shares multiplied by the number of issued shares. The **fundamental theory of share values** states that the realistic market price of a share can be derived from a valuation of estimated future earnings. The share price should therefore **rise** if the company is to undertake a project with a **positive net present value**.

Efficient market hypothesis

The **semi-strong form** of the efficient market hypothesis says that share prices will swiftly and rationally reflect all information that is **publicly available**. ABC is quoted on a major international stock exchange which is likely to exhibit semi-strong form efficiency.

When the proposed investment becomes public knowledge, it can therefore be expected that the share price will rise in line with the additional earnings expected from the investment. However, this does depend on the market's view of the proposed investment and its associated risk profile.

Rights issue

£340 million is to be raised through a rights issue which will be at a discount of 15% on the current share price. This discount will probably mean that the **share price will fall**, at least in the short term, unless the earnings enhancing nature of the project is sufficient to compensate for the discounted issue.

There is a danger that the market reacts so negatively to the investment that the share price falls by more than 15% which would jeopardise the rights issue.

Market sentiment

Market sentiment is a major factor in the behaviour of share prices and much depends on investors' views of the **change in business risk** that is involved in this project.

Other factors may be affecting share prices at the same time and, as a well diversified company, the share price of ABC is likely to reflect the overall movement in the share index. For example, general gloomy market sentiment and worries over economic growth prospects could adversely affect all share prices.

38 BZ

> **Text references.** WACC and the CAPM are covered in Chapter 8 and sources of finance in Chapters 5 and 6.
>
> **Top tips.** This question covers various parts of the syllabus so a little knowledge is needed about a lot of areas. The calculation of the WACC in part (a) should be straightforward. The only complication is the calculation of the market value of debt but don't worry if you did not think to adjust it, very few marks would be lost.
>
> The discussions in the rest of the question need to be carefully planned and headings used to give a structure to your answer. Use your common sense and general business knowledge to come up with ideas, particularly in part (c).
>
> Don't forget to do an APV calculation in part (c).
>
> **Easy marks.** There are easy marks available in the straightforward calculation in part (a) and plenty of marks for common sense discussion points.

(a)   Calculation of WACC

The market value of equity is the number of shares in issue multiplied by the market price:

$$V_E = 39m \times €4$$
$$= €156m$$

The interest rate of 8% on the debt is lower than the current cost of debt so the value of debt has to be adjusted to reflect this difference to give the market value of debt.

$$V_D = €121.5m \times 0.08/0.09$$
$$= €108m$$

$$V_E + V_D = 156 + 108 = €264m$$

$$K_e = 11\%$$

$$K_d = 9\% \times (1 - 28\%)$$
$$= 6.48\%$$

$$WACC = k_e \left[\frac{V_E}{V_E + V_D} \right] + k_d \left[\frac{V_D}{V_E + V_D} \right]$$

$$= 11 \left[\frac{156}{264} \right] + 6.48 \left[\frac{108}{264} \right]$$

$$= 6.5\% + 2.65\%$$

$$= 9.15\%$$

(b)   Determining an appropriate discount rate for the US subsidiary proposal

Using the WACC

The WACC that has been calculated reflects the **average cost** of acquiring funds. Use of the WACC as the **discount rate** is the normal approach in appraising potential new investments. However, this is based on the assumption that the new investments are **small** in relation to the size of the company, and that they carry a **similar level of risk** to the existing business.

The new US investment is a **large** investment that uses a **new type of finance** and will carry a **different level of risk**. The WACC would therefore **not** be an appropriate discount rate to use.

Risk-adjusted cost of capital

The discount rate that should be used for the US investment is a **project specific** cost of capital. This would reflect the different **business risk** and **financial risk** of the new investment.

The project specific cost of capital would be calculated using the **capital asset pricing model** and a **proxy entity's published beta** which has been **adjusted** to reflect gearing differences.

Exchange rate risk

An overseas investment carries the **additional risk** from adverse movements in exchange rates. There are two methods that can be used to appraise international investments which use different discount rates. Firstly, the project cash flows could be converted into euros and then discounted at a **euro discount rate** to calculate the NPV in euro terms. Alternatively, the dollar cash flows could be discounted using an **adjusted dollar discount rate** and the resulting NPV converted at the spot exchange rate.

The approach to be chosen will depend on the available information and the extent to which **forecasts are reliable**.

(c)   Using government subsidies

Advantages

The main advantage is the subsidised interest rate which makes the finance **cheaper**. There is no mention of **security** being needed for the loan which leaves assets free to be used as security for other debt finance. If a government is willing to provide subsidised finance, it may offer **additional help** to the business, for example, training support, obtaining planning permissions or winning public sector contracts.

Disadvantages

The **interest rate** being offered by the State is currently **lower** than the domestic rate but this may **change** over the five-year investment period. The **exchange rate** could also change during this time. If the dollar strengthens against the euro, the interest payments would become more expensive.

There is **political risk** involved in international investments. In this situation, the US State Government may fail to honour its commitment to the project or change the tax position. There may also be **terms and conditions** attached to the financing package which make it commercially unacceptable.

Calculation of value of subsidy

Value of loan in €s	= $50/1.2	
	= €41.67m	
Interest benefit	= (9% - 3.5%) × €41.67	
	= €2.29m	
Tax shield lost	= 28% × €2.29m	
	= €0.64m	
Net benefit	= 2.29 – 0.64	
	= €1.65m	

Annuity factor for five years @ 9% = 3.89

9% is used as this is the opportunity cost of debt.

Present value of subsidy   = €1.65 × 3.89 = €6.42m

(d)   Financing of US business operations

Once the US loan has been repaid, there are a number of alternative financing methods that could be available.

Bonds

New debt finance could be raised in the form of long-term bonds. This will depend on what level of **gearing** is acceptable for this entity. BZ currently has a debt ratio of 41% (108/264 × 100 from part (a)) which may already be considered high enough. Using debt finance would further increase **financial risk** on top of increased business risk from a new venture into a new market.

Equity

BZ's shares are not listed but shares occasionally change hands in private transactions. It would probably be difficult to raise funds through a **rights issue** in view of the limited marketability and fees could be expensive.

A **venture capitalist** might be interested in providing finance but the amount involved is probably too small. There would also be a requirement for a representative from the venture capitalist to sit on the board which may be an unacceptable condition.

Cash

BZ has an **overdraft facility** for short-term financing requirements, so presumably does not have any cash assets. There may be **surplus non-current assets** which could be sold to raise cash.

Other companies

A successful distribution network in the USA could be attractive to other companies who may be able to supply finance, for example, **suppliers** of BZ's textiles. A **joint venture** with another company could be an option.

Recommendation

There is no obvious perfect financing method in these alternatives and options could have changed in five years when the loan is due to be repaid. The best option is to wait and see if the venture is a success before looking at what happens next.

39 GUC

Text references. Cost of equity is covered in Chapter 8 and yield to maturity is dealt with in Chapter 6. Different sources of debt and equity finance are covered in Chapters 5 and 6 respectively.

Top tips. Make use of the information you have in order to calculate the cost of equity in part (a)(i) – don't panic because you can't use the CAPM!

Part (b) makes use of the information you have calculated in part (a) and helps with the comparison between the three alternatives. Remember to look for future implications of each method of finance rather than just looking at the current cost.

Easy marks. You should be able to pick up some straightforward marks in part (a)(ii) when calculating the yield to maturity. There are also some relatively easy marks available in part (b) when comparing the alternative sources of finance.

Examiner's comments. This question was poorly attempted, with calculation of cost of equity often not attempted at all. Part (a)(ii) was generally answered satisfactorily although candidates frequently did not include the conversion premium. Many answers to part (b) failed to recognise the specific issues raised by the scenario and provided a discussion of everything the candidate knew about raising new debt and equity.

(a)   (i)   Current cost of equity

> **Tutorial note**. Very often the natural reaction when faced with a cost of equity question is to try to use the CAPM. When you have read through the question you will realise that you do not have the necessary information to do so therefore you have to find data that can help you find the cost of equity.

Earnings for the following period (ie E_1) per share = P\$864m × 1.06 = P\$915.8m

Earnings per share = P\$915.8m/785m shares = P\$1.17 per share

Current share price = P\$7.70

Cost of (return on) equity = P\$1.17/P\$7.70 = 15.2%

(ii) <u>Gross yield to maturity</u>

The yield to maturity is effectively the IRR of the bond's cash flows.

	0 P\$	*1 - 5* P\$	*5* P\$
Initial investment	(100)		
Cash inflows (interest – 3% of P\$100)		3.00	
Redemption value (W1)			113.30
Discount factor (6%)	1.000	4.212	0.747
DCF	(100)	12.64	84.64

Net present value = P\$(2.72)

> **Tutorial note.** We started with a discount rate of 6% as that is close to the yield to maturity of bonds without conversion rights.

Try 4% to obtain a higher NPV

	0 P\$	*1 - 5* P\$	*5* P\$
Initial investment	(100)		
Cash inflows (interest – 3% of P\$100)		3.00	
Redemption value (W1)			113.30
Discount factor (4%)	1.000	4.452	0.822
DCF	(100)	13.36	93.13

Net present value = P\$6.49

Using interpolation we can find the yield to maturity

Yield to maturity = 4 + [6.49/(6.49 + 2.72)] x (6 – 4) = 5.41%

Workings

(1) <u>Redemption value</u>

Every P\$100 invested will convert into 11 ordinary shares

Share price at redemption date (5 years' time) = P\$7.70 x 1.06^5 = P\$10.30

Total value of shares at redemption = 11 x P\$10.30 = P\$113.30

Conversion premium = current market value (P\$113.30) – current conversion value (P\$100)

= \$13.30

(b) <u>Evaluation of alternative methods of finance</u>

The three alternative methods under consideration are

(i) New equity by means of a rights issue

(ii) A five year bond with a yield of 0.5% below industry average

(iii) A convertible bond, coupon rate 3% issues at par (convertible into ordinary shares in five years' time)

Before the three methods are considered individually it is worthwhile making some **general observations** about GUC.

Share price has fallen by P\$0.50 (or 6.1%) in the last two months. This might send signals that the organisation is not a good investment as its shares are not being received well by the market.

The **P/E ratio** of GUC is 7 [(785m shares x P\$7.70)/P\$864m]. This is considerably below the industry average, again suggesting that GUC is not a good investment for potential shareholders.

GUC's **gearing ratio** of 34% is only approximately three quarters of the industry average. This suggests that there is further scope for using debt finance to finance future investments.

Profile of shareholders will have a significant impact on the method of finance that is finally used. Institutional investors make up the vast majority of shareholders in GUC.

These issues should be taken into consideration when evaluating the individual methods of finance.

Rights issue

A rights issue is a means of raising additional capital by giving existing shareholders the right to subscribe to new shares in proportion to their current holdings. This particular rights issue gives shareholders the chance to purchase shares at a 15% discount to current share price (that is a share price of P$6.55).

One of the main issues with this type of finance is that it will **dilute the power of current holdings**. As the vast majority of shares is held by institutional investors, this might not be very popular. It also follows that EPS will be diluted, at least for a time.

An increase in shares will improve the gearing ratio but gearing is not really a problem for GUC given that its **current gearing ratio is significantly below the industry average**.

GUC will have to make a decision regarding dividends. A rights issue obviously increases the number of shares in issue which will therefore increase dividend payout in monetary terms. If GUC intends to keep the total funds available for dividends constant (which will thus reduce dividend per share) it must make its intentions clear. However it must also be mindful of the **signals** that this may give to the market.

Of its total shareholders, 28% are small investors who may not be able to afford to take up the rights issue. If this is the case, underwriting costs may be substantial.

As mentioned in the general observations above, GUC's share price has fallen by 6% in the last two months. There is no apparent reason for this. Such a reduction may make shareholders think twice about taking up their rights if GUC does not look like a good investment in the future.

In addition to GUC looking like a potential poor future investment, any further reductions in share price may mean that GUC – under the current terms of the rights issue – may be in danger of **not raising the necessary funds**, even if the rights are fully subscribed. Any further rights issue might send signals that the original issue was not successful and thus make any further issues even less attractive.

Based on earlier calculations, any issue of equity carries a cost of approximately 14.3%. Even without further evaluation, it is clear that this is the most expensive option.

Five year bond, 6% coupon (that is, 0.5% below industry average yield)

The after-tax cost of issuing this bond is 4.2%, considerably cheaper than the 14.3% cost of equity discussed above.

The fact that the coupon rate of the bond is less than industry average suggests that the market sees GUC as being **less risky than the average company** in the same industry. This may be due to GUC's lower than average level of gearing.

If further debt is introduced into the capital structure, GUC should be aware of the need for any collateral to secure the bonds.

Convertible bond

The yield to maturity of the convertible bond is 5.41% (see calculations above) which makes it cheaper than the five year bond (by 0.59%) pre-tax and obviously much cheaper than the rights issue.

Although it appears cheaper on paper, GUC should bear in mind that at the end of five years it will have to pay dividends on a higher number of shares once conversion takes place. This is likely to prove **more expensive** than the five year 'ordinary' bond in the long run.

Once the conversion premium (capital gain) has been taken into consideration the use of a convertible bond is not quite as cheap as it might appear at first glance. However it should be borne in mind that the share price might not perform as well as predictions might suggest, in which case this source of finance might become cheaper.

On the other hand – linked to the point above – if the share price does not perform as well as expected, the potential debt holders may not want to take the risk of having to convert their debt holding into shares that actually have a lower value than their initial investment.

Recommendation

The rights issue appears to be **prohibitively expensive** compared with the other alternatives and should therefore be discarded. GUC has no apparent need to try to reduce its gearing through a rights issue therefore there is no need to take on the extra cost of issuing equity.

The choice is now between the 'ordinary' bond and the convertible bond. Pre-tax, the convertible bond is cheaper but has the problem of resulting in more shares being in circulation at the end of five years. Its continued attraction will depend on current shareholders' attitude towards the inevitable dilution of EPS in five years' time.

40 ADS

Text references. Capital structure is covered in Chapter 9. Cost of capital (including WACC) is dealt with in Chapter 8.

Top tips. In part (a) don't just concentrate of MM's theory – you are trying to show how this theory differs from the traditional approach therefore you must be prepared to discuss the features of both. Use the diagrams to illustrate your points.

In part (b) (ii), don't forget to deduct the value of debt from the total value of the geared firm (using MM formulae from the formulae sheet) in order to arrive at the value of equity. You should be able to check if your results are reasonable as you go along as you should be expecting the cost of equity to increase as debt is introduced but overall WACC should be lower for a geared firm (using the MM theory)

Whatever your results for part (b), make sure you demonstrate that you understand that cost of equity for a geared firm should be higher than an all-equity firm and that WACC should be lower. Don't forget to address the directors' concerns about lowering the value of equity.

Easy marks. There are easy marks to be gained in part (b) as the formulae are given in the exam.

Examiner's comments. This question tended to be answered very well or very poorly. In part (a)(i) few candidates gained more than token marks for the MM graphs. Answers to part (b)(i) frequently multiplied the share price by the number of shares in issue rather than using the DCF approach. Part (b)(ii) required the use of MM's model with taxes. Many candidates attempted valuation of ADS's equity using a variety of other methods. However on the 'own answer' principle, most candidates gained marks for the WACC calculation. Part (c) was particularly poorly attempted and most candidates failed to address the question asked.

(a)   How Modigliani and Miller's (MM) capital structure theory differs from the traditional theory

The traditional view

The traditional view of capital structure and its effect on WACC is as follows.

(i)   It assumes that, as the level of gearing increases, the cost of debt will remain unchanged up to a certain gearing level. Beyond this level it will increase as interest cover falls, risk of bankruptcy increases and the amount of assets available for security falls.

(ii)   Cost of equity will rise as gearing levels increase, reflecting the increased financial risk. Increased financial risk means that, as interest payments rise, the earnings available to pay dividends to shareholders will become more uncertain as interest takes precedence over dividend payments.

(iii) WACC does not remain constant, but falls initially as the proportion of debt increases. It will begin to rise as the increases in cost of equity (and possibly cost of debt) becomes more significant.

(iv)   The optimum level of gearing is where the company's WACC is minimised.

      The traditional view about cost of capital can be illustrated by the following diagram.

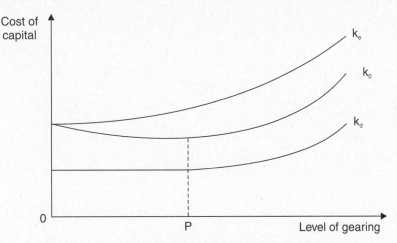

Where k_e is the cost of equity in the geared company

    k_d is the cost of debt
    k_0 is the weighted average cost of capital

Point P illustrates the level of gearing at which WACC is at its lowest. This is known as the optimal capital structure.

MM view of WACC (net operating income approach)

The MM view is similar to the traditional view in that it also assumes that cost of equity will increase as the level of gearing increases (again due to increased financial risk).

However MM proposed that the total market value of a company, in the absence of tax, will be determined by only two factors.

(i)   The total earnings of the company
(ii)   The level of business risk attached to these earnings

The capital structure of the company would have no effect at all on the company's WACC. This can be illustrated in the following diagram.

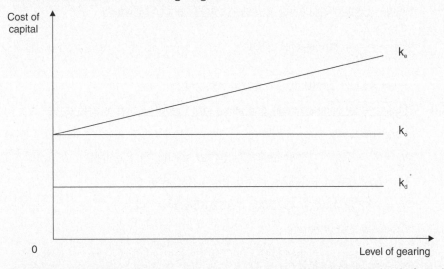

The diagram illustrates that the cost of debt remains unchanged as the level of gearing changes and the cost of equity rises in such a way as to keep the WACC constant.

However the above model ignores taxation. If tax was introduced into the model, debt can be beneficial to the company due to the tax shield available on interest. MM admitted that tax relief on interest payments makes debt capital cheaper to a company and thus reduces WACC when gearing is increased. They claimed that WACC would continue to fall up to a gearing level of 100%. This differs from the traditional view which states that there is an optimal capital structure after which WACC will start to rise.

The following diagram illustrates the MM approach with taxation.

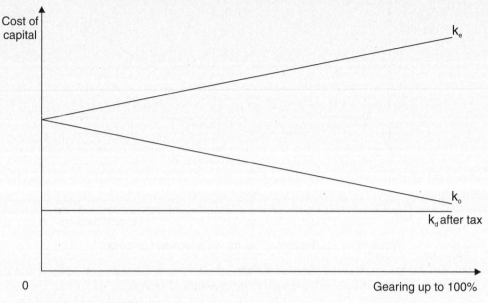

<u>Limitations in the real world</u>

Whilst MM's theory is widely recognised, it has restrictions when applied to the real world.

(i)   MM assumes that capital markets are perfect (for example a firm will always be able to raise funds for worthwhile projects). It ignores the increasing danger that very high levels of gearing can lead to financial distress costs and agency problems (where managers may be reluctant to invest if gearing levels are already high).

(ii)   The absence of transactions costs ensured that the arbitrage process worked. In practice transactions costs will restrict this process.

(iii) The theory assumes that individual and corporate gearing will be the same. This is unlikely to be the case in the real world as even smaller companies are likely to have a superior credit rating to individual investors.

(b)   (i)   <u>Value of equity assuming new stores are financed by equity</u>

$$PV = \frac{1}{r-g} \times \text{earnings for 2011}$$

$$PV = A\$127.1m/(0.09 - 0.04) = A\$2,542m$$

(ii) <u>Financed by undated bond and using MM theory with corporate taxes</u>

Value of equity

$V_g = V_u + TB_c$ (where TB_c is the tax savings on the debt)

$V_g = A\$2,542m + (A\$250m \times 0.25) = A\$2,604.5m$

$V_E = A\$2,604.5m - A\$250m = A\$2,354.5m$

Expected cost of equity

$$k_{eg} = k_{eu} + [k_{eu} - k_d]\frac{V_D[1-t]}{V_E}$$

$k_{eg} = 9 + (9 - 5) \times [(250 \times 0.75)/2,354.5]$

$k_{eg} = 9.3\%$

WACC

$$WACC = k_e \left[\frac{V_E}{V_E + V_D} \right] + k_d (1 - t) \left[\frac{V_D}{V_E + V_D} \right]$$

WACC = 9.3 x (2,354.5/2,604.5) + (5 x 0.75) x (250/2,604.5)

WACC = 8.41 + 0.36

WACC = 8.77%

(c)   Explanation of results

MM theory with taxation proposes that cost of capital will fall when debt is introduced into the capital structure. The results in part (b) show this to be the case. Cost of capital with no debt was 9% (from the question) whilst WACC when debt is introduced is 8.86%.

The value of the company increases when debt finance is introduced into the capital structure. With all-equity finance, value of the company will be A$2,542m whilst with debt it increases to A$2,604.5m. This increase is due to the value of the tax shield on the debt.

However it can be seen that the value of equity falls when debt is introduced (from A$2,542m to A$2,354.5m. This is because the equity shareholders do not contribute any funds in the investment project if debt is used but will contribute the full A$250m if equity finance is used. However the overall value of the firm is increased when debt is brought in.

Shareholders' wealth if equity finance is used will actually be A$2,542m – A$250m = A$2,292m but with debt finance this increases to A$2,354.5m. The benefit of the tax shield (which is the difference between the two figures) is enjoyed entirely by the equity shareholders.

Directors should not be concerned about the fall in the value of equity as they will be able to demonstrate that the equity shareholders will ultimately benefit from the introduction of debt due to the **tax shield** available.

41 FF

Text references. Capital structure and Modigliani and Miller theory and formulae are all covered in Chapter 9.

Top tips. In part (b) don't be put off by the unusual requirement to draw graphs. When drawing the graphs you should noticed that they are in line with Modigliani and Miller's capital structure theory with taxation.

Easy marks. You should be able to pick up a number of easy marks for the calculations in part (a) (i).

Examiner's comments. Many candidates made the same error when calculating the value under funding structure A by not adding in the present value of the future cash flows of the project of $110 million. The graphs, were generally poor and some candidates provided a graph showing results other than those asked for in the question.

(a)   (i)   Value of company

Funding structure A

F$11 × 30 million + Project value of F$110 million = F$440 million

Funding structure B

Value of ungeared company + value of the tax shield = 440m + (0.25 × 80m) = F$460m

Funding structure C

Value of ungeared company + value of the tax shield = 440m + (0.25 × 32m) = F$448m

(ii)   <u>WACC</u>

Funding structure A

WACC = cost of equity = 9%

Funding structure B

WACC = $k_{eu}(1 - tL)$ = 9% × (1 – (0.25 × 80/460)) = 8.61%

Funding structure C

WACC = $k_{eu}(1 - tL)$ = 9% × (1 – (0.25 × 32/448)) = 8.84%

(b)

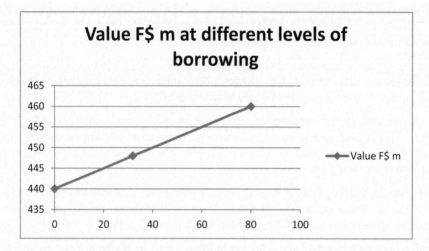

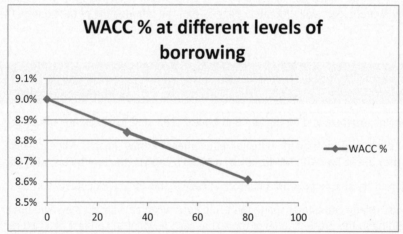

Under MM theory (with taxation) the value of the company will increase as a result of the tax relief on the debt. The increase in value associated with the tax relief on additional debt will belong to the providers of equity and therefore shareholder wealth is increased.

As a result of introducing debt finance, the WACC falls. This is due to the fact that the impact of the tax shield on the debt more than compensates for the increase in the cost of equity as a result of taking on the additional debt.

(c)   FF should chose funding structure B as it adds most to shareholder wealth without creating **significant danger of financial distress**, since financial gearing remains relatively low as the amount of debt is approximately 20% of the company value.

The increase in the value of FF is due to the tax benefit in perpetuity from the use of the debt financing.

It should be noted that MM theory is based on a number of assumptions that do not necessarily hold in reality. These include the existence of perfect capital markets and perfect information. MM theory also ignores the impact of financial distress (for example threat of bankruptcy), which would increase the cost of equity such that WACC would increase.

42 DAN

Text references. Portfolio theory is covered in Chapter 10 and the capital asset pricing model in Chapter 8. Dividend policy is discussed in Chapter 4.

Top tips. The calculations in part (a) have not been examined in this format before. They are logical and straightforward and even if you struggle, there are plenty of marks available later in the question which do not depend on a correct answer to part (a).

Make sure you apply theory to the specific circumstances in this question. Planning your answers to parts (b) and (c) will help.

Easy marks. Part (b)(i) is a straightforward regurgitation of textbook knowledge.

Examiner's comments. This question was poorly handled by many candidates. Many clearly lacked the necessary technical knowledge.

(a)   <u>Required return on existing portfolio</u>

Average beta of existing portfolio = 1.2

$$\begin{aligned} \text{Return} &= R_f + (R_m - R_f)\beta \\ &= 5\% + ((11\% - 5\%) \times 1.2) \\ &= 12.20\% \end{aligned}$$

<u>Entity B beta</u>

$$\begin{aligned} \text{Return} &= R_f + (R_m - R_f)\beta \\ 15.8\% &= 5\% + ((11\% - 5\%) \times \beta) \\ 6\% \times \beta &= 10.8\% \\ \beta &= 1.8 \end{aligned}$$

<u>Expected return</u>

The expected return of a portfolio will be a **weighted average** of the expected returns of the investments in the portfolio, weighted by the proportion of total funds invested in each.

$$\begin{aligned} \text{Total funds} &= £100,000 + (£40,000 \times 0.975) \\ &= £139,000 \end{aligned}$$

	Proportion	%	β	Weighted average β
Existing portfolio	100/139	72	1.2	0.86
Entity A	19.5/139	14	1.1	0.15
Entity B	19.5/139	14	1.8	0.25
		100		1.26

$$\begin{aligned} \text{Expected return} &= R_f + (R_m - R_f)\beta \\ &= 5\% + ((11\% - 5\%) \times 1.26) \\ &= 12.56\% \end{aligned}$$

(b)   (i)   The risk involved in holding securities divides into risk **specific** to the company which is **unsystematic** and risk due to **variations in market activity** which is **systematic.**

<u>Unsystematic risk</u>

Provided the investor **diversifies** his investments in a suitably wide portfolio, the investments which perform well and those which perform badly should tend to cancel each other out and much risk can be diversified away. This is **unsystematic risk**.

<u>Systematic risk</u>

Systematic or market risk cannot be diversified away and is due to factors affecting the **whole market** eg macroeconomic factors. In return for accepting systematic risk a risk-averse investor will expect to earn a return which is **higher** than the return on a risk-free investment.

Beta factors

Systematic risk is measured using **beta factors**. The beta factor measure a share's **volatility** in terms of market risk ie relative to the market portfolio. If a share price were to rise or fall at double the market rate, it would have a beta factor of 2.0. If the share price moved at half the market rate, the beta factor would be 0.5.

Beta is measured by analysing returns from a security and from the average market return over time. The results can be plotted on a scattergraph and a line of best fit drawn. The slope of this line is the beta.

(ii)   Dan's investment decision

Portfolio theory states that the investor should be concerned with his overall position, not with the performance of individual investments. This is because a diversified portfolio will **remove unsystematic risk.**

Dan already has 15% of his portfolio invested in Entity A's industry sector so he will **reduce diversification** if he buys shares in Entity A. Entity A has a beta of 1.1 which is **lower** than his current portfolio, so is of lower risk but this implies a reduced return. Entity A's sector shares will constitute 25% (34.5/139) of his new portfolio so he must have a very good reason to want to do this.

Entity B has a **higher beta** of 1.8 than the portfolio average. This increases the risk of the portfolio and also increases the expected average return to 12.56% from the existing 12.20%. Shares listed on the Alternative Investment Market are **riskier** than those on the main stock market but this investment will **increase** the diversification of the portfolio.

Directors of Entities A and B

Beta factors are useful for investors who are deciding whether or not to buy an entity's shares. They are therefore more useful in the **secondary market** for shares. However if an entity wants to issue **new shares**, for example a **rights issue** is planned by Entity A, the share value and its beta become more important. The entity would want to consider the **price** of the issue and the beta factor will be an element to include in the calculation.

Beta values can also be used when an entity is considering an investment which involves diversification into a new business area. A **project-specific** discount rate can be calculated which incorporates a new beta value.

All of this assumes that beta values calculated using historic information are a **reliable** indicator of current and future risks.

(c)   Entity A

Entity A is planning a **rights issue** to raise new funds. Modigliani and Miller stated that the method of financing of a business would have **no impact** on its cost of capital or shareholder value except for the value of the tax shield from debt.

However, in reality, a rights issue can affect shareholder value. After the announcement of a rights issue **share prices generally fall**. This temporary fall is due to **uncertainty** in the market about the consequences of the issue. After the issue has been made, the share price will normally fall because there are more shares in issue and the new shares were issued at a **discount price**.

The theoretical ex-rights price (TERP) is:

	p
4 shares @ 250p	1,000
1 share @ 200p	200
	1,200

TERP = 1,200/5 = 240p

The value of the rights is 40p per new share or 10p per old share.

This assumes that the funds generated by the rights issue will generate the **same rate of return** as existing funds. If not, a **yield-adjusted** theoretical ex-rights price should be calculated showing the effect on shareholder value.

<u>Entity B</u>

Entity B is planning to offer a choice to investors of a cash or scrip dividend. This is its usual policy so there is no change to the **signal** it is giving to investors.

A **scrip dividend** effectively converts retained earnings into issued share capital. It enables the entity to retain funds within the business and is particularly useful for a young, risky, rapidly growing business which may have problems obtaining debt finance.

If the entity is able to use the funds to generate growth, shareholder value will be enhanced.

<u>Dan's investment decisions</u>

<u>Entity A</u>

Dan is planning to invest £19,500 in Entity A which will buy 7,800 shares (19,500/2.50). This will entitle him to buy 1,950 new shares (7,800/4) in the rights issue which will cost £3,900 (1,950 × £2). If he does not want to spend this additional money, he has a number of options.

- **Do nothing**. Rights are sold on the shareholder's behalf by the company
- **Sell the rights**. He will then have a lower percentage holding and the total value of the shares will be less
- **Buy fewer shares in entity B** and use the funds to buy the rights

<u>Entity B</u>

Dan is planning to buy 3,900 shares (£19,500/£5.00) which will entitle him to a dividend of £1,755 ($0.45 × 3,900) or 390 shares.

His decision will depend on his **tax situation** as to whether he would prefer income or capital gains.

His decision to invest in this type of entity presumably indicates his belief in the **potential growth** in value of the shares therefore he is likely to prefer extra shares.

43 CD

> **Text references**. The function of treasury departments is covered in Chapter 10.
>
> **Top tips**. Part (a) is not a straightforward question on the functions of treasury departments in general. You are expected to answer the question in the context of the scenario so don't be tempted to write a general answer on the benefits of a centralised treasury department and how such a department would operate. Although hedging techniques are not covered in detail in this paper (they are covered in more detail in Paper P3), you can briefly acknowledge the issue of foreign exchange risk.
>
> There are actually three parts to part (b) – evaluate the current objective and the proposed new objectives, discuss alternative objectives and conclude with a recommendation based on your evaluation and discussion. Put forward a balanced view of each of the objectives and remember to discuss *appropriate* alternatives – that is, your discussion must focus on what might be suitable objectives for CD, rather than a general discussion.
>
> **Easy marks**. Part (b) offers some easy marks from the evaluation of the various objectives. You should also be able to pick up some marks in part (a) from your knowledge of the pros and cons of debt and equity as sources of finance.

(a)   CD has a **centralised** treasury department which is responsible for the treasury requirements of all the different parts of the entity.

The centralised treasury department will be responsible for determining the **optimal methods of financing** for the entity, given current economic conditions, as well as **hedging policies** to protect against foreign exchange risk.

<u>Capital structure</u>

The current situation is that CD has a debt/equity ratio of 25% (20/80). The debt is made up of 7% fixed-rate secured bonds and unsecured overdraft with a rate of 8%. Finance theory suggests that at least some of the capital structure should include debt. **Debt is a cheaper form of finance** than equity, given the tax shield provided by the interest payments and the lower returns that debt providers tend to expect.

<u>Use of fixed-rate debt in current economic climate</u>

In the current economic climate, inflation is near zero and interest rates are expected to fall. The treasury department will therefore be questioning the wisdom of using **fixed-rate debt** as a form of financing, for some or all of the following reasons:

(i)   CD is expecting **no better than modest growth** therefore fixed amounts of interest will have to be paid out of potentially falling profits. Returns to shareholders will decrease as a result. This will be in direct contravention of the corporate objective of increasing dividends.

(ii)   When inflation is near zero, the **real value of debt does not decrease**, hence the benefits of debt finance are diminished.

(iii)   If interest rates fall below the fixed rate attached to the bonds, CD will be paying **more in interest than is necessary** (although it could be argued that this is one of the risks of taking on fixed-rate debt). This will effectively reduce the funds available for distribution as dividends, which again fails to meet the objective of increasing payments to shareholders.

<u>Equity as a source of finance</u>

With the **corporate objective** of increasing dividends each year being threatened by the current debt structure, the treasury department may consider the wisdom of **raising additional equity**. As profits are at best going to remain static (or actually fall), equity may be preferable given that there is no legal obligation to pay dividends. However one of the problems CD has is that it is not listed on a stock exchange. Private entities tend to have more problems trying to raise equity – for example, how should shares be valued, should CD apply for a public listing and by what means should equity be raised?

<u>Foreign currency obligations</u>

Other issues that the treasury department might consider are how any **foreign currency obligations** are financed and how exchange rate risk is hedged. Whilst it appears that only inventory is purchased in different foreign currencies, the entity may be affected by fluctuations in exchange rates, particularly if a reasonably long credit period is given (such as 60 days). If CD is losing money through exchange rate movements, the treasury department may wish to consider **hedging instruments** such as forward contracts or options.

<u>Dividend policy and capital structure decisions</u>

Given the economic conditions, current finance structure and the objective of increasing dividends, the treasury department will have to consider **which combination of dividend policy and capital structure** will be most beneficial to the shareholders (that is, will maximise the present value of their cash flows). Can the current fixed-rate bonds be repaid early and replaced with either lower fixed-rate bonds or variable rate loans? One issue that will have to be considered here is the possibility of early repayment penalties that must be set against the potential benefits of paying lower rates of interest.

The issue of **return on investment** will also have to be considered. If the entity negotiates lower interest rates, this may reduce its perceived risk, leading to a lower cost of capital and thus lower expected returns to shareholders. A compromise will have to be reached between the desire for high rates of return and the potential for lower interest payments.

(b)   Maximisation of shareholder wealth is the **theoretically ideal** corporate objective. However most organisations now recognise that having this as their sole objective is unrealistic. Whilst there is still the philosophy that shareholders' wealth should be improved as much as possible, this is usually within the **constraints of other objectives**, such as **legal obligations** relating to the environment, **ethical considerations** (not using 'sweat-shop' labour for example) and **health and safety issues**.

CD has the additional problem of trying to **value** shareholder wealth. It is not listed on the stock exchange and thus has no quoted share price set by market forces. If there are problems valuing wealth, how can the entity determine how to maximise it?

<u>Increasing dividends v maximising shareholder wealth</u>

The objective of increasing dividends each year does not necessarily support the maximisation of shareholder wealth. If there are profitable investments available that would increase future wealth, then the entity should ideally be using its funds to finance such investments. By increasing dividends each year, the entity is **restricting the funds available** for profitable investments and thus its ability to improve shareholder wealth. Most organisations have a **target payout ratio** (dividends as a percentage of profit available to shareholders) which means that dividends will move in relation to fluctuations in profit. This makes more sense than a situation where dividends are increasing whilst profits are actually falling!

Accounting ratios

Some of the directors have suggested accounting ratios such as **Return on Investment** (ROI) as more suitable objectives. One of the main benefits of such accounting ratios is that they are **easy to understand** and are **comparable** across time and between other similar entities in the same industry. However there are several issues with using accounting ratios as objectives, including:

(i)   The numbers are easy to manipulate, even when governed by accounting standards

(ii)   The ratios are based on historic numbers rather than future cash flows, which can cause problems with comparisons if the entity is about to undergo, or has just undergone, a substantial change in structure

(iii)   Lack of consideration for non-financial objectives

Target profit after tax is another objective being considered. As with accounting ratios, profit figures are **easy to understand** and determining whether target has been achieved is a straightforward comparison exercise. However the problem with such a measure is that **taxation policies** are beyond the control of individual entities. Changes in such policies render comparisons between years useless unless time-consuming (and potentially inaccurate) restatement of figures takes places.

Alternative objectives

As a private entity, it is difficult for CD to have objectives related to shareholder wealth given the difficulties described above in determining value. Dividends alone are unlikely to be a good measure of shareholder wealth and should perhaps be considered in conjunction with other measures such as earnings growth. Ratios measuring growth are likely to be more meaningful than absolute measures such as 'increasing dividends' every year and are more likely to make sense. There is no point having such an objective if profits from which dividends are paid are falling.

Conclusion and recommendation

Given the above evaluation it would seem more sensible for CD to have a range of complementary objectives rather than focusing on just one. It may be worthwhile consulting the shareholders themselves to determine what they are trying to get out of their involvement with CD. From the results of this consultation the directors may be able to come up with suitable objectives for the entity that meet the needs of the majority.

44   Claudia

Text references. WACC calculations are covered in Chapter 8. Investment appraisal is covered in Chapter 11.

Top tips. This is a relatively straightforward question so don't be put off by this! Don't forget to adjust the equity figure in part (c) for the NPV of the project, as you are calculating post-project WACC.

Easy marks. Part (a) offers 3 very easy marks.

(a)   WACC

The formula for WACC is given in the exam formula sheet as follows.

$$WACC = k_e\left[\frac{V_E}{V_E + V_D}\right] + k_d(1-t)\left[\frac{V_D}{V_E + V_D}\right]$$

K_e = 6.2%   (given in question)

MV_E = 20 million shares x $2.50 = $50 million

Kd (after tax) = 5.4 x (1 – 0.35) = 3.51%

MVD = $33 million

WACC = 6.2 x [50/(50 + 33)] + 3.51 x [33/(50 + 33)] = 5.13%

(b) Evaluation of project

Tutorial note. The fact that the cash flows will occur indefinitely indicates that you can use the PV of perpetuity formula.

	$
Increase in pre-tax earnings (annual)	770,000
Less tax at 35%	(269,500)
Increase in post-tax earnings	500,500

PV of cash flow in perpetuity	500,500/0.0513 = $9.756m
Discount back one year (as cash flows do not start until year 2)	9.756m/1.0513 = $9.280m
Initial investment	$10m
NPV of project	$(0.720)m

The project has an NPV of $(0.720)m therefore Claudia should not invest in the new computer system.

(c) Post-project WACC

Ke and kd (after tax) remain unchanged (6.2% and 3.51% respectively)

MV_D = $33m + $10m = $43m

MV_E = $50m – 0.720m = $49.28m

Debt + equity = $43m + $49.28m = $92.28m

WACC = 6.2 x (49.28/92.28) + 3.51 x (43/92.28) = 4.95%

Suitability of pre-project WACC for discounting the computer system project

The post-project WACC is slightly smaller than pre-project WACC but the difference is quite insignificant. There is no reason to suggest that the outcome of the project would have been substantially different if the post-project WACC had been used.

There is no significant risk associated with the project. The update of a computer system is not unusual for this business and will have no impact of the business risk.

In conclusion the current WACC is deemed to be a suitable discount rate to use in the appraisal of the computer system project.

(d) (i) Key factors in assessing customer requirements

The web site is being designed to bring Claudia's sales system into line with her main competitors. In order to ensure no sales are lost – and indeed to encourage increased sales – the sales web site must be as easy and quick to use as possible. Before deciding on her own web site requirements, Claudia should review her competitors' systems for attractive features and also review the way in which her customers use her own system.

During the review of her system, Claudia should consider the following.

- **Language**. The messages given on web sites should be as concise and informative as possible, using easy to understand language and as little technical jargon as possible.

- **Security**. It is essential that payments made by customers are secure with no means of access by outsiders to their personal and payment details.

- **Speed**. Customers will soon become frustrated if the system is very slow and transactions take a long time to process, therefore it is crucial that the web site operates quickly.

- **Easy to use**? If customers find the system cumbersome and information difficult to find, they will quickly take their custom elsewhere. The web site should be easy to navigate.

It may be worthwhile asking customers using the current system for feedback on the language, speed and ease of use issues. This could be in the form of a short questionnaire that either pops up on screen or is e-mailed to them after they have placed an order. If there is a common theme running through the responses – for example, the web site is difficult to navigate through – it will give an indication of necessary improvements.

(ii)   Key factors in drawing up an implementation plan

Timing is a key issue when drawing up an implementation plan. Claudia should draw up a timetable of key factors to be achieved and the dates by which they should be completed.

Responsibilities of key staff should be made clear and any issues regarding timings and expertise should be discussed prior to the process starting. Any necessary training should be identified and given as soon as possible.

Progress review. At frequent intervals throughout the process, the progress of the project should be reviewed and timings revised if necessary in the light of findings.

Monitoring costs. This should be carried out regularly to identify any potential budget over-runs. Any corrective action should be taken as soon as possible.

System testing. Before the system goes live, it is essential to test that it is working properly and doing what it is supposed to. Trial orders should be put through to test the entire ordering process and assessments made on security, ease of use and accuracy.

Moving from old to new system. If possible, Claudia would be wise to keep the old system running in parallel with the new system until she is satisfied that the new system is performing properly and any implementation issues have been resolved.

45   Dominique

Text references. International NPV is covered in Chapter 12. The impact of tax on NPV decisions is covered in Chapter 11.

Top tips. Don't forget that there is no tax relief on residual value in Year 5 and remember to state any assumptions you make about tax relief on the additional logistics planning costs in Year 0. T$ are **depreciating** against D$ therefore you will **multiply** the current D$/T$ exchange rate by the rate of depreciation to show that D$1 will buy a greater amount of T$.

Easy marks. There are easy marks to be gained in part (a) when calculating NPV. Make sure you use the NPV format that is given in Chapter 11 of the Study Text.

(a)   NPV using Forecast A exchange rate

	Year 0 T$m	Year 1 T$m	Year 2 T$m	Year 3 T$m	Year 4 T$m	Year 5 T$m
Initial investment	(150)					
Residual value						40.0
Cash inflows		45.0	54.0	64.8	68.7	72.8
Tax at 20%		(9.0)	(10.8)	(13.0)	(13.7)	(14.6)
Tax dep allowance (W1)		6.0	4.8	3.8	3.1	4.3
Net cash remitted to Country D	(150)	42.0	48.0	55.6	58.1	102.5
Country D tax 5% (W2)		(2.1)	(2.4)	(2.8)	(2.9)	(3.1)
Net cash flow	(150)	39.9	45.6	52.8	55.2	99.4
Discount factor 12%	1.000	0.893	0.797	0.712	0.636	0.567
DCF	(150)	35.6	36.3	37.6	35.1	56.4
NPV	51					
Exchange rate	2.1145					
NPV in D$	24.1					
Additional logistics planning	(0.38)					
Net result	**23.72**					

Working 1

Year	Cost/written down value T$m	Tax relief at 20% T$m
0 – Cost	150.0	
1 – 20% reducing balance	(30.0)	6.0
	120.0	
2 – 20% reducing balance	(24.0)	4.8
	96.0	
3 – 20% reducing balance	(19.2)	3.8
	76.8	
4 – 20% reducing balance	(15.4)	3.1
	61.4	
5 – 20% reducing balance	(12.3)	2.5
	49.1	
Residual value	(40.0)	
Balancing allowance	9.1	1.8

Working 2

Residual value in year 5 is not subject to tax therefore additional tax paid in year 5 is calculated on the cash flows net of residual value – that is T$102.5m – T$40m = T$62.5m (tax = 5% of T$62.5m = T$3.1m).

Assumption

There is no tax relief on the additional logistics planning costs.

NPV using Forecast B exchange rates

	Year 0 T$m	Year 1 T$m	Year 2 T$m	Year 3 T$m	Year 4 T$m	Year 5 T$m
Net cash flow (as above)	(150)	39.9	45.6	52.8	55.2	99.4
Exchange rate (W3)	2.1145	2.2287	2.3490	2.4758	2.6095	2.7504
	D$m	D$m	D$m	D$m	D$m	D$m
Net cash flow D$	(70.90)	17.9	19.4	21.3	21.2	36.1
Additional logistics planning	(0.38)					
Discount factor 12%	1.000	0.893	0.797	0.712	0.636	0.567
DCF	(71.28)	15.9	15.5	15.2	13.5	20.5

NPV = D$9.32m

Working 3 – exchange rates

Year	Exchange rate (D$/T$)
0	2.1145
1	2.1145 x 1.054 = 2.2287
2	2.2287 x 1.054 = 2.3490
3	2.3490 x 1.054 = 2.4758
4	2.4758 x 1.054 = 2.6095
5	2.6095 x 1.054 = 2.7504

Alternative working

Instead of calculating the individual exchange rates for each year, you could have adjusted the discount rate for the depreciation in currency. The following formula is given in the formula sheet.

$$\frac{1 + \text{annual discount rate B\$}}{1 + \text{annual discount rate A\$}} = \frac{\text{Future spot rate A\$/B\$ in 12months' time}}{\text{Spot rate A\$/B\$}}$$

Where   B\$ can be substituted for T\$

                A\$ can be substituted for D\$

This can be rearranged as follows.

1 + annual discount rate T\$ = (1 + annual discount rate D\$) x

$$\frac{\text{Future spot rate D\$ / T\$ in 12months' time}}{\text{Spot rate D\$ / T\$}}$$

1 + annual discount rate T\$ = 1.12 x (2.2287/2.1145)

Annual discount rate T\$ = 18%

This discount rate takes into account the currency depreciation of 5.4% and the investment appraisal rate of 12%. You would use this rate to discount the **T\$ cash flows** back to Year 0. You would then convert the NPV to D\$ using the spot rate.

	Year 0 T\$m	Year 1 T\$m	Year 2 T\$m	Year 3 T\$m	Year 4 T\$m	Year 5 T\$m
Net cash flow (as above)	(150)	39.9	45.6	52.8	55.2	99.4
Discount factor 18%	1.000	0.847	0.718	0.609	0.516	0.437
DCF	(150)	33.8	32.7	32.2	28.5	43.4
NPV	20.6					
Spot rate	2.1145					
NPV (D\$M)	9.7					
Additional logistics planning costs	(0.38)					
NPV (D\$M)	9.32					

This is the same result as that calculated above using the individual exchange rates.

Comments on results

The project shows a **positive NPV** regardless of the forecast exchange rate, although if the exchange rate remained stable Dominique's shareholders would enjoy a greater increase in wealth (D\$23.72m rather than D\$9.32m).

Dominique should **accept the project** and go ahead with the proposal of opening a number of supermarkets in Country T. Even if the exchange rate does fluctuate, shareholder wealth will still increase by D\$9.32m. In fact, it may increase by much more than that amount, given that forecasts have only been made for five years and the residual value is quite low. Given the likelihood that the supermarkets will remain open beyond five years, the NPV may be considerably higher and residual value likely to be greater than the figure estimated.

In addition, Dominique would be complimenting its existing considerable international spread of supermarkets therefore it seems wise to proceed with the project on both financial and geographical grounds.

(b)   Impact of changes in exchange rates and tax rates on Dominique's performance

Exchange rates

The majority of Dominique's borrowings are in its **home currency** (D\$). This means considerable exposure to exchange rate movements as foreign currency costs are being funded by home currency. In addition, all foreign currency cash flows are converted back into D\$. The above analysis of the proposed project shows the extent of Dominique's **exposure** to exchange rate movements – the NPV will fall by approximately 61% if T\$ depreciated against D\$ by 5.4% per annum.

Exchange rate movements will have an effect of the cost of goods purchased in one country (and paid for using that country's currency) and sold in another country. Dominique should use **hedging instruments** to reduce exposure to currency risk – try to fix the currency rates of predictable cash flows to limit losses due to currency movements.

Profits repatriated from foreign countries will also be affected by exchange rate movements. Dominique should again use hedging instruments for predictable cash flows to reduce the potential impact of an appreciation of the D$.

The cost of any foreign currency debt will be affected by exchange rate movements as Dominique will be required to convert D$ into the appropriate foreign currency. Any depreciation in D$ will result in more expensive foreign debt payments as it will cost more in D$ to buy the same amount of foreign currency. To reduce this exposure, Dominique should try to arrange for foreign currency dividend and interest receipts are matched with foreign currency debt payments.

Tax rates

Tax rates in different countries will also impact on Dominique's performance given the geographical diversity of its operations. One of the ways Dominique could reduce this impact is to aim to earn **higher revenues** in **lower tax countries**. It should also ensure it keeps itself informed of **changes in government policies** in the countries of interest and have a contingency plan to reduce the effect of any increases in tax rates (for example, increasing profit margins). **Tax planning** is also important to ensure that funding is structured in such a way as to be as tax-efficient as possible.

46 CTC

> **Text references**. Investment appraisal is covered in Chapter 11 and project management in Chapter 14.
>
> **Top tips**. The examiner's comments emphasise the importance of being able to recognise sunk costs, and it's worth setting these out. Although the unusual form of the question may be offputting, in the end it is breakeven analysis, comparing the extra costs with revenue per student and finding the missing figure which is number of students required. (b) emphasises various important factors in project control including staff support and monitoring.
>
> **Easy marks**. Using knowledge from earlier management accounting papers together with project control principles should have helped you answer (b).
>
> **Examiner's comments**. Many candidates included sunk costs and excluded benefits such as students taking other courses. Another fundamental error was misallocating costs to time frames. Many candidates failed to answer the question in (b) and few calculated revised break-even numbers.

(a)   Number of student enrolments on ITC course required for viability

The costs and revenues given can be divided into the following groups:

<u>Costs which are irrelevant to the decision</u>

These are:

- **Book value of computers** (not a cash flow)
- **Market research cost** (sunk cost)
- **Existing staff costs** (common to all alternatives)
- **Apportionment of college overheads** (not an incremental cost, total will be common to all alternatives)

<u>Initial investment costs, year 0</u>

	€
Sale of computers foregone: 20 × €100	(2,000)
Upgrade of computers	(15,000)
Staff training and course development	(30,000)
	(47,000)

Annual incremental revenues/costs for the course as a whole

In advance	€
Additional fees for the 150 'baseline' students @ 360 – 350 = €10	1,500
Additional costs for the 150 @ 60 – 50 = €10	(1,500)
	– These cancel out

In arrears

Additional directly attributable course costs	(1,000)

Potential additional cost, in advance

Additional staff member, if students > 200	(10,000)

Incremental revenues/costs per student over 150

In advance	€
Fees	360
Additional benefits to college (assumed in advance)	20
Books and consumables	(60)
	320

Case 1: Student numbers not > 200

	Years	€	8% factor	PV €
Investment costs	0	(47,000)	1	(47,000)
Annual incremental course costs	1 - 4	(1,000)	3.312	(3,312)
				(50,312)
Incremental benefit per student over a four year period	0 - 3	320	3.577	1,145

The **number of additional students** over 150 to cover the investment costs and annual incremental costs is 50,312 / 1,145 = 43.9.

Thus the number of students required on the ITC course for it to be financially beneficial is 150 + 44 = 194 or more up to 200, when the additional staff cost sets in.

Case 2: Student numbers > 200

	Year		8% factor	PV
Investment costs	0	(47,000)	1	(47,000)
Additional staff cost (in advance)	0 - 3	(10,000)	3.577	(35,770)
Annual incremental course costs	1 - 4	(1,000)	3.312	(3,312)
				(86,082)

The **number of additional students** over 150 to cover the investment costs, additional staff cost and annual incremental costs is 86,082/1,145 = 75.2.

This is 150 + 76 = 226 students.

Summary

The ITC course will be financially viable if enrolments are between 194 and 200 or greater than 226.

(b) Advice to the governing body of the college

(i) **Effective monitoring and control of the costs** requires the following approach:

(1) The course should be the **clear responsibility** of a course director who should account to the governing body for its financial results (as well as quality, success, etc).

(2) The course director will need **proper back-up** from the course enrolments department and the accounting department to provide assistance in budgeting, a check on numbers enrolling, cost collection and control over expenditure.

(3) **Budgeting** should be **realistic, not over-optimistic** or **pessimistic**. The course director should involve all relevant parties to gain their views.

(4) The enrolments department and the accounting department should be prepared to **provide daily information** on enrolments and costs during the run-up to the start of the course. In addition to actual results, periodic **'feed-forward' estimates** of the likely final results would be extremely useful for the course director.

(5) **Possible candidates** for the extra part-time staff member should be identified well in advance, so that recruitment can take place swiftly if numbers warrant it.

(6) The course director should **hold regular meetings** with all relevant parties to assess progress. Swift decisions should be made in response to enrolments above or below targets or other unbudgeted factors.

(ii) <u>Options available if enrolments are 150 by the enrolment deadline</u>

The options available are to **cancel the course** or to **run it.** Cancelling is probably not an option if 150 students have enrolled, as it will cause much bad will. It would be better to run the course for one year only and then review the situation as to whether it should be continued.

By the time the **enrolment deadline** has been reached, the money will already have been spent on the course investment costs: **upgrading the computers** and staff training and development, total €45,000. These therefore become sunk costs, and the number of additional students per year over 150 to cover the remaining costs falls to (50,312 – 45,000) / 1,145 = 4.6 students. Thus enrolments of 155 will now cover relevant costs.

The additional 5 students (and more) can probably easily be found by **extending the enrolment deadline** or by some **low-cost advertising**.

47 KH

Text references. NPV calculations are explained in Chapter 11 and risks of international investment are discussed in Chapter 12.

Top tips. To conform with the information given in the question bullet points, calculations in (a) must be based on nominal cash flows converted to dollars and discounted at 20%. The recommendation to proceed should be accompanied by a brief description of the purchasing power parity theory of exchange rates and notes on the estimation uncertainties and lengthy project payback period.

The most important elements of the calculations in (a) were the determination of the net present value and the SA cash flows in US $ (worth two marks).

(b) is a fairly typical example of a discussion question where you would be awarded up to three to four marks for every relevant point. However a short list of political risks would not be enough. The examiner will expect you to discuss them in enough detail to show why they're relevant, linking into the scenario (for example it's quite justifiable to suggest that exchange rate volatility indicates potential economic problems), and suggesting appropriate remedies (risk reduction by hedging techniques or borrowing in the country).

Don't be surprised to see a similar question to (b) in the Paper P3 exam, as the risks of international investment is an area where the syllabuses definitely overlap.

Easy marks. You should be able to gain 6-7 marks by discussing common economic and political risks, though you need to think a bit more widely (and use your Enterprise Strategy knowledge) to come up with the other risks.

Examiner's comments. Attempts at (a) were generally satisfactory, although few were completely correct. Some answers had very confused calculations and lacked recommendations; other, more specific mistakes, included failure to inflate South American cash flows to nominal values before conversion, using real rather than nominal rates and failure to consider terminal values. (b) was generally answered better by non-UK candidates; some answers discussed hedging to the exclusion of other risks (a brief mention of hedging would have been fine, but no more.)

To: Finance Director
From: Financial Manager
Date: 4 December 20X1
Subject: Evaluation of potential acquisition of South American stores group

(a)   Net present value of the investment

The financial evaluation of the South American project is based on estimates of the future nominal cash flows of the investment, in both South America and USA. All foreign cash flows are **converted to dollars** and the total is **discounted** at a **risk adjusted cost of capital** of 20% per annum. The theory of **purchasing power parity** has been used to estimate future currency exchange rates. This predicts that if currencies are allowed to float freely on the market, they will **adjust in the long run to compensate** for differences in countries' **inflation rates**. The results show that the project has an **expected net present value** of nearly $30 million, which indicates that it is worthwhile and should add to shareholder value.

Risks and uncertainties

However, the risks and uncertainties which need to be appreciated include:

(i)   **Large margins** of **potential error** in the **exchange rate predictions**
(ii)   A **slow payback**: in present value terms the project will probably not break even until year 6 or 7
(iii)   The **political risks** discussed below

Calculations

Computation of expected future exchange rates using the theory of Purchasing Power Parity

The current exchange rate is $1 = SA30. If the rates of inflation in South America and the USA are estimated as 40% and 4% indefinitely, future exchange rates will be expected to increase by the factor 1.4/1.04 each year:

| | Year | | | |
	0	1	2	3
Exchange rate (previous year × 1.4/1.04)	30.00	40.38	54.36	73.18

Discounted cash flows for first three years

| | Year | | | |
	0	1	2	3
South American cash flows (in '000):				
In real terms	(1,000,000)	250,000	350,000	450,000
In nominal terms (40% pa inflation)	(1,000,000)	350,000	686,000	1,234,800
Exchange rate	30	40.38	54.36	73.18
Converted to dollars	(33,333)	8,668	12,620	16,873
US cash flows ($'000)				
In real terms	(10,000)	(300)	(400)	(500)
In nominal terms (4% pa inflation)	(10,000)	(312)	(433)	(562)
Total nominal cash flow ($'000)	(43,333)	8,356	12,187	16,311
20% discount factors	1	0.833	0.694	0.579
Present value	(43,333)	6,961	8,458	9,444
Net present value (0-3)				(18,470)

Years 4 to perpetuity

Taking cash flows from year 4 as a constant $16.311 million, the present value of the perpetuity will be:

Valued as at year 3: $16.311m/0.2 = $81.555m

Discounted back to year 0: $81.555 × 0.579 = $47.220m

Total net present value is therefore $47.22m – $18.47m = **$28.75m**

(b)   Main political risks

The main political risks that might be faced by the company in the South American country are discussed below, together with suggested counter-strategies.

(i) Political instability

Extreme **political problems** include civil war, prolonged terrorist activities, or expropriation of private (especially foreign-owned) assets by the government. If these situations are likely, investment is unwise, and an alternative country in the region should be chosen. It is recommended that a **detailed political analysis** is undertaken, covering the stability of the present government and the policies of likely alternatives. To counter the risk of extreme threats suddenly arising, it is wise to negotiate as much **loan finance** as possible from institutions in the South American country. This would allow a **swift bankruptcy** and withdrawal from the country in the event of severe difficulties. To counter this strategy, the host government/institutions may require guarantees from our parent company, however.

(ii) Economic sanctions

If the South American government experiences economic difficulties, it may attempt to solve them by taking short term action which is detrimental to our investment.

(1) Raising local taxes

Our best counter-strategies are to **negotiate tax concessions** in advance and to **use transfer pricing strategies**, including royalties and management charges, to minimise the South American taxable profits and dividends.

(2) Imposition of exchange controls

Examples include non-convertibility of the local currency, or prevention of repatriation of funds. There are a number of measures we can take to minimise this risk, including making **extensive use of local currency loans** for financing, and **arranging currency swaps** and **back-to back loans** with other multinational companies and banks with complementary cash needs.

(iii) Lack of protection for intangible assets

As in a number of regions we may experience a **lack of political will** to assist us in enforcement of our intellectual property rights. We need to ensure that **appropriate patents and trade marks** are taken out and to be prepared to take **legal action** against those who attempt to infringe them. However our major strategy in this area should be to build a strong **barrier to entry** by competitors by **promoting our brand image** strongly.

(iv) Action groups

There is also a potential risk posed by the growing number of action groups who are opposed to our company and/or multinational corporations generally. These may succeed in influencing **local public opinion** and/or the host government. Difference in customs, laws and language may also lead to problems. Our counter-strategy should involve **development of a public relations campaign**, including charitable donations, and the appointment of competent local partners to assist us with interpretation of the regulatory and cultural environment.

48 DAC

Text references. NPV calculations and risk is covered in Chapter 11.

Top tips. This question tests your ability to evaluate foreign income cash flows and the management of the risks involved.

In (a), as the UK inflation rate is not given, but the risk-free interest rates are given for both countries, you have to use the interest rate parity theory to calculate the year-end exchange rates. The answers to (a)(i) and (ii) should be the same, barring a small difference due to rounding.

A common failing of answers to questions such as (b) is failure to mention DAC at all, and providing a discussion of the risks and management of foreign investment in general terms. DAC's situation is more significant in (ii) as you need to make some sort of an assessment of the level of the risks the company faces. Again a question like (b)(ii) could also crop up in P3. Be careful in (iii) not to repeat in detail what you said in (ii) about risks; you should focus on the risks relating to finance rather than the risks relating to the company's market.

Easy marks. Most of the arguments in (b)(i) are fairly standard points about the WACC, but the answer does acknowledge how they relate to DAC.

(a) (i) **To calculate the sterling NPV of the project**, it is necessary to estimate the year end £/US$ spot rates for the duration of the project. This can be done using the interest rate parity theory as follows.

	Rate at start of year £/$	Adjust by	Closing rate
Year 1	1.6000	× 1.04/1.05	1.5848
Year 2	1.5848	× 1.04/1.05	1.5697
Year 3	1.5697	× 1.04/1.05	1.5547
Year 4	1.5547	× 1.04/1.05	1.5399
Year 5	1.5399	× 1.04/1.05	1.5252

The US$ cash flow can now be converted to sterling and discounted at the sterling required rate of return (14%):

	Year 0	Year 1	Year 2	Year 3	Year 4
Cash flow in US$m	(4.50)	1.75	1.95	2.50	3.50
Closing spot rate	1.6000	1.5848	1.5697	1.5547	1.5399
Cash flow in £m	(2.813)	1.104	1.242	1.608	2.273
14% discount factors	1.000	0.877	0.769	0.675	0.592
Discounted cash flow	(2.813)	0.968	0.955	1.085	1.346

Net present value   **£1.541m**

(ii) To discount the annual cash flows in US$, it is necessary to calculate the appropriate discount rate to use. This can be done as follows.

Using the adjusted discount rate formula

$$\frac{(1+\text{annual discount rate \$})}{(1+\text{£ discount factor})} = \frac{\text{Future spot rate £ / \$ in 12 months' time}}{\text{Spot rate £ / \$}}$$

(1 + annual discount rate $) = (1.5848/1.6000) × 1.14

Annual discount rate $ = 12.92%, say 13%

The NPV calculated in US$ is as follows.

	Year 0	Year 1	Year 2	Year 3	Year 4
Cash flow in US$m	(4.50)	1.75	1.95	2.50	3.50
13% discount factors	1.000	0.885	0.783	0.693	0.613
Discounted cash flow	(4.500)	1.549	1.527	1.733	2.146

Net present value ($m)   2.455

NPV in sterling at £/$1.6   **£1.534m**

(b) (i) The **WACC** is valid for use in investment appraisal, given the following **assumptions**.

(1) **New investments** must be **financed by new sources of funds**.

(2) The **cost of capital** to be **applied** to project evaluation must **reflect the marginal cost of new capital**.

(3) The WACC **reflects the company's long-term future capital structure** and capital costs.

Argument in favour of the use of the WACC in investment appraisal

A company's capital structure **changes only very slowly over time**, and therefore the marginal cost of new capital should be roughly equal to the weighted average cost of current capital. If this is correct, then by selecting investments that offer a return above the WACC, the company will increase the market value of its ordinary shares in the long run.

Arguments against the use of the WACC

(1) New investments undertaken by a company might have **different business risk characteristics** from the existing operations. In this situation, the return required by investors might go up or down as a result.

(2) The new finance raised to fund the project might **significantly change the capital structure** and the perceived financial risk of investing in the company.

(3) Where there is a significant proportion of floating rate debt, the WACC will be **constantly varying**, and therefore the WACC at any one point in time will only be an approximation of the true cost of capital.

In an **international situation**, such as that faced by DAC, the drawbacks arising from variations in risk are likely to become more significant. However, it is always difficult to quantify these types of risks objectively, and it is likely that the WACC will continue to be the most appropriate measure. Where quantifying risk is a problem, the company could use additional measures, such as sensitivity analysis, to direct attention to the key areas of concern surrounding the decision.

(ii) The **main risks** that are likely to be encountered by a company moving into a new international market include the following.

(1) Foreign exchange risks

Transaction risk. Costs and revenues may be **more volatile** than predicted due to unforeseen movements in exchange rates between the home country and that in which the investment is located. This can be managed by matching costs and revenues as far as possible, and using hedging techniques such as forward exchange contracts.

Translation risk. The **valuation** of the assets to be included in the consolidated statement of financial position may **vary** due to **movements in exchange rates**. This is unlikely to be important in the investment decision unless the company is highly geared and close to breaching any borrowing covenants.

(2) Economic risks

These arise when **events** occur in the economy of the country that **impact upon the performance of the investment**. For example, a sharp rise in the level of personal taxation may cause a fall in demand for the project. This risk is unlikely to be significant in DAC's case, and there is little that can be done to manage such a situation.

(3) Geographical separation

This causes a number of problems in the areas of **communication and control**, and the **recruitment of the appropriate local specialists**. Since DAC is proposing to invest in the USA, these problems are likely to be less significant than in a more remote, less developed, non-English speaking country.

(4) Political risk

Where a multinational invests in another country, it may face political risk of **action by that country's government**, which restricts the multinational's freedom. An example is the import restrictions imposed by the USA on the British cashmere industry in retaliation for the EU

restrictions on banana imports in 1999. This can be a risk in any country, and again there is little that the company can do to avoid it.

(iii) **DAC** should consider various options when it decides how to obtain finance for its overseas operations.

Retained cash surpluses

DAC could use retained cash balances for investment. The advantages are that there would be no **formalities or issue costs**. The obvious disadvantage is that cash surpluses may not be large enough to finance the level of expansion the directors wish to undertake. The value of the investment may also decline due to exchange movements.

Borrowing in domestic market

Borrowing in DAC's own market may be a cheap source of finance, and DAC will be able to take advantage of **tax shield effects**, being able to claim loan interest on debt. However the terms and amounts available will depend on DAC's credit rating, and DAC will also be subject to **exchange risk.** DAC may however be able to arrange a **currency swap** to mitigate these problems.

Borrowing in US

The main advantage of borrowing in the US is that DAC will limit exchange risk by **matching,** because the **borrowing** is in the **same currency** as the expected revenues. The directors may wish to gear up quite highly on US borrowing. However the availability and terms of finance may be less favourable as DAC is not a well-known borrower

Borrowing in euro-debt

Borrowing on the euromarkets will be cheaper, and DAC would look to borrow dollars in this market, dealing again with the problem of **exchange risk**. Other terms may also be favourable as often euroloans do **not require any security.** It may be quicker to raise the sums required than on the US market. However DAC will require a **good international credit rating** and must have **access to enough hard currency** to be able to **make repayments**.

49 CD

> **Text references.** Investment appraisal methods are covered in Chapter 11.
>
> **Top tips.** You need to look carefully for the important information in this question. You are given inflation rates in both countries so your first step should be to calculate expected exchange rates using the purchasing power parity formula. The net cash flows are in **real** terms so need to be converted into **nominal** cash flows.
>
> Use your knowledge of business strategy from P6 in the discussion in part (c).
>
> **Easy marks.** The twelve marks for the calculations in part (a) are relatively easy to achieve if you have done enough practice on questions involving inflation and exchange rates and are confident with MIRR.
>
> **Examiner's comments.** This was a popular question on which the well prepared candidate could gain good marks. Part (b) was very poorly answered with candidates unable to explain what the calculations meant. The main faults in part (c) were discussion of irrelevant issues and too lengthy discussion of too many other criteria.

(a) Appraisal of alternative 2

Exchange rates

The future £/$ exchange rates for years 1 to 3 can be predicted using the purchasing power parity formula.

Future spot rate £/$ = Spot rate £/$ $\times$ [(1 + US inflation rate)/(1 + UK inflation rate)]^n where n is the number of years in the future.

Thus, future exchange rate £/$ = $1.600 \times [1.04/1.03]^n$

Year	0	1	2	3
Exchange rate forecast £/US$	1.600	1.616	1.631	1.647

Net present value computation

Year	0	1	2	3
US$m real cash flows	(25.00)	2.60	3.80	4.10
US$m nominal cash flows (inflation 4% pa)	(25.00)	2.70	4.11	4.61
Exchange rate	1.600	1.616	1.631	1.647
US nominal cash flows in £m	(15.63)	1.67	2.52	2.80
£m real cash flows		3.70	4.20	4.60
£m nominal cash flows (inflation 3% pa)		3.81	4.46	5.03
Total nominal cash flows in £m	(15.63)	5.48	6.98	7.83
9% discount factors	1	0.917	0.842	0.772
Present value £m	(15.63)	5.03	5.88	6.04
Net present value	1.32			

The NPV of the project is **£1.32 million** positive.

Internal rate of return

The IRR can be found by trial discount rates and interpolation. If the discount rate is 15%, the NPV is £(0.43) million.

Year	0	1	2	3
Total nominal cash flows in £m	(15.63)	5.48	6.98	7.83
15% factors	1	0.870	0.756	0.658
PV	(15.63)	4.77	5.28	5.15
NPV	(0.43)			

By interpolation the IRR is 9% + (15% – 9%) × 1.32/(1.32 + 0.43) = **13.5% pa**

Modified internal rate of return

This is found by compounding the cash inflows forward to the end of the project at the cost of capital, 9%.

		£m		Year 3 value £m
Outlay:	Year 0	(15.63)		
Inflows:	Year 1	5.48	× 1.09^2	6.51
	Year 2	6.98	× 1.09	7.61
	Year 3	7.83		7.83
				21.95

The 3 year rate that links the 15.63 outlay and the 21.95 inflow is found from the discount tables.

15.63 / 21.95 = 0.712, which represents a discount rate of 12% for 3 years.

Thus the MIRR is **12%**.

Alternatively, the MIRR can be found by calculating the return achieved on an investment of £15.63m over three years, ie $\sqrt[3]{\dfrac{21.95}{15.63}} - 1 = 12\%$.

(b)   Advantages of MIRR

MIRR has the advantage over IRR that it assumes the **reinvestment rate** is the **company's cost of capital**. IRR assumes that the reinvestment rate is the IRR itself, which is usually untrue.

In many cases where there is conflict between the NPV and IRR methods, the MIRR will give the same indication as NPV, which is the **correct theoretical method**. This helps when explaining the appraisal of a project to managers, who often find the concept of rate of return easier to understand than that of net present value.

Disadvantages of MIRR

However, MIRR, like all rate of return methods, suffers from the problem that it may lead an investor to reject a project which has a **lower rate of return** but, because of its size, generates a **larger increase in wealth**.

In the same way, a **high-return** project with a **short life** may be preferred over a **lower-return** project with a longer life.

(c) Evaluation of the two alternatives

Before making a decision there are a number of other important non-financial factors that must be taken into consideration.

Alternative 1

- Alternative 1 has a high risk of lowering the firm's reputation for quality and causing confusion among the customer base. The overall effect may be to **lose existing customers** but not to gain many new ones.

- It also removes the **focus** from the business. Marketing a wider range of products may be more difficult than is anticipated and may stretch resources.

Alternative 2

- Alternative 2 represents a fundamental change in the nature of the business from a niche manufacturer to a **value added** distributor.

- The firm may be able to add successfully its **brand reputation for quality** to mass market products, but this will only be possible if the US 'flat packs' are of guaranteed quality and consistency, and the varnishing and assembly work are carried out to a high standard.

- The change in the nature of the firm's work may require **substantial new equipment**.

- This alternative may also result in a **loss of skilled workers**, with the risk of lower quality.

  Given the similarity in the NPVs between the two projects, the decision will almost certainly depend on non-financial factors

Summary of the financial results

Alternative	1	2
NPV at 9%	£1.45m	£1.32m
IRR	10.5%	13.5%
MIRR	13.2%	12.0%

All other things being equal, the project to be accepted should be the one with the higher NPV, that is Alternative 1. NPV shows the absolute amount by which the project is forecast to **increase shareholders' wealth**, and is theoretically more sound than the IRR and MIRR methods.

In this case the MIRR method backs up the NPV, but the IRR gives the opposite indication. This 'conflict' arises because IRR makes the wrong **assumption** about reinvestment rates (see (ii) above).

Recommendation

Although non-financial factors are important, we do not have enough information to make a definite decision about the strategic suitability of the two alternatives. The project with the higher NPV is therefore recommended, alternative 1.

50 UVW

Text references. International investment appraisal is covered in Chapter 12, certainty equivalents in Chapter 11 and treasury management in Chapter 10.

Top tips. This question starts off as a straightforward international investment appraisal for which you can use a standard method of workings and proforma NPV. You then need to know how to apply certainty equivalents.

Part (a) (ii) gives specific instructions about what is and is not needed. Use headings in your answer to ensure you answer the specific requirements.

Part (b) asks specifically about the decentralisation of management of working capital so don't be tempted to write everything you know about treasury departments!

Easy marks. The initial calculations should provide some easy marks and the discussion sections should allow you to use your basic knowledge and common sense to gain marks, provided you answer the specific question.

Examiner's comments. Common errors included using 10% as a discount rate instead of 3% in the certainty equivalent calculations; including sunk costs; discussing only financing as an 'other factor'; discussing method of valuation weaknesses rather than other factors; getting the focus wrong in part (b).

(a)   (i)   NPV without certainty equivalents

Exchange rates

Year 0:   20.00
Year 1:   20.00 × 1.08/1.04 = 20.77
Year 2:   20.77 × 1.08/1.04 = 21.57
Year 3:   21.57 × 1.08/1.04 = 22.40

	Year 0 $m	Year 1 $m	Year 2 $m	Years 3 to 8 $m
Costs of Asian operation	(100.00)	(70.00)	(65.00)	(60.00)
Exchange rate	20.00	20.77	21.57	22.40
Costs in £s	(5.00)	(3.37)	(3.01)	(2.68)
Capital eqt for Asian operation	(2.00)			
Comparable UK costs		1.50	4.50	4.75
Net cost savings	(7.00)	(1.87)	1.49	2.07
Discount factor @10%	1.000	0.909	0.826	3.599 (5.335 – 1.736
Present value	(7.00)	(1.70)	1.23	7.45
NPV	**(0.02)**			

NPV with certainty equivalents

	Year 0 $m	Year 1 $m	Year 2 $m	Years 3 to 8 $m
Net cost savings	(7.00)	(1.87)	1.49	2.07
Certainty equivalent	1.00	1.20	0.75	0.70
Risk adjusted cost saving	(7.00)	(2.18)	1.12	1.45
Discount factor @ 3% risk free rate	1.000	0.971	0.943	5.107 (7.020 – 1.913)
Present value	(7.00)	(2.12)	1.06	7.41
NPV	**(0.65)**			

(ii)   Internal factors

The calculations indicate that there is a **cost advantage** from manufacturing in Asia. However, a number of other factors must be considered.

Quality

Car manufacturers require an extremely **high standard** of components delivered on a **just-in-time** basis. Penalties will often be imposed if components are sub-standard or delivered late, so UVW will have to be totally convinced that the Asian operation will be able to deliver components of an **acceptable quality** and on time. In a highly competitive market, any damage to reputation will be very costly.

Employees

UK employees are likely to **react badly** to the news of an Asian manufacturing base. This may negatively affect productivity in the UK and will probably result in **adverse publicity** for the company.

There may be a loss of **key manufacturing** skills in the UK production facility which could lead to a lack of flexibility in production in the future.

UVW also needs to be sure that there is **sufficient technical expertise available** in the Asian workforce. Training can be provided by the UK senior managers but the workforce still needs to have the necessary basic skills.

The use of certainty equivalents

Certainty equivalents are an approach to **dealing with risk**. The greater the risk of an expected cash flow, the smaller the certainty equivalent value. They are particularly useful when a small change in one of the variables can act with other variables and create significant falls in predicted benefits.

The disadvantage of the certainty equivalent approach is that the amount of the adjustment to each cash flow is decided **subjectively** by management.

Why the 'rough calculations' might have been wrong

The **exchange rate trend** may have been ignored in the Finance Manager's calculations and this would lead to a significant negative NPV.

He may also have included the costs of the **feasibility study** which is a sunk cost and should not be included in the project appraisal.

The cost of the **salaries** of the senior managers from the UK should not be included as they would be incurred anyway. Only their accommodation and travel is relevant to the project appraisal.

(b)   Management of working capital

The management of working capital involves ensuring that the company has the liquid funds that it needs and maximises its profitability. It involves the management of receivables, payables and inventory levels, as well as either the investment of surplus funds or ensuring there are sufficient cash resources.

Centralised function in the UK

A centralised function in the UK would be able to achieve **economies of scale** by, for example, obtaining better borrowing rates or netting-off balances.

The difference in inflation rates between Asia and the UK will result in changing exchange rates which will need to be planned for and hedging techniques used. A centralised function in the UK is more likely to have the **exchange rate management expertise** required.

Management of receivables would probably be better achieved in the UK as there will again be experience and expertise in dealing with the particular type of motor trade customers.

Management of working capital in Asia

Management of inventory would be easier if undertaken in the Asian country. The geographical distance involved in managing inventory from the UK would make it much more difficult, especially as very little is manufactured for inventory. The aim should be for minimum holdings to maximise profitability and this requires careful control and management locally.

Management of payables will depend on where the necessary parts are sourced from. Local sourcing in the Asian country could help to avoid exchange rate issues and then local knowledge would again make payables management more efficient.

Government restrictions

UVW will need to undertake research to determine if there any **restrictions on funds** being taken out of the Asian country or any **property taxes** on inventory holdings. This may affect the strategy chosen for working capital management.

51 CM

> **Text references**. Investment appraisal is covered in Chapter 11.
>
> **Top tips**. The calculations in this question are very time pressured, but if you are familiar with the techniques, they provide plenty of opportunities to gain marks. A clear layout and workings are essential. The average annual accounting return (AAAR) is another name for the accounting rate of return.
>
> Use your common sense and business strategy knowledge in your answer to part (b).
>
> **Easy marks**. There are plenty of easy marks available in these calculations even if you get stuck on the harder parts.
>
> **Examiner's comments**. There were numerous acceptable alternatives to providing the calculations and markers used the 'own figure' principle.

(a)   Investment 1

    Tax depreciation

	£'000
	1,100
Year 1 WDA @ 40%	(440)
	660
Year 2 WDA @ 40%	(264)
	396
Year 3 WDA @ 40%	(158)
	238
Residual value	300
Balancing charge	62

    Tax depreciation in Year 3 = 158 – 62 = 96

    Tax calculation

	Year 1	Year 2	Year 3
	£'000	£'000	£'000
Revenue	375	450	575
Production costs	(131)	(158)	(201)
Tax depreciation	(440)	(264)	(96)
Taxable profit/(loss)	(196)	28	278
Tax @ 25%	49	(7)	(70)
Profit/(loss) before tax	(23)	25	108
Profit after tax	26	18	38

    (i)   Average annual accounting return

$$\text{Average profit after tax} = \frac{26+18+38}{3}$$

$$= 27.3$$

$$\text{Average investment} = \frac{1,100+300}{2}$$

$$= 700$$

$$\text{AAAR} = \frac{27.3}{700} \times 100$$

$$= 3.9\%$$

(ii) <u>NPV</u>

Real cost of capital = 8%
Inflation rate = 2.75%

(1+ money cost of capital) = (1 + real cost of capital) (1 + inflation rate)
= (1+ 0.08) (1 + 0.0275)
= 1.1097

Discount rate = 11%

	Year 0 £'000	Year 1 £'000	Year 2 £'000	Year 3 £'000
Capital expenditure	(1,100)			
Residual value				300
Revenue		375	450	575
Production costs		(131)	(158)	(201)
Tax		49	(7)	(70)
Net cash flow	(1,100)	293	285	604
Discount factor @ 11%	1.000	0.901	0.812	0.731
Present value	(1,100)	264	231	442

Net present value **(£163,000)**

<u>Investment 2</u>

<u>Tax calculation</u>

	Year 1 A$'000	Year 2 A$'000	Year 3 A$'000
Revenue	1,300	1,450	1,650
Production costs	(260)	(290)	(330)
Tax depreciation	(2,900)		
Taxable profit/(loss)	(1,860)	1,160	1,320
Tax @ 10%	186	(116)	(132)
Profit/(loss) before tax	73	193	354
Profit after tax	259	77	222

(i) <u>Average annual accounting return</u>

Average profit after tax $= \dfrac{259 + 77 + 222}{3}$

$= 186$

Average investment $= \dfrac{2,900 + 0}{2}$

$= 1,450$

AAAR $= \dfrac{186}{1,450} \times 100$

$= 12.8\%$

(ii) If we convert cash flows into sterling and then discount at the sterling discount rate:

	Year 0	Year 1	Year 2	Year 3
A$'000 cash flows				
Capital expenditure	(2,900)			
Revenue		1,300	1,450	1,650
Production costs		(260)	(290)	(330)
Tax		186	(116)	(132)
Net cash flow	(2,900)	1,226	1,044	1,188
Exchange rate (£/A$)	2.00	*1.91	1.82	1.74
£'000 cash flows	(1,450)	642	574	683
Discount factor @ 11%	1.000	0.901	0.812	0.731
Present value	(1,450)	578	466	499

Net present value **£93,000**

* Exchange rate is falling by 4.5% pa so in Year 1 = 2.00 × 0.955

Alternative method

Discount the foreign cash flows at an adjusted discount rate.

$$\frac{(1 + \text{annual discount rate A\$})}{(1 + \text{annual discount rate £})} = \frac{\text{Future spot rate £/A\$}}{\text{Spot rate £/A\$}}$$

$(1 + \text{annual discount rate A\$}) = (1.91/2.00) \times 1.11$

Annual discount rate A\$ = 6%

	Year 0 A\$'000	Year 1 A\$'000	Year 2 A\$'000	Year 3 A\$'000
Net cash flow	(2,900)	1,226	1,044	1,188
Discount factor @ 6%	1.000	0.943	0.890	0.840
Present value	(2,900)	1,156	929	998
Net present value	183			

Convert @ spot rate $= \dfrac{\text{A\$183}}{2}$

= **£91,500** (difference due to rounding)

(b)   Summary of calculations

	Investment 1	Investment 2
AAAR	3.9%	12.8%
NPV	(£163,000)	£93,000

Recommendation

CM's **expected accounting return on investment** is 15% so **neither** investment meets this criteria. Investment 1 also fails to achieve a **positive NPV**. On pure financial terms, Investment 1 would be rejected and Investment 2 would be considered very carefully. However, a number of other factors need to be taken into consideration.

The **average annual accounting return** has the serious drawback that it does not take account of the **timing** of the profits from an investment. It is based on **accounting profits,** not cash flows, which are subject to differing accounting treatments. It takes no account of the **length** of the product life cycle and it ignores the **time value** of money.

The NPV calculations are dependant on the **discount rate** which may not be accurate, especially for Investment 2 which will be **riskier** as it is a **foreign** investment. It could be argued that a **higher** discount rate should be used which makes the investment even less attractive.

Further calculations could be carried out such as **sensitivity analysis** and **payback**. However it would be difficult to recommend either investment given the figures presented.

Non financial factors

The oil industry is notoriously risky and subject to a wide range of economic, political and social factors.

For example, **political stability** is of crucial importance, especially in the Asian market. This will need to be considered before deciding to undertake Investment 2.

CM also needs to consider whether it has the necessary **skills** and **resources** available to undertake Investment 2 in a new market.

52 RST

Text references. CAPM is covered in Chapter 5 and NPV in Chapter 11. Real options are considered in Chapter 13 whilst debt finance is covered in Chapter 6.

Top tips. This is an unusual style of NPV question because there are no calculations involved. For part (a) (i) make sure you include the limitations of the methods used in the appraisal. Part (a) (ii) requires you to appraise the conclusion reached by the finance manager.

In part (c) you need to address the idea that the appraisal could be performed using the cost of debt as the discount rate and also issues with using a foreign currency denominated loan when there are no cash flows in that currency.

Easy marks. You should be able to pick up some easy marks in part (b) through explaining real options that are applicable and applying them to the scenario.

Examiner's comments. Some candidates did not understand real options and instead discussed general factors to be considered when making an investment decision, which received no credit. Others managed to list the three types of real option and attempted to link them to the scenario, but did not comment on how the options could be factored into the initial investment decision.

Marking scheme

			Marks
(a)	(i)	Up to 2 marks per issue max	4
	(ii)	Up to 3 marks per issue max	4
(b)		Up to 4 marks per type of option max	9
(c)		Up to 4 marks per comment max	8
			25

(a) (i) Validity of using a proxy company and CAPM to determine discount rate

There are issues arising from using a proxy company to estimate a cost of equity. The proxy company may have significant differences with RST in terms of its operations and also its business risk. In addition the cost of equity used to calculate the WACC may **not have been adjusted** to reflect the financial risk of RST.

The use of CAPM is questionable given that the model makes several **simplifying assumptions,** which may not hold in the real world. An equity beta is also difficult to obtain and assess for a private company. However this approach does have more theoretical basis than using a crude adjustment to the basic cost of capital.

Validity of using NPV

The use of NPV as a method of investment appraisal is theoretically sound as it takes into account the time value of money and also the riskiness of the project. Higher risk projects can use a risk-adjusted discount rate to build in the higher risk. If the discount rate used is **appropriate** and the cash flows have been accurately predicted, then a positive NPV means that the project will **increase shareholder wealth**.

(ii) Validity of finance manager's conclusion

The finance manager's conclusion is based on the fact that the expected value of the NPV is positive by applying probabilities to a number of possible outcomes. This is **not an appropriate method** for a one-off project of this nature.

Since the expected NPV of AUD 21.6 million is not actually achievable, this figure does **not have any great significance**. This figure cannot be used solely to accept the project.

The key factor here is the risk appetite of the Board. For this project there is an **80% chance of a positive NPV** and a 20% chance of making a negative NPV. The decision whether to accept the project will depend on whether the Board considers this level of risk to be acceptable. It is important that the Board is aware that there is a 20% chance of shareholder wealth falling. Other factors that should be considered include **quantitative factors** such as sensitivity analysis.

(b)   When making an investment decision there are three types of different real options to be considered. These three options are the option to abandon, the option to follow-on and the option to wait.

Option to abandon

If in the early stages of a project there is the possibility of abandoning the project for a low cost, then this option has a value which should be considered at the decision making stage. Therefore the value of this option should be included in the NPV appraisal.

The option to abandon a project can be valuable where there is uncertainty over the outcome of the project. In this case there are three possible outcomes and one has a negative NPV. If there is a way of determining if RST will suffer the worst case scenario early on in the project, then it may be better to abandon the project and reduce losses.

Option to follow-on

Once a project is undertaken, it might lead to opportunities for further projects. Where these opportunities exist, there should be a value attached to them and this should be included in the original decision making. Follow-on projects may exist for a project that has a negative NPV itself, but by **including the follow-on projects a positive NPV** is generated and therefore the initial project is worthwhile.

For RST, the Perth-based project may provide new contacts at companies which may lead on to additional work in the same area, in other parts of Australia or even abroad.

Option to wait

This option would allow RST to wait and see how the market develops before starting the project. This may be useful as there is **significant uncertainty** about the outcome of the project. The option to wait could be used to see if the worst case scenario occurs and so is potentially of significant value to RST as it could prevent the acceptance of a project with a negative NPV.

However, if a competitor decides to take advantage of the opportunity while RST is waiting then the opportunity may be completely lost to RST and the option to wait would be of little value.

(c)   Using a lower discount rate, such as the cost of debt, will make the project more attractive as the NPV will be higher. However, it is **not appropriate** to use the cost of debt as a discount rate for project appraisal. The project should be viewed from the context of the whole company. The returns will need to satisfy the providers of all capital and not just the debt providers. This is why the weighted average cost of capital is adjusted for any specific business risk.

Director S is concerned about the level of gearing. This is valid if gearing is at a relatively high level for the industry. In this case as **gearing increases**, the risk of **bankruptcy** increases due to the mandatory interest payments. This increased risk means that equity providers require a higher level of return. RST relies heavily on debt finance and so it is likely that any increases in the level of debt will have a significant impact on WACC.

Interest payments may currently be lower for USD debt than for AUD debt. However, **expectations theory** predicts that over the long term the benefits from lower interest rates would be offset by an equivalent movement in the exchange rate. Any overall benefit would be eliminated or negligible.

Exchange rates may not necessarily move as predicted by theories. As a result the use of USD debt will expose RST to **currency risk.** The exposure to currency risk would be reduced if there are any USD cash flows within RST. The three types of currency risk that RST would be exposed to are:

(i)   **Transaction risk** from converting interest payments and the capital repayment.

(ii)   **Economic risk** if competitor companies do not also suffer similar currency risks.

(iii)   **Translation risk** on accounting for the debt at financial reporting dates.

If the USD strengthened against the AUD, then RST may be faced with a significant currency exposure. As this exposure would be **unnecessary** it is recommended that RST uses AUD denominated debt instead.

53 PP

Text references. Investment appraisal is covered in Chapters 11 -14.

Top tips. In part (b) (i) it is important to think about the difference between an IT system and other capital investment projects, such as the fact that the IT system may contain intangible costs and benefits as well as tangible ones.

Easy marks. The net present value calculation is fairly straightforward and students should be able to contribute good discussion points in part (b) (ii).

Examiner's comments. Only a few candidates were able to calculate the break even value required in part (a)(ii). In part (b)(i) many candidates failed to recognise the difficulty of identifying intangible benefits and determining an appropriate discount rate for them. A common mistake in part (b)(ii) was to discuss shareholders and/or dividend policy when the question scenario states that PP is a partnership.

Marking scheme

			Marks	
(a)	(i)	Initial investment, redundancy and maintenance	1.5	
		Annual staff saving	1.0	
		Discounting	1.5	
		Negative NPV	1.0	
				5
	(ii)	Use of annuity	3	
		Conversion to equivalent revenue	3	
				6
(b)	(i)	Discussion of pros	2	
		Discussion of cons	2	
		Appropriate discount rate difficult to obtain	2	
				6
	(ii)	Up to 2 marks per relevant point max		8
				25

(a) (i) Net present value before new business cash flows

Year	0	1-4
	USD '000	USD '000
Initial investment	(600)	
Maintenance		(50)
Redundancy costs	(200)	
Annual cost saving		100
Net cash flow	(800)	50
Discount factor at 12%	1.000	3.037
Present value	(800)	151.9
NPV	(648.1)	

(ii) To break even, the project will need cash flows with a present value of USD 648,100. If we assume that the cash inflows are spread evenly across the four year period we can use the four year annuity factor to calculate the annual cash flows required from the new business.

From part (a) (i) we know the four year annuity factor at 12% is 3.037. Therefore the annual net cash inflow required is 648,100 / 3.037 = USD 213,401.

The net cash inflows are expected to be 52% of the cash inflows (revenue) from the new business. Therefore the annual cash inflow would be 213,401/0.52 = USD 410,387

This is the annual cash flow required in order for the project to break even.

(b) (i) There are both benefits and drawbacks from using a conventional discounted cash flow approach to appraise an IT project.

Benefits

The conventional approach means that all projects are **assessed on the same basis**. It also means subjective judgements are largely avoided. This can be a problem when other 'softer' criteria are included in project appraisal such as 'improved information.'

Drawbacks

Unlike most other types of capital projects, costs and benefits from IT projects may be intangible as well as tangible. An example of this is increased efficiency. It can be difficult to give these costs/benefits a realistic or meaningful value.

Since the risks involved in an IT project are not easy to ascertain this makes it difficult to **determine the appropriate discount rate** for the project.

Adjustments should be made to incorporate risk into the evaluation. A risk adjusted discount rate that reflects the specific risk of the IT project is one option. Alternatively an expected value approach could be used by assigning probabilities to possible outcomes. Both of these involve subjective judgements. Another approach is to use sensitivity analysis to assess the impact on the evaluation of changes to the key variables.

(ii) There are a number of other factors to consider before accepting or rejecting this project.

Fit with overall strategy and operational plans

The IT project should fit within the overall strategy for PP and it must be understood how it will contribute to meeting operational performance targets.

PP also needs to be consider whether there are **alternative systems** that would have a better fit with PP. There are two issues to this consideration, whether this system meets the needs of PP best and whether it is the most cost effective system for PP.

Alternatively if this system is required as an essential part of operations, then there is no real choice and it has to be accepted. There may be some scope for fine-tuning and ensuring that the system is the best one for PP.

Reputation and market position

The position in the market of PP is important. It is more likely to be successful if it has a good reputation and a strong competitive position. This is particularly important if PP operates in a **competitive industry**.

Economic conditions

The general state of the economy as well as conditions in PP's own industry are relevant. New business is less likely to be attracted in difficult trading conditions.

Employees

PP should ensure that its staff have the skills needed to be able to operate the new system effectively. Training may be required to ensure this and these costs should be included in any evaluation.

Conclusion

Analysis should be performed to ensure that the proposed IT system meets the needs of the business at both the strategic and operational level. The discounted cash flow analysis may be of less importance if the project is essential to the business. Market research may be helpful to accurately predict levels of new business. Staff should be assessed to ensure that they have the necessary skills and training to be able to use the new system effectively.

54 MR

Text references. NPV, IRR and MIRR are all covered in Chapter 11.

Top tips. Don't forget to use the NPV proforma that is given in the Study Text. Be careful with your treatment of the initial investigation costs. Although they haven't yet been paid, there is an obligation to pay them therefore you should be treating these costs as sunk costs.

Easy marks. You should be able to pick up a number of marks in part (a) via the NPV calculations and the general comparison between MIRR and NPV/IRR.

Examiner's comments. Some candidates performed extremely well on this question whilst others struggled with the calculations. Common errors included:

– omitting residual value of non-current assets
– including the costs of the initial investigation (this is a sunk cost)
– including depreciation rather than tax relief on depreciation in the DCF calculation
– errors in MIRR calculation: many candidates calculated a present value rather than a future value

Marking scheme

				Marks
(a)	(i)	NPV – initial investment	1	
		Residual values non-current and current assets	1	
		Tax calculations	1	
		Capital allowances and tax relief	2	
		Discounting and NPV calculations	1	
		IRR	3	
		MIRR	<u>4</u>	
				13
(a)	(ii)	Advantages and limitations – up to 2 marks per valid issue discussed		Max 6
(b)		Meeting financial objectives – calculations and discussion	Max 2	
		Comparison with target gearing ratio (calculations and discussion)	Max <u>4</u>	
				Max <u>6</u>
		Total		<u>25</u>

(a) (i) <u>Net present value (NPV)</u>

As the project is considered to be riskier than average, use the risk-adjusted rate of 9% to discount the cash flows.

	0 US$m	1 US$m	2 US$m	3 US$m
Net operating cash flows		14.0	17.0	22.0
Taxation (25%)		(3.5)	(4.25)	(5.5)
Non-current assets	(30.0)			3.0
Working capital	(16.0)			16.00
Tax relief on non-current assets (W1)	_____	<u>2.25</u>	<u>2.25</u>	<u>2.25</u>
Cash flow after tax	(46.0)	12.75	15.00	37.75
Discount factor (9%)	1.000	0.917	0.842	0.772
DCF	(46.0)	11.69	12.63	29.14

Net present value = US$7.46m

Working 1 – tax relief

Tax relief on non-current assets = [(90% of US$30m)/3] x 0.25 = US$2.25m

Internal rate of return (IRR)

$$IRR = a + \frac{NPV_a}{NPV_a - NPV_b} (b - a)$$

NPV at 20%

	0	1	2	3
	US$m	US$m	US$m	US$m
Cash flow after tax	(46.0)	12.75	15.00	37.75
Discount factor (20%)	1.000	0.833	0.694	0.579
DCF	(46.0)	10.62	10.41	21.86

NPV = US$(3.11)m

IRR = 9 + [7.46/(7.46 + 3.11)] x (20 – 9) = 16.8%

Modified internal rate of return (MIRR)

Year	Cash inflows	Interest rate multiplier	Amount when reinvested
	US$m		US$m
1	12.75	1.1881	15.15
2	15.00	1.0900	16.35
3	37.75	1.0000	37.75
			69.25

$$MIRR = \sqrt[3]{\frac{69.25}{46.0}} - 1 = 0.1461 \text{ or } 14.61\%$$

(ii) Advantages and limitations of MIRR compared with NPV and IRR

MIRR does not suffer from the problem of **multiple returns** that is an issue with IRR. A project will only ever have one MIRR which reduces confusion. It also assumes that an organisation will reinvest its capital at its **own cost of capital**, rather than at the IRR itself. This brings the **reinvestment assumption** into line with that of NPV and ensures that the MIRR decision outcomes are **consistent** with those of NPV. IRR does not always give the same result as NPV.

One of the **limitations** of MIRR that it may lead an investor to **reject** a project with a **low rate of return** but which actually generates high levels of wealth. This may occur if the MIRR is greater than the cost of capital – the technique will **underestimate** the project's true return.

Also if the difference between the IRR and the organisation's cost of capital is large, the project's length can have a significant effect on actual MIRR.

In a similar way to IRR, MIRR favours projects with **short paybacks** whereas NPV looks at the cash flows over the entire life of the project. It could be argued that this approach will release funds earlier for reinvestment but it gives no indication of the **size** of the project or the **likely increase in shareholders' wealth** (whereas NPV does give such information).

(b) Impact of the project on MR's ability to meet its financial objectives

MR has two primary financial objectives:

(i) To earn a return on shareholders' funds of 11% per annum on average over a three year period
(ii) To keep the gearing ratio below 35%

Return on shareholders' funds

The project – when discounted at a discount rate that specifically reflects its own risk – generates a positive NPV. Both the IRR and MIRR are greater than the risk-adjusted cost of capital of 9% therefore the project should contribute towards the objective of achieving a return on shareholders' funds of 11%.

Gearing

MR will be required to borrow 50% of the initial investment cost – that is US$23m. Gearing would therefore change as follows.

Gearing = Debt/(Debt + Equity)   (based on market values)
Gearing = (350m + 23m)/(350m + 23m + 760m)
Gearing = 33%   (existing gearing = 31.5%)
The project will bring MR extremely close to its maximum required gearing ratio of 35%.

Points to note on the project's impact on the primary financial objectives

(i)   **Market values** change daily and are affected by factors both internal and external to the company. Gearing based on book values is less volatile than the current gearing formula and would be a useful supplement to the primary gearing objective.

(ii)   The project is evaluated over a **very short timescale** (3 years) which is too short for an investment of this nature. To obtain a more accurate NPV result, the project should be evaluated over a longer period.

(iii)   PV relies heavily on the **residual value** of the non-current assets and working capital. Linked to (ii) above, these values may be considerably different if a longer time horizon was used to evaluate the project which will have a significant impact on the final NPV figure.

(iv)   It should be remembered that NPV of the project might be considerably different from MR's calculations once the project has been evaluated by the external market.

55 GOH

Text references. NPV is covered in Chapter 11. WACC is covered in Chapter 8. Financial and non-financial objectives are covered in Chapter 1.

Top tips. Note that 16 out of the 25 available marks are for discursive elements – make sure you give yourself the best chance of gaining good marks by relating your comments directly to the scenario. In part (a)(ii) don't forget to refer to financial and non-financial objectives as required by the question.

The NPV calculation in part (b)(i) is straightforward but remember to include the opportunity cost of the land.

When calculating the WACC, you will have to find the current pre-tax cost of debt based on current market value and then convert to a post-tax rate.

Easy marks. The calculation of NPV is very straightforward so you should be aiming for high marks in this section.

Examiner's comments. Many candidates demonstrated a good understanding of the various issues faced by a public sector organisation in an investment appraisal situation and how these might be different to those faced by a private sector organisation. A high proportion of candidates scored high marks in this question.

(a)   (i)   <u>WACC</u>

Cost of equity = 9%

Value of equity = 24.5m shares x G$13 = G$318.5m

Cost of debt

Pre-tax cost of debt = 5.5 x (100/95) = 5.79%

Post-tax cost of debt = 5.79 x (1 – 0.3) = 4.05%

Value of debt = G$100m x 0.95 = $95m

$$WACC = k_e\left(\frac{V_E}{V_E + V_D}\right) + k_d\left(\frac{V_D}{V_E + V_D}\right)$$

WACC = 9 x [318.5/(318.5+95)] + 4.05 x [95/(318.5+95)] = 6.93 + 0.93 = 7.86% (say 8%)

(ii)   Appropriateness of using JKL's WACC as the discount rate in GOH's project appraisal

Private sector v public sector

The main issue with JKL's WACC is that JKL is a private sector organisation. Such entities have different financial and non-financial objectives to public sector entities like GOH.

As a public sector organisation, GOH is more likely to have a greater focus on non-financial objectives such as:

- Social issues (for example, education)
- Value for money
- Environmental issues

A private sector organisation like JKL will be primarily focused on the objective of **maximising shareholders' wealth**. This involves focusing on shareholder returns in the form of dividends and capital gains – that is, financial targets. Shareholders in private sector organisations require higher rates of return to compensate for the additional risk they take.

Given the above, GOH should **use a lower discount rate** as its stakeholders will not expect the high returns that are more typical of the private sector.

Measures of returns and benefits

A public sector organisation is likely to incorporate non-financial issues such as social and environmental improvements into its project appraisal. Private sector organisations are unlikely to include estimates of such non-financial benefits.

When the above issues are taken into consideration, the use of JKL's discount rate for appraising GOH's project is not appropriate.

(b) (i) <u>Calculation of project NPV</u>

Year	0	1	2	3	4 - 15	15
	G$m	G$m	G$m	G$m	G$m	G$m
Initial investment	(950)					150
Opportunity cost of land	(250)					600
Net benefits		90	110	120	130	
Discount factor (4%) – (W1)	1.000	0.962	0.925	0.889	8.343	0.555
DCF	(1,200)	86.58	101.75	106.68	1,084.59	416.25

NPV = G$595.85m

The project is feasible and from a financial point of view should go ahead.

Working

Annuity factor for years $4 - 15 = AF_{15} - AF_3 = 11.118 - 2.775 = 8.343$

(ii) <u>Other issues to be taken into consideration</u>

Availability of government funding

This project requires a substantial injection of cash by the government – not just for the initial investment but also running costs. Before proceeding, GOH should evaluate whether such **levels of funding are likely to continue** to be available throughout the life of the project.

Alternative uses of government funds

It should be determined whether this project is the **best use of government funds**. Where would the funds be used if the project did not go ahead? Which project should be given priority on the basis of healthcare benefits?

Sensitivity analysis

It is important to carry out a sensitivity analysis of NPV to changes in the key variables. The analysis includes the opportunity cost of not selling the land for example – how feasible would the project be if the developer dropped his price or withdrew the offer entirely? What would happen if net benefits were not as high as initial estimates suggest? What about the proportion of services that are likely to be free – is this likely to be higher than previously thought?

Social benefits of the project

The social benefits of the health centre have been accounted for in the 'net benefits' figures. However social benefits are **difficult to quantify** without a formal basis of identification. It is therefore uncertain how reliable these figures are – further evaluation is necessary.

Length of appraisal period

A 15 year appraisal period does not seem very long for a new health centre. A **longer time period** should be considered, particularly as there are likely to be further expenses once the current evaluation period is over.

Other strategic approaches

Before making a final decision, GOH should consider other strategic approaches such as:

*   Transferring provision of the service to the private sector or another government body

*   Location and size of the health centre – are there other alternatives?

*   Are there any existing facilities that could be refurbished rather than building a completely new health centre?

*   Joint venture with other health agencies to share costs and facilities

*   The potential for using voluntary organisations to support the healthcare services offered

56   CMec

Text references. International investment decisions are dealt with in Chapter 12. Post-completion audits are covered in Chapter 14.

Top tips. This question covers both approaches to calculating the NPV of an international investment. The first issue to deal with is the exchange rate – you are given risk-free interest rates for both Country A and the UK which should suggest the use of interest rate parity. Use the formula given in the exam and the calculations are quite straightforward.

In part (c) don't be tempted to write all you know about the various risks involved in international investment appraisal. You are asked how the project evaluation could be adapted to take this risks into account – make sure you answer the question.

Part (d) is similar – you are not asked to write about a post-completion audit in general but the extent to which an audit of a domestic project could be helpful when planning the implementation of the overseas investment. Make sure you provide a balanced argument if you can.

Easy marks. There are numerous easy marks to be picked up in part (a).

Examiner's comments. Part (b) was often not attempted by candidates. This requirement needed an explanation of the theory of interest rate parity. Some candidates recognised this but few were able to offer sensible explanations of the theory.

In part (c) candidates tended to discuss risks in general, but did not suggest how the project evaluation should be adapted to incorporate any risks identified.

Part (d) candidates tended to offer a discussion of all aspects of PCAs instead of answering the set requirement.

(a) (i) Discounting GBP cash flows at GBP discount rate

Year	1st Jan 20X2 A$m	31st Dec 20X2 A$m	20X3 A$m	20X4 A$m
Store purchase	(415.0)			
Re-branding and re-fitting	(170.0)			
Residual value of stores				450.0
Operating cash flows		200.0	250.0	350.0
Working capital (10% growth pa)	(150)	(15.0)	(16.5)	181.5
Net cash flow	(735.0)	185.0	233.5	981.5
Exchange rate GBP/A$ (W1)	1.3000	1.3701	1.4440	1.5219
	£m	£m	£m	£m
Country A cash flows in GBP	(565.38)	135.03	161.70	644.92
UK cash flows		(14.00)	(14.00)	(14.00)
Total cash flows	(565.38)	121.03	147.70	630.92
Discount factor (10%)	1.000	0.909	0.826	0.751
DCF	(565.38)	110.02	122.00	473.82

NPV = £140.46m

Workings

(1) Exchange rates

Using interest rate parity and risk-free rates in Country A and UK:

Year	Exchange rate (GBP/A$)
1st January 20X2	1.3000
31st December 20X2	1.3000 x (1 + 0.075)/(1 +0.02) = 1.3701
31st December 20X3	1.3701 x (1 + 0.075)/(1 + 0.02) = 1.4440
31st December 20X4	1.4440 x (1 + 0.075)/(1 + 0.02) = 1.5219

(ii) Discounting A$ cash flows at a corresponding A$ discount rate

Year	1st Jan 20X2 A$m	31st Dec 20X2 A$m	20X3 A$m	20X4 A$m
Store purchase	(415.0)			
Re-branding and re-fitting	(170.00)			
Residual value of stores				450.00
Operating cash flows		200.00	250.00	350.00
Working capital (10% growth pa)	(150.0)	(15.00)	(16.50)	181.50
Net cash flow	(735.00)	185.00	233.50	981.50
UK cash flows in A$ (see W1 for rates)		(19.18)	(20.22)	(21.31)
Net cash flow	(735.00)	165.82	213.28	960.19
Discount factor 16% (W2)	1.000	0.862	0.743	0.641
DCF	(735.00)	142.94	158.47	615.48

NPV = A$181.89m

Translating at spot rate of GBP1 = A$1.3000:

NPV = £139.92m

Workings

(2) Adjusted discount rate

(1 + Country A rate)/(1 + UK rate) = (Future spot rate GBP/A$ in 12 months' time)/(Spot rate)

(1 + Country A rate)/1.10 = 1.3701/1.3000

Country A rate = 15.9% (say 16%)

(b) Why we would expect the NPVs to be the same

The exchange rate is calculated using interest rate parity, which uses the risk-free rates in Country A and the UK to predict future exchange rates. This rate is used to translate A$ cash flows into GBP which are then discounted at the GBP discount rate.

With the alternative approach you will notice that the adjusted discount rate is calculated using the predicted future spot rate (which was calculated using interest rate parity as above). The movements in exchange rates are therefore incorporated into the adjusted discount rate, rather than being incorporated into the translated cash flows.

The two approaches **should give the same results** provided that interest rate parity holds true. There are likely to be some differences due to rounding issues and the markets not perfectly matching with the interest rate parity rules.

(c) <u>Adapting the project evaluation to take additional foreign investment risks into account</u>

There are a number of additional risks that are present in a foreign investment. These include:

- Exchange rate risk

- A greater risk that forecast costs and revenues are not accurate due to a lack of knowledge about the market

- Uncertainty about management time in overseeing the project and in subsequent operations. There will be costs associated with this.

These issues can be addressed through the following methods/techniques.

Sensitivity analysis can be used on **key variables**, such as exchange rate values and the property values after 3 years to see if the project will increase shareholder wealth in a number of different situations.

Certainty equivalents could be used to lower returns from the project and so adopt a more prudent approach.

A risk-adjusted discount rate could be used which has factored in the additional risk of the overseas investment and also the equity betas of similar businesses.

Expected value analysis could be used by applying probabilities to the outcome of each possible scenario.

(d) <u>Post-completion audit</u>

A post-completion audit is an objective, independent assessment of the success of a capital project in relation to plan. It covers the whole life of the project and provides feedback to managers to aid the implementation and control of future projects.

A post-completion audit for a previously completed UK project will be of some use but it will be limited.

It may identify weaknesses in the forecasting and estimating techniques used to predict cash flows and therefore a certain amount of 'slack' may be built into this international investment. If the same techniques are used to forecast cash flows for UK and international projects then this is useful information to have.

Post-completion audits may **identify general inefficiencies** in the capital investment process that can be reduced or eliminated in subsequent projects. The identification of such issues can be fed into this project to ensure similar mistakes are not repeated.

However there are **considerable differences between UK-based projects and international projects**. International projects bring their own problems, such as trying to deal with overseas legislation and culture, which will not be present in UK-based investments. As a result the post-completion audit will not identify how these issues could be dealt with.

CMec has never invested in a foreign country therefore they will have **no experience of the problems** such investments can bring. Basing their approach to a foreign investment on their UK experience could be dangerous as managers may think they can engage the same procedures as for home-based projects. This can lead to costly mistakes and inefficient use of resources.

Whilst a post-completion audit may be useful for identifying general issues, using a UK-based audit for an international project (which is not comparable) will be of little use and could encourage managers to assume that they can take a similar approach to international projects as to home-based investments.

57 TM

> **Text references.** The ratios to help you calculate the operating cycle are given in Chapter 3. Working capital financing is covered in Chapter 4. International investment is dealt with in Chapter 12.
>
> **Top tips.** This question demonstrates the importance of having knowledge of topics covered in previous papers. The operating cycle is covered in detail in Paper P1 so make sure you revise this area.
>
> **Easy marks.** There are some easy marks to be gained in part (a).

(a)   Effect of exchange rate movements on second quarter results

Quarter 1

Export sales = A\$5,750,000 x 30% = A\$1,725,000

This is equivalent to A\$1,725,000 x €0.4000 = €690,000

Quarter 2

Export sales = €690,000 x 4/3 = €920,000

At the current exchange rate, sales of €920,000 convert to

€920,000/0.4000 = A\$2,300,000

At the revised exchange rate, sales of €920,000 convert to

€920,000/0.4600 = A\$2,000,000

The impact on revenue that is due entirely to exchange rate movements is A\$300,000. This equates to 4.7% of revenue in Quarter 2.

TM should also think about the impact this will have on accounts receivable, given that credit terms are being increased by 30 days to 90 days.

(b)   (i)   Operating cycle

> **Tutorial note.** The operating cycle calculation is covered in Paper P1 *Performance Operations*. If you are unsure about these calculations, please refer back to the P1 study materials to refresh your memory.

The operating cycle can be calculated as follows:

	Ratio
Raw materials – inventory days	(Raw materials/Purchases) x 365 days
Less	
Payables days	(Accounts payable/Purchases) x 365 days
Add	
Receivables days	(Accounts receivable/Credit sales revenue) x 365 days
Add	
Production days	(Work in progress/Cost of sales) x 365 days
Add	
Finished goods inventory days	(Finished goods/Cost of sales) x 365 days

	Quarter 1	Q1 Days	Quarter 2 (A$1 = €0.4000)	Q 2 Days
Raw materials-inventory days	[1,500/(2,150 X 4)] X 365	63.7	[1,700/(2,350 X 4)] X 365	66.0
Payables days	[1,800/(2,150 X 4)] X 365	(76.4)	[2,600/((2,350 X 4)] X 365	(101.0)
Receivables days	[5,000/(5,750 X 0.93* X 4)] X 365	85.3	[7,000/(6,325 X 0.93 X 4)] X 365	108.6
Production days	[740/(3,163 X 4)] X 365	21.3	[860/(3,529 X 4)] X 365	22.2
Finished goods inventory days	[420/(3,163 X 4)] X 365	12.1	[500/(3,529 X 4)] X 365	12.9
Operating cycle		106.0		108.7

*Revenue multiplied by 0.93 to represent credit sales ie 90% of home sales and 100% of overseas sales. (0.7 × 0.9) + 0.3 = 0.93

Tutorial note. You would receive credit if you used other relevant ratios and calculations.

Operating cycle if exchange rate is A$1 = €0.4600

As calculated in (a) above, a change in exchange rate at the beginning of Quarter 2 would reduce revenue by A$300,000 to A$5,582,250 [(A$6,325,000 × 0.93) – 300,000]. Similarly accounts receivable would fall by A$300,000 to A$6,700,000.

Receivables days = [6,700/(5,582 X 4)] X 365 days = 109.5 days

This is only fractionally higher than the previous figure of 108.7 days. There would be no significant change to the operating cycle (it would increase by only 0.8 days).

(ii) Comparison of Quarter 1 and Quarter 2 operating cycle components

Whilst the total operating cycle has not increased significantly from Quarter 1 to Quarter 2, two components have changed quite considerably.

Payables days have increased from 76.4 days to 101 days, indicating that TM is taking almost 25 days longer to pay its suppliers. It is not clear whether this has been agreed with suppliers in advance but TM is **foregoing prompt payment discounts** and supplier goodwill.

Receivables days have increased by approximately 23 days from 85.3 days to 108.6 days. An increase in the time taken for customers to pay TM should be expected, given that TM offered an extra 30 days credit to its export customers. Export sales make up the following percentage of total sales in Quarter 2:

Quarter 1 export sales	30% of A$5,750 = A$1,725
Quarter 2 export sales	A$1,725 X (4/3) = A$2,300
Quarter 2 export sales as % of total sales	(A$2,300/A$6,325) X 100 = 36.4%

We would therefore expect Receivables days to increase by no more than (36.4% of 30 days) 11 days – half of what the actual increase is. This suggests that customers in general are going to take longer to pay – a situation that TM should wish to avoid. It should consider offering **incentives for customers** to pay either early or on time – for example, discounts or interest being charged on overdue accounts.

Whilst the increase in Payables days cancels out the increase in Receivables days this situation means that the extra time it takes customers to pay is being financed by the extra time TM is taking to pay its suppliers. As mentioned above, TM may have agreed the extra credit period with its suppliers but it is unlikely.

Production days and inventory days have not increased significantly but should nevertheless be investigated to avoid any further increases that may become problematic.

(c) Appropriate financing structure

TM currently funds its net current assets (permanent and fluctuating) using **short-term funding** in the form of an overdraft. This is a particularly aggressive policy which tends to yield the highest expected return (due to short-term debt being generally cheaper than long-term debt). However such a policy is **extremely risky** and should be amended to a more moderate form.

TM should consider financing its permanent current assets with medium- or long-term funds and using short-term funds to finance fluctuating current assets. As the greater need for finance has arisen due to the expansion of export sales, it might be worthwhile considering a euro-denominated loan.

Benefits and potential problems of using euro-denominated finance

The main advantage of using euro-denominated finance is that it **matches** with the export sales' currency. This reduces foreign currency risk as adverse movements in loan repayments due to changes in exchange rates will be offset by favourable movements in euro-based sales revenue. Another advantage is that euro loans are **widely available** therefore TM should not have any problems obtaining such a loan.

One of the issues with using euro-denominated finance is its **inflexibility** in hedging foreign currency risk. As currency rates fluctuate, so too will the value of the euro-denominated accounts receivable. However the loan is not easily adjustable to reflect these fluctuations which will limit the advantage of matching receivables with the loan finance.

Another problem with euro-denominated finance is that it only hedges currency risk on accounts receivable. TM is more likely to be concerned with the effect of currency risk on operating profits. A more appropriate method of hedging currency risk in this situation would be forward contracts. Such contracts will hedge translation exposure which means that the use of euro-denominated finance would not be appropriate.

58 FBQ

> **Text references.** Adjusted present value is covered in Chapter 13 and the capital structure decision in Chapter 9.
>
> **Top tips.** This is a straightforward NPV question which gives you practice at adjusting the beta and then calculating the APV. We have given two methods to calculate the ungeared cost of equity as either method is acceptable here. Clear workings an layout are essential in this type of question. In part (b) remember the mix should be suitable, acceptable and feasible.
>
> **Further question practice.** If you struggled with the APV part of this question, you should try Question 47 next.

(a)   Calculation of K_e

$$\beta_u = \beta_g \left[\frac{V_E}{V_E + V_D\left[1-t\right]} \right] + \beta_d \left[\frac{V_D\left[1-t\right]}{V_E + V_D\left[1-t\right]} \right]$$

$$\beta_u = 1.35 \left[\frac{2}{2 + 1\left[1 - 0.3\right]} \right]$$

$$= 1.35 \times 0.741$$

$$= 1.00$$

Ungeared K_e $= R_f + [R_m - R_f]\beta$
$\qquad = 4 + (10 - 4)1$
$\qquad = 10\%$

Alternative method:

Existing cost of equity $K_e = R_f + [R_m - R_f]\beta = 4 + (10 - 4)1.35 = 12.1\%$

Cost of debt $= 4\%$

$$WACC = k_e \left[\frac{V_E}{V_E + V_D} \right] + k_d \left[1-t\right] \left[\frac{V_D}{V_E + V_D} \right]$$

$$= (12.1 \times 2/3) + (4 \times 0.7 \times 1/3)$$

$$= 9\%$$

Ungearing the WACC:

$$k_{adj} = k_{eu}[1 - tL]$$

$$L = \left[\frac{V_D}{V_E + V_D}\right]$$

$$9 = k_{eu}(1 - (0.3 \times 1/3))$$

$$k_{eu} = 9/0.9 = 10\%$$

NPV calculation

Year	0	1	2	3	4
	$'000	$'000	$'000	$'000	$'000
Contribution (W1)		1,220	1,563	2,003	2,567
Fixed costs (W2)		(919)	(965)	(1,013)	(1,064)
		301	598	990	1,503
Taxation (30%)		(90)	(179)	(297)	(451)
		211	419	693	1,052
Purchase of machine	(900)				
Proceeds from sale					200
Tax benefits (W3)		67	51	38	54
After-tax cash flows	(900)	278	470	731	1,306
10% discount factor	1.000	0.909	0.826	0.751	0.683
Present value	(900)	253	388	549	892
Net present value	**1,182**				

Workings

(1)   Contribution

Year	1	2	3	4
	$	$	$	$
Selling price ($/unit)	51.50	53.04	54.63	56.27
Variable cost ($/unit)	16.64	17.31	18.00	18.72
Contribution ($/unit)	34.86	35.73	36.63	37.55
Sales volume	35,000	43,750	54,688	68,360
Total contribution	1,220,100	1,563,188	2,003,221	2,566,918

(2)   Fixed costs

Total fixed production overhead cost in current price terms = 35,000 units × $25
= $875,000

Inflated at 5% per year:

Year	1	2	3	4
	$	$	$	$
Fixed costs	918,750	964,688	1,012,922	1,063,568

(3)   Tax benefits

Year	Capital allowances	Tax benefits @30%
1	900,000 × 0.25 = 225,000	67,500
2	225,000 × 0.75 = 168,750	50,625
3	168,750 × 0.75 = 126,563	37,969
4	Balancing figure = 179,687	53,906
	900,000 − 200,000 = 700,000	

Adjustment for financing

Interest payable = 4% × $600,000 = $24,000
Tax shield = $24,000 × 30% = $7,200
Discount factor at 4% cost of debt over 4 years = 3.630
Present value of tax shield = 3.630 × $7,200 = $26,136

Issue costs = $15,000

APV = $(1,182,000 + 26,136 – 15,000) = $1,193,136

The project should therefore be accepted.

(b)   Equity and debt

(i)   The **cost of debt capital**. Tax relief will be available to FBQ on interest costs, but not on dividends. Debt capital is therefore cheaper than equity, and is consequently often preferred by management.

(ii)   FBQ's board of directors might try to **keep gearing** within a **target range** that shareholders and lenders might regard as 'normal' or '**acceptable**' for the company.

(iii)   Gearing policy might be affected by board policy on **retained profits**. When retained profits are fairly high, a company might have little recourse to external financing, and so would have a very low gearing level.

(iv)   Gearing might be influenced by **management's views on interest rates**. Borrowing might be avoided when market interest rates are considered high, or in the case of variable rate borrowing if interest rates are expected to rise.

Long-term and short-term debt

(i)   **Non-current assets** should normally be **financed** by **long-term sources** of **finance** and **current assets** by a **mixture of long-term and short-term sources**. If a company finances illiquid assets from short-term debt it faces the risk of insolvency in the event of its being unable to renegotiate the loans when they fall due.

(ii)   **Transaction** costs **vary** according to the type of finance being raised, for example it will be cheaper for FBQ to arrange a medium-term bank loan than a public issue of dated loan notes. Short-term debt will need to be renegotiated more frequently and this will give rise to recurring transaction costs.

(iii)   The **relative interest rates** carried by long-term and short-term debt will **vary over time** according to supply and demand and to market expectations of interest rate changes. Rates are generally higher on long-term loans than on short-term since the level of risk faced by the lender that interest rates may rise before repayment is due is higher.

(iv)   FBQ's directors may find it easier to **raise short-term finance** with **low security** than long-term finance.

(v)   In opting for short-term debt, FBQ would face the risk that it may **not** be able to **renegotiate the loan** on such good terms, or even at all, when the repayment date is reached. Long-term loans are thus less risky.

(vi)   Long-term debt may carry **early repayment penalties** if it is found that the loan is no longer needed or a more attractive form of finance becomes available. Short-term debt is **more flexible** since it allows the firm to react to interest rate changes and to avoid being locked into an expensive long-term fixed rate commitment at a time when rates are falling.

59 CIP

Text references. Cost of capital is covered in Chapter 9. NPV is covered in Chapter 11 and APV in Chapter 13.

Top tips. Don't forget to include the administration costs of raising the loans in the APV calculation.

Easy marks. The calculation of NPV in (a)(i) is extremely straightforward. If you have learned the steps for calculating adjusted WACC you should be able to pick up another few easy marks.

Examiner's comments. Many candidates were unable to successfully complete the APV calculation.

(a)   (i)   <u>NPV using existing WACC</u>

Year	0	1	2	3	4 - 6
	€000	€000	€000	€000	€000
Cash flow	(6,500)	750	950	1,400	2,100
Discount factor	1.000	0.909	0.826	0.751	2.487 x 0.751 = 1.868
DCF	(6,500)	681.75	784.70	1,051.40	3,922.8

NPV = €(59,350)

(ii)   <u>NPV using a risk-adjusted WACC</u>

Proxy company equity beta = 1.95

Ungear proxy company equity beta:

$$\beta_u = \beta_g \frac{V_E}{V_E + V_D(1-t)} + \beta_d \frac{V_D(1-t)}{V_E + V_D(1-t)}$$ (we are not told the debt beta therefore assume it is zero)

$\beta u = 1.95 \times (4/[(1 \times 0.7) + 4])$

$\beta u = 1.66$

Regear beta for CIP's capital structure:

$$\beta_g = \beta_u \frac{V_E + V_D(1-t)}{V_E}$$

$\beta g = 1.66 \times [(3 + 0.7)/3] = 2.05$

Cost of equity using CAPM:

$ke = 4 + (9 - 4) \times 2.05 = 14.25\%$

Risk-adjusted WACC:

$$WACC = k_e \left(\frac{V_E}{V_E + V_D}\right) + k_d \left(\frac{V_D}{V_E + V_D}\right)$$

$WACC = 14.25 \times (3/4) + (6 \times 0.7) \times (1/4)$

$WACC = 11.74\%$ (say 12%)

NPV

Year	0	1	2	3	4 - 6
	€000	€000	€000	€000	€000
Cash flow	(6,500)	750	950	1,400	2,100
Discount factor	1.000	0.893	0.797	0.712	2.402 × 0.712 = 1.710
DCF	(6,500)	669.75	757.15	996.80	3,591.0

NPV = €(485,300)

(iii)   <u>Adjusted Present Value (APV)</u>

Base case discount rate

This is the cost of equity for an all-equity financed company. We calculated the asset beta that would be appropriate for the project in (ii) above – that is, 1.66. We can then use the CAPM to establish the cost of equity of an ungeared company.

$keu = 4 + (9 - 4) \times 1.66 = 12.3\%$ (say 12%)

This is the same as the adjusted WACC above therefore we know that the NPV at this discount rate is €(485,300).

Tax relief on loan interest

This will be discounted at the pre-tax cost of debt.

Subsidised loan (40% of total finance required)

= 40% × €6,500,000 × 1% x 30% × 4.917

= €38,353

Bank borrowings (20% of total finance required)

= 20% × €6,500,000 × 6% × 30% × 4.917

= €115,058

Total PV of tax relief = €153,411

PV of subsidy on loan:

= 40% × €6,500,000 × [(6% – 1%) × (1 – 0.3)] × 4.917

= €447,447

Administrative costs

= 60% × €6,500,000 × 1%

= €39,000

APV

	€
Base case NPV	(485,300)
PV of tax relief on loan interest	153,411
PV of subsidy on loan	447,447
Administrative costs	(39,000)
APV	76,558

(b) Evaluation of potential financial benefits of the project

Summary of results and decisions

	€	*Decision*
NPV	(59,350)	**Reject**
NPV with adjusted WACC	(485,300)	**Reject**
APV	76,558	**Accept**

There is a contradiction in the decision to be made depending on the appraisal technique chosen. We will therefore consider the appropriateness of each technique to the project under consideration.

NPV using existing WACC

This is **not an appropriate technique** as the business and financial risks associated with the project are different from the existing risks of CIP.

The project's business risk is higher than that of CIP's current business operations. Also the benefits of the subsidised loan and access to higher levels of debts are specific to the project and have not been taken into consideration.

NPV using risk-adjusted WACC

This technique is better than the previous one as it takes the **business risk** of the project into account by adjusting the WACC.

However the technique still does not take the benefits of the financing used that were discussed above.

APV

APV is useful in situations where a project has special financing features or subsidies, which is the case here. Using NPV for this project means that the tax benefits of the subsidy and bank loan and the administration costs associated with arranging the loans can be taken into account.

The APV calculation uses the ungeared cost of equity which was derived from the proxy company. This means that the results are based on **project risk** rather than CIP's current business risk.

(c)   Advice to the Directors

APV is the most appropriate technique for appraising this project. Based on the APV results the project should be accepted.

However it should be borne in mind that one of the underlying assumptions of APV is that it is appropriate to use the actual gearing level for the project where different projects within the organisation have different levels of debt. This appears to be the case here therefore a decision based on APV seems to be robust.

60 PEI

Text references. NPV is covered in Chapter 11. Capital rationing and PI are dealt with in Chapter 13. International investment appraisal is covered in Chapter 12.

Top tips. When calculating the £/A$ exchange rate, remember that it is A$ that is weakening therefore you should be multiplying the previous year's rate by 1 + the rate of depreciation to find the next year's exchange rate. Don't forget the funding limitations in place when you evaluate your results and make a recommendation in part (a)(ii).

Part (b) is a roundabout way of asking you to calculate the adjusted discount rate that would be suitable for Project C's home currency.

Easy marks. Part (a)(i) offers some very easy marks and if you are familiar with the issues that arise from overseas investments then part (c) does too.

Examiner's comments. This question was generally well answered, especially the calculations for part (a)(i), although a minority of candidates did not calculate profitability indices. Part (b) was frequently ignored or misunderstood. In part (c) many answers discussed all types of key factors whereas the question required a focus on financial factors.

(a)   (i)   Project A

Discount factor 8% perpetuity = 1/0.08 = 12.5

NPV = (12.5 x £1.75m) - £15.5m = £6.38m

PI = NPV of project/initial investment = £6.38m/£15.5m = 41.2%

Project B

	0	1	2 - 7	7
	£m	£m	£m	£m
Initial investment	(10.20)	1.15	3.10	2.5
Discount factor (8%)	1.000	0.926	(5.206 – 0.926) = 4.28	0.583
DCF	(10.20)	1.06	13.27	1.46

NPV = £5.59m

PI = £5.59m/£10.2m = 54.8%

Project C

Exchange rates

Year	£/A$	Cash flows (£m)
0 (beginning of 20X1)	2.00	(9.50)
1	2.03	A$9.30/2.03 = 4.58
2	2.06	A$9.30/2.06 = 4.51
3	2.09	A$9.30/2.09 = 4.45
4	2.12	A$9.30/2.12 = 4.39
5	2.15	A$9.30/2.15 = 4.33

BPP
LEARNING MEDIA

	0 £m	1 £m	2 £m	3 £m	4 £m	5 £m
Initial investment	(9.50)					
Cash flow		4.58	4.51	4.45	4.39	4.33
Discount factor (9%)	1.000	0.917	0.842	0.772	0.708	0.650
DCF	(9.50)	4.20	3.80	3.43	3.11	2.81

NPV = £7.85m

PI = £7.85m/£9.5m = 82.6%

<u>Summary of results</u>

	NPV	PI	Ranking NPV	Ranking PI
Project A	£6.38m	41.2%	2	3
Project B	£5.59m	54.8%	3	2
Project C	£7.85m	82.6%	1	1

(ii)   Evaluation of results

On the basis of the summary of results above, Project C is ranked number 1 by both appraisal methods. NPV and PI give conflicting results for Projects A and B. Although NPV is generally considered to be the superior technique for investment appraisal, PI is useful in capital rationing situations as it can be used to determine the best combination of projects to undertake.

Combination of results

Only two combinations have to be considered as Project C has been ranked first by both techniques. This means that this project is certain to be undertaken. In addition, the A + B combination is too expensive – only £25m is available whereas the cost of these two projects is £25.7m.

Combination	Initial investment	NPV	PI	Ranking NPV	Ranking PI
A + C	£25m	£14.23m	56.9%	1	2
B + C	£19.7m	£13.44m	68.2%	2	1

Again we have conflicting results. Both combinations include Project C therefore we should really focus on the relative merits of Projects A and B to make a final decision.

Project A lasts for an indefinite period whereas Project B only lasts for 7 years. Bearing in mind that investors prefer to receive returns sooner rather than later it would appear than Project B is preferable in terms of duration. Both projects have been discounted at the same cost of capital, suggesting that they are viewed as being equally risky. It would therefore appear that Project B is preferable to Project A due to the shorter time span involved.

The combination of **Projects B and C** would appear to be preferable to the A and C combination and allows PEI to invest the remaining capital elsewhere. However this recommendation is based on the assumption that the remaining £5.3m is actually invested at a comparable rate of return.

(b)   <u>Alternative method of evaluating Project C</u>

The alternative method of evaluating Project C involves discounting A$ cash flows at an adjusted cost of capital that will be suitable for the foreign currency.

We can calculate an appropriate discount rate for A$ using the following formula (known as the International Fisher Effect).

$$\frac{(1+\text{annual discount rate A\$})}{(1+\text{annual discount rate £})} = \frac{\text{Future spot rate £ / A\$ in 12 months' time}}{\text{Spot rate £ / A\$}}$$

We know that future spot rate/spot rate = 1.015 (that is the A$ is weakening against the £). Therefore:

(1 + annual discount rate A$) = 1.015 x 1.09

Discount rate A$ = 10.6%

(c)   <u>Key financial factors</u>

Foreign exchange risks. Any movement in exchange rates will have an impact on future cash flows. PEI may have to consider hedging against any foreign exchange risks that result from investing overseas in Project C.

Political and country risks. PEI should investigate any potential political issues it may encounter when investing in Project C's home country. There may be pressure from the government to keep any profits from Project C in that country for example – this could have an effect on the attractiveness of this project. In addition, PEI will have to consider the challenges in finding suitable staff that speak the home language of the country of Project C. There may be an issue of quality control if local staff do not fully appreciate the levels at which services should be delivered.

Shareholders' attitudes towards risk. Current shareholders may be averse to investing in an overseas country, depending on the mix of shareholders in the organisation.

Funds required. Whilst internal funds are available to invest in Project C (see above calculations) it may not be the most appropriate way in which to finance a foreign investment. PEI might want to consider taking out an A\$ loan to match with the currency in which the expenditure will take place. This will provide an instant hedge against foreign currency movements.

Tax implications. PEI should investigate whether there is a tax treaty in place with the foreign country that will protect its earnings against being taxed twice.

61 REM

Text references. CAPM calculations are explained in Chapter 8. Post-completion audits are discussed in Chapter 14.

Top tips. (a) requires an application of the formula relating asset and equity betas. We have used the adjusted cost of capital formula in (a) (iii) to reflect the financing effects of undertaking the new investment. This represents a revised WACC, as opposed to the ungeared cost of equity (8.85%) or the geared cost of equity 5 + 1.098 (9 – 5) = 9.36%.

The main problem with using a proxy company to find an asset beta is that most quoted companies are diversified and finding one in the same 'industry' as the project is difficult. In the course of your discussion, don't forget to 'work in' some limitations of the capital asset pricing model, which will gain you a few more marks.

Post- completion audits are easier to write about if you think of it as debriefing or post mortem: Did we achieve our objective? What did we do right and what went wrong?

Easy marks. Post-completion audits may come up in this paper or Paper P3, and it's easy to earn half a dozen marks discussing them.

Examiner's comments. (a) was generally done quite well. Errors some candidates made included a failure to adjust for tax, and lack of discussion, including failure to justify use of the equity beta. In (b) answers tended to be stronger on use of a proxy company than the alternative approaches. Candidates appeared unclear on what was meant by use of an adjusted discount rate. The main problem with (c) was that candidates spent too long on this part of the question.

(a)   (i)   We need first to find the **ungeared (asset) beta** of the courier company, a company with similar business risk to the project REM is undertaking. Its beta is 1.3, at a debt equity ratio (V_D/V_E) of 1:2 and it is assumed this is an equity beta and not an asset beta.

If tax is 30%, and debt is risk free, the beta of debt is zero, and the asset beta β_u for the courier company is given by:

$$\beta_u = \beta_g \left[\frac{V_E}{V_E + V_D[1-t]} \right]$$

Thus $\beta_u = 1.3 \times 2/[2 + 1(1 - 0.3)] = 1.3 \times 2/2.7 = 0.963$

Since REM is considering investing in a courier-type project, the asset beta for this project appraisal can be assumed to be **0.963**. (Note that this will be different from REM's existing asset beta).

(ii) We need to **adjust the asset beta** to take account of REM's finance risk and hence find its equity beta. REM's debt equity ratio is 1:5.

Equity beta will be given by:

$$\beta_g = \beta_u + \left[\beta_u - \beta_d\right]\frac{V_D\left[1-t\right]}{V_E}$$

$\beta_g = 0.963 + 0.963 \times [(1 - 0.3)/5] = 1.098$

The equity beta for REM when appraising this project is **1.098**.

> This equity beta can be used to calculate a geared cost of equity using the following formula:
>
> $K_e = 5 + (9 - 5) \times 1.098 = 9.392\%$

(iii) *Use asset beta to find ungeared cost of equity*

$k_{eu} = 5 + 0.963 (9 - 5)$
$\phantom{k_{eu}} = 8.85\%$

We then need to adjust the ungeared cost of equity to arrive at a cost of capital that reflects REM's financial risk.

Use $k_{adj} = k_{eu}[1 - tL]$ to find k_{adj} to be used as discount rate

$k_{adj} = 8.85 [1 - (0.3 \times 1/6)]$
$\phantom{k_{adj}} = 8.4\%$

> Alternatively use the geared cost of equity to calculate REM's WACC.
>
> $$WACC = k_e\left[\frac{V_E}{V_E + V_D}\right] + k_d\left[1-t\right]\left[\frac{V_D}{V_E + V_D}\right]$$
>
> $ = 9.392 \times (5/6) + (5 \times 0.7) \times (1/6) = 8.4\%$

(iv) *NPV of the project*

Year	$m	Discount factor 8.4%	PV $m
0	(12.50)	1	(12.500)
1–4	3.15	3.283	10.341
5	5.85	0.668	3.908
			1.749

The net present value of the project is **$1.749 million**, indicating that the project is worthwhile.

Working: 8.4% discount factors

4 year cumulative discount factor $= \dfrac{1-(1+r)^{-n}}{r}$

$ = (1 - (1/1.084^4)/0.084 = 3.283$

Five year PV factor $= 1/1.084^5 = 0.668$

(b) <u>Advantages of using a proxy company</u>

(i) Beta factors for company's shares can only be **directly measured** if the companies are **quoted** and have **market prices**. For companies that do not have a quoted share price, the use of a proxy company is a reasonably good method of determining a beta factor and hence a cost of capital.

(ii) The betas of proxy companies are also useful if a company decides to invest in a project that is in a **different risk class** from its normal business. The proxy company is chosen because its business is **similar to the new project**, not to the investing company's existing business.

Since both cases are true for REM – it is unquoted and it is investing in a project of a different risk class – the identification of the courier company as a quoted proxy company with a known beta is useful.

Problems with using a proxy company

(i)   The courier company is **unlikely** to be **fully representative** of REM's new project.

(ii)   Few quoted companies operate in just one business field. **Diversification** affects a company's beta.

(iii)   **Beta factors** are affected by **gearing**. To adjust for the different gearing levels of REM and the proxy company requires two computations, as shown.

(iv)   The computations and indeed the CAPM are based on a number of **simplifying assumptions**, and estimates of betas are subject to **large statistical errors**, which mean that the estimates can only be approximate. They are also based on **historical data**.

(v)   The **relevance** of the CAPM to the cost of capital of an unquoted company is doubtful. The CAPM assumes that shareholders **eliminate unsystematic risk** by holding **diversified portfolios**. The shareholders of REM probably do not hold large portfolios outside their investment in REM. Hence the investment's **total risk** may be more relevant than its systematic risk.

Alternative methods of adjusting for risk

(i)   The project cash flows could be **reduced subjectively** to certainty-equivalents, and the project **discounted at the risk free rate**.

(ii)   If sufficient appropriate data could be found, the cost of equity could be estimated using **arbitrage pricing theory**. This assumes that the cost of equity is based on a number of **independent factors,** to each of which a particular **risk premium** is attached. These could include unanticipated inflation, changes in production levels, changes in the risk premium on bonds and changes in the term structure of interest rates.

(iii)   The **marginal cost of new finance** could be used.

(c)   Benefits of post-completion audits

    (i)   Better forecasting techniques

        The audit can identify **weaknesses** in the forecasting and estimating techniques used to evaluate projects, and should help to improve the **discipline and quality** of forecasting. In particular by **classifying variances** as controllable (for example efficiency of operations) or non-controllable (for example weather, interest rates), the evaluation can be used to improve future project appraisals, and encourage a more realistic approach to project uncertainties.

    (ii)   Better future investment decisions

        Post-completion evaluation of the project will help determine whether a **continuation of the project**, or similar future projects, is likely to be worthwhile. The post-completion audit can also identify where **mistakes** have been made, so that similar mistakes can be avoided in the future. It may also identify **successes** that might be created in future projects.

    (iii)   Better current investment decisions

        Awareness that an audit will be carried out at a later date may encourage managers to be **more realistic** and not unduly optimistic in their judgements. However this might tempt managers towards prudence, which may be counter-productive if it leads to rejection of a good project.

    (iv)   Contribution to performance evaluation

        A post-completion audit can provide feedback to project managers and to senior management which is of use in the process of **management control** and **performance** assessment.

62 GHI

Text references. Adjusted present value is covered in Chapter 13 and project control in Chapter 14.

Top tips. Part (a) is a complicated calculation with numerous opportunities to make mistakes! Make sure you use an **ungeared** cost of equity in the NPV calculation and carefully calculate each part of the APV calculation. The examiner also accepted an approach where additional tax of 10% on UK profits is charged after translating £ cash flows into €s.

Easy marks. Part (b) is a straightforward discussion where it is relatively easy to pick up marks. Make sure you carefully revise the discussion aspects of project control.

Examiner's comments. This was a very popular choice of question to do but many candidates failed to fully understand how to progress from NPV to APV and few candidates used an ungeared cost of equity in the NPV base calculation.

(a)   Calculation of K_e:

Adjusted present value:

WACC = $(10.7 \times 0.6) + (3.25 \times 0.4) = 7.72$

$K_{adj} = K_{eu}\left[1 - tL\right]$

$K_{eu} = \dfrac{K_{adj}}{[1 - tL]} = \dfrac{7.72}{[1 - (0.35 \times 0.4)]} = 9\%$

NPV calculation:

Year	0	1	2	3	4	5
	£m	£m	£m	£m	£m	£m
Project cash flows	(10.00)	5.00	5.00	4.00	3.00	3.00
UK tax @ 25%		(1.25)	(1.25)	(1.00)	(0.75)	(0.75)
After tax cash flow	(10.00)	3.75	3.75	3.00	2.25	2.25
Exchange rate						
(weakening at 3% pa)	1.60	1.55	1.51	1.46	1.42	1.37
	€m	€m	€m	€m	€m	€m
Cash flows in €	(16.00)	5.81	5.66	4.38	3.19	3.08
Extra French tax						
@ 35% – 25% = 10% (W)		(0.78)	(0.76)	(0.58)	(0.43)	(0.41)
After tax cash flow	(16.00)	5.03	4.90	3.80	2.76	2.67
9% discount factor	1.000	0.917	0.842	0.772	0.708	0.650
Discounted cash flow	(16.00)	4.61	4.13	2.93	1.95	1.74

Net present value   €(0.64m)

Working

Project cash flows in £m					
taxed at the extra 10%	0.50	0.50	0.40	0.30	0.30
Exchange rate as above	1.55	1.51	1.46	1.42	1.37
Extra tax in €m	0.78	0.76	0.58	0.43	0.41

Alternative solution (taxing the overseas project at the domestic rate of tax as this is ultimately what will have to be paid)

Year	0	1	2	3	4	5
	£m	£m	£m	£m	£m	£m
Project cash flows	(10.00)	5.00	5.00	4.00	3.00	3.00
Tax @ 35%		(1.75)	(1.75)	(1.40)	(1.05)	(1.05)
After tax cash flow	(10.00)	3.25	3.25	2.60	1.95	1.95
Exchange rate	1.60	1.55	1.51	1.46	1.42	1.37
	€m	€m	€m	€m	€m	€m
Cash flows in €	(16.00)	5.04	4.91	3.80	2.77	2.67
9% discount factor	1.000	0.917	0.842	0.772	0.708	0.650
Discounted cash flow	(16.00)	4.62	4.13	2.93	1.96	1.74

Net present value   €(0.62 million)

Adjusted present value:

Tax relief on debt interest = €16m × 5% × 35% = €280,000 per annum
Present value of tax relief for 5 years @ 5% (cost of debt) = €280,000 × 4.329 = €1,212,120

Issue costs = €16m × 2% = €320,000
Tax relief on issue costs = €320,000 × 35% = €112,000

Adjusted present value = NPV if all equity financed + PV of the tax shield
APV = €((640,000) + 1,212,120 – 320,000 + 112,000) = €364,120

The project has a **negative** base case NPV but it is not particularly large. After allowing for the tax relief on debt, the NPV is positive and the project could be recommended. However, the limitations of the NPV and APV calculations may make this advice **unreliable**.

The **limitations** of an APV approach in this context are as follows.

- Establishing a suitable cost of equity for the initial DCF computation is difficult and subjective and may not fully reflect the risk of the project
- It is difficult to accurately identify all the costs and benefits associated with the method of financing
- It is assumed in the calculations that all of the €16m loan will be needed for this project

(b)   (i)   The project committee of GHI will play a vital role in the **planning** of the project. Effective planning, particularly the **design** of the product, is an essential contributor to the success of this project. A good design is a very important way of making products **distinctive**. It not only draws attention to the company's products, it also improves performance and cuts production costs.

           The project committee will collect information about the UK market using detailed **market research** of UK customers. The UK phone market is highly **competitive** and **saturated** so the strategic market position must be considered. GHI could **differentiate** their product according to price, design or service, depending on the outcome of the market research.

   (ii)   The implementation stage is concerned with **co-ordinating** people and other resources to carry out the project plan. The project committee will prepare a plan for implementation, which may first involve a trial implementation in selected areas which are thought to be representative of the total market. They will then plan for the full launch of the product, ensuring that the product is in the right place at the right time and that customers know about it. Launch plans may have to be modified if competitors change their response.

           The project committee will be responsible for **evaluating the performance** of the project in terms of costs incurred, sales volumes and sales prices compared to budget. This will feed into a **control mechanism** as deviations from budget are investigated throughout the implementation and action taken as necessary.

On completion of implementation, the project committee will be responsible for carrying out a post-completion appraisal designed to provide information to aid the implementation and control of future projects.

63 QE

> **Text references.** The profitability index method is explained in Chapter 13 and acquisition issues are discussed in Chapter 16.
>
> **Top tips.** You would normally get a couple of marks for using an appropriate format, that is the answer should be a report, divided into the four bullet point headings in the question, and including main computations as an appendix.
>
> In (a) the profitability index method would be used to decide which investment to undertake, as capital is rationed for the period in which the decision is taken. (b) represents important knowledge about alternative uses of funds. (c) stresses the importance of finding the right level of gearing. (c) and (d) also bring in non-financial factors (will acquisitions take up too much management time? Will synergies be realised?)
>
> **Easy marks.** Organic growth vs acquisition should be a very straightforward discussion.

Marking scheme

			Marks
(a)	Calculations	7	
	Discount rate	3	10
(b)	One mark per use		4
(c)	Up to 2 marks per relevant point max		6
(d)	Up to 2 marks per relevant point max		5
			25

To: Board of Directors
From: Financial Manager
Date: 12 May 20X0

(a)   Evaluation of potential acquisitions

This report reviews the three potential acquisitions which are at present under consideration and comments on aspects relating to them.

Financial appraisal of the investments

Given that there is a ceiling of £1.4 million available for investing in three potential businesses which have a total cost of £2.3 million, the principles of investment appraisal using **capital rationing** should be applied. The following results summarise calculations which are attached in the Appendix:

Company	Initial outlay £'000	Net present value £'000	NPV/outlay
AB	1,100	192	17.5%
CD	550	52	9.5%
EF	650	108	16.6%

Highest NPV

The goal is to achieve the **highest net present value (NPV)** from a combination of projects that can be afforded. The profitability index (NPV/outlay) shows that AB offers the highest NPV per £ invested. If AB is accepted, both others must be rejected. The only other alternative is to accept both of CD and EF, which would give a total NPV of £160,000, which is significantly less than the £192,000 generated by AB.

Conclusion. Accept the acquisition of AB and reject the other two investments.

Discount rates

In making this decision it is assumed that 12% per annum in real terms is a **valid discount** rate for all the projects. Although this is the normal 'hurdle rate' applied to all our company's projects, in practice the **discount rate used** should vary with each project, depending on its risk. Also, in a situation of capital rationing, the **opportunity cost of capital increases**, representing the rate of return foregone on investment opportunities that must be rejected because of the shortage of cash. The computations may therefore need to be reworked using different discount rates.

(b)   Use of surplus cash not needed for investment

If AB is acquired, there will be a £300,000 cash surplus left over, which cannot be invested in CD or EF. This should not be left idle, but should be applied in the best possible way(s) from the following:

(i)   **Repaying** some of the **company's debt** which, we agree, is at a high level at the moment

(ii)   **Placing** some of the **cash on deposit** or in short term investments to produce enough for the required investment in Company AB in one year, which is estimated at £100,000; although an investment in the money market produces a return below the company's cost of capital, this is acceptable if it eases a further cash restriction in one year's time

(iii)   **Investing in increased working capital,** if this is thought to be beneficial

(iv)   **Increasing the dividend** to shareholders

(c)   Comments on previous Board decisions relating to this investment

I have been asked to comment on:

(i)   Invest rather than to repay debt

There is no harm in having a higher gearing ratio than other companies in the industry unless it is thought that there is a significant chance of difficulty in **meeting debt obligations** in the event of a downturn in profits. Debt servicing costs have the advantage of **attracting tax relief**, whereas dividend payments do not. Since you have weighed up the risks involved and have decided that the present gearing level is acceptable, and I have no grounds on which to disagree with your judgement.

(ii)   Reject a further issue of funds to finance the remaining investment opportunities

All investments with a positive NPV will increase shareholder wealth. There is therefore **no financial reason** for rejecting the acquisition of CD and EF, which could be financed by a further issue of shares or debt. Bearing in mind the company's high level of gearing, the most suitable financing method would be a **share issue**. In this way, the three companies could be acquired by suitable **combinations of cash and shares** offered to their shareholders. However, there are organisational and managerial grounds for rejecting too many acquisitions at the same time. They might **divert management time** and **adversely affect the core business**. I ask you to consider further these investment opportunities in the light of these suggestions.

(d)   Advantages of growth by acquisition

Acquiring an **existing company** is a speedier method of entering a new business than setting up a project using internal resources, because an acquired business will already have **customers** and, hopefully, **goodwill**. An acquisition also effectively **eliminates a competitor** and may **allow higher profitability**. Other advantages may come from the **combination of complementary resources** of the acquiring and acquired companies.

Problems of growth by acquisition

Frequently a **significant premium** must be **paid** in order to **encourage existing shareholders** to sell, or to outbid a rival. This may make it difficult to show a **respectable return** on the cost of the acquisition.

The acquired company may **not produce the exact product or service** that the acquirer needs, or may need **significant investment** before it conforms to quality requirements.

Management problems are also quite common, particularly when the acquiring and acquired companies have different organisational cultures. **Disputes** may case the loss of key staff members, resulting in reduced quality or even in the establishment of competing businesses.

Appendix – computation of NPV and profitability index

	Year				NPV	Profitability index*
	0	1	2	3		
12% factors	1.000	0.893	0.797	0.712		
AB	£'000	£'000	£'000	£'000		
Cash flows	(1,100)	-100	750	1100		
DCF	(1,100)	-89	598	783	192	17.5%
CD						
Cash flows	(550)	125	275	380		
DCF	(550)	112	219	271	52	9.5%
EF						
Cash flows	(650)	200	325	450		
DCF	(650)	179	259	320	108	16.6%

* Profitability index = NPV/initial outlay.

64 RST

> **Text references**. Capital rationing is covered in Chapter 13.
>
> **Top tips**. Be careful with the timing here. The capital rationing is in Year 1 so the profitability index should be based on net Year 1 cash flows. Make sure you relate your discussion in part (b) to the **public** sector.
>
> **Easy marks**. The calculations are quite straightforward provided you get the timings right. You can use your common sense and financial knowledge to gain good marks in part (b).
>
> **Examiner's comments**. This question was generally well answered with most candidates being able to make a reasonable attempt at the NPV calculations and draw basic conclusions from results. However, few were able to calculate appropriate PI' or identify the best overall combination of projects.

(a) (i) NPV of cash flows:

Project		NPV $m
A	−9 + (−16 × 0.87) + (4/0.15)	3.75
B	−10 + (−10 × 0.87) + (4/0.15 × 0.87)	4.50
C	−10 + (−12 × 0.87) + (5 × 5.019)	4.66
D	Cumulative discount factor when n is 7 = 4.16, when n is 2 = 1.626 −8 + (−5 × 0.87) + (6 × (4.16 − 1.626))	2.85
E	Cumulative discount factor when n is 15 = 5.847, when n is 5 = 3.352 −9 + (−8 × 0.87) + (2 × 3.352) + (5 × (5.847 − 3.352))	3.22

On the basis of NPV of cash flows, the **ranking of the projects** is **C, B, A, E, D**.

With the capital constraint of $30m, this will mean that projects **C, B and A** should be **accepted** with a total net cash outflow in Year 1 of $29m (16 + 10 + 12 − 5 − 4) and a total NPV of $12.91m.

(ii) Profitability index:

Project	NPV	Year 1 net outflow	Profitability Index
A	3.75	12	0.31
B	4.50	10	0.45
C	4.66	7	0.67
D	2.85	5	0.57
E	3.22	6	0.54

On the basis of the profitability index, the **ranking of the projects** is **C, D, E, B, A**.

With the capital constraint of $30m, this will mean that projects C, D, E and B should be accepted with a total net cash outflow in Year 1 of $28m and a total NPV of $15.23m.

In conclusion, RST should accept projects **C, D, E and B** as this will give the highest possible NPV given the capital constraint in Year 1.

(b) (i) RST is a publicly-owned entity and is therefore subject to debate as to whether capital rationing techniques based on maximising NPV are appropriate.

NPV is a very useful technique for **privately owned** entities whose prime objective is the **maximisation of shareholder wealth**. The NPV of a project produces an estimate of the amount by which shareholder wealth will be increased. A publicly-owned entity will have **other non-financial objectives**, such as maximising service, so maximising NPV may not be the most appropriate prime objective.

However, publicly-owned entities are subject to **capital rationing** as funds, and therefore spending, are restricted. This makes it even more important for them to have an effective way to measure which projects are the most financially attractive, as they are unlikely to be able to borrow additional funds as a private entity could.

(ii) Other factors that RST should consider would be firstly, which are the key variables in the calculations carried out. A **sensitivity analysis** could then be conducted to look at the impact of changes in these key variables. Each project's NPV can be recalculated using alternative assumptions, for example the timing of the cash-flows.

Options theory could be applied to the development projects. For example, there may be follow-on investments as options or an option to wait on some of the projects.

As a publicly-owned entity, RST will need to consider non-financial factors such as targets and priorities for service levels. For example, which geographical areas or types of patients have particular needs. They may also need to be concerned with environmental and human resources issues. There is a significant element of political risk for RST as health care priorities can change.

65 HIJ

> **Text references.** Capital rationing and APV are covered in Chapter 13.
>
> **Top tips.** There are some very tough parts to this question. There is an unusual use of annuities to calculate an equivalent cash flow per annum. A common sense approach would have worked here even if you were not sure of the technique.
>
> There is a lot of work to do in part (b) for 6 marks and you need to look at the value of each part of the financing effects.
>
> **Easy marks.** The calculation of the profitability index and discussion of capital rationing should have provided the easiest marks in this question.
>
> **Examiner's comments.** This question was generally very poorly answered. Many candidates could not calculate EAAs and few recognised the need to combine the projects to determine rankings.

(a) (i) <u>Profitability index</u>

In a situation of **single period capital rationing**, the objective should be to **maximise the net present value** per $ invested. A computation of NPV/initial investment for each project shows the following.

Project	NPV/initial investment $m	Ranking
A	2.75/15.4 = 0.18	3
B	3.60/19.0 = 0.19	2
C	3.25/12.8 = 0.25	1

This implies that the company should choose to invest first in Project C, then in Project B and finally in Project A. However there is not enough money to invest in all of them, and the projects are **indivisible**, which implies that only one can be accepted. This method of evaluation is therefore not very useful in this situation.

Equivalent annual annuities

The discount rate to be used is 12%.

Project	Duration Years	Annuity factor	Equivalent annual annuity	Ranking
A	6	4.111	2.75/4.111 = 0.67	2
B	7	4.564	3.60/4.564 = 0.79	1
C	Indefinite	1/0.12 = 8.333	3.25/8.333 = 0.39	3

The equivalent annual annuity expresses the value of each project as a cash flow per annum and allows projects with **unequal lives** to be compared. This method implies that the company should invest first in Project B and then Project A.

However, this does not incorporate the advantage of Project C having **indefinite cash flows**. It is only an acceptable basis of comparison if Projects A and B could be renewed when they come to the end of their useful life.

Recommendation

The only way to undertake two projects and to use the most of the capital available is to choose **Projects A and C**. This will use $28.2 million of the $30 million of capital available. Neither of the methods of evaluation come up with this solution.

As Project B would be chosen using the equivalent annual annuity method, it would be worth investigating whether it would still be an acceptable project at a higher rate of interest.

(ii)   Capital rationing may be necessary in a business due to **internal factors** (soft capital rationing) or **external factors** (hard capital rationing).

Soft capital rationing

This may arise because management may be **reluctant to issue additional share capital** because of concern that this may lead to outsiders gaining control of the business. In this case, HIJ is a private entity so even if shares could be sold, it is unlikely that the current owners would choose to do so.

Management may **not want to raise additional debt capital** because they do not wish to be committed to large fixed interest payments. This is true for HIJ as borrowing above $30 million will be at a much higher rate of interest.

Hard capital rationing

This may arise if there are **restrictions on bank lending** due to government control or **lending institutions** consider an organisation to be too risky to be granted further loan facilities. There is no indication that these factors apply here.

(iii)   Nominal and real cash flows

In an inflationary environment, cash flows in a project may be given in **nominal terms** (the actual cash that will arise) or **real terms** (in today's currency).

Similarly, the required rate of return on an investment may be given as a **nominal** rate of return (including an allowance for a general rate of inflation) or as a **real** rate of return (the return required over and above inflation).

In this case, if the cash flows have been calculated in real terms, they should be discounted using a **real discount rate.** This rate will be calculated using the Fisher formula: (1 + real rate of return) = (1 + nominal rate of return)/ (1 + rate of inflation). This will result in a **lower discount rate** which will produce **higher NPVs**. It will not affect the **relative values** of each project however as each will be affected by a proportionate amount.

(b)   Base case NPV of Project B = $3.60m

Adjustments to allow for the side-effects of financing

Tax shield on subsidised loan

Amount of subsidised loan = 50%× (19.0 – 3.5) = $7.75m

Annual interest = 8% × $7.75m = $0.62m

Tax relief = 30% × $0.62m = $0.186m

Cumulative discount factor at 10% for 8 years = 5.335

NPV of tax shield = 5.335 × 0.186 = **$0.99m**

Tax shield on rest of loan

Annual interest = 10% × $7.75m = $0.775m

Tax relief = 30% × $0.775m = $0.2325m

Cumulative discount factor at 10% for 8 years = 5.335

NPV of tax shield = 5.335 × 0.2325 = **$1.24m**

Value of subsidy

Interest benefit = (10% - 8%) × $7.75m = $0.155m

Tax shield lost = 30% × 0.155m = $0.0465m

Net benefit = 0.155 – 0.0465 = $0.1085m

Cumulative discount factor at 10% for 8 years = 5.335

NPV of subsidy = 5.335 × 0.1085 = **$0.58m**

Adjusted present value

Value of grant = $3.50m

APV = 3.60 + 3.50 + 0.99 + 1.24 + 0.58 = **$9.91m**

Project B now becomes a much more attractive prospect with a **profitability index** rating of 0.52 (9.91/19) and an **equivalent annual annuity** of 2.17 (9.91/4.564). This change means that it is now the top ranked project using both methods of evaluation.

66   BA

Text references. Acquisition issues are covered in Chapter 16.

Top tips. A briefing note need not be as formally laid out as a report. In (a) you need to compute the values of both companies before the announcement, which you can do by using their earnings and P/E ratios. You are then told how the share prices react to the announcement: good news for YZ shareholders but not for BA.

The normal arrangement on a cash or shares offer is that the cash equivalent is lower, because cash is less risky. This does not appear to be the case here, though, for reasons that are difficult to understand. When discussing the factors to consider, you should include BA's motives and plans for the merger, and whether large shareholders in YZ plc wish to retain their influence on the board of directors.

Easy marks. (a) is a tough question, and it's useful to work through the stages to see how our answer fits together. (b) is a fairly mainstream discussion, but it does need to be tailored to the needs of shareholders to secure a good mark.

Examiner's comments. This question proved to be the least popular question on the paper, surprisingly because it covered familiar ground and a key syllabus topic. In general calculations were either non-existent or confused; although candidates did use the dividend valuation model, they failed to use any other model that would have provided a basis for comparison. EPS calculations were also poor. Many candidates ignored the requirement in (c) to give advice.

Briefing note on proposed offer by BA for the shares of YZ

Prepared by: A. Shareholder
Date: 9 December 20X2

(a)   Evaluation of the share-for-share offer from BA

Value of the companies' shares before the announcement

	BA	YZ	Combination
	$m	$m	
Earnings before tax	126.60	112.50	
Tax (30%)	(37.98)	(33.75)	
Earnings after tax	88.62	78.75	
P/E immediately before announcement	11	7	
Total value of equity shares before announcement:			
(= earnings after tax × P/E): $m	974.82	551.25	$1526.07m
No. of shares (= share capital/par value): million	250	180	
Value per share before announcement (cents)	390c	306c	

These share prices are in within the range of the 20X2 maximum and minimum share prices given. The value of the two companies together, before the announcement of the share offer, is $1,526 million.

Value of shares if merger takes place

Assuming the companies are fairly valued and that there is no hidden synergy in the combination (which is unlikely), the value of the combination will remain unchanged by the merger, at $1,526 million. If we accept the merger terms of 5 shares in BA for every 6 shares in YZ, the number of shares in BA will increase by 5/6 × 180 million = 150 million. This will give a total of 250 +150 = 400 million shares in BA, giving a share price for BA after the merger of $1,526/400 = 381 cents.

This values YZ shares at 5/6 × 381 cents = 317 cents. On the basis of these computations shareholders in BA lose (down 2.3%), while those in YZ gain (up 3.6%).

However, these computations are made redundant by the extreme reaction of the stock market against BA's offer:

	BA	YZ	Combination
Change in share price on announcement of offer:	−10%	+14%	
Value per share after announcement: cents			
BA: 390 × 0.9	351		
YZ: 306 × 1.14		349	
No of shares m	250	180	
Total value of equity shares after announcement: $m	877.50	628.20	1505.70m
Total value of shares before announcement: $m	974.82	551.25	1526.07m
Total gain/(loss) by shareholders: $m	(97.32)	76.95	(20.37m)
Gain/(loss) per share: cents	(39)	43	

The shareholders of BA have lost more than the shareholders of YZ have gained, creating a net loss in the total value of the two companies.

Valuation using the dividend valuation model

As a benchmark, we can value both companies using the dividend valuation model

	BA	YZ
Dividend yield just before announcement	2.40%	3.10%
Share price before announcement	390c	306c
Therefore, latest dividend, d	9.36c	9.49c
Growth forecast, g	4%	4%
Cost of equity capital, k_e	13%	11%
Thus, value per share by DVM: $d(1+g)/(k_e - g)$	108c	141c

The share values obtained by the dividend valuation model are significantly lower than the current market prices. We need to consider carefully what future **dividend policy** would be if we accepted shares.

(b) <u>Factors to consider when deciding whether to accept or reject the bid</u>

<u>Raising the offer</u>

We need to assess the chances that BA will make a **better offer** if we reject their current offer. We should assess whether there are other potential targets for which BA might bid.

<u>The value of the offer</u>

An alternative to accepting the offer is to sell our shares on the market. Although we will probably not be able to sell our large shareholdings at the current market price, the **comparison** of the two values is of prime importance.

<u>Our influence as shareholders</u>

As we hold large blocs of shares, we are in a position to influence the board of YZ through our 'protest group'. Our shareholdings will be **diluted** if we accept the share-for-share offer by BA and we may prefer to reject the offer.

<u>BA's motive for the merger</u>

BA has developed a reputation **for rapid growth**, but appears to have slowed down recently. If we accept the offer, it should be because we believe that BA can achieve the results that we have been seeking for YZ. There is a danger, however, that BA is merely seeking to **increase its earnings per share** by acquiring us – this can be easily done because our P/E is lower than BA's. BA may also be hoping to take advantage of our share price being near its lowpoint for the year.

<u>BA's plans for the merged companies</u>

We need to examine the plans for **management** of the combination and strategic plans which justify the combination, and to determine whether long-term gains are likely for shareholders in the merged company.

<u>Market viewpoint</u>

The market gives us a low **price-earnings ratio compared** with our competitors. We should consider whether the market has **underestimated the value in the company,** particularly the **intellectual expertise** or whether the market does not believe in YZ's ability to turn the company around.

<u>Shares or cash?</u>

Cash is **more certain in value** than shares because, as we have seen, shares in listed companies can fall very quickly. BA's shares dropped by 10% following announcement of the merger, illustrating the potential risk involved. To compensate us for accepting the risk, BA should have offered a higher value in shares than the cash alternative. However, their share offer to us was worth 5/6 × 390c = 325c for each of our shares, which is *less* than the cash offer to us (unless the 345c cash is per BA share).

A disadvantage of accepting the cash offer is that this counts as **a disposal of shares**, resulting in a charge to capital gains tax, whereas accepting a share-for-share offer does not count as a disposal.

If we accept shares that we intend to keep in the long-term, the likely **dividend policy** of the group will be significant.

(c) <u>Advice on action to take</u>

On the basis of my calculations, I make the following recommendations:

(i) **Do not accept the current share-for share offer** made by BA. Our share price is now standing at 349c, against BA's 351c. At 5 of their shares for 6 of ours you would make a clear loss.

(ii) You should consider **accepting the cash offer** of 345 cents per share. Although our share price is slightly higher, you would be unlikely to be able to sell large shareholdings at full market price. Since our share price appears high compared with the company's fundamental valuation (as shown by the dividend valuation model calculation), it may be a good time to accept the cash offer and take your profit.

(iii) If you do not wish to sell at the moment, then **reject BA's offer**. The market appears to be signalling that the **proposed terms** were **not good enough**. BA may yet return with a better offer, or another offer may come elsewhere.

(iv) You should consider a **fall-back strategy** if BA do not improve their offer of trying to appoint a new board who are more likely to unlock the value in YZ.

67 PDQ

Text references. Business valuations are explained in Chapter 15. Management buyouts are discussed in Chapter 16.

Top tips. You may have suggested equally plausible valuations to the ones we have suggested in (a). To score good marks, you would need to suggest various measures, and examine critically their limitations, (assumptions, lack of information, range of values suggested, further factors) considering how useful they would be in the circumstances described in the question.

(b) needs to be examined from the viewpoints of the managers/employees, and also the venture capitalists. The venture capitalists will be looking to obtain a good price if possible.

Easy marks. Remember that the calculations in (a) will only account for a small number of marks; it's equally important to discuss the non-financial factors and to provide a reasonable recommendation.

Examiner's comments. Generally (a) was not answered well, as candidates struggled to place a value on a company that was lossmaking. Most DCF calculations did not go beyond 20X4. Common weaknesses included failing to allow for tax, failing to estimate cash flows beyond 20X7, and not bringing the value of the perpetuity calculated back to the present. Generally (b) was answered well, except by those candidates who ran out of time after (a).

(a) Offer price for management buy-out

Bases of valuation

The shares in the company can be valued by various methods, which fall into two main categories: **assets** and **expected income**.

Assets basis

For a going concern, using the value of the **net assets** will normally understate the value of PDQ, as there is no clear way of valuing the intangible asset of **goodwill**, other than by examining expected future income. The figures obtained should therefore be seen as providing a **minimum value**.

Using **net assets**, after deducting all liabilities, this method gives a book value of:

£0.95 million, or £3.80 per share as at 31 December 20X3 and

£3.70 million, or £14.80 per share as at 31 December 20X4.

Expected income – dividend valuation model

One method of estimating the value of the company's shares is to **estimate future dividends** and to **discount them at the shareholders' cost of capital**, using the dividend valuation model.

However no dividends have yet been paid, and will not be paid in 20X3, and we lack information about what the future dividend policy might be. Because of this lack of information it is unrealistic to use the dividend valuation model, as too many doubtful assumptions would be involved.

Expected valuation – earnings

Using earnings rather than dividends has the advantage that we do not need to speculate about dividend policy. It may also be a more realistic reflection of the venture capitalists' viewpoint since they hold the majority of shares.

A number of calculations can be made using the dividend valuation formula, but substituting E_0, earnings, for D_0, dividends:

$$P_0 = \frac{E_0(1+g)}{(r-g)}$$

The problems of using this method in the initial few years is that the growth rate 20%, **exceeds** the cost of capital.

Hence the calculation has to be in two parts:

	Post tax cash flow £ million	Discount factor 15%	Discounted cash flow £ million
20X4	2.75	0.870	2.39
20X5	2.31	0.756	1.75
20X6	2.77	0.658	1.82
20X7	3.33	0.572	1.90
			7.86

20X5 figure = 2.75 (1.2) (1 – 0.3); 20X6 and 20X7 earnings increase by 20% and for 20X8 onwards:

$$\frac{3.33(1+0.05)}{0.15-0.05} \times 0.572 = £20 \text{ million, where 0.572 is the Year 4 discount factor for 15%.}$$

Combining the two gives a company valuation of £27.86 million and a valuation of the venture capitalists' shares of £15.32 million.

A more pessimistic calculation would be to take the 20X4 earnings figure, adjust for tax in subsequent years $(2.75 \times (1 – 0.3)) = 1.925$, assume that 5% rather than 20% was a more realistic growth rate after 20X4, and use the formula:

$$P_0 = \left(\frac{1.925(1.05)}{0.15-0.05} \times 0.870\right) + 2.39 = £20m$$

This gives a valuation for the venture capitalists' shareholding of around £11 million.

Expected income – p/e ratio method

Using the (notional) post tax earnings for 20X4 of £1.925m, we can multiply by a p/e ratio that is regarded as suitable for PDQ. The **industry average p/e** is 28.4, which would give a company value of £54.67 million. If the venture capitalists share was to be valued at the original purchase price, £12 million, this would imply use of a p/e ratio of

$$\frac{(£12 \text{ million}/0.55)}{£1.925 \text{ million}} = 11.3$$

However, the P/E method is **simplistic** and takes **no specific account of growth expectations** or **risk** of the specific company. P/es for listed companies in the industry vary from 7.5 to 51.5, which would value PDQ at anywhere between £14 million and £99 million, if it was an established listed company. However, as the company is unlisted, a p/e ratio lower even than 7.5 may therefore be appropriate. We would need to know what sort of expectations of growth were generating the higher p/e ratios in the sector, and the reasons for those expectations.

Other considerations

The venture capitalists may well be unwilling to accept a **price lower** than the £12 million they initially paid, and may be looking for a **premium** on their initial investment.

The venture capitalists should have a **good knowledge** of the company, and may well be in a good position to assess the likely accuracy of the directors' forecasts. They will not necessarily assume that the directors are being over-optimistic in their predictions. Particularly in the later years, it is possible that the directors are being over-conservative, as a forecast of lower growth would imply a lower purchase price.

They will also examine **market data** on listed companies that are similar in profile to PDQ, and base their valuation on the share prices of such companies, with perhaps some allowance for the fact PDQ is unlisted.

If the finance can be raised quickly, the venture capitalists may be willing to accept a lower price in return for a sale to a willing buyer.

Offer terms

The founders and employees may wish to start by offering the price of £12 million that the venture capitalists paid, since the earnings method suggests this figure is reasonable and it can also be calculated using a p/e ratio above the sector minimum.

(b)   Management buy-out versus sale to another investor

Advantages of management buy-out

(i)   The management team already **knows** the **strengths and weaknesses** of the business and does not need time to evaluate it. The managers may be better able to focus the business on its **core activities**.

(ii)   Assuming finance is available, the buy-out may be **arranged quicker** than a sale to another party.

(iii)   Widening the equity ownership to employees of the company gives them the opportunity of **participating in large equity gains**. This is likely to increase motivation and strengthen the commonality of objectives with top management during the crucial growth period of the next few years.

(iv)   The company's **independence** will be **preserved**, whereas a sale to a competitor may result in effective closure of the business to eliminate competition.

Disadvantages of management buy-out

(i)   The statement that a management buy-out will be speedy is based on the assumption that the **necessary finance** will be **readily available**. Managers and employees may find it difficult to contribute enough equity, and any lender would be influenced by the **limited security available** and the fact that PDQ has not yet actually **moved into profit**. Obtaining the funds may thus prove problematic.

(ii)   The main disadvantages of a buyout to existing equity shareholders is that the **price** obtained from the **sale of shares** may be **lower** than that **obtainable from another buyer** for various reasons. Another buyer may overlook various problems with the company that are fully perceived by the management team.

(iii)   Another buyer may be able to **create synergetic gains** by combining the company with their own business, which would not be available to the management team.

(iv)   From the **employees' viewpoint**, the main disadvantage of a buyout is that their **savings**, in the form of shareholdings in the company, are subject to the same risks as their job. It is safer to save in a **diversified portfolio** than to put 'all one's eggs in one basket' in the company.

(v)   Although they suffer from the risks resulting from lack of diversification, many employees will not be in a position to **exercise influence** on company decisions. It appears that the founding shareholders will remain in charge. This can create substantial tension if the outcome of company plans is not successful.

68 YY

Text references. MBOs are covered in Chapter 16. Business valuations are covered in Chapter 15. Venture capital is covered in Chapters 5 and 16.

Top tips. You can get away with a fairly generic answer to part (b) but make sure you relate the rest of your answers to the scenario (particularly in part (c)).

Note that there are more marks available for part (c) so be prepared to provide more depth in your answer, including any relevant calculations.

Easy marks. If you are familiar with MBOs and venture capital, there are some easy marks to be gained in parts (a) and (b).

Examiner's comments. Candidates' knowledge of MBOs and Venture Capitalists was often quite shallow. Many candidates appeared to reproduce a memorised list of all possible issues relating to these topics rather than focusing on the actual requirements and scenario set out in the question.

Briefing notes

For use in: TS Management Team meeting

Date: 1st October 20X1

Subject: Possible MBO of TS

(a) <u>Mr A – Managing Director of TS</u>

Mr A is concerned that YY's Board will not recognise the value that TS's management team can add to the subsidiary. He would also like to demonstrate to the Board that an MBO would be more advantageous to YY than an open sale.

Value added by the TS management team

The TS management team is likely to be able to add value to the subsidiary for the following reasons:

(i) They will have a **thorough understanding of the telecommunications equipment industry**, more so than YY's Board. They will be able to set their own agenda, realistic objectives and goals without being subject to scrutiny by a Board with less knowledge of the industry than those making the decisions.

(ii) If managers and employees have a 20% stake in the business they are more likely to be **motivated** to improve performance.

(iii) There will be **no central administration costs** charged by YY which should reduce overheads. However there is the risk of losing some economies of scale which may cancel out this benefit.

(iv) Top management will be focused solely on TS rather than on a larger group therefore decision-making is likely to be more timely and flexible.

MBO v trade sale

The main benefit to YY of an MBO as opposed to a trade sale is that there will be **no need to search for a potential buyer** – TS's management team has already expressed a willingness to purchase the business. A further benefit is that the administrative costs will be borne by TS's management rather than by YY.

As the management team of TS is familiar with the strengths and weaknesses of the business it may take less time to agree on a suitable selling price.

(b) <u>Mr B – Financial Manager of TS</u>

Mr B is interested in getting a venture capitalist involved and would like to know about the advantages and disadvantages of venture capital financing. He would also like to find out about any realistic alternatives to venture capital as a source of funding.

Advantages of venture capital financing

(i) The venture capitalist will **share the risk** of the investment with the managers and employees of TS.

(ii) Venture capitalists can be an **invaluable source of advice** to the management team when dealing with banks and stock markets – particularly during the early stages of the investments and if there is an intention to move towards an IPO in the future.

Disadvantages of venture capital financing

(i) Venture capitalists expect **very high returns** on investment therefore management of TS will have to ensure that their growth and earnings forecasts are achievable and sufficient to fulfil these high expectations.

(ii) There would be a **significant loss of control** as the venture capitalist would own up to 80% of the business. This may cause problems when important decisions have to be made, due to potential conflicting views and attitudes towards risk.

(iii) Venture capitalists will only invest for a **short period of time** – they always require an exit route. This tends to be selling their shares on the open market, either via a placing or an IPO. If an IPO is used, the management team of TS will not realise much in the way of returns – the majority of these will go to the venture capitalist.

It may be possible for the management team to negotiate an 'earn out' agreement, whereby the venture capitalist will sell back shares to the team based on achievement of specified returns.

Realistic alternatives

(i) Persuading YY to continue to own a shareholding in the business. This may prove difficult if YY wants to sell the subsidiary but if it does not have a readily available investment opportunity it may consider a gradual reduction in its shareholding rather than an immediate sale.

(ii) An **investment bank**. It is unlikely that an investment bank will be willing to provide finance for an 80% stake in the business. The cost of this debt would be too high to be realistically considered.

(iii) A **combination of finance methods**. Although a realistic possibility such an arrangement would be expensive and time-consuming to put together.

(c) Mr C – Marketing Manager of TS

Mr C is concerned about the valuation of TS and has raised several issues.

(i) *Asset valuation is considerably less than actual valuation*

The valuation of $1,000m is based on YY's P/E ratio which has then been applied to TS's earnings of $75m.

YY's current market capitalisation = 525m shares × $31.20 = $16,380m

Earnings = $1,260m

P/E ratio = $16,380m/$1,260m = 13

This would give a valuation for TS of $13 \times \$75m = \$975m$

There is thus a differential of $25m. We are given limited information so we can only make suggestions for this difference. TS may have a different gearing ratio to YY and may have a greater tangible assets base (common in manufacturing companies).

(ii) *Net asset value*

The book value of TS's net assets is $735m but this is of **little relevance** when valuing the business. It excludes any intangible assets such as brands or goodwill and will really only be of any relevance if the business was being liquidated or broken up. Neither of these situations apply here as TS is being sold as a going concern.

The book value of net assets will also exclude any inter-group debt which would have to be added back to obtain the total figure that YY would have to raise from the sale of TS. Any external debt which is to be assigned to the new owners does not need to be added back.

(iii) *More appropriate methods of valuation?*

It could be argued that using **YY's P/E ratio is not appropriate** for valuing TS, as the latter is in a different business to YY and its shares are not listed. The normal approach to valuing an unlisted company if the earnings-based method is used is to find a similar quoted company and start with its P/E ratio.

The industry average is 15 which would give an even higher valuation of $1,125m. However TS operates in only one part of the telecommunications industry hence this P/E ratio is unlikely to be appropriate either.

Probably the most appropriate method of valuation would be for TS to discount its cash flows using a discount rate that reflects the risk of the business. Again it is not easy to determine such a discount rate – it may be necessary to use a similar company's information as an approximation (for example, a company in the same business as YY).

69 PCO

Text references. Acquisition issues are covered in Chapter 16.

Top tips. This question covers most of the significant areas on mergers and acquisitions and includes a mix of calculations and discussion of non-financial issues. Remember when doing the calculations that you are not looking for a single right answer but different possibilities to use to suggest a range of possible offers.

Part (a) covers the main methods which are covered in many other questions in this kit. Don't be surprised incidentally if the dividend growth rate exceeds the cost of equity capital, as it does here. If this happens, you need to suggest how to adjust the valuation.

In (b) remember that the target is a listed company, so the results of (a) should be compared with the current market values (which rules out the net asset valuation method as providing any sort of guide). Once you've decided the rough offer price, funding that offer needs to be considered. As we're not told anything here, you have to consider both a cash and shares offer, and calculate the effect on gearing if a cash offer is made and borrowing is required.

Easy marks. (b) (i) and (iii) are standard discussion areas on financing and strategic issues relating to an acquisition. You should make sure you can score well in these areas.

(a) <u>Pre-acquisition data</u>

			PCO	OT
(i)	Shares in issue (million)		40	24
	Share price (pence)		967	1,020
	Market value of shares (£m)		386.8	244.8
	Earnings per share (pence)		106	92
	P/E ratio		9.12	11.09
(ii)	Beta of equity		0.9	1.2
	Cost of equity [4% + (8% - 4%)β]		7.6%	8.8%
(iii)	Dividend per share (pence)		32	21
	Growth rate		5%	9%
	Prospective share price (pence) $\dfrac{\text{Dividend per share} \times \text{Growth rate}}{\text{Cost of equity - Growth rate}}$		1,292	See below
	Prospective market value of company (£m)		516.8	See below

For OT, the dividend growth model is not valid as the forecast growth rate, 9% is higher than its cost of equity 8.8%. The formula would give a negative value to the shares. A forecast of lower growth after an initial high-growth period would be more realistic.

(b) (i) <u>Minimum price</u>

The current market value (£244.8m, at 1,020 pence per share) is probably the **minimum value** that OT's shareholders will accept for their company. This is significantly higher than its net tangible asset value of £145 million, which is not a realistic going concern value.

<u>Maximum price</u>

Because the bid is likely to be treated as hostile by OT's directors, PCO will probably need to offer a **premium** over OT's current market value. In doing so, they must be careful not to offer too high a price, thus gaining a subsidiary at the expense of creating a loss in value for their own shareholders.

		Share value £m
Pre-acquisition figures:		
PCO		386.8
OT		244.8
Total		631.6
Financial advisors' post acquisition estimate		720.0
Estimated gain from merger synergy		88.4

The **maximum price** that PCO could offer for OT's shares would be if it gave away the whole of the synergetic gains from the merger to OT. This would imply a premium of £88.4 million over the current market value of £244.8m, representing a bid price of (£244.8m + £88.4m) / 24m = 1,388 pence per share. At this maximum price PCO's shareholders would expect to make no gain or loss from the merger.

Price to be offered

Clearly both parties need to negotiate within the minimum and maximum offer prices of 1,020 and 1,388 pence per share for OT. PCO should make an initial offer towards the low end of this range and be prepared to negotiate upwards, say 1122p, a 10% mark-up on the current market price.

(ii)   Funding the bid

PCO would consider offering either cash or shares as purchase consideration for the acquisition.

Cash offer

To OT shareholders the **advantage** of receiving a cash offer is that the price, once offered, is **not subject** to **stock market fluctuations**. Because of this relative certainty, PCO may feel that it need not offer such a high price as it might if it were offering shares. However, the **disadvantage** of a cash offer to the OT director-shareholders is that they will **no longer have** an **equity stake** in their business. This may cause them to reject a cash offer unless the price is very high. A cash offer will also fail if the market bids the price of OT's shares above that of the cash offer.

Need for borrowing

Assuming PCO is going to pay approximately £279 million for OT, it can only make a cash offer if it borrows most of these funds. The existing cash balance is £105 million, so PCO will need to borrow, say, £200 million to finance the acquisition and leave some cash in the bank. This will cause gearing to rise significantly.

Existing gearing by market values is given in the data:

		PCO	OT
Current market value of equity	£m	386.8	244.8
Debt ratio		17%	14%
Debt market value (Equity market value × 17/83)	£m	79.2	39.9

Thus the total debt in the firm following the merger would be approximately £79m + £40 + £200 = £319m. **The value of equity** is estimated by the advisors as £720m. This would give a debt ratio $V_D/V_D + V_E$) of 319/1039 = 31%. In other words gearing will nearly double if the acquisition is made with cash.

There is a possible advantage in increasing gearing (**tax relief** on debt interest). However the likelihood is that the large gearing increase needed to finance the acquisition of OT would result in **excessive financial risk** and cause a **significant rise in the cost of capital** and **reduction in share value**.

Share offer

To PCO, a share offer has the **advantage** that it need not borrow cash and the **disadvantage** that existing shareholdings will be diluted.

Increase in authorised capital

A share offer by PCO will require it to increase its authorised share capital. At present there are only 10m shares left unissued, and any reasonable offer will require more shares than this. Note

that the increase in authorised share capital is likely to act as a **signal to the market** that an acquisition is being contemplated.

Terms of offer

If PCO (share price 967p) initially values OT shares at, say, 1,100 pence, the initial offer would be 1,100/967 = 1.14 shares in PCO for every share in OT.

Suppose this offer is eventually accepted. PCO would need to issue 1.14 × 24 million = 27.4 million new shares.

The total number of PCO shares in issue would then be 40 + 27.4 = 67.4 million in a company with a value of £720 million. In theory the PCO share price would move up to 720/67.4 = 1,068 pence per share.

OT shareholders would then hold shares worth 1.14 × 1,068p = 1,218p in exchange for their original OT shares which were worth 1,020p. Thus both sets of shareholders would gain from the share exchange.

Cash and shares

In reality, the choice may not just be between a purely cash offer and a purely shares offer. PCO could consider offering a combination of cash and shares, also an element of debt as well.

(iii)   Business implications

Effect on existing operations

An areas of concern here is that OT provides services to companies that are rivals of PCO. There is the danger that these rivals will react adversely to the acquisition and may, over time, move their distribution business away from OT. This needs to be carefully assessed. PCO should consider how it would react if its distribution business was being handled by a rival firm.

Future prospects

Because the combination is a form of vertical integration, there is no clear link between the management issues of the two organisations. It may take some time before directors and employees from the two different companies understand each others' business needs. One of the major risks of the merger is that a conflict may emerge between the **management styles and objectives** of employees of the two original companies.

Synergies

From the financial analysts' report, there appear to be opportunities for fairly significant gains (approximately 14%) if the businesses are combined. Referred to as synergy, these gains may come from a number of areas, including:

- **Economies of scale**. Elimination of duplicated resources, ability to sell surplus land and premises, rationalisation of head office and administration costs.
- **Economies of vertical integration**. Achieving lower operating costs by owning both distribution channels and sales outlets. It may be possible to use OT's distribution expertise to eliminate outside contractor delivery costs for PCO's petroleum and other products, although the flexibility to change supplier will disappear,

In acquiring OT and paying more than the current market price per share, PCO will need to be confident that such synergetic gains are **achievable**. Unless the new organisation effectively translates its plans into actions, profits and share prices will fall below expectations. In particular, the management of the enlarged company will need to ensure that key management and technical skills are retained.

More information

The directors need to consider further how the **business** and **financial risks** of the company will change if the merger takes place, and in particular how the costs of capital might alter. They may also wish to investigate whether there are better **targets for takeover**.

70 BiOs

> **Text references.** Business valuation techniques are covered in Chapter 15. Venture capital and equity finance is discussed in Chapter 5.
>
> **Top tips.** Questions or parts of questions like (a) are likely to occur in most exams. You could have calculated a more precise P/E ratio based on forecast growth rates but this would be complicated and unnecessary. (b) brings out the sort of knowledge you need to have about different finance sources. However the last paragraph brings out the possibility that there is not a 'right' answer; it may be that what is most suitable for the company (delaying listing?) may not be so acceptable to shareholders who wish to realise their investments.
>
> **Easy marks.** The discussion of the advantages and disadvantages of a stock exchange listing is a standard one that you must be able to reproduce.

(a) Range of values for the company

Valuation methods

A company can be valued in terms of:

- The **underlying value** of its assets
- Its **ability to generate future profits** and cash flows (economic value).

Net asset valuation

Asset values are mainly of relevance if the company is to be broken up for disposal. BiOs Ltd's net asset value is **£395,000**, which, we are told, reflects the realisable value of its assets. This gives a 'floor level' value for the company, but is far too low to be of relevance to negotiations with the investment bank, because:

- The company is a **going concern** and is not about to be broken up.
- As BiOs is a consultancy company, most of its **assets** (know-how, skills, contacts) are **intangible** and their value is not included in the net asset value.

It is more relevant to estimate the **economic value** of BiOs, which can be done in a number of ways.

Price/earnings (P/E) ratio method

In this method, which gives a quick approximation to economic value, equity earnings are multiplied by a suitable P/E ratio taken from quoted companies in the same industry.

BiOs' earnings in 20X3 = 756p × 100,000 shares
= £756,000

P/E ratio	12	18	90
Valuation (£'000)	9,072	13,608	68,040

The problem with P/E ratios is that they are affected significantly by the expected growth rate of the company. In the industry examined, P/Es vary between 12 and 90. Given that BiOs is predicted to **grow fast**, we would expect its value to be in the top half of this range, at least, but the P/E ratio method does not adequately allow for the growth rate in the computation.

This approach to valuation is therefore relevant but simplistic and subject to large margins of error.

Present value of future cash flows

This method estimates a stream of future cash flows rather than just one profit figure and discounts the cash flows at a **cost of capital** suitable for the risk of the company's operations.

Using the assumptions that profit after tax equals cash flow, that this will grow in years 2 and 3 at 30% per annum, followed by 10% per annum after that, and that the industry average cost of capital is suitable, we can estimate the company's value as follows:

20X3 = year 0, 20X4 = year 1 etc.

	£'000	12% factor	PV £'000
20X4 earnings	1,487	0.893	1,328
20X5 earnings: 30% higher	1,933	0.797	1,541
20X6 earnings : 30% higher	2,513	0.712	1,789
			4,658
20X7 to perpetuity: 10% growth (Working)	2,764		98,398
Present value of future cash flows:			103,056

Working

20X7 cash flow = 2,513 × 1.1 = 2,764. Present value (at 20X6) of the perpetuity from year 4 onwards, growing at 10% per annum = 2,764/(12% – 10%) = 138,200. To find the PV as at year 0, discount by the 3 year factor: 138,200 × 0.712 = 98,398.

The value of BiOs by this method is **£103 million**. Although there is a substantial margin of error on this valuation estimate, the method is considerably more useful than the P/E approach because it allows for **earnings growth estimates**. The company's growth projections are dependent on the ability to find skilled consultants, who are in short supply.

Conclusion

On the basis of the figures given, the company's value is probably in the range £65 million to £130 million. Further information is needed on the following areas:

- The **assumptions** on which earnings forecasts are based, in particular the assumption that staffing resources can deliver the **predicted growth rates**
- The **company's cost of capital** would help to make a more accurate assessment.

(b) Advantages of using venture capital

Venture capital funding

Venture capital funds specialise in financing **early stage, risk-oriented ventures** like BiOs. They will offer finance and assistance once a company has started to generate revenue and shows that it has high growth prospects. The funds offered are typically for **five to seven years**. At the end of this period it is presumed that the company will have grown and will be looking for more permanent sources of funds, at which point the venture capital fund will seek an exit route.

Exit route

The most profitable exit route for a venture capital company is when the company in which it has invested achieves a **stock exchange listing** (see below). Alternatives are to sell their shares to another investor (which might be another venture capital fund, but could be a potential acquirer of BiOs) or back to the original owners.

Disadvantages of using venture capital

Selection of investments

Extensive research is carried out on potential companies for **venture capital investment** and only a very small percentage of applications are accepted. The fact that BiOs has been approached by the marketing department of an investment bank is no guarantee that a venture capital fund will find the company an acceptable proposition.

Participation of venture capitalist

The venture capital fund becomes an equity participant in the company through a structure typically comprised of a combination of a substantial proportion of shares, warrants, options, and convertible securities. It also provides a representative who sits on the **company's board**, offers strategic advice to the management team and assures that the fund's interests are considered. If the directors of BiOs would not welcome this level of **investor involvement**, they should not consider venture capital.

Stock market flotation

The alternative under consideration by BiOs is to continue with existing sources of funds and to go for a stock exchange flotation within two to three years. To achieve a listing, the company needs to

demonstrate that, in addition to good growth prospects, it has a **strong management team**, **strong financial controls** and **good management reporting systems**. These last factors will probably need improvement, as most of BiOs' administration systems are currently outsourced.

<u>Advantages of obtaining a stock exchange listing</u>

- Existing owner directors can **realise** some or all of **their investment**
- **New equity finance** is easier to raise
- The company's **status** is **raised**
- The company's shares can be used as **consideration for an acquisition**

<u>Disadvantages of obtaining a stock exchange listing</u>

- **Accountability is increased**: directors must be seen to be accountable to outside shareholders and there is more scrutiny over the company's activities
- **Costs** are incurred for the initial flotation and as ongoing annual fees

<u>The choice</u>

Whichever method is adopted, the end result is probably a **stock exchange flotation**. The directors of BiOs need to decide whether they are happier reaching this end with funding and advice from a venture capital company or whether they are better off seeking an **earlier listing** and thus encouraging equity investors through the stock market. To make their decision they need first to consider their **personal and business objectives**, for example do they wish to realise their wealth in the shortest time or to develop a dominant force in their market sector.

71 FS

> **Text references.** The calculation of cost of capital using the capital asset pricing model is explained in Chapter 8. Acquisition issues are discussed in Chapter 16.
>
> **Top tips**. Part (a) requires use of the more complicated asset beta formula which is in your formula sheet, but if you find the formula difficult to use, make sure that you tackle the other elements of the question (worth 20 marks).
>
> **Easy marks**. Parts (b) and (c) are fairly standard discussions using the common valuation methods to assess an acquisition and discussing the main implications of cash versus shares (borrowing versus loss of control). Remember you must **relate** your discussion to the scenario.
>
> **Examiner's comments.** This question was generally quite poorly attempted with many not realising the approach that was required. In part (b) most candidates managed to provide some discussion of a range of valuation methods. Common errors included showing net assets as total assets; not recognising that assets will be increased by retained earnings; not providing a range of valuations based on different growth forecasts; providing calculations but inadequate discussion. Discussion must always be **related** to the scenario details.

(a) <u>Cost of capital for valuing MT</u>

FS wishes to make an offer for the share capital of MT and therefore **needs to value MT's shares**. This can be done by **discounting MT's equity dividends** at a cost of equity that reflects the business and financial risk of MT. This cost of equity is not provided and cannot be easily observed as it is a private company. MT's cost of equity will therefore be **estimated** from **FS's asset beta,** making the assumption that the business risk of the two companies is the same. This will then be adjusted to reflect MT's gearing.

FS's equity beta is 1.1, its debt beta is 0.2 and its capital structure in market values is:

	€m
Debt (trading at par)	750
Equity (420m × €3.57)	1,500
	2,250

$$\beta_u = \beta_g \left[\frac{V_E}{V_E + V_D\left[1-t\right]} \right] + \beta_d \left[\frac{V_D\left[1-t\right]}{V_E + V_D\left[1-t\right]} \right]$$

Ignoring tax, FS's β_u is $(1.1 \times 1,500/2,250) + (0.2 \times 750/2,250) = 0.8$.

Thus MT's asset beta is also 0.8, its debt beta is 0.2 and its capital structure is:

	€m
Debt	300
Equity	900
	1,200

MT's equity beta β_g is estimated as $[0.8 - (0.2 \times 300/1200)] \times 1200/900 = \mathbf{1.00}$.

The **cost of equity** for MT is **estimated** from the **capital asset pricing model**. As the equity beta is 1, the cost of equity will be the same as the expected return on the market – 8%.

Note. No adjustment has been made for the fact that MT's bonds are paying a higher interest rate than FS's bonds. This is assumed to be because they are unsecured and MT is a private company. Thus MT's bonds are also assumed to have a fair value equal to their nominal value.

(b) Bidding strategy for MT's shares

Valuation by dividend valuation model

The value of MT's shares to FS can be estimated by **discounting MT's expected future dividends** (as a stand-alone company) at 8% and adding on the value of identified synergy from the merger. The calculations below use MT's estimates.

	20X6
Earnings	€88.9m
Dividends (50%)	€44.45m
K_e	8%
Growth	4%

$$P_0 = \frac{d_1}{k_e - g} = \frac{44.45}{0.08 - 0.04}$$

$$= €1,111m$$

The picture is very different if FS's less optimistic growth projections are used.

	20X5	20X6
20X5 MT earnings	€71.5m	€71.5m
20X6 growth	2%	4%
Earnings	€72.93m	€74.36m
Dividends (50%)	€36.465m	€37.18m
K_e	8%	8%

$$P_0 = \frac{d_1}{k_e - g} \qquad \frac{36.465}{0.08 - 0.02} \qquad \frac{37.18}{0.08 - 0.04}$$

$$= €608m \qquad = €930m$$

Adding the estimated synergy of €200 million gives a value for MT as **€1,311** million (based on MT's forecasts) or **€1,130** (based on FS's forecasts).

Earnings basis valuation

An alternative method of valuing MT is to apply a **suitable P/E ratio** to its latest earnings. FS's earnings per share in 20X5 is $128.5 / 420 = €0.306$. The P/E ratio is $€3.57/€0.306 = 11.67$.

Applying this ratio to MT's 20X5 earnings gives $11.67 \times €71.5\,m = €834$ million. Adding synergy gives a maximum value of €1,034 million. This method is simpler and less satisfactory as it stands than the discounting method as it does not specifically account for growth expectations. It might be possible to factor in growth using earnings yield, if necessary.

Assets basis valuation

In practice this would need to take into account **revaluation of assets to fair values**, but since no information is available, the value of MT's equity on this basis would equal book value, ie €900 million and adding synergy would give €1,100 million. Since this is lower than the P/E valuation, FS should ask for more detail on MT's asset values.

Conclusion

On the basis of the above figures, the maximum FS should be prepared to offer MT would be €1,311 million, but only if it accepts MT's **projections of earnings growth**. More information would be useful, if possible. The initial price to be offered would probably have to be around €1,100 million unless new information showed that some of the company's assets are overvalued.

(c)   Purchase consideration

Cash offer

FS shares are trading at roughly their book value, €1,500 million. The acquisition of MT would involve purchase consideration nearly as high as this and an offer for cash would therefore have to be financed by **increasing borrowing.** Since FS's gearing is already quite high at D/E = ½, a cash offer for MT can probably be taken as out of the question.

Nevertheless if a cash offer were possible, it would have the advantage to MT's shareholders that it is a **more secure form of purchase consideration** and the advantage to FS's shareholders that there would be no dilution of shareholdings.

Share for share offer

It is far more likely that the FS would offer a **share for share swap.** Thus if MT were valued at €1,200 million, say, giving a value per share of €1,200 / 440 = €2.73, given that the share price of FS is €3.57, the offer would have to be of the form 2.73 shares in FS for 3.57 shares in MT, ie approximately 10 shares in FS for 13 in MT.

The advantage to FS is that there would be no need to borrow, but the great disadvantage is that the **existing shareholders** would **lose control** of the group. There are likely to be large shareholders on the board of MT who would end up as the major shareholders in the combined group. This would have knock-on consequences for the composition of the board of directors and may result in disputes that are impossible to reconcile.

72   AB

Text references. Business valuation is covered in Chapter 15.

Top tips. This looks like a relatively standard business valuation question and, if you concentrate on the more straightforward areas, it should be possible to secure a strong pass mark. There were up to 3 marks for dealing with intellectual capital, but this is a tricky area and should not have dominated your answer.

Easy marks. Part (b) requires a straightforward explanation of business valuation methods but you **must** make sure you explain the **relevance** to AB.

Examiner's comments. This question was answered less well than other optional questions. Many candidates provided too few types of valuation and/or did not calculate per share figures. Very few candidates made a serious attempt at calculating the value of intellectual capital. The level of discussion in part (b) was weak.

(a)   Asset valuations

The net realisable value of AB's net assets at 20X6 is equal to the book value of its equity: **€233 million**.

However, this value excludes one of AB's main assets, its intellectual capital value. One way of estimating this is to use the industry information on return on total assets.

$$\text{Average pre-tax earnings} = \frac{(67.5 + 74.2 + 56.9)}{3}$$

$$= €66.2\text{m}$$

Average tangible assets $= \dfrac{(198+229+263)}{3}$

$= €230m$

Return on assets $= \dfrac{66.2}{280} \times 100$

$= 28.8\%$

Return that an average entity would earn from €230m tangible assets $= 15\% \times €230m$
$= €34.5m$

Premium attributable to intangible assets $= (66.2 - 34.5)$
$= €31.7m$

After-tax premium $= €31.7m - 30\%$
$= €22.2m$

NPV of premium $= €22.2 \times \dfrac{1}{0.1}$
$= €222m$

Thus the net asset value, including intellectual capital value, is 233 + 222 = **€455 million**.

P/E basis valuation

The telecommunications average P/E has been 12.5, but it is thought that AB's P/E may be up to 30% higher, ie 16.25. These two P/E's are applied to AB's after tax earnings in the table below: the actual results for 20X6 and the forecast results for 20X7.

		20X6	20X7
		€m	€m
Pre-tax earnings		56.9	72.0
Tax		17.1	22.0
After tax earnings		39.8	50.0
Apply P/E	12.5	497.5	625.0
Apply P/E	16.25	646.8	812.5

Using this method, the value of the company is between **€498 million** and **€813 million**.

Present value of free cash flow

There are several definitions of free cash flow, and the calculation shown here is one illustrative approach.

The cash flows for 20X7, 20X8, 20X9 and beyond are shown below.

	20X7	20X8	20X9 and beyond
	€m	€m	€m
Pre-tax earnings	72	91	
Tax 30%	(22)	(27)	
After tax earnings	50	64	
Add back depreciation	48	48	
After tax cash flows	98	112	115.36 growing at 3% pa indefinitely

In 20X9 onwards the after tax cash flows are assumed to grow at 3% per annum (given). As the company has no borrowings, the present value of these cash flows is found by discounting at the cost of equity capital, 10% pa

The perpetuity from 20X9 onwards has a present value at the end of 20X8 of $\dfrac{\text{Earnings}\,(1+g)}{r-g}=$

115.36/(0.10 – 0.03) = €1,648 million. The present value at end of 20X6 of the cash flows from 20X7 onwards is:

		€m	10% factors	€m
Year 1:	20X7	98.0	0.909	89.1
Year 2:	20X8	112.0	0.826	92.5
	Perpetuity	1648.0	0.826	1361.2
				1542.8

After tax cash flows are available for reinvestment and distribution. As depreciation is assumed to be constant to perpetuity, it may be assumed that capital investment each year is equal to depreciation. Thus the present value of capital investment cash flows is 48/0.1 = €480 million.

The present value of free cash flow available to equity is 1,543 – 480 = **€1,063 million**

Range of values for AB

Using different valuation bases, the range of values for AB is summarised as follows:

	Total	Per share
Value of tangible net assets	€233 million	€7.77
Value of net assets including intellectual capital	€455 million	€15.17
Price/earnings ratio based valuation	€497.5 to €812.5 million	€16.58 to €27.08
Present value of free cash flows	€1,063 million	€35.43

(b)   Valuation methods

All assets, including businesses, can be valued on several bases, the chief of which are **realisable value**, **replacement cost** and **economic value**.

The economic value of an business is the net present value of cash flows expected to be generated by the business. For a going concern this will usually be considerably **higher** than the net realisable value or the replacement cost of the business assets, and this is the justification for staying in business.

This is borne out by the figures for AB, where asset based valuations are low compared with the economic values, represented by the P/E and free cash flow valuations.

Tangible net assets

The **value of tangible net assets** gives a **minimum value** for the business and represents the cash that could be raised if the business was wound up, tangible assets sold and cash collected and paid out to creditors. As such it is only relevant to AB's potential flotation value to the extent that it shows investors this minimum value in the event of a severe downturn in business.

Assets including intellectual capital

The **asset value including intellectual capital** is an attempt to recognise that for consultancy companies much of the value is tied up in the **knowledge and skills of its employees**, rather than in plant and machinery. Hence the value is significantly higher than that of the tangible net assets alone. The relevance of intellectual capital value to the business value depends on the extent to which it belongs to the business as opposed to individual employees. If AB wishes to obtain a flotation, it is wise to tie in key employees with contracts and to ensure that all key processes are patented or copyrighted where possible.

Price-earnings ratio

The most **popular** method for making a going concern valuation is to multiply estimated equity earnings by an agreed Price/Earnings ratio. For AB this gives a wide range of possible values, depending on the estimates of earnings and on the P/E ratio used. The method is **simplistic** and makes only crude adjustments for key valuation factors such as expected growth rate, business risk and financial risk.

Free cash flow

The **free cash flow method** attempts to compute the **present value of cash available** to equity after making specific adjustments for investment in fixed assts and working capital. In practice, the method would be carried out more rigorously, with capital expenditure budgets specifically examined. As AB is an all equity company and its risk profile is assumed to be unchanged in the future, the discount rate used is the cost of equity capital, which is the minimum required rate of return on equity. This valuation method therefore produces an estimate of the **maximum** price that new investors would pay for the company.

Conclusion

An average of the range of values would be approximately €600m or €20 per share and this is arguably as valid a valuation as any that have been presented.

In practice all business values are subject to **negotiation**, and the figures calculated are only **guides** for investors and the company managers. If the directors of AB decide that they would like to float the company, the ultimate price would depend on supply and demand, which in turn depends on market-wide conditions as well as the availability of specific alternative routes, such as potential sale of the business to other companies.

73   VCI

Text references. Venture capital is covered in Chapters 5 and 16 and business valuation in Chapter 15.

Top tips. Your difficulty with this question may be knowing where to start! The easiest way is to set out the results for YZ and then use the value of dividends in the dividend valuation model to work out the value of the company.

Easy marks. The discussions in parts (a) (ii) and (b) are straightforward. Ensure you are able to discuss venture capital, it is commonly examined.

Examiner's comments. The main failure was in calculating dividends although on the 'own answer' principle many candidates then scored good marks. In part (b) many candidates did not address the scenario or the question as asked.

(a)   (i)   Issue of shares to VCI

A summary of YZ's results for the year ended 31 March 20X6 shows the following:

	$m
Revenue	105.00
Profit before interest and tax	28.83
Interest: 7% × $15m	1.05
Profit before tax	27.78
Tax: 28%	7.78
Profit after tax	20.00
Dividends: 40%	8.00
Retained earnings	12.00

Valuing the company on the basis of the dividend valuation model, and a constant growth rate of 6% per annum gives the following:

Cost of equity	Company value = $\dfrac{d_0(1+g)}{k_e - g}$	No of shares	Value per share
10%	$8m × 1.06/(0.1 − 0.06) = $212 million	22.5	$9.42
15%	$8m × 1.06/(0.15 − 0.06) = $94 million	22.5	$4.18

To raise an additional $25 million, the number of shares issued to VCI will be as follows:

If cost of equity is 10%: $25m/$9.42 = 2.65 million shares, say **2.7 million** (= 11% of equity).
If cost of equity is 15%: $25m/$4.18 = 5.98 million shares, say **6.0 million** (= 21% of equity).

The above calculation for the value of the company, and hence the number of new shares that would be issued to VCI, is subject to **considerable uncertainty**, both for the **growth rate** (6% to

perpetuity is high) and for the **cost of equity** capital (which needs to be investigated in more detail).

Ultimately the number of shares issued has to be **negotiated** with VCI, which seeks a 30% pre-tax rate of return on equity. Based on last year's pre-tax profits of $27.78 million, this would imply a rough company valuation of 27.78/0.3 = $93 million, ie the lower of the two figures above. However, the existence of alternative financing strategies for YZ will have a major influence on the negotiation process.

(ii) <u>Possible exit strategies available to VCI</u>

Like all venture capital companies, VCI will look for an 'exit route' for its investment within the medium term, in this case 5 years. This may take a number of forms:

(1) <u>Flotation of the equity shares</u>

This would be on a stock exchange or other equity market (eg over the counter market). This will involve placing VCI's shares, and probably some of the shares of existing shareholders, with institutional shareholders who take longer term equity interests than venture capital companies. This is likely to be feasible if YZ **maintains its growth rate** and will enable the existing shareholders to maintain control if they wish, or to sell out if they wish. This is likely to be acceptable to YZ's shareholders.

(2) <u>Sale of the company to another company</u>

A reasonable bid from, say, a competitor will enable VCI to realise its investment. This will cause the existing shareholders to lose control, which may or may not be in line with their personal objectives, depending on the price offered and the possibility of continuing involvement with the company.

(3) <u>A management buy-in</u>

A new management team may wish to purchase VCI's shares on condition that they have significant **influence** over company management. This is likely to cause a loss of management control as discussed above.

(4) <u>Sale of VCI's stake to the company's existing shareholders and managers</u>

A management buy-out may be feasible for YZ if results have not been as good as expected and VCI has decided to **liquidate** its investment.

(b) <u>Venture equity capital</u>

Venture capital companies are in business to take **medium term interests** (say 5 years) in **growing** companies. At least part of the finance offered is usually an **equity stake**, combined with a seat on the board of directors.

The **advantage** of equity finance is that the **financial risk** of the company in relation to fluctuations in profits is kept to a minimum. In good years, shareholders receive high dividends, but in poorer years, there is **no liability** to keep paying high dividends. This enables the board of directors to take reasonable **business risks** without worrying about the short term costs of finance. Use of equity also makes future borrowing easier, if it is required at some stage.

Venture capital companies can also introduce their client firms to valuable business contacts, including potential customers and joint venture partners, and can offer their experience with similar companies to assist in the design of business strategy for YZ.

However, venture capital companies normally look for companies with **high growth potential**. This is unlikely to be the case for YZ in its present state. To satisfy the venture capital company, which will have a **significant influence over board policy**, YZ would probably need to embark on a strategy of **acquisition for growth** combined with **cost savings** from economies of scale. This may not be in line with the current thinking of the board, who might prefer the steadier growth strategy that they have at the moment.

<u>Debt finance</u>

As an alternative, the company has considered raising more **long term debt finance**. The advantages of debt are that (i) **management control** does not change; and (ii) it has a **cheaper** direct cost than equity, especially because interest is a tax deductible expense. Against this is the problem that too much debt

increases financial risk, forcing the directors to be become more **risk averse** in their business strategies. Also lenders may require a **charge** on the company's assets, especially if overall borrowing is high.

AB's existing long term borrowing is $15 million and its total assets less current liabilities are about $35 million. The motor vehicles, which are the life-blood of the company's business, are not owned, but on short **term operating leases**. Consequently, raising $25 million entirely by **borrowing would probably be unwise**.

Although the existing gearing ratio (Debt/Debt + Equity) is less than 10% in market values, it is 43% in book values which may deter lenders.

Recommendation

The recommendation is that for the proposed $25 million expansion the company should consider **increasing its equity capital**. Unless existing shareholders are able to finance a rights issue, this is likely to mean seeking venture capital finance from a venture capital company or from private investors.

74 GG

Text references. Business valuations are covered in Chapter 15 and divestment in Chapter 16.

Top tips. The calculations in this question are quite straightforward provided you read the information carefully and realise that you need to do two calculations for each valuation method, pre- and post-synergistic benefits.

Easy marks. Ungearing and regearing the proxy company's beta in part (a) should provide an easy three marks.

Examiner's comments. Calculation of valuations was generally good but there was very limited discussion of the validity of results obtained.

(a) $\beta_u = \beta_g \left[\dfrac{V_E}{V_E + V_D(1-t)} \right]$ can be used as debt is risk-free, and $\beta_d = 0$

$\beta_u = 1.4 \left[\dfrac{4}{4 + 1(1-0.3)} \right]$

$= 1.1915$

Regearing for BB

$\beta_g = \beta_u + [\beta_u - \beta_d] \dfrac{V_D[1-t]}{V_E}$

$= 1.1915 + [1.1915 \times (1 \times (1-0.3)/2.5]$

$= 1.525$

Substituting in CAPM

$k_e = 3\% + (8-3)\,1.525$
$= 10.63\%$

(b)   (i)   The synergistic benefits to HH of the acquisition are expected to be a 10% improvement in BB's annual earnings. The value of this is 10% × $1 million = $1.1 million.

P/E valuation

	Pre-synergistic benefits Earnings = $1m	Post-synergistic benefits Earnings = $1.1m
	$m	$m
Using a P/E of 13 (proxy P/E)	13.0	14.3
Using a P/E of 11 (HH P/E)	11.0	12.1

Dividend valuation model

$$P_0 = \frac{d_0(1+g)}{(k_e - g)}$$

	Pre-synergistic benefits $m	Post-synergistic benefits $m
Based on a 50% payout	$\frac{(50\% \times 1) \times (1+7\%)}{(10.63\% - 7\%)} = 14.74$	$\frac{(50\% \times 1.1) \times (1+7\%)}{(10.63\% - 7\%)} = 16.21$
Based on a 40% payout	$\frac{(40\% \times 1) \times (1+7\%)}{(10.63\% - 7\%)} = 11.79$	$\frac{(40\% \times 1.1) \times (1+7\%)}{(10.63\% - 7\%)} = 12.97$

No information is available for a **net assets basis of** valuation.

The **range of valuations** is:

Pre-synergistic benefits: $11.00 million to $14.74 million
Post-synergistic benefits: $12.10 million to $16.21 million

(ii)   Potential synergistic benefits

HH expects to be able to use its good reputation and strong market presence to improve BB's annual earnings by 10% but many takeovers **fail** to achieve their full potential. H may be being **over-optimistic** about future market conditions and assuming that post-acquisition integration will be successful. Any offer price should therefore reflect the uncertainty of these synergistic benefits.

P/E valuation

The validity of the P/E valuation depends on the validity of the P/E ratio that is used. The proxy company may not be a good match to BB in terms of **business or risk profile** and an **industry average** P/E may be more reliable.

The P/E of HH is lower and may be more appropriate to use if it reflects the likely risk profile of the new entity.

GG's share price has increased by 15% recently, probably as a result of speculation in response to the divestment announcement. If this rise is removed from the P/E ratio of GG, its P/E ratio would be 11.9 (14 × 85%), giving a revised valuation for BB of $11.9 million, lower than that of the valuation using the proxy P/E.

P/E ratios are based on **historic performance** and take no account of the likely impact of the takeover on performance of the company or of its earnings projections.

This approach to valuation is relevant but simplistic and subject to large margins of error.

Dividend valuation model

The dividend valuation model has the central assumption that the market value of shares is **directly related** to the **expected future dividends** on those shares.

The **highest valuation** in the range calculated is based on a **50% dividend payout**, which assumes the same payout as GG and the proxy company. This is higher than the 40% payout rate of HH and in practice it is very difficult to determine the allocation of dividends from a holding company to a subsidiary.

The main **weakness** of this approach to valuation is the **method used to estimate the growth rate.** This assumes that the **historic rate** of dividend growth will continue at a constant rate into the future, but the current rate of growth could well change following the acquisition. However, the model does attempt to relate the share price to the future stream of earnings from the business and so is more realistic than the P/E ratio basis of valuation. It is also appropriate to use when valuing a **small shareholding.**

Factors affecting offer price

The offer price will depend on the **relative bargaining position** of the shareholders of GG and HH. There may also be **competing bids** which could push the price up. The estimated **costs of integration** and other **acquisition co**sts should also be deducted from the offer price.

The offer price

HH needs to determine the **maximum price** it is prepared to pay which will include a proportion but not all of the anticipated synergistic benefits and which incorporates a 7% growth rate if the Directors are completely confident they can achieve this growth.

An **initial offer** should be made of $13 million with a maximum price of $14 million.

(c) Potential benefits arising from the divestment

Core business

The aim of the divestment is so that GG can **concentrate on its core business** of major infrastructure developments. This is where its strengths lie and so the maximum added value for shareholders can be achieved.

Investment opportunities

The sell-off will raise approximately $13 million of cash, which can be used to **invest in suitable business opportunities** or solve any cash flow problems GG may have.

Ease of control

Concentrating management effort on core parts of the business may **reduce any control problems.**

Protection against takeover

The rest of the business may be **protected from takeover** if a particularly attractive part is sold.

Potential drawbacks arising from the divestment

Disruption

A sell-off can **disrupt** the rest of the organisation, especially if key players disappear as a result.

Removal of scale economies

There may be **shared operations**, such as treasury management, which benefited from **economies of scale**. These will be reduced when part of the organisation is sold off.

Takeover threat

The business may be **more vulnerable to a takeover** in the short-term whilst it is cash rich and until a suitable re-investment opportunity can be found. There is a risk that **no suitable opportunity** will be identified.

Impact on earnings

BB was a relatively higher growth business (7% forecast earnings growth) compared to GG (6% forecast earnings growth) and the divestment may result in **lower earnings** for GG.

75 Q & Z

Text reference. Competition regulation is covered in Chapters 2 and 16, post-acquisition integration in Chapter 14 and capital structure theories in Chapter 9.

Top tips. This is a hard question with no calculations to give you a starting point. An answer plan is essential to make sure you stick to the point and answer the specific question requirements. You will need to bring in your knowledge from other subjects.

Easy marks. Part (c) is the easiest part of the question if you are confident in your knowledge of capital structure theories.

Examiner's comments. Common errors in part (b) were superficial discussion and over-concentration on just one or two issues. There was generally a good understanding and presentation of MM's theory. A large number of candidates did not discuss the impact of potential changes in capital structure in the context of the scenario.

(a) <u>The role of competition authorities</u>

Competition authorities such as Country Y's Competition Directorate are set up by a government to **promote and protect competition** in an economy. It will make in-depth enquiries into mergers and markets to ensure that one company cannot dominate a market.

<u>Effect of market domination</u>

Market domination can result in **higher prices** being imposed on consumers and a lack of **incentive to improve** products or offer a wider range of products.

<u>Criteria used</u>

Where a **potential merger** is sufficiently large to warrant an investigation, the competition authority will look at whether the merger will be **against the public interest** in terms of:

(i) Effective competition within the industry

(ii) The interests of consumers, purchasers and users of the goods and services of that industry in respect of quality, price and variety

(iii) The reduction of costs and the introduction of new products and techniques

<u>Other policies</u>

The other strand of competition policy is concerned with preventing the development of anti-competitive practices such as **price-fixing agreements** (cartels).

(b) <u>Potential problems in merging management structures</u>

<u>Retention of Z's current management</u>

Z is a small entity with much of its value derived from the **intellectual capital** of its managers who have vital knowledge of specialist manufacturing techniques. The takeover will enable them to realise their capital gains from their shares in Z and they may be tempted to leave the company as soon as possible. A condition of the bid is the retention of the management team of Z but they will still need to be managed carefully to ensure their co-operation and future contribution.

<u>Location of entities</u>

Country Y is a large country and the two entities are at opposite ends of it. Furthermore, Entity Q is in a remote area so travelling between the two sites is likely to be **time consuming** and **unpopular** with employees. Long distance management can lead to **poor communication and control**.

It will not be easy to come up with an **acceptable location for the merged entity**. There is spare capacity in Q's head office building but the management of Z may be unwilling to re-locate to a remote part of the country. Property in the capital city is likely to be more expensive and/or limited in supply so a move to Z's location could be equally unacceptable.

<u>Possible solutions</u>

<u>Staff retention</u>

The current management of Z need to be looked after by ensuring clear **communication** of goals, **flexibility** in approach and **service contracts** tying them to the company for a certain time. The service contracts must be attractive in the form of **increased salaries** and benefits. In the longer term, their knowledge must be **captured** perhaps using a form of **knowledge management system.**

<u>Relocation</u>

Research will need to be undertaken into which key employees would be prepared to re-locate. Again, **communication** is essential to ensure that worried employees do not become de-motivated and leave the organisation. **Reducing uncertainty** as far and as quickly as possible can preserve morale.

The organisation also needs to examine which operations could be centralised and the optimum **cost effective** location.

Potential problems in merging systems

Differences in systems

The computer systems of Q were written especially for the entity whereas Z's systems are much smaller scale using basic accounting and spreadsheet packages. They are therefore **very different** and merging the two systems is likely to be **very problematic**.

Lack of flexibility

Q's system is **in need of replacement** to one which is more flexible and adaptable to changing circumstances but it is very unlikely that Q would be able to operate using a network of PCs as used by Z. Z specialises in niche markets so Q's bespoke system is unlikely to provide the **flexibility** needed to respond and adapt quickly to rapidly changing customer demands.

Possible solutions

Parallel running

Initially, the two systems could **continue to run independently** supplemented by requests for additional reports to ensure adequate information and control flows between the two management bodies.

Common system

As the integration process proceeds, the best aspects of each of the entities' systems can be identified and a **common system developed.**

(c) Capital structure theory

Capital structure refers to the way in which an entity is financed by a combination of debt and equity.

Traditional approach

The **traditional approach** is that there is an **optimal capital structure** or combination of debt and equity finance that **minimises the overall cost of capital** and therefore **maximises the overall value** of the entity.

Modigliani and Miller

The **Modigliani and Miller approach** is that the entity's overall weighted average cost of capital, and therefore its value, is **not influenced** by changes in its capital structure. Their argument is that the issue of debt causes the cost of equity to rise in such a way that the benefits of debt on returns are exactly offset.

However these conclusions change once **taxes** are included. As debt increases, the tax relief on interest payments, the **tax shield**, lowers the average weighted cost of capital, effectively gives the entity more cash and increases its value. The additional amount if value in a geared entity is the value of the tax shield.

Debt capacity

There is a limit to the amount of debt finance that an entity can support, its **debt capacity**. Beyond this level of debt, the **risk of bankruptcy** leading to higher required returns and **agency costs** as a result of action taken by concerned debt holders, will undermine the tax advantages of debt finance. **Tax exhaustion** may also set in where there are not enough profits from which to obtain all available tax benefits.

Q and Z

Q has relatively **low levels of debt** as a result of high earnings in earlier years so could **increase its value** by increasing gearing. The development of Z's business has largely been funded by **high levels of borrowing** at high rates of interest and with security requirements. Z is therefore borrowing in excess of its debt capacity and would benefit from reducing gearing.

Combining the capital structures of the two entities would therefore be beneficial to both and increase the value of the combined entity.

76 SB

(a) (i) <u>Asset valuation</u>

Total net book value and current realisable value of assets = **£22.6m**

Value per share = £22.6m/5m = **£4.52**

<u>P/E ratio valuation</u>

Earnings are £20.2 million as given in the question.

P/E ratio	Total value	Value per share
	£m	£
6*	121.2	24.24
9	181.8	36.36
12	242.4	48.48
25	505.0	101.00

* This is the lowest P/E ratio in the range multiplied by 2/3 to reflect the unlisted status of SB.

<u>Cash flow valuation</u>

	20X4	20X5	20X6	20X7
	£m	£m	£m	£m
Revenue	52.25	62.70	75.24	79.75
Operating costs @ 60%	(31.35)	(37.62)	(45.14)	(47.85)
Profit before tax	20.90	25.08	30.10	31.90
Tax @ 28%	(5.85)	(7.02)	(8.43)	(8.93)
Net cash flow	15.05	18.06	21.67	22.97
Annuity factor for Year 20X7 onwards*				16.667
				382.84
Discount factor @ 12%	0.893	0.797	0.712	0.712
Present value	13.44	14.39	15.43	272.58
Total value	**315.84**			
Value per share	**£63.17**			

* Annuity factor = 1/(0.12 - 0.06) = 16.667

(ii) <u>Asset valuation</u>

The asset valuation reflects **current realisable values** rather than out of date book values, but it still undervalues the business. This method is most commonly used to arrive at a **break-up value** for businesses with a significant amount of non-current assets. However, it is **less appropriate for service businesses**, and in particular for those in which the majority of the value is in the form of human and/or intellectual capital. In the latter type of company, a net assets valuation can be attempted if the intangibles are included as assets in the statement of financial position. However, a significant part of the value of SB resides in its expertise, and this is not reflected in the company's net asset value.

P/E ratio valuation

This method **compares the earnings information** of SB with that of other **entities of similar size** and characteristics that operate in the same markets, to arrive at an appropriate market price for the shares.

The problem here is deciding **which P/E ratio** to use as there is a wide range of possibilities.

The **lowest value** uses the bottom of the range and multiplies it by 2/3 to reflect the fact that SB is unquoted. If the shares were to be offered on the open market in an IPO, it would be prudent to price them at a **discount** to reflect the fact that the company would be a new entrant to the stock market, despite a fifteen year trading history. Pricing at a discount will also make the issue more attractive to investors and thereby help to obtain a good take-up of shares.

If SB were **taken over by a competitor**, the P/E ratio of that competitor could be used under the assumption that the new entity would have the same growth potential.

Historical data is being used which is not necessarily a good indicator of what will happen in the future.

Cash flow valuation

This method uses the **expected future cash flows** and a suitable **cost of capital** to discount them. It gives the **highest** valuation as it is based on **optimistic** forecasts.

There are a number of **uncertainties** surrounding the growth that has been predicted for SB. For example, the concessions in the Caribbean have not yet been finalised.

The cost of capital which has been used in the calculations is the **average cost of capital for the industry** and this may not be appropriate for SB. The **business risk** may be different, especially for growth into a new region. The method of finance to be used may be different to the average entity in this industry, thus changing the level of **financial risk**. It is likely that a **higher cost of capital** should we used to reflect the extra risk of SB's business and this would lower the valuation.

(iii)   Recommendation

The recommended valuation figure is **£300m** or **£60** per share. This is approximately a 5% reduction on the cash flow valuation and reflects the higher end of the range of P/E ratios for the industry. It allows for potential **downside** from the risk associated with SB and potential **upside** from the growth expected. It would be sufficiently attractive for investors in an IPO and also to competitors wanting to take over SB.

(b)   A trade sale

This would effectively be a **takeover** of SB by a competitor. The directors of SB would **receive cash** and/or **shares** in the competitor which could be an attractive proposition. They would however be subject to **capital gains tax**.

As so much of the value of the company comes from the expertise of its directors and employees, the directors could expect to be **tied into a contract** with the competitor for a period of time.

The main problem is that the founding directors would **lose control** of their business and have to follow the strategy and policies of the competitor, for better or worse.

An initial public offering (IPO)

The main attraction of an IPO is that the original owners of a company are able to **realise the value of their holding**. It also **enables future growth** of the company by allowing access to a wider pool of finance, enhancing the public image of the company, improving the marketability of the shares and making it easier to seek growth by acquisition.

However, IPOs **cost money**, including **brokerage commissions** and **underwriting fees.** Their success is dependant on **trading conditions** in the market at the time of flotation. There will be **significantly greater public regulation**, accountability and scrutiny and a **wider circle of investors** with more exacting requirements will hold shares.

Recommendation

If the directors are confident that future growth will be achieved and market conditions are favourable, they should go for an IPO. If however, the future looks risky, it would be better to sell out to a competitor and maximise the value of their holding now.

77 RV

> **Text references.** Business valuation is covered in Chapter 15.
>
> **Top tips.** The calculations in part (a) are straightforward provided you can remember how to use the Modigliani and Miller formula. The key part is to remember to use earnings after tax and before interest in perpetuity. There will still be plenty of marks if you use the wrong figures but remember to calculate the value of the tax shield and use the correct formula.
>
> You can discuss the limitations of the methods on part (a) (ii) even if you struggle with the calculations in part (i).
>
> You may struggle with finding enough to say in part (b). Make sure that your answer remains relevant to a private entity and don't be tempted to discuss the merits of flotation. The question does not ask how the entire entity could be sold.
>
> **Easy marks.** The calculations in part (a) have some easy marks available but this question is not as easy as it looks at first.

(a) (i) <u>Calculations of value of equity</u>

Number of shares $= 4m \div 0.20$

$= 20m$

Dividend valuation model

Dividend in 20X9 $= £10m \times 0.7 \times 0.25 = £1.75m$

Growth in earnings and dividends are expected to be zero for the foreseeable future.

$P_0 \quad = d_0/k_e$

$= 1.75/0.12$

$= \textbf{£14.58m}$ in total

Value per share $= 14.58/20$

$= 72.9p$

Modigliani and Miller

$V_g = V_u + TB_c$

V_u = Earnings after tax and before interest in perpetuity, assuming 6% growth from 20Y0 onwards.

Earnings in 20X9 (E) $= £10m \times 0.95 \times 0.7$

$= £6.65m$

$V_u \quad = E(1 + g)/k_e$

$= 6.65(1 + 0.06)/0.12$

$= £58.74m$

This represents the PV in one years' time, so the current present value is

$= £58.74 / 1.12$

$= £52.45m$

> **Tutorial note.** When using earnings instead of dividends in the dividend growth formula, the growth rate is not included in the bottom part of the formula. This is because the earnings number will normally be higher than the dividend because not all earnings are paid out as dividends. It can be assumed that re-invested earnings are generating future growth. So if we were to also include growth in the bottom part of the formula then this would be including growth twice, ie double-counting.
>
> Also note that the discounting by one year of £58.74m to obtain a present value is not essential.

$$TB_c = £20m \times 30\%$$
$$= £6m$$
$$V_g = 52.45 + 6$$
$$= £58.45m$$

Value of equity $= V_g -$ value of debt
$$= 58.45 - 20$$
$$= \textbf{£38.45m}$$

Value per share $= £38.45/20$
$$= 192p$$

> **Alternative method** The following alternative valuation using the dividend valuation model could be used.
>
> **Using current payout policy**
>
> Current dividend £1.75m
>
> $D_1 = £1.75m \times 1.06 = £1.855m$
>
> Amount in perpetuity $= 1.855/(0.12 - 0.06) = £30.917m$
>
> Discount at 12% to get PV now $= 30.917/1.12 = £27.60m$
>
> As above the present value of tax relief is £6m and debt is £20m.
>
> Value of equity $= £27.60m + £6m - £20m = £13.60m$
>
> Value per share $= £13.60m/20m = 68p$ per share

(ii) <u>Limitations of methods</u>

Dividend valuation model

The value of RV's shares according to this technique is 72.9p each. The asset value is 125p (£25m/20) per share so this indicates that the dividend valuation model seriously **undervalues** the business.

This model is more appropriate for valuing a **minority shareholding** where the holder has no influence over the level of dividends to be paid than for valuing a whole company, where the total cash flows will be of greater relevance.

The practical problems with the dividend valuation model lie mainly in its **assumptions**. Even accepting that the required 'perfect capital market' assumptions may be satisfied to some extent, in reality, the formula used assumes constant growth rates and constant required rates of return in perpetuity.

<u>Modigliani and Miller</u>

Modigliani and Miller's theory is more appropriate for valuing the entire business but it does rely on a number of **assumptions**.

The real world is inevitably different to the perfect market of Modigliani and Miller's theory. **Market imperfections** such as transaction costs and irrational shareholder behaviour exist. It ignores the fact that some earnings may be **retained** for future investment and also that **growth in earnings** may change and vary.

A more appropriate method

It would be advisable to **forecast cash flows** more accurately using as much data as possible. These future cash flows could then be **discounted** at a **risk-adjusted discount rate** which would reflect more realistically the risks of the new investment opportunities.

Another suitable method could be to use the **P/E ratio** of a **listed** entity operating in the same service industry. RV's earnings could then be multiplied by this P/E ratio to give a more accurate approximation of its value. The valuation would however be limited by the differences that would inevitably exist between RV and the other entity.

(b)   Value of a small shareholding

It has been stated that the **dividend valuation model valuation** is the most appropriate for a small shareholding. It uses the value of the income steam that these small shareholders receive. A higher dividend results in a higher business valuation and, if dividend income is the primary concern of these shareholders, this is logical. RV is a **private company** so the opportunity for **capital gains** from buying and selling the shares will be limited.

The **signalling effect** of dividends, whereby shareholders see changes in dividend policy as an indication of the company's prospects, is not as relevant for a private company.

The employees who wish to sell their shares would probably find an **asset valuation** the easiest to understand and accept but this is likely to **undervalue** a service industry business with significant intangible assets.

A **valuation of the whole entity** would be much more complex and involve considerably more information. As mentioned in part (a), this would involve forecast cashflows and P/E ratios of similar listed entities, as well as economic prospects and potential buyer information.

Selling the shares

Private companies' shares are obviously not as easy to sell as the shares of listed companies. The **company** itself could buy back its shares if it has sufficient cash. 5% of the asset value is £1.25m. This is a significant amount of cash which RV would probably prefer to spend on the new investment opportunities.

The **venture capital trust** might be willing to purchase the shares, especially if it has an optimistic view of the growth prospects of RV.

Alternatively there may be **connected external buyers** such as customers or suppliers who would be interested in obtaining an equity stake.

The buyer of the shares would pay cash in exchange for a share transfer which would then be officially documented.

78   LP

Text references. Acquisitions are covered in Chapter 16 and debt finance in Chapter 6.

Top tips. This is not a straightforward business valuation question and you will need to think carefully about how to answer part (a). Part (b) however requires a straightforward discussion with a few calculations. You make need to make some assumptions for the calculations if you struggled with part (a).

In part (b) (ii) there are only 5 marks available so don't write everything you know about sources of finance and make sure your suggestions are appropriate for this type of entity. A rights issue is highly unlikely in these circumstances and venture capital is inappropriate.

Easy marks. The easiest marks in this question are for the discussion parts so don't spend too long on the trickier calculations.

(a)   <u>The opening bid</u>

The opening bid was two LP shares for one MQ share. At current market prices, two LP shares are worth 610 pence (2 × 305) which is 70 pence less than the current share price of MQ. The share price of MQ was 610 pence one month ago so the market could have been **anticipating a higher bid**.

The share price of LP has fallen by 5 pence since one month ago but this often happens to a predator's share price in a bid situation.

At current market prices, the bid is **highly unlikely to succeed**.

<u>Revised terms</u>

LP will need to **raise the bid** in order for it to succeed. The problem is deciding on a bid that is sufficiently high to attract MQ's shareholders but not so high that the merger does not succeed.

If the market considers the revised bid to be too high, LP shares will fall in value and the bid will again become unattractive to MQ's shareholders.

<u>Valuing MQ</u>

P/E ratio of LP = 310/95 = 3.26

P/E ratio of MQ = 610/120 = 5.08

The **predator's** P/E ratio is therefore **lower than the target's** which implies that there is an expectation that MQ's EPS will grow more rapidly in the future.

The value of MQ's **earnings in perpetuity (**using LP's cost of equity)

= 130m × 1.2/0.1 = £1,560m

This compares to a **current market capitalisation** of £884m (6.8 × 130m), indicating high potential for growth.

<u>Recommended terms</u>

At current share prices, the bid would need to be at least 2.23 (680/305) LP shares for every MQ share. In view of the future earnings potential, it would make sense to offer at least a **20% premium** on MQ's pre-bid share price. This values the shares at 732 pence (610 × 1.2) , which equates to an offer of **2.4 LP** shares (732/305) for every one MQ share.

(b)   (i)   <u>Advantages of a cash alternative</u>

To MQ shareholders the advantage of receiving a cash offer is that the price is **not subject to stock market fluctuations.**

Existing shareholdings will be **less diluted** if there is a cash alternative and **future gains** from the merger will be obtained by a **higher proportion** of LP's shareholders.

<u>Disadvantages of a cash alternative</u>

Existing MQ shareholders may suffer an immediate liability to **tax** on the **capital gain** but shareholders in this position could choose to take the share exchange option instead.

The main disadvantage is potentially the **impact on gearing**. The cash will have to be raised and this is likely to be from debt finance.

<u>Amount of cash required</u>

Assuming that the bid is 2.4 LP shares for every MQ share and a share price of 732 pence, the total value of the bid would be £952m (£7.32 × 130m).

If 60% of MQ's shareholders accept the cash offer, approximately £571m (60% × £952m) will be needed.

The combined cash balances of the two companies are £355m (330 + 25). Additional cash would therefore be needed amounting to **£216m** (571 − 355).

<u>Impact on gearing</u>

A **highly geared** company may not be able to issue further bonds to obtain cash for a cash offer.

Using the book values of debt given and the current market value of equity:

Current gearing of LP $= 350/(350 + 1{,}464)$
$= 19.3\%$

Gearing for new group if there is a full share exchange $= 455/(455 + 1{,}464 + 952)$
$= 15.8\%$

Gearing for new group if £216m is raised $= (455 + 216)/(455 + 2{,}164 + 1{,}464 + 952)$
$= 21.7\%$

The gearing obviously increases if the bid is financed by raising cash through debt finance.

(ii) How the cash alternative might be financed

As stated above, the most probable way in which cash would be raised is via **debt finance**. This could take a number of different forms.

Redeemable secured bond

This would be a **long-term bond** which would be redeemed in 10 to 15 years. The current debt for both companies is redeemable in 3 to 4 years so longer dated bonds would be sensible to avoid any cash flow problems.

The bonds could be **secured** via a **fixed or floating charge** on assets. This security would enable a **lower** coupon rate to be offered on the bonds than if the bonds were unsecured.

Convertible bonds

These allow the bond holder to **convert** the bonds into **ordinary shares** at some future date. This **debt sweetener** again enables a lower coupon rate to be offered. This lower yield is the price the investor has to pay for the conversion rights. It is, of course, also one of the

reasons why the issue of convertible bonds is attractive to a company, particularly one with tight cash flows around the time of issue, but an easier situation when the bonds are due to be converted.

Bonds with warrants

Share **warrants** are another form of debt sweetener which give their holder the right to apply for new shares at a specified exercise price in the future. Warrants are usually issued as part of a package with unsecured bonds: an investor who buys bonds will also acquire a certain number of warrants. The purpose of warrants is to make the bonds more attractive.

Once issued, warrants are detachable from the bonds and can be sold and bought separately before or during the 'exercise period' (the period during which the right to use the warrants to subscribe for shares is allowed). The market value of warrants will depend on expectations of actual share prices in the future.

79 XK

Text references. Divestments are covered in Chapter 16.

Top tips. In part (b), try to be topical and don't be afraid to bring in real-life economic issues such as recession. However make sure you keep your points relevant to the industry in which XK operates. Part (c) is asking you to look at the advantages and disadvantages of each part of the financing structure (venture capital etc). Don't forget to make recommendations of alternative financing structures, ensuring that they are feasible for the scenario in the question. Bear in mind that there are marks for calculations so make sure you provide some relevant figures.

Easy marks. You should pick up a few marks in part (b) by discussing the economic and market factors impacting on the negotiations.

Examiner's comments. This question was answered satisfactorily although few candidates managed to provide many (if any) calculations to support their answer to (c). Common errors included discussing too few types of shareholders in part (a) or actually writing too much on this part, discussing advantages and disadvantages of MBOs in general rather than those of the structure proposed in the scenario, assuming that a divestment was the subsidiary going out of business and not understanding that Y is a wholly owned subsidiary.

Marking scheme

			Marks
(a)	Up to 3 marks per group of stakeholders discussed		Max 7
(b)	Up to 3 marks per economic or market factor discussed		Max 7
(c)	Calculations	Max 5	
	Advantages and disadvantages – 1 mark per valid point	Max 4	
	Recommendations	Max 2	
			Max 11
		Total	25

(a)   Interests of the various stakeholder groups

Shareholders in XK

The removal of Company Y's earnings – which account for 6% of group earnings – may have an effect on the risk of the group and thus on the required return for investors. In response to these changes the market value of XK might be adversely affected, thus impacting on shareholders' wealth.

XK's directors and employees

If directors have **share options**, the value of these may be affected if share price falls. Also any profit-related earnings may be adversely affected if the divestment of Y causes group earnings to fall. If directors have neither of these benefits the effects of the divestment are likely to be minimal. Employees should feel few effects unless their jobs were in some way related to Company Y (for example, head office services). A few **redundancies may occur** if this is the case.

Company Y's directors and employees

The executive directors of Company Y are funding part of the MBO and as a result are taking on **significantly more risk** than they had been exposed to. However with the increase in risk comes the increase in control.

Non-director employees may be at risk of redundancy or revised terms and conditions if the MBO results in a restructuring of Company Y or a review of costs. In the long-term the MBO should result in increased employment if the executive directors' ambitions to respond to market challenges are successful.

Customers

Company Y's customers may be **subjected to revised terms and conditions** and may lose some benefits of their supplier being part of a large group (for example, after sales service). However any loss of earnings

as a result of customers going elsewhere will have a greater effect on Company Y's shareholders and staff than on the customers themselves.

Suppliers and providers of debt finance

In a similar way to customers, Company Y's suppliers may experience revised terms and conditions, particularly if purchasing policy is currently controlled by Group Head Office. Any major changes to terms of trade could result in suppliers withdrawing their services or being less generous with credit terms and discounts.

The removal of Company Y from the group statement of financial position should not cause XK's bank any great concern. The **bonds are secured on non-current assets** and even the removal of Company Y's US$220m non-current assets will not affect the bonds' security (US$1,000m secured on the remaining US$2,030m of non-current assets).

XK should be careful with its current assets : current liabilities ratio. It is required to maintain a ratio of at least 1.5 : 1. At the moment the ratio stands at 1.65 : 1 (700/425) but this may be affected by the removal of Company Y's figures from the statement of financial position.

Other stakeholders

Local government and national government may be affected by the divestment although lack of information precludes us from predicting the extent of the effect. Local government will be anxious to maintain employment levels in their community whilst national government may focus on the effect of the divestment on corporation tax receipts.

The group that is most likely to be affected is the **executive directors** involved in the buyout. XK's employees may suffer redundancies whilst suppliers may experience changes in terms and conditions.

(b) Economic and market factors

Recession

The current recession could have a significant impact on the negotiations. It may have been a factor in encouraging the divestment in the first place. XK's bargaining position may be **weakened** by the possibility that it is just wanting to remove Company Y from the group, resulting in a lower price being obtained for the sell-off.

Inflation

As inflation starts to rise, this will erode the real value of the company and also make it more difficult to estimate future cash flows (and thus NPV). Such uncertainty may reduce the price the 'financing syndicate' is prepared to pay for Company Y. This will have an obvious negative impact on XK's cash flow in the event of a sell-off.

Interest rates

Should interest rates increase consumers will be **less inclined to spend money** on items deemed 'non-necessity'. Company Y's cash flows are likely to suffer as a result which could have an impact on perceived risk and cost of capital. An increase in the cost of capital will reduce the NPV of Company Y and thus the amount that the 'financing syndicate' will be willing to pay.

Alternative investment opportunities

Before XK makes a final decision on whether to divest Company Y, it should consider what it might do with the **cash** (currently estimated to be US$325m). There is no point just having this substantial sum sitting in the bank – there should be some potential ideas of how the money might be **invested**. XK could consider paying off some of its debt (although the debt situation gives no cause for concern) or perhaps returning some money to its shareholders in the form of a special dividend or share buyback. If there are no feasible or attractive options available XK should ask whether it should be divesting itself of the profitable Company Y.

Stock market sentiment

It is unclear how XK's perceived risk will be affected by the divestment of Company Y. If the divested subsidiary has a greater perceived risk than that of XK then XK's risk should fall. However without further information on risk profiles no predictions can be made.

The fact that XK's share price has risen by 5% in the last three months (against a general stock market decline of 3%) suggests that the stock market has some **inside knowledge** of the potential divestment. Shareholders have not been informed nor their views sought therefore their reaction to the proposed divestment is not yet known.

The share price is likely to increase further when details of the divestment are revealed. XK will be divesting 6% of group earnings for a price that equates with approximately 10% of total market value [325/(375 x 8.75)].

(c)   Advantages and disadvantages of proposed buyout structure

Venture capitalists

The main advantage of having venture capitalists involved is that they are willing to take a substantial amount of risk. However this risk-taker approach does not come without a price – in this case, the venture capitalists require all earnings to be retained in the business for five years and an **average return of 25%** over that period. If all funds are retained in the business this will help to promote capital growth. The required return is not unusual for venture capitalists.

However delivering a 25% return will not be easy. The following calculations illustrate the point.

(i)   Net earnings per annum after interest

	US$m
Previous year's earnings (6% of US$510m)	30.6
Contribution to financing by investment bank = 90% of 220 = 198m	
Interest on financing by investment bank = (6% of 198m) x (1 – 0.25)	(8.91)
Net earnings for the year	21.69

(ii)   Venture capitalists' contribution to funding Company Y buyout

	US$m
Total cost of buyout	325.0
Directors' contribution	(5.0)
Investment bank's contribution (90% of US$220m)	(198.0)
Venture capitalists' contribution	122.0

(iii)   Return on venture capitalists' investment

	US$m
Investment	122.00
Net earnings per annum	21.69
Return on investment (21.69/122)	17.8%

Given the figures above, venture capitalists are only likely to receive a maximum of 17.8% return on their investment (assuming no returns are given to the directors), as opposed to the 25% they require. The venture capitalists will only invest in Company B if they think the directors can **deliver on their goal of rapid growth**.

Investment bank

The maximum investment from the investment bank will be US$198m, resulting in high interest payments. However the main advantage of debt funding is that **equity shareholders retain a greater share of the business**.

The high interest payments will reduce the earnings of Company Y which will in turn reduce the value of the company and increase its risk. An increase in risk means higher cost of capital.

Interest cover can be calculated as follows.

	US$m
Profit before interest and tax: 6% of [(510 x 100/75) + (7.5% x 1,150)]	45.98
Interest on Y's debt: 6% of US$198m	11.88
Interest cover: 45.98/11.88	3.87 times

Interest cover is not very high. If earnings cannot be sustained at the level above then Company Y may struggle to cover interest payments.

A **substantial amount of earnings is being consumed by interest payments**, leaving little for investment for growth. Given the difficulties in trying to meet the venture capitalists' required return (see above), the directors need as much investment as possible to grow the business otherwise the venture capitalists will start asking questions.

A further issue that cannot be ignored is the matter of repaying the US$198m loan at the end of five years. The directors will need to accumulate **sufficient cash** within the business to allow them to do so. If a significant proportion of earnings is being taken up with interest payments then this may not be possible.

Directors

The directors are the last to be considered when it comes to earning returns. The calculations of venture capitalists' returns (see above) were based on the assumption that the directors received no returns – which is **not sustainable**. However no returns will be possible until the other investors' requirements have been met and sufficient growth has taken place.

Alternative financing structures

There are several serious **reservations** with the current proposed financing structure. As has been illustrated above, the venture capitalists will not receive the required 25% return on their investment if current predictions regarding earnings and interest rates are correct. In addition, there will be little or no opportunity for company growth to remedy this problem as interest payments comprise a substantial proportion of predicted earnings.

It may be worth negotiating with the venture capitalists to see if they would be willing to take a **larger share of the company**. This would reduce the debt finance required from the investment bank and thus the interest payments, leaving more funds available to provide a return to the venture capitalists.

Another possibility would be to source another debt provider, perhaps with a more favourable rate of interest. If that is not possible, the current lender might be prepared to provide an alternative to straight debt – for example, convertible debt or warrants. However this may not be acceptable given the resultant dilution of equity in the long-term.

80 WW

Text references. Cost of equity and WACC are covered in Chapter 8. Business valuations are covered in Chapter 15.

Top tips. Make sure you label each of your calculations – there are numerous calculations required in this question and it is easy to get them mixed up.

In part (b)(ii) you are expected to discuss the validity of the methods in relation to the scenario – don't be tempted to produce a generic discussion, although you can make use of general issues surrounding each method when constructing your answer.

Easy marks. You should have been able to pick up a number of easy marks in part (a). Calculations of the range of values in (b)(i) also offer some easy marks.

Examiner's comments. Some candidates failed to understand the need to ungear and regear the beta. If they did recognise the need, they often failed to do so correctly.

(a) (i) Cost of equity

Using CAPM:

$k_e = R_f + (R_m - R_f)\, \beta$

$k_e = 5 + (6 \times 1.5)$

$k_e = 14\%$

(ii) <u>WACC</u>

$$WACC = k_e(\frac{V_E}{V_E + V_D}) + k_d(\frac{V_D}{V_E + V_D})$$

WACC = (14 x 0.6) + (6 x (1 – 0.30) x 0.4)

WACC = 10.08%

(iii) <u>Adjusted WACC for Specialist Division</u>

Ungear YY's beta

$$\beta_u = \beta_g \frac{V_E}{V_E + V_D(1 - t)} + \beta_d \frac{V_D(1 - t)}{V_E + V_D(1 - t)}$$

β_u = 0.8 x 75/(75 + 25 x 0.7)   (Note: debt beta is zero)

β_u = 0.65

Regear for XX

$$\beta_g = \beta_u + (\beta_u - \beta_d)\frac{V_D(1 - t)}{V_E}$$ (Note: debt beta is zero)

β_g = 0.65 + 0.65 ((0.4 x 0.7)/0.6)

β_g = 0.95

k_e = 5 + 6 x 0.95

k_e = 10.7%

Calculate adjusted WACC for Specialist Division

$$WACC = k_e(\frac{V_E}{V_E + V_D}) + k_d(\frac{V_D}{V_E + V_D})$$

WACC = (10.7 x 0.6) + (6 x 0.7 x 0.4)

WACC = 8.1%

(b) (i) <u>Range of values for the Specialist Division</u>

Asset-based valuation

As per the figures in the question, the book value of the assets employed in the Specialist Division is A\$15m and the replacement value of these assets is A\$20m.

Cash flow basis

Discount the Specialist Division's annual cash flows of A\$2.5m at XX's WACC of 10.08%. Annual growth rate in perpetuity is 1%.

Value of Specialist Division = (A\$2.5m x 1.01)/(0.1008 – 0.01) = A\$27.8m

Using WACC based on proxy company YY

Value of Specialist Division = (A\$2.5m x 1.01)/(0.081 – 0.01) = A\$35.6m

(ii) <u>Validity of the methods suggested by the Directors</u>

Director A

Asset-based valuations are only appropriate for break-up scenarios – XX is acquiring the Specialist Division as a going concern. In addition, net assets basis of valuation is likely to undervalue the division as it does not take intangible assets into consideration.

The use of book values will mean that the valuation will depend on the methods and rates of depreciation used.

Assets-based valuations are useful for providing a **lower limit** for the value of the division but will not give a **realistic** value.

Director B

Director B has suggested using XX's existing WACC to discount the tax-adjusted future cash flows. This values the division before considering how it is being funded. This approach is appropriate for the Specialist Division as it does not have any debt of its own.

A problem with this approach is that it does not take the Specialist Division's **business risk** into consideration, which is different from the business risk of XX. This can be rectified by using the ungeared beta of YY, the proxy company.

Director C

Director C suggested discounting the tax-adjusted cash flows of the Specialist Division using an adjusted WACC. This means that the issue of business risk (which was a problem with Director B's approach) has been dealt with. The proxy company YY's beta can be ungeared and then regeared to take account of XX's capital structure and risk profile – this gives a separate cost of equity and WACC for the Specialist Division.

When this approach is used, it gives a **much higher valuation** for the Specialist Division, which reflects the lower risk of YY relative to XX. Note that YY, with its sole activity of publishing specialist magazines, is more likely to have repeat business whereas XX is in the book publishing trade (more risky). This explains YY's lower beta.

Director D

Director D has suggested using an earnings-based valuation approach. This creates an immediate problem, as this approach requires both earnings figures and cost of equity, neither of which is available for the Specialist Division. This is because the division is not a subsidiary and therefore does not have its own capital structure, share price and dividend history.

Even if the figures were available, the earnings-based valuation **only values equity**. Any debt valuation would have to be added to the value of equity to obtain an estimate of the value of assets being acquired by XX.

(iii)   Advice on appropriate price

If XX required an **initial bargaining position** it could use the price suggested by the asset-based valuation method.

It is more likely that XX would view Director C's proposal as being most valid. This method is based on pre-debt cash flows, which makes sense as the Specialist Division does not have any of its own debt. This gives a value of A\$35.6m.

However this value is at the upper limit of what should be paid for the Specialist Division and it is not recommended that XX offers this figure initially. It may be that XX might be willing to pay even more than A\$35.6m if it is thought that growth rates could exceed the current estimates of 1% per annum.

It is recommended therefore that XX starts bidding at a price of, say, A\$27.8m (the value estimated using the cash-flow basis suggested by Director B). Negotiations should not go beyond A\$35.6m as this value reflects the lower-risk profile of the Specialist Division compared to XX.

81 MMM

Text references. Business valuations are covered in Chapter 15. Amalgamations and restructuring are covered in Chapter 16.

Top tips. In part (a) you are expected to compare the current situation of both MMM's shareholders and JJJ's shareholders with their situations in the event of the share based bid and the cash bid. In simple terms what the question is asking is under which bid or bids will each group of shareholders be better off.

In part (b)(i), remember that JJJ's shareholders will still receive the full cash offer regardless of whether synergistic benefits are realised or not.

Easy marks. Whilst your answer must relate to the scenario, there are some easy marks to be gained in part (b)(ii) when discussing integration issues.

Examiner's comments. Although this is a mainstream topic, many candidates struggled with the numerical calculations and relied on the discursive elements to pick up the majority of the marks awarded.

(a)   (i) and (ii) Evaluation of bid offers

Prior to offer

MMM:

Number of shares = 30m

Share price = $6.90

Total value = $207m

JJJ:

Number of shares = 5m

Share price = $12.84

Total value = $64.2m

Total:

Total value of combined companies (including synergies) = $207m + $64.2m + $8m = $279.2m

Bid offer A

MMM:

Number of shares = 30m

Total value = 30/40 x $279.2m = $209.4m

Share price = $209.4m/30m = $6.98

JJJ:

Number of shares = 10m

Total value = $279.2m - $209.4m = $69.8m

Share price = $6.98

Total:

Total value of company = 40m shares worth $279.2m

Bid offer B

Cash offer is worth 5m (JJJ's shares) x $13.50 = $67.5m

MMM:

Number of shares = 30m

Total value = $279.2m - $67.5m = $211.7m

Share price = $7.06

JJJ:

JJJ's shareholders will receive $67.5m in cash.

Total:

Total value of company = $279.2m

Impact on MMM's shareholders

MMM's shareholders start with a shareholding that is worth $207m. They will be better off under either of the bids, but will gain most from the cash offer where the share price will rise by $0.16 per share. This represents a total gain of $4.8m. With the share offer, MMM's shareholders will gain $2.4m in total.

The cash offer protects MMM's shareholders' **proportionate ownership** as the number of shares in issue does not change. With the share offer, the number of shares increases to 40m, meaning that MMM's shareholders only have a 75% ownership of the combined company.

It is important for MMM's management to manage business activities acquired from JJJ to ensure that the higher growth rate of 9% predicted for JJJ is realised. If these activities are simply absorbed into the normal operations of MMM there is a risk of the **higher growth rate not being achieved**, due to MMM's own predicted growth being considerably lower at 6%.

A major problem with the cash offer is gaining access to the not inconsiderable sum of $67.5m. This amount represents almost 33% of MMM's current market capitalisation and management will have to consider the impact on gearing levels and earnings per share.

An issue with the share offer is the cash flow implications of future dividends being paid on a larger number of shares.

Impact on JJJ's shareholders

JJJ's shareholders also gain regardless of the bid offer. The greater gain is made from the share offer where share value increases by 8.7% from $64.2m to $69.8m. However if the cash offer is accepted there is a guaranteed gain of $3.3m. The share price gain carries a risk of being less than expected due to a potential fall in MMM's share price if the market fails to react positively to the takeover or the synergistic gains are not realised.

The shareholders also have to consider the risks of accepting a shareholding in a company that has much **lower growth prospects** than their own company, which may in turn lead to much lower long-term gains.

(b) (i) Impact on shareholders of not realising synergistic gains

If none of the gains are realised the value of the combined company will fall by $8m.

	Before offer Total value ($m)	After share offer Total value ($m)	After cash offer Total value ($m)
MMM	207.0	209.4 – (30/40 x 8) = 203.4	203.7
JJJ	64.2	69.8 – (10/40 x 8) = 67.8	67.5
Total	271.2	271.2	271.2

The above figures show that if the synergistic benefits are not realised then only JJJ's shareholders will benefit from the takeover, regardless of the type of bid. They will still receive an **immediate gain** of $3.3m if the cash offer is accepted which has no risk attached. The theoretical gain of $3.6m from the share offer will depend on whether the market reacts positively to the takeover (in the form of a higher share price for MMM). It is also subject to the risk of having a shareholding in a company that has lower growth prospects than JJJ.

MMM's shareholders will not benefit from the takeover if the synergistic benefits are not realised. They will lose $3.6m from the share offer and $3.3m from the cash offer. The bid will only be

attractive to MMM's shareholders if the additional benefits from JJJ's IT and IS systems are realised or if MMM experiences higher than expected growth through the combined business.

(ii) <u>Minimising risk of not realising estimated synergistic benefits</u>

The realisation of synergistic benefits depends on a number of factors. Regardless of how good estimates are of the perceived benefits, it is important to ensure that the **integration process is handled with sensitivity** and careful planning otherwise these benefits may be much smaller than anticipated or actually non-existent.

The key benefits are perceived to come from JJJ's **IT and IS systems**. However it is important that MMM's systems are not shut down immediately – both systems should be run in parallel to ensure that MMM's processes fit in with those of JJJ. If possible, test data should be run.

MMM's **key personnel** will have to be trained in the operation of the new systems and this training should then be passed on to others in the organisation who would benefit from it.

If possible, MMM should try to retain key personnel from JJJ who are fully trained in how the systems work – this knowledge will be invaluable in training MMM's staff.

It is essential that relations between MMM's staff and those of JJJ are **handled sensitively** as MMM's staff may feel threatened by the new processes. Also, JJJ's staff may feel intimidated by coming into a new company and being faced with potential hostility from existing personnel at MMM.

Careful planning is a key factor – introduction of major changes to IT and IS systems cannot happen overnight. Timetables and responsibilities must be established and adhered to and targets set for interim stages of completion.

Proper management is essential – not just of the changeover from one set of processes to another but of the entire integration process.

82 Groots

Text references. Net present value calculations are explained in Chapter 11. Acquisitions issues are discussed in Chapter 16.

Top tips. There are a number of issues that you have to work through in (a) (i) and 7 marks seems a fairly low mark allocation. Note the figures have to be inflated because we are using money cost of capital. Note also the examiner's comment about calculation of forward exchange rates. Although purchasing power parity may be a technically better method than interest rate parity, the scenario specifies interest rate parity, so you must use it. Don't worry too much if you used another method for the perpetuity calculation: others are possible and that part would only have been worth 2 marks.

(a) (ii) clearly confused a lot of candidates. It is technically correct to say that the two methods should be the same; the approach we take is to try to speculate why in practice calculations might have distortions

There are also problems with the requirements in (a) (iii), if your two answers were the same (as they should have been in theory), but just use whatever your answer was. Also there may be conflict between using the answer in (a) (i) and attempting to maximise shareholder wealth.

The discussions in (b) need to bring out the curious market value that the shares currently have. As Groots is listed it is possible to expand the shareholder base. There are a number of points in the scenario that can be drawn on in the discussion in (b) (iii).

Easy marks. The easiest part of the discussion should have been post-completion audits, which is a standard question.

Examiner's comments. In (a) calculations were often wrong and comments not provided. Forward rates were often calculated using purchasing power parity rather than interest rate parity, and showing the Caribbean $ appreciating rather than depreciating against the Euro. Candidates also failed to use two methods, adjust for inflation and calculate post year 4 cash flows. Some incorrectly deducted tax from post-tax cash flows and added rather than deducted repayment of debt. The most common error in (a) (iii) was to use the nominal value of shares.

Answers to (b) (i) often lacked discussion of the methods used, and most candidates failed to mention the significance of market values. Some answers incorrectly calculated net asset value. Answers to (ii) were better, although some candidates made the basic mistake of stating that retained earnings could be used to finance the acquisition. Other mistakes included suggesting inappropriate methods eg venture capital and factoring, and failing to support answers with calculations. Some answers failed to take into account the fact that both companies were listed.

(b) (iii) was often answered badly or not at all. (iv) was done reasonably well, but candidates often failed to take into account the fact that this was a takeover situation, and suggested incorrectly that the results of the post-completion audit would be publicised to shareholders.

(a) (i) Maximum price that Groots would pay for Cocomos

This is the **present value** of the expected future cash flows of Cocomos.

For each method, the computation involves looking at the cash flows given for years 1 to 4 and a perpetuity from year 5 onwards.

The cash flows for the first 4 years are:

Year	1	2	3	4
Post tax net cash flow C$ mill. (real terms)	31.5	37.5	41.5	47.2
Nominal cash flow (inflate at 4.5% per year)	32.92	40.95	47.36	56.29

Exchange rates

First evaluate the estimated future exchange rates, using interest rate parity:

Future spot rate C$/€ = Spot rate C$/€ x (1 + ECCA interest rate)/(1 + Caribbean interest rate)

Year	C$/€	
0	0.300	
1	0.292	[0.300 × 1.035 / 1.065]
2	0.283	[0.292 × 1.035 / 1.065]
3	0.275	
4	0.268	
5	0.260	

Method 1 – forecasting the exchange rate

Year	1	2	3	4
Nominal cash flow C$ (as above))	32.92	40.95	47.36	56.29
Exchange rate C$/€	0.292	0.283	0.275	0.268
Nominal cash flow in € million	9.61	11.59	13.02	15.09
10% discount factor (Groots € cost of capital)	0.909	0.826	0.751	0.683
Discounted cash flow	8.735	9.573	9.778	10.306
NPV	38.39			

The present value of the perpetuity as at year 4 $= \dfrac{15.09(1.02)}{0.10 - 0.02} = €192.40$ million

The present value of the perpetuity as at year 0 (using the 4 year discount factor) = 192.40 × 0.683 = €131.41 million.

Total NPV by method 1 = 38.39 + 131.41 = €169.80 million.

Subtracting Cocomos' debt (value converted at spot = 135 × 0.3 = 40.5), gives the maximum price for Cocomos' equity as 169.80 – 40.5 = **€129.3 million.**

Method 2 – leaving the cash flows in the overseas currency

Cost of capital

Groot's nominal discount rate in euros k(€) is 10%. Its discount rate in C$ can be found by using the **adjusted discount rate** formula.

$$\frac{(1 + \text{annual discount rate€})}{(1 + \text{annual discount rate C\$})} = \frac{\text{Future spot rate C\$ / €in 12 months' time}}{\text{Spot rate C\$ / €}}$$

1.1/(1 + annual discount rate C$) = 0.292/0.300

(1+ annual discount rate C$) = 1.1 x 0.300/0.292

Annual discount rate C$ = 0.13 (or 13%)

This is higher than the 12% which Cocomos estimates as its cost of capital, and which Groots believes is too low.

Year	1	2	3	4
Nominal cash flow C$ (as above)	32.92	40.95	47.36	56.29
Discount factor 13%	0.885	0.783	0.693	0.613
Discounted cash flow	29.13	32.06	32.82	34.51
NPV C$	128.52			
Spot rate	0.300			
NPV €	38.56			

The present value of the perpetuity as at year 4 $= \dfrac{56.29(1.02)}{0.13 - 0.02} = C\$521.96$ million

The present value of the perpetuity as at year 0 (using the 4 year discount factor)

    = 521.96 × 0.613
    = C$319.96 million

Converted to € at spot = 319.96 × 0.3 = €95.99

Total NPV by method 2 = 38.56 + 95.99 = €134.55 million.

Subtracting Cocomos' debt (value converted at spot = 135 × 0.3 = 40.5), gives the maximum price for Cocomos' equity as 134.55 – 40.5 = **€94.05 million.**

(ii)   <u>Same rates</u>

The difference between the two results above should be due to **rounding** of the **discount rates** and **growth rates** used in the computations.

<u>Practical reasons for differences</u>

<u>Methods used</u>

In practice the **estimates of future exchange rates** and **cost of capital** may be made in different ways, resulting in differences between the two answers. For example, the future exchange rates may be estimated using **purchasing power parity** (based on estimates of inflation rates), and the cost of capital for Groots in C$ may be based on data in the East Caribbean stock market.

<u>Assumptions</u>

Because the theories used for making these estimates make **simplifying assumptions**, and because they depend on **statistical analysis** for estimation of parameters, there are in practice bound to be differences between the results of the two different approaches unless they use exactly the same underlying assumptions.

The **key assumption** made in both methods was that the growth rate after Year 4 was 2% in both €s and $s and this is unlikely. If the $ cash flows are increasing by 2%, the effect on € cash flows will be influenced by exchange rate weakening of approximately 3%. This means that € cash flows will not increase in line with $ cash flows. A more accurate analysis in part (a) would recognise this and bring the two methods in line with each other.

(iii)   <u>Value of Cocomos</u>

From the above calculations, the **value of Cocomos shares** is **€129.3 million**, which is above its current market value, which is 55 million × 6.95 × 0.3 = approximately €115 million.

Groots shares are worth €6.85 today, which implies that the number of shares to be issued as purchase consideration is 129.3/6.85 = 18.88 million (ie 1 new Groots share for approximately 2.9 shares in Cocomos).

There are many assumptions behind this computation, including:

- There is **no synergy** when the two companies are merged; this would raise the maximum price that Groots might be prepared to pay

- Groots' **share price does not change** as a result of information and rumours concerning the takeover bid

- **New events** do **not change the value of Cocomos:** eg new opportunities, currency changes, new bidders

(b)   Report to the directors of the Groots Group

From: Financial Manager

<u>Proposed acquisition of Cocomos</u>

This report discusses and makes **recommendations** on the **maximum price** that should be paid for the prospective new acquisition Cocomos Limited and the most appropriate type of financing for the acquisition. In addition, it analyses strategies for enhancing the value of the combined firm and discusses the benefits and limitations of a post-completion audit and review.

(i)   <u>Recommendation on price to be offered to Cocomos</u>

The table below shows the value of Cocomos per share and for the whole 55 million shares, using four different bases of valuation.

Price	Per share €	All shares € m
(1) Cash flows (see (a) above)	2.35	129
(2) Current earnings Groots P/E ratio (see workings below)	2.32	127
(3) Current market value of shares	2.08	115
(4) Net asset value (book value of equity shares)	0.84	46

(1)   Cash flows

Methods (1) and (2) show the value of the **future cash flows** and **earnings** of Cocomos to Groots. Method (1) is based on the **discounted value of future cash flows** arising from Cocomos. It **provides the most logical analysis** of the available data and, because the discount rate is the minimum required return for the investment, this gives the **maximum price** that we consider paying.

The value arrived at is of course **only an estimate,** and subject to appreciable estimation error, because the method is based on **simplified assumptions** about future exchange rates and interest rates, and about the **future cash flows** of Cocomos and the risk that the investment carries. In particular, it is **very sensitive** to **estimates of cash flow** beyond year 5. If we are able to gain more information about these factors, we will be able to have more confidence in the figure.

(2)   Earnings-based measure

Method (2) is a more traditional earnings-based method. The price/earnings ratio of Groots has been used as to multiply the current profitability of Cocomos, resulting in a broad estimate of earnings-based value, as seen in the workings below.

Workings for method (2)

	Groots	Cocomos
Profit after tax	193.5 – 46.9 = €146.6 m	48.6 – 11.5 = C$37.1 m × 0.3 = €11.13 m.
Earnings per share	€146.6 m / 245 m. = €0.598	€11.13 m / 55m = €0.202
P/E ratio	€6.85 / €0.598 = 11.455	

Applying Groots' P/E to Cocomos earnings:

11.455 × €11.13 m = €127.5m. (€2.32 per share).

This method is subject to significant inaccuracies because it **fails to recognise the possible difference in growth rates** between Groots and Cocomos, and because it is based on earnings, which contain significant non-cash items such as depreciation.

(3)   Current market value of shares

Method (3) is simply the **current market value of the shares** on the East Caribbean Stock Exchange. The fact that this is so far below estimates we have made of the value of Cocomos to Groots needs further investigation. At best, it shows the hidden value that be unlocked from Cocomos as part of the Groots Group. At worst it may mean that our estimates of Cocomos' value are over-optimistic.

(4)   Net assets method

Finally method (4) shows the **value of the net assets** of the company. This is very low compared with the other methods because it does not attempt to value the business as a going concern, but merely shows the value of its assets as a base-line in the event of poor performance.

Other factors affecting valuation

We need to consider the impact of other factors not allowed for above, in particular the impact of **currency changes** and whether the value may be affected if the franchisees object, and the bid in effect has to become hostile.

Conclusion

In summary, we recommend that the **maximum price payable** for Cocomos is €2.35 per share. We should, of course, not offer this price but should offer a premium over current market price that is sufficient to attract the shareholders of Cocomos (eg €2.20 per share).

(ii) <u>Alternative forms of consideration</u>

<u>Cash-share issue decision</u>

The shares of Cocomos can be acquired by **cash** or by an **issue of Groots shares**, or by a combination of the two, including allowing the shareholders of the acquired company to opt for shares or cash.

The general principles are:

(1) If shares are offered, the **expected value of the purchase consideration** will need to be higher than if cash is offered, because cash is risk free to the former owners of Cocomos, whereas shares in Groots may fall in value.

(2) Whichever method is used, **nearly all of the existing cash balance** will be needed to **repay the €40.5 million debt** of Cocomos when the acquisition is made. Therefore, if cash is offered, Groots will need to borrow, and this will raise company gearing (and hence financial risk for Groots shareholders). If shares are issued, gearing and financial risk will decrease.

(3) A **share issue** will tend to **dilute shareholdings** whereas a cash acquisition will not. Key shareholders will be interested in the disposition of shareholdings after the merger.

(4) If borrowing (in order to pay cash) is carried out in the **currency of the acquired company,** this can act as a hedge against exchange rate risk.

<u>Share issue</u>

A **share issue** would require 19 million new shares (ie 1 new Groots share for approximately 2.9 shares in Cocomos – see part (a) above). This would increase Groots share capital by nearly 8% to 264 million. Assuming no change in share value, the gearing will drop from 23% debt to 22%, as seen in the table below.

Before issue	*No*	*Price*	*Value €m*	*Gearing*
Shares	245	6.85	1,678	77%
Loan stock	475	105.5%	501	23%
			2,179	
After issue				
Shares	264	6.85	1,808	78%
Loan stock			501	22%
			2,309	

The major shareholders of Groots will see their shareholdings diluted by about 7%, also a **dilution of earnings per share** and the directors of Cocomos and their families, who own 51% of Cocomos, will end up owning approximately 3.5% of Groots' shares, a proportion comparable with the existing board of Groots, whose holding will drop to approximately 7.4% from 8%. A share issue will therefore probably imply that Cocomos' management are given a significant role on the board of Groots.

<u>Cash purchase</u>

A **cash acquisition** would mean the purchase consideration could be less, say €120 million instead of €130 million. This would have to be financed by borrowing, which would therefore raise gearing significantly to about 27% debt as shown below.

	Value €m	*Gearing*
Shares	1,678	73%
Loan stock (501+ 120)	621	27%
	2,299	

<u>Use of debt</u>

The advantage of **debt financing** is that it is cheap and attracts **tax relief on interest**, and the disadvantage is that shareholders' financial risk increases. If we follow the **Modigliani-Miller** approach to analysing this problem, at the level of gearing in question (which is not unduly high) the most significant factor is the beneficial one of tax relief on debt, which will create an increase in shareholder value of approximately €120m × 25% (the tax rate), that is €30m. However

Modigliani and Miller assume fixed interest debt: a variable rate loan would increase interest rate risk.

If the company can raise Caribbean dollars debt finance, this would be a good way of **reducing the currency risk** of owning a Caribbean investment.

Attitude of shareholders

The different groups of shareholders in Cocomos are likely to have **different attitudes** to the **offer of cash or shares**.

(1)   The **local pension fund and most small shareholders in** the Caribbean will probably **not want shares** in a British company, as this will bring currency risk. They will therefore prefer cash.

(2)   The **wealthy individual investors** will probably be **less averse to a share issue**, but may prefer to keep this part of their portfolio in the Caribbean.

(3)   The **directors of Cocomos** and their families may be **very interested** in a share issue by Groots as this may enable some of them to gain board positions and exert influence on a much larger trading unit. For the acquisition to succeed it is probably necessary that some of the Cocomos directors receive shares in Groots.

On balance therefore, we recommend that Groots makes an offer involving a share issue with a cash alternative, such that investors can choose the method that is beneficial to them.

(iii)   Strategies for enhancing the combined value of the company following the acquisition

These strategies should be **developed** and **agreed** before the acquisition is finalised. It is essential that the board is able to communicate its plans to all interested parties as soon as possible in order to maintain the confidence of investors and staff.

The strategies that need to be pursued are:

Management of the group

There needs to be **quick agreement** on the **composition of the board of directors** and **action taken where necessary** to prevent any disputes. **Management of the segments** within the business will need to be **agreed**, taking account of the changes introduced, as discussed below. **Corporate objectives** will need to be **agreed** and **harmonised,** and there may be cultural differences in methods of operation that need to be understood, and either welcomed or eliminated.

Elimination of duplicated costs and sale of duplicated assets

These will occur across the **business functions** of the combined organisation – not just in the acquired company - including purchasing, marketing, finance and administration. A list of these **duplicated activities** is needed, together with a plan for **actioning their elimination**, including redundancies, closure of offices, sales of duplicated buildings and other assets. This plan should be carried out in a controlled fashion, especially **redundancies** and **ending of franchises,** where necessary. The importance of this aspect of the merger is that it has a direct 100% effect on the 'bottom line' and will be expected by shareholders.

Decision on the core business: elimination or sale of fringe activities

Sometimes businesses maintain sections of their business simply to increase their **turnover or status** or because of **directors' special interests.** Frequently these activities consume much management time. Because it makes the firm larger, the merger provides an excuse for **eliminating such fringe activities** and provides the opportunity for **focusing on the core business.** Thus, for example, it may be that certain parts of Groots or Cocomos are worth more to other companies and can be beneficially sold at this stage.

Marketing strategy and the business model

This needs so far as possible to be **harmonised** across the group. Specifically in Cocomos' case, a decision needs to be made on whether the **franchising of outlets** will be **continued,** or whether all outlets will be brought in-house. There will be opportunities for cross-selling products between customers of the two companies. In a 'fashion' business, this is very powerful.

Business and risk management strategies

There will be opportunities to **streamline all business strategies** in the group (eg supply chain, finance, administration, information technology). These should all be reviewed. The directors also need to carry out a detailed **risk management programme,** assessing the group's revised **risk appetite**, and analysing key risks such as economic, political and cultural.

Stakeholder relationships

All **stakeholder groups** (eg investors, employees, customers) should be managed by appointed directors. A communication plan should be produced and actioned for each group.

(iv)   Benefits and limitations of a post-completion audit and review

Post-completion audits

A post completion audit (PCA) is an independent appraisal of a project after it is completed, with the objective of evaluating the strengths and weaknesses during the various project stages.

Key issues

Specifically in the case of an acquisition decision, the many questions the company will need answered include:

- Were the **estimates and arguments** that led to the **acquisition realistic?** Or were they over-optimistic or pessimistic?
- Were the **budgets** set before and after the **acquisition realistic?** Did managers have a fair chance of implementing the necessary plans?
- Were there **some plans** which managers were too reluctant to carry out and why?
- What factors were **left out of the original plans** that proved to be significant?
- What **positive factors arose** which meant that performance was better than expected?
- Were there **short term gains** which prevented longer term advantages?

Information requirements

The success of a PCA depends on the **availability of information** that, in turn, depends on the quality of records that have been kept and on the availability of staff, who may have left if a project turned out a failure.

Advantages of PCAs

(1)   A PCA forces assessment of why actual results might have differed from expected results. This may impact upon how the **acquired company** is **managed.**

(2)   A PCA will **document lessons** that need to be learned and can potentially greatly **assist in improving the appraisal, implementation and control** of future projects.

(3)   A PCA can also evidence for **appraising the performance of managers** and **training** future managers.

Disadvantages of PCAs

(1)   A PCA can be **time-consuming.**

(2)   A PCA can be **costly in terms of the time** of the senior staff needed to carry out the audit, and the time of the managers in responding to the audit.

(3)   A PCA can be sometimes **demotivational** when managers have already learned their lessons and do not want to be reminded of the mistakes they made.

(4)   A PCA may have difficulty identifying **controllable** and **non-controllable** factors.

(5)   The **strategic benefits** of the merger may only **materialise** after the PCA has been carried out.

83 GAS

Text references. Investment appraisal calculations and risk are explained in Chapter 11. Equity issues and share markets are covered in Chapter 5.

Top tips. The calculations in (a) don't seem to have much relevance for the rest of the answer. The tax assumption could alternatively have been taking a tax credit for the year 1 loss. (b) is a list of many of the main risks you will have seen in Paper P3 *Performance strategy*. (c) requires a good knowledge of the efficient markets hypothesis, particularly the semi-strong version, and how share price models can be affected.

Easy marks. Hopefully use of your P3 knowledge should have enabled you to score heavily in (b).

Examiner's comments. In part (a), candidates made a good attempt at scheduling the cash flows and calculating NPV but some had difficulties in differentiating between profit and cash flows.

Part (b) was generally done quite well but few candidates picked up the key issue of high dependency of the result on the estimated realisable value of the plant and equipment. The calculations in part (c)(ii) were not done well and there was limited discussion.

(a)   Investment criterion 1: Accounting rate of return

Year	1	2	3	4 - 10
	B\$ m	B\$ m	B\$ m	B\$ m
Net operating cash flows	20	150	250	300
Depreciation	(35)	(35)	(35)	(35)
Accounting profit before interest and tax	(15)	115	215	265

There is no interest associated with the project.

Average accounting profit is [-15 + 115 + 215 + (7 × 265)] / 10 = B\$ 217 million.

Project investment	Year 0	Year 10
	B\$ m	B\$ m
Plant and equipment	700	350
Working capital	50	40
	750	390

Average investment in the project = (opening value + closing value) / 2 = (750 + 390) / 2 = B\$ 570 million

Accounting rate of return = 217 / 570 = **38%**. This is well above the minimum investment criterion of 25% per annum.

Investment criterion 2: Net present value at 10.5% discount rate

Tax allowances on the plant and equipment are the **same** as the accounting depreciation. Because GAS plc has no other projects in Bustan, it is assumed that its loss in year 1 will be carried forward to year 2, resulting in the following tax payments (B\$ million):

Year 1:	Zero
Year 2:	20% × 100 = 20
Year 3:	20% × 215 = 43
Years 4–10:	20% × 265 = 53.

GAS plc's project discount rate in pounds k(£) is 10.5%. There are two ways of finding the NPV:

1   **Converting cash flows to £ and discounting at 10.5%;** or

2   **Discounting the B\$ cash flows at the equivalent discount rate in** B\$ and then converting the NPV to £ at the spot rate.

Although the first method sounds easier, it results in the need to treat each of the 10 years separately, because the exchange rate will change each year. The second method will therefore be used, as it allows the use of annuity factors.

GAS plc's **project discount rate in Bustan dollars k(B\$)** can be found by using the **adjusted discount rate formula** given in the formula sheet. This compares the future spot rate in 12 months' time with the current spot rate and applying to the UK discount rate of 10.5%.

Future spot rate £/B$ = Spot rate £/B$ x [(1 + Bustan interest rate)/(1 + UK interest rate)]

Future spot rate £/B$ = 0.7778 x (1.1/1.048)

Future spot rate £/B$ = 0.8164

Adjusted discount rate

$$\frac{(1 + \text{annual discount rate B\$})}{(1 + \text{annual discount rate £})} = \frac{\text{Future spot rate £/B\$ in 12 months' time}}{\text{Spot rate £/B\$}}$$

$$\frac{(1 + \text{annual discount rate B\$})}{1.105} = \frac{0.8164}{0.7778}$$

(1 + annual discount rate B$) = (0.8164/0.7778) x 1.105

Annual discount rate B$ = 15.98% (say 16%) which is the discount rate that will be used on the post tax project cash flows in B$.

NPV of Bustan cash flow (B$ million)

Year	0	1	2	3	4 - 10	10
Plant and equipment	(700)					350
Working capital	(50)					40
Net operating cash flows		20	150	250	300	
Tax payable			(20)	(43)	(53)	
Net cash flow	(750)	20	130	207	247	390
Discount rate 16%	1.000	0.862	0.743	0.641	2.587	0.227
PV	(750)	17.2	96.6	132.7	639.0	88.5
NPV B$	224.0					

The NPV in £ is found by converting at the spot rate, B$ 0.7778 = £1:

NPV of Bustan cash flows in £ million = 224.0 / 0.7778 = 288.0.

The remaining cash flows of the project are the UK tax payments. Because of the double tax agreement, these will be 30% – 20% = 10% of the taxable profits. Thus UK tax will be half of the tax paid in Bustan, but one year later.

For convenience of calculation, the UK tax payments are treated as if they are in B$ and their NPV is converted at the spot rate.

Year	3	4	5 - 11
Additional tax payable in UK	(10.0)	(21.5)	(26.5)
Discount rate 16%	0.641	0.552	2.231
PV	(6.4)	(11.9)	(59.1)
NPV B$	(77.4)		

PV of UK tax payments in £ million = (77.4) / 0.7778 = (99.5)

Thus the net present value of the project in £ million is 288.0 – 99.5 = **£189 million**.

This is a high positive net present value, indicating that investment criterion 2 is satisfied.

(b) Major risk issues

When evaluating the project there is a wide range of risks that need to be considered. Although overlapping, these can be grouped into operating risks, commercial risks, political risks and financial risks.

Operating risks

These are the risks associated with **electricity generation** and **power supply systems.** GAS plc has experience of this business across Europe and will factor in its normal business risks, but there may be **additional operational risks** when working in Bustan, for example from lower skill levels, unknown geographical terrain, non-availability of materials and poor infrastructure. These risks should be **quantified** and **minimised** by carrying out as much research as possible and building appropriate estimates into the analysis where necessary.

The **realisable value estimated for plant and equipment** is a major assumption and there is a significant risk that this could prove to be over-optimistic. The present value of this disposal value is $350m × 0.227 = $79.45m = £102m. This means that even if the disposal value was zero, the project would still have a positive NPV.

Commercial risks

Most of these result from **competition** (both direct and for substitute sources of power) and need to be evaluated. **Pricing estimates** need to be **examined carefully**, particularly because the Bustan dollar is likely to decline (see financial risks below).

Cultural risks

Other commercial risks may result from **differences in the law and culture** of Europe and Bustan. For example, misunderstandings or conflicting business protocols may cause delays.

Political risks

The government of Bustan (or a future government headed by another political party) may take action that is **detrimental to the profitability** of GAS's operations. For example, it may **impose price controls** on electricity supplies, **increase taxation** or **introduce exchange controls** on repatriated profits. These risks should be minimised so far as possible by conducting research and signing agreements with the government (eg on tax rates and profit repatriation).

Financial risks

The financial risks that GAS will face will be an extension of what it already faces in Europe: gearing, interest rate risk and currency risk. Since the project is all equity financed, the directors have chosen **not to increase gearing** or **interest rate risk.** This policy increases the **currency risk** of their operations in Bustan, because the whole value of their operating profit from Bustan will vary with fluctuations in the Bustan dollar. Declines in the value of the B$ will need to be countered by **price increases,** which may be politically unacceptable in some circumstances. An alternative method of financing which could hedge some of this currency risk is to take out a **substantial loan** in **Bustan dollars**.

(c)   To: The Board of Directors of GAS plc
        From: Management Consultants

Report on share price volatility and estimation of a fair valuation of the shares of GAS plc

You have asked us to provide some possible explanations for the increased volatility of GAS plc's share price in 20X4 and 20X5, to advise on a fair market price for the shares, and to explain how and to what extent the directors can influence the price of the company's shares.

(i)   Volatility of share price movements

No perfect models of share valuation or share price movements exist. The following notes are therefore intended as partial explanations for the share price volatility. They are based on the **efficient market hypothesis** and the **capital asset pricing model**, two areas of theory that, despite their imperfections, have provided useful analyses of many financial management problems.

Efficient markets hypothesis

The **efficient market hypothesis** (semi strong form) postulates that share prices **swiftly and rationally reflect all information** that is **publicly available**. During this whole period, the market has reacted to any favourable or unfavourable information about the Bustan economy by marking GAS shares up or down accordingly. In addition, in the period to June 20X4 there were uncertainties as to the company's future expansion plans.

June 20X4 announcement

The announcement in June 20X4 ended speculation on the company's intentions but added to market uncertainties for many reasons including:

- The **proposed project** was **so large**
- It would require a **major rights issue**, which is unpopular with some shareholders
- There was **no proposed mechanism** for hedging currency risk on the project

- The proposal could have been **rejected or delayed** by the Bustan government. Thus in the period to January 20X5, further sources of information about Bustan or Gas plc had an increased effect on share price

On 1 January 20X5, the Board's press release **clarified the company's success** in winning the project but the accompanying dividend forecast has been treated with some scepticism, resulting in further uncertainties and fluctuations in the share price.

Capital asset pricing model

The **capital asset pricing model** suggests that much of the company's share price volatility that has been experienced is **irrelevant** to investors who hold diversified portfolios, because specific company risks are cancelled out when a broad portfolio of investments is held. Thus you should not be too concerned about overall share price volatility, but base your decisions on the company's systematic risk (represented by its beta factor).

(ii) Fair market price for GAS plc's shares in January 20X5

The **fairest** valuation for a company's shares would be based on **all relevant information** at the time. However, the implication of the efficient market hypothesis (semi-strong form) is that the actual share price will be based on **public information only.**

The market does not have the cash flow forecast for the Bustan project and analysts will therefore either use **other available information**, such as the directors' dividend forecast, or else try to use available public information to construct their own cash forecast for the project.

Effect of the rights issue on the share price

The share price at 31 December 20X4 was 335 pence ex div. The effect of the 1 for 4 rights issue on this price (in isolation of any project effects) can be easily computed.

The number of shares issued to fund the plant and equipment (1 for 4 rights issue) is $\frac{1}{4} \times 1,200$ million = 300 million. This implies an issue price of approximately:

$$\frac{700 \div 0.7778}{300} = 300 \text{ pence (ignoring issue costs)}$$

The theoretical ex rights price of the shares (ignoring the project NPV which is not public information) is **328 pence**, as shown below (4,920m / 1,500m).

Shares	Number (million)	Value £	Total £m
Original	1,200	3.35	4,020
New	300	3.00	900
Total	1,500	3.28	4,920

Effect of the project NPV

If the market was told that the **proposed project** has a **positive expected NPV** of £189 million, and if this figure were believed by the market, then the shares should increase in value by £189 million to a total value of £5,109 million, that is a value per share of **341 pence**. This is the closest we can get to a fair value of the shares.

Effect of the directors' dividend forecast

The market can use the revised dividend forecast to estimate a share value, using the company's cost of equity. The estimate you have given us of the shareholders' required return on equity is 9.4% per annum.

Using the **dividend valuation model**, based on the dividend of 14 pence and the company's share price of 335 pence at 31 December 20X4, and assuming that the market expected a 5% growth rate in dividends (equal to the historical growth rate), the company's cost of equity capital can be estimated as:

$$\left(\frac{14 \times 1.05}{335}\right) + 0.05 = 0.094 \text{ or } 9.4\%. \text{ We therefore concur with your estimate.}$$

If the directors' revised dividend forecast on 1 January 20X5 is believed by the market, the revised value per share, based on the dividend valuation model can be estimated in two stages:

Stage 1: PV of first three years' constant dividends

Year	Div (pence)	DF at 9.4%	PV (pence)
1 (20X5)	14	0.914	12.80
2 (20X6)	14	0.836	11.70
3 (20X7)	14	0.764	10.70
			35.20

Stage 2: PV of the perpetuity from year 4 of dividends growing at 7% per year.

The present value as at *end of year 3* = $(14 \times 1.07) / (0.094 - 0.07) = 624.17$ pence.

This has a present value as at year 0 of $624.17 \times 0.764 = 476.87$ pence.

Thus the total value per share = $35 + 477 = $ **512 pence**.

Our conclusion is that the dividend forecast provided by the directors is over-optimistic. An estimate of 7% growth *to perpetuity* when the cost of funds is only 9.4% is impossible in practice. The closest figure to the fair market value is **341 pence**.

(iii)   The extent to which directors can influence their entity's share price

Importance of confidentiality

Directors of public companies cannot make all information about their entities available to the market without running the risk of giving away information to competitors. It is therefore vital that directors can be **trusted to keep information secret** when necessary. However, risk aversion or a sense of management power will often lead directors to withhold company information from the market when it would be better for it to be disclosed.

Consequences for shareholders

In public companies, therefore, shareholders suffer from a **lack of inside knowledge** about company performance and plans, and this can result in decisions to buy or sell shares (and resulting share prices) based on false or partial information.

Impact of directors' statements

In this situation, directors can **greatly influence share prices** by the statements they make to the market, combined with their reputation for accuracy and truth (or otherwise). Because directors are in a position to make far-reaching strategic decisions using information that is not available to shareholders, their reputations can have a significant effect on share value. In some cases a director can improve a company's share price simply by joining the board.

In the situation of GAS plc it would have been better to issue a **forecast NPV** of the new project than to issue a vague dividend forecast that is clearly over-optimistic.

84 PM

Text references. Business valuation is covered in Chapter 15 and post-merger value enhancing strategies in Chapter 16.

Top tips. You must read this question very carefully as it is easier than you might at first think! It is not a general valuation question so only use the earnings and P/E information given to you. In part (b), you must include supporting calculations to your report (in appendices) and there are marks for good presentation and structure.

Easy marks. The discussion areas in part (b) are a source of easy marks. You should make sure you do not spend so much time on part (a) that this part of the question is rushed.

Examiner's comments. This question was particularly poorly attempted, mainly because candidates did not read the scenario properly. Many completely misunderstood the question and assumed it was a general valuation question. They therefore wasted valuable time calculating values using net assets, dividend valuation models etc.

(a)   Workings

Terms of offer   = 1 PM share for 2 NQ stock units

$$= \frac{850m}{2} \text{ new PM shares}$$

$$= 425m$$

Total number of PM shares = 425m + 950m = 1,375m

To get market capitalisation of £6,905m, implies a **share price** of 6,905/1,375 = 502p

EPS = 31.65p so **P/E** = $\dfrac{502}{31.65}$ = 15.86

Current EPS

PM	NQ
273/950 = 28.7p	300/850 = 35.3c @ 1.85 = 19.1p

Current P/E ratios

PM	NQ
456/28.7 = 15.9	450/35.3 = 12.75

An EPS of 31.65 pence implies combined post merger earnings of 31.65p × 1,375 = £435m.

Combined earnings for y/e 31/3/X6 = 273 + (300/1.85) = £435m

Current market capitalisation

PM	NQ
950 × 4.56 = £4,332	850 × 4.5 = $3,825 @1.85 = £2,068

Number of shares in merged entity

PM	NQ	Post-merger
950	425	1,375
69%	31%	100%

(i)   The post merger values are estimated as a **market capitalisation** of £6,905 million and **EPS** of 31.65 pence. As can be seen in the workings, the total number of PM shares after the merger would be 1,375 and combined earnings with an exchange rate of £/$1.85 are £435m. This gives the EPS of approximately 31.65 pence.

A **P/E ratio** of 15.86 has been used to generate a market capitalisation of £6,905m. The current P/E of PM is 15.9 and that of NQ is 12.75. It has therefore been assumed that a P/E ratio similar to that of PM rather than NQ will apply post-merger. This is consistent with the CEO of PM's view that PM's growth rating can be applied to NQ's earnings.

(ii)   If we assume that the forecast market capitalisation of £6,905m will apply post-merger, the share prices will be:

PM: £6,905/1,375m shares = £5.02 (current price is £4.46 per share)
The market capitalisation of PM's shares will increase to 950m shares × £5.02 = £4,769m

NQ: £5.02 (see above) × 0.5 (1 PM share is offered for each 2 NQ shares) = £2.51
This is $4.64 (£2.51 × 1.85) compared to $4.50 today.

The market capitalisation of NQ's shares will increase to 850m × £2.51 = £2,134m.

The shareholders of both companies will therefore **benefit** from this proposed merger, but only if the P/E ratio of PM can be applied to the group after the acquisition. Much will depend on the market's views of the proposed merger and whether it believes that synergies will result from it.

(iii) The forecast market capitalisation of £6,905m and the sale of the software licences for £100m would produce a total **maximum value** for the merged entity of £7,005m. The value of NQ as part of this entity would be £7,005m – £4,332m (the current value of PM) = £2,673m. This gives a value of 314p for each stock unit, equating to approximately 1 PM share for 1.5 (456/314) NQ shares.

(b) To: The Board of PM
From: Financial adviser
Re: Issues concerning the merger of PM Industries plc with NQ Inc
Date: May 20X6

1 Introduction

This report will evaluate and discuss the merger of PM with NQ. The following issues will be discussed:

- How the merger might contribute to the achievement of PM's financial objectives
- External economic forces that might help or hinder the achievement of the merger's financial objectives
- Post-merger value enhancing strategies that could increase shareholder wealth

2 The achievement of PM's financial objectives

The current financial objectives are:

- To increase EPS by 5% per annum
- To maintain a gearing ratio below 30%
- To maintain a P/E ratio above the industry average

2.1 EPS

Earnings for the past 5 years have increased by 4.95% for PM per annum and by 4.66% for NQ (see Appendix 1). If this were to continue after the merger, this **objective would not be achieved**. However, the expectation from the merger is that higher growth can be achieved. This would presumably come from NQ rather than PM, as PM has already divested the poor performing business units and it is debateable how much more growth can come from volume in a relatively mature market.

PM has higher margins than NQ and the expectation would be that higher margins could be achieved post-merger at NQ. However, earnings as a percentage of revenue have been falling year on year for both companies as would be expected in a mature market, so the 5% growth in EPS looks ambitious.

2.2 Gearing

Appendix 2 shows the calculation of current gearing for the two companies and that of the merged entity. Both companies have gearing below the financial objective level of 30%. A share exchange would reduce the gearing ratio to 21.8%. However, a cash offer would involve substantial borrowing and PM's current gearing percentage of 27.9% does not leave much room for manoeuvre. Any fall in share price as a result of the bid will also **endanger the achievement of this objective**.

It is however a relatively low level of gearing in today's financial climate and the Board might want to consider changing this financial objective should it become necessary.

2.3 P/E ratio

PM's P/E ratio is currently 15.9 with an industry average of 14 and therefore meets the objective. NQ's P/E ratio is 12.75 with an industry average of 13 and therefore does not meet the objective. However the bid calculations all involve an assumption that the P/E of the combined company will be nearer to that of PM. Appendix 3 shows that the P/E of the merged entity may be a weighted average of approximately 15, still above the industry average. This will depend entirely on the **market's perception of the merged company** and whether it believes that synergies will be obtained. Potential downside risks include integration problems and exchange rate volatility.

3 External economic forces

3.1 Economic conditions

PM has widespread commercial and industrial interests worldwide and as such has a **diversified portfolio** in terms of industrial sectors and geographic regions. This should mean that the risks from downturns in economies should be reduced as not all economies and sectors will be affected to the same extent. However, NQ obtains 75%, and the combined company would have around

50%, of its revenues from the US and would therefore be heavily affected by any problems with the US economy.

A general crash in stock markets could affect the gearing and P/E ratios.

3.2 Exchange rates

A globally trading organisation will be subject to the risks associated with movements in exchange rates. Changes in inflation and interest rates can affect exchange rates and cause uncertainty. For example, higher costs or lower revenues and accounting losses as a result of adverse movements in exchange rates may have a serious impact.

A policy to deal with the risks associated with exchange rates needs to be in place. **Economic exposure** from exchange rate movements can be hedged by matching assets and liabilities and by diversification. **Transaction risk** can be hedged by matching receipts and payments, invoicing in own currency and leading and lagging the times that cash is received and paid.

The organisation may decide to use money market hedges and specialist personnel will be needed.

3.3 Government interference

The merged entity may be subject to competition controls, particularly in the pharmaceutical materials sector, where PM is already market leader in the UK and Europe.

Strategies to limit the effects of political risk include negotiation with host governments, re-locating production or threatening withdrawal.

4 Post-merger value enhancing strategies

Many mergers fail to achieve their full potential because of lack of attention paid to **post-acquisition integration**. A clear programme therefore needs to be in place, designed to re-define objectives and strategy and take appropriate care of the human element.

The first stage would be to conduct a **position audit** to enable a clear understanding of the culture and operations of NQ. Both physical and human assets should be examined in order to get a clear picture. An **integration strategy** should then be devised before the merger is finalised. There needs to be a clear plan for the integration of the two organisations. This plan should deal with problems such as differences in management styles, information technology incompatibilities and resistance to the merger from employees.

Synergies will result from efficiency gains and/or asset sales, which will probably involve redundancies. These will need to be carefully considered and managed in terms of their effect on the workforce. Successful post-acquisition integration requires careful management of the human factor to avoid loss of motivation.

PF Drucker suggested **five golden rules** for the process of post-acquisition integration:

Rule 1	There should be a 'common core of unity' shared by the acquiror and acquiree. The ties should involve overlapping characteristics such as shared technology and markets, and not just financial links.
Rule 2	The acquiror should ask 'What can we offer them?' as well as 'What's in it for us?'
Rule 3	The acquiror should treat the products, markets and customers of the acquired company with respect, and not disparagingly.
Rule 4	The acquiring company should provide top management with relevant skills for the acquired company within a year.
Rule 5	Cross-company promotions of staff should occur within one year.

Corporate objectives may need to be re-defined and strategic plans developed for the merged entity. The **cost of capital** should also be re-evaluated as it may be reduced as a result of the merger.

5   Conclusion

This report has demonstrated that the three stated objectives will probably be achieved post-merger. Earnings growth may be boosted by synergies and savings achieved from the merger, PM's P/E ratio is likely to stay above the industry average and gearing will fall if shareholders accept a share exchange. However there are significant downside risks relating to all three objectives.

Appendix 1

Earnings growth:

PM	NQ
$273 = 225(1 + g)^4$	$300 = 250(1 + g)^4$
$1 + g = 1.0495$	$1 + g = 1.0466$
$g = 4.95\%$	$g = 4.66\%$

Appendix 2

PM	NQ	Merged entity
Debt = 1.05 × 1,150 = £1,208	Debt = $550	Debt = 1,208 + (550/1.85) = £1,505
Equity = 950 × 4.56 = £4,332	Equity = 850 × 4.5 = $3,825	Equity = £6,905
Gearing % = 1,208/4,332 = 27.9%	Gearing % = 550/3,825 = 14.4%	Gearing % = $\dfrac{1,505}{6,905} = 21.8\%$

Appendix 3

Weighted average P/E:

PM	NQ	Merged entity
15.9 × 69% = 11	12.75 × 31% = 4	15

85 SHINE

Text references. Investment appraisal methods are covered in Chapter 11 and the role of the Treasury department in Chapter 10.

Top tips. Parts (a) and (b) are straightforward calculations that need a logical, methodical approach. Save time by only doing the calculations necessary. For example, do not write out a complete NPV calculation for every scenario. Part (c)(iii) is **not** asking you to write everything you know about treasury and finance departments. Make sure you answer the actual question.

Easy marks. Part (a) consists of very straightforward NPV calculations for twelve marks. Part (b) has some unusual calculations but is straightforward as long as you can remember what to do with an exchange rate gain.

Four marks are available for structure and presentation so use clear tables for the calculations and a proper format in part (b).

Examiner's comments. Part (a) was generally answered very well but the report sections for part (c) were generally quite poor. A fundamental problem was an inability to apply knowledge to the scenario provided.

(a) NPV of the cash flows for the investment

Scenario 1: Constant exchange rate; tax rate 10%

	Year	$m	Ex. rate €/$	€m	12% discount factors	PV €m
Initial investment	0	(200)	1.10	(181.8)	1.000	(181.8)
Residual value	4	50	1.10	45.4	0.636	28.9
Pre-tax operating net cash inflows	1 to 4	70	1.10	63.6	3.037	193.2
Tax on operating cash flows	1 to 4	(7)	1.10	(6.4)	3.037	(19.4)
NPV						20.9

The NPV is positive: **€20.9 million**.

Scenario 2: Constant exchange rate; tax rate 25%

The figures will be the same except that the tax on operating cash flows is 150% (15/10 × 100) higher. Thus the NPV will be 20.9 – [19.4 × 15/10] = 20.9 – 29.1 = **€(8.2 million)**.

Scenario 3: Euro strengthens against dollar by 7% a year; tax rate 10%

The exchange rate is found by multiplying by 1.07 each year.

	Year	$m	Ex. rate €/$	€m	12%	PV
Initial investment	0	(200)	1.10	(181.8)	1.000	(81.8)
After tax cash flows (90%)	1	63	1.18	53.4	0.893	47.7
"	2	63	1.26	50.0	0.797	39.9
"	3	63	1.35	46.7	0.712	33.2
"	4	63	1.44	43.8	0.636	27.8
Residual value	4	50	1.44	34.7	0.636	22.1
NPV						(11.1)

The NPV is negative: **€(11.1 million)**.

Scenario 4: Euro strengthens against dollar by 7% a year; tax rate 25%

	Year	$m	Ex. rate €/$	€m	12%	PV
Initial investment	0	(200)	1.10	(181.8)	1.000	(181.8)
After tax cash flows (75%)	1	52.5	1.18	44.5	0.893	39.7
"	2	52.5	1.26	41.7	0.797	33.2
"	3	52.5	1.35	38.9	0.712	27.7
"	4	52.5	1.44	36.5	0.636	23.2
Residual value	4	50	1.44	34.7	0.636	22.1
						(35.9)

The NPV is negative: **€(35.9 million)**.

(b) Forecast statement of financial position of the SHINE group at 31 December 20X6

1 Financing with long term borrowings denominated in euros

Scenario	A € million	B € million
Total assets	28,182 (W1)	28,143 (W2)
Equity		
Share capital	3,000	3,000
Retained earnings (balance)	8,300	8,261
	11,300	11,261
Non-current liabilities		
Floating rate borrowings: Euros	4,182 (W3)	4,182 (W3)
Current liabilities	12,700	12,700
Total equity and liabilities	28,182	28,143
Gearing: Debt / (Debt + Equity)	27%	27%

2   Financing with long term borrowings denominated in US dollars

Scenario	A	B
	€ million	€ million
Total assets	28,182 (W1)	28,143 (W2)
Equity		
Share capital	3,000	3,000
Retained earnings (balance)	8,300	8,300
	11,300	11,300
Non-current liabilities		
Floating rate borrowings: Euros	4,000	4,000
US dollars	182	143 (W4)
	4,182	4,143
Current liabilities	12,700	12,700
Total equity and liabilities	28,182	28,143
Gearing: Debt / (Debt + Equity)	27%	27%

Workings

1   28,000 + (200/1.1) = €28,182m
2   28,000 + (200/1.4) = €28,143m
3   4,000 + (200/1.1) = €4,182m
4   200/1.4 = €143m

(c)   To: Board of Directors, SHINE Group
From: Finance Director

Evaluation and implementation of the proposed wind farm project

Introduction

The proposed wind farm project enables SHINE to further the key objective of developing renewable energy sources. The purpose behind this objective is not just to make high financial returns but also to **protect and enhance our reputation** as a socially and environmentally caring global energy organisation. As such, the project is assured extensive media coverage following recent television and investor campaigns.

This report offers advice and opinions on three areas:

- Constraints affecting the investment decision
- The alternative proposed financing structures
- The inter-related roles of the treasury and finance departments when making decisions of this type

(i)   Internal and external constraints affecting the investment decision

Within the SHINE organisation, the investment decision is constrained by internal constraints:

(1)   Gearing

The group has an objective to keep gearing below 40%. This is a potential constraint affecting any investment that will result in extra debt.

(2)   The need to achieve a reasonable financial return from the project

Although the financial returns are not required to be high, we cannot, as a public company, **afford to make high losses** on projects of this type. This would damage shareholder confidence.

(3)   Incomplete knowledge and skills

We are dealing with technological areas that are relatively new to us and we also suffer from a **lack of knowledge** of the local laws and culture. Steps will need to be taken to fill this information gap.

(4)   <u>Management time and resources</u>

Development of these cutting-edge projects uses up considerable amounts of management time at all levels. It is difficult to quantify this effect, but the danger is that existing profitable business suffers. Effective project management is essential.

A number of **external constraints** on the project are emerging:

(1)   Local protest – farmers

A group of farmers is concerned with the possibility of acid water from boreholes, and we need to explore ways in which this can be **prevented**, and the associated **costs** of doing so.

(2)   <u>Local protest – executive homeowners</u>

The damage done to the previously unspoiled views from these homes cannot be avoided. We need to **defuse** this protest before it gains momentum in the local community, and this may require compensation or purchase of some of the properties.

(3)   <u>Risk of future tax increases</u>

The tax on this type of project is at the moment at a preferential rate of 10%, but the local government is seriously considering abolishing this concession, which would raise the tax rate to 25%. Our calculations (see part (a)) show that this would be likely to cost between €25 – €30 million and would **remove any chance of a positive financial return**. We need to consult with local experts and make a strategic decision whether to live with this risk or to take positive steps to **mitigate** it, for example by setting up or assisting a local lobby group, or by negotiating a project-specific tax concession.

(4)   <u>Exchange rate risk</u>

As with all foreign projects we run the risk that the currency in which we expect to earn profits (US dollars) will decline against our home currency (Euro). Our calculations show that a steady strengthening of the euro against the dollar of 7% per year for four years would cost between €28 – €30 million. This risk can be **mitigated** by financing the project with a US dollar loan, as explained in (ii) below.

(5)   <u>Volatility of energy prices</u>

Risks for this project are estimated to be normal for our business.

(ii)   <u>Proposed alternative financing structures</u>

Two financing structures have been proposed by treasury department: long term borrowing in either euros or US dollars. Both of these methods pass the test that **gearing** (debt divided by the total of equity plus debt) should not become greater then 40%.

The differences between these methods are:

- They may have different **interest costs** in real terms; and
- They certainly have different effects on overall **exchange rate risk**.

<u>Interest costs</u>

As regards **interest costs**, a careful comparison must be made before making a decision. If borrowing in one currency appears cheaper than in another, this effect can and will often be removed by movements in the exchange rate between the currencies. Nevertheless there can be differences between the real interest costs of the loans, for example because the company may have a **comparative advantage** when borrowing in its own main currency, the euro.

<u>Exchange rate risk</u>

As regards **exchange rate risk**, a US dollar loan will be subject to substantial exchange gains or losses in response to **currency movements**, and these show up as **translation** gains or losses in the statement of financial position and real gains or losses in **cash flows** (economic exposure).

However when the US dollar loan is used to finance a project that generates income in the same currency (US dollars), exchange losses on the earnings are substantially offset by exchange gains on the loan. Similarly exchange gains on the earnings are substantially offset by exchange losses on the loan. This compensating effect is known as a '**currency hedge**' and has the effect of making

overall cash flows more predictable and less risky if the company borrows in the same currency as the project earnings.

By contrast, the euro loan has no risk in itself but fails to provide any hedge against exchange risk on the US dollar earnings of the project, so that the overall combination of project and finance is more **risky** if the company borrows in euros than if it borrows in dollars.

Recommendation

The **objective** of this project is to **avoid making losses** rather than to make high profits. The hedging effect of the US dollar loan will help achieve this and we therefore recommend that the project should be financed by borrowing in US dollars.

(iii)   Roles of treasury and finance departments in appraisal and implementation of the project

The roles of these two departments are interrelated during the appraisal of the project, and during project planning and implementation.

Project appraisal

During the project appraisal stage, the role of the finance department is to use information from the project forecasts to make projections of annual cash flows and profits, over the whole of the project life. These are then analysed in statements of profitability, cash flow and project appraisal, including net present value computations. Project and activity forecasts are assessed against alternatives in order to decide the **best course of action** at each stage.

During the appraisal stage, the treasury department considers the financial implications of alternative sources of project finance. The treasury department attempts to balance the cost of finance against its risk, including the appropriate mix between long term and short term finance, equity and debt (gearing) and financial risk, interest rate risk and currency risk.

The decision information produced by these two departments is inter-related. For example, foreign projects are often best financed by loans in the same currency (see (ii) above), and the borrowing capacity of a project can make it worthwhile even if its base case NPV is not good.

Project planning

Once a project has received permission to proceed, the finance department will assist with **preparation of detailed budgets** and devising an accounting and monitoring system that will produce the required **performance information** for all stakeholders.

The treasury department will make arrangements for **raising** the necessary finance, as decided during the appraisal stage, and for setting up procedures for monitoring and handling cash, managing working capital and currency and interest rate risk.

Project implementation

During project implementation, the finance department monitors financial records of actual operations against budgets and feeds back information to project managers, in order to seek explanations of variances and to encourage improvements or changes to plan where necessary.

The treasury department similarly monitors cash, working capital, currency risk and interest rate risk. It reviews financing options throughout the project. For example there may be opportunities to terminate loans and refinance, or to enter into swaps

86 Sandyfoot

> **Text references.** Investment appraisal is covered in Chapter 11, debt finance in Chapter 6 and real options in Chapter 13.
>
> **Top tips.** Be careful with the exchange rate information in part (a), it is easy to get confused as there are three types of $s. In part (b) make sure you answer each of the detailed elements of the question, there are a lot of discussion marks in this question. Don't be tempted to spend too much time on the analysis of a loan involving the sacrifice of profits. You do not need to discount the values as we are comparing like with like. As always, if you get stuck, move on.
>
> **Easy marks.** The investment appraisal in part (a) is straightforward and should provide plenty of easy marks if you use a logical approach and lay out the calculations clearly. There are three marks available for structure and presentation so use a report format and write clearly with plenty of headings.
>
> **Examiner's comments.** A key weakness was failing to read the question properly. Candidates frequently suggested home currency debt due to tax relief but the scenario stated Sandyfoot does not pay tax. Too much time was often devoted to part (a) resulting in weak part (b) answers. Many candidates were unable to evaluate and provided little more than a series of bullet points. Very few candidates provided calculations to support their method of funding answer.

(a)   <u>NPV of proposed investments</u>

<u>Alternative 1</u>

Year	0	1	2	3	4 and beyond
	Esco	Esco	Esco	Esco	Esco
	$'000	$'000	$'000	$'000	$'000
Land purchase	(6,000)				
Building costs	(3,000)				
Equipment costs	(1,000)				
Fees		1,750	2,250	2,700	2,781
Operating costs (60% of fees)		(1,050)	(1,350)	(1,620)	(1,669)
Opportunity cost of travelling (1% of fees)		(18)	(23)	(27)	(28)
Net cash flows	(10,000)	682	877	1,053	1,084
Annuity factor (W)					11.111
					12,044
12% discount factors	1.000	0.893	0.797	0.712	0.712
Present value	(10,000)	609	699	750	8,575
NPV	**633**				

<u>Working</u>

To calculate the present value in year 4 of the net cash flows in perpetuity, the net cash flow in Year 4 is multiplied by:

$$\frac{1}{r-g} = \frac{1}{0.12 - 0.03} = 11.111$$

Alternative 2

Year	0	1	2	3 to 15
	Midco	*US*	*US*	*US*
	$'000	*$'000*	*$'000*	*$'000*
Leasehold	(20,000)			
Building costs	(10,000)			
Equipment costs	(5,000)			
Fees		4,650	5,350	6,450
Operating costs (60% of fees)		(2,790)	(3,210)	(3,870)
	(35,000)	1,860	2,140	2,580
Exchange rate (W1)	6.500	1.817	1.834	1.852
	Esco	*Esco*	*Esco*	*Esco*
	$'000	*$'000*	*$'000*	*$'000*
Cash flows in Esco $s	(5,385)	1,024	1,167	1,393
Opportunity cost of lost fees		(250)	(250)	(250)
Net cash flows	(5,385)	774	917	1,143
16% discount factors (W2)	1.000	0.862	0.743	3.970
Present value	(5,385)	667	681	4,538
NPV	**501**			

Workings

1   The exchange rates are calculated using the interest rate parity formula.

Future spot rate Esco $/US$ = 1.8 × [1 + (nominal US interest rate/nominal Esco interest rate)]

$$\text{Year 1} = 1.8 \times \frac{1.05}{1.04} = 1.817$$

$$\text{Year 2} = 1.817 \times \frac{1.05}{1.04} = 1.834$$

$$\text{Year 3} = 1.834 \times \frac{1.05}{1.04} = 1.852$$

2   The discount factor for years 3 to 15 is calculated as the cumulative discount factor for t15 − cumulative discount factor for t2 = 5.575 − 1.605 = 3.970

(b)   Report

To: Chief Executive
From: Financial Manager
Re: Evaluating the investment decision and its funding
Date: May 20X7

Introduction

This report will evaluate and discuss the two alternative investment opportunities available to Sandyfoot and the methods of funding. The following issues will be discussed:

• An evaluation of the two investments
• A discussion of the advantages and disadvantages of the three methods of funding
• Recommendations about the choice of investment alternative and method of funding

(i)   An evaluation of the two investments

On the basis of the NPV calculations, Alternative 1 has an NPV of Esco $633,000 and Alternative 2 has an NPV of Esco $501,000 so Alternative 1 should be chosen. However, a number of other factors need to be considered.

(1) Risk factors

Staff issues

Staff issues are a major risk factor for both alternatives. The quality of teaching staff is a key **intangible asset** in educational establishments and both alternatives require changes to working practices and locations which teachers may find unacceptable. This could result in a **lack of availability** of good teaching staff.

Costs of travelling time for Alternative 1 may also have been **underestimated**.

Government action

Government action is a risk factor for both alternatives. Alternative 1 relies on planning permission being granted by the local authority which may not be granted, but there may be a positive impact if the area is turned into a development zone.

Alternative 2 is at risk from **political instability** and **government interference**. For example, the government may in future put restrictions on repatriation of cash flows. There is uncertainty over interest rates and inflation and these could affect the forecast cash flows.

Buildings

Buildings are a further area of risk. Alternative 1 involves the purchase of land and building of a new facility. These costs are **subject to change** and **future refurbishment costs** should also be considered.

The building costs for Alternative 2 are subject to even more uncertainty due to a **different operating environment** and there is also the risk of the unspecified price of the potential acquisition of the freehold in 15 years' time.

Forecast fees

Forecast fees may not be reliable for either alternative. As already mentioned, Midco is a new and uncertain operating environment in Alternative 2. For example, there may be effective competitors who will respond to Sandyfoot's new offering by undercutting prices for courses.

For Alternative 1, the benefits of the increased catchment area for part-time students in Esco may have been **over-estimated**. It could be useful to conduct a **sensitivity analysis** of the forecast fees and also the costs of operation.

Exchange rate risk

Exchange rate risk cannot be ignored for Alternative 2. Fees will be payable in US $s which is depreciating against the Esco $ on the basis of interest rate parity. Exchange rates are **very difficult to forecast** 15 years into the future and any change could have a significant effect on forecast cash flows.

(2) Choice of discount rates

The discount rate for Alternative 1 needs to incorporate business and financial risk and the directors believe that 12% is an adequate return. A premium of 4% has been added to the discount rate for Alternative 2 to reflect the extra risks outlined above.

This discount rate may however be too high if the inflation, political and operational risks discussed above turn out to be low.

(3) Real options

An option is the right to make a choice, a major capital investment may not always be set in stone. The real option features that are implied in the two investments are the option to abandon, the option to wait and the follow-on options. The value of such an option can be assessed and added to the appraisal computation as a benefit.

Option to abandon

An abandonment option refers to the ability to abandon the project at a certain stage in its life. If large sums are being spent, and prospects do not appear healthy, an abandonment option may be available. If the benefit streams from a project are highly **uncertain**, an

option to abandon the project if things go wrong could be highly valuable. The **riskiness** of the project is reduced and the expected NPV increased.

In this situation, Alternative 2 involves a long-term leasehold with **break clauses** in the contract at five year intervals. This cannot currently be valued as an option as the full costs are not specified. Alternative 1 does not have an option to abandon available so this makes it less valuable in this respect.

Option to wait

An option to wait is a timing option which allows resolution of uncertainty. Investments are rarely 'now or never' opportunities but we do need to consider the cash flows foregone in the period of postponement. The cost of this is balanced against the value of waiting.

Alternative 1 offers an option to wait to see if development status is granted but there is no guarantee that the Esco government will make a decision in six months' time. There has been a lot of interest in the land that is for sale so this could be a 'now or never' opportunity. The deposit paid to the seller is effectively a **call option** with a six month timescale.

Follow-on option

A follow-on option is a strategic option when the investment opportunity leads to follow-on wealth generating opportunities. For example buying new equipment could enable an organisation to develop experience and skills with the latest technology which may allow opportunities that would otherwise have been unavailable.

Alternative 1 offers the possibility of increased business in the catchment area and Alternative 2 offers the opening up of new business opportunities.

(ii)   Methods of funding

Alternative 1 has funding identified but Alternative 2 would require a choice between three methods. The amount of funding required is Esco $2,385,000 (Esco $5,385,000 capital outlay less Esco $3 million accumulated cash reserves).

(1)   Borrow in the currency of the home country

For any income generating foreign investment there is an **economic risk** that the foreign currency **depreciates**, resulting in a reduced value of income when converted to the home currency. This is particularly damaging if borrowing is in the home currency as such risk is **not hedged**. There may also be problems if the Midco government puts restrictions on repatriation of cash flows as mentioned in part (i).

A lender may not be prepared to lend with **foreign assets as security** so existing assets may need to be valued so that they can be used to raise the debt. This can be expensive and time consuming.

A normal advantage of debt finance is that interest payments are tax deductible. However Sandyfoot does not pay tax so the interest will have to be paid in full without any tax shield. The interest will amount to Esco $3,577,500 (10% of Esco $2,385,000 each year for 15 years).

(2)   Borrow in the currency of the host country

The Midco government is effectively accepting a **transfer of the economic risk** by making the loan interest-free and requiring a share of profits. Further information would be required on what would happen if profits fell to nil or a very low level. For example, assets could be seized if the 'dividend' was too low.

Assuming that profits are as predicted, the cost of the borrowing is Esco $2,984,000 (see workings below) so this is a cheaper option than the first method outlined above. However, if profits are higher than expected, this could become a more expensive option.

Working

Year	1	2	3	4–15 (12 years)
	Esco	Esco	Esco	Esco
	$'000	$'000	$'000	$'000
Cash flows	1,024	1,167	1,393	16,716
Depreciation (35,000/15/6.5)	359	359	359	4,308
Profit	665	808	1,034	12,408
Dividend @ 20%	133	162	207	2,482
Total dividend payment	2,984			

(3) Borrow in the most favourable market

Borrowing markets are becoming increasingly internationalised, particularly for larger organisations. A **eurobond** is a long-term loan raised by international organisations and sold to investors in several countries at the same time. The term of a eurobond is typically 10 to 15 years. Although Eurobond funds may be raised at **lower cost** than direct borrowing from banks, issue costs are generally **higher** than the costs of using the eurocurremcy markets.

The current favourable borrowing rates compared to Esco $ bonds and US $ bonds are presumably due to expectations of low inflation and a strong currency. This means that the future debt repayment in Esco $s will be greater than when the debt was first taken out.

Borrowings can be taken out in the same currency as that in which the income is generated in order to **hedge** against unfavourable currency movements. This could mean that borrowing in US $s could be a better option but no further information is available to enable a cost comparison.

(iii) Recommendations

(1) Further work

Carry out **further investigation** of the risk areas identified in Section (i) (1) of this report and recalculate the NPVs as necessary to enable a more fully informed evaluation. This may result in Alternative 2 becoming a more attractive option, particularly as it offers a better **strategic fit** with Sandyfoot's objective of developing its student market internationally

(2) Delay the decision

Consider **delaying a decision** for six months so that more information is available on the implementation of a development area in Esco.

(3) Midco funding

If a decision is made to invest in Alternative 2, the **Midco government's offer** of funding should be used as it is probably the cheapest option and minimises the risks of borrowing.

(4) Joint venture

Consider the use of a **joint venture** to enable both investments to be undertaken as they both offer a positive NPV and contribute to Sandyfoot's objectives.

87 PT

Text references. Business valuation is covered in Chapter 15 and acquisitions in Chapter 16.

Top tips. This question is very time-pressured and it would be all too easy to spend far too long on all of the calculations. If you get stuck on part (a) move on and don't waste time doing endless calculations at the expense of easier to obtain marks in other parts of the question.

In part (b) (ii) you can make assumptions to shorten the time you need to spend on the calculations and give yourself more time for the written sections.

Easy marks. The discussion parts of part (b) have plenty of opportunities for easy marks, particularly in parts (iii) and (iv). There are 4 marks available for structure and presentation so make sure you use a report format.

Examiner's comments. The general performance of candidates in valuing the intangible assets was very poor. In part (b) candidates are expected to apply book knowledge to the scenario. A general discussion without reference to the scenario will earn few marks.

(a) Valuation of intangible assets

Calculated intangible value

Average return on net tangible assets = 20%

Average return for ITPT from €1,300m tangible assets = 20% × €1,300m = €260m

Return that an average entity would earn from €1,300m tangible assets = 12% × €1,300m
= €156m

Premium attributable to intangible assets   = (260 – 156)
= €104m

NPV of premium = €104 × 1/0.15
= €693m

The intangible assets of ITPT can therefore be valued at **€693m.**

This method uses an industry average return and cost of capital which may be **distorted by extreme values**.

Market-to-book value

Market value = €7.80 × 300 = €2,340
Book value = €777m
Value of intangible assets = 2,340 – 777 = €1,563m

This method is **simplistic** and ignores other factors affecting the share price. It is a one-off observation based on just one share price. It also uses **book valuations** for tangible assets which may be totally unrealistic.

Market-to-replacement cost value

Market value = €7.80 × 300 = €2,340
Replacement value = 777 + (1,500 – 1,021) = €1,256m
Value of intangible assets = 2,340 – 1,256 = €1,084m

This method allows for a more realistic valuation of the tangible assets but is still very **simplistic**.

Total value

Asset valuations

The **net realisable value** of ITPT's net assets in 20X7 is equal to the book value of its equity: **€777m.**

The net assets basis of valuation can be used to provide a **minimum value** of the company but it does ignore any future profitability expectations, which could be important here as growth is expected to fall. This valuation also ignores the value of intangible assets.

However, if we use the **current replacement value** of the property, plant and equipment, an additional €479m (1,500 – 1,021) can be added to the total valuation giving a value of **€1,256m**, again ignoring the value of intangible assets.

Dividend valuation model

Total dividend = $0.34 × 300m shares = €102m

Dividend in 20X8 = 102 × 1.12 = €114.2m
Present value = 114.2 × 0.885 = €101.1m (using the cost of equity for ITPT of 13%)

Dividend in 20X9 = 102 × $(1.12)^2$ = €127.9
Present value = 127.9 × 0.783 = €100.1m

Dividend in 20Y0 = 102 × $(1.12)^3$ = €143.3
Present value = 143.3 × 0.693 = €99.3m

$$P = \frac{d_0(1+g)}{(k_e - g)}$$

$$P = \frac{143.3 \times (1 + 0.05)}{0.13 - 0.05}$$

$$= €1,880.8m$$

Multiply by year 3 discount factor = 1,880.8 × 0.693 = €1,303.4

Total value = 1,303.4 + 101.1 + 100.1 + 99.3 = **€1,603.9m**

The dividend valuation model attempts to relate the value of the business to the future stream of earnings but it is more useful for **valuing small parcels of shares** rather than an entire controlling interest. It does depend on an **accurate forecast** of the rate of growth of earnings which may be difficult to provide.

(b) To: Directors of PT Group
     From: External consultant
     Re: Proposed acquisition of ITPT

Introduction

The aim of the proposed acquisition of ITPT is to enable PT to improve its growth prospects. This report offers advice and opinions on four areas:

- The appropriateness of the proposed bid price
- Whether the acquisition would enable achievement of PT's financial objectives.
- The structure and finance of the bid offer
- The strategic implications of the acquisition

(i) The appropriateness of the proposed bid price

At current share price

At the current share price, the market value of ITPT is €2,340m so a bid of €2,500m would probably **be sufficient to attract the shareholders of ITPT**, especially if the share price has risen in anticipation of the bid.

The estimated synergies are €60m per annum which is equivalent to additional value of €400m, if this is assumed to be post tax and discounted to infinity at 15%. This gives a total value of **€2,740m** and so the offer looks to be acceptable.

Using replacement values

However, if we use the valuation based on the replacement value of the assets, the bid price looks **high**. This values the business at €1,256m so there would have to be at least an additional €1,244m of value from the intangible assets and synergistic gains. Intangible assets are notoriously hard to value and synergies are only estimates which are often over-stated.

Need for strong growth prospects

If an acquisition strategy involves buying a company on a **higher P/E ratio**, it is essential for continuing EPS growth that the acquired company offers prospects of **strong profit growth** and this is debateable for ITPT.

(ii)　Achievement of financial objectives

To increase group earnings by an average of 10% per annum over the next three years

	20X7 €m	20X8 €m	20X9 €m	20Y0 €m
ITPT		262.1	293.5	328.8
PT	703.3 (W)	766.9	839.2	921.1
Synergies		60.0	60.0	60.0
Group total	703.3	1,089.0	1,192.7	1,309.9
% change		54.8%	9.5%	9.8%

Working

$0.78 \times 300 = 234.0$
$0.695 \times 1,012 = 703.3$

Average growth over the three years = $(\sqrt[3]{1,309.9/703.3} - 1) \times 100\% = 23\%$

Cash offer

If we assume that €2,500 is borrowed to finance the bid, annual interest payment net of tax = $2,500 \times 10\% \times 80\% = €200m$

	20X7	20X8	20X9	20Y0
Group total earnings	€703.3m	€1,089.0m	€1,192.7m	€1,309.9m
Additional finance charge		€ (200.0)m	€ (200.0)m	€ (200.0)m
Net earnings	€703.3m	€889.0m	€992.7m	€1,109.9m
% change		26.4%	11.7%	11.8%

Average growth over the three years = $(\sqrt[3]{1,109.9/703.3} - 1) \times 100\% = 16.4\%$

This objective is therefore achieved under either financing structure.

To increase EPS to above 110c within three years

Cash offer

If we assume that €2,500 is borrowed to finance the bid, annual interest payment net of tax = $2,500 \times 10\% \times 80\% = €200m$

	20X7	20X8	20X9	20Y0
Group total earnings	€703.3m	€1,089.0m	€1,192.7m	€1,309.9m
Additional finance charge		€ (200.0)m	€ (200.0)m	€ (200.0)m
Net earnings	€703.3m	€889.0m	€992.7m	€1,109.9m
Number of shares	1,012	1,012	1,012	1,012
EPS	69.5c	87.8c	98.1c	109.7c

The objective is not achieved.

Share-for-share offer

	20X7	20X8	20X9	20Y0
Group total earnings	€937.3m	€1,089.0m	€1,192.7m	€1,309.9m
Number of shares (1,012 + (2,500/4.80))		1,533	1,533	1,533
EPS		71.0c	77.8c	85.4c

The objective is not achieved.

To maintain a gearing ratio of less than 40%

Cash offer

PT dividend payout ratio = $29.0/69.5 \times 100\% = 41.7\%$

Retained profit % is therefore $100 - 41.7\% = 58.3\%$

	20X7 €m	20X8 €m	20X9 €m	20Y0 €m
Group total earnings less interest	937.3	889.0	992.7	1,109.9
Total debt	2,855.0	5,355.0	5,355.0	5,355.0
Total equity:				
Issued capital	1,012.0	1,012.0	1,012.0	1,012.0
Reserves	7,970.0	8,488.3 (W)	9,067.0 (W)	9,714.1 (W)
Total capital		14,855.3	15,434.0	16,081.1
Gearing		36.0%	34.7%	33.3%

The objective is achieved.

Working

7,970 + (0.583 × 889.0) = 8,488.3
8,488.3 + (0.583 × 992.7) = 9,067.0
9,067.0 + (0.583 × 1,109.9) = 9,714.1

Share-for-share offer

	20X7 €m	20X8 €m	20X9 €m	20Y0 €m
Total debt	2,855	2,855.0	2,855.0	2,855.0
Total equity:				
Issued capital	1,012	1,533.0	1,533.0	1,533.0
Reserves (W)	7,970	11,105.7	11,801.0	12,564.7
Total capital		15,493.7	16,189.0	16,952.7
Gearing		18.4%	17.6%	16.8%

Working

7,970 + (0.583 x 1,089.0) + (521m shares x €4.80) = 11,105.7
11,105.7 + (0.583 × 1,192.7) = 11,801.0
11,801.0 + (0.583 × 1,309.9) = 12,564.7

The objective is achieved.

(iii)   The bid offer structure and finance

Cash offer

Control implications

A cash bid will not alter the **balance of control** in PT whereas a share offer will create 521m new shares, an increase of about 50% which will be in the hands of the shareholders of ITPT.

EPS

The cash bid will result in a **better earnings per share** which will meet the objective of an increase to above 110 cents per share.

Gearing

If the cash bid is financed via borrowing, the **gearing** will still be within **acceptable limits** and the moderate amount of increased financial risk is unlikely to have a detrimental effect on the share price. Debt finance is generally viewed as being a cheaper source of finance than equity and it can be argued that it should be chosen in preference to a share issue in order to maximise the value of the company.

Cutting the dividend

Financial impact

The total dividend to be paid in 20X8, assuming a continuation of a 41.7% dividend payout ratio for PT, would be €454.1m (41.7% × €1,089.0m). This would be **insufficient to fund the bid** and the company would still need to borrow funds.

Impact on shareholders

A cut in dividends is likely to be highly unpopular with shareholders who would view this as a **negative signal** about the strength of future profits. When a company's dividend policy changes, investors may sell their shares, resulting in a fall in the share price.

Conclusion

It can therefore be concluded that borrowing to finance a cash offer would be a better option than cutting dividends.

Share-for-share offer

Cash is **more certain in value** than shares because the price of shares in listed companies can fall very quickly. To compensate for the risk, PT may find that a share offer would have to be higher than the cash alternative. This would **further dilute** the current shareholders' holdings and exacerbate the loss of control issues.

(iv)   Broader strategic implications

Cost of entry

Acquisitions may provide a means of entering a market at a **lower cost** than would be incurred if the company tried to develop its own resources, or a means of acquiring the business of a competitor. ITPT is a competitor in the Eurozone and has an excellent reputation as well as efficient, modern IT and distribution resources.

Growth opportunities

A strategic opportunity would occur where a company such as PT is growing steadily but in a **mature market with limited growth prospects** and it acquires a company such as ITPT in a younger market with a higher growth rate. However, this is not entirely the case. ITPT is in the same European market as PT and the growth is actually going to be in the **Chinese market** with a slowdown in growth anticipated for ITPT.

Widening capability

An alternative strategic opportunity could be if PT needed to **widen its capability** and could do so by acquiring a company with the key talents and/or technology. The acquisition of ITPT would bring **technical and commercial expertise,** an existing customer base and other aspects of goodwill that will take a long time to achieve through internal development.

Systems and employees

However, there is no guarantee that the IT systems and distribution operation of ITPT would be able to cope with worldwide delivery on a much **bigger scale**. Furthermore, a reputation for good customer service depends on **employees** and they may become disillusioned and demotivated as a result of becoming part of a large conglomerate.

Customer views

Customers of ITPT may not be happy to use the services of a combined group which would again have a negative impact on forecast growth figures.

Interpretation

There may be significant **problems of integration** if the two companies' systems are merged. For example, the IT systems may be incompatible, particularly if the systems of ITPT are much more modern.

Recommendation

It is recommended that PT does not proceed with the proposed acquisition of ITPT. It is likely that an unacceptably high price would have to be paid for the company with no guarantee that future growth and synergistic gains will be delivered.

PT should look to acquire a company with expertise in Chinese markets in order to capitalise on the growth in that region.

88 Ancona

> **Text references**. The cost of capital is covered in Chapter 8, divestment in Chapter 16 and business valuation in Chapter 15.
>
> **Top tips**. This question is broken down into lots of small parts so a logical, sensible approach with a careful eye on the time will enable you to pick up marks throughout. Your knowledge of enterprise strategy will really help in part (b). You are given a value for Zola Agencies in part (c) so make sure you use this.
>
> **Easy marks**. Part (a) provides easy marks for simple calculations and explanations. Don't forget to use a report format in part (b) to get the marks for presentation. Common sense and careful time management will earn you plenty of marks in this question.
>
> **Examiner's comments**. Part (a)(i) of the question was generally done very well but part (ii) was less well handled and many candidates missed the main point of the question, simply describing the general limitations of CAPM. Part (b) was generally done well but some candidates spent too much time on this section at the expense of subsequent sections. Part (c)(i) was poorly answered with few appropriate calculations. In part (ii) many candidates did not apply their answer to the scenario.

(a)   (i)   <u>Zola Agencies</u>

Discount rate (k_e) $= R_f + (R_m - R_f)\,\beta$
$= 5\% + [(9\% - 5\%) \times 2.5]$
$= 15\%$

	15%	12%
Discount factor for 20Y1 – 20Y3:		
Cumulative discount factor for Year 5	3.352	3.605
Cumulative discount factor for Year 2	(1.626)	(1.690)
	1.726	1.915

	20X9 US$m	20Y0 US$m	20Y1–20Y3 US$m
Cash flow	138	172	250
Discount factor @ 15%	0.870	0.756	1.726
	120.06	130.03	431.50
Total present value	681.59		

<u>Ancona USA</u>

	20X9 US$m	20Y0 US$m	20Y1–20Y3 US$m
Cash flow	118	131	210
Discount factor @ 12%	0.893	0.797	1.915
	105.37	104.41	402.15
Total present value	611.93		

   (ii)   <u>Zola Agencies</u>

A discount rate of 15% has been used which assumes that it has policies and a risk profile similar to the entity mentioned in the scenario. This may however be inaccurate.

<u>Ancona USA</u>

A discount rate of 12% has been used which is the **weighted average cost of capital** of Ancona International. The weighted average cost of capital can be used if the **existing capital structure** will be maintained and the same **business risk** will apply.

Debt: equity ratios can be used to compare capital structures of Ancona USA and Ancona International.

	Ancona International $m		Ancona USA $m
Debt	2,050		200
Equity (350 × $18)	6,300	(assume NPV = market value)	612
Debt/equity gearing ratio	32.5%		32.7%

The capital structure of the two entities is very similar and the policies and business risk would remain similar. The use of a 12% discount rate is therefore appropriate.

(b) To: Directors of Ancona International
From: Independent Financial Adviser
Date:
Re: Sale of USA operations

Introduction

This report will consider and advise on the sale of the USA operations of Ancona International. The report will deal with:

(1) The interests of the various stakeholder groups.
(2) The economic and market factors that might impact on negotiations.
(3) A recommendation of an appropriate valuation for the USA operations.

(i) Stakeholder groups

The main stakeholders who will be concerned here are the shareholders of Ancona International, the directors and employees of Ancona USA, suppliers, bankers, customers and governments.

Ancona International shareholders

Shareholders have invested in Ancona on the basis of its **current risk profile**. Revenue growth has been satisfactory but unspectacular and it has concentrated on quality and customer loyalty.

The **divestment** would remove approximately 10% of the business and the revenue and profits lost (15% of after-tax earnings) would need to be replaced with suitable alternative income streams.

Institutional shareholders are expected to support the divestment so must therefore be satisfied that alternative sources of profits can be found.

Directors and employees of Ancona USA

The **directors** of Ancona USA and 'other employees' are planning to take over the USA operations and are therefore presumably prepared to take on the **risks** involved in a **management buyout**.

These risks include potential **business failure** and **loss of jobs**. The types of contracts that Mr de Z wants to tender for are **fiercely competitive** and time consuming and there is no guarantee of success. Existing employees may not have the necessary skills or be willing to work in this new environment.

Suppliers

The new entity may wish to negotiate **different contracts** with suppliers and have different purchasing strategies.

In terms of **liquidity**, the current ratio is 1.6 (95/60) for Ancona USA so there is currently no problem with liquidity. There is no guarantee that this will continue under a new regime.

Customers

Existing US customers may notice a significant change if resources are concentrated on **winning new contracts** rather than ensuring customer loyalty.

Bankers

There is no significant debt for existing bankers to be concerned about. The bonds are secured on Ancona International's non-current assets and this will only have an impact if some of these assets are to be divested as part of the management buyout.

DW Bank will become a significant stakeholder in Zola Agencies if financing alternative 2 is chosen.

Governments

The UK government is likely to have no interest in Ancona other than the usual tax implications. The US government may be concerned about **employment implications** but only if operations are sufficiently large or geographically concentrated in one area.

(ii) Economic and market factors

The main economic and market factors that might impact on negotiations are interest rates, inflation, stock market movements and sentiment, alternative investment opportunities and regulations.

Interest rates

Alternative 2 financing is predominantly based on **debt finance** (75%) and interest rates could therefore have a significant impact. $250m of the debt is at a fixed interest rate but the remainder is at a **variable rate** so subject to change.

Interest rates affect **cash flows** in the form of borrowing costs but also affect **demand** for services such as advertising. A rise in interest rates will affect other entities' cash flows who are then likely to spend less on non-essentials such as advertising. This would reduce the value of Ancona USA.

A rise in interest rates would also **increase the discount rates** issued in NPV calculations and reduce NPVs.

Higher interest rates may arise due to **higher inflation** where governments use interest rates as a weapon to curb demand. Higher inflation will impact on future cash flows and again will lead to a lower valuation for Ancona USA.

Stock markets

Ancona International's CEO is confident he would get support for the divestment proposal from the institutional shareholders. However, **sentiment** can easily change and will depend on shareholders' reaction to **news of negotiations**.

As mentioned above much will depend on the ability of Ancona to replace lost profits with new investment opportunities. Investors will also be concerned with the **risk profile** of new investments.

Alternative investment opportunities

The divestment of the USA operations will generate a **large cash balance** which can be invested. The issue will be finding a suitable investment opportunity. If no opportunity exists, a **share repurchase** could be considered which would increase gearing from a relatively low level. It can be seen, however, as an admission that the company cannot make better use of the funds than the shareholders.

Regulation

Amalgamations and restructuring are subject to regulatory control in the UK and the US but this proposal is unlikely to be of any concern to competition authorities in either country.

(iii) Recommendation of an appropriate valuation

Net asset value

	$m
Total assets	435
Total liabilities	(260)
	175

The net asset value provides a 'floor level' value but is likely to be much too low, especially for a business with a high level of intellectual capital.

Cash flow based value

The present value of future cash flows if the subsidiary remains part of the group is **$612m** and if it is sold off as Zola Agencies is **$682m**.

These values are however based on **subjective estimates** of growth and cash flows **beyond 20Y3** have been ignored. This has been done because of the uncertainties involved but it will seriously **undervalue** the entity.

The **discount rates** used are also subjective and alternative assumptions could significantly alter the valuations.

As stated in part (ii) **cash flows** could be affected by a number of economic factors and this could again significantly change the valuations.

Sensitivity analysis would help to analyse the risk surrounding each of the variables.

P/E ratio value

$$\text{Ancona International EPS} = \frac{\$680}{350}$$
$$= \$1.94$$

$$\text{P/E ratio} = \frac{18}{1.94}$$
$$= 9.3$$

Using Ancona International's P/E ratio and the earnings from the US operation in 20X8, the P/E ratio value is **$948.6m** (9.3 × $102m). This is the valuation assuming the subsidiary remains part of the Ancona International group and carries on with the same policies and business risk.

However, P/E ratio valuations are based on **historic performance** and take no account of earnings projections. They are **simplistic** and subject to large **margins of error**.

Conclusion

A recommended valuation is based on the cash flow based values of between $612m and $682m and this would be a useful range for negotiation. It is strongly recommended that the directors of Ancona International consider investment opportunities for the cash raised from the divestment, before agreeing that it should go ahead.

(c)   (i)   Alternative 1

PE Capital requires a 30% compound average return by 31 March 20Y3 (5 years).

If we assume that the proposed Zola Agencies is valued at $650m, PE capital will provide 95% of this amount ($618m).

$$\text{Final value of investment} = \$618m \times (1 + 30\%)^5$$
$$= \$2,295m$$

$$\text{Total required value of Zola Agencies} = \frac{100}{95} \times \$2,295m$$

$$= \$2,416m$$

Alternative 2

Again, assuming the value of Zola Agencies is $650m, $488m (75% of $650m) will be needed from DW bank.

Interest payments

	$m
$250m × 10% × (1– 0.3)	17.50
$238m × 11% × (1– 0.3)	18.33
	35.83

Earnings

	20X9	20Y3
	$m	$m
Earnings	138	250
Interest	(36)	(36)
	102	214
No of shares	50m	50m
EPS	$2.04	$4.28

(ii) <u>Alternative 1</u>

<u>Advantages</u>

PE Capital is a **private equity** investor who will bear most of the **risk** of the new venture. In return, PE Capital will require a **very high return** but no **interest** or **dividends** will need to be paid. The **reinvestment** of earnings into the business should result in a good level of growth.

<u>Disadvantages</u>

PE Capital will require that a director of PE sits on the board of Zola Agencies and Mr de Z may have **conflicting views** on strategy.

The exit route by IPO means that PE Capital will reap most of the benefits of flotation. The success of an IPO is subject to prevailing market conditions which could be a problem in five years' time.

<u>Alternative 2</u>

<u>Advantages</u>

The main advantage is that Mr de Z and his colleagues will **retain control** and will be free to pursue their new business strategy. They will also have more **exit strategy options** available if they decide to float or sell Zola Agencies in the future.

Interest cover is sufficient and increases from 3.8 in 20X9 (138/36) to 6.9 in 20Y3 (250/36).

<u>Disadvantages</u>

The majority of the funding is in the form of **debt finance** which will incur significant **interest payments**. These will **reduce earnings** and **increase financial risk** which will **increase the cost of equity**. This will result in a **lower value** of the business by 20Y3 compared to **Alternative 1**.

The consortium of private investors will require a **dividend** of 20% which is very high. This may be negotiable if an IPO is a possibility.

<u>Recommendation</u>

Mr de Z appears to be keen to raise the risk profile of the business so is more likely to prefer Alternative 2. He would retain control and maximise potential returns for himself and his colleagues.

89 KEN

Text references. Cash flow forecasts are covered in Chapter 3; Economic factors in Chapter 2; Treasury function in Chapter 10; Investment appraisal in Chapter 11; Real options in Chapter 13; Merger issues in Chapter 16.

Top tips. This is a wide ranging question covering a number of areas of the syllabus. The requirements are broken into six separate sections so you will need to allocate your time carefully. If you get stuck on any part, move on. For example, it is tempting to make part (a) much more complicated than it needs to be, but remember there are only four marks available.

Set out your NPV in part (d) (ii) so that it is easy for the marker to follow your logic.

Make sure your written answers focus on the specific requirements and relate to the specific circumstances of KEN.

Easy marks. Don't forget to use a report format in part (d) for three easy marks. Use your common sense and general business knowledge to gain easy marks in part (b). Part (c) is straightforward use of textbook knowledge.

Examiner's comments. Part (a) was generally answered well although there were a number of candidates who only calculated the total figure for after-sales receipts after the fall in selling prices rather than the fall in receipts.

The most common error in part (b) was to discuss issues relating to the credit crunch rather than making comments relevant to the scenario.

In part (c) some candidates discussed all aspects of treasury management rather than just liquidity and funding management.

The NPV of the sale of land in part (d) caused problems with many candidates unable to identify relevant cash flows or make a reasonable attempt at the tax calculation. Few candidates highlighted the importance of the cash/liquidity position of the merger candidate in part (iii).

(a)   20X4

    Number of houses to be sold in 20X4 = 70

    10% deposit will be received in 20X4

    Average selling price before fall in house prices = A$350,000

	A$
Total after-tax sales receipts = 10% × 70 × A$350,000 × (1 – 30%) =	1,715,000
New selling price = A$350,000 × 80% = A$280,000	
Total after-tax sales receipts = 10% × 70 × A$280,000 × (1 – 30%) =	1,372,000
Fall in after-tax sales receipts	**343,000**

    20X5 (Phase 2 only)

    90% is due on completion

    Average selling price before fall in house prices = A$350,000

	A$
Total after-tax sales receipts = 90% × 70 × A$350,000 × (1 – 30%) =	15,435,000
New selling price = A$350,000 × 80% = A$280,000	
Total after-tax sales receipts = 90% × 70 × A$280,000 × (1 – 30%) =	12,348,000
Fall in after-tax sales receipts	**3,087,000**

(b)   Industry factors

    Property development is a potentially **highly profitable** industry which attracts speculators and entrepreneurs. It is **highly competitive** with a wide range of entity sizes.

    However, property development is also **risky**. Companies usually have to **borrow finance** to make asset purchases with no guarantee that expected cash flows will be achieved. The risk involved means that **finance costs** may be higher than other industries.

Timing of cash flows can also be problematic. The land and building materials have to be purchased some time before any revenue is received. For example, KEN has to wait a year from the time of sale until 90% of the sale price is received. In the meantime, the company has to pay 70% of the construction costs. This can create problems with **liquidity**, with a requirement for **expensive short-term finance** such as overdrafts. **Overtrading** is a risk in this situation.

Economic factors

The building industry is notorious for being one of the first industries **adversely affected** by an **economic downturn** and also to benefit from an upturn in the economy. A **recession** means more unemployment and a loss in consumer confidence. A house purchase is a major decision and will soon be postponed in such circumstances.

Interest rates are an economic weapon used to influence demand in the economy and an increase will have a rapid adverse effect on house purchase decisions. Any increase in the time taken to sell houses will have a negative impact on a property developer's cash flow. This is a problem for KEN at the moment as interest rates have recently risen.

The increase in interest rates may also **increase** KEN's **finance costs**.

Market factors

Customer demand needs to be carefully monitored. Changes in housing needs may result from heightened environmental concerns, or changes in demographics (eg average family sizes). **Worsening economic factors** may result in smaller houses, or perhaps apartments, being preferred. If KEN fails to monitor these trends then it will experience a worsening financial situation. For example for the project under discussion, if the 300 houses are not of a type that is in demand, if the economy slows down they will be difficult to sell.

Reputation is a valuable commodity in the housing market and a reputation for quality and reliability will help to protect KEN from some of the problems in the market.

(c) ### The Treasury function

CIMA Official Terminology describes the treasury function as 'the function concerned with the provision and use of finance'. Broadly, the treasury department **raises and manages company funds** and liquid assets.

Liquidity management

This will involve using the cash flow forecasts provided by the finance department to ensure that **sufficient cash is available to meet the needs of the business.**

If there is a forecast **cash surplus**, the Treasury Department will arrange for the funds to be invested. Typically these investments will be in **low risk**, **highly liquid** assets so that the funds are available when needed.

If there is a forecast **cash deficit** the Treasury Department will arrange for funds to be available using appropriate funding sources (see below).

Funding management

Here the Treasury Department will consider appropriate funding sources. Consideration will be given to:

- **How much debt to use** – this will reflect the stability of the businesses cashflows. If these are volatile (as is likely here) then gearing should be kept to a low level
- **Where to borrow from** – if debt is to be used, strong relationships should be developed with the chosen bank to ensure that the bank is supportive if the business experiences financial difficulties
- **What type of debt to use** – short term debt may be cheaper than long term debt
- **How to raise equity finance** – if equity finance is needed, the Treasury Department will assist in the organisation of a rights issue, or may recommend a change in dividend policy to free up funds

(d)   To: The Board of Directors of KEN
       From: Finance Director
       Re: Strategic choices facing KEN

Introduction

KEN is facing potential liquidity problems following the recent fall in house prices. This report offers advice and opinions what the strategic response should be at this time. It will consider three areas:

- The net present value of the Phase 3 cash flows after the fall in house prices, compared with the net present value associated with selling the land
- Whether or not to proceed with Strategy 1 and what real options are available
- Reasons for considering a merger and potential problems

(i)   NPV of Phase 3 cash flows

Year	20X5 A$'000	20X6 A$'000	20X7 A$'000	20X8 A$'000
Sales revenue (W1)				
10% deposit	2,560	1,280		
90% on completion		23,040	11,520	
Construction costs (W2)				
70% on sale	(13,440)	(6,720)		
30% following year		(5,760)	(2,880)	
Sales office costs	(170)	(110)		
Net profit	(11,050)	11,730	8,640	
Tax @ 30%		3,315	(3,519)	(2,592)
Net cash flows	(11,050)	15,045	5,121	(2,592)
12% discount factors	0.797	0.712	0.636	0.567
Present value	(8,807)	10,712	3,257	(1,470)
NPV	**3,692**			

Workings

1   *Sales revenue*

    Selling price of Phase 3 house after fall in price = $400,000 × 80% = $320,000

Year	20X5	20X6
Number of houses to be sold	80	40
Sales revenue (A$'000)	25,600	12,800

2   *Construction costs*

    Construction costs = 60% × A$400,000 = A$240,000 per house

Year	20X5	20X6
Number of houses to be sold	80	40
Construction costs (A$'000)	19,200	9,600

NPV of selling the land

	20X4 A$'000	20X5 A$'000
Sale of land	4,400	
Redundancy costs	(60)	
Pre-tax cash flow	4,340	
Tax (W)		(522)
Net cash flow	4,340	(522)
Discount factor @ 12%	0.893	0.797
Present value	3,876	(416)
NPV	**3,460**	

Note. The costs of obtaining planning permission are a sunk cost and are not relevant for decision making.

Working

Taxation

$(4,400 - 2,600 - 60) \times 30\%) = 522$

The comparison of the net present values indicates that the better option is to **continue with Phase 3.**

(ii) Strategy 1 – abandon Phase 3 and sell the land

The net present value comparison above indicates that in purely **financial terms**, KEN should continue with Phase 3 rather than sell the land.

This financial analysis relies on a number of **assumptions** which may not be accurate.

- **House prices** could fall even further than the 20% expected
- **Costs** could be higher than anticipated
- The **discount rate** could be too low, especially given the rise in interest rates

Real options

An option is the right to make a choice which can be very valuable when applied to capital investments. The real options which apply to this decision are the option to abandon and the option to wait. The follow-on option when the investment opportunity leads to follow-on wealth generating opportunities does not apply here.

Option to abandon

An abandonment option refers to the ability to abandon the project at a certain stage in its life. If large sums are being spent, and prospects do not appear healthy, an abandonment option may be available. If the benefit streams from a project are highly **uncertain**, an option to abandon the project if things go wrong could be highly valuable. The **riskiness** of the project is reduced and the expected NPV increased.

In this situation, the option to abandon involves abandoning Phase 3 and selling the land. This option is likely to exist until construction work begins.

Option to wait

An option to wait is a **timing option** which allows resolution of uncertainty. Investments are rarely 'now or never' opportunities but we do need to consider the cash flows foregone in the period of postponement. The cost of this is balanced against the value of waiting.

KEN could **delay construction** of Phase 3 until the housing market picks up again. The sales staff would still need to be paid but there would be no construction costs to pay. The risk is that the value of the land could fall further in the meantime. The planning permission may also have a finite timescale.

The value of this option is that KEN would be in a position to recommence construction as soon as the housing market looks more positive. KEN would then be under less financial pressure in the 1st year of Phase 3, where it will experience significant cash outflows.

Other factors

KEN has built a **strong reputation** and needs to protect this for the future success of the company. Any action which undermines this reputation should be avoided. A decision to abandon a project may make KEN appear **vulnerable** and could encourage more aggressive behaviour from KEN's rivals.

Sales office staff may have valuable skills which will be needed in a future upturn. By making these people redundant, these skills are lost.

Sales of Phase 2 houses could be adversely affected by the abandonment of Phase 3. There are still 70 houses to be sold and purchasers may be put off by the prospect of a change in plans for the rest of the site. This could cause prices for Phase 2 to fall further and further damage the liquidity and profitability of KEN.

KEN's current financial situation is unknown but is a relevant factor here. If KEN is worried about its cash position in the short to medium term, it would be more likely to seize the opportunity to free up cash by selling the land.

If **other projects exist** (for example overseas) that offer more attractive returns, then KEN should consider Strategy 1 to free up the required funds.

(iii)   <u>Strategy 2 – a merger</u>

A merger is a business combination of two or more companies, of which **none obtains control** over the other. Mergers have tended to be more common in industries with a history of little growth and low returns. Highly profitable companies tend to seek acquisitions rather than mergers.

The reason for a merger is to obtain **synergistic benefits.**

- Operating economies from the elimination of duplicate facilities such as a sales office
- A larger, merged company may find it easier to **raise finance** and the **liquidity** position may be improved
- The other property development entity may have less risky earnings and a larger asset base
- The merger could be defensive ie stop a competitor obtaining advantage or to reduce rivalry in the industry

<u>Potential problems</u>

Given the economic and market conditions, it is likely that the other property development entity is facing the **same issues** with house sales and liquidity. A merger would not necessarily improve the situation for either entity.

Valuing the two entities and agreeing on a suitable **share exchange** is likely to be problematic.

If the merger does go ahead, **post-acquisition integration** could be a problem, particularly if the **culture** of the two entities varies. For example, the other property development entity may focus on high volume, low cost building rather than the high build quality of KEN.

<u>Conclusion</u>

Given that KEN has been highly successful as an independent company in recent years, **Strategy 2 (a merger) looks like a risky option and is not recommended**. However, the merger could still be explored to see what terms are being offered and what the risks are.

Strategy 1 should only be considered if KEN is experiencing **liquidity problems**. If not, then the best option would be for KEN to wait until the housing market picks up again and then to commence construction of Phase 3; **so Strategy 1 is not recommended.**

90   T Industries

Text references. Business valuations are covered in Chapter 15 whilst amalgamations are dealt with in Chapter 16.

Top tips. Parts (a) and (b) involve relatively straightforward calculations but make sure you use the current share price to calculate the market capitalisation in (a)(i). It would be easy to pick up the share price at 30 June 20W9 which would give the wrong result. Before you start answering the question, establish what 'today's date' is.

Part (c) involves making a number of assumptions therefore the answer given here is not necessarily the one that you come up with. If your assumptions are reasonable, you will get credit for your answers. This emphasises the need to state your assumptions as they actually affect your final answer.

Make use of the information you are given in the question requirements as well as in the scenario. In (c)(ii) for example you are given the methods of finance to consider and in (c)(iii) you are told that interest and inflation rates are low and falling. The examiner will expect you to apply your knowledge to these particular issues.

Note that you are specifically told at the end of the requirements that you should make assumptions for part (c) if you are unable to complete calculations for (a) and (b). This is an approach we recommend for all questions – there is no point losing marks for the want of particular figures when you can demonstrate your ability in certain parts of the question with 'assumed' figures.

Easy marks. There are quite straightforward marks to be gained in parts (a) and (b).

(a) (i) P/E ratio and current market capitalisation

	T Industries	L Products
Current market capitalisation	670p x 120m = £804m	375p x 60m = £225m
P/E ratio (Current MV/Earnings)	£804m/£65m = 12.37	£225m/£22.5m = 10

Alternative calculation for P/E ratio

	T Industries	L Products
Earnings per share (EPS)	£65m/120m = 0.542	£22.5m/60m = 0.375
P/E ratio (Current share price/EPS	£6.70/0.542 = 12.37	£3.75/0.375 = 10

(ii) Cost of equity using CAPM

$$K_e = R_f + (R_m - R_f)\beta$$

T Industrioes

$$K_e = 3 + (9 - 3) \times 1.17 = 10.02\% \text{ (say 10%)}$$

L Products

As there is no beta coefficient for L Products we have to ungear the beta of the company in a similar business and then regear to reflect the level of L Products' gearing.

Ungear beta

$$\beta_u = \beta_g \left[\frac{V_E}{V_E + V_D (1-t)} \right] + \beta_D \left[\frac{V_D (1-t)}{V_E + V_D (1-t)} \right]$$

$$\beta_u = (1.4 \times 0.6) + (0.2 \times 0.4) = 0.92$$

Regear beta

$$\beta_g = \beta_{u+} (\beta_u - \beta_d) \frac{V_D (1-t)}{V_E}$$

$$\beta_g = 0.92 + (0.92 - 0.2) \times (220/225) = 1.62$$

Cost of equity using CAPM

$$Ke = 3 + (9 - 3) \times 1.62 = 12.72\% \text{ (say 13%)}$$

(iii) Estimated value using DCF method

	20X0 £m	20X1 £m	20X2+ £m
Earnings	65.0	66.95	69.63
Discount factor (10%)	0.909	0.826	13.77
DCF	59.09	55.30	958.81

NPV = £1,073.2m

Note that the discount factor for 20X2+ is the growing perpetuity (discount rate 10%, growth rate 4%) discounted back two years.

Discount factor = $[1/((0.1 - 0.04)] \times 0.826 = 13.77$

L Products

	20X0 £m	20X1 £m	20X2+ £m
Earnings	21.38	23.52	24.11
Discount factor (13%)	0.885	0.783	7.46
DCF	18.92	18.42	179.86

NPV = £217.2m

Discount factor 20X2+ = $[1/(0.13 - 0.025)] \times 0.783$

(b)   Increase in value generated by combining the two businesses

Sum of current values of the individual businesses = £1,073.2m + £217.2m = £1,290.4m

Value of combined business

PV of earnings 20X0 and 20X1

	20X0	20X1	Total
	£m	£m	£m
T Industries	59.09	55.3	114.39
L Products	18.92	18.42	37.34
	78.01	73.72	151.73

PV of earnings 2012+

Total earnings 2011 (T Industries and L Products) = £66.95m + £23.52m = £90.47m

Increase by 4% = £94.09m

PV of perpetuity = £94.09m x [1/(0.1 – 0.04)] x 0.826 = £1,295.62m

Total PV of combined business

= £151.73m + £1,295.62m

= £1,447.35m

Increase in value = £1,447.35m - £1,290.4m = **£156.95m**

(c)   REPORT

To: T Industries' Board of Directors
From: Finance Director
Subject: Proposed acquisition of L Products

This report evaluates the various issues that must be considered in the proposed acquisition of L Products. Whilst the acquisition would broaden T Industries' business base and provide access to scarce technical expertise, it is likely to be a hostile bid and the initial approach may result in a bidding war.

Range of values within which T Industries should be prepared to negotiate

There are various ways in which shares may be valued for acquisition purposes.

(i)   **Asset valuation basis**, which tends to provide a minimum value for a business. The value of a share in a particular class is equal to the net tangible assets divided by the number of shares. Intangible assets tend to be excluded from this valuation. This method of valuation is not really relevant in this particular situation although valuation of the scarce technical expertise that T Industries would acquire from L Products would be useful.

(ii)   **Earnings valuation basis**, which usually gives the highest business valuation. It values the earnings of the entity under new ownership and makes use of the P/E ratio which shows the stock market's view of the growth prospects of the company.

(iii)   **Dividend valuation basis**, which provides a mid-range valuation of the entity. However it is not really relevant in this acquisition situation as it tends to be more useful for small shareholdings.

(iv)   **Cash flow valuation bases**, which include DCF method, shareholder value analysis, economic value added and market value added. These methods focus on the present value of the future cash flows that will be generated by the new management. They are suitable when one company plans to buy the assets of another company (as in the case of T Industries and L Products) and make further investments to improve future cash flows.

Efficient markets

There are three forms of market efficiency:

(i)   **Weak** – where the current share price is derived from the study of past share prices
(ii)   **Semi-strong** – where the current share price also reflects all published information.
(iii)   **Strong** – where the current share price reflects all information, both published and unpublished

Generally stock markets display **semi-strong form tendencies** therefore it can be assumed that the current share price of T Industries reflects all published information about the company. However caution should be taken when interpreting L Products' share price as the AIM tends to be less 'efficient' than the full stock market.

Premium paid for acquisitions

As both companies are listed on a stock market, the current share price will be the **minimum price** that shareholders of the target company will be willing to accept (unless they had knowledge that the share price was going to fall in the near future). Generally, a premium of approximately 20% is paid on top of the share price for an acquisition, rising to 50% during a hostile bidding war.

Share exchange

The current share price of T Industries is 670p and 375p for L Products. If a 20% premium is paid for L Products this would give a share price of 450p. If T Industries is considering a share exchange, this would equate approximately to 1 T Industries share for 1.5 L Products shares (or 2 for 3).

Cash flow basis

As previously calculated, the increase in value achieved by combining the two companies is £156.95m. Bearing this in mind, T Industries might consider a bid as follows.

	£m
Market value of L Products (60m shares x 375p)	225.00
Increase in value	156.95
Total	381.95

This would equate to a share price of £381.95m/60m shares = 637p

A share price of 637p seems **excessive** as this would amount to a premium of approximately 70% on current share price and would equate to a share exchange of approximately 1 : 1. If this share price was used, most of the gains from acquisition would go to L Product's shareholders – a situation that is unlikely to go down well with T Industries' shareholders.

Factors to be taken into consideration

Before a formal offer is made, the Board should take a number of factors into consideration.

(i)   **L Products' technical expertise**. The offer should include the value that T Industries places on the scarce technical expertise that would be acquired from L Products. This is more difficult to value than tangible assets and does not tend to be included in the valuation methods mentioned above. However it is an valuable asset and its benefits should not be ignored when considering an offer price.

(ii)   **Bidding war**. As L Products' share price has fallen over the past five months, there is an opportunity to obtain the company more cheaply than might otherwise be the case. However other companies are likely to be having similar thoughts and an initial approach by T Industries may start a bidding war. There is therefore a danger than the price is pushed beyond the real worth of L Products as different parties try to secure the acquisition.

(iii)   **L Products' shareholders**. It is important to reassure L Products' shareholders than the acquisition would lead to a more secure and settled future for the company. Even if L Products' directors are hostile to the bid, the shareholders might support it.

(iv)   **Underlying assumptions**. Valuations of L Products should be treated with caution as they are underpinned by a number of assumptions. Growth rates might not be realised, resulting in an over-valuation and the company might actually increase the risk of T Industries, which means that the cash flows might be discounted at a lower-than-appropriate rate. It will be worthwhile to try out several different scenarios to determine the impact on valuation.

If we use L Products' 20W9 earnings and assume that its P/E ratio will be the same as that of T Industries, we arrive at a more realistic share price.

2009 earnings = £22.5m

T Industries P/E ratio = 12.37

Market value of L Products = £22.5m x 12.37 = £278.33m

Price per share = £278.33m/60m shares = £4.64 (or 464p)

This represents a premium of approximately 23.7% on the current share price, which is a more realistic figure. If a share exchange was used, the offer would be 1 : 1.44 (that is, one T Industries share for 1.44 shares in L Products).

Recommendation

It is recommended that an initial bid of 464p – 488p should be made. This represents a 24% - 30% premium on the current share price which is a reasonable uplift. It means that if a bidding war takes place the starting price is not ridiculously high.

The most appropriate method of financing the proposed acquisition

Two main methods of financing the bid have been identified – share exchange and the issue of new debt.

If a share price of 464p was offered (which would result in a 1 : 1.44 share issue) this would amount to an issue of approximately 41.7 additional shares. Such a large issue of new shares will require authorisation before the bid can go ahead.

If T Industries decides to finance the offer by issuing new debt, it will be required to raise £278.4m (60m shares x 464p).

Estimated effect on gearing

Current gearing levels

	T Industries	L Products
	£m	£m
Debt	450	220
Equity (market value)	804	225
Total debt + equity	1,254	445
Level of gearing [debt/(debt + equity)]	35.9%	49.4%

Combined entity gearing

	Share exchange	Issue of new debt
	£m	£m
Debt (combined)	670	670+278.4 = 948.4
Equity (market value)	1,029	1,029
Total debt + equity	1,699	1,977.4
Level of gearing [debt/(debt + equity)]	39.4%	48%

The above figures for the combined gearing calculations assume that the market value of the combined entity is simply the sum of the individual market values of T Industries and L Products. However these figures will change depending on how the **market actually values the combined entity**.

It can be seen that gearing is much higher if the bid is financed by the issue of new debt. A 48% gearing figure may be deemed unacceptable by the Board of the combined entity. There is also a danger that such a high gearing figure will increase the perceived risk of the entity which will in turn increase the cost of capital.

Estimated effect on EPS

	Share exchange	Issue of new debt
Combined earnings	£87.5m	£87.5m
Number of shares in issue	160m	120m
EPS	54.7p	72.9p

One of the financial objectives of T Industries is to increase the EPS year on year. A bid financed by share exchange would increase the EPS only slightly (20W9 EPS = 54.1p) whereas a cash bid would result in a much higher figure. However this is simply due to the fact that earnings are being split between fewer shares and the **two figures cannot really be compared**. In addition, future movements in EPS under a cash bid will be affected by interest rate movements.

Recommendation

A cash bid is probably a more secure option for T Industries but it may increase the hostility of L Products' shareholders as they will be unable to participate in the profits of the combined entity. Before making a final decision, acceptable levels of gearing should be determined – if the cash bid pushes gearing above these predetermined levels then it cannot be considered to be a viable option.

Implications of the proposed acquisition for achievement of T Industries' financial objectives

T Industries' two financial objectives are as follows.

(i)   To increase EPS year on year
(ii)   To improve shareholder value by an average of 8% pa over a rolling 5 year period

Although these objectives have been achieved over the last 9 years, economic conditions in general and the construction industry in particular have become much more volatile. It has been recognised that these **objectives may have to be reviewed** which makes sense in the current climate. It would be extremely optimistic – and perhaps foolhardy – to continue to expect an 8% growth in shareholder value in times of economic volatility.

How the proposed acquisition might help

The acquisition of L Products will give access to scarce technical ability which may improve T Industries' own products and thus lead to improved earnings. The earnings situation may also be improved by access to new markets and L Products' own customer base.

If L Products is acquired, the combined entity will have a better chance of **raising additional finance** due to the increased asset base that can be used as security. Such additional funding will allow the combined entity to take advantage of more profitable investment opportunities as they arise, resulting in improved earnings and the potential for dividend growth.

If T Industries can fulfil its objective of 4% growth, not just for its own earnings but those of L Products too, this will not only increase the possibility of dividend growth but also share price rises.

Financing policies

The theoretical order in which different methods of financing should be used is

(i)   Retained earnings
(ii)   Debt
(iii)   Equity

In times of low interest rates and low inflation debt would initially appear to be very attractive. However this may not be the case. When the economy is volatile, earnings are likely to be the same and fixed **interest payments have to be met from potentially lower profits**. This will reduce the EPS and the likelihood of dividends being paid at all, never mind growing.

The value of the tax shield offered by debt finance is reduced when profits are falling. In theory this is the only element of the capital structure of an organisation that affects its value. As the value of the tax shield declines, so does the attractiveness of debt.

The above factors may encourage T Industries to lean towards share exchange as the preferred method of financing the acquisition of L Products. However the markets may view the issue of equity differently. As equity is generally the 'finance of last resort' the markets may see its use as a sign of **liquidity problems** within the organisation. Share prices will be reduced as a result and the objective of increasing shareholder value will become more difficult to achieve.

Another problem with the use of equity is trying to persuade investors to take up the offer. In times of recession, investors 'tighten their belts' and may be less willing to buy additional shares, preferring the capital gain instead. In this event, debt may be not just the preferred option but the **only option**.

Dividend policies

Current results show that T Industries pay 40% of earnings as dividends and L Products almost 51%. As interest rates are so low it would make sense for dividend payments to be reduced which would allow the company to reinvest the funds in profitable projects with higher returns. However directors should consider the **signals** this may send to the market. It may be that the market receives the news favourably and assumes that the funds are being used for profitable opportunities (thus increasing share price). However there is the chance that the opposite signal is sent and the share price falls.

In the current climate, many companies are reducing dividend payouts, therefore any decision to follow this trend might be met with less resistance from the company's shareholders.

If you would like to discuss any of the above issues, please do not hesitate to contact me.

91 Power Utilities

Text references. This question covers various areas of the syllabus. Investment appraisal techniques and international investment appraisal (including foreign currency risk) are covered in Chapters 11 and 12 respectively. Divestment (exit) strategies are covered in Chapter 16.

Top tips. It is easy to become overwhelmed with a long question such as this one. Make sure you read the requirements carefully so that you understand what you are required to do. In part (a) there are four different NPVs to calculate. Be careful to identify any sunk costs (some of the environmental costs have already been paid or committed to) and don't forget to convert the construction costs to the domestic currency. One of the complications with exchange rates is that you are given the rate for May 20X9 which is part of the way through the year. To find the rate for 20Y0 you will have to inflate by more than 5%.

You must read the unseen material carefully to ensure you treat each cash flow correctly (for example, tax relief is not available on the environmental study). Don't forget to use annuity factors otherwise you will waste a lot of time!

In part (b) you must use a report format and don't forget to answer both sub-sections. Your answer must relate to the figures you calculated in (a) – even if these figures are incorrect you will still gain marks if your explanation and evaluation are sensible for your own answers. Avoid the temptation of writing everything you know about foreign currency risk in part (b)(ii) – you are expected to relate it to the scenario and remember to make a recommendation based on your calculations.

The answer to part (c) should again be specific to PU. Even if you are familiar with the various methods for divestment, make sure they are viable options for PU.

Easy marks. There are easy marks to be gained throughout the question. In part (a) you should be able to identify sunk costs and calculate NPV without any changes in exchange rates or tax rates. Part (c) should also present some easy marks if you are familiar with divestment strategies.

(a)   Scenario 1 – no change to the exchange rate or tax rate

Year	20Y0	20Y2	20Y3	20Y4		
Time	1	3	4	5	5–24	6–25
	P$m	P$m	P$m	P$m	P$m	P$m
Environmental study (W1)	(32.0)					
Construction costs (W2)		(383.7)	(383.7)			
Pre-tax net op. Cash flows					150.0	
Tax saved (W3)			115.1	115.1		
Tax paid						(45.0)
Net cash flow	(32.0)	(383.7)	(268.6)	115.1	150.0	(45.0)
Discount factor @ 10% (W4)	0.909	0.751	0.683	0.621	5.815	5.286
DCF	(29.1)	(288.2)	(183.5)	71.5	872.3	(237.9)

NPV = P$205.1m

Workings

(1)   *Environmental study*

Environmental study in PS$m = US$(5)m × exchange rate of P$6.3958 = P$(32)m

Note that the payments made in 20X8 and 20X9 for the environmental study are not included as these are sunk costs (not relevant).

(2)   *Construction costs*

Construction costs in P$m = US$(60)m × exchange rate of P$6.3958 = P$(383.7)m

(3) *Tax saved*

Tax saved = 30% of construction costs = P\$383.7m × 30% = P\$115.1m

Tax saved is deferred by one year. No tax relief is available on the environmental study.

(4) *Annuity factors*

Annuity factor (years 5 – 24) = Annuity factor (1 – 24) – annuity factor (1 – 4)

= 8.985 – 3.17

= 5.815

Annuity factor (years 6 – 25) = Annuity factor (1 – 25) – annuity factor (1 – 5)

= 9.077 – 3.791

= 5.286

<u>Scenario 2 – new 10% tax rate from 20Y4 onwards</u>

Year	20Y0	20Y2	20Y3	20Y4		
Time	1	3	4	5	5–24	6–25
	P\$m	P\$m	P\$m	P\$m	P\$m	P\$m
Pre-tax net op. Cash flow					150.0	
Tax 10%						(15.0)
Net cash flow	(32.0)	(383.7)	(268.6)	115.1	150.0	(15.0)
Discount factor @ 10%	0.909	0.751	0.683	0.621	5.815	5.286
DCF	(29.1)	(288.2)	(183.5)	71.5	872.3	(79.3)

NPV = P\$363.7m

<u>Scenario 3 – exchange rate changes (tax rate stays the same)</u>

Year	20Y0	20Y2	20Y3	20Y4		
Time	1	3	4	5	5-24	6-25
	P\$m	P\$m	P\$m	P\$m	P\$m	P\$m
Environmental costs (W2)	(34.5)					
Construction costs (W2)		(457.0)	(479.9)			
Pre-tax net op. Cash flow					150.0	
Tax saved			137.1	144.0		
Tax paid						(45.0)
Net cash flow	(34.5)	(457.0)	(342.8)	144.0	150.0	(45.0)
Discount factor @ 10%	0.909	0.751	0.683	0.621	5.815	5.286
DCF	(31.4)	(343.2)	(234.1)	89.4	872.3	(237.9)

NPV = P\$115.1m

Workings

(1) *Exchange rate*

The 20Y0 exchange rate is found as follows:

Exchange rate (May 20X9) = US\$/P\$6.3958

May 20X9 is 1 year and 7 months from the end of 20Y0 so the exchange rate is forecast as

$6.3958 × 1.05^{(1 + 7/12)} = 6.3958 × 1.0803 = 6.909$

Exchange rates for 20Y1 – 20Y3 are as follows:

20Y1 $6.909 \times 1.05 = 7.254$

20Y2 $7.254 \times 1.05 = 7.617$

20Y3 $7.617 \times 1.05 = 7.998$

(2)   Environmental costs and construction costs

Convert costs to P$ using the exchange rates calculated in working 1 above.

20Y0   Environmental costs = US$(5)m $\times$ 6.909 = P$(34.5)m

20Y2   Construction costs = US$(60)m $\times$ 7.617 = P$(457.0)m

20Y3   Construction costs = US$(60)m $\times$ 7.998 = P$(479.9)m

Scenario 4 – new exchange rate and new tax rate of 10% from 20Y4 onwards

> **Tutorial note.** The figures for times 1, 3, 4 and 5 will be the same as scenario 3.

Year	20Y0	20Y2	20Y3	20Y4		
Time	1	3	4	5	5-24	6-25
	P$m	P$m	P$m	P$m	P$m	P$m
Environmental costs	(34.5)					
Construction costs		(457.0)	(479.9)			
Pre-tax net op. Cash flow					150.0	
Tax saved			137.1	144.0		
Tax paid						(15.0)
Net cash flow	(34.5)	(457.0)	(342.8)	144.0	150.0	(15.0)
Discount factor @ 10%	0.909	0.751	0.683	0.621	5.815	5.286
DCF	(31.4)	(343.2)	(234.1)	89.4	872.3	(79.3)

NPV = P$273.7m

(b)   REPORT

To: Directors of PU
From: Finance Director
Date: September 20X9
Re: Hydroelectric power station – project appraisal

Introduction

This report addresses the issue of the proposed hyrdroelectric power station, focusing on the following points:

(i)   The extent to which the project is likely to improve PU's financial position (and thus shareholders' wealth)

(ii)   Other factors that may need to be considered before the final investment decision is made

(iii)   An appropriate financing structure for the project, including an evaluation of the costs and risks arising from the use of foreign currency borrowings

Part (i)

Financial appraisal of the project

The NPV of the project in each of the four possible scenarios can be summarised as follows:

	Tax rate 30%	Tax rate 10%
	P$m	P$m
Constant exchange rate	205.1	363.7
US$ strengthening by 5% per annum	115.1	273.7

The NPV of the project is positive in all possible scenarios therefore it would appear that accepting the project would increase shareholder wealth. However before a final decision is made there are a number of relevant factors that should be taken into consideration.

Part (ii)

Movement in tax rates

If the exchange rate remains constant but the tax rate falls from 30% to 10%, NPV increases by 77% from P$205m to P$363.7m. The tax rate decision has yet to be approved by Parliament but the company should continue to lobby in its favour.

Movement in exchange rates

An appreciation of 5% in the value of the US$ would have the effect of reducing NPV by 44% from P$205.1m to P$115.1m (assuming a tax rate of 30%), due to construction costs and environmental costs increasing in P$ terms. This P$90m reduction represents a large exchange rate risk and PU should consider the use of such instruments as forward or future contracts to hedge against this risk. As such instruments 'lock in' the exchange rate, the project can be appraised using the agreed rate. This will remove the uncertainty of exchange rate movements, thus giving PU a better idea of what NPV is likely to be.

Impact on gearing – financial risk

PU's corporate financial objectives include maintaining group gearing **below 40%** based on market values. If PU decides to finance this project entirely by debt we have to determine the effect this will have on gearing levels.

	Current position	If project is debt-financed
Debt (market value)	P$9,560	Increase in debt of US$130m Exchange rate in 20Y2 of approximately 7.617 Increase = P$990.21m Total debt = P$10,550.21m
Equity (market value)	5,525m shares × P$2.80 = P$15,470	Assume that this will increase by the most pessimistic NPV of the project (P$115.1m) New total = P$15,585.1m
Gearing [debt: (debt + equity)]	$\dfrac{9,560}{(9,560+15,470)} = 38.2\%$	$\dfrac{10,550.21}{(10,550.21+15,585.1)} = 40.4\%$

If the project is financed entirely by debt, the gearing ratio will be pushed beyond the upper limit of 40%. In order to avoid this, PU will have to find **other sources of finance** to supplement any debt used.

Reliability of data

PU has no previous experience of the type of project being proposed therefore the data being used for investment appraisal purposes may be significantly inaccurate. The construction costs and operating cash flows are estimates, as is the life of the dam. The cost of capital used to appraise the project is the 'normal' rate used by PU. It could be argued that a **higher cost of capital** should be used to reflect the higher risk of an unfamiliar project.

It may be worth carrying out **sensitivity analysis** to determine the impact of changes to these factors on the financial worth of the project.

Risk of damage to corporate reputation

There is a significant risk of opposition to the project from the local community, due to the impact that it will have on housing and farmland. Unless steps are taken to minimise the disruption and impact, the reputation of PU could be seriously compromised. This is a particular problem at the moment as PU's profile is likely to increase with the proposed acquisition of DP.

Political risk

At the moment there appears to be support from the government for this type of project in the form of potential tax benefits. However PU should consider the potential impact of a change in government – would a new government be equally supportive or might the project's future be jeopardised?

Technological risk

PU has never undertaken a project like this before therefore there is a risk that there is insufficient expertise to see it through to completion and subsequent success. Given the importance of the project – and the attention it is receiving from the public – PU should seriously consider this issue and whether it might be wise to enter into a **joint venture** with another, more experienced, party.

Other projects

PU should assess whether undertaking this project will compromise its ability to invest in **other forms of technology** or other initiatives such as the potential acquisition of DP.

Real options

PU should consider whether the new technological expertise that is being developed in the dam's construction can be put to good use in the **future**. Similar projects might be developed either in the domestic market or further afield, and the current project might have scope for future expansion.

There is an option to withdraw from the project by the end of 20X9 should PU decide that further development is not desirable. Should such a decision be taken after the end of 20X9, PU will be required to pay the final instalment of the environmental study costs.

Advice on whether or not to proceed

This project should help PU in its objective to improve efficiency of energy production and is likely to provide a good return to shareholders.

The extra risk involved – such as the **foreign exchange risk** – should be managed appropriately and it is strongly recommended that a construction company with expertise in this area should be found.

There are potential future opportunities arising from this project, including the expansion of the proposed power station and the development of similar projects in other markets and/or countries.

Part (iii)

Costs and risks of using foreign currency borrowings

As noted above, there is a high exchange rate risk associated with a movement in the US$/P$ exchange rate. This section of the report considers the difference between financing the project using a domestic loan (with fixed interest of 5% before tax) and financing the project using a foreign currency-denominated loan.

Costs

We will compare the two alternatives using IRR.

	1 January	
	20Y2	*20Y7*
	Time 0	*Time5*
	P$m	*P$m*
Cash flow (W1)	(831.5)	927.4
Discount factor (5%)	1.000	0.784
DCF	(831.5)	727.1

NPV = P$(104.4)m

Working - Conversion of US$ to P$

> **Tutorial note.** We are assuming a constant exchange rate for this calculation.

1 January 20Y2 = US$(130)m x 6.3958 = P$(831.5)m
1 January 20Y7 = US$145m x 6.3958 = P$927.4m

To find the IRR we need another NPV. Try 2%.

	1 January	
	20Y2	20Y7
	Time 0	Time 5
	P$m	P$m
Cash flow (W1)	(831.5)	927.4
Discount factor (2%)	1.000	0.906
DCF	(831.5)	840.2

NPV = P$8.7m

$$IRR = 2 + \frac{8.7}{(8.7 + 104.4)} \times (5 - 2) = 2.2\%$$

Risks

The problem with the above calculations and results is that they assume a constant exchange rate. If we assume that the US$ is going to appreciate by 5% per annum (using the exchange rates we calculated for Scenario 3 above), the loan actually becomes much more expensive.

	1 January	
	20Y2	20Y7
	Time 0	Time 5
	P$m	P$m
Cash flow (W1)	(943.0)	1,342.4
Discount factor (5%)	1.000	0.784
DCF	(943.0)	1,052.4

NPV = P$109.4m

Working

Conversion of cash flows from US$ to P$

> **Tutorial note**. Remember to use the exchange rate calculated for 20Y1 for the 1 January 20Y2 cash flows as the exchange rates refer to the end of the year.

1 January 20Y2 = US$(130)m × 7.254 = P$(943)m
1 January 20Y7 = US$145m × 7.254 x 1.055 = P$1,342.4m

To find IRR we need another NPV. Try 10%.

	1 January	
	20Y2	20Y7
	Time 0	Time 5
	P$m	P$m
Cash flow (W1)	(943.0)	1,342.4
Discount factor (10%)	1.000	0.621
DCF	(943.0)	833.6

NPV = P$(109.4)m

$$IRR = 5 + \frac{109.4m}{(109.4 + 109.4)} \times (10 - 5) = 7.5\%$$

The IRR has increased significantly with the prospect of a 5% per annum appreciation of the US$. The effective cost of 7.5% compares unfavourably with a known cost of 5% if a domestic loan was used to finance the project.

If the risk of a much higher effective cost is unacceptable to PU, the company should only consider a US$ loan if the foreign exchange risk can be managed using such instruments as forward or future contracts. There are no US$ receipts against which the loan could be netted off.

Financing structure for the loan - recommendation

If the foreign exchange risk could be **hedged** using appropriate instruments, the US$ loan is worth considering. However PU would have to compare the cost of the hedged debt with the cost of the domestic loan.

PU should also consider the fact that it is already close to its upper limit of 40% gearing and as such should consider financing at least part of the project using a **rights issue** rather than debt. A **maximum of 40%** of the project should be financed by debt to maintain the current gearing ratio. If hedging is not possible, PU should use domestic debt finance rather than foreign currency debt.

Should you wish to discuss any part of this report further please do not hesitate to contact me.

(c)   Potential reasons for disposing of the hydroelectric power station

Refocus the business

PU might want to refocus its attention on coal-fired power stations which is the main area of **expertise**. The hydroelectric power station may no longer fit in with PU's portfolio.

Raise cash

PU might have a need for cash, either due to economic conditions or to finance a new project. The sale of the hydroelectric power station may be the most sensible strategy to **raise funds**.

Increase efficiency

Hydroelectric power was not part of PU's expertise. Management may have found it too difficult to run given their limited knowledge and concluded that it would be in PU's best interests to sell the power station to another company.

Accepting a bid

PU may have received a bid for the power station that it would be in the best interests of the shareholders to accept.

Reduce cost of capital

The hydroelectric power station posed a considerable risk to PU and a strategic decision may have been taken to sell it to reduce this risk and thus the company's **cost of capital**.

Ways in which the divestment could be achieved

Management buyout (MBO)

Employees, usually in association with venture capitalists, take over the running of the power station. This reduces the need for **redundancies**.

Sell-off

The power station could be sold as a going concern to another company, usually in return for cash. However if this move resulted in redundancies, PU's reputation could be damaged.

Spin-off (demerger)

A separate listing could be sought for PP which would lead to a clearer management structure. Management of PP could concentrate on the hydroelectric power station whilst management of PU devote their attention to the coal-fired business.

Closure

The power station could be closed completely, although this is unlikely as most of the costs will be sunk costs by year 6.

92 Aybe (1)

Text references. This question covers various areas of the syllabus. Investment appraisal techniques and international investment appraisal (including foreign currency risk) are covered in Chapters 11 and 12 respectively. Divestment (exit) strategies are covered in Chapter 16.

Top tips. Use the NPV proforma provided in Chapter 11 – this will make your answers to part (a) easier to follow (both for you and the marker). Make sure you treat the currency in the correct way. It is the US DOLLAR that is appreciating (and therefore the C$ is depreciating, which means you will be dividing the spot rate by 1.05 each time). Reading the question carefully is essential to ensure you pick up the different tax treatments and discount rates for each project.

Part (b) is essentially a sensitivity analysis exercise but don't forget to interpret your calculations (there are 8 marks available for discussion, 6 for calculations).

In part (c) you should be looking at the issues surrounding the financing decision for foreign investment, such as translation risk and matching .

Don't be tempted just to give a generic answer to part (d). There are general issues that should be suggested but the question has also specifically asked for discussion of issues that are specific to each project.

Easy marks. You should be able to pick up a number of easy marks in part (a) when calculating the NPV of the projects.

Examiner's comments. Overall the performance was good on this question. The better candidates managed to make some reference to the pre-seen material but many failed to make any connection.

Common errors:

Part (a)

– Incorrect calculation of forward exchange rates (showing a weakening rather than a strengthening US$)

– Incorrect tax calculations, typically ignoring the balancing allowance, or incorrect timing of tax relief cash flows

– Ignoring tax relief on development in Project 2

– Timing errors on cash flows in Project 2, especially in the cost of land and development

A sizeable minority of candidates could not set up their NPV calculations in the prescribed tabular/columnar format. This made marking difficult and candidates often failed to gain credit for structure and presentation of figures.

In part (b) many candidates identified relevant factors but often failed to relate the points that were being made to the choice of project. Some candidates discussed the sensitivity of the NPV result to changes in individual inputs but failed to discuss the implications of their results.

The main weakness in part (c) was misreading the question and discussing possible methods of financing rather than the choice of currency.

Part (d) was generally well attempted although many answers lacked focus on the question asked.

Marking scheme

	Marks	
(a) Capital allowances and tax relief	2.0	
Exchange rates and cash inflow conversion	2.0	
Project 1		
Cash inflows	0.5	
Cash outflows	0.5	
Loss on current products	0.5	
Residual value	0.5	
Tax	1.0	
Discounting and NPV	1.5	
Project 2		
Grant - timing	0.5	
Total cash flow	0.5	
Timings of land, development costs and residual values (0.5 marks each)	1.5	
Tax calculations and timings	2.0	
Conversion of cash flows to C$	1.0	
Discounting	<u>1.0</u>	
		17
(b) Up to 3 marks per factor discussed	<u>Max 8</u>	
Calculations – up to 3 marks per relevant calculation	<u>Max 6</u>	
		14
(c) Advantages of US$ borrowings – 0.5 marks per relevant point	<u>Max 2</u>	
Advantages of C$ borrowings – 0.5 marks per relevant point	<u>Max 2</u>	
Recommendation based on evaluation	<u>2</u>	
		6
(d) General issues, project 1, project 2 – up to 3 marks per issue discussed	Max 11	
Structure and presentation	<u>Max 3</u>	
	Total	<u>50</u>

REPORT

To: The Directors of Aybe
From: External consultant
Date: 27 May 20X0
Re: Production facilities for new state-of-the-art products

Introduction and purpose

The purpose of this report is to evaluate the two projects that have been proposed for the production of the new state-of-the-art products. It focuses on both the financial and strategic aspects of each of the proposals and recommends which project should be undertaken.

Investment appraisal financials

> **Tutorial note** – this forms the answer to part (a).

Project 1 – factory refit in Country C

Year	20X1 C$m	20X2 C$m	20X3 C$m	20X4 C$m	20X5 C$m
Cash inflow (W1)	Nil	44.1	46.3	48.6	51.1
Cash outflows		(30.0)	(30.0)	(30.0)	(30.0)
Loss on current products	(4.0)				
Net operating cash flow	(4.0)	14.1	16.3	18.6	21.1
Tax at 25%	1.0	(3.5)	(4.1)	(4.7)	(5.3)
Factory refit	(35.0)				
Residual value					4.0
Tax relief on refit (W2)	4.4	1.1	0.6	0.8	0.9
Net cash flow	(33.6)	11.7	12.8	14.7	20.7
Discount factor 8%	0.926	0.857	0.794	0.735	0.681
DCF	(31.1)	10.0	10.2	10.8	14.1

NPV = C$14.0m

Workings

1   Exchange rate and cash inflow conversion

Year	C$/US$	Cash inflow (C$m) – Project 1
20X0	4.000	
20X1	3.810	
20X2	3.629	US$160 ÷ 3.629 = 44.1
20X3	3.456	US$160 ÷ 3.456 = 46.3
20X4	3.291	US$160 ÷ 3.291 = 48.6
20X5	3.134	US$160 ÷ 3.134 = 51.1

2   Tax allowances – factory refit in Country C

Year	Tax allowances C$m	Tax relief at 25% C$m
20X1 – Cost	35.00	
FYA (50%)	(17.50)	4.4
	17.50	
20X2 – WDA (25%)	(4.38)	1.1
	13.12	
20X3 – WDA	(3.28)	0.8
	9.84	
20X4 – WDA	(2.46)	0.6
	7.38	
20X5 – Residual value	(4.00)	
Balancing allowance	3.38	0.9

Project 2 – new factory in the USA

Year	20X0 US$m	20X1 US$m	20X2 US$m	20X3 US$m	20X4 US$m	20X5 US$m
Grant			15.0	15.0	15.0	
Net pre-tax operating cash flows			<u>50.0</u>	<u>50.0</u>	<u>50.0</u>	<u>50.0</u>
Total cash flow			65.0	65.0	65.0	50.0
Tax at 30%			(19.5)	(19.5)	(19.5)	(15.0)
Land	(20.0)					
Development cost		(60.0)	(60.0)			
Residual value of project						40.0
Tax relief (W3)		<u>18.0</u>	<u>18.0</u>			(6.0)
Net cash flow	(20.0)	(42.0)	3.5	45.5	45.5	69.0
Dis. factor 11%	1.000	0.901	0.812	0.751	0.659	0.593
DCF	(20.0)	(37.8)	2.8	34.2	30.0	40.9
Exchange rate C$/US$ (W1)	4.00	3.810	3.629	3.456	3.291	3.134
	C$m	C$m	C$m	C$m	C$m	C$m
DCF	(5.0)	(9.9)	0.8	9.9	9.1	13.1

NPV = C$18.0m

Workings

3   <u>Tax allowances</u>

Year	Tax allowance US$m	Tax relief at 30% US$m
20X1 – Cost	60	
100% FYA	<u>(60)</u>	18
	<u>Nil</u>	
20X2 – Cost	60	
100% FYA	<u>(60)</u>	18
	Nil	
20X5 – Residual value (excl land)	20	
Balancing charge	20	(6)

Assumptions

1   Inflation remains at the assumed level, as do costs and revenues

2   The US$200,000 fee has been treated as a sunk cost

3   Exchange rates move as predicted. Any differences will be hedged using futures or forwards

4   Tax rates and capital allowance rates will not change throughout the life of the project

5   Real options are included in the residual value

6   Any supervisory costs and further consultants' costs are immaterial to the project and will not affect the outcome

Tutorial note – this forms the answer to part (b).

<u>Analysis of the projects</u>

Summary

Investment appraisal using NPV indicates that building a new factory in the USA (with NPV = C$18.0m) is preferable to refitting the current factory in Country C (NPV = C$14.0m).

Changes to planning horizon

For such a major investment, the planning horizon is **very short** (5 years, with only 4 of these in actual production). The planning horizon is a fundamental issue in the appraisal of the two projects. If the US dollar continues to strengthen at a rate of 5% per annum, the C$ value of cash inflows will decline. If we look at the post-tax operating cash flows in 20X5

Project 1   C$15.8m
Project 2   C$11.2m   (US$35m / 3.134)

we can see a difference of C$4.6m. However if this was projected further, the annual 5% appreciation of the US$, together with the higher discount rate being used in Project 2, this difference would be **quickly eroded**.

If we ignored the currency movements and analysed the 20X5 post-tax operating cash flows in perpetuity, the results would be as follows.

Project 1   C$15.8m/0.08 = C$197.5m
Project 2   C$11.2m/0.11 = C$101.8m

Project 1 would be preferable to Project 2 by quite a considerable margin, even without allowing for other factors.

Based on the evidence above, the planning horizon is **critical** to the appraisal of the two projects. If it is likely that the production horizon will be greater than 5 years, this should be built into the appraisal process. Failure to do so could produce a misleading – and ultimately expensive – result.

Consultants' fees

There is no information on the extent of the consultants' fees. The likely cost of these fees should be investigated as soon as possible as it could have a **significant impact** on the feasibility of Project 1.

It is also unclear as to why there are no external consultants' fees for Project 2. It should be determined as soon as possible whether any such fees are likely to be incurred as this will have an effect on the project NPV.

Discount rates

No information is available regarding how the respective discount rates were determined. Any change in discount rates will obviously have an effect on the NPV of each project and potentially on the recommendation of which project to adopt. By conducting a sensitivity analysis on the discount rate for each project, we can determine the extent to which the rates can change before the NPVs become negative.

Project 1

Year	20X1	20X2	20X3	20X4	20X5
	C$m	C$m	C$m	C$m	C$m
Net cash flow	(33.6)	11.7	12.8	14.7	20.7

NPV at 8% = C$15.1m

NPV at 30% = C$(3.1)m

$$IRR = a + \frac{NPV_a}{NPV_a - NPV_b} (b - a) = 8 + [15.1/(15.1 + 3.1)] \times (30 - 8) = 26.3\%$$

The discount rate can increase by 18.3 percentage points (229%) before NPV reaches zero. Project 1 is therefore not overly sensitive to changes in the discount rate.

Project 2

Year	20X0	20X1	20X2	20X3	20X4	20X5
	US$m	US$m	US$m	US$m	US$m	US$m
Net cash flow	(20.0)	(42.0)	3.5	45.5	45.5	69.0
Exchange rate C$/US$ (W1)	4.00	3.810	3.629	3.456	3.291	3.134
	C$	C$	C$	C$	C$	C$
Net cash flow in C$	(5.0)	(11.02)	0.96	13.17	13.83	22.02

NPV at 11% = C$17.6m

NPV at 45% = C$(1.3)m

$$\text{IRR} = a + \frac{\text{NPV}_a}{\text{NPV}_a - \text{NPV}_b} (b - a) = 11 + [17.6/(17.6 + 1.3)] \times (45 - 11) = 42.7\%$$

The discount rate can increase by 31.7 percentage points (288%) before NPV becomes zero. This project is even less sensitive to discount rate movements than Project 1.

It may be advisable to compare these results with those using alternative approaches to **risk adjustment** (such as expected values). Before proceeding with either project it is strongly recommended that the factors that contributed to the determination of the discount rates are thoroughly investigated and verified. If the discount rates are found to be reasonable, it is unlikely that these rates will be significant factors in the final decision, given the extent to which they would have to increase before the projects became infeasible.

Exchange rates

It has been assumed that the US$ will appreciate steadily by 5% each year. There is a strong likelihood that this will not be the case. Aybe should be conscious of exposure to exchange rate risk, although there is a possibility that the US cash inflows will provide a hedge against US cash outflows. If the US$ only appreciated by 4% per annum, NPV would be

Year	20X0	20X1	20X2	20X3	20X4	20X5
	US$m	US$m	US$m	US$m	US$m	US$m
Net cash flow	(20.0)	(42.0)	3.5	45.5	45.5	69.0
Exchange rate C$/US$ (W1)	4.00	3.85	3.70	3.56	3.42	3.29
	C$	C$	C$	C$	C$	C$
Net cash flow in C$	(5.0)	(10.91)	0.95	12.78	13.30	20.97
Dis. factor 11%	1.000	0.901	0.812	0.751	0.659	0.593
DCF	(5.0)	(9.83)	0.77	9.60	8.76	12.44

NPV = C$16.74m

For every 1% change in the exchange rate, NPV moves by 7%. Project 2 is sensitive to changes in the exchange rate and this should be factored into any decision that is made. Aybe may have to think about using such **hedging techniques** as futures or forwards to protect itself from exposure to foreign currency risk.

Gearing

Aybe has indicated that there will be no further issue of equity shares for the next five years. As a result, the project will have to be funded by debt, subject to the loan covenant that the debt/equity ratio should not be greater than 0.75. The effect on gearing will be as follows.

Current gearing ratio	40/(180 x 0.64) =	34.7%	(where 0.64 is the market value/share)
Project 1	(40 + 35)/(180 x 0.64 + 14.8)	=	57.7%
Project 2	[40 + (140/4)]/(180 x 0.64 + 18.3)	=	56.2%

Gearing does not change significantly from Project 1 to Project 2 and remains within the acceptable limits, although there is a considerable increase in gearing as a result of investing in either of the projects. However gearing should **not be a major factor** in the final decision.

BPP
LEARNING MEDIA

Project 1 – production disruption

The effect of the disruption to production on future business should be **investigated further**. It may not be realistic to assume that this disruption will not result in customers permanently moving their business to other competitors. If it is found that there will be some lasting impact on current business, this will have to be accounted for in the appraisal of Project 1.

Residual value of projects

The residual value of both projects is a fundamental part of the appraisal process. For Project 1, the residual value is approximately 11% of the refit cost whilst for Project 2, residual value is a very significant 33% of the development costs. Should the residual values be considerably different from estimates, this could have a significant effect on the feasibility of the projects. A sensitivity analysis is given below to show the extent to which NPV will change when residual value is changed.

Project 1

Current estimated residual value   C$4m

Current NPV   C$14.8m

If residual value fell by 1% to C$3.96m the effect would be as follows.

	C$m	
Residual value	3.96	
Balancing allowance	0.86	[(7.38 – 3.96) x 0.25]
Total value	4.82	
Total current value	4.90	(4 + balancing allowance of 0.9)
Difference	(0.08)	
Discounted at 8%, five years)	(0.05)	

This represents a 0.3% change in NPV for a 1% change in residual value.

Project 2

Current residual value (including land)   US$40.0m

Current NPV   US$18.3m

If residual value was reduced by 1% the effect on NPV would be as follows.

	US$	
Residual value	39.60	
Balancing charge	(5.94)	(19.8 x 0.3)
Net value	33.66	
Current value	34.00	(40 – 6)
Difference	(0.36)	
Discounted at 11%, five years	(0.21)	

This represents a 1.1% reduction in NPV for a 1% reduction in residual value of land and buildings.

Political risk

It has been assumed that tax rates and capital allowance rates will **stay the same** throughout the duration of the projects. These rates may change as a result of such factors as change of government, trying to reduce budget deficits or trying to encourage investment. Any changes in tax rates will obviously have an effect on the tax relief given on the investments which will in turn affect the NPV.

Another political issue that should be considered is the possibility of changes to the rules on grant entitlement. If Aybe no longer qualifies for a grant – or qualifies for a reduced grant – the NPV of Project 2 will be affected, which may reverse the recommendation of which project is likely to be most profitable.

Recommendation on how to proceed

Based on the financial appraisal of both projects, Project 2 is recommended for several reasons.

(i)   This project has the highest NPV and is therefore likely to be the most profitable. This position has been helped by the US$15m grant.

(ii)   There are no expected disruptions to current production in Country C. This eliminates the risk of customers failing to return to Aybe when normal production resumes.

(iii)   As products are priced in US$, basing production in the US will reduce currency risk. Costs will be incurred in US$ which may be set against US$ revenue.

(iv)   Specialist consultants are based in the USA. If production was also based there, it should mean more rapid responses to issues and also the cost of travel between Country C and the USA.

However the above recommendation is subject to the investigation of the issues that were highlighted in the analysis of the projects above.

> **Tutorial note** – this forms the answer to part (c).

Choice of currency for Project 2

Given that Aybe would be operating in both Country C and the US if Project 2 was selected, it should be straightforward to raise finance in either C$ or US$. The main advantage of using C$ is that the interest can be **paid easily from income denominated in C$**. There will be no exchange rate risk in converting C$ income to US$ in order to service the debt.

If the loan was taken out in US$, this has the advantage of matching the finance currency with the investment currency. This helps to **reduce foreign currency risk** and also ensures that not all of the profits from the US establishment will be repatriated back to Country C.

The problem with raising finance in US$ is that there may be insufficient income in US$ to fully service the debt. However this should not be a major issue given that the new products will be priced in US$ for all world-wide sales. The US$ debt can be serviced using this income from other parts of the business.

One factor that should not be ignored is what the **shareholders might want** or expect from the business. They may prefer to have the lower risk offered by financing US debt in US$. Expectations also depend on the extent to which Aybe has been exposed to foreign currency risk in the past. Will shareholders expect results to be affected by movements in the US$ exchange rate or will this be an unfamiliar issue? If Aybe is suitably hedged against foreign exchange risk, results should not be affected to any great extent. If US debt is used, steps should be taken to ensure suitable hedging policies have been implemented.

Recommendation

The benefits of financing US investments in US$ are likely to exceed the risks of doing so therefore it is recommended that US$ are used to finance the new US subsidiary.

> **Tutorial note** – this forms the answer to part (d).

Efficient management and control of implementation of the projects

Past capital budget overspends means that close management and control of the project's implementation is essential. As well as general implementation issues common to both projects, there are specific factors to each project that must be considered when putting the project into practice.

General issues

Before either project can commence, a suitable **support team** should be set up to oversee progress. A suitably qualified project manager should be in post and remain in this position for the duration of the project. It is important to set up a reliable team of **professionals** to deal with the day-to-day progress of the project, including contractors and site managers, and build up a good working relationship with the members of the team.

From the outset, the project teams should be fully aware of the **legal and environmental issues** surrounding the project and ensure that work being carried out does not breach any regulations. Reputable contractors should already be aware of such issues but it is worth reminding all parties of factors that may be specific to the project.

Although a financial appraisal of the projects has been conducted the issues raised in the *Analysis of the projects* section of this report must be investigated. If not already conducted, research into the potential market for the new product should take place to ensure that the quoted revenue figures used in the NPV calculations are valid.

As well as focusing on physical resources for the project, it is essential that any specific employee training needs for any new production processes are identified and addressed at the earliest opportunity. Doing so will ensure minimum disruption to the production of the new products when the facilities become available.

It is important that Aybe learns from past capital investment overspends. The project team should review any post completion audits from previous projects where such problems occurred to identify where mistakes had been made. Appropriate steps can be taken to ensure that such mistakes do not occur in the implementation of this project, particularly given the magnitude of investment involved.

Project 1 – factory refit in Country C

The main issue with Project 1 is the disruption to current business. It is crucial that such disruption is kept to a minimum therefore careful management of the process will be required. **Forward planning** might help – for example, building up inventory in the time leading up to the disruption period so that existing customers are still receiving their orders.

Regular checks on the progress of the refit will be necessary, not only to ensure it is on schedule but also that it is within budget. As overspending has been a problem in the past Aybe cannot afford, either financially or strategically, to have a similar situation with a C$35m project.

Project 2 – new factory in the USA

Distance will be a problem when trying to manage the US project. However as Aybe already operates in the US this may not be a significant issue. It should be ensured that project managers are familiar with the legal and environmental requirements in force in the US to **ensure compliance**. Aybe should arrange for a project manager to be based in the US for the duration of the project.

As US$200,000 has already been paid for the option of purchasing full ownership rights, it is essential that Aybe gains the necessary **planning permission** within the eight month window. Effective management will be necessary to oversee the progress of the planning permission application and to ensure that any issues are dealt with promptly.

The revenue grant is subject to certain conditions. In order to avoid having to repay the grant (and thus effectively render the project infeasible) the project manager should be monitoring progress to ensure **compliance with the terms and conditions**.

Construction of a manufacturing facility will inevitably involve major changes to the land and the construction site. As mentioned above, environmental factors must be considered and it will be a major task of the project manager to ensure that regulations are being adhered to.

93 Aybe (2)

Text references. Business valuations are covered in Chapter 15 whilst issues surrounding acquisitions are dealt with in Chapter 16.

Top tips. The examiner's answers included a number of assumptions in part (a) and applied several, seemingly ad hoc, percentages when trying to determine valuations for NN. It is unlikely that you would come up with exactly the same percentages but as long as the figures you come up with are reasonable you will gain the available marks.

Part (b) should be in the form of a report so make sure you gain maximum presentation marks by structuring your answer accordingly.

It is important in this part of the question to continue to refer to the specific scenario. Part (b)(i) asks you to evaluate the situation from the viewpoint of the two sets of shareholders. Remember that NN's shareholders will be wanting to receive the maximum possible price whilst Aybe's shareholders will want to pay as little as they can get away with. Aybe's shareholders will be interested in the net effects of integration and synergy therefore you can calculate a more realistic valuation of NN by including these items.

It is easy to get carried away with your answer to (b)(ii) due to the temptation to write all you know about the problems with acquisitions. By all means use your generic knowledge of these problems but relate them to the specific situation of Aybe and NN. Key points may include differences in culture between listed and private companies and the issue of maintaining market awareness of NN's products without having a 'them and us' attitude.

You can also use your generic knowledge of bonds v bank borrowings to fund acquisitions in (b)(iii) but at the same time apply this knowledge to the companies in the scenario. The covenant problem can be dealt with by doing straightforward comparisons between Aybe's current gearing and interest cover situations and the post-acquisition figures.

Easy marks. You should be able to pick up some marks when valuing NN using DCF. In addition there are numerous marks that can be gained through your general knowledge of acquisition and funding issues.

Examiner's comments. In general, this question was well answered, although lack of understanding of key finance topics in (b)(iii) gave cause for concern. Layout varied considerably between candidates and some of the DCF calculations were particularly difficult to follow.

In part (a)(i) there was a large number of disappointing answers on the choice of debt finance, which suggested some serious misconceptions about the nature of bonds and bank debt.

Common errors included:

–   Using WACC rather than cost of equity to value the company

–   Incorrectly calculating net assets

–   Omitting advice on an appropriate price

–   Saying that bonds are preferable to bank debt as they do not impact on gearing or do not need to be repaid as they could be converted into shares

Marking scheme

				Marks
(a)	(i)	Parcel of shares	1	
		P/E basis – 1 mark per different basis used	Max 2	
		DCF basis – CAPM (including risk adjustment) for discount rate	3	
		Calculation of profits	1	
		Present value calculations	3	
		Specification of range of value	1	
				11
(a)	(ii)	Suitability of each method specified in (a)(i) – up to 3 marks each		Max 6

(b)	(i)	NN's shareholders' viewpoint		3	
		Aybe's shareholders' viewpoint: calculations		4	
		discussion		3	
		Advice on offer price		<u>1</u>	
					11
(b)	(ii)	Integration issues – up to 3 marks per issue discussed			Max 7
(b)	(iii)	Issues relating to debt finance – up to 2 marks per point	Max 6		
		Calculations regarding bank covenants	Max 4		
		Discussion and conclusion	<u>2</u>		
					Max 12
Structure and presentation					<u>3</u>
				Total	<u>50</u>

(a) <u>Price achieved in recent sale of shares</u>

5% parcel of shares was sold for EUR3 million six months ago. This translates to a **market capitalisation** of EUR60 million.

Exchange rate is C$/EUR3.000 therefore this represents a cost to Aybe of C$20 million.

The main problem with this valuation is the fact that the sale was made **six months ago**, hence the price is likely to be out of date. It was also a relatively small proportion of the company rather than a controlling interest which would usually attract a premium.

However EUR60 million could give a reasonable representation of the minimum price that NN's shareholders might be willing to accept (excluding the premium). If a premium of, say, 15% was added, this would give a valuation of EUR69 million.

<u>P/E basis of valuation</u>

The proxy company for NN's results, QQ, has a P/E ratio of 9 which is a useful starting point for valuing NN. However QQ is a more mature company, whereas NN has not yet completed the initial **rapid growth period** of its lifecycle. Aybe might have to be prepared to pay a higher price based on a P/E ratio of, say, 11 or 12.

However it could also be argued that the P/E should be lower, given that private companies' P/E ratios tend to be lower than those of quoted companies (as it is more difficult to find a market for selling shares). There may be grounds for using a P/E ratio of 70 – 75% of QQ's ratio – that is, 6.3% - 6.75%.

Aybe's P/E ratio = (180m shares x C$0.64)/C$23m = 5

This figure might be applied which would indicate the reluctance of Aybe's shareholders to pay a higher price for NN's shares.

The P/E ratio (whichever one is chosen) could be applied either to the 2009 profit of EUR10m or the estimated 2010 profit of EUR11m. Possible valuations are included in the table below.

P/E	Earnings EUR million	Value of NN EUR million	Value of NN C$ million (C$/EUR3)
5	10	50	16.67
5	11	55	18.33
6.3	10	63	21.00
6.3	11	69.3	23.10
12	10	120	40.00
12	11	132	44.00

Any of these valuations could be feasible.

<u>Discounted cash flow basis</u>

The valuation of a business based on discounted free cash flows is highly sensitive to the choice of **discount rate**. Given the information available it makes most sense to use the cost of equity of QQ (the proxy company) as a starting point for NN's discount rate.

Using the CAPM

$K_e = R_f + (R_m - R_f)\beta$

   $= 2 + 6 \times 1.7$

   $= 12.2\%$

Increase by 15% to reflect greater risk = 14.03% (say 14%)

Net present value

	2011 EUR million	2012 EUR million	2013 EUR million	2014+ EUR million
Profit (W1)	11.88	12.83	13.86	14.28
Discount factor (14%) (W2)	0.877	0.769	0.675	6.136
DCF	10.42	9.87	9.36	87.63

Net present value = EUR117.28m

At the current spot rate, this is equivalent to C$39.09m

Working 1

Profit grows by 8% in the first three years and then by 3% thereafter

	Profit EUR million
2011	11.00 x 1.08 = 11.88
2012	11.88 x 1.08 = 12.83
2013	12.83 x 1.08 = 13.86
2014+	13.86 x 1.03 = 14.28

Working 2

Discount factor (2014 onwards) = Perpetuity factor (14%, growth 3%) discounted back 3 years
                                      = [1/(0.14 − 0.03)] x 0.675
                                      = 6.136

As specified in the requirement, this excludes any effects of synergy benefits and integration costs.

Summary of valuations

	Range of values EUR million
Private sale	60 – 69
P/E ratio basis	50 – 132
DCF basis	117.28

Suitability of valuation methods

Share price basis

On average, based on the above summary, the share price gives the lowest valuation, which is consistent with the assumption that the current share price is usually taken to be the minimum offer price. Given that NN is a private company, obtaining a share price is quite difficult. The only price available is six months old relating to a private sale of a small proportion of shares.

Issues with the share price basis

(i)   Any valuation of a company based on six month old data is bound to be **out of date**, particularly if performance forecasts have changed during that time.

(ii)   There are no details regarding how the private sale was conducted. Were the shares sold at a premium or a discount? If so what was it? Or was the agreed price an arm's length price? Without knowing these details we can't determine how accurate the share price was at the time of the sale.

P/E basis

This is a common basis for valuing a controlling interest in a company and is particularly useful for private companies where no market-determined share price is available.

However the P/E ratio was based on a listed company's ratio which is of limited use. We are told that QQ has the same capital structure as NN – which helps – but they are at very different stages in their life cycles. NN is a 'young' company that is still to experience high levels of growth whilst QQ is a more mature company which is less risky (indicated by the fact that its cost of equity has to be uplifted by 15% to reflect the return required from NN).

The adjustments made to QQ's P/E ratio (uplifting from 9 to 11 or 12) helps to reflect NN's higher growth potential and gives higher valuations. However this adjustment is **completely subjective** and is not supported by the discounted cash flow valuation.

Discounted cash flow basis

The main benefit of using this valuation basis is that it is based on predicted cash flows of NN itself, rather than relying on approximations from the proxy company QQ. However caution should be exercised in the interpretation of the results whose usefulness will depend on the **accuracy of the predictions**. 8% growth in NN's cash flows has been predicted for each of the next three years, and 3% growth after that, neither of which may not be realised in practice.

(b)   REPORT

To: Directors of Aybe

From: External consultant

Re: Proposed acquisition of NN

The purpose of this report is to evaluate the proposed acquisition of NN and to offer advice on the next steps in the process.

Evaluation of proposed initial offer price

NN's shareholders

An initial offer price of EUR75 million has been proposed for the transfer of ownership of NN to Aybe. The results of valuing NN using various bases are summarised below.

Summary of valuations

	Range of values EUR million
Private sale	60 – 69
P/E ratio basis	50 – 132
DCF basis	117.28

The private sale basis figures are based on the sale of a 5% stake in NN six months ago. The initial offer price represents a 25% premium on this valuation. However this valuation will be distorted by the fact that the private sale took place six months ago (therefore the figures are likely to be out of date) and represented only a **small proportion of shares**.

The valuations obtained via the P/E and DCF bases are considerably higher than the private sale basis and also significantly exceed the initial offer price of EUR75 million. It is therefore unlikely that NN's shareholders will accept this price.

However NN' shareholders should be aware that they are unlikely to achieve full price for their shares as the company is still in a period of rapid growth. Any potential investor should be expected to discount the price they are prepared to pay to compensate for the possibility that **growth prospects do not actually materialise**. NN's shareholders need to consider whether it is worth waiting a few years in order to realise the full value of their shares or to take what they can now and have immediate access to the funds.

Aybe's shareholders

Aybe's shareholders will also be concerned with the expected benefits from synergy and any integration costs that must be incurred when NN is acquired. These items have been built into the calculations below to give a better picture of net present value of the acquisition. **Synergy benefits** are likely to lead to a 14% growth in earnings in the first three years (rather than 8% predicted by NN) and 3% growth thereafter.

	2010 EUR million	2011 EUR million	2012 EUR million	2013 EUR million	2014+ EUR million
Cash flow	(2.5)	12.54	14.30	16.30	16.79
Discount factor (14%)	1.000	0.877	0.769	0.675	6.136
DCF	(2.5)	11.00	11.00	11.00	103.02

NPV = EUR133.52 million (C$44.51 million)

If Aybe is confident that the synergy benefits can be **sustained** at the predicted levels and that integration costs are unlikely to rise above EUR2.5 million, then the offer price of EUR75 million (C$25 million) will be extremely acceptable to Aybe's shareholders.

However in order to gain some interest from NN's shareholders – and not have them reject the initial offer out of hand – it might be a good idea to raise the initial offer price. EUR75 million is still significantly below the DCF valuation of EUR117.28 million (before synergy benefits) and EUR133.52 million (after benefits and integration costs). If the offer price is raised to say EUR95 – 100 million, Aybe has a better chance of putting itself in a strong bargaining position. Aybe's shareholders will still benefit from increased wealth but the higher bid may be met with less hostility from NN's shareholders.

Recommendation on initial offer price

Based on the above evaluation it is recommended that the initial offer price is raised from the proposed EUR75 million to EUR95 – 100 million. It should be borne in mind that there is limited flexibility for Aybe to increase the offer further should negotiations require it.

Potential problems and issues arising from integration of NN into Aybe

The integration of one company into another is always going to give rise to certain issues and problems. To minimise the impact of integration, it is important to be aware of these issues and problems and have steps in place to deal with them as **quickly and effectively** as possible.

Merging corporate cultures and objectives

This is one of the main issues surrounding acquisitions. When two companies come together there is likely to be some element of 'our way is best' and a **reluctance to embrace cultural changes**. As NN is a private company, its staff may have different ideals and approaches to business – for example, they may be used to a more 'personal' approach by its directors rather than the more formal structure of a listed company.

Integration of management and systems

The directors of NN have probably been used to having a fairly 'free rein' with how business is conducted, implementation of strategies, dictating the direction of the business and other such major issues. They may struggle with the nature of their role within the SC division of Aybe. It is important to establish their roles (if any) within the new structure as soon as possible. Issues that should be addressed include the importance of NN's directors' knowledge, securing continuity if these directors decide not to stay, financial and other motivation for NN's directors to remain with Aybe if their continued contribution is crucial to future success.

In addition to integration of management, **harmonisation of IT systems** is a major issue that should be resolved quickly. Purchasing and sales systems for example must be made compatible. It is important to implement the systems that work best for the company as a whole. Just because the SC division has used a particular system for a long time does not necessarily mean it is the most efficient. If some of NN's systems are considered to be better for business then these should be adopted.

Realisation of projected growth in NN's earnings

NN has been valued based on its projected future earnings and these projections have in turn affected the offer price. A key issue that has to be addressed is ensuring that these growth projections are realised. Shareholders will expect to see financial benefits from the acquisition of NN otherwise questions will be asked as to why the company was acquired in the first place.

Linked with this issue is the risk of new entrants into NN's relatively new product market. If projected growth relies on no new major competitors coming into the market, it will be worthwhile researching how realistic these projections are.

NN's borrowings and financing the bid

NN is highly geared and the **repayment of their bank loan** could be an issue. This, together with how to finance the bid itself, could raise cash flow and further debt issues. This problem can be linked with the importance of realising projected earnings growth mentioned above. If earnings potential is not realised this could give rise to cash flow issues, thus raising problems of how to pay interest on this additional debt.

Branding

Part of NN's success so far is in no doubt due to its ability to meet the specific needs of individual customers. To help realise the projected growth in NN's earnings, it is important that this service continues. However to ensure successful integration, there should be no distinction between what was once NN's products and those of the SC division – there is a fine line to be drawn between retaining image and the integration of NN's products into the SC division's catalogue.

Choice of debt finance to fund the proposed acquisition

Factors affecting the choice of issuing bonds or arranging bank borrowings

Bond issue and bank borrowings will have the same impact on Aybe's gearing and offer the benefit of tax relief on interest. The factors that affect the choice of debt finance will therefore not include gearing and tax issues.

A major issue regarding bonds is the depth of maturity of the C$ and EUR bond markets. Will it be possible for Aybe to raise a potential C$33 million (EUR100 million) in bonds? If not, it may be necessary to either combine the two methods of debt financing or to opt entirely for bank borrowings.

Linked with the possibility of being unable to secure financing via the bond markets is the likelihood that an application for a C$33 million (or EUR100 million) loan would be approved. More information is needed regarding the **creditworthiness** of Aybe and its ability to service a loan of this magnitude. Will fixed interest payments on such a loan pose a liquidity risk for example?

Before a bank will consider granting a loan of such magnitude, it is likely to ask for security or impose additional covenants on the loan. Aybe should consider whether it has sufficient security to back such a loan and if it is willing to be subject to further restrictive covenants.

The success of a bond issue will depend to a large extent on how Aybe is **perceived in the market place** and current market conditions. Is Aybe well known and well received in the markets? Is there sufficient market liquidity to make the success of a bond issue more likely? What is Aybe's credit rating? All these questions have to be addressed before making a final decision on whether to use bonds to raise finance.

Aybe must also consider whether it wishes to finance the acquisition in C$ or EUR. The advantage of using EUR is that it matches the financing currency with the investment currency, thus reducing foreign exchange risk. However Aybe will be subjected to EUR interest rates and will be required to repay the loan in EUR, therefore it will be relying to a large extent on earnings from NN to service these payments.

Current restrictive covenants

Aybe is currently subject to two restrictive covenants:

(i)   Interest cover must not fall below 5
(ii)   Ratio of non-current liabilities to equity must not increase beyond 0.75 : 1

Aybe's current situation is as follows (based on market values).

	C$m
Non-current liabilities	45
Equity (180m x C$0.70)	126

Non-current liabilities : MV of equity = 45/126 = 35.7%

The **current gearing situation** is well within the bank covenant.

Post-acquisition situation

In order to fund the acquisition, Aybe is expected to have to raise a minimum of EUR75 million to pay for NN plus EUR45 million to fund NN's outstanding debt (total of EUR120 million or C$40 million at the current exchange rate).

By acquiring NN, Aybe will obtain net assets with a market value of C$40 million.

Revised gearing ratio would be as follows.

	C$m
Non-current liabilities (45 + 40)	85
Equity (126 + 40)	166

Non-current liabilities : Equity = 85/126 = 51.2%

The revised gearing situation is also comfortably within the bank covenant.

Interest cover covenant

Interest cover = PBIT/Interest charge

Current interest cover = (37 + 4)/4 = 10.25

Post acquisition situation

Assume that the acquisition is financed by new debt of C$40 million at an interest rate of 8%. NN's finance costs (based on the 2009 Income Statement) are EUR4 million (C$1.33 million). Its PBIT is EUR20 million (C$6.67 million).

Revised PBIT = C$41m + C$6.67m = C$47.67 million

Revised interest costs = C$4 million + (C$40 million x 8%) = C$7.2 million

Revised interest cover = 6.6 times

This is still within the bank covenant therefore it is possible to fund the acquisition **entirely by bank borrowings** without breaching the current bank covenant.

If you have any further queries regarding the proposed acquisition of NN please do not hesitate to contact me.

94 DEF (1)

Text references. Cash flow forecasts are covered in Chapter 3. Business valuations are dealt with in Chapter 15 and objectives of organisations in Chapter 1.

Top tips. In part (a) remember that you are not producing cash flows for discounting purposes. This means that you should include interest payments and receipts.

In part (b)(i), make use of the information in the question as it will guide you on the valuation bases you can use. You have sufficient information for DCF calculations and net asset totals. You have an unusual situation of the net assets valuation being greater than the DCF valuation which can be raised in the discussion element. Recommendations about price are always arbitrary so any reasonable figures based on your own calculations will gain marks.

Part (b)(ii) reflects one of the main challenges facing an acquiring company – dealing with different objectives and cultures. You should demonstrate the 'great divide' between the objectives of public sector and private sector companies and show how the objectives of DEF are unlikely to be acceptable to private sector shareholders.

The strategic objectives relevant to part (b)(iii) are included in the pre-seen information. You should not ignore the pre-seen case study during the exam – just because you have seen it in advance doesn't mean that information from it will not be used in the exam itself.

Easy marks. The cash flow forecast in part (a) is quite straightforward and you should pick up a number of easy marks here.

Examiner's comments. This question was generally well answered, although many candidates produced a profit and loss account rather than a cash flow statement and/or failed to provide a statement of cash and cash equivalents. Relatively few candidates were able to incorporate any of the pre-seen information into their answers. In the discussion sections many candidates provided comprehensive answers that would have been improved by greater focus on the scenario.

(a)   Net cash flow forecast

	Year ended 30th June	
	2012	2013
Number of passengers	3.675m	3.969m
	D$	D$
Aviation income (W1)	12.27	13.77
Car parking income (W1)	4.04	4.80
Retail concessions (W1)	5.01	5.36
Other income (W1)	4.26	4.56
Total cash inflows	25.58	28.49
Less operating costs (W2)	(21.27)	(22.12)
Net operating cash flow	4.31	6.37
Add interest received (W3)	0.12	0.21
Less interest paid (W3)	(1.59)	(1.59)
Taxable cash flows	2.84	4.99
Tax at 30%	(0.85)	(1.50)
Capital allowances (W4)	0.23	0.17
Net cash flow for the year	2.22	3.66

Workings

(1)   Underline: Cash inflows

	2012	2013
Number of passengers	3.5m × 1.05 = 3.675m	3.675m × 1.08 = 3.969m

Aviation income

Aviation income per passenger	D$3.21 × 1.04 = D$3.34	D$3.34 × 1.04 = D$3.47
Total aviation income	D$12.27m	D$13.77m

Car parking income

Per passenger	D$1 × 1.1 = D$1.10	D$1.10 × 1.1 = D$1.21
Total	D$4.04m	D$4.80m

Retail concessions

Increase of 7% each year	D$4.68m × 1.07 = D$5.01m	D$5.01m × 1.07 = D$5.36m

Other income

Increase of 7% each year	D$3.98m × 1.07 = D$4.26m	D$4.26m × 1.07 = D$4.56m

(2)   Operating costs

	2012	2013
Exclude depreciation and increase by 4% per annum	(D$25.45m – D$5m) × 1.04 = D$21.27m	D$21.27m × 1.04 = D$22.12m

(3)   Interest received and paid

	2012	2013
	D$m	D$m
Interest received		
Opening balance	3.03	5.25*
Interest of 4%	0.12	0.21
Interest payable		
Borrowings	22.7	22.7
Interest of 7%	(1.59)	(1.59)

* The opening balance for 2013 comes from the statement of opening and closing balances which is further down the page.

(4)   Capital allowances

	Capital allowances D$m	Tax relief at 30% D$m
2012 Opening balance	3.00	
25% WDA	(0.75)	0.23
Tax written down value	2.25	
2013 25% WDA	(0.56)	0.17
Tax written down value	1.69	

Statement of opening and closing balances for cash and cash equivalents

	2012 D$m	2013 D$m
Opening balance	3.03	5.25
Net cash flow (from cash flow forecast)	2.22	3.66
Closing balance	5.25	8.91

(b)   REPORT

To: Board of Directors, DEF Airport
From: External consultant
Re: Potential takeover bid from TUV Airport

This report focuses on issues that result from a potential takeover bid for DEF Airport (DEF) by TUV Airport (TUV). It covers three main areas.

(i)   Ranges of values for DEF which will be useful to gauge the reasonableness of any bid received

(ii)   The main differences in financial objectives of public and private sector organisations, focusing on the stated financial objectives of DEF and TUV

(iii)   The strategic implications of the proposed sale for the LSGs and the other major stakeholder groups

Range of values for DEF

One of the main problems with trying to value DEF arises from its status as a non-listed organisation. This means that there is no market-determined share price available to value DEF. In the absence of a share price, total value can be estimated using one of several available techniques.

Net assets basis

The net assets basis, as the name suggests, values the organisation on what its net assets are worth..

	Year ended 30 June 2011 D$m
Total assets	162.68
Less current liabilities	(9.45)
Non-current liabilities	(22.70)
Net assets	130.53

Discounted cash flow basis

This valuation basis calculates the present value of **all future cash flows** of DEF. The calculation can either include the benefits of synergy that TUV would gain from the acquisition of DEF or exclude these benefits.

	2012 D$m	2013 D$m	2014 D$m	2015 D$m	2016 D$m	2017+ D$m
Cash flow before synergy benefits	2.22	3.66	6.00	8.00	9.00	9.45
Synergy benefits	3.00					
Total cash flows	5.22	3.66	6.00	8.00	9.00	9.45
Discount factor (11%)	0.901	0.812	0.731	0.659	0.593	9.883*
DCF	4.70	2.97	4.39	5.27	5.34	93.39

Net present value (with synergy benefits) = D\$116.06m

Net present value (without synergy benefits) = D\$116.06m – (D\$3m x 0.901) = D\$113.36m

*Growing perpetuity discount factor (11%, growth rate 5%) = [1/(0.11 – 0.05)] x 0.593 = 9.883

Dividend valuation basis and earnings valuation basis

These techniques are also available for valuing a business. The earnings valuation basis values earnings under new ownership (using the P/E ratio) but there is insufficient data available to allow us to use this technique. The dividend valuation basis is really only used for organisations that are paying dividends.

Discussion of results

DEF's value ranges from D\$113.36m (DCF without synergy benefits) to D\$130.53m using the net assets basis. This is unusual as the net assets basis generally gives the **minimum valuation** for an organisation. At face value, it would be tempting to say that DEF's shareholders would be better off if the organisation ceased trading and the assets sold off.

However it is worthwhile considering the situation in more detail. If DEF closed down, who would realistically buy the assets (apart from another airport)? The assets have a very specific purpose and are unlikely to be put to any alternative use. The area has been specifically developed as an airport and the cost of making it fit for any other purpose is likely to be prohibitive. When these issues are taken into consideration, the 'close down and sell off' option is neither attractive nor feasible.

The difference in valuations warrants further scrutiny. The fact that DEF's discounted future cash flows are lower than the value of its net assets might suggest that some of the non-current assets are over-valued. There is insufficient information to look at the individual classes of non-current assets on their own merit but there may be a case for further impairment of the assets.

There is a substantial **revaluation reserve** figure on the statement of financial position for 2011 (D\$89.1m). There is no comparative figure for 2010 but if assets have recently been revalued it might be worth revisiting the reasons for doing so. Without revaluation of non-current assets, the net assets figure would only be D\$41.43m. Even if only half of the revaluation figure was required, net assets would still only be D\$85.98m. This might be a more realistic value but without further information it is not possible to say for certain.

Recommended valuation figure for use in negotiations

DCF valuations suggest that DEF could be valued between D\$113.36m and D\$116.06m. However variations in growth estimates should be built into the valuations. A valuation of between D\$105m and D\$120m appears to be realistic, depending on economic conditions and the likelihood that forecast growth rates will be achieved.

Differences in financial objectives of public and private sector organisations

Private sector organisations

Private sector organisations with numerous large and small shareholders usually focus on **maximising shareholder wealth**. This can be achieved via internal means – such as distributing a proportion of earnings as dividends – or via external means (for example, acquisitions).

TUV's stated financial objectives echo the above - they are focused on maximising shareholder wealth through internal and external means. The potential acquisition of DEF would be designed to increase the value of TUV which will in turn benefit its shareholders.

Public sector organisations

Public sector organisations do not have shareholders to be concerned with but tend to be more focused on getting the best value for money and at least breaking even where possible. Such organisations provide goods and services without the commercial pressure of competition and are therefore not so driven by the need to keep costs down and price competitively. This may at times conflict with the objective of getting the best value for money.

Public sector organisations may be driven more by **non-financial objectives**, such as the welfare of employees or relationships with suppliers.

DEF's stated financial objectives are closely aligned to the general objectives given above.

(i)   The airport does not run at a loss

(ii)   All creditors are paid on time

(iii)   Gearing levels must not exceed 20% (where gearing = debt to debt + equity) and all long-term borrowings are financed from sources approved by the four LSGs

The LSGs also require that DEF at least achieves financial self-sufficiency – very different from the shareholder wealth maximisation objective of TUV.

One of the main issues that TUV will have to consider when deciding whether to bid for DEF is whether it will be easy or possible to integrate such different organisational cultures. If we look at how each of DEF's objectives would have to change in order to fit in with the wealth maximisation focus of TUV it will make these challenges clear.

The first objective would not be acceptable to shareholders in a going-concern organisation. They are expecting **returns on their investments** which cannot be achieved by simply breaking even. The only time such an objective would be acceptable is if the organisation was emerging from a period of loss-making.

Paying creditors on time does not tend to be high on the agenda of a private sector organisation. Whilst it ensures an on-going good relationship with suppliers, it is not conducive to maximising profits or shareholder wealth.

The **gearing restriction** does not offer much scope for debt-financed investment. The current level of gearing (based on book values) is

D\$22.7m/(D\$22.7m + D\$130.53m) = 14.8%

At book values, debt could only increase to a total of D\$32.64m before maximum gearing was reached – an relatively small increase of just under D\$10m. Such a restriction is unlikely to be attractive to shareholders who are used to large expansion plans designed to increase the value of the company (and thus their wealth).

Strategic implications for LSGs and other stakeholders in DEF

LSGs' current investment

Apart from debt owed to external parties (D\$6.3m) the LSGs own the whole of DEF. If a current market value of D\$113.36m is assumed for the whole organisation, this represents a stake of D\$107.06m. The only return they receive on this investment is the interest (7%) on their loans to DEF of D\$16.4m. This amounts to D\$1.15m per annum – a return on investment of only 1.07%. This is a **very low return** for such a risky business as airport provision and one that is unlikely to be acceptable in the long-term.

Risk is likely to increase further with the planned expansion of DEF by 2015. Funding will be required for such expansion – probably debt, although the calculations above show that only a relatively small increase in debt is sustainable if the gearing target is not to be exceeded.

Although the investment does not look attractive, the LSGs have to consider the wider-reaching implications of the potential sale of DEF. It would mean a valuable public service moving into private hands and its provision (or otherwise) would no longer be under government control. If DEF continues to make losses under private ownership, there is the chance it will be closed altogether, which would have a devastating effect on the local area. This would **undermine the strategic objective** of maintaining or increasing employment opportunities in the airport vicinity.

Other stakeholders

Residents in the vicinity of the airport

If DEF changes to private ownership there is a chance that the needs of the local residents will take lower priority. Two of the strategic objectives of the development plan relate to local residents' welfare – the reduction to a minimum of visual and audible impacts of the airport and the minimisation of pollution effects. If TUV takes over the priority of these objectives may be reduced or even scrapped, although it will have to adhere to any relevant legislation on these issues.

Airlines that make use of DEF

DEF is mainly used by holiday airlines and the facilities are assumed meet the needs of this particular market. TUV might try to 'upgrade' the airport if there is sufficient potential increased revenue, which might force these airlines out. However an improved 'scheduled' service might benefit the local economy

and the proposed expansion might be altered to provide facilities for the types of passengers using such services.

A North American carrier is considering using DEF, which would necessitate the provision of facilities expected by first and business class passengers. The airline is insisting on paying in US$ which raises currency exchange risk. TUV might be better equipped to deal with such risk by such means as the purchase of hedging instruments or offsetting any US$ expenditure it currently has against this revenue.

Airport employees

As is often the case with acquisitions, there may be a threat to airport employees in terms of potential job cuts. However this might not be a huge issue if the proposed expansion goes ahead.

Airport passengers

As mentioned above in relation to airlines that make use of DEF, there might be a move to reduce holiday charter services towards the more prestigious scheduled international services. Passengers currently using the airport may find that services are reduced or terminated for certain destinations and future passengers may be forced to pay higher prices for such facilities as car parking in order to help finance the expansion and improvement plan.

Recommendation – should a sale to TUV be negotiated?

Given the analysis above, selling the airport would seem to make financial sense. The LSGs are currently earning a very poor return on their investment which is not sustainable in the long term. If they do not sell now there is a strong possibility that the airport will continue to lose money and become less attractive to future potential buyers.

Whilst maintaining control of the airport may be attractive strategically – by ensuring that services are maintained and disruption to local residents is kept to an minimum – the airport just **does not offer good investment opportunities**. It is unlikely that the proposed development will be viewed as giving 'value for money' and the LSGs will therefore be reluctant to provide any further financing. The interests of local residents can be protected via suitable legislation or conditions attached to the sale.

It is therefore recommended that DEF should commence negotiations with TUV regarding a potential sale.

95 DEF (2)

Text references. Cash flow forecasts are covered in Chapter 3. NPV is covered in Chapter 11 and leasing in Chapter 7. Read about real options in Chapter 13.

Top tips. Make sure you follow the instructions in part (a) as you are only asked to refer to the forecast results for the year ended 30th June 20X1 only. Don't waste time calculating any further results as you will not gain any additional marks.

Part (b) requires numerous repetitive calculations and you cannot use annuities. Turn your page sideways if you have to in order to give yourself plenty of space for all the columns. It is worthwhile laying out your workings first rather than trying to put everything into one table – this keeps calculations separate and lessens the change of you choosing incorrect figures. Don't forget that the capital allowances in (b)(ii) are claimed at the end of the year so will be included in the 20X2 column rather than 20X1.

The way in which part (d)(i) was asked might have confused you initially. Remember that maximum lease payments are linked to the perceived cash benefit of the project as a whole. Remember to convert the overall cash benefit (NPV of the project + after-tax cost of investment) to a pre-tax figure before calculating the annual lease payments using annuities.

Easy marks. There are some easy marks to be gained in part (b) when calculating the NPVs. You should also ensure that you gain the presentation marks by laying out your calculations and report professionally.

(a) Forecast results for year ended 30th June 20X1

	Total	Car parking	Non-car parking
	D$m	D$m	D$m
Revenue	23.40	3.5	19.90
Operating costs	(25.45)	(2.7)	(22.75)
Net operating loss	(2.05)	0.8	(2.85)

Car parking revenue = (50% of 1.4m) cars × D$5 per car = $3.5m

The analysis above shows that the car parking section of the business makes an overall profit whilst the remainder of the business makes a loss. If the car parking section was discontinued, the net operating loss would increase by 39% - a significant effect considering car parking revenue accounts for only 15% of total revenue.

If we look at **cash flow** (assumed to be operating profit + depreciation), the effect is similar.

	Total	Car parking	Non-car parking
	D$m	D$m	D$m
Revenue	23.40	3.5	19.90
Operating costs	(25.45)	(2.7)	(22.75)
Add depreciation	5.00	0.2	4.80
Net cash flow	2.95	1.0	1.95

Without the car parking activity, net cash flow would fall by 34% (for a 15% reduction in revenue). From the figures given it is clear that car parking is relatively cheaper (and more efficient) in terms of operating costs compared with the non-car parking activities. This is perhaps understandable as the general running costs of a car park should be fairly minimal and depreciation low.

The figures demonstrate the importance of the car parking business to DEF for the year ended 30th June 20X1. This is likely to change in the future given the forecasts for DEF's share of the overall car parking business and limited increases in fees compared with costs. However for the current year the car parking business has a significant financial impact on DEF's results.

(b) Present value of DEF's car parking business

  (i) *No investment in upgrading on-site car parking facilities*

  Workings

  (1) Number of cars using DEF's parking facilities

20X1	50% of 1,400,000	= 700,000
20X2	(1,400,000 x 1.06) x 40%	= 593,600
20X3 onwards	(1,400,000x 1.06^2) x 35%	= 550,564

  (2) Average car parking fee per car

20X1	$5.00
20X2	$5.00 x 1.03 = $5.15
20X3	$5.00 x 1.03^2 = $5.30
20X4	$5.00 x 1.03^3 = $5.46
20X5	$5.00 x 1.03^4 = $5.63
20X6	$5.00 x 1.03^5 = $5.80
20X7	$5.00 x 1.03^6 = $5.97
20X8	$5.00 x 1.03^7 = $6.15
20X9	$5.00 x 1.03^8 = $6.33
20Y0	$5.00 x 1.03^9 = $6.52
20Y1	$5.00 x 1.03^{10} = $6.72

NPV of project assuming no investment

		20X2 D$m	20X3 D$m	20X4 D$m	20X5 D$m	20X6 D$m	20X7 D$m	20X8 D$m	20X9 D$m	20Y0 D$m	20Y1 D$m
Total parking income		3.06	2.92	3.01	3.09	3.19	3.29	3.39	3.49	3.59	3.70
Operating costs		-2.60	-2.70	-2.81	-2.92	-3.04	-3.16	-3.29	-3.42	-3.56	-3.7
Net income		0.46	0.22	0.20	0.17	0.15	0.13	0.10	0.07	0.03	0.00
Tax	-0.30	-0.14	-0.07	-0.06	-0.05	-0.05	-0.04	-0.03	-0.02	-0.01	0.00
After tax income		0.32	0.15	0.14	0.12	0.11	0.09	0.07	0.05	0.02	0.00
Discount factor 12%		0.893	0.797	0.712	0.636	0.567	0.507	0.452	0.404	0.361	0.32
DCF		0.285	0.120	0.100	0.083	0.057	0.046	0.032	0.020	0.007	0.000

NPV (D$m)   **0.750**

(ii) *Proposed upgrade takes place*

Workings

(1) Number of cars using DEF's car parking facilities

20X1	50% of 1,400,000 = 700,000
20X2	$(1,400,000 \times 1.06) \times 50\%$ = 742,000
20X3 onwards	$(1,400,000 \times 1.06^2) \times 50\%$ = 786,520

(2) Average car parking fee per car

20X1	$5.00
20X2	$5.00 \times 1.04 = \$5.20$
20X3	$5.00 \times 1.04^2 = \$5.41$
20X4	$5.00 \times 1.04^3 = \$5.62$
20X5	$5.00 \times 1.04^4 = \$5.85$
20X6	$5.00 \times 1.04^5 = \$6.08$
20X7	$5.00 \times 1.04^6 = \$6.33$
20X8	$5.00 \times 1.04^7 = \$6.58$
20X9	$5.00 \times 1.04^8 = \$6.84$
20Y0	$5.00 \times 1.04^9 = \$7.12$
20Y1	$5.00 \times 1.04^{10} = \$7.40$

(3) Capital allowances

20X2 – D$4m $\times$ 30% = D$1.2m

Tutorial note

Remember you are claiming the allowance at the end of the year therefore you are claiming in 20X2 rather than 20X1.

NPV of project if investment takes place

	20X1 D$m	20X2 D$m	20X3 D$m	20X4 D$m	20X5 D$m	20X6 D$m	20X7 D$m	20X8 D$m	20X9 D$m	20Y0 D$m	20Y1 D$m
Parking		3.85	4.26	4.42	4.60	4.78	4.98	5.18	5.38	5.60	5.82
Op costs		(3.10)	(3.22)	(3.35)	(3.49)	(3.63)	(3.77)	(3.92)	(4.08)	(4.24)	(4.41)
Net income		0.75	1.04	1.07	1.11	1.15	1.21	1.26	1.30	1.36	1.41
Tax (30%)		(0.23)	(0.31)	(0.32)	(0.33)	(0.35)	(0.36)	(0.38)	(0.39)	(0.41)	(0.42)
After-tax income		0.52	0.73	0.75	0.78	0.81	0.85	0.88	0.91	0.95	0.99
Initial investment	(4.00)										
Cap. All.		1.20									
Total cash flow	(4.00)	1.72	0.73	0.75	0.78	0.81	0.85	0.88	0.91	0.95	0.99
Dis factor 12%	1.000	0.893	0.797	0.712	0.636	0.567	0.507	0.452	0.404	0.361	0.322
DCF	(4.000)	1.536	0.582	0.534	0.496	0.459	0.431	0.398	0.368	0.343	0.319

NPV = D$1.466m

(c) **REPORT**

To: Board of Directors, DEF Airport

From: Financial Controller, DEF Airport

Re: Proposed investment in on-site car parking facilities

Introduction

This report focuses on the proposed investment in on-site car parking facilities. It will advise on whether the investment should go ahead and if so which of the alternative operation schemes should be implemented. In addition, potential lease payments are considered and the alternative schemes compared with reference to DEF's financial and strategic objectives.

Should DEF proceed with the proposed investment? *(answer to part (c))*

If the proposed investment does take place, shareholders will be better off by D$0.716m (the difference between the NPV of undertaking the investment and the NPV of not investing). Although the financial viability of the project is only measured over a **10 year time horizon**, it is likely that the benefits will continue beyond that.

In addition, net operating loss would be D$0.8m lower if the car parking business was included (which represents a reduction of approximately 28% on non-car parking losses). Clearly the car parking business makes a **significant contribution** to DEF's overall business.

From a financial point of view, it would be worthwhile undertaking the proposed investment to upgrade the car parking facilities as it will increase shareholder value. In addition, on-site car parking facilities are likely to make the airport more attractive to existing and potential users.

Appropriate annual lease payment under Scheme B *(answer to part (d)(i))*

An appropriate annual lease payment can be determined by using the perceived value of the cash flows from the car parking business to ABC.

After tax value of cash flows

	D$m
NPV	1.466
Cost of investment net of tax [(D$4m – (D$1.2m x 0.893)]	2.930
After tax cash flows	4.396

Perceived pre-tax cash value to ABC = D$4.396m/0.7 = D$6.28m

The annual lease payment can be calculated by converting the perceived pre-tax cash value into a 10 year annuity using the discount rate of 12%.

Annual lease payment = D\$6.28m/5.650 = D\$1.11m

Note that this is the **maximum annual payment** and does not offer ABC the opportunity to make a profit on the deal or any compensation for the risk of taking responsibility for the car park's operation.

Comparison and contrast of Schemes A and B *(answer to part (d)(ii))*

This section of the report compares and contrasts the two schemes with reference to DEF's financial and strategic objectives.

Financial objectives

The financial objectives stated by DEF are as follows.

- The airport should not run at a loss

- All creditors should be paid on time

- Gearing levels must not exceed 20%

(1) The airport should not run at a loss

Scheme A

Under this scheme DEF retains full control of the car parking business and therefore also retains 100% of the profits. It is unlikely that ABC's payment in return for control of car parking will **match the profits** earned by the business.

Scheme B

As mentioned above, the payment from ABC in return for control of the car parking business is likely to be lower than the profits earned by the business (and thus the profits DEF could have retained). ABC will obviously want to make a profit from the deal therefore the annual payment must be sufficiently low to allow this to happen and to **compensate ABC for the additional risk** it is undertaking.

In order to fulfil the objective of not running at a loss, Scheme A at first appears to be preferable. However the reduced risk in Scheme B should not be overlooked. DEF will receive a guaranteed payment from ABC under Scheme B whereas the level of profits under Scheme A are less certain.

(2) All creditors should be paid on time

Scheme A and Scheme B

There is no evidence to suggest that either scheme would have a more favourable impact on when creditors are paid.

(3) Gearing levels must not exceed 20%

Current gearing level = D\$22.7m/(D\$22.7m + D\$130.53m) = 14.8%

Scheme A

If we assume that the D\$4m investment will be financed by a loan, gearing will increase to:

(D\$22.7m + D\$4m)/ (D\$22.7m + D\$4m + D\$130.53m) = 17%

This does not give much space for further debt-funded investment as 17% is extremely close to the gearing limit. DEF must consider whether increasing gearing levels to a point where further investment might be jeopardised is appropriate for the long-term success of the business.

Scheme B

There may be potential for DEF to capitalise the lease payments from ABC. If so this will increase the non-current asset base which will in turn help to lower the gearing levels to compensate for the extra D\$4m debt.

Strategic objectives

DEF's strategic objectives are more likely to be fulfilled by the car parking business if it **retains complete control** of the business (Scheme A). If ABC takes control of the business, DEF will have no say in how car parking facilities are operated.

However before the business could be leased to ABC, the upgraded facilities would have to be built – an activity that DEF will control. Therefore the quality of the facilities will be the same regardless of the management scheme chosen. Land based access to the airport should therefore be achieved, as should meeting the demands of forecast passenger numbers.

It is the management and day-to-day operations of the car parking facilities that will differ depending on the scheme chosen. DEF may have plans to employ local people in the upgraded car parking business (thus fulfilling objective 6) but there is no guarantee that ABC will do the same. There are no available details about any minimum staffing levels that ABC must adhere to so there is a danger that the facility might be understaffed. Whilst it is possible – and indeed recommended – that a minimum level of service is agreed prior to the leasing agreement, there is no guarantee that service levels can be adjusted sufficiently to meet changing customer demands.

As mentioned under 'Financial objectives' above, Scheme B is less risky in that the amount DEF receives from the car parking facility is guaranteed. This amount will contribute towards ensuring that the **airport is financially viable**. The profits received under Scheme A will also help to fulfil this objective, although the extent of the financial contribution is less certain.

Real options

The car parking business offers several real options to DEF.

(1) There is the option to abandon the upgrade the car parking facilities which could be complimented by an alternative strategy of offering lower quality facilities but at a lower parking fee.

(2) The upgrade project could be delayed until a later date in an attempt to keep gearing levels down.

(3) There is the option to follow on with a further redevelopment project or perhaps a change of use of the existing facilities.

The abandonment and delay options are really only possible under Scheme A where DEF retains complete control of the facility. The follow on option is still possible under Scheme B as DEF might decide to regain control after the 10 year lease period has expired. DEF then has the opportunity to redeploy the land for an alternative money-making use.

Advice on whether to choose Scheme A or Scheme B

Risk

The preference for Scheme A or Scheme B will depend on part on the **attitude towards risk** of DEF's directors. If there is an aversion to risk, Scheme B will be preferable as this provides a guaranteed income stream for the next 10 years. However risk takers will prefer Scheme A as this has the potential for higher returns.

Shareholders' wealth

Scheme A has the potential to give the **better return on investment** (and greater increase in shareholders' wealth) although this will ultimately depend on how profitable the car park is. This scheme offers a better opportunity for DEF to adjust the car parking facilities to meet the changing needs of its customers. Also the success of the project can be influenced by the management team, who should be aware of the financial and strategic objectives of DEF, and the directors may prefer Scheme A for this reason. However the scheme may be infeasible due to **lack of availability of necessary finance**.

Scheme B offers less flexibility but should still increase shareholders' wealth if an annual lease payment of D$1.11m is agreed. However, in order to build in compensation for risk and the ability of ABC to make a profit from the deal, the agreed payment is likely to be lower. This means that shareholders' wealth may suffer compared with Scheme A.

Availability of finance

If Scheme A was chosen, DEF would have to raise D$4m but the bank may have concerns over collateral. The guaranteed income stream from Scheme B could be used as collateral for the loan, thus reducing the perceived risk by the bank and increasing the likelihood of the loan being granted.

Conclusion

Given the analysis above, it is recommended that Scheme B is adopted if the DEF directors are averse to risk and/or the funds are not made available for Scheme A.

If there are any queries or any items requiring clarification, please do not hesitate to contact me.

96   F plc (1)

Text references. International investment appraisal is covered in Chapter 12. Real options are covered in Chapter 13. Payback is covered in Chapter 11.

Top tips. Make sure you separate the Euro-denominated cash flows from the sterling cash flows in your NPV calculations to enable you to make the necessary conversions to sterling. You are told that sterling is strengthening against the Euro therefore you would expect £1 to be worth more in Euros each year (this is a useful check when calculating the exchange rates).

With the calculations for the abandonment option, don't forget to include only those cash flows that occur on or after the possible abandonment date. Any cash flows that occur before that date are not relevant to the decision (they are sunk costs).

Easy marks. There are easy marks to be gained from the calculation of the payback period in (a)(ii). You should be able to pick up marks by interpreting your results in part (a)(iii) – remember you will get marks for the interpretation of your own figures, regardless of whether they are correct or not.

Examiner's comments. This question was generally very well answered. The greatest weakness was part (c) where many candidates showed poor understanding of real options and/or did not fully address the question asked. The structure and presentation of figures were not appropriate in many cases.

REPORT

To: The Divisional Board of the F plc Snacks Division

From: Management Accountant of Snacks Division

Date: 26th May 2011

Re: Proposed product launch

Introduction and purpose

The Snacks Division launched a new premium brand of chocolate bars (MATT SNACKS) in 2010. The Divisional Marketing Manager has put forward a proposal to launch the full range of MATT SNACKS in France. This report considers the details of this proposal based on various scenarios and evaluates what action, if any, should be taken.

The report also considers the wider implications of the proposal – that is, the effects on the company as a whole and the Snacks Division in particular – and concludes with a recommendation.

Tutorial note. The following information forms the solution to part (a)(i).

We have so far spent £0.5m on initial market research for the potential French launch. As we have spent this money already it is not a relevant cost in our appraisal, regardless of the scenario.

Scenario A

NPV calculation

Year	01/01/12 €m	2012 €m	2013 €m	2014 €m	2015 €m
Sales revenue (growing at 5% per annum)		10.0	10.50	11.03	11.58
Costs (growing at 5% per annum)		(1.0)	(1.05)	(1.10)	(1.16)
Net euro cash flows		9.0	9.45	9.93	10.42
Exchange rate (£/€) – W1	1.200	1.224	1.248	1.273	1.298
	£m	£m	£m	£m	£m
Converted euro cash flows		7.35	7.57	7.80	8.03
Sterling costs (growing at 5% pa)		(2.00)	(2.10)	(2.21)	(2.32)
		5.35	5.47	5.59	5.71
Tax on cash flows		(1.87)	(1.91)	(1.96)	(2.00)
Capital allowances – distribution centre (W2)		2.45			(1.40)
Capital allowances – market research and launch		1.05			
Distribution centre cost (W2)	(7.00)				
Market research and launch costs	(3.00)				
Distribution centre sale (€5.2m/1.298)					4.01
Net cash flows	(10.00)	6.98	3.56	3.63	6.32
Discount factor (15%)	1.000	0.870	0.756	0.658	0.572
DCF	(10.00)	6.07	2.69	2.39	3.61

NPV = £4.76m

Workings

(1) *Exchange rate*

	£/€
01/01/12	1.200
2012	1.200 x 1.02 = 1.224
2013	1.224 x 1.02 = 1.248
2014	1.248 x 1.02 = 1.273
2015	1.273 x 1.02 = 1.298

(2) *Capital allowances*

£ value of distribution centre on purchase = €8.40m/1.2000 = £7m

2012 tax relief = £7m x 35% = £2.45m

2015 balancing charge = (€5.2m/1.298) x 35% = £(1.4)m

Market research and launch costs tax relief = (£2m + £1m) x 35% = £1.05m (received 2012)

Scenario B

Year	01/01/12 €m	2012 €m	2013 €m	2014 €m	2015 €m
Sales revenue (growing at 5% per annum)		5.50	5.78	6.07	6.37
Costs (growing at 5% per annum)		(1.00)	(1.05)	(1.10)	(1.16)
Net euro cash flows		4.50	4.73	4.97	5.21
Exchange rate (£/€) – W1	1.200	1.224	1.248	1.273	1.298
	£m	£m	£m	£m	£m
Converted euro cash flows		3.68	3.79	3.90	4.01
Sterling costs (growing at 5% pa)		(1.50)	(1.58)	(1.66)	(1.74)
		2.18	2.21	2.24	2.27
Tax on cash flows		(0.76)	(0.77)	(0.78)	(0.79)
Capital allowances – distribution centre (W2)		2.45			(1.40)
Capital allowances – market research and launch		1.05			
Distribution centre cost (W2)	(7.00)				
Market research and launch costs	(3.00)				

Year	01/01/12 €m	2012 €m	2013 €m	2014 €m	2015 €m
Distribution centre sale (€5.2m/1.298)					4.01
Net cash flows	(10.00)	4.92	1.44	1.46	4.09
Discount factor (15%)	1.000	0.870	0.756	0.658	0.572
DCF	(10.00)	4.28	1.09	0.96	2.34

NPV = £(1.33)m

Expected value of project = (0.7 × £4.8m) + (0.3 × £(1.33)m) = £2.96m

---

Tutorial note. The following information forms the solution to part (a)(ii).

Payback period

We are trying to determine how long it takes to recoup our net investment (after capital allowances have been taken into account).

Net investment = £10m – £2.45m – £1.05m = £6.5m

Scenario A

Year	Net cash flow £m	Accumulated cash flow £m
1st January 2012	(6.5)	(6.5)
2012	5.35 – 1.87 = 3.48	(3.02)
2013	5.47 – 1.91 = 3.56	0.54

Payback period = 1 + (3.02/3.56) years = 1.85 years

Scenario B

Year	Net cash flow £m	Accumulated cash flow £m
1st January 2012	(6.5)	(6.5)
2012	2.18 – 0.76 = 1.42	(5.08)
2013	2.21 – 0.77 = 1.44	(3.64)
2014	2.24 – 0.78 = 1.46	(2.18)
2015	2.27 – 0.79 + 4.01 = 5.49	3.31

Payback period = 3 + (2.18/5.49) years = 3.4 years

Tutorial note. The following information forms the solution to part (a)(iii).

Interpretation of results

	Scenario A	*Scenario B*	*Expected value*
NPV	£4.8m	£(1.33)m	£2.96m
Payback	1.9 years	3.4 years	

Based on the results above we have an expected NPV of £2.96m therefore we could deduce that we should proceed with the project. However we will **never actually realise the 'expected' result** – we will either receive £4.8m or lose £1.33m.

The problem we have is that the project is a one-off and it is not wise to base investment decisions on expected values for one-off projects. If we did this would imply we are indifferent between the two scenarios occurring which we may not be. It will depend on whether we are willing to take the 30% risk of Scenario B occurring and losing £1.33m in exchange for the 70% possibility of Scenario A occurring which would result in a gain of £4.8m.

If we look at Payback, the results enforce the risk associated with Scenario B. The net investment is not recouped until the project is almost at an end (3.4 years). This demonstrates that the project will struggle to pay back the investment at all, never mind make a profit.

Scenario A shows very positive results and there is a very good chance that this will occur. However we also have to consider the risk that Scenario B might occur, resulting in quite significant losses. The final decision will depend on our **attitude towards the 30% risk of losing money** on the project.

Tutorial note. The following information forms the solution to part (b).

Evaluation of the option to abandon the project

There is an option to abandon the project after one year – that is, on 1st January 2013. The distribution centre could be sold for an estimated €7m (£5.72m = €7m/1.224) which would result in a balancing charge of £2m (£5.72m × 35%) at the end of 2013.

In order to evaluate the option to abandon, we can ignore anything that occurs before 1st January 2013 (the date when the abandonment could take place). We can then compare the NPV of the project if it is abandoned with the NPV if we continued with the project.

Scenario B – abandon the project

	1st January 2013 £m	31st December 2013 £m
Sale of distribution centre	5.72	
Balancing charge		(2.00)
Discount factor (15%)	1.000	0.870
DCF	5.72	(1.74)

NPV = £3.98m

Scenario B – do not abandon

31st December	2013 £m	2014 £m	2015 £m
Net cash flows	1.44	1.46	4.09
Discount factor (15%)	0.870	0.756	0.658
DCF	1.25	1.10	2.69

NPV = £5.04m

From a purely financial viewpoint it would appear to be more profitable to let the project continue rather than abandon it.

However other issues must be considered before making a final decision. The cash flows may be quite sensitive to the maturity of the project – they may be low in early years and increase as the products become more well-known. There may also be an adverse effect on the company's reputation if it pulls out of the market early or if a competitor subsequently decides to enter the market. Finally the company has a strategic objective of increasing its market share in both domestic and overseas markets – this project may be key to achieving this objective.

Conclusion

Given the evaluation above there appears to be a strong case for continuing with the project rather than abandoning it at the beginning of 2013, even if Scenario B holds for the remainder of the project.

Tutorial note. The following information forms the solution to part (c).

How real options and other strategic financial issues might influence the initial investment decision

Given the financial evaluation above it is unlikely that the project will be abandoned, therefore the availability of the option will have **little influence over the decision** and thus little value at the start of the project. However this assumes that cash flows behave as predicted which is not guaranteed. If initial investment costs (including the marketing and launch costs) are greater than anticipated then the abandonment option may be exercised.

The abandonment option acts as security (or insurance) for the company and its value will depend on the extent of the losses it is securing against. If the company is risk-averse, then the option will have greater value for each level of potential loss.

Other types of real options include the option to **follow-on** or the option to **wait**.

The option to follow-on is a strategic option when the investment opportunity leads to follow-on wealth-generating opportunities. This would appear to be the most likely option in this case. If MATT products prove to be successful in France, there may be other opportunities to launch further products in that country, or perhaps try to launch the products in other countries. The considerable potential value of this option should be built into the investment appraisal calculations.

It is not advised to incorporate a 'wait' option as this would give competitors time to break into the market ahead of F plc.

There are other strategic financial issues that may be incorporated into the decision-making process.

Attitude towards risk

Whilst there is a 70% chance that the investment will make money, there is still a **significant chance of losses** being made. If shareholders are averse to risk the chance of making losses may be too great. However it is worth exploring whether these losses could be absorbed by other parts of the group.

Effect on Earnings per Share

In the event of Scenario B occurring, EPS would be adversely affected due to losses being made. However with Scenario A, the project offers more than the required 15% rate of return therefore EPS would increase. As above, shareholders' attitude towards potential effects on EPS will depend on attitude towards risk.

Effect on gearing

The investment required in the project is relatively small compared to the company as a whole. However as **gearing of the group is quite high** there may be a future issue if expansion is planned into new product ranges and markets. This option to follow-on might not be so attractive if it would mean an increase in gearing to exceptionally high levels.

Risk of overtrading

Overtrading occurs when a company tries to do too much too quickly and with too little long-term capital. If expansion into the French market is too rapid, there could be an adverse effect on cash flow. It is essential to ensure that sufficient cash will be available to fund a successful launch (such as extra inventories and receivables).

Is sufficient finance available to fund the investment?

Before the investment can go ahead, necessary funding has to be in place. By studying the company's current financial statements it can be seen that there are very low retained earnings but high levels of debt. Will financial institutions be **prepared to lend further funds** to a company whose creditworthiness may be in question? Will it be necessary to sell off existing parts of the business to raise the necessary capital?

Tutorial note. The following information forms the solution to part (d).

Recommendation

Given the evaluation above it is difficult to give a definite recommendation. There are considerable uncertainties surrounding the cash flows and whether the project will actually make money. Whilst the potential outcome of the project is likely to be clearer in a year's time, it will be too late by then to abandon the project (which must be done on 1st January 2013. Analysis of the option to abandon shows that, even with the loss-making Scenario B, the company would be better off continuing with the project.

An option to follow-on does exist in the event that the product launch is successful. It may be that the company is prepared to take the risk of moving ahead with the project with the potential for further future profits. However it should also be borne in mind that current markets may be unprofitable or market share is lost due to competitors' expansion activities. The option to follow-on might not make more money for the company – it may simply replace the money lost in current markets.

It is important that no decision is made in isolation. The company should consider the availability of other less risky projects before making a final decision as these may allow more efficient use of what appears to be relatively scarce capital.

97 F plc (2)

> **Text references**. Cash flow forecasts are covered in Chapter 3 and exchange rate issues in Chapter 12. Different sources of finance are considered in Chapters 5 and 6 whilst the three financial management decisions are covered throughout the text (and are introduced in Chapters 1 and 2).
>
> **Top tips.** Try to make use of proformas as much as possible in parts (a)(i) and (ii) – it makes it easier for the marker to follow and for you to ensure that you have included all relevant cash flows. Remember that you are producing cash flow forecasts rather than NPV calculations – this means you will have to include interest.
>
> Once you have produced the cash flow forecasts, the rest of the question depends on the results. Don't worry if you have made mistakes in your calculations – you will receive marks for your answers based on your own figures.
>
> **Easy marks**. You should be able to pick up a number of easy marks in part (a) when preparing the cash flow forecasts.
>
> **Examiner's comments.** Many candidates appeared to be ill-prepared for a cash forecasting question. Despite one of the most useful outputs of cash forecasts being an identification of likely future borrowing requirements, this was often overlooked. In the evaluation section there was evidence of reasonable understanding of alternative dividend policies and sources of finance but there was not always sufficient reference back to the results of the cash forecast or adequate application of the theories to the scenario presented.

REPORT

To: Board of Directors, F plc

From: Finance Director

Date: 1st October 2011

Re: Proposed expansion plans and future strategies

Introduction

The purpose of this report is to evaluate proposed expansion plans into new product ranges in the next two or three years. The report also considers the proposal to increase annual dividend by 8% per annum which is intended to reflect increased confidence in future performance.

The report will focus on the effects of movements in exchange rates on future performance and share price, the sustainability of the proposed dividend policy and the additional financing requirements for the project and increased dividend payout.

> **Tutorial note.** The following information forms the solution to part (a).

Cash flow forecast – 1st January 2011 to 31st December 2013

(Assume a constant exchange rate)

	2011 £m	2012 £m	2013 £m
Cash inflows (W1)	215.40	284.60	338.50
Net £ cash outflows	(148.00)	(218.00)	(241.00)
Net operating cash flows	67.40	66.60	97.50
Interest received on cash balance (3% of £20m)	0.60	0.60	0.60
Interest paid on borrowings (7% of borrowings b/f)	(16.38)	(15.24)	(16.28)
Net cash flow after interest	51.62	51.96	81.82
Tax (35%)	(18.07)	(18.19)	(28.64)
Net cash flow after tax	33.55	33.77	53.18
Dividend (W2)	(17.28)	(18.66)	(20.15)
Investment net of tax	Nil	(30.00)	(20.00)
Net operating cash flow	16.27	(14.89)	13.03
Opening cash balance	20.00	20.00	20.00
Borrowings brought forward	234.00	217.73	232.62
Adjust borrowings with net operating cash flow	(16.27)	14.89	(13.03)
Borrowings carried forward	217.73	232.62	219.59
Comprising:			
Long-term borrowings	160.00	160.00	160.00
Revolving credit facility (RCF) – difference	57.73	72.62	Nil
Additional finance required			59.59

Note that the RCF expires on 31st December 2013 therefore there will be no RCF available at the end of that year.

Workings:

(1) Conversion of € cash flows to £

2011 = €280m/1.3000 = £215.4m

2012 = €370m/1.3000 = £284.6m

2013 = €440m/1.3000 = £338.5m

(2) Dividend per annum

2011 = 1.08 × £16m = £17.28m

2012 = 1.08 × £17.28m = £18.66m

2013 = 1.08 × £18.66m = £20.15m

Cash flow forecast – 1st January 2011 to 31st December 2013

(Assume that the Euro weakens against sterling by 6% per annum)

	2011 £m	2012 £m	2013 £m
Cash inflows (W4)	203.19	253.30	284.18
Net £ cash outflows	(148.00)	(218.00)	(241.00)
Net operating cash flows	55.19	35.30	43.18
Interest received on cash balance (3% of £20m)	0.60	0.60	0.60
Interest paid on borrowings (7% of borrowings b/f)	(16.38)	(15.80)	(18.29)
Net cash flow after interest	39.41	20.10	25.49
Tax (35%)	(13.79)	(7.04)	(8.92)
Net cash flow after tax	25.62	13.06	16.57
Dividend (W2)	(17.28)	(18.66)	(20.15)
Investment net of tax	Nil	(30.00)	(20.00)
Net operating cash flow	8.34	(35.60)	(23.58)
Opening cash balance	20.00	20.00	20.00
Borrowings brought forward	234.00	225.66	261.26
Adjust borrowings with net operating cash flow	(8.34)	35.60	23.58
Borrowings carried forward	225.66	261.26	284.84
Comprising:			
Long-term borrowings	160.00	160.00	160.00
Revolving credit facility (RCF)	65.66	80.00	Nil
Additional finance required		21.26	124.84

Note that the maximum RCF is £80m.

Workings:

(3) Exchange rate

2011 = 1.3000 × 1.06 = €1.3780

2012 = 1.3780 × 1.06 = €1.4607

2013 = 1.4607 × 1.06 = €1.5483

(4) Conversion of cash flows

2011 = €280m/1.3780 = £203.19m

2012 = €370m/1.4607 = £253.30m

2013 = €440m/1.5483 = £284.18m

Tutorial note. The following information forms the solution to part (b)(i).

Evaluation of the possible impact of exchange rate movements on cash flows

From the analysis above it is clear that exchange rate movements have a significant effect on annual and cumulative cash flows.

A 6% weakening of the Euro against sterling leads to the following financial differences:

(1) By 2013 net cash flows before interest and tax will be £43.18m rather than £97.5m, a reduction of almost 56%.

(2) Cash flows after interest, tax and dividends will be negative rather than positive (as would be the case if exchange rates remained constant). This is **before** the deduction of the capital investment and RCF repayments.

(3) Funding required by 2013 will be 30% higher than if exchange rates remained constant (£284.84m rather than £219.59m).

We have not built in the possibility of **increasing export prices** to compensate for the exchange rate movement. However any price increases may have a negative effect on sales therefore the anticipated increase in cash inflows might be cancelled out by reductions in quantity sold. However it may be that our competitors are facing

similar issues with exchange rates which could lead to a general increase in prices throughout the market. Before taking any action on price movements we need to understand any exchange rate risks being faced by our competitors.

Evaluation of the possible impact of exchange rate movements on share price

Any downward effect on cash flows is bound to have an effect on our **share price**. The share price is determined by the market based on the perceived value of the company. As predicted cash flow is one way of valuing a company, any movements in future cash flows will feed through to the share price.

The **semi-strong form of market efficiency** means that share prices should move to reflect any publicly available information. Exchange rate movements and proportion of export sales – both of which will have an effect on cash flows – will be known (exchange rates via the financial markets and export sales in F plc's financial statements).

> **Tutorial note.** The following information forms the solution to part (b)(ii).

Sustainability of proposed dividend policy and alternative dividend policies to be considered

Dividend signalling means that any changes in dividend policy may send certain signals to the market (whether intentional or unintentional). It is therefore essential that we consider any changes to our current policy very carefully.

Current dividend yield (based on 2010 dividend payouts) is £16m/(560m shares x £0.60) = 4.8%

We are suggesting an 8% per annum increase in dividend payout. If exchange rates remain constant (as per our first forecast calculations) this increase is sustainable. We should also consider the effects of inflation when determining the sustainability of this nominal growth – the higher inflation is, the lower real growth will be (if nominal growth remains constant).

If exchange rates move (as per our second set of calculations) and inflation remains unchanged, then the proposed growth rate of 8% **does not appear to be sustainable**. Net operating cash flows are only positive in 2011 and then become increasingly negative in 2012 and 2013. We will have to ensure that any further changes in dividend policy as a result of potential movements in share price are fully communicated to the market and to the shareholders to prevent any adverse effects on share price.

A feasible alternative to the current proposal would be to **reduce the growth rate** to say 2 or 3% which is more sustainable than 8%. This represents a considerable reduction but if we communicate the information properly to the shareholders and the market, giving details of why the reduction is taking place, there should be little or no short-term effects on the share price.

> **Tutorial note.** The following information forms the solution to part (b)(iii).

Additional financing requirements and additional sources of finance

From our analysis above it can be seen that additional financing will be required regardless of movements in exchange rates. However if exchange rates remain constant, additional funding will not be required until the end of 2013 (£59.59m) due to the repayment of the RCF. We may have to re-negotiate the RCF when it comes up for renewal at the end of 2013. Given the amount of the shortfall, we do not require such a significant RCF – perhaps £65m - £70m to give us a financial cushion above the £59.59m required.

If exchange rates move against us, we would require additional funding from 2012 onwards, even with the RCF drawn down to its maximum amount. The total additional funding required by the end of 2013 is £124.84m.

With such a large amount required, gearing would have to increase significantly even if the share price remained at the 2010 level. It may not be possible to raise the additional funds and the future of the company may be threatened.

Additional sources of finance

In addition to the RCF there are other sources of finance we could consider.

(1)   **Rights issue** – as share price is starting to recover and confidence in the company seems to be rising it may be a good time to raise additional equity via a rights issue. If the issue price is set at an appropriate level and investors are kept informed of the benefits, this may be an effective source of long-term financing to support the proposed investments.

(2)   **Overdraft** – instead of re-negotiating the RCF we could consider arranging an overdraft facility. This would be particularly appropriate where the exchange rate remains constant and the need for additional finance is lower. However we must consider the possibility that an overdraft facility can be withdrawn at any time and is therefore not a secure method of finance. An RCF arrangement is safer.

(3)   At the moment we are considering financing the Euro-based investment in sterling. It may be worth considering the arrangement of a **Euro-denominated loan** to provide a natural hedge against exchange rate movements.

Tutorial note. The following information forms the solution to part (c).

<u>Advice on overall impact of possible exchange rate movements and liquidity constraints on F plc's financial and strategic decisions</u>

This report has emphasised the considerable impact any movements in exchange rates could have on cash flow, liquidity and share price. However there are other relevant factors that must be analysed when considering the results of the cash forecasts.

Liquidity issues include the following:

(1)   A much **lower increase** in dividend payout – would an increase of say 2 – 3% have a significant adverse effect on how the market views the company? It would be difficult to justify a rapidly increasing dividend payout when there is no matching increase in profits and cash flows.

(2)   Given our current highly geared position, and the end of the current RCF agreement in 2013, will we be able to obtain sufficient additional finance to fund the shortfall in funds and the dividend payout increase? If not we may have to postpone the proposed product launches.

(3)   We may have to reduce the amount of future investment to keep cash in the company, as mentioned in (2) above. It may be better to wait until the Euro starts to recover before considering any further investment in Euro-based operations.

Exchange rate issues include the following:

(1)   Is there any link between the strength/weakness of the Euro and the volume of sales?

(2)   If competitors are having similar issues with exchange rate movements is it likely that general Euro prices will increase (thus preventing a loss in market share due to our individual price rises)?

(3)   Regardless of what competitors are doing, will sales volume drop significantly if we increased our Euro prices in response to the weak exchange rate?

(4)   Are any other exchange rate movements likely (either better or worse than those we have anticipated at the moment)?

<u>Conclusion</u>

Before we can make any investment, financing or dividend decisions we will have to consider the factors highlighted above. It is unlikely that the proposed dividend increase is sustainable due to its likely effect on liquidity and financing requirements. However no firm decisions should be taken until a full evaluation of the factors above has been conducted.

If you have any questions regarding the contents of this report please do not hesitate to contact me.

98 M plc (1)

Text references. Business valuations are covered in Chapter 15.

Top tips. As always, make sure you maximise your chances of gaining the presentation marks by structuring your answer as a report and making it as easy to follow as possible.

In order to answer part (a) you will have to return to the pre-seen material to find the strategic and financial objectives. Whilst this is not specifically stated, you should be aware that the appropriateness of each use of funds will depend on how well (or otherwise) they help the company to achieve its stated objectives. The pre-see material remains very important in the exam itself – don't assume that all the information to answer the question will come from the unseen material.

Part (b)(i) is worth 18 marks therefore you should expect to perform a number of calculations and use each of the main valuation techniques. You are actually told to include a discounted FCF valuation using PP's WACC which should make things slightly easier. Whilst the calculations are numerous you should hopefully not find them too difficult if you have revised this area thoroughly.

Whilst it is tempting in part (b)(ii) to give a general critique of the appropriateness of each valuation technique, make sure you relate it to the scenario. Remember you are writing a report to the Board of M plc therefore you have to make it relevant. Try to pick up on any unusual valuations (ones that are significantly different from the others) as this might suggest the technique giving such a valuation is not appropriate.

Part (c) should again relate to the particular scenario but you can do so by using your knowledge of general risks and then applying them to the proposed sale of FR.

Easy marks. Part (b)(i) should provide some easy marks if you are familiar with the various valuation techniques available.

Examiner's comments. Candidates tended to struggle with requirements b(ii) and b(iii) in relation to the valuation of a division for disposal. There were a number of common errors, including: using of book values instead of market values when calculating WACC; Unnecessary de-gearing/re-gearing of the proxy company beta; miscalculating free cash flows; Failing to include the synergistic benefit as a perpetuity; Failure to calculate free cash flow as a growing perpetuity; Poor discussion of the valuation methods used.

In part (c) many candidates discussed the general risks of a monopoly rather than the specific risks to a selling company posed by an investigation by the competition authorities. Another common error in this part of the question was a misinterpretation of the question requirement as a need to evaluate the risks of takeovers in general.

REPORT

To: Board of Directors, M plc

From: Financial Adviser

Date: 1st December 2011

Re: Potential sale of FR

Introduction

This report focuses on the potential sale of the French subsidiary FR.

Several possible uses of the funds from the sale have been cited and these are evaluated in the first part of the report and a recommendation made regarding the best use of the funds.

The report also calculates a range of possible values for FR and discusses how appropriate each of the valuation approaches is to the company. There is also advice on an appropriate minimum and maximum value to set for FR to ensure M plc is not overcharging potential buyers but at the same time is not letting FR be sold too cheaply.

There is the possibility of an investigation by competition authorities if PP makes a bid for FR, due to the former company's current strength in the European publications market. The possible risks that could arise from such an investigation are evaluated in the final part of this report.

> **Tutorial note**. The following information forms the solution to part (a).

Three possible uses of the funds raised from selling FR have been identified.

Reinvest in a new project

If the funds could be reinvested in a project that has a positive NPV, this will **increase** M plc's **shareholders' wealth** and help the company to **achieve its growth targets**. M plc's main shareholders are putting pressure on the Board to devise a strategic plan aimed at achieving the stated financial objectives and any investment in profitable projects will help in achieving these objectives.

Profit growth target of 4% between 2011 and 2012 has been achieved but the revenue growth target (also 4%) has not been achieved. Analysis is as follows:

	2012	2011	*Actual growth*	*Target growth*
Revenue	280	274	2.2%	4%
Operating profit	73	68	7.4%	4%

Note: Operating Profit for 2011 = Op. profit for Newspapers, Web and Advertising less Headquarters op.costs

It is important that M plc researches **suitable projects** with positive NPVs and the contribution they may make towards meeting the company's strategic and financial objectives.

If M plc sells FR it will lose control over FR's pan European publication which currently helps to fulfil the **third strategic objective** (*as identified in the pre-seen information*). In order to compensate for this, M plc might wish to consider the possibility of providing an alternative service to native English speakers in countries where English is not the first language (for example a web-based news service). This will help to fulfil strategic objectives 2 and 3 2 whilst at the same time fill the gap left by the loss of the pan European publication.

Repay outstanding debt or reduce debt levels

Loan capital of £83m is due to be paid off on 1st April 2013. The money raised from the sale of FR could be put towards the repayment of this debt on the redemption date or possibly earlier if there are no penalties from doing so. Alternatively it could be used to pay off any other outstanding debts and other arrangements made to repay the £83m.

Gearing

M plc's current gearing level can be calculated as follows:

Market capitalisation = £3.50 x 140m shares = £490m

Current debt = £250m

Gearing = 250m/(250m + 490m) = 33.8%

This is well within the stated financial objective of a gearing level of less than 40%, meaning there is no urgent need to pay off the debt to meet this target. This may allow M plc to seek a renewal of the loan.

If M plc received the full anticipated value of €75m and used the entire amount to pay off debt then gearing would be revised as follows:

Proceeds in £ = €75m x 0.89 = £66.75m

Gearing = (250 – 66.75)/(250 – 66.75 + 490) = 27.2%

The above gearing calculation assumes that M plc's share price will remain unchanged. This is unlikely when gearing changes, due to changes to risk and return.

Pay one-off dividend to shareholders

Whilst a one-off dividend payment to shareholders may appear to be an attractive option, it only has long-term benefit to the shareholders if they can **reinvest** the funds **at a higher rate** than the company itself. If this is not the case then the money should be retained within the company and reinvested in profitable projects that will increase shareholders' wealth at a higher rate than they themselves can manage.

The Board should also guard against the possible **signals that a one-off payment might send to the market**. It may be viewed as being an indication that there are no profitable projects in which to invest the funds which could have an adverse effect on share price. Alternatively it might create an expectation that dividends will be higher in the future. M plc has a financial objective of achieving a stable growth in dividends but creating unrealistic expectations may cause problems if it is unable to meet them.

Recommendation

Of the three suggested used for the funds it is recommended that the Board reinvests the money in projects that yield a positive NPV in order to increase future earnings.

Tutorial note. The following information forms the solution to part (b)(i).

This section of the report uses various valuation techniques to estimate the value of FR.

Net assets basis

	€m
Non-current assets (market value)	56
Net current assets	2
Net asset value	**58**

P/E basis (earnings valuation)

Using PP's P/E ratio:

P/E ratio = 13 *(given in the question)*

Valuation = Earnings x P/E ratio = €4m x 13 = €52m

Total value (including debt of €25m) = €77m

Using M plc's P/E ratio:

Share price = £3.50 *(given in the question)*

EPS = £44m/140m shares = £0.314

P/E ratio = £3.50/£0.314 = 11.15

Valuation = €4m x 11.15 = €44.6m

Total value = €69.6m

Discounted free cash flow valuation

This method will use PP's WACC as the discount rate. We have to calculate the WACC first.

Cost of debt

Year	0	1 - 3	3
	€	€	€
Market value	(103.00)		
Net interest (6% x [1 – 0.30])		4.20	
Redemption value			100.00
Discount factor (5%)	1.000	2.723	0.864
DCF	(103.00)	11.44	86.40

NPV = €(5.16)

Discount at 3%

Year	0	1 - 3	3
	€	€	€
Market value	(103.00)		
Net interest (6% x [1 – 0.30])		4.20	
Redemption value			100.00
Discount factor (3%)	1.000	2.829	0.915
DCF	(103.00)	11.88	91.50

NPV = €0.38

Post-tax cost of debt = 3 + [0.38/(0.38 + 5.16)] x (5 – 3) = **3.1%**

WACC

	Cost of capital	Market value	Cost of capital x MV
		€m	
Bond (W1)	3.1%	123.6	3.83
Preference shares (W2)	5.93%	27.0	1.60
Ordinary shares (W3)	10.5%	290.0	30.45
		440.6	35.88

WACC = 35.88/440.6 = **8.143%**

Workings

(1)   Market capitalisation of bond = €120m x 1.03 = €123.6m

(2)   Cost of preference shares = (8/135) x 100 = 5.93%

        MV of preference shares = 20m shares x €1.35 = €27m

(3)   Cost of equity (using CAPM) = 3 + (1.5 x 5) = 10.5%

        MV of ordinary shares = €5.80 x 50m shares = €290m

Free cash flow

	€m
Operating profit	6.70
Less: tax charge	(1.30)
Less: tax relief on finance charge (30% of €1.4m)	(0.42)
Add: depreciation	0.50
Less: funds reinvested in working capital	(1.80)
Pre-financing free cash flows	3.68

Alternative approach	
	€m
Earnings	4.00
Add: finance charge	1.40
Less: tax relief on finance charge (30% of €1.4m)	(0.42)
Add: depreciation	0.50
Less: funds reinvested in working capital	(1.80)
Pre-financing free cash flows	3.68

Growth rate is 2% in perpetuity

Discount rate is 8.143%

Valuation =(€3.68m x 1.02)/(0.08143 – 0.02) = **€61.1m**

Additional value from synergistic benefits

Annual benefit is €0.7m (after tax)

In perpetuity, the present value of these benefits = €0.7m/0.08143 = €8.6m

Summary of valuations

	Value pre-synergistic benefits €m	*Value post-synergistic benefits* €m
Net assets basis	58.0	66.6
P/E ratio (PP)	77.0	85.6
P/E ratio (M plc)	69.6	78.2
DCF	61.1	69.7

> **Tutorial note.** The following information forms the solution to part (b)(ii).

Appropriateness of each of the valuation methods used

Net assets method

This method gives the minimum price that M plc should be prepared to accept for FR (pre-synergistic benefits valuation is €58m).

However this method is **not appropriate** when the business is being sold as a going concern. It is based on market values of non-current assets whereas it is assumed that the acquiring company intends to keep these assets within the business.

Another issue with this method is that it does not include the value of intangible assets, such as the brand name of the newspaper. The value of FR is thus underestimated.

Earnings valuation method based on P/E ratios

Historic earnings figures from a single year have been used in this valuation. Unfortunately there is insufficient data available to determine whether these figures are a good representation of **sustainable future earnings**.

We have used both PP's and M plc's P/E ratios in the valuation process. Using PP's P/E ratio gives a pre-synergistic benefits valuation of €77m whilst M plc's ratio gives a valuation of €69.6m.

PP's P/E ratio is likely to be more appropriate as PP operates in the same market as FR. M plc operates in numerous market sectors and geographical locations and is thus likely to have a different risk and earnings profile.

We have assumed that PP can achieve the same rate of return from FR as from its own current business operations. Whether this assumption is true depends on the extent to which FR's relatively poor performance has been due to poor management on M plc's part rather than on the popularity and future growth potential of the newspaper titles themselves. The former appears to be true – when M plc acquired foreign titles it was unable to develop them to their full potential, possibly due to lack of local knowledge or management supervision. The valuation using PP's P/E ratio assumes that PP can turn this situation around and also assumes that PP and FR carry the same levels of risk.

DCF valuation method

This method is generally considered to be the most appropriate valuation technique as it is based on actual **forecast free cash flows** of the business (before interest). These cash flows have been discounted at PP's WACC and gives a valuation of €61.1m.

The DCF approach gives a lower value than the P/E approach which casts doubt on the validity of using either P/E ratio as a basis of valuation.

Using WACC and pre-financing cash flows makes more sense than using cost of equity and post-financing cash flows as FR's gearing is determined by M plc in line with group requirements rather than reflecting how this type of business should be financed. Without a share price it is not possible to calculate FR's WACC.

> **Tutorial note.** The following information forms the solution to part (b)(iii).

Appropriate minimum and maximum price for FR

PP is likely to offer a reasonable price towards the **lower end** of the valuation scale. This will allow them to maximise their profits but at the same time provide some space for negotiation. This will give an indication of the likely minimum price that M plc may achieve.

The net assets valuation method (before synergistic benefits) gives the minimum price that M plc should be prepared to accept – that is €58m. The DCF valuation gives a price of €61.1m. The opening offer is likely to be somewhere between these two figures.

The maximum price M plc might expect is the DCF valuation including synergistic benefits – that is €69.7m. However it is **unlikely that PP will be prepared to pay such a high amount** as synergistic benefits are extremely difficult to realise in practice, regardless of how confident the company is of being able to turn FR around into a much more profitable operation.

M plc hopes to achieve a price of €75m. Given the evaluation above, this appears to be much too high and the company should be prepared to accept a lower price.

> **Tutorial note.** The following information forms the solution to part (c).

Risks arising from investigations by competition authorities into planned takeovers

The competition authorities will investigate a proposed takeover bid if it feels the takeover may not be in the public interest or if there could be a substantial reduction in competition (which could result in less competitive pricing).

We already know that there could be a referral of the proposed takeover bid for FR by PP to the competition authorities in France due to PP's dominant position in the market. The main risks of this are as follows.

(i) Investigations are often **lengthy** during which period the takeover is put on hold. There is therefore the risk that PP will abandon its bid as it may not want to be involved in a time-consuming investigation. This means that we will lose the most serious bid we currently have and have to go through the lengthy and costly process of securing another bid.

(ii) If the authorities find that the takeover would result in a potential monopoly, they will commence proceedings which are likely to be lengthy. Once again PP may abandon its bid due to the proceedings and/or the delay and we would once again have to start looking for another interested party.

(iii) There is the risk that the authorities may ask PP to sell off some of its other business operations in order to acquire FR. Whether the takeover will then go ahead will depend on how **amenable PP is** to this requirement.

(iv) Investigations by competition authorities may result in the natural equilibrium of the market being upset. Companies may become more wary about entering into takeover bids which could result in **otherwise viable businesses** being left to fail.

Conclusion

This report has evaluated the proposed sale of FR. The most appropriate use of the funds obtained from this sale will be to reinvest in projects with positive NPVs as this will help to boost earnings towards the growth targets stated.

However it is extremely unlikely that the expected price of €75m will be achieved as the valuation methods suggest a maximum price of under €70m. The Board should therefore be prepared to accept a lower price rather than risk losing potential interested bidders.

The Board should also be aware of the risks associated with a potential investigation by competition authorities if PP bids for FR. There may be a considerable delay in the bid being accepted (if at all) and PP may pull out of the bid before the investigation is complete.

If you have any questions relating to any part of this report please do not hesitate to contact me.

99 M plc (2)

Text references. Cost of equity is covered in Chapter 8 and business valuations in Chapter 15. Financial objectives are considered in Chapter 1 whilst defensive tactics for a takeover are looked at in Chapter 16.

Top tips. In part (b) (i) you should only produce valuations that are applicable in the circumstances ie a P/E ratio multiple is not valid due to the differences in the two businesses. In part (b) (ii) the advice should be based on earlier calculations. Don't worry if you have made mistakes in your calculations – you will receive marks for your answers based on your own figures.

Although a few marks are available for calculations in part (c) do not get too caught up in this as the majority of marks are available for comments. Also do not neglect the other relevant factors by only concentrating on the financial objectives.

Easy marks. You should be able to pick up a number of easy marks in part (d) when suggesting actions of GG to defend against the takeover and also when calculating the three costs of equity in part (a).

Examiner's comments. In part (b)(ii) many candidates implemented a formulaic approach and discussed at length net asset valuations, P/E valuations and dividend valuations even though they weren't relevant to this scenario. The knock-on effect was that not enough time was spent on the DCF valuation and therefore answers were generally weak. Also, many candidates did not realise that the market capitalisation value should be used as the starting point for negotiation since GG is a listed company.

REPORT

To: Board of Directors, M plc

From: Finance Director

Date: 1st April 2012

Re: Proposed takeover of GG

Introduction

The purpose of this report is to evaluate the proposed takeover of GG, including recommending an appropriate bid value, advising on whether M plc should proceed with the bid and recommending actions to help ensure a positive response to the bid.

Tutorial note. The following information forms the solution to part (a) (i).

Cost of equity calculations

Using the CAPM formula the following costs of equity can be calculated.

M plc's current k_e	$= 1.1\% + 1.8 \times 4.0\% = 8.3\%$
GG's current k_e	$= 3.0\% + 2.5 \times 4.0\% = 13.0\%$
M plc's k_e adjusted for GG's business risk	$= 1.1\% + 2.5 \times 4.0\% = 11.1\%$

GG's equity beta does not need to be adjusted for financial risk as both companies have approximately the same gearing ratio.

Tutorial note. The following information forms the solution to part (a) (ii).

There is a difference of 4.7% between the two current costs of equity. 1.9% of this is due to the difference in the risk free return rates in the UK and the USA. This difference is eliminated when GG's cost of equity is **adjusted into a GBP basis**. This serves to highlight the exchange risk that M plc would be subject to if GG is acquired, if interest rate differentials are not mirrored in exchange rate movements.

The remaining difference of 2.8% is due to the higher returns expected by GG's shareholders due to the greater risk in GG's operations. This is indicated by the **higher equity beta**. The 2.8% is the difference in equity betas multiplied by the market premium of 4%. It indicates the extent to which GG's operations are riskier than M plc. Effectively it is the restatement of GG's cost of equity on a GBP basis.

Tutorial note. The following information forms the solution to part (b) (i).

Valuations of GG

Market capitalisation of GG

GG has 40 million shares and a current share price of USD 7.50. This gives a **total market capitalisation** of USD 300 million. Converting at the current exchange rate of GBP1 = USD 1.63, this is GBP 184 million or GBP 4.60 per share of GG.

For **comparison** the current market capitalisation of M plc is 140 million shares at GBP 3.77 per share, which is GBP 527.8 million. This demonstrates the significance of the acquisition to M plc.

Discounted cash flow basis

The free cash flow of GG for the last year was 60% of earnings.
Free cash flow = 60% USD × 30 million = USD 18 million
This is expected to **increase** at 8% per year in perpetuity.

Year ended		31 March 2013	31 March 2014	31 March 2015	Future years
		USDm	USDm	USDm	USDm
Free cash flow	(W1)	19.44	21.00	22.68	790.14
Exchange rate	(W2)	1.6626	1.6959	1.7298	1.7298
		GBPm	GBPm	GBPm	GBPm
Sterling cash flows		11.69	12.38	13.11	456.78
Discount factors	(W3)	0.900	0.810	0.729	0.729
Present value		10.52	10.03	9.56	332.99

Total present value = GBP363.1m

This is GBP 9.08 per share.

Workings

W1   Free cash flow of USD 18m inflating at 8% per annum

31 March 2013	31 March 2014	31 March 2015	Future years
USDm	USDm	USDm	USDm
19.44	21.00	22.68	790.14

The value of the cash flow in perpetuity from 31 March 2016 at 31 March 2015 is calculated as
(22.68 × 1.08) / (0.111 – 0.08) = 790.14

W2   Exchange rates
2013 = 1.63 × 1.02 = 1.6626
2014 = 1.6626 × 1.02 = 1.6959
2015 onwards = 1.6959 × 1.02 = 1.7298

W3   Discount factors
The cost of equity for M plc adjusted for GG's equity beta will be used as the discount rate
2013 = 1/1.111 = 0.900
2014 = $1/1.111^2$ = 0.810
2015 = $1/1.111^3$ = 0.729

Note
There is insufficient information to calculate either an asset based value or a dividend based valuation for GG.

A bootstrapping P/E valuation is considered to be unsuitable for this acquisition, since the two companies are so dissimilar. M plc has a P/E ratio of 12 and GG has a P/E ratio of 10. Given the lack of expertise of M plc in GG's industry it seems unlikely that M would increase GG's performance up to its own P/E ratio. A P/E ratio calculation based on GG's earnings and P/E ratio should be the same as the market capitalisation.

> **Tutorial note**. The following information forms the solution to part (b) (ii).

Validity of valuations calculated

Market capitalisation

As a listed entity GG has a current market value share price, which represents the market's current view of the value of the company. However this share price is only likely to be valid for a **relatively small holding of shares** as this is what is typically traded on the market. M plc will have to pay a **premium** above this price to encourage existing shareholders to sell, as if they wanted to sell their shares at the existing price, then they are able to anyway.

GG's current share price is USD 7.50 (equivalent to GBP 4.60 at the current spot rate). This share price has **risen 10% recently** due to speculation about the takeover bid. This is common in a takeover situation where the target company is not keen on the deal.

DCF valuation based on free cash flow

This valuation is based on the future cash flows generated by GG and as such provides an indication of its overall value. However, there are a **number of variables** and assumptions within the model which mean that the valuation is unlikely to be accurate. The future growth rates and movements in the exchange rate are **estimates** and these figures may be different in reality. Since appreciation of GBP against USD is expected, but has not been built into the valuation beyond three years, this valuation is **likely to be overstated**.

Initial offer price

The initial offer will need to be at a **premium** to the current share price of GG for the following reasons:

(i)   It recognises the additional value of the whole business over the value of a small shareholding.
(ii)   To be attractive enough for GG's shareholders to sell their shares
(iii)   In order to overcome hostility from the Board of GG.

In the event of the takeover becoming hostile, this may **encourage rival bids** from other companies and so M plc may have to pay an even higher premium, which increases the risk that M plc pays too high a price for GG and the takeover would be more likely to be unsuccessful.

The DCF valuation indicates a value per share of GBP 9.08, which is GBP 4.48 (or 97%) higher than the GBP value of the current share price of GG. This valuation is based on optimistic growth prospects and a strengthening of sterling against the US dollar, both of which may not happen in reality. This **valuation** therefore is likely to be **too high**. M plc should attempt to agree a price at a lower level than this.

As a recommendation M plc should start negotiations with an initial offer price at a **premium of 15%** to the current share price. This would be a price of USD 8.63 per share, which is worth GBP 5.29 at the current exchange rate. It should be noted that the final price may be higher if shareholders do not find this offer **sufficiently attractive**. A lower price may risk antagonising GG's shareholders, making them less likely to accept future offers, leading to a higher final price.

Terms of the offer

Using a value of GBP 5.29 per share for GG, combined with an existing market price for M plc's shares of GBP 3.77, share exchange terms of 7 M plc shares for 5 GG shares is roughly equivalent so would appear to be a good starting point.

> **Tutorial note**. The following information forms the solution to part (c)

Impact of the takeover on financial objectives

Objective 1

GG has an expected growth rate of 8% for earnings, but since the USD is expected to depreciate against sterling by 2% a year, this is **net growth of 6%** in GBP terms. This is significantly higher than the target growth rate for revenue and profit of 4%. It is likely that the takeover will help with achieving this objective.

Objective 2

Since GG's growth rate is in excess of M plc's, the acquisition of GG is **likely to help achieve growth** in dividends.

BPP
LEARNING MEDIA

Objective 3

GG has approximately the same level of gearing as M plc, which currently has a gearing level of 32%, calculated as 250m / (250m + (3.77 × 140)) = 32%

As a result the gearing of the group should remain at the **same level** immediately following the acquisition, assuming a share exchange bid. Gearing, based on market values, in the long term will depend on future performance.

Other relevant factors

Following a successful takeover M plc would be subject to increased risks as follows.

(i)   **Business risks** would be higher as GG operates in a different business sector. M plc has no expertise in this area making it harder for M plc to manage the business successfully.

(ii)   The **equity beta** of the new company would be higher than M plc's. Since GG has a higher equity beta than M plc, the overall equity beta of the new company will be higher.

(iii)   **Foreign exchange risk** will also be higher as GG is a US business which has USD cash flows, which M plc does not have.

M plc may also suffer issues during the **implementation stage** when attempting to merge systems or through a clash of management styles/culture. This is especially a risk as GG is located overseas. This means all of the usual risks associated with setting up in a **foreign country** apply, such as different regulatory frameworks, customer preferences, infrastructure and the cost of providing management support to the overseas country.

Due to the share exchange, the shareholders of M plc will suffer **dilution of their control**. Assuming the 7 shares for every 5 shares in GG offer is successful, then 7/5 × 40m = 56 million shares will be issued to GG's shareholders. This would give GG's shareholders 56/(140 + 56) = 29% control of the combined business.

M plc shareholders may consider the takeover to be unwise and therefore may sell their shares, leading to a **fall in the share price** of M plc.

Recommendation

There is a **huge risk** attached to this proposed takeover. GG is a very **large business in comparison** to M plc and the takeover would fundamentally change the nature of M plc's operations. M plc may struggle to manage the new business effectively and adverse foreign exchange movements could cause the group to make significant losses. The market has **signalled** that the takeover would not be in the interest of M plc through the recent fall in the share price. Given all of this it is recommended that M plc **does not proceed** with the takeover of GG.

Tutorial note. The following information forms the solution to part (d)

The Board of GG may take the following actions to defend what it considers to be a hostile bid

(i)   Appeal to GG's shareholders by using publicity to explain that the **value** will be **greater** under the **current ownership**. This could include research ideas, management potential or making shareholders aware of GG's achievements.

(ii)   Attack M plc by being **critical** of its management style, strategy or lack of capital investment depending on the circumstances relevant to the situation. This is more likely to be successful where a share exchange is proposed.

(iii)   A **White Knight** strategy may be employed, which involves trying to identify an alternative bidder who would be friendlier. This might be a US company that GG feels has a better fit with its operations.

(iv)   GG could make a **counterbid** for M plc.

(v)   The bid could become referred to the **competition authorities** in order to delay and potentially block the takeover.

The Board of M plc could take the following actions in the face of a hostile reception from GG

(i)   Appeal to GG's shareholders by using **publicity to advertise its strength**.

(ii)   Offer a **higher price** to attract the less enthusiastic shareholders of GG.

(iii)   Include a **cash alternative** to the share exchange offer. However, this would have an adverse impact on gearing as the cash required would need to be borrowed.

If you have any questions regarding the contents of this report please do not hesitate to contact me.

100 B Supermarkets (1)

Text references. International investment appraisal and risk are covered in Chapter 12. Financial analysis is covered in Chapter 3. Issues dealing with integration are covered in Chapter 16.

Top tips. For part (a) (ii) students should comment on B's ability to meet its stated financial objective of growing earnings per share by 7%.

In part (b), note that the investment cash flows are all fully allowable for tax purposes so they can be included before tax in the appraisal.

Easy marks. You should be able to pick up a number of easy marks from the calculations in part (a) (i) provided that you know how to do these calculations. The net present value calculation in part (b) is also fairly straightforward.

Examiner's comments. In part (a) (iii) some candidates merely repeated what had been said earlier. A similar weakness was to limit discussion to learned theory of dividend policy issues such as the "clientele effect" and "signalling" and did not recognise that the share price has remained resilient since 2008, indicating that the company was able to support the dividend payouts. Indeed, the company has a substantial amount of cash and cash equivalent in the Statement of Financial Position.

In part (b) (ii) many candidates were unable to identify the key issues. Some candidates just provided a check list of political, economic, cultural risks etc with general discussion that was not sufficiently related to the scenario.

(a) (i)

Year	Earnings €m	No of shares (m)	EPS €	Share price €	P/E ratio
2007	3,945	1,284	3.07	47.38	15.4
2008	2,818	1,284	2.19	25.45	11.6
2009	3,097	1,350	2.29	28.68	12.5
2010	3,366	1,350	2.49	29.44	11.8
2011	3,591	1,350	2.66	31.37	11.8

Year	Dividend per share €	Dividend paid (€m)	Dividend payout
2007	1.54	1,977	50%
2008	1.54	1,977	70%
2009	1.54	2,079	67%
2010	1.62	2,187	65%
2011	1.65	2,228	62%

(ii) Additional calculations

Year	Earnings €m	EPS €	Change in earnings	Change in EPS
2007	3,945	3.07	-	-
2008	2,818	2.19	(29%)	(29%)
2009	3,097	2.29	10%	5%
2010	3,366	2.49	9%	9%
2011	3,591	2.66	7%	7%

Performance of B

There was a significant fall in earnings between 2007 and 2008 of 29%. This coincided with the **downturn of the global economy**, which could have been amplified by a shortage of available credit and increased price competition in a bid to attract consumers who became increasingly cost conscious.

There has been some recovery in earnings since then, with an initial 10% increase in 2009, but this growth rate has been falling since, with growth of only 7% in 2011. In 2011 earnings have not yet recovered to their 2007 level.

Share price and P/E ratio

The share price fell significantly from €47.38 to €25.45 in 2008 reflecting a lack of market confidence in the prospects for the group. The share price has since **improved year on year** and is currently €31.37, suggesting a growing confidence in the prospect for B. The P/E ratio also fell significantly in 2008 before recovering slightly in 2009 before dropping slightly in 2010 and stabilising in 2011. This stabilisation demonstrates that there is **confidence in the future prospects** in spite of the current difficult trading conditions.

Objective of growth in earning per share

There is a financial objective to grow earnings per share at 7% per year. This was only met in 2010 and 2011. In 2009 earnings grew by 10%, but due to an issue of shares, earnings per share only increased by 5%.

(iii) Dividend per share was maintained at the 2007 level for 2008 and 2009 despite a significant fall in B's earnings. This is likely to be due to the signalling effect of dividends and B not wanting to panic the market. The consequence of this is that the dividend payout ratio was much higher than the target of 50%. In 2008 the ratio was 70%. The payout ratio continues to be above the 50% target. This means that there are significantly less funds available for investment than would have been expected, which may compromise long-term growth. This increases the likelihood of additional debt finance being required, which may be problematic when credit is in short supply due to the current economic conditions and banks being required to maintain higher capital levels.

A stable dividend is often used to **reassure shareholders**, but this did not work in 2008 for B as there was still a significant fall in the share price. Overall shareholders saw a negative return in 2008 despite the stable dividend.

The reasons for the dividend increases in 2010 and 2011 are not immediately clear, but B may want its shareholders to have increasing returns. However the dividend payout ratio would return to the target level quicker if a stable dividend had been maintained. This would also make more funds **available for capital investment**.

(b) Briefing paper for the Board of B Supermarkets
From: Financial Director
Date: 24 May 2012
Re: Proposed acquisition of Alpha Supermarkets

Purpose

The purpose of this briefing paper is to provide information concerning the proposed acquisition of Alpha Supermarkets and to assess the potential financial benefits as well as other opportunities and risks associated with the acquisition.

Calculation of net present value for an average store

Year	0	1	2	3
	A\$m	A\$m	A\$m	A\$m
Investment*	(35.00)	(3.00)	(3.00)	30.00
Revenue		30.00	33.60	37.63
Costs		(13.00)	(14.04)	(15.16)
Net cash flow before tax	(35.00)	14.00	16.56	52.47
Tax	11.20	(4.48)	(5.30)	(16.79)
Tax credit	(11.20)	4.48	5.30	1.42
Net cash flow	(35.00)	14.00	16.56	37.10
Discount factor at 15%	1.000	0.870	0.756	0.658
PV	(35.00)	12.18	12.52	24.41

NPV (A\$ million)	14.11
Spot rate (A\$/€1)	7.5
NPV (€ million)	1.88

* **Tutorial note:** Investment balances are included before tax, because these are all fully allowable deductions for tax purposes, although this is not usually the case with investment appraisal questions.

Using this NPV per average store, the total added value from 15 stores would be

€1.88m × 15 = €28.2 million

Potential risks and opportunities

The acquisition of Alpha Supermarkets would bring **entry into a new market**, that of Country A, and with it a number of risks and opportunities.

An offer at a 20% premium to the previous takeover bid would be valued at around €150 million. This is **not likely to be material** in overall terms for B Supermarkets. Even if Alpha Supermarkets lost 50% of this purchase value that would be just 2% of the 2011 annual profit of €3,591 million.

There is the potential for damage to the reputation of B Supermarkets if the acquisition is unsuccessful. This reputation damage may then have further knock-on effects in other markets and affect the plans for expansion into Asia. This risk is difficult to quantify.

There are other smaller risks as part of developing a business in a new country, although B Supermarkets does already have some experience of this in both Asia and North America, with the Asian experience particularly relevant here. These risks include:

(a)   Customers may be unhappy with a **foreign owner** and may choose to take their custom elsewhere.

(b)   **Foreign exchange risk** arises from exposure to the A$, including translation risk on the net investment cost and transaction risk from the changing value of remittances back to B Supermarkets.

(c)   The position of the Government of Country A is important. If the current government is **unstable**, this may affect future prospects. There could also be changes to the tax regime or government intervention in the project.

(d)   **Exchange controls** may be in place, restricting the amount that can be remitted to B Supermarkets, or taxes may be charged on these remittances.

(e)   **Unfamiliarity** with the market brings additional risk of an unsuccessful expansion, which is reduced here slightly due to the small scale of the acquisition.

(f)   Competitors could be concerned about the impact of B Supermarkets entering the market. **Local companies may co-operate** in an attempt to make the expansion unsuccessful. This could be in the form of a price war or other forms of intense competition.

(g)   The expansion will require **financing for each stage**. There is a risk that the funding will not be available when it is required, due to poor creditworthiness of B Supermarkets or a lack of liquidity in the capital markets.

(h)   **Integrating the systems** of Alpha with those of B could create problems. There are also further integration issues with local employees and it will be necessary for them to be willing to embrace new systems and a different corporate culture.

On the opportunities side, there is significant **potential for substantial future growth in earnings and dividends** as a result of further expansion in the region. This will support B Supermarket's financial objective 1. These opportunities are follow-on options after Alpha Supermarkets has been acquired.

Whether to proceed

It is recommended that B Supermarkets proceeds with the acquisition of Alpha Supermarkets. The initial financial return from the acquisition of the 15 stores is not expected to be large in the short-term, but it will give rise to further expansion options in the long term. In addition there is potential for significant further growth in this region, which makes the expansion plans worth pursuing.

The above advice is based on the assumption that B Supermarkets has **enough resources** (both staff and financial) to implement the expansion plan. It is also assumed that local staff in Country A will be willing to co-operate with required changes and that any other challenges noted above do not prove to be impossible to overcome

There is an increased chance of a successful overseas expansion as a result of the experience B Supermarkets already has in establishing an overseas presence in Asia.

MOCK EXAMS

CIMA – Pillar F

Paper F3

Financial Strategy

Mock Examination 1

Instructions to candidates:

You are allowed three hours to answer this question paper.
In the real exam, you are allowed 20 minutes reading time before the examination begins during which you should read the question paper, and if you wish, make annotations on the question paper. However, you will **not** be allowed, **under any circumstances**, to open the answer book and start writing or use your calculator during this reading time.
You are strongly advised to carefully read the question requirement before attempting the question concerned.
Answer the compulsory questions in Section A.
Answer TWO of the THREE questions in Section B.

DO NOT OPEN THIS PAPER UNTIL YOU ARE READY TO START UNDER EXAMINATION CONDITIONS

SECTION A

Question 1

Pre-seen case material

Clothing manufacturing in Europe

Since the 1960s there has been a decline in the number of UK and European clothing manufacturers due to competition from cheaper, and sometimes higher quality, imported clothes. The clothing industry generally has become much more fashion conscious and price sensitive. This has led to a reduced number of companies that are still in business in Europe. Some companies have moved all or part of their manufacturing processes to other countries to achieve a cheaper operating base, and up until recently this has allowed them to continue to compete on price.

Many companies have had contracts to supply High Street retailers for over four decades and are highly dependant on retaining these key customers who wield immense buying power over the small manufacturers. A number of family owned manufacturing companies, that had been highly profitable once, have ceased trading, or are operating at very low margins, as a direct result of the High Street retailers being able to dictate terms of business and prices.

An additional factor that has put the main High Street retailers under more price pressure has been the appearance and market growth of new High Street retailers and their new brands, who have procured their goods mainly from overseas sources

The result is that the few companies that are based in the UK and Europe which are left in the business of clothing manufacturing are having to look very hard at their strategic plans in order for them to manage to maintain their business over the next few years.

History of Kadgee Fashions (Kadgee)

Kadgee was formed in post-World War Two in a European country, and has remained as an unlisted company, although its shares are now held by others outside of the founding family. Kadgee quickly established itself as a high quality manufacturer of both men's and ladies clothes. By the 1960s Kadgee had a turnover equivalent to €25 million, and had nine factories operating in two European countries.

During the late 1960s Kadgee suffered its first major fall in sales, and found that it had large stocks of men's clothes that had been manufactured without specific sales contracts. Kadgee managed to sell off some of the stocks, albeit at below cost price. However, the management decided that it should not manufacture clothes without a firm contract from a retailer in future.

In the early 1970s the range and design of its men's clothing was changed several times, but it continued to make little profit. In 1973, Kadgee sold its men's clothing range and designs and some of its manufacturing equipment to a large listed company. Kadgee decided to concentrate on expanding its ranges of ladies' clothing to meet the growing demands of its main customers (see below).

During the next few years, Kadgee consolidated its position and its profitability increased again. In the early 1980s its then Chief Designer persuaded the Managing Director to expand its clothing range to include a range of girls' clothes. This new limited range was launched in 1982 and was immediately sold out. Kadgee has positioned itself at the upper price range of clothing, and has never tried to mass produced low cost clothing.

During the 1980s Kadgee continued to expand its ranges of ladies and girls' clothes. A further change that occurred was that many of Kadgee's customers were starting to dictate the styles and types of clothing required and Kadgee's designers had to manufacture to customers' specifications.

However, during the 1990s Kadgee suffered a number of setbacks. It also saw many of its competitors suffer losses and cease trading. Kadgee had been able to stay profitable only because of its particular customer base and because it sold high quality clothes that commanded a premium price. However, Kadgee saw its margins on many product lines reduced greatly and also it started to lose many of its smaller customers, who choose to import, at much lower prices, clothing produced in Asia.

Kadgee's shareholders

Kadgee has remained an unlisted company. At the end of 20X5 29% of its shares were held by the company's founder who is no longer on the board, 60% by current directors, 11% by employees. The company has 200,000 shares of €0·10 each in issue and has a total of 400,000 authorised shares. The shares are not traded but the last time the shares were exchanged was eight years ago, when shares were purchased at €8·00 each.

Kadgee's customer base

Kadgee manufactures clothing for a number of European and international clothing retailers, including many well known High Street retailers. It manufactures clothing in the medium to higher price ranges and its customers require top quality designs and finishing to maintain their brand reputation.

The majority of Kadgee's clothing is manufactured for its customers under the customers' own label, for example, clothing manufactured for one of its customers called Portrait is labelled as 'Portrait'.

In 20X5, Kadgee's customer base, analysed by sales value, was as follows:

	20X5 revenue	% of Kadgee's total sales
	€ million	%
Portrait	24·0	32·3
Forum	16·8	22·6
Diamond	13·5	18·1
Zeeb	5·1	6·9
JayJay	4·5	6·0
Other retailers of ladies' clothes	7·3	9·8
Haus (children's clothes only)	3·2	4·3
Total	74·4	100·0

Most of Kadgee's contracts are renewed at the start of each fashion season. Kadgee is currently negotiating for clothing sales for the summer season of 20X7.

Human Resources

In the clothing manufacturing business one of the most crucial aspects to achieve customer satisfaction is quality. Kadgee has been very fortunate in having a skilled, very dedicated workforce who have always adapted to new machinery and procedures and have been instrumental in suggesting ways in which quality could be improved. This has sometimes involved a very minor change in the design of a garment and the designers now work much more closely with the operational staff to ensure that the garments can be assembled as quickly and efficiently as possible.

Losses made by Kadgee

Kadgee has suffered from falling operating profit margins due to the pressure exerted by its customers over the last ten years. For the first time in Kadgee's history, it experienced losses for five years through to, and including, 20X2. During this time Kadgee increased its loans and its overdraft to finance operations.

In 20X0, Kadgee refinanced with a ten year loan, which was used to repay existing debt, and also to invest in the IT solutions discussed below, as well as to purchase some new machinery. Kadgee also invested in its design centre (see below), which was completed in 20X1.

During 20X1, the company invested in new IT solutions enabling its customers to be able to track all orders from the garment cutting process right through to completion of garments and through to the delivery to customers' premises.

The IT solutions also enabled Kadgee to monitor its production processes including machine usage, wastage at various stages of production and speed of production through the various stages. This has enabled Kadgee's management to reduce areas that did not add value to the finished garment. The use of TQM throughout the business has also increased Kadgee's efficiency and enabled it to eliminate some other areas which did not add value to the finished garments.

While margins are still low, Kadgee has been operating profitably again since 20X3, albeit at lower margins to those achieved in the past.

Changes in the supply chain

Many of Kadgee's customers have needed to speed up the process of supplying clothing to their shops, so as to meet the demands of the market and to remain competitive. Kadgee has worked closely with its customers in order to achieve shorter lead times from design to delivery of finished products.

In 20X1, Kadgee introduced a new design centre, centralised at its Head Office. The design centre uses computer aided design techniques, which has helped Kadgee's customers to appreciate the finished appearance of new designs. This seems to have helped Kadgee to win new business and to retain its current customers. It has also contributed to Kadgee's ability to speed up the process from design board to finished article. Kadgee has also benefited from working closer with its customers and this has resulted in additional orders, which Kadgee's customers' would otherwise have procured from overseas sources.

Growing competition from China

During the 1990s and into the 21st century China has had a massive impact on the textile industry. China's manufacturing base is forecast to grow further and this will have a negative impact on many companies operating at a higher cost base elsewhere.

Many European companies have spent millions of Euros establishing manufacturing bases outside their home countries in the last 15 years. Many have opened factories in countries which have much lower operating costs. These include countries such as Turkey, Sri Lanka and Pakistan, as well as Eastern European countries.

The companies which have set up operations in these low cost countries did so in an effort to cut costs by taking advantage of low overheads and lower labour rates, but still managed to maintain quality. However, even the companies that have moved some, or all, of their manufacturing bases and have taken steps to reduce their costs, now have to reconsider their cost base again. This is because of the very low cost of Chinese imports, which they are having difficulty competing against.

Following the relaxation of trade barriers, there has recently been a deluge of Chinese clothing imports into Europe, the UK and the USA.

The quality of Chinese manufactured clothing is improving rapidly and it is now globally recognised that the 'Made in China' label represents clothing of a higher quality than many European manufactured garments. Furthermore, the Chinese manufactured garments are being produced at a substantially lower manufacturing cost.

Kadgee has so far been operating in a market that has not been significantly affected by imported goods, as it produces medium to higher priced clothing, rather than cheaper ranges of clothes. However, many of Kadgee's customers are now looking to reduce their costs by either buying more imported clothes or by negotiating substantial price cuts from their existing suppliers. The purchasing power of European retailers being exerted on its suppliers is immense and Kadgee is under much pressure to deliver high quality goods at reduced operating profit margins from all of its customers.

Date

It is now 1 November 20X6.

Appendix 1

Kadgee's Statement of financial position, Income Statement and Statement of changes in equity

Statement of financial position

	20X5		20X4	
At 31 December	€'000	€'000	€'000	€'000
Non-current assets (net)		9,830		11,514
Current assets				
Inventory	8,220		6,334	
Trade receivables and rent prepayments	19,404		18,978	
Cash and short term investments	119		131	
		27,743		25,443
Total assets		37,573		36,957

Equity and liabilities

	20X5		20X4	
At 31 December	€'000	€'000	€'000	€'000
Equity				
Paid in share capital	20		20	
Share premium reserve	450		450	
Retained profits	21,787		20,863	
		22,257		21,333
Non-current liabilities				
Loans: Bank loan at 8% interest per year (repayable in 2010)		4,500		4,500
Current liabilities				
Bank overdraft	1,520		940	
Trade payables and accruals	8,900		9,667	
Tax	396		517	
		10,816		11,124
Total equity and liabilities		37,573		36,957

Note. Paid in share capital represents 200,000 shares of €0·10 each at 31 December 20X5

Income Statement

	Year ended 31 December	
	20X5	20X4
	€'000	€'000
Revenue	74,420	75,553
Total operating costs	72,580	73,320
Operating profit	1,840	2,233
Finance costs	520	509
Tax expense (effective tax rate is 24%)	396	517
Profit for the period	924	1,207

Statement of changes in equity

	Share capital €'000	Share premium €'000	Retained earnings €'000	Total €'000
Balance at 31 December 20X4	20	450	20,863	21,333
Profit for the period	–	–	924	924
Dividends paid	–	–	–	–
Balance at 31 December 20X5	20	450	21,787	22,257

Appendix 2

Kadgee's Cash Flow Statement

	Year ended 31 December			
	20X5		20X4	
	€'000	€'000	€'000	€'000
Net cash inflow from operations				
Operating profit		1,840		2,233
Add back depreciation	1,965		1,949	
(Increase)/Decrease in inventory	(1,886)		(535)	
(Increase)/Decrease in trade receivables	(426)		(1,526)	
Increase/(Decrease) in trade payables and accruals	(767)		(604)	
		(1,114)		(716)
Net cash flow from operations		726		1,517
Finance costs paid		(520)		(509)
Taxation paid		(517)		(390)
Purchase of tangible fixed assets		(281)		(350)
Dividends paid		–		–
Cash Inflow/(Outflow) before financing		(592)		268
Increase/(Decrease) in bank overdraft		580		(194)
Increase/(Decrease) in cash and short term investments		(12)		74

Unseen case material

Kadgee's Board has decided that the solution to falling operating margins is to diversify into highly profitable upmarket men's clothing. To do this, the company would need to establish a new manufacturing plant. There are two options available in either Kadgee's home country in Europe or Bizan, a country in Asia with a rapidly growing textile industry. Ideally, the Board would like to open the new facility at home as well as expanding into Asia, but it does not believe it has the financial or management resources to do both at the same time.

The estimated cost for the European investment is €3 million. These initial investment costs will be written off over a period of 5 years. To establish operations in Bizan will cost an estimated BZ$7.5 million. This Asian investment, combined with capital expenditure already committed, would exceed the company's capital investment limit if it were to be enforced.

Forecast pre-tax operating nominal cash flows for the first three years of operations are as follows:

		Year		
		1	2	3
Asian investment	BZ$m	2.25	2.45	2.65
European investment	€m	0.63	0.90	1.05

- All operating cash flows may be assumed to occur at the end of each year. The initial capital investment will be made at the beginning of year 1 (year 0).

- Estimated cash flows beyond year 3 are highly uncertain, but for purposes of evaluation, the company assumes 5% per year growth on year 3's pre-tax operating sterling cash flows until the end of year 5. Cash flows beyond year 5 are ignored.

Exchange rate information

	Forecast inflation rates per annum constant %
Bizan	1.5
Eurozone	2.5

The spot $/€ exchange rate as at today is 1.70.

Taxation

Corporate tax rates in the two countries are as follows:

	%
Bizan	25
Eurozone	30

Assume for the purposes of evaluation:

- Both countries allow 100% first year allowance tax relief on capital investments of this type.
- There is a double taxation treaty in existence.
- Tax is payable (or refundable) at the end of the year in which the liability or refund arises.
- Kadgee pays tax at the national tax rates.

Cost of capital and adjustment for risk

For domestic investments Kadgee uses a risk-adjusted discount rate using the CAPM to calculate this rate where possible. The expected nominal, pre-tax risk free rate in Europe is 5% and the return on the market is 9%. The quoted equity beta of a suitable proxy company with a similar capital structure to Kadgee is 1.3.

However, Kadgee's Finance Director recognises that the risks involved in the overseas proposal are different. Determining an appropriate discount rate to reflect risk is difficult in the circumstances. She has therefore recommended that the post-tax cash flows for the Bizan venture be adjusted using estimates of probability applied to sterling cash flows, discounted at the risk free rate. These estimates of probability are as follows:

	Year		
	1	2	3
Probability	0.9	0.87	0.82

Beyond year 3, a probability factor of 0.7 is estimated.

Methods of investment appraisal

Kadgee uses NPV analysis in the investment appraisal process, but the company also expects new investments to contribute to all the company's objectives.

Objectives

The Board has recently agreed the following objectives

- Increase earnings per share by 10% per annum
- Post-tax accounting rate of return on shareholders' funds of 20% per annum
- Maintain a leading global presence in its operating markets

P/E ratio

The average P/E ratio of listed companies in a similar industry is 10.53

Required

Assume you are the Capital Investment Analyst at Kadgee.

(a) Calculate the discount rate to be used in the evaluation of the European investment and discuss briefly on the limitations of using this rate in the investment being proposed here for Kadgee. Assume Kadgee's debt is trading at par and has a beta of zero. **(5 marks)**

(b) Calculate the NPV, Profitability Index and estimated Accounting Rate of Return (ROCE) for each investment. For the purposes of calculating the ROCE, assume that cumulative sterling post-tax cash flows at the end of year 5 equal cumulative post-tax profits before depreciation. **(20 marks)**

(c) Write a report to the board evaluating the proposed investments. Include the following sections in your report:

(i) An evaluation of how each of the two investments will contribute to the achievement of the company's stated objectives. **(10 marks)**

(ii) An analysis of the various types of risk involved in these investments and advice on a strategy for managing those risks. Include comments on the methods the Finance Director has recommended to adjust the cash flows for risk. **(8 marks)**

(iii) A recommendation as to whether the company should invest in either or both projects. Include comments on the potential financing. **(7 marks)**

(Total = 50 marks)

SECTION B – 50 marks

Answer TWO of the three questions

Question 2

PQD is an unquoted company aiming for a stock exchange listing. Its directors have commissioned a firm of consultants to conduct a wide-ranging review of the company's public image and market position. Although this is not predominantly a financial review, the consultants need to examine the company's financial performance. The company has the following summary information for the last five years.

	Year 1 £m	Year 2 £m	Year 3 £m	Year 4 £m	Year 5 £m
Revenues	51.2	58.3	63.9	75.2	78.2
Cost of sales	20.5	22.2	24.3	30.1	30.5
Salaries and wages	15.4	16.8	17.2	15.8	15.2
Other costs	6.1	7.9	9.9	16.3	17.9
Profit from operations	9.2	11.4	12.5	13.0	14.6
Interest	1.5	1.6	1.3	0.3	0.2
Tax	2.5	3.2	3.7	4.2	4.8
Profit after interest and tax	5.2	6.6	7.5	8.5	9.6
Dividends payable	2.1	2.6	3.0	3.4	4.8
Average receivables	10.5	11.7	13.3	14.8	15.2
Average payables	3.8	4.2	5.1	6.7	6.9
Average total assets	41.2	45.2	46.7	63.3	67.1
Shareholders' funds	26.2	30.2	34.7	59.8	64.6
Long-term debt	15.0	15.0	12.0	3.5	2.5
Number of shares in issue (millions)	6.0	6.0	6.0	8.0	8.0
P/E ratio:					
Company	8.0	8.5	9.0	9.2	9.5
Industry	8.5	9.0	9.1	9.0	9.1
Number of employees	1,720	1,750	1,820	1,720	1,690

Notes

1   Each P/E ratio is the average for the year.

2   The increased equity in year 4 was the result of a 1-for-3 rights issue at 1,000p per share which took place at the beginning of the year. Some of the money raised was used to reduce debt.

For the past five years, PQD has stated its objectives as: 'To maximise shareholder wealth whilst recognising the responsibility of the company to its other stakeholders'.

As one of the consultants working on this assignment, you have been asked to assess whether the company has achieved its objectives in the five-year period under review and to discuss the key factors which have determined your assessment.

Required

(a)   (i)   Discuss whether the company has met its objectives, based solely on the information available.

(12 marks)

(ii)   Explain what other financial information you would need in order to provide your client with a more accurate assessment.
(8 marks)

(b)   Describe the role of the financial managers if PQD decides to seek a flotation.
(5 marks)

(Total = 25 marks)

Question 3

AB manufactures products for children. The company's turnover and earnings last year were $56 million and $3.5 million respectively. Its shares are not listed but they occasionally change hands in private transactions. AB's weighted average cost of capital (WACC) is 13% net of tax. The directors believe that an appropriate gearing ratio (debt to debt + equity) for a company such as AB is 30%, which is the industry average. Currently, AB's gearing ratio is slightly higher than this at 35%. Its debt comprises two secured long-term bank loans and a permanent overdraft, secured by a floating charge on the company's current assets. The current cost of debt to a company such as AB is 10% before tax.

The company is considering expansion abroad, in particular in an Eastern European (EE) country where its products have become popular. The EE government has offered AB plc a financing deal to establish a manufacturing operation. The financing would take the form of an EE marks 30 million 6-year loan at a subsidised rate of only 2.5% each year interest. The current exchange rate is EE marks 20 to the $.

Interest would be payable at the end of each year and the principal repaid at the end of 6 years. The exchange rate of EE marks to the $ would be fixed at the current rate for the whole 6-year period of the loan. The marginal tax rate in both countries is 25%.

Required

(a)   Calculate the company's present cost of equity and the present value of the EE government subsidy implicit in the loan. Comment briefly on the method used and any assumptions you have made in your calculations.   **(7 marks)**

(b)   Discuss the relevance of both the cost of equity you have calculated in answer to (a) above and the WACC given in the scenario, to the company's investment decision. Include comment on an alternative discount rate that could be used appropriately in the scenario's circumstances.   **(6 marks)**

(c)   (i)   Discuss the advantages and disadvantages of using the EE government subsidy in AB's international investment decision.

        (ii)   Recommend alternative methods of financing that might be suitable for AB in the circumstances of the scenario.   **(12 marks)**

(Total = 25 marks)

Question 4

KM is a company that has expanded overseas over a number of years and now has operations in many countries. KM is organised in a divisionalised structure and historically the divisions have enjoyed considerable autonomy, including deciding what specialists they should employ. Head office functions are categorised as support functions such as the financial control and accounting function that has overseen all financial activity, and profit centres such as the information technology function that are required to charge divisions with a full market price for their services.

The directors have recently become concerned about various aspects of financial management within the group as one division has recently lost considerable money through trading on the derivatives market. The returns from the investment of surplus funds by other divisions appear to be unsatisfactorily low. There has also been criticism that the financial control function lacks resources to supervise all aspects of the group's financial management satisfactorily.

The finance director is therefore considering removing certain responsibilities from the financial control function, and establishing a separate treasury function, based at Head Office.

Required

(a)   Describe the main responsibilities of the treasury function, and explain why the director is considering separating the treasury and financial control functions.   **(11 marks)**

(b)   Explain the advantages and disadvantages of operating the treasury function as a profit centre rather than a cost centre.   **(6 marks)**

(c)   Explain the advantages of centralisation of the treasury function.   **(8 marks)**

(Total = 25 marks)

Answers

DO NOT TURN THIS PAGE UNTIL YOU HAVE
COMPLETED MOCK EXAM 1

Plan of attack

We know you've been told to do it at least 100 times and we know if we asked you you'd know that you should do it. So why don't you do it in an exam? 'Do what in an exam?' you're probably thinking. Well, let's tell you for the 101st time. **Take a good look through the paper before diving in to answer questions.**

First things first

What you must do in the first five or ten minutes of the exam is **look through the paper** in detail, working out **which questions to do** and the **order** in which to attempt them. So turn back to the paper and let's sort out a plan of attack.

We then recommend you spend the remaining time analysing the requirements of Question 1 and highlighting the key issues in the question. The extra time spent on (a) will be helpful, whenever you intend to do the question, If you decide to do it first, you will be well into the question when the writing time starts. If you intend to do it second or third, probably because you find it daunting, the question will look easier when you come to back to it, because your initial analysis should generate further points whilst you're tackling the other questions.

The next step

You're probably either thinking that you don't know where to begin or that you could have a very decent go at all the questions.

Option 1 (if you don't know where to begin)

If you are a bit **worried** about the paper, it's likely that you believe that case study **Question 1** looks daunting. We therefore recommend that you do one or both of the optional questions before tackling the case study. Don't however fall into the trap of going over time on the optional questions because they seem easier. You will need to spend half the time available on the case study.

- In order to pass **Question 2** comfortably you will need to include a number of ratios, most of which you should hopefully remember not just from this paper but lower level papers as well. Don't though just concentrate on these, as the discussion will be worth more than half marks.

- There are some easy marks to be had in the discussion parts of **Question 3** even if you are not sure how to do all of the calculations.

- You can score very well on **Question 4** if you can produce a planned and well written answer.

- Don't be put off if there are one or two aspects of the calculations you struggle with in parts (a) and (b) of **Question 1**. There are some easier marks available as well.

Option 2 (if you're thinking 'I can do all of these')

It never pays to be over confident but if you're not quaking in your shoes about the exam then **turn straight to compulsory Question 1**. You've got to do it so you might as well get it over and done with.

Once you've done the compulsory question, choose two of the questions in Section B.

- You should find the calculations in **Question 2** fairly straightforward, but remember that the discussion will account for more than half the marks.

- If you're happy with the area of cost of capital, you may well choose **Question 3,** although bear in mind it does involve some complicated calculations.

- If you choose **Question 4**, make sure you have enough knowledge to answer such a comprehensive question.

No matter how many times we remind you...

Always, always **allocate your time** according to the marks for the question in total and for the parts of the questions. And always, always **follow the requirements exactly**.

You've got free time at the end of the exam.....?

If you have allocated your time properly then you **shouldn't have time on your hands** at the end of the exam. If you find yourself with five or ten minutes spare, however, go back to **any parts of questions that you didn't finish** because you ran out of time.

Forget about it!

And don't worry if you found the paper difficult. More then likely other students would too. If this were the real thing you would need to forget the exam the minute you leave the exam hall and **think about the next one**. Or, if it's the last one, **celebrate!**

Question 1

Text references. CAPM calculations are explained in Chapter 8, NPV calculations in Chapter 12 and capital rationing in Chapter 13.

Top tips. Note the data that is relevant to the calculation in (a), including risk-free rates and price-earnings ratios for the market values. In (b) it is easiest to do the purchasing power parity calculation. Because there is no timing difference between paying tax in Bizan and Europe, it is easiest to convert the pre-tax dollar cash flows to Euros and then to compute the 30% tax liability.

(c) (i) does not specify that you will need calculations; however remember that the discussion parts of Section A often require calculations to support the discussion, even if you are not asked to provide them. Certainly here you need to show whether the quantitative objectives have been fulfilled.

(c) (ii) highlights one of the weaknesses of CAPM; the possibly unwarranted assumption that investors are well-diversified. The 7 marks available in (c) (iii) indicates that you needed more than 2-3 lines recommendation.

Easy marks. (c) (ii) offers plenty of scope to score half a dozen reasonable marks, provided you mention solutions as well as risk.

(a) Cost of capital

The company will use a **risk adjusted weighted average cost of capital** to appraise its European investment.

The **risk adjusted cost of equity capital** can be found using the **capital asset pricing model**, where R_f is 5% and R_m is 9%. The beta of the proxy company, 1.3, can be used as this company has a similar capital structure to Kadgee.

Thus $k_{eu} = 5\% + 1.3 (9\% - 5\%) = 10.2\%$.

Because Kadgee's debt beta is zero, its after tax cost will be the same as the after tax risk free rate. The pre-tax rate is 5%, so the post-tax rate will be $5\% \times (1 - 0.3) = 3.5\%$.

Market values of equity and debt

Total equity earnings = €924,000 and P/E can be assumed to be average, 10.53.

Thus value of equity = €924,000 × 10.53 = €9.7m.

Debt is at par, value €4.5m. Therefore total value of equity plus debt = €14.2m.

Weighted average cost of capital $= [\dfrac{9.7}{14.2} \times 10.2\%] + [\dfrac{4.5}{14.2} \times 3.5\%] = 8.08\%$, say 8%.

Assumptions of calculation

This computation uses a number of broad approximations, thus:

- The risk adjustment assumes that the new project is of **average risk** for Kadgee
- The valuation of Kadgee's equity assumes that Kadgee is of **average risk** for its sector
- The proxy company's beta may not be appropriate as there may be important differences impacting upon risks
- The CAPM itself is only an **approximate model**
- Kadgee is a **private company**: its shareholders are likely to have a large proportion of their assets tied up in Kadgee, and will be more affected by the unsystematic risk of Kadgee than is predicted by the CAPM.

(b) Proposed European investment

NPV

The after tax operating cash flows are 70% of the pre-tax figures, and the capital allowance results in a tax reduction at the end of year 1. No residual value after 5 years.

	0	1	2	3	4	5	Total profit
	€m	€m	€m	€m	€m	€m	
Initial outlay	(3.00)						
First year allowance		0.90					
Operating cash flows (× 0.7 yrs 1–3, 5% growth yrs 4–5)		0.44	0.63	0.74	0.77	0.81	
Cash flows	(3.00)	1.34	0.63	0.74	0.77	0.81	1.29
Discount factor 8%	1.000	0.926	0.857	0.794	0.735	0.681	
Discounted cash flows	(3.00)	1.24	0.54	0.59	0.57	0.55	0.49

The NPV of €0.49 million is positive, indicating the investment is worthwhile.

Profitability index

The profitability index is $\dfrac{\text{NPV}}{\text{outlay}} = \dfrac{0.49}{3} = 0.163$

ROCE

Cost of investment = €3m

Average capital employed $= \dfrac{\text{€3m}}{2} = \text{€1.5m}$

Cumulative after-tax operating cash flows total €3.39 million (0.44 + 0.63 + 0.74 + 0.77 + 0.81). With the capital allowance tax reduction, the cumulative after tax cash flow is €3.39m + €0.9m = €4.29m

Total accounting depreciation is €3 million, so total accounting profit is €1.29 million (see above). Per year, this is:

$\dfrac{\text{€1.29}}{5} = \text{€0.26m}$

So, average ROCE is: $\dfrac{\text{€0.26m}}{\text{€1.5m}} = 17.3\%$ per annum

Proposed Asian investment

Use **purchasing power parity** to compute the predicted exchange rates for BZ$/€.

Predicted exchange rate next year (BZ$/€)

= spot rate (BZ$/€) x (1 + BZ$ inflation rate)/(1 + € inflation rate).

Rate in year 0 is $1.70 = €1. Rates in each succeeding year are found by multiplying by: $\dfrac{1.015}{1.025}$

	Year			
	0	1	2	3
Exchange rate	1.700	1.683	1.667	1.651

NPV

Taxation

Tax is charged on profits at 25% pa in Bizan. The same profits are taxed at 30% in Europe, but the 25% paid in Bizan is offset. Thus the net tax paid is 30% of profits.

	Year						Total profit
	0	1	2	3	4	5	
Capital outlay $m	(7.50)						
Pre-tax operating cash flows $m		2.25	2.45	2.65			
Exchange rate	1.700	1.683	1.667	1.651			
Cash flow €m	(4.41)	1.34	1.47	1.61	1.69	1.77	
Tax – capital allowance		1.32					
Tax – op cash flows		(0.40)	(0.44)	(0.48)	(0.51)	(0.53)	
After tax cash flows	(4.41)	2.26	1.03	1.13	1.18	1.24	2.43
Probability factor	1.00	0.90	0.87	0.82	0.7	0.7	
5% discount factor	1.000	0.952	0.907	0.864	0.823	0.784	
Risk adjusted PV	(4.41)	1.94	0.81	0.80	0.68	0.68	0.50

Risk adjusted net present value: €0.5m.

Again the net present value is positive, and project appears worthwhile.

Profitability index

The 'profitability index' is $\dfrac{NPV}{outlay} = \dfrac{0.5}{4.41} = 0.113$

ROCE

Cost of investment = €4.41m.

Average capital employed = $\dfrac{€4.41m}{2} = €2.21m$

Total accounting profit is €2.43m (see above), giving an average per year of $\dfrac{€2.43}{5} = €0.49m$

So, ROCE is $\dfrac{€0.49m}{€2.21m} = 22.2\%$ per annum

(c) To: Board of Directors
From: Capital Investment Analyst
Date: 12 April 20X5
Subject: Report on proposed investments in Europe and Asia

I have carried out computations (see attached) to establish the financial viability of the two proposed investments. This report uses these results and other factors to evaluate the investments and to assist you in deciding whether to proceed with them.

(i)   Contribution to the achievement of the company's objectives

The company has three stated objectives:

(1)   To increase earnings per share by 10% per annum

Both of these investments easily achieve and beat this target which calls into question whether the figures are perhaps over-optimistic, especially in the current market conditions.

European investment

Year	After tax operating cash flow	After tax depreciation	Accounting profit	Company total after tax profit	% increase
0				0.92	
1	0.44	(0.42)	0.02	0.94	2.2
2	0.63	(0.42)	0.21	1.15	22.3
3	0.74	(0.42)	0.32	1.47	27.8
4	0.77	(0.42)	0.35	1.82	23.8
5	0.81	(0.42)	0.39	2.21	21.4
			1.29		

Asian investment

Year	After tax operating cash flow	After tax depreciation	Accounting profit	Company total after tax profit	% increase
0				0.92	
1	0.94	(0.62)	0.32	1.24	34.8%
2	1.03	(0.62)	0.41	1.65	33.1%
3	1.13	(0.62)	0.51	2.16	30.9%
4	1.18	(0.62)	0.56	2.72	25.9%
5	1.24	(0.62)	0.62	3.34	22.8%
			2.42		

(2) A post-tax accounting rate of return on shareholders' funds of 20% per annum

The company's **current post-tax accounting rate of return on shareholders' funds** is 924/22,257 = 4.2%, which is considerably below the required target. The European investment, showing an average accounting rate of return of 17.3%, improves this performance but does not meet the target rate of return. The Asian investment shows an expected accounting rate of return that is higher than target, at 22.2% per annum. Again the realism of the forecasts must be questioned as forecast returns are so much higher than current returns.

The company should be cautious when using the accounting rate of return as it **uses profits** rather than the preferable alternative of cash flows. The measure doesn't take into account timing and differences in cash flows, nor the impact of different project length of lives.

(3) Maintain a leading global presence in its operating markets

The textile industry now responds and changes rapidly to meet customer needs. A leading global presence is achieved by maintaining customer-desired innovations and quality of production and delivery. This will require a significant investment programme. The two investments should be rated in terms of these qualities rather than by where the products are manufactured. Nevertheless, the investment in Asia may help to build the company's market in that region.

Net present value

As indicated, both investments have a **positive net present value** and both could be undertaken if financed for example by **increased borrowing.** If they are mutually exclusive, the Asian investment should be selected as it has the higher NPV.

(ii) Analysis of risks and strategies for risk management

Reputational risk

Any failures relating to quality, supply, etc could damage this business, which has built up such a strong reputation and goodwill over many years. This is more of a risk with the Asian investment as Kadgee has no previous experience of manufacturing in this region, and could be a key reason for choosing the European investment.

Political risk

The Asian investment will involve a certain amount of political/cultural risk caused by **differences in laws** (eg property, labour, tax) and business custom. Advice must be sought on these matters and political risk factored into the decision.

Financial risks

Currently Kadgee does not appear to be excessively geared. However the cost of servicing debt has placed so much pressure on cash flows that last year that the overall amount of cash available to the firm decreased. This situation is not sustainable in the long run, and must be remedied by improving the cash generation from operational activities (ie margins).

If the new investment is financed by borrowing, this will increase gearing and finance costs further (see part (iii) below).

Foreign exchange risk

The Asian investment carries **foreign exchange risk**, which is the risk that project cash flows are adversely affected by changes in the $/€ exchange rate. For example dollar cash inflows converted to euros would be eroded by a weakening of the dollar, and this would hit particularly hard if a substantial proportion of costs was in euros.

Exchange risk can be reduced by various **hedging strategies.** Specific transactions (purchases or sales) can be hedged using **forward contracts, futures or options**. The ongoing (economic) exchange risk of the net operating cash flows is best managed by **matching income against costs** in dollars where possible. This implies sourcing components locally rather than supplying from head office, and borrowing in dollars to finance the capital investment costs.

CAPM

The methods of allowing for risk suggested by the Finance Director are based on the capital asset pricing model (CAPM), which distinguishes between **market risk** and **specific risk** of investments. When investors hold diversified portfolios of shares, only market risk needs to be considered, because the specific risk of investments is neutralized by the other investments in the portfolio. However:

(1) Kadgee is a **private company**, financed by some major shareholders whose investment in the company represents a substantial part of their wealth. They may not hold diversified portfolios as assumed by the CAPM and will probably require a higher return to compensate for specific risk of the company's investments.

(2) Although the Asian investment carries more foreign exchange risk than the European investment, and might be financed in a different way, it would perhaps be better to **appraise both investments** by the same technique, ie appraise both by the adjusted present value method, either adjusting the discount rate for both, or by using the 'certainty equivalent cash flow' method for both. This would make comparison and sensitivity analysis easier to carry out.

(3) The planned investment will take Kadgee into a **new area of business** whether the manufacturing is carried out in Europe or Asia. It could therefore be argued that a **higher discount rate** should be used to reflect the additional risk of entering a new market.

(iii) Recommendations

The financial appraisal of the investments shows the following

Investment	Europe	Asia
Outlay €m	3	7.5
PV €m	0.49	0.50
Profitability index (NPV/outlay)	0.163	0.113
ROCE	17.3%	22.2%

The discounted cash flow appraisal of these two investments shows that both have **positive expected net present values**, and that consequently they would be expected to increase shareholder value if accepted and properly managed.

Strategic opportunity

The Asian investment represents an opportunity for Kadgee to break out of the cycle of **falling margins**, due its suffering a high cost base in a market where prices are being forced down by cheaper imported product. The experience of European clothing makers has been that sourcing from Asia is **essential for survival**. Reductions in costs by moving production to lower cost economies may be essential for the survival of Kadgee.

Financing

Kadgee would find it very difficult to raise sufficient finance for both investments and a choice has to be made between the two. On financial grounds, the **Asian investment** should be accepted because it has the marginally higher NPV and a higher ROCE.

Significant additional finance would be required for either project. If borrowing were used, gearing would increase from 16.8% (4,500/22,257 + 4,500) to 33% for the European investment or 35% for the Asian project.

Alternatively, **financing by a share issue** would enable the company to invest and reduce gearing. Unfortunately this may not be easy under the current private company set-up: shareholders may not have the resources to increase their equity investments. There are two main alternatives:

- **Make the company public again** and float on the stock exchange; or
- **Seek a capital investment** from a venture capital fund, thereby delaying eventual flotation by, say, five years

Recommendations

Assuming that the optimistic projections can be relied upon, Kadgee should go ahead with the investment opportunity in Asia.

The company must balance the need to **invest in growth** (maintaining competitiveness) against its ability to **manage new investments** as well as the existing business, and against the financial risks that come from rapid growth financed by borrowing.

Question 2

Text references. Financial performance measures are revised in Chapter 3.

Top tips. In (a) it is helpful to start with the point that the measures of financial performance are primarily to show shareholders whether their wealth is being maximised.

Allocating your time in (a) is very important; your answer needs to contain detailed discussion as well as ratios, so you cannot spend all your time calculating ratios. We give more comparisons than you would have time to do; when you choose which ratios to calculate, you need to come up with a selection that measures shareholder value, profitability and working capital (liquidity), and also calculate some ratios that will be of interest to stakeholders other than shareholders.

The discussions in (a) concentrate on shareholders as we have most information about their interests. Certainly though you need a paragraph on each of the other major stakeholders, and need to make some mention of them when discussing the further information required. You should consider what information is not provided in the financial accounts, and where that information can be obtained.

In (b) you need to bring out the **personal skills** as well as the **technical skills** that financial managers need to have.

Easy marks. The ratios may appear easier, but in fact you will score very few marks for ratios that are not connected with your commentary. You'll get more marks if you calculate fewer ratios (if you provide some coverage of the areas mentioned above) and comment on all your calculations.

(a) (i) Analysis of PQD's performance

A numerical analysis of the **financial performance** of PQD is shown below. The figures provide the basis for making a traditional evaluation of the performance of the company from the point of view of the shareholders. However, there is only limited information on which to assess performance from the standpoint of the other stakeholders.

Calculation of key variables

		Year				
		1	2	3	4	5
Shareholders' ratios						
(1)	Payout ratio (%)	40.38	39.39	40.00	40.00	50.00
(2)	Dividend per share	£0.35	£0.43	£0.50	£0.43	£0.60
(3)	Share price					
	P/E × earnings/no of shares in issue	£6.93	£9.35	£11.25	£9.78	£11.40
(4)	Dividend yield (%)	5.05	4.60	4.44	4.40	5.26
(5)	Earnings/share	£0.87	£1.10	£1.25	£1.06	£1.20
(6)	Market capitalisation (£'000)	41,580	56,100	67,500	78,240	91,200

	Year				
	1	2	3	4	5
Profitability					
(1) Post tax profit/sales (%)	10.16	11.32	11.74	11.30	12.28
(2) ROCE					
(PBIT: total assets) (%)	22.33	25.22	26.77	20.54	21.76
(3) Sales growth (%)		13.87	9.61	17.68	3.99
(4) PBIT growth (%)		23.91	9.65	4.00	12.31
(5) Interest: debt (%)	10.00	10.67	10.83	8.57	8.00
Working capital					
(1) Receivable days	75	73	76	72	71
(2) Payable days					
(based on cost of sales)	68	69	77	81	83
Average wages/person	£8,953	£9,600	£9,451	£9,186	£8,994

Shareholders

(1) <u>Payout ratio</u>

From the point of view of the shareholders, financial performance has been good. The **payout ratio** has been maintained at 40% and in year 5 increased to 50%.

(2) <u>Dividend per share</u>

Dividend per share has increased throughout the period with the exception of year 4 when their was some **dilution** due to the rights issue. This reflects the overall trend of growth in sales and profits, albeit somewhat less erratically.

(3) <u>Return on capital employed</u>

Return on capital employed fell after the rights issue although it shows signs of renewed improvement in year 5.

(4) <u>Sales</u>

It appears that in the earlier part of the period under review, growth in earnings was achieved from growth in sales. The figures suggest that the part of the proceeds of the rights issue not used to redeem debt was **invested in assets** which may have been used to generate the further sales growth in year 5.

(5) <u>Workforce</u>

At the same time there was a **significant reduction** both in the **number of people employed** and the **average level of remuneration** in years 4 and 5, which may suggest that PQD has been replacing labour by capital to achieve both sales growth and cost savings. The drop in the average earnings level could also suggest either a switch to more part-time working (assuming that the number employed figure is not a full-time equivalents figure) or that there has been rationalisation in the management structure which has reduced the proportion of more highly paid employees.

(6) <u>Return to shareholders</u>

The actual **return to the shareholders** over the period can be calculated as follows.

	£m
Increase in market capitalisation (£91.2m – £41.58m)	49.62
Less cost of rights issue	(20.00)
Dividends (Yrs 1-4)	11.10
	40.72

This equates to a total return over four years of 98%.

Stakeholders

Other stakeholders in the business include customers, suppliers, employees, providers of debt finance and the tax authorities. The performance of PQD from their points of view can be evaluated as follows.

(1)   Customers

The **volume of goods and services provided** has increased by 52.7% over the period, presumably to their benefit. However, the period of credit allowed has **reduced from 75 to 71 days**.

(2)   Suppliers

The **volume of business** has also increased by 48.8% based on the **cost of goods sold**. However, the period of credit taken by PQD has increased from 68 to 83 days, presumably to the detriment of the suppliers.

(3)   Employees

The **numbers employed increased** from years 1 to 3 before being cut back. **Average earnings** similarly increased to year 3 before falling back. Assuming that there was some degree of wage inflation in the economy during the period, the employees do not appear to have fared particularly well. Possible reasons for the movement in the figures were outlined above.

(4)   Providers of debt finance

There has been a steady **repayment of debt** capital during the period with the major repayment being made at the same time as the rights issue in year 4. At the same time the average rate of interest paid has reduced from 10% to 8%.

(5)   Tax authorities

They have benefited from **payments** of £18.4m over the five year period.

Shareholders' position

In conclusion, it can be seen that the major benefit over the period has accrued to the **ordinary shareholders**. Some assessment of the position of the other stakeholders has been made but it is not possible to make a full evaluation of their relative position from the information given. Since the objective is not expressed in quantitative terms it is not possible to provide a definitive appraisal as to whether or not it has been successfully met.

(ii)   The other financial information that would be helpful include the following areas.

(1)   Financial projections and investment proposals

The wealth of the shareholders as represented by the **market value** of the shares is very dependent upon **future earnings** and **dividend projections**. It would therefore be helpful to have access to more detailed information on these areas in order to assess the likely movements in both financial performance and the share price. The fact that the P/E ratio has been increasing at a faster rate than the industry average suggests that the market takes a positive view of PQD's current performance and projections.

(2)   Factors external to the firm

These include factors such as the **current rates of interest and inflation** which would allow a better appraisal to be made of the performance of the company in real terms from the point of view of the shareholders. It would also be helpful to have information on the **size and projected growth of the markets** in which PQD operates, its current and projected market share and the competitive structure of the industry.

(3)   Detailed management accounts and reports

It would be helpful to have access to a more detailed analysis of the customer and supplier base, the breakdown of the sales figures by market sector, volume and price, credit policies etc. Similar information on the status of the fixed asset base would also be helpful. Human resources information on the grading, turnover and salary levels of the various groups of employees would enable a better analysis to be made of the position of this particular stakeholder group.

Internal targets

The objective as stated is not expressed in terms of **measurable targets**. It would therefore be helpful to have any internal information relating to any internal targets that are set, as well as discussion documents relating to this process. A further stakeholder group that has not been

mentioned so far is the **wider community** and the **environment**; details of charitable giving, social and environmental projects would allow an appraisal to be made of performance in this area.

(b) Role of financial management

(i) The financial managers must understand the **listing requirements** and be able to liaise with the banks and institutions advising on the flotation.

(ii) The financial managers must also be **able to provide information** on the likely valuation of the shares and to advise on the proposed capital structure of the quoted company.

(iii) If the flotation is being made due to the need for **access to a wider pool of funds** to finance expansion, then many of the points made in part (a) will also be relevant.

(iv) If the purpose of the flotation is to enable the owners to realise the value of their investment then the financial managers must be able to **persuade potential investors** that the company will be as successful under a new ownership and control structure as it was as a private company.

(v) The managers must be good at **communicating information** about the company to the wider public, and must be able to present **financial information in a clear and accessible format**.

Question 3

Text references. Weighted average cost of capital is covered in Chapter 8 and the capital structure decision is discussed in Chapter 9.

Top tips. In (a) you have to manipulate the weighted average cost of capital and take careful note of what the question says about the weighting of debt and equity. Also don't forget that the cost of debt has to be adjusted for tax (the question states that the WACC is post-tax).

It is easy in (b) to repeat yourself; the most important points are that the project may not have the same business risk, and the change in financing will also affect the financial risk. The information given in the scenario is insufficient for you to be able to quantify what an appropriate discount rate might be.

Note in (c)(i) that taking the subsidy exposes AB to various risks; it certainly isn't a risk-free investment.

The wording in (c) (ii) appears to suggest that no one source of finance will be completely appropriate. The wording of the question is unusual; you might expect that a recommendation would normally be for a single course of action rather than alternatives.

Easy marks. (c)(ii) is a fairly standard sources of finance question so you need to make sure you leave enough time to gain the six or so marks that would be available.

Examiner's comments. (a) was generally well done, although some students had problems with the calculation of the present value of the subsidy; a few calculated the value of the loan rather than the subsidy. Marking for (c) was evenly split between (i) and (ii); some answers to (ii) just provided a list of sources of finance without discussion or recommendations.

(a) Using the formula

$$k_0 = k_{eg}\left[\frac{V_E}{V_E + V_D}\right] + k_d\left[\frac{V_D}{V_E + V_D}\right]$$

where k_0 = weighted average cost of capital
         k_{eg}, k_d = cost of equity, cost of debt (post-tax)
         V_E, V_D = value of equity, value of debt

$13 = k_{eg}\,0.65 + 10(1 - 0.25)\,0.35$
$k_{eg} = 16.0\%$

Annual interest savings = $(30,000,000/20)\,(0.1 - 0.025)\,(1 - 0.25)$
                             = \$84,375

Discounted at pre tax cost of debt 10%

Interest savings   =   84,375 × Year 1-6 cumulative present value factor
               =   84,375 × 4.355
               =   367,453

Assumptions

The method assumes:

(i)   The **cost of debt** on additional borrowing will be 10%.
(ii)   The **cost of equity** remains static.
(iii)   The company has **sufficient profits** against which to set interest charges.
(iv)   The **debt ratio** will **remain unchanged**.

Use of WACC

Instead of being **discounted** at the **cost of debt**, the subsidy could be **discounted** at the **weighted average cost of capital** as this would be used to discount the benefits of alternative scenarios.

(b)   Cost of equity

The **cost of equity** would not be appropriate as:

(i)   Equity is **only one** of the **sources of finance** for the new project.
(ii)   The **cost of equity** may change as equity shareholders desire different returns as a result of the company expanding into Eastern Europe.

The **weighted average cost of capital** given in the question would not be appropriate.

(i)   It does not take into account the **cost of the subsidised EE government loan**.
(ii)   The **capital structure** and thus the **financial risk** of the company will change. As the company already has a gearing ratio in excess of the industry average, the additional risk may be significant.
(iii)   **AB's overall business risk** may change as a result of investing in Eastern Europe. Whether it will increase or decrease is difficult to say. Returns from Eastern Europe may be more uncertain than from current sales areas; on the other hand, **diversification** into Eastern Europe may lower business risk if returns from that area are not positively correlated with returns from other areas.

Marginal cost of capital

AB should use a **marginal cost of capital** to appraise the investment. This should be based on the risks and incremental cost of investing in Eastern Europe. AB could find the beta of a similar company that invested into Eastern Europe and use CAPM to **calculate the discount rate**, taking into account the **differences in gearing**.

(c)   (i)   Advantages of using subsidy

        1   The loan represents **long-term finance** matched against the returns from a long-term manufacturing project.
        2   AB does not need to **provide security** for the loan.
        3   Government involvement may mean that AB **faces fewer administrative problems** when setting up its investment, such as planning permission.

        Disadvantages of using subsidy

        1   There may be **onerous conditions** attached to the subsidy, for example a requirement to have **local managers** involved in directing the project.
        2   A change of government may lead to a **change** in the **terms** of the loan.
        3   The **exchange rate** may **move adversely;** if EE marks become more expensive, the interest costs will be greater.
        4   The interest savings will be **less attractive** if domestic rates decrease over the **six year period.**
        5   If the investment quickly proves **unviable**, AB will be **locked into interest and repayment commitments** for some years afterwards.

(ii)   Other possible methods of finance

    1   Rights issue

        An issue of shares to existing shareholders would have the advantages of **maintaining the existing ownership structure** and **reducing** the **company's gearing levels.** The main problem may be whether **sufficient funds** can be raised by this method.

    2   Stock market

        AB could seek a **listing on a stock exchange** in order to be able to offer its shares to the general public. It should be able to raise the money it needs by this means and the share issue would **reduce gearing**; however the current shareholders would face a **loss of influence** on the company's affairs and **publicity and disclosure requirements** will be greater. These drawbacks may imply that the amount of funding required is too small to justify seeking a listing.

    3   Debt finance

        Although more debt finance would **worsen AB's gearing**, the directors should investigate the possibility of issuing **loan stock** secured on fixed assets. The **cost of loan stock** may be **lower** than the current cost of bank finance, and AB would not have to fulfil the onerous conditions that the overseas government might impose.

    4   Asset disposal

        AB may be able to raise significant sums of money by selling off surplus assets or spinning off for sale certain parts of its business.

    5   Venture capital

        Venture capitalists may well be interested in this type of new venture. However if they provide debt finance, **gearing** will be **worse**; if they provide equity finance, AB will have to consider the **level of return** they require. Either way venture capitalists are likely to demand a **degree of control** (perhaps a seat on the board) and AB may have to **match the finance** that the venture capitalists provide by obtaining funding from other sources.

Recommendations

AB should consider obtaining a **mix of finance** to finance the project, as no single source seems to be completely suitable. A combination of debt and equity finance, with the aim of at least maintaining current gearing levels, would be best.

Question 4

Text references. Chapter 10 discusses the work of the treasury function.

Top tips. This is a fairly comprehensive question on the role of the treasury department, covering the major areas that you are likely to be asked about. Questions in this area tend to demand breadth of knowledge, so you will need to make a good number of points in order to pass the question. Note what exactly the treasury department does manage. Your answer should refer to the circumstances of KM.

Easy marks. If you revised this area this should have been a straightforward question.

(a)   Definition

    Treasurership has been defined as 'the function concerned with the provision and use of finance. It includes provision of capital, short-term borrowing, foreign currency management, banking, collections and money market investment'.

    Responsibilities of treasury function

    The main responsibilities of the treasury function include:

    (i)   Strategic decisions

        Treasury is likely to be consulted on the **establishment of corporate financial objectives, aims and strategies** and be responsible for establishing policies and systems (outlined further below).

(ii) <u>Liquidity management</u>

This involves making sure that the organisation has the **liquid funds** it needs and invests any surplus funds, even for very short terms. The treasurer should maintain a good relationship with one or more banks to ensure that negotiations are as swift as possible, and that rates are reasonable. It includes **working capital and money transmission management, banking relationships** and **arrangements** and **money management**.

(iii) <u>Funding management</u>

Funding management is concerned with all forms of **borrowing**, and alternative sources of funds, such as leasing and factoring. The treasury function includes **establishing funding policies and procedure, obtaining the right types of funds** from the **best sources**.

(iv) <u>Currency management</u>

The treasury department should have the expertise to be able to deal with the problems and substantial risks involved in trading abroad and in particular dealing in foreign exchange markets. Treasury should establish **exposure policies and procedures** and have responsibility for exchange dealing, including futures and options.

(v) <u>Corporate finance</u>

The treasury department will be involved with major **equity funding decisions** and **dividend policies**, and **major investment decisions** including business acquisitions and disposals, project finance and joint ventures. It will also be involved in attempts to obtain a **stock market listing**.

(vi) <u>Other functions</u>

Treasury may also be responsible for a variety of decisions including effective management of the organisation's **tax liability**, **risk management and insurance** and **pension fund investment management**.

<u>Reasons for separating the financial control and treasury functions</u>

(i) <u>Different roles</u>

As indicated above, the treasury department's role is concerned developing financial strategy and fund management, functions demanding specialist skills. The finance function's role is focused on **recording and reporting skills**, which requires management and financial accounting knowledge. The financial control function may also be responsible for managing the **payroll** and **internal audit** functions and hence will require specialist skills in these areas.

(ii) <u>Relationships with stakeholders</u>

The financial control function is concerned with **determining whether** the **various activities** of the organisation are meeting their **financial objectives**. This function will therefore be interested in a **wide variety of stakeholder relationships,** for example, with customers, suppliers and employees. By contrast, the treasury function is mainly concerned with the relationship of the company to the **providers of finance**.

(iii) <u>Geographical dispersion</u>

In a geographically dispersed company such as KM, it is likely that financial control functions will exist at a variety of local levels, while the **treasury department** will be centralised at the head office.

(b) <u>Advantages of operating treasury department as profit centre</u>

(i) This approach recognises the fact that some companies are able to make **significant profits** from their treasury activities. Treating the department as a profit centre may make treasury staff more motivated to achieve the best possible return for the company.

(ii) If it is treated as a profit centre, the department will have to **charge for its services** to other parts of the organisation. This may make the subsidiaries more aware of the true cost of the services they use, and encourage them to use the department more efficiently.

<u>Disadvantages of operating treasury department as profit centre</u>

(i) Treasury staff may be tempted to **speculate**, and to ignore the risk criteria that they should be using. The company may suffer **large losses** as a result.

    (ii)   **Internal charging** may mean that **some subsidiaries go outside the** organisation for treasury services and thus reduce the overall benefit to the organisation of having a centralised treasury function.

    (iii)   **Performance evaluation** may be difficult. The success of the function may sometimes involve the avoidance of costs rather than the maximisation of profits.

    (iv)   **Administrative costs** may be **increased**.

(c)   <u>Advantages of a centralised treasury department</u>

    (i)   Centralised liquidity management avoids having a **mix of cash surpluses and overdrafts in different localised bank accounts**, particularly in a company such as KM, which now includes a number of overseas operations.

    (ii)   **Bulk cash flows** are possible, allowing lower bank charges to be negotiated.

    (iii)   **Larger volumes of cash** are available to invest, giving better **short-term** investment opportunities.

    (iv)   Any borrowing can be arranged in **bulk**, at **lower interest rates** than for smaller borrowings.

    (v)   **Foreign currency risk management** should be improved, with matching of cash flows in different subsidiaries being possible. This means that there should be less need to use expensive hedging instruments such as option contracts. This is particularly valuable in a company such as KM plc where there are a number of overseas operations.

    (vi)   A large centralised department can employ **staff with a greater level of expertise** than would be possible in a local, more broadly based, finance department.

    (vii)   Centralisation will allow the company to benefit from the use of **specialised cash management software**.

    (viii) Access to treasury expertise should improve the quality of **strategic planning and decision making**.

CIMA – Pillar F

Paper F3

Financial Strategy

Mock Examination 2 (September 2012)

Instructions to candidates:

You are allowed three hours to answer this question paper.
In the real exam, you are allowed 20 minutes reading time before the examination begins during which you should read the question paper, and if you wish, make annotations on the question paper. However, you will **not** be allowed, **under any circumstances**, to open the answer book and start writing or use your calculator during this reading time.
You are strongly advised to carefully read the question requirement before attempting the question concerned.
Answer the compulsory questions in Section A.
Answer TWO of the THREE questions in Section B.

DO NOT OPEN THIS PAPER UNTIL YOU ARE READY TO START UNDER EXAMINATION CONDITIONS

SECTION A

Question 1

Pre-seen case study

Introduction

B Supermarkets (B) was founded as a grocery retailer in a European country in 1963. Its sales consist mainly of food and household items including clothing. B now owns or franchises over 15,000 stores world-wide in 36 countries. The company has stores in Europe (in both eurozone and non-eurozone countries), Asia and North America. B's head office is located in a eurozone country. B has become one of the world's largest chains of stores.

B's Board thinks that there are opportunities to take advantage of the rapid economic growth of some Asian countries and the associated increases in demand for food and consumer goods.

Structure

The B Group is structured into a holding company, B, and three subsidiary companies which are located in each of the regions of the world in which it operates (Europe, Asia and North America). The subsidiary companies, referred to as "Regions" within B, are respectively B-Europe, B-Asia and B-North America.

Store operations, sales mix and staffing

B operates four types of store: supermarkets, hypermarkets, discount stores and convenience stores. For the purpose of this case study, the definition of each of these types of store is as follows:

A *supermarket* is a self-service store which sells a wide variety of food and household goods such as washing and cleaning materials, cooking utensils and other items which are easily carried by customers out of the store.

A *hypermarket* is a superstore or very large store which sells the same type of products as a supermarket but in addition it sells a wide range of other items such as consumer durable white goods, for example refrigerators, freezers, washing machines and furniture. Hypermarkets are often located on out-of-town sites.

A *discount store* is a retail store that sells a variety of goods such as electrical appliances and electronic equipment. Discount stores in general usually sell branded products and pursue a high-volume, low priced strategy and aim their marketing at customers who seek goods at prices which are usually less than can be found in a hypermarket.

A *convenience store* is a small shop or store in an urban area that sells goods which are purchased regularly by customers. These would typically include groceries, toiletries, alcoholic beverages, soft drinks and confectionery. They are convenient for shoppers as they are located in or near residential areas and are often open for long hours. Customers are willing to pay premium prices for the convenience of having the store close by.

B sells food products and clothing in its supermarkets and hypermarkets at a higher price than many of its competitors because the Board thinks that its customers are prepared to pay higher prices for better quality food products. B also sells good quality consumer durable products in its supermarkets and hypermarkets but it is forced to sell these at competitive prices as there is strong competition for the sale of such goods. B's discount stores sell good quality electrical products usually at lower prices than those charged in its supermarkets and hypermarkets, B only sells electronic equipment in its discount stores. Customers have a greater range from which to choose in the discount stores as compared with supermarkets and hypermarkets because the discount stores specialise in the goods which they sell. B's convenience stores do not have the availability of space to carry a wide range of products and they charge a higher price for the same brand and type of goods which it sells in its supermarkets.

Although B owns most of its stores, it has granted franchises for the operation of some stores which carry its name.

Nearly 0.5 million full-time equivalent staff are employed world-wide in the Group. B tries when possible to recruit local staff to fill job vacancies within its stores.

Value statement and mission

In recognition of the strong competitive and dynamic markets in which it operates, B's Board has established an overall value statement as follows: "We aim to satisfy our customers wherever we trade. We intend to employ different generic competitive strategies depending on the market segment in which our stores trade."

The Board has also produced the following mission statement:

"B practises sustainable investment within a healthy ethical and thoughtful culture and strives to achieve customer satisfaction by giving a courteous and efficient service, selling high quality goods at a reasonable price, sourcing goods from local suppliers where possible and causing the least damage possible to the natural environment. By this, we aim to satisfy the expectations of our shareholders by achieving consistent growth in our share price and also to enhance our reputation for being an environmentally responsible company."

Strategic objectives

The following objectives have been derived from the mission statement:

1. Build shareholder value through consistent growth in the company's share price.

2. Increase customer satisfaction ratings to 95% as measured by customer feedback surveys.

3. Increase commitment to local suppliers by working towards achieving 40% of our supplies from sources which are local to where B stores trade.

4. Reduce carbon emissions calculated by internationally agreed measures by at least 1% per year until B becomes totally carbon neutral.

5. Maximise returns to shareholders by employing different generic competitive strategies depending on the market segment in which B stores trade.

Financial objectives

The Board has set the following financial objectives:

1. Achieve consistent growth in earnings per share of 7% each year.

2. Maintain a dividend pay-out ratio of 50% each year.

3. Gearing levels as measured by long-term debt divided by long-term debt plus equity should not exceed 40% based on book value.

Governance

The main board comprises the Non-executive Chairman, the Chief Executive and nine Executive directors. These cover the functions of finance, human resources, corporate affairs (including legal and public relations), marketing, planning and procurement. There is also one executive director for each of the three regions, being the Regional Managing Directors of B-Europe, B-Asia and B-North America. There are also nine non-executive main board members in addition to the Chairman.

The main Board of Directors has separate committees responsible for audit, remuneration, appointments, corporate governance and risk assessment and control. The Risk Assessment and Control Committee's tasks were formerly included within the Audit Committee's role. It was agreed by the Board in 2009 that these tasks should be separated out in order not to overload the Audit Committee which has responsibilities to review the probity of the company. B's expansion has been very rapid in some countries. The expansion has been so rapid that B has not been able to carry out any internal audit activities in some of these countries to date. The regional boards do not have a committee structure.

Each of the Regional Managing Directors chairs his or her own Regional Board. All of the Regional Boards have their own directors for finance, human resources, corporate affairs, marketing, planning and procurement but their structure is different for the directors who have responsibility for the stores. In B-Asia, one regional director is responsible for the hypermarkets and supermarkets and another is responsible for discount stores and convenience stores. In B-North America, one regional director is responsible for the hypermarkets and supermarkets and another is responsible for discount stores (B does not have any convenience stores in North America). In B-Europe there is one regional director responsible for supermarkets and hypermarkets, one for discount stores and one for convenience stores. In all regions the regional directors have line accountability to their respective regional managing director and professional accountability to the relevant main board director. There are no non-executive directors on the regional boards. Appendix 1 shows the main board and regional board structures.

Treasury

Each of B's three regions has a regional treasury department managed by a regional treasurer who has direct accountability to the respective Regional Director of Finance and professional accountability to the Group Treasurer. The Group Treasurer manages the central corporate treasury department which is located in B's head office. The Group Treasurer, who is not a main board member, reports to the Director of Finance on the main board.

Shareholding, year-end share prices and dividends paid for the last five years

B is listed on a major European stock exchange within the eurozone and it wholly owns its subsidiaries. There are five major shareholders of B, including employees taken as a group, which between them hold 25% of the 1,350 million total shares in issue. The major shareholders comprise two long term investment trusts which each owns 4%, a hedge fund owns 5%, employees own 5% and the founding family trust owns 7% of the shares. The remaining 75% of shares are owned by the general public.

The year-end share prices and the dividends paid for the last five years were as follows:

	2007	2008	2009	2010	2011
	€	€	€	€	€
Share price at 31 December	47.38	25.45	28.68	29.44	31.37
Net Dividend per share	1.54	1.54	1.54	1.62	1.65

Planning and management control

B has a very structured planning process. Each regional board produces a five year strategic plan for its region relating to specific objectives set for it by the main board and submits this to the main board for approval. The main board then produces a consolidated strategic plan for the whole company. This is reviewed on a three yearly cycle and results in a revised and updated group five year plan being produced every three years.

B's management control system, which operates throughout its regions and at head office, is well known in the industry to be bureaucratic and authoritarian. Strict financial authority levels for development purposes are imposed from the main Board. There is tension between the main Board and the regional boards. The regional board members feel that they are not able to manage effectively despite being located much closer to their own regional markets than the members of the main Board. The main Board members, on the other hand, think that they need to exercise tight control because they are remote from the markets. This often stifles planning initiatives within each region. This tension is also felt lower down the organisation as the regional board members exercise strict financial and management control over operational managers in their regions in order to ensure that the main Board directives are carried out.

Competitive overview

B operates in highly competitive markets for all the products it sells. The characteristics of each of the markets in which it operates are different. For example, there are different planning restrictions applying within each region. In some countries, B is required to operate each of its stores in a partnership arrangement with local enterprises, whereas no such restriction exists within other countries in which it trades. B needs to be aware of different customer tastes and preferences which differ from country to country. The following table provides a break-down of B's stores in each region.

	B Europe	B Asia	B North America
Supermarkets and hypermarkets	3,456	619	512
Discount stores	5,168	380	780
Convenience stores	4,586	35	

B is one of the largest retailing companies in the world and faces different levels of competition in each region. B's overall market share in terms of retail sales for all supermarkets, hypermarkets, discount stores and convenience stores in each of its regions is as follows:

	Market share
Europe	20%
Asia	1%
North America	1.5%

The following table shows the sales revenue and net operating profit earned by B in each of its regions for the year ended 31 December 2011:

	B Europe € million	B Asia € million	B North America € million
Revenue	89,899	10,105	9,708
Net Operating Profit	4,795	743	673

B is constantly seeking other areas of the world into which it can expand, especially within Asia where it perceives many countries have an increasing population and strengthening economies.

Corporate Social Responsibility (CSR)

B is meeting its CSR obligations by establishing environmental targets for carbon emissions (greenhouse gas emissions), careful monitoring of its supply chain, undertaking sustainable investments and investing in its human capital.

Environmental targets for carbon emissions:

B's main board is keen to demonstrate the company's concern for the environment by pursuing continuous improvement in the reduction of its carbon emissions and by developing ways of increasing sustainability in its trading practices. A number of environmental indicators have been established to provide transparency in B's overall performance in respect of sustainability. These published measures were verified by B's statutory auditor and are calculated on a like-for-like basis for the stores in operation over the period measured.

In the year ended 31 December 2011, B reduced its consumption of kilowatt hours (kWh) per square metre of sales area as compared with the year ended 31 December 2008 by 9%. The target reduction for that period was 5%. In the same period it reduced the number of free disposable plastic bags provided to customers per square metre of sales area, by 51% against a target of 60%. Its overall greenhouse gas emissions (measured by kilogrammes of carbon dioxide per square metre of sales area) reduced by 1% in 2011 which was exactly on target.

B provides funding for the development of local amenity projects in all of the countries where B stores operate. (An amenity project is one which provides benefit to the local population, such as providing a park, community gardens or a swimming pool.)

Distribution and sourcing:

Distribution from suppliers across such a wide geographical area is an issue for B. While supplies are sourced from the country in which a store is located as much as possible, there is nevertheless still a requirement for transportation across long distances either by road or air. Approximately 20% of the physical quantity of goods sold across the group as a whole is sourced locally, that is within the country in which the goods are sold. These tend to be perishable items such as fruit and vegetables. The remaining 80% of goods are sourced from large international manufacturers and distributors. These tend to be large items such as electrical or electronic equipment which are bought under contracts which are set up by the regional procurement departments. B, due to its size and scope of operations, is able to place orders for goods made to its own specification and packaged as under its own brand label. Some contracts are agreed between manufacturers and the Group Procurement Director for the supply of goods to the whole of the B group world-wide.

B's inventory is rarely transported by rail except within Europe. This has resulted in lower average reductions in carbon emissions per square metre of sales area by stores operated by B-Asia and B-North America than for those stores operated by B-Europe. This is because the carbon emission statistics take into account the transportation of goods into B's stores.

Sustainable investments:

B aspires to become carbon neutral over the long term. The Board aims to reduce its carbon emissions by investing in state of the art technology in its new store developments and by carrying out modifications to existing stores.

Human Resources:

B prides itself on the training it provides to its staff. The training of store staff is carried out in store by specialist teams which operate in each country where B trades. In this way, B believes that training is consistent across all of its stores. In some countries, the training is considered to be at a sufficiently high level to be recognised by national training bodies. The average number of training hours per employee in the year ended 31 December

2011 was 17 compared with 13 hours in the year ended 31 December 2010. In 2011, B employed 45% more staff with declared disabilities compared with 2010.

Information systems and inventory management

In order to operate efficiently, B's Board has recognised that it must have up-to-date information systems including electronic point of sale (EPOS) systems. An EPOS system uses computers or specialised terminals that can be combined with other hardware such as bar-code readers to accurately capture the sale and adjust the inventory levels within the store. EPOS systems installation is on-going. B has installed EPOS systems in its stores in some countries but not in all its stores world-wide.

B's information systems are not perfect as stock-outs do occur from time-to-time, especially in the European stores. This can be damaging to sales revenue when stock-outs occur during peak sales periods such as the days leading up to a public holiday. In Asia and North America in particular, B's information technology systems sometimes provide misleading information. This has led to doubts in the minds of some head office staff about just how robust are B's inventory control systems.

As is normal in chain store groups, there is a certain degree of loss through theft by staff and customers. Another way that loss is suffered is through goods which have gone past their "sell-by" date and mainly relates to perishable food items which are wasted as they cannot be sold to the public. In most countries, such food items which cannot be sold to the public may be sold to local farmers for animal feed.

Regulatory issues

B's subsidiaries in Asia and North America have sometimes experienced governmental regulatory difficulties in some countries which have hindered the installation of improved information systems. To overcome some of these regulatory restrictions, B-Asia and B-North America have, on occasions, resorted to paying inducements to government officials in order for the regulations to be relaxed.

Appendix 1

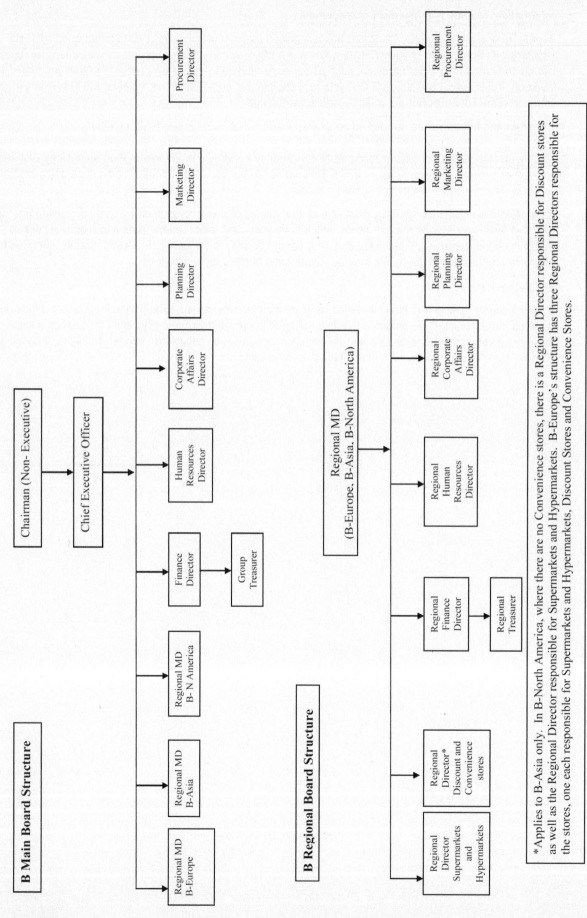

B Main Board Structure

Chairman (Non- Executive) → Chief Executive Officer

Chief Executive Officer →
- Regional MD B-Europe
- Regional MD B-Asia
- Regional MD B- N America
- Finance Director → Group Treasurer
- Human Resources Director
- Corporate Affairs Director
- Planning Director
- Marketing Director
- Procurement Director

B Regional Board Structure

Regional MD (B-Europe, B-Asia, B-North America) →
- Regional Director Supermarkets and Hypermarkets
- Regional Director* Discount and Convenience stores
- Regional Finance Director → Regional Treasurer
- Regional Human Resources Director
- Regional Corporate Affairs Director
- Regional Planning Director
- Regional Marketing Director
- Regional Procurement Director

*Applies to B-Asia only. In B-North America, where there are no Convenience stores, there is a Regional Director responsible for Discount stores as well as the Regional Director responsible for Supermarkets and Hypermarkets. B-Europe's structure has three Regional Directors responsible for the stores, one each responsible for Supermarkets and Hypermarkets, Discount Stores and Convenience Stores.

<u>Appendix 2</u>

B's income statement and statement of financial position.

Income statement for the year ended 31 December 2011

	Notes	€ million
Revenue		109,712
Operating costs		(103,501)
Net operating profit		6,211
Interest income		165
Finance costs		(852)
Corporate income tax		(1,933)
PROFIT FOR THE YEAR		3,591

Statement of financial position as at 31 December 2011

		€ million
ASSETS		
Non-current assets		57,502
Current assets		
Inventories		7,670
Trade and other receivables		1,521
Cash and cash equivalents		3,847
Total current assets		13,038
Total assets		70,540
EQUITY AND LIABILITIES		
Equity		
Share capital	1	2,025
Share premium		3,040
Retained earnings		18,954
Total equity		24,019
Non-current liabilities		
Long term borrowings		15,744
Current liabilities		
Trade and other payables		30,777
Total liabilities		46,521
Total equity and liabilities		70,540

Notes:

1   There are 1,350 million €1.50 shares currently in issue. The share price at 31 December 2011 was
€31.37.

Unseen case material

Today is 1 September 2012.

The directors of B Supermarkets (B) are considering establishing a chain of convenience stores in the USA following the success of such stores in Europe. Food sales in the USA are currently dominated by large supermarket chains in out-of-town locations. The general pattern is for consumers to go shopping for food once a week. However, with increasing pressure on leisure time, a greater number of single person households and an increasing preference for fresh food, there is a growing trend for more frequent, local, food shopping. The Regional Managing Director for North America hopes that by establishing a chain of convenience stores that B can take advantage of this trend. The aim is to attract customers by building a reputation for fresh produce and the convenience of ready prepared meals.

An opportunity has arisen for B to purchase and develop 50 empty retail properties. The properties are considered to be of an appropriate size and location for running small convenience stores. The price, USD 30 million for all 50 of the retail properties, is also very attractive.

Details of proposed project

A project team has been set up to manage the project. The project would commence on 1 January 2013 and is to be evaluated over a four year time period from that date.

The stores would be empty when acquired and would need to be re-fitted at an approximate one-off total cost of USD 10 million for re-fitting all 50 stores.

Both the purchase cost of the properties and the cost to renew the store fittings can be assumed to be paid on 1 January 2013. The store fittings are estimated to have a residual value of USD 4 million on 31 December 2016. There is some uncertainty over the value of the stores themselves on that date. The project team has decided to evaluate the project on the basis that the properties, excluding fittings, could be sold for cash on 31 December 2016 at a price that is 20% greater, in nominal terms, than the original purchase cost.

The Management Accountant has produced some estimates of the total expected revenue and cost figures for the first year of the project as shown below. Note that these are aggregated figures across all 50 stores.

Revenue	USD 90 million
Purchase costs	USD 35 million
Other operating costs	USD 40 million

Each of the above revenue and costs is expected to grow by 12% a year for the duration of the project.

The project team is planning to adopt an aggressive strategy for managing working capital. Target working capital days for the project are given below, together with historical data for B for comparative purposes. Both accounts payable and inventory days are based on purchase costs.

Working capital days	Project	B
Accounts receivable	Nil	Nil
Accounts payable	100 days	139 days
Inventory	30 days	53 days

Additional information:

- Working capital values for accounts payable and inventory at the beginning of each year are to be calculated by applying the target working capital days to the appropriate forecast revenue and/or cost figures for the coming year.

- Working capital adjustments should be assumed to arise at the start of each year.

- The final accounts payable and inventory balances at the end of the project should be assumed to be realised in full at that time.

- After working capital adjustments, project revenue and costs should be assumed to be cash flows and to be paid or received at the end of the year in which they arise.

- Corporate income tax is payable at 33% at the end of the year in which it is incurred. Tax depreciation allowances are available on the store fittings costs on a reducing balance basis at 25% a year. No corporate capital taxes apply to the purchase and sale of the properties.

- The EUR/USD spot rate is expected to be EUR/USD 1.1000 on 1 January 2013 (that is, EUR 1 = USD 1.1000). Interest rates for the EUR and USD are 3% and 5% respectively and the EUR/USD spot rate is expected to move in line with the interest rate differential for the duration of the project.

- A discounted cash flow approach is to be used in evaluating the project, based on B's EUR based weighted average cost of capital of 11%.

Required

Assume you are a member of the project team and are preparing a briefing paper for the local Regional Board of B regarding the proposed project in which you:

(a)   (i)   Describe two possible reasons, other than the use of an aggressive strategy to manage working capital levels, for the differences in working capital days between those expected for the project and historical data for B.   **(3 marks)**

      (ii)   Discuss the benefits and potential drawbacks of the proposed aggressive strategy for managing working capital for the project.   **(6 marks)**

      (iii) Calculate the forecast accounts payable and inventory balances for each year of the project.
                                                                                                      (5 marks)

(b)   (i)   Calculate the forecast project net present value (NPV), in EUR, as at 1 January 2013. **(14 marks)**

      (ii)   Calculate the change in the project NPV if the value of the properties, excluding fittings, on 31 December 2016 is 20% lower than the original purchase cost of USD 30 million.   **(3 marks)**

(c)   Advise whether or not to proceed with the project, taking into account:

      - Your results in (b)(i) and (b)(ii) above.

      - The reasonableness of the key input variables used in the NPV appraisal.

      - The potential risks to B of establishing a new business in a foreign country.   **(16 marks)**

Additional marks available for structure and presentation: **(3 marks)**

                                                                                      (Total = 50 marks)

SECTION B

Question 2

SPORT is a UK-based charity, a 'not for profit' organisation which does not have any shareholders. Its main objective is to provide specialised low cost sports equipment to people with disabilities living in the UK to help them participate in a range of sporting activities. The charity raises funds through an extensive network of its own charity stores, by individual donations and by special fund raising events. The stores sell clothing and other goods which have been donated by the public and are largely staffed by volunteers. All of the store premises are leased rather than owned by SPORT.

SPORT has recently appointed a new Finance Director (FD), who previously worked in the commercial sector for a large sports equipment retailer. The FD is currently reviewing the objectives of SPORT and, in order to assist with this process, the FD has compiled the following list of objectives based on a review of the annual reports of various retail companies which supply sports equipment in the 'for profit' sector.

Extract financial and non-financial objectives for 'for profit' sports equipment retailers:

Financial objectives	Non-financial objectives
Increase earnings per share by 5% a year	High customer satisfaction
Achieve steady growth in dividends	Retain market position in top 3 suppliers
Maximum debt to debt plus equity of 50%	Reduce carbon footprint

The Chair of the Trustees has suggested that the charity considers issuing a GBP 10 million bond in order to finance an ambitious expansion of its retail and fundraising operations. The proceeds of the issue would be used to open a further 100 stores across the UK. Currently, SPORT has 300 stores. The FD has reacted favourably to this proposal and he has been quoted in the press as saying: 'Charities should be run on commercial lines to maximise social good'.

Required

(a)   Describe the main differences between the overall objectives of 'for profit' organisations and 'not for profit' organisations.   **(4 marks)**

(b)   (i)   Advise on the extent to which each of the financial and non-financial objectives listed above could be adapted for use by SPORT.   **(9 marks)**

        (ii)   Discuss what additional objectives might be appropriate for SPORT.   **(5 marks)**

        (iii)   Advise whether the proposed bond issue to finance an increase in charity stores is appropriate for a charitable organisation such as SPORT. Include reference to the recent press comment from the FD in your answer.   **(7 marks)**

(Total = 25 marks)

Question 3

Today is 1 September 20X2.

LL is a company based in Asia which uses L$ as its functional currency. The company has adopted International Financial Reporting Standards.

LL is currently preparing a bid for a government contract to operate a train service on a new high-speed rail link between the capital city and another city in the same country. The investment appraisal of the project has been completed and shows that the project is financially beneficial. The focus of attention has now shifted to considering how best to finance the initial investment required in the new rolling stock (that is, locomotives and carriages) that is needed to run on the line.

The rail link would be operated by LL for a period of ten years commencing on 1 January 20X3. The new rolling stock required would cost L$50 million if bought outright. There is an active market in second hand rolling stock and it is estimated that the rolling stock could be sold at the end of the ten year period for L$22 million.

The following two alternative financing approaches are being considered:

- Bank borrowing from its primary bank for a ten year term together with the outright purchase of the rolling stock.

- A ten year operating lease provided by the supplier of the rolling stock.

Bank borrowing and outright purchase:

- LL would buy the new rolling stock on 1 January 20X3.

- LL can borrow from its primary bank at a 2.5% credit margin above the bank's published base interest rate. The bank's base rate is currently set at 3.5% but can be expected to change in line with changes in market interest rates.

- Maintenance costs are expected to be of the order of L$1.5 million per year if LL purchases the rolling stock outright.

Operating lease:

- An initial up-front payment of L$5.8 million would be payable at the start of the lease on 1 January 20X3.

- Ten further lease payments of L$5.8 million each would be payable on 31 December in each year starting on 31 December 20X3.

- The lessor retains responsibility for maintaining the rolling stock throughout the period of the lease and has included the cost of maintenance services within the lease payments.

Additional information:

- LL's financial year runs from 1 January to 31 December.

- LL pays corporate income tax at a rate of 33%, payable annually at the end of the year following that in which the tax charge or tax saving arises.

- 100% tax depreciation allowances are available at the time of acquiring an eligible asset such as rolling stock.

- Lease payments made by LL would be allowable for tax when they are incurred.

Required:

(a) Evaluate, using a discounted cash flow approach as at 1 January 20X3, whether it would be cheaper for LL to buy and borrow or enter into an operating lease for the new rolling stock. **(12 marks)**

(b) Advise on the impact of each of the two alternative financing approaches on LL's statement of financial position. **(4 marks)**

(c) Advise LL which type of financing approach to choose, taking into account:

- Your findings in (a) and (b) above.
- Other relevant factors. **(9 marks)**

(Total = 25 marks)

Question 4

WIDGET is a listed group which operates a number of manufacturing facilities within its home country, Country F. The currency of Country F is the F$.

WIDGET has F$700 million funds available for capital investment in new product lines in the current year. Most products have a very limited life cycle. Four possible projects have been identified, each of which can be started without delay.

Initial calculations for these projects are shown below:

Project	Initial investment (F$ million)	Net annual cash inflows after the initial investment (F$ million)	Project term (years)	PV of cash flows arising after the initial investment (F$ million)	NPV (F$ million)
A	100	151.2	1	135	35
B	150	82.3	4	250	100
C	300	242.6	2	410	110
D	350	124.0	6	510	160

Notes:

1.   The projects are non-divisible and each project can only be undertaken once.
2.   Apart from the initial investment, annual cash flows are assumed to arise at the end of the year.
3.   A discount rate of 12% has been used throughout.
4.   Ignore taxation.

Required

(a)   (i)   Prioritise the projects according to each of the following measures:

- Net present value (NPV)
- Profitability index (PI)
- Payback (undiscounted)   **(5 marks)**

(ii)   Explain the strengths and weaknesses of each of the prioritisation methods used in (a)(i) above as the basis for making investment decisions in the context of capital rationing for non-divisible projects.   **(9 marks)**

(b)   (i)   Advise what combination of projects maximises shareholder wealth within a maximum total initial investment of F$700 million.   **(3 marks)**

(ii)   Explain how the optimal combination of projects would need to be reassessed under EACH of the following circumstances:

- 'Soft' rather than 'hard' single period capital rationing applies.

- The same level of capital rationing and range of projects is expected in the following year.   **(8 marks)**

(Total = 25 marks)

Answers

DO NOT TURN THIS PAGE UNTIL YOU HAVE
COMPLETED MOCK EXAM 2

502

Plan of attack

We know you've been told to do it at least 100 times and we know if we asked you you'd know that you should do it. So why don't you do it in an exam? 'Do what in an exam?' you're probably thinking. Well, let's tell you for the 101st time. **Take a good look through the paper before diving in to answer questions.**

First things first

What you must do in the first five or ten minutes of the exam is **look through the paper i**n detail, working out **which questions to do** and the **order** in which to attempt them. So turn back to the paper and let's sort out a plan of attack.

We then recommend you spend the remaining time analysing the requirements of Question 1 and highlighting the key issues in the question. The extra time spent on (a) will be helpful, whenever you intend to do the question, If you decide to do it first, you will be well into the question when the writing time starts. If you intend to do it second or third, probably because you find it daunting, the question will look easier when you come to back to it, because your initial analysis should generate further points whilst you're tackling the other questions.

The next step

You're probably either thinking that you don't know where to begin or that you could have a very decent go at all the questions.

Option 1 (if you don't know where to begin)

If you are a bit **worried** about the paper, it's likely that you believe that case study **Question 1** looks daunting. We therefore recommend that you do one or both of the optional questions before tackling the case study. Don't however fall into the trap of going over time on the optional questions because they seem easier. You will need to spend half the time available on the case study.

- **Question 2** deals with objectives of 'for profit' and 'not for profit' organisations. You should be able to pick up some general marks on part (a) if you are really stuck. Part (b) requires specific application of the scenario to consider objectives that are suitable for SPORT.

- Although lease vs buy questions may seem daunting, you should be able to perform discounted cash flow calculations quite easily by now so there are some easy marks to be gained in **Question 3**. Part (c) offers some easy marks by relating your answer to whatever you have calculated and by making relevant points about the different financing methods.

- **Question 4** is quite a discursive question about investment appraisal and capital rationing. You should be able to explain the strengths and weaknesses and perform the calculations in part (a) to pick up marks.

- **Question 1** actually offers quite a number of easy marks so don't be put off by the total marks available. You should be able to pick up some marks in part (a) when calculating and commenting on working capital. You should also pick up some marks through a clearly laid out NPV calculation.

Option 2 (if you're thinking 'I can do all of these')

It never pays to be over confident but if you're not quaking in your shoes about the exam then **turn straight to compulsory Question 1**. You've got to do it so you might as well get it over and done with.

Once you've done the compulsory question, choose two of the questions in Section B.

- **Question 2** is a good question if you are confident about objectives in different types of organisation. Whilst part (a) has some generic elements, don't forget to relate your answer to the scenario in part (b).

- **Question 3** tests investment appraisal and leasing. However if you have studied discounted cash flow analysis in detail (and you should have!) you should be able to make a good attempt at this question.

- **Question 4** focuses on investment appraisal and capital rationing. You should be able to pick up some quite straightforward marks in parts (a)(ii) but don't spend so long on these that you run out of time on part (b), which tests you on how hard and soft capital rationing are different and the difference between single and multi-period capital rationing.

No matter how many times we remind you...

Always, always **allocate your time** according to the marks for the question in total and for the parts of the questions. And always, always **follow the requirements exactly**.

You've got free time at the end of the exam.....?

If you have allocated your time properly then you **shouldn't have time on your hands** at the end of the exam. If you find yourself with five or ten minutes spare, however, go back to **any parts of questions that you didn't finish** because you ran out of time.

Forget about it!

And don't worry if you found the paper difficult. More then likely other students would too. If this were the real thing you would need to forget the exam the minute you leave the exam hall and **think about the next one**. Or, if it's the last one, **celebrate!**

Question 1

Text references. International investment appraisal is covered in Chapter 12, working capital policy is covered in Chapter 4.

Top tips. For (b)(i) make sure you have read the question properly and understand that tax depreciation is only available on the shop fittings, not on the properties. You will save time if you realise the costs and revenues are all increasing at the same rate and therefore only a net operating cash figure is required.

In part (c) you should recognise that you need to question some of the assumptions made for the variables in part (b)(i). In particular comment on the residual value of the property and whether it is sensible to assume the property prices will increase.

Easy marks. The reasons behind the inventory and payables days should be straightforward as should the benefits and drawbacks of the aggressive working capital strategy.

Examiner's comments. In part (a)(i) there were a number of students who did not read the requirement properly.

In part (b)(i) a common error was that students failed to include working capital cash flows.

There was a general lack of depth in answers to part (c). In general for this paper there are up to 2 or 3 marks for each issue discussed (being half a mark for a simple bullet point, 1 if the issue is raised in an appropriate full sentence and another 1 or 2 if this is developed).

BRIEFING PAPER

To: The Regional Board

From: Project team member

Date: 1 September 2012

Proposed project investment appraisal

The purpose of this paper is to provide an initial assessment on whether or not to proceed with the proposed expansion with a chain of convenience stores in the USA.

> **Tutorial note** – this forms the answer to part (a) (i)

The target working capital days are as follows

	USA Stores	B group	Difference
Accounts receivable	Nil	Nil	Nil
Accounts payable	100 days	139 days	-39 days
Inventory	30 days	53 days	-23 days

The differences can be partly explained by the fact that convenience stores in the US will have a **different profile of goods** to the average store operated by B. Convenience stores are likely to have a greater percentage of **fresh foods** available, which perish quickly and therefore require a quicker turnover. The B group stores contain a higher proportion of non-perishable items, which can be held in inventory for a longer period of time, which is why its inventory days figure is higher.

The lower accounts payable days could be caused by B having a **smaller presence** in North America and not having the size or trading history that B has elsewhere, which can be used to negotiate longer credit periods. It could also reflect the fact that a greater service level is needed because of the faster inventory turnover.

> **Tutorial note** – this forms the answer to part (a) (ii)

The aggressive working capital strategy will mean that **inventory is kept to a minimum** and **accounts payable will be maximised** as far as suppliers will tolerate. It is assumed that 100 days is the maximum tolerance for suppliers. Since no accounts receivable are expected, they do not need to be considered in the benefits and potential drawbacks.

BPP
LEARNING MEDIA

Benefits of the aggressive strategy

Cash flow is increased by having a small investment in inventory and paying suppliers as late as possible. This will reduce the amount of finance needed to support working capital, which in turn reduces finance costs.

There will also be **reduced inventory holding costs**, although this may be partly mitigated by increased delivery costs as a result of more frequent deliveries.

Potential drawbacks of the aggressive strategy

There will be an increased risk of **stock outs** as a result of holding low levels of inventory, which could lead to customer dissatisfaction and potential loss of customers.

Suppliers may be dissatisfied with slow payment and either **stop supplying** B or reduce the quality of their service.

Suppliers may seek to **increase their prices** to compensate for the later payment.

Tutorial note – this forms the answer to part (a) (iii)

---

		0 USD'000	1 USD'000	2 USD'000	3 USD'000	4 USD'000
Purchases	12% growth		35,000.00	39,200.00	43,904.00	49,172.48
Acc. Payable	100 days	9,589.04	10,739.73	12,028.49	13,471.91	
Inventory	30 days	(2,876.71)	(3,221.92)	(3,608.55)	(4,041.57)	
Net Balance		6,712.33	7,517.81	8,419.94	9,430.34	0.00
Movement	(used in (b)(i))	6,712.33	805.48	902.13	1,010.40	(9,430.34)

Tutorial note – this forms the answer to part (b) (i)

---

		0 USD'000	1 USD'000	2 USD'000	3 USD'000	4 USD'000
Net cash	12% growth		15,000.00	16,800.00	18,816.00	21,073.92
Tax at 33%			(4,950.00)	(5,544.00)	(6,209.28)	(6,954.39)
Working capital	From (a)(iii)	6,712.33	805.48	902.13	1,010.40	(9,430.34)
Investment	(30 +10)	(40,000.00)				
Residual value	(30 × 1.2) + 4					40,000.00
Tax benefit	(W1)		825.00	618.75	464.06	72.19
Total USD flows		(33,287.67)	11,680.48	12,776.88	14,081.18	44,761.38
Exchange rate	(W2)	1.1000	1.1214	1.1432	1.1654	1.1880
		EUR'000	EUR'000	EUR'000	EUR'000	EUR'000
Total in EUR		(30,261.52)	10,415.98	11,176.42	12,082.70	37,677.93
11% discount factor		1.000	0.901	0.812	0.731	0.659
PV		(30,261.52)	9,384.80	9,075.25	8,832.45	24,829.76

NPV = 21,860.75 in EUR'000

Workings

1   Tax depreciation

	1	2	3	4
	USD'000	USD'000	USD'000	USD'000
Fittings balance b/f	10,000.00	7,500.00	5,625.00	4,218.75
25% Tax depreciation	(2,500.00)	(1,875.00)	(1,406.25)	(218.75)
Tax relief at 33%	825.00	618.75	464.06	72.19
Balance c/f	7,500.00	5,625.00	4,218.75	4,000.00

Balancing allowance in year 4.

2   Exchange rates

Year 0 = 1.1000

Year 1 = 1.1000 × 1.05/1.03 = 1.1214

Year 2 = 1.1214 × 1.05/1.03 = 1.1432

Year 3 = 1.1432 × 1.05/1.03 = 1.1654

Year 4 = 1.1654 × 1.05/1.03 = 1.1880

Tutorial note – this forms the answer to part (b) (ii)

The properties are assumed to be sold at USD 36 million (30m × 1.2). If they were sold instead at USD 24 million (30m × 0.8) there would be a difference of USD 12 million.

The present value in EUR of this cost from year 4 would be USD 12 million/1.1880 × 0.659 = 6,656,566

Therefore NPV would be reduced by EUR'000 6,656.57

Revised NPV (EUR'000) = 21,860.74 – 6,656.57 = 15,204.17

Tutorial note – this forms the answer to part (c)

The initial financial analysis of the investment in the USA shows significant returns are expected with a net present value of approximately EUR 21.9 million. On this basis alone it is **recommended that B undertakes the investment** in the 50 new convenience stores.

However, it should be noted, that this result depends on the **accuracy of the predicted variables** used in the analysis. This is shown in part by the result in part (b) (ii). Changing the assumption behind the residual value of the property from an increase of 20% to a decrease of 20% means the total NPV is reduced by approximately EUR 6.7 million, which is a fall of 31% (6.7/21.9). Given the unpredictable nature of property prices and the fact that significant falls are possible there is a strong argument that the 20% decrease is the more **prudent** approach and should be used in for the decision making process.

Other variables

There are other variables in the analysis which may prove to be inaccurate. These include:

The **growth rate**. Growth is estimated at 12%, although this appears to include expected inflation it is reasonably high and may well be unsustainable.

Revenue. This will depend on anticipating customer demand and having the goods that customers want to buy.

Labour costs. This depends on estimated staffing levels being correct and also salary levels being sufficient to attract enough staff.

The **cost of capital** used is the rate that applies to B as a whole. Given that this project is overseas and could be perceived as being riskier than B's ongoing business it could be argued that a higher rate would be more appropriate.

The analysis assumes that working capital investment occurs at the beginning of each year. It may be more **prudent** to assume that it happens at the end of each year, since cash is released from working capital in this instance.

There may also be **significant foreign exchange risk** to this investment. The actual result could be significantly lower if the US dollar depreciates significantly against the euro. The predicted rates have been generated by considering the interest rate differential between the USA and Europe and they may not be particularly reliable estimates. Shareholders may have taken the foreign exchange exposure risk of B into account when deciding to invest, and the majority of B's cash flows will still be in euros. Investors may have invested to obtain exposure to exchange rates and expect their investment to reflect exchange rate movements as a result.

Overseas risks

There are a number of additional risks that arise from investment in a foreign country, which includes:

Foreign exchange risk, this has been covered above.

Litigation risk arising from US regulations and legislation. This is not likely to be a significant problem for B given its existing American operations.

There is a risk that economic or political measures could be put in place by the US government affecting the operation of the stores, but again this appears unlikely.

B already has some experience of operating in American, but not in this particular market. Therefore it will be important to understand any local **protocol** in this market and also to **understand** customer **preferences**. There may also be reluctance from customers to buy from foreign-owned stores.

B will have to ensure that its culture fits in with the American market, but again this is partly mitigated through its experience of operating other types of stores in North America.

B may need to find people from its existing staff to manage the convenience stores in the USA, at least at the beginning. Finding the right member of staff who would be willing to move, even for a temporary period, could be problematic.

Conclusion

From the above analysis, the investment appears to be worthwhile. The main risk to B will be whether the convenience store concept can work in the US. B may want to consider opening a small number of stores on a trial basis to test the convenience store concept in the US and confirm that they can be run at a profit before expanding to the full 50 stores.

Question 2

Text references. Organisational objectives are discussed in Chapter 1.

Top tips. The key to this question is not to spend too long on any part of the question. It would be easy to write too much in one part and run out of time. Therefore make sure you allocate the time correctly and do not overrun on any part of this question.

In part (b) (iii) it is important to consider that a charity is not able to take on risk in the same way that a company can.

Easy marks. Part (a) provides some straightforward discussion marks about the differences in objectives between for-profit and not-for-profit organisations.

Examiner's comments. Part (b)(ii) was the requirement that caused the most difficulty and in some cases students did not attempt it. Many answers were a vague list of ideas that were not formulated into specific objectives.

Not all students picked up the idea of whether it was appropriate for a charity to take on significant levels of risk regarding the FD's comments.

Marking scheme

				Marks
(a)		Identify main objectives	2	
		Describe differences	2	
				4
(b)	(i)	Adaptation of financial objectives	4.5	
		Adaptation of non-financial objectives	4.5	
				9
	(ii)	Up to 2 marks per relevant point max		5
	(iii)	Discussion on FD's comments	4	
		Advice on bond issue	4	
			Max	7
				25

(a) A 'for profit' organisation is run for the benefit of its shareholders who are the owners of the organisation. The main objective for such an organisation is usually the **maximisation of shareholder wealth**. This is measured by dividend payments to shareholders and the capital gain through increases in the share price. Other financial objectives will tend to **support this main objective**. There may be non-financial objectives as well, but these are typically given less importance.

Since a not-for-profit organisation does not have shareholders a profit objective is not appropriate. The main purpose will be a charitable objective such as improving the environment or the welfare of a certain group in society. As a result the key objective will be based on the **benefits provided by the organisation**. Not-for-profit organisations measure their objectives in terms of the three Es: efficiency, economy and effectiveness rather than profit measures.

(b) (i) <u>Financial objectives</u>

Growth in earnings per share

Since SPORT does not have any shareholders, this objective is not appropriate. However the idea of **increasing income and reducing expenses** (which would mean an increase in earnings) is relevant to SPORT. SPORT has commercial activities that should be operated along commercial lines as far as possible. This will help to **maximise the surplus** (income minus expenses) of SPORT, which is used to provide the sports equipment. SPORT may look to adapt this objective into two different objectives covering for example

- Reducing costs in charity stores
- Increasing public donations

Financial gearing target

Financial gearing is a measure of **risk** and therefore can be used for not for profit organisations as well. Clearly there is **no equity figure** to be used for SPORT so this target would take the form of an absolute figure as a limit for debt. This is based on the assumption that the surplus in each year is spent in full on equipment.

Dividend growth

As there are no shares, this is not an appropriate objective for SPORT. However it could be redefined in terms of **growth in the level of surplus**/amount spent on sports equipment generated by SPORT.

Non-financial objectives

Non-financial objectives are more likely to be applicable to both for profit and not-for-profit organisations.

Customer satisfaction

The **customer satisfaction target** could be used with both the store customers and the people who are supplied with the sports equipment.

Market position

Retaining market position is unlikely to be so important to SPORT. Although it will seek to maintain and grow its public profile to ensure donations and public support continue. An alternative objective may be to **maintain its level of donations** relative to other charities.

Carbon footprint

Reducing carbon footprint is an important objective for **all organisations** and should be encouraged for SPORT.

(ii)   SPORT may want to have additional objectives which cover other stakeholders such as employees, suppliers and local communities. As a charity, SPORT will understand the social aspect of business and will recognise the need to focus on **all stakeholders**.

Examples of objectives which may be suitable for SPORT include:

- Provide a fair salary for employees.
- Provide equal treatment for employees and volunteers.
- Fair treatment for all of SPORT's suppliers.
- Ensure a high level of service to store customers.
- Ensure goods sold meet quality and safety standards.
- Ensure sports equipment supplied is of a high quality and is safe to use.
- Expand the range of recipients of the sports equipment.

(iii)   The FD makes a valid point about running a charity on commercial lines. For example costs should be controlled and **waste should be minimised**. Members of the public who have made donations will not want to see their money being **wasted**. They would the maximum feasible amount to supply sports equipment. A charity should seek to operate stores at to maximise profits and therefore maximise the funds available for the charitable purpose. Some charities do have loss making trading arms and if this were to fail then the charity could be brought down with it.

It is not appropriate for a charity to take **excessive risk** to try to increase its surplus. Commercial operations should be conducted in a professional manner, and the Trustees of the charity have a higher duty to reduce risk than Directors do to shareholders. In the UK, Trustees can be personally liable for mismanaging a charity. Therefore Trustees will **need to be sure** that the return on the funds generated by the bond issue will exceed the interest payments and that funds can be realised to repay the bond on maturity.

Conclusion

If the Trustees are confident that the expansion will generate sufficient funds and increase net income without significantly increasing the risk then the bond issue could be considered further,

Question 4

(a)   (i)

Project	Investment F$m	PV of post year 1 cash flows F$m	NPV F$m	PI	Annual cash flows F$m	Term (Years)	Payback (Years)
A	(100)	135	35	35%	151.2	1	0.7
B	(150)	250	100	67%	82.3	4	1.8
C	(300)	410	110	37%	242.6	2	1.2
D	(350)	510	160	46%	124.0	6	2.8

Payback calculations

Project A $100/151.2 = 0.7$

Project B $150/82.3 = 1.8$

Project C $300/242.6 = 1.2$

Project D $350/124 = 2.8$

Ranking of projects

Project	NPV	PI	Payback
A	4	4	1
B	3	1	3
C	2	3	2
D	1	2	4

(ii)   The **NPV method** gives an absolute figure which shows the increase in shareholders' funds as a result of the investment in a particular project. If capital is unlimited then this is the measure that should determine the projects to be invested in. If capital is limited then it is also necessary to consider the amount of limited capital required by the project.

The **profitability index** is a measure that can be used when capital rationing is in place. It is most useful where projects are divisible, but is **less useful**, as in this case, **where projects are indivisible**. It can be of some help to rank non-divisible projects and can help to identify the optimum combination of projects, or at least a combination that is close to the optimum. However in this particular case it has not produced such a combination.

The **payback method** takes into account the **timing of the cash flows**. Project A is therefore prioritised as it returns the initial investment within the first year. This can be useful in a multi-period scenario as it will indicate that funds could be reinvested in a different project in the following year. This may be an advantage where projects planned for the following period will deliver greater shareholder wealth than those in the current period. However, if capital rationing is

only in place for the current period, then this is less useful. Payback helps to **identify riskier projects** as the uncertainty of future cash flows increases with time and therefore a project with a lower payback period will be less risky.

All of these methods have drawbacks. Capital rationing decisions are often **more complicated** than identifying the ranking by such methods. Some of the complications of capital rationing problems are as follows:

(1) If capital is restricted in one period that it is highly likely to also be restricted in the next and **subsequent periods** as well. A multi-period model will therefore be required.

(2) Projects are unlikely to possess the same characteristics. For example, some projects may contain real options with follow on opportunities. Other projects may have greater **strategic significance**, which outweigh other financial considerations.

(3) Some projects may be **'one-off' opportunities** which can only be undertaken in a particular period. Other projects may be able to be delayed and then commence in the following period.

No one method is likely to provide the best solution to a capital rationing scenario on its own. Each method provides useful information which can help the decision making process

(b) (i) <u>Project combinations</u>

Combination	Investment	NPV
	F$m	F$m
ABC	550	245
ABD	600	295
CD	650	270

The best combination is from projects A, B and D. This only uses F$600m of the available funds.

(ii) <u>Soft or hard capital rationing?</u>

Soft capital rationing occurs when the capital restriction is internally imposed by the company, usually for budgeting purposes. The capital limits are targets and there is the **potential to adjust them according to particular circumstances**.

Hard capital rationing is externally imposed, for example due to restrictive debt covenants, and the **limits cannot be adjusted**.

If WIDGET applies soft capital rationing, it may seek to increase the limit on capital to F$800 million as this would mean that projects B, C and D could be undertaken. They would generate an NPV of F$370 million which is F$75 million higher than the current optimum combination of F$295 million. This is an increase of 25%, with an increase in capital of 14% (100m/700m).

If the limit could be increased further, it would be **beneficial** to the shareholder to **undertake all of the available projects**.

<u>Capital rationing in the following year</u>

The optimal combination depends on **whether capital is rationed in the following year**. If this is the case, project A becomes more attractive as the payback period is less than one year and so this capital is **available to be reinvested in the next year**.

Assuming that the limit of F$700 million applies again in the next year, this will then greatly enhance the funds available for investment at that time.

Tutorial note: Multi-period capital rationing can be solved by using an alternative method such as linear programming, but this is outside the scope of the F3 syllabus.

CIMA – Pillar F

Paper F3

Financial Strategy

Mock Examination 3 (November 2012)

Instructions to candidates:

You are allowed three hours to answer this question paper.
In the real exam, you are allowed 20 minutes reading time before the examination begins during which you should read the question paper, and if you wish, make annotations on the question paper. However, you will **not** be allowed, **under any circumstances**, to open the answer book and start writing or use your calculator during this reading time.
You are strongly advised to carefully read the question requirement before attempting the question concerned.
Answer the compulsory questions in Section A.
Answer TWO of the THREE questions in Section B.

DO NOT OPEN THIS PAPER UNTIL YOU ARE READY TO START UNDER EXAMINATION CONDITIONS

SECTION A

Question 1

Pre-seen case study

V, a private limited company in a European country (SK), which is outside the Eurozone, was founded in 1972. The currency in SK is SK$. V is a travel business that offers three holiday (vacation) products. It has a network of 50 branches in a number of major cities throughout SK.

History of the company

V achieved steady growth until six years ago, when it found that its market share was eroding due to customers increasingly making online bookings with its competitors. Direct bookings for holidays through the internet have increased dramatically in recent years. Many holidaymakers find the speed and convenience of booking flights, accommodation or complete holidays online outweighs the benefits of discussing holiday alternatives with staff in a branch.

V's board had always taken the view that the friendly direct personal service that V offers through its branch network is a major differentiating factor between itself and other travel businesses and that this is highly valued by its customers. However, V found that in order to continue to compete it needed to establish its own online travel booking service, which it did five years ago. Until this point, V's board had never engaged in long-term planning. It had largely financed growth by reinvestment of funds generated by the business. The large investment in IT and IS five years ago required significant external funding and detailed investment appraisal.

Much of V's business is now transacted online through its website to the extent that 60% of its revenue in the year ended 30 June 2012 was earned through online bookings.

Current structure of V's business

V offers three types of holiday product. These are known within V as Package, Adventure and Prestige Travel. V only sells its own products and does not act as an agent for any other travel companies. It uses the services of other companies engaged in the travel industry such as chartered airlines and hotels which it pays for directly on behalf of its customers.

Package

"Package" provides holidays mainly for families with children aged up to their late teens. These typically are for accommodation in hotels (where meals are part of the package) or self-catering apartments (where no meals are provided within the package).

Adventure

"Adventure" caters for people aged mainly between 20 and 30, who want relatively cheap adventure based holidays such as trekking, sailing and cycling or who wish to go on inexpensive back-packing holidays mainly in Europe and Asia.

Prestige Travel

"Prestige Travel" provides expensive and bespoke holidays mainly sold to couples whose children have grown up and left home. The Prestige Travel product only provides accommodation in upmarket international hotel chains in countries across the world.

All three of these products provide holidays which include flights to and from the holiday destinations and hotel or self-catering accommodation. V has its own customer representatives available at the holiday destinations to provide support to its customers. All-inclusive holidays (in which all food and drinks are provided within the holiday price) are offered within each of the three product offerings.

Support products

V supports its main products by offering travel insurance and foreign currency exchange. The travel insurance, which is provided by a major insurance company and for which V acts as an agent, is usually sold along with the holidays both by branch staff and by staff dealing with online bookings.

Currency exchange is available to anyone through V's branches irrespective of whether or not the customer has bought a holiday product from V. A new currency exchange product is provided by V through which a customer purchases an amount of currency, either in SK's home currency (SK$) or else in a foreign currency and this is credited on to a plastic card. The card is then capable of being read by automated teller machines (ATM's) in many countries across the world allowing the customer to withdraw cash in the local currency up to the amount that has been credited on to the card.

Marketing of products

V relies for the vast majority of its business on the literature, available in hard copy and online, which it provides on the holiday products it sells. Exceptionally, V is able to offer some of its existing holiday products at discount prices. These may be offered under any of the three main products offered but they are mostly cut-price holiday deals which are available under the Package holiday product label.

Sales structure

Staff in each of the 50 branches accept bookings from customers and all branches have direct IT access to head office. Online enquiries and bookings are received and processed centrally at head office, which is located in SK's capital city.

Branch managers have some discretion to offer discounts on holidays to customers. V offers a discount to customers who buy holidays through its online bookings. The branch managers have authority to reduce the price of a holiday booked at the branch up to the amount of the online discount if they feel it is necessary to do so in order to make the sale.

Financial information

V's revenue, split across the holiday and support products offered, for the financial year ended 30 June 2012 is summarised as follows:

	Revenue SK$ million
Package	90
Adventure	60
Prestige Travel	95
Support products	5

The overall net operating profit generated in the financial year to 30 June 2012 was SK$35 million and the profit for the year was SK$24 million, giving a profit to sales ratio of just under 10%. V's cash receipts fluctuate because of seasonal variations and also because V's customers pay for their holidays shortly before they depart.

Further details, including extracts from V's income statement for the year ended 30 June 2012 and statement of financial position as at 30 June 2012 are shown in Appendix 1.

Financial objectives

V's key financial objectives are as follows:

1. To grow earnings by, on average, 5% a year.
2. To pay out 80% of profits as dividends.

Foreign exchange risk

V has high exposure to foreign exchange risk as its revenues received and payments made are frequently in different currencies. It normally settles hotel bills and support costs, such as transfers between hotels and airports in the local currencies of the countries where the hotels are located. It normally pays charter airlines in the airline's home currency. Scheduled airline charges are settled in the currency required by the particular airline.

V is exposed to fluctuations in the cost of aircraft fuel incurred by airlines which are passed on to travel businesses. It has often been necessary for V to require its customers to make a supplementary payment to cover the cost of increases in aircraft fuel, sometimes after the customer had thought that the final payment for the holiday had been made.

Board composition and operational responsibilities

The Board of Directors comprises five people: an Executive Chairman (who also fulfils the role of Chief Executive), a Finance Director, an Operations Director, an IT Director and a Human Resources Director. The

Executive Chairman founded the business in 1972. He has three grown-up children, two of whom successfully pursue different business interests and are not engaged in V's business at all. The third child, a son, is currently taking a "year out" from study and is going to university next year to study medicine.

The branch managers all report directly to the Operations Director. In addition, the Operations Director is responsible for liaising with airlines and hotels which provide the services offered by V's promotional literature. The IT Director is responsible for V's website and online enquiries and bookings. The Finance Director is responsible for V's financial and management accounting systems and has a small team of accountancy staff, including a part-qualified management accountant, reporting to her. The Human Resources Director has a small team of staff reporting to him.

Shareholding

There are 90 million SK$0.10 (10 cent) shares in issue and the shareholdings are as follows:

	% holding
Executive Chairman	52
Finance Director	12
Operations Director	12
IT Director	12
Human Resources Director	12

Employees

V employs 550 full-time equivalent staff. Turnover of staff is relatively low. High performance rewards in terms of bonuses are paid to staff in each branch if it meets or exceeds its quarterly sales targets. Similarly, staff who deal with online bookings receive a bonus if the online bookings meet or exceed quarterly sales targets. V's staff, both in the branches and those employed in dealing with online bookings, also receive an additional bonus if they are able to sell travel insurance along with a holiday product to customers.

Employee development for staff who are in direct contact with the public is provided through updates on products which V offers. Each member of branch and online booking staff undertakes a two day induction programme at the commencement of their employment with V. The emphasis of the induction programme is on customer service not on details relating to the products as it is expected that new staff will become familiar with such product details as they gain experience within V.

Safety

V publicly states that it takes great care to ensure that its customers are as safe as possible while on holiday. To date, V has found that accidents while on holiday are mainly suffered by very young children, Adventure customers and elderly customers. There has been an increase in instances over the last year where customers in resort hotels have suffered severe stomach complaints. This has particularly been the case in hotels located in resorts in warm climates.

Executive Chairman's statement to the press

V's Executive Chairman was quoted in the national press in SK in January 2012 as saying, "We are maintaining a comparatively high level of revenues and operating profit. This is in a period when our competitors are experiencing very difficult trading conditions. We feel we are achieving this due to our particular attention to customer service. He cited V's 40 years of experience in the travel industry and a previous 99% satisfaction rating from its customers as the reasons for its success. He went on to state that V intends to expand and diversify its holiday product range to provide more choice to customers.

Board meeting

At the next board meeting which took place after the Executive Chairman's statement to the press, the Operations Director expressed some concern. He cast doubt on whether V was able to provide sufficient funding, marketing and IT/IS resources to enable the product expansion to which the Executive Chairman referred. The Operations Director was of the opinion that V places insufficient emphasis on customer relationship marketing. The Finance Director added at the same meeting that while V presently remained profitable overall, some products may be more profitable than others.

The Executive Chairman responded by saying that V's high level of customer service provides a sufficiently strong level of sales without the need to incur any other marketing costs. He added that since V achieved a high profit to sales ratio, which it has managed to maintain for a number of years, it really didn't matter about the profits generated by each customer group.

Retirement of the Executive Chairman

The Executive Chairman formally announced to the Board in July 2012 that he intends to retire on 30 June 2013 and wishes to sell part of his shareholding in the company. The Board members believe the time is now right for V, given its expansion plans, to enter a new stage in its financing arrangements, in the form of either debt or equity from new providers.

Extracts from V's income statement and statement of financial position

Income statement for the year ended 30 June 2012

	Notes	SK$ million
Revenue		250
Operating costs		(215)
Net operating profit		35
Interest income		3
Finance costs		(4)
Corporate income tax	1	(10)
PROFIT FOR THE YEAR		24

Statement of financial position as at 30 June 2012

	Notes	SK$ million
ASSETS		
Non-current assets		123
Current assets		
Inventories		3
Trade and other receivables		70
Cash and cash equivalents		37
Total current assets		110
Total assets		233
EQUITY AND LIABILITIES		
Equity		
Share capital	2	9
Share premium		6
Retained earnings		60
Total equity		75
Non-current liabilities		
Long-term borrowings	3	50
Revenue received in advance		3
Current liabilities		
Trade and other payables		35
Revenue received in advance		70
Total liabilities		158
Total equity and liabilities		233

Notes:

1. The corporate income tax rate can be assumed to be 30%.

2. There are 90 million SK$0.10 (10 cent) shares currently in issue.

3. 30% of the long-term borrowings are due for repayment on 30 June 2014. The remainder is due for re-payment on 30 June 2020. There are debt covenants in operation currently which restrict V from having a gearing ratio measured by long-term debt divided by long-term debt plus equity of more than 50%.

Unseen case material

Assume today is 22 November 2012.

The Board of Directors of V has recently met to discuss ambitious plans to expand the business and to float the company on the local Stock Exchange by means of an IPO (initial public offering). An IPO would help give V access to large amounts of additional funding, at a time when new bank funding and capital market issues are difficult to achieve due to restricted credit conditions in the financial markets. In addition, an IPO would give existing shareholders, the current directors, the opportunity to realise part or all of their investment. With his imminent retirement, the Executive Chairman, in particular, is eager to realise part of his investment. There has been positive feedback following preliminary discussion with market analysts regarding the possibility of an IPO.

Details of the proposed IPO

Certain directors of V wish to sell some of their shares as part of the IPO. In addition, the Board has decided to offer a further 10 million new 10 cent shares in V as part of the IPO.

The number of shares to be sold by each director is as follows:

Executive Chairman	8 million shares
Finance Director	1 million shares
IT Director	3 million shares
Human Resources Director	1 million shares

A total of 23 million shares would therefore be sold under the IPO if the issue is fully subscribed. Further sales of shares by current directors will be permitted after pre-defined time periods. The Operations Director has no plans to dispose of any shares as part of the IPO.

It was agreed that, in the event that the IPO is undersubscribed, the sale of shares held by directors would take priority over the issuing of new shares.

Activities in July 2012

An Investment Bank was appointed in July 2012 to help with the IPO process.

The Board of V considered that, based on financial information for V as at 30 June 2012, a reasonable target price per share for the IPO would be SK$ 3.40. It was then agreed that, under the IPO, offers for the purchase of shares should be requested on a tender basis in the guide price range of SK$ 2.90 to SK$ 3.60 per share. Under the tender bid, potential investors are asked to specify the number of shares they wish to purchase and the maximum price that they are prepared to pay for those shares.

Financial information for V

The income statement and statement of financial position for V for the last financial year can be found on page 6 of the pre-seen material.

Additional relevant financial information as at 30 June 2012:

- Net operating profit for V for the year ended 30 June 2012 has been arrived at after charging depreciation of SK$ 3 million.

- Capital expenditure for V in the year ended 30 June 2012 was SK$ 5 million, which is typical of the level of annual capital expenditure needed to maintain operations.

- The market value of V's non-current assets is estimated to be SK$ 150 million.

- V pays corporate income tax of 30% on taxable profits and tax is paid in the year in which the taxable profit arises.

- V is estimated to have an equity beta of 1.9.

- The risk free rate is 2% and the market return is 6% in Country SK, the country in which V is based.

There have not been any recent private transactions in V's shares that could be used as a guide to the value of V. However, a review of the financial statements of competitor companies has shown that industry P/E ratios tend to be between 11 and 14.

The travel business in which V operates is highly cyclical but an underlying trend can be identified by adjusting for the cyclical nature of the business cash flows. Until now, the business has shown consistent but unspectacular nominal growth in after-tax cash flows of approximately 2% per annum after adjusting for cyclical effect. However, it is hoped that expansion plans would result in an increased nominal annual growth rate of 3% in the 2 years to 30 June 2014 and then 5% from 1 July 2014 for the foreseeable future. It is estimated that an upfront investment of SK$ 50 million would be required to finance the expansion plans; this would partly be funded by proceeds from the IPO.

Outcome of the tender offer

An open invitation to submit offers to subscribe for shares in V under a tender bid was published on 1 October 2012 with a deadline for submission of offers by 15 November 2012.

Interim results for the quarter ended 30 September 2012 were published on 20 October 2012 and indicated lower growth than had been forecast in the information published at the launch of the tender offer and resulted in a lower than expected demand for shares.

The tender offers actually received by the deadline date are summarised below:

Maximum price offered (SK$ per share)	Number of shares requested at this price (millions)
2.90	4
3.00	3
3.10	2
3.20	3
3.30	3
3.40	6
3.50	5
3.60	4

In the light of the disappointing response, the following two alternative pricing strategies in respect of the IPO are being considered by the Board of V:

Pricing strategy A: Set the selling price at the original target price of SK$ 3.40 per share and accept that the offer will then be undersubscribed and a lower value of new finance raised.

Pricing strategy B: Set the selling price at a level at which the issue is fully subscribed.

Required

Assume you are the Finance Director of V and have been asked to write a report to the Board of V in which you:

(a)   **Describe** the role of an Investment Bank in an IPO by tender bid.   **(4 marks)**

(b)   (i)   **Calculate** a range of possible values for the equity of V based on financial information as at 30 June 2012.   **(13 marks)**

(ii)   **Discuss** the validity of each method used in (i) above as a basis for valuing the equity of V.
   (6 marks)

(iii)   **Discuss**:

- The nature and extent of V's intangible assets.   **(4 marks)**

- The implications of a large value of intangible assets on setting a target offer price.
   (2 marks)

(iv)   **Advise** whether the target share price of SK$ 3.40 was set at an appropriate level based on financial information as at 30 June 2012.   **(6 marks)**

(c)   **Evaluate** the implications of each of the pricing strategies A and B, based on the offers for shares received by 15 November 2012, on:

- The directors of V.
- The new shareholders of V.

Up to 7 marks are available for relevant calculations.   **(12 marks)**

Additional marks available for structure and presentation: **(3 marks)**

(Total = 50 marks)

SECTION B

Question 2

BBD is a listed company, based in Canada, which specialises in extracting natural gas for sale to national distribution networks. Wholesale gas is priced globally in US dollars.

A possible new project to build four new gas drill rigs is being considered. The rigs would use fracking, a relatively new and controversial method of extracting natural gas.

Fracking involves drilling a well hundreds of metres into the ground and pumping it full of water, sand and chemicals to fracture the rock and release gas for sale. There have recently been some reports of fracking causing small earthquakes which result in damage to properties nearby the drill rigs. There is also some concern about the possibility of pollution of the water supply as a result of fracking.

BBD is confident of being able to raise sufficient debt finance for the project based on forecast future earnings from selling the extracted gas. The company is already relatively heavily geared, with a gearing ratio of 50% (debt/debt + equity). 80% of the equity is owned by 6 major institutions, including 2 pension funds.

BBD has recently been the subject of a review by a major rating agency which has unexpectedly put the company on 'negative outlook', implying that there is a high chance that its rating could be reduced. Further discussion has revealed that the rating agency is concerned about the risk involved in the new project and about the increase in gearing that this would create.

A rating downgrade could have major implications for BBD. Therefore the directors have been discussing and investigating courses of action open to them in respect of the planned project in light of the threat of a credit downgrade. The following three possible responses have been identified:

A   Cancel the project.

B   Proceed with the project and accept the risk of a downgrade.

C   Cancel this year's dividend and use the cash saved to help finance the project, thereby hoping to avoid a credit downgrade.

Required

(a)   **Discuss** the potential exposure of BBD's financial results to external factors such as economic variables, market prices and external constraints.   **(7 marks)**

(b)   (i)   **Advise** BBD on the possible implications for the company of a credit downgrade.   **(5 marks)**

        (ii)   **Evaluate** each of the three possible responses A, B and C identified by the directors from the viewpoint of shareholder wealth.   **(9 marks)**

        (iii)   **Recommend** which possible response A, B or C should be adopted by BBD.   **(4 marks)**

                                                                                                    (Total = 25 marks)

Question 3

Assume today is 1 October 2012.

XRG is a long established manufacturer of paper and plastic products, mainly for use in the packaging industry. XRG is based in the UK, where it is the market leader, but it sells worldwide. Its shares are listed on a UK stock exchange.

XRG has three financial objectives:

- Gearing at or below 50% (calculated as the ratio of debt to debt plus equity and based on book values).
- Earnings per share of at least GBP 0.30.
- Dividend per share of at least GBP 0.10.

XRG needs to refinance GBP 1,250 million of 5% secured borrowings that mature on 1 January 2013. The board of XRG has been discussing whether to renegotiate the debt and continue with a relatively high level of gearing or, alternatively, to issue shares via a rights issue and use the proceeds of the issue to repay the debt on 1 January 2013.

In summary, the two alternative financing strategies being considered are:

Renew the debt for 10 years at an interest rate of 6%. As before, it would be secured on the company's non-current assets.

FINANCING STRATEGY 1

Renew the debt for 10 years at an interest rate of 6%. As before, it would be secured on the company's non-current assets.

FINANCING STRATEGY 2

Issue new shares at a discount of 25% on today's share price of GBP 3.33 by means of a rights issue.

Forecast equity and debt balances for XRG as at 31 December 2012:

		GBP million
EQUITY		
	Share capital (50 pence ordinary shares)	500
	Reserves	1,550
DEBT		
	5% secured, maturing 1 January 2013	1,250
	7% unsecured, undated	1,250

Additional information:

- The new financing strategy will be implemented on 1 January 2013.
- Profit before interest and tax for the year ended 31 December 2013 is forecast to be GBP 650 million.
- Corporate income tax is payable at 30% of the profit before tax figure.
- The dividend payout ratio will be maintained at 35% of earnings.
- Industry average gearing is 40%.

Required

(a) For EACH of the two alternative financing strategies under consideration, **construct**:

- A forecast income statement for the year ending 31 December 2013.
- A forecast schedule of equity and debt balances as at 31 December 2013. **(8 marks)**

(b) **Evaluate** the impact of EACH of the two alternative financing strategies 1 and 2 on:

(i)   The likely attainment by XRG of each of its three financial objectives. **(9 marks)**

(ii) XRG's shareholders and debt providers. **(8 marks)**

(Total = 25 marks)

Question 4

APT is a manufacturing company based in a country in the eurozone. The company's shares are listed on a European stock exchange and its current market capitalisation is EUR 1,200 million. APT's debt funding comprises a secured bond of EUR 250 million carrying interest at 6.5% and repayable in 2020.

APT is considering a new product line that would require initial investment in machinery and working capital totalling EUR 500 million. The residual value of the machinery and working capital is expected to be EUR 170 million in total at the end of the project. Net annual cash flows for the proposed project, after tax, for the five years of the project are forecast as follows:

Year	1	2	3 - 5
Net after tax cash flows (EUR million)	70	100	115

50% of the new capital required would be raised by a loan from a banking consortium. This loan would carry interest at 7% and a floating charge on the project's assets. The duration of the borrowing would match the duration of the investment, with the full amount of the borrowing repayable at the end of the five year term. APT has sufficient cash to fund the other 50% of the capital expenditure.

The proposed project is in a market which has a different risk profile from APT's current operations. YYY is a company that operates exclusively in this market. YYY's market capitalisation is currently EUR 660 million and it has EUR 250 million of outstanding debt.

Other information:

1   APT's current weighted average cost of capital (WACC) is 11%.

2   Equity betas for APT and YYY are 1.6 and 1.3 respectively. The risk free rate of return and market rate of return are expected to be 4.5% and 9.5% respectively for the foreseeable future.

3   Assume both APT and YYY have a debt beta of 0.2.

4   The market value of APT's bond can be assumed to be the same as its face value.

5   All initial capital expenditure occurs at the beginning of the project. Assume all other cash flows occur at the end of each year.

6   The corporate income tax rate applicable to the taxable profits of both APT and YYY is 28%. Tax is paid at the end of the year in which the taxable profit arises. There are no tax depreciation allowances available for the investment in machinery.

Required

(a)   **Calculate** the Net Present Value (NPV) of the project being considered by APT at the following discount rates:

    (i)   APT's current weighted average cost of capital (WACC). **(3 marks)**

    (ii)   A project specific risk adjusted discount rate based on the gearing of the project. **(8 marks)**

(b)   **Calculate** the Adjusted Present Value (APV) of the project being considered by APT. **(6 marks)**

(c)   **Advise** APT on the appropriateness of each of the valuation methods used in (a) and (b) above to value this project. **(8 marks)**

(Total = 25 marks)

Answers

DO NOT TURN THIS PAGE UNTIL YOU HAVE
COMPLETED MOCK EXAM 3

528

Plan of attack

We know you've been told to do it at least 100 times and we know if we asked you you'd know that you should do it. So why don't you do it in an exam? 'Do what in an exam?' you're probably thinking. Well, let's tell you for the 101st time. **Take a good look through the paper before diving in to answer questions.**

First things first

What you must do in the first five or ten minutes of the exam is **look through the paper** in detail, working out **which questions to do** and the **order** in which to attempt them. So turn back to the paper and let's sort out a plan of attack.

We then recommend you spend the remaining time analysing the requirements of Question 1 and highlighting the key issues in the question. The extra time spent on (a) will be helpful, whenever you intend to do the question, If you decide to do it first, you will be well into the question when the writing time starts. If you intend to do it second or third, probably because you find it daunting, the question will look easier when you come to back to it, because your initial analysis should generate further points whilst you're tackling the other questions.

The next step

You're probably either thinking that you don't know where to begin or that you could have a very decent go at all the questions.

Option 1 (if you don't know where to begin)

If you are a bit **worried** about the paper, it's likely that you believe that case study **Question 1** looks daunting. We therefore recommend that you do one or both of the optional questions before tackling the case study. Don't however fall into the trap of going over time on the optional questions because they seem easier. You will need to spend half the time available on the case study.

- **Question 2** deals with financial objectives and their achievement. This is a good question for you to do if you prefer discussion type questions to calculation-based ones.

- **Question 3** is a question on forecasting, which offers some quite straightforward calculations to build your confidence. The question is broken down quite nicely into manageable sections and sub-sections so you should be able to pick up some quite easy marks. However if you are not confident about forecasting you should probably avoid this question.

- **Question 4** is an investment appraisal question. You should be able to have a good attempt at all of the calculations as they are not too complex. The discussion in part (c) should also offer some marks for some straightforward observations about the methods used.

- There are actually quite a few marks that you can pick up quite easily in **Question 1**, particularly in part (b)(i) if you are familiar with valuation techniques.   The net assets valuation method is quite easy and should give you a couple of marks. Part (a) is basically textbook knowledge and you should be able to make some sensible comments in parts (b)(ii) and (iii) to pick up some marks. For part (b)(iv) ensure your conclusion is supported by your earlier work. Remember you will be marked on your comments based on your own results so don't worry if you make mistakes in the valuation section. Part (c) is harder, but it should still be possible to pick up some marks, even if you are not sure how the tender offers works.

Option 2 (if you're thinking 'I can do all of these')

It never pays to be over confident but if you're not quaking in your shoes about the exam then **turn straight to compulsory Question 1**. You've got to do it so you might as well get it over and done with.

Once you've done the compulsory question, choose two of the questions in Section B.

- **Question 2** is a good question if you are confident about financial management decisions and how they might conflict with each other. However, don't get carried away with one section at the expense of other parts of the question.

- **Question 3** is quite a straightforward question if you are comfortable with forecasting as there are numerous easy marks to pick up. Remember to make your answer to part (b)(ii) relevant to the scenario for each of the groups.

- **Question 4** should allow you to pick up a number of calculation marks in parts (a) and (b). You should be familiar with DCF calculations using each of the approaches required. However don't forget the marks available for discussion in part (c).

No matter how many times we remind you...

Always, always **allocate your time** according to the marks for the question in total and for the parts of the questions. And always, always **follow the requirements exactly**.

You've got free time at the end of the exam.....?

If you have allocated your time properly then you **shouldn't have time on your hands** at the end of the exam. If you find yourself with five or ten minutes spare, however, go back to **any parts of questions that you didn't finish** because you ran out of time.

Forget about it!

And don't worry if you found the paper difficult. More then likely other students would too. If this were the real thing you would need to forget the exam the minute you leave the exam hall and **think about the next one**. Or, if it's the last one, **celebrate!**

Question 1

Text references. IPOs are covered in Chapter 5. Business valuations are covered in Chapter 15.

Top tips. As always, make sure you maximise your chances of gaining the presentation marks by structuring your answer as a report and making it as easy to follow as possible.

Part (b)(i) is worth 13 marks. Therefore you should expect to perform a number of calculations and use each of the main valuation techniques. This requires you to work out which types of valuation are possible. Hopefully you can see that apart from the net assets and P/E ratio valuations it is also possible to do a DCF valuation too. Whilst the calculations are numerous you should hopefully not find them too difficult if you have revised this area thoroughly. In part (b) (ii) it is important to ensure your answer relates to the scenario rather than being a generic list of weaknesses of each method.

Part (b)(iii) requires you to think of the types of intangible asset that may exist within V. Typically within service industries these lie in the existing staff and with customer goodwill.

Part (c) may seem unusual, but can offer some easy marks, even if you have struggled with the rest of the question. The key is understanding what the tender bid means. At any given price the number of shares requested at that price and at **higher** prices can be sold.

Easy marks. Part (a) should provide some easy marks as it is textbook knowledge.

REPORT

To: Board of Directors, V

From: Finance Director

Date: 22 November 2012

Re: IPO considerations

Introduction

This report focuses on the proposed IPO by tender of V.

It initially briefly covers the role of the appointed Investment Bank in an IPO by tender bid.

The report also calculates a range of possible values for the equity of V and discusses how appropriate each of the valuation approaches is to the company. There is also separate consideration of the intangible assets of V and their impact on the equity value. This is followed by an analysis of whether the previously suggested target price for the IPO of SK$3.40 was set at a reasonable level.

Finally the report considers the implications of the two pricing strategies suggested as a result of the receipt of the tender offers.

> **Tutorial note**. The following information forms the solution to part (a).

In this case, the appointed Investment Bank will act as the **issuing house**. The IPO will entail the acquisition by the Investment Bank of the 23 million shares of V to be issued, with a view to offering them for sale to the public. The Investment Bank will typically advising on the process involved, an appropriate issue price, stock exchange requirements and whether any other specialists should be appointed. The Bank will also hap to draw up the prospectus and could also underwrite the offer.

The Investment Bank then publishes an invitation to the public to apply for shares on a tender basis. The issuing house accepts responsibility to the public, and gives the support of its own reputation and standing to the issue. The Investment Bank will then typically allot the available shares at the **highest price** at which they will all be taken up. This is known as the **striking price**. In our case we were looking for a target price of SK$3.40.

> **Tutorial note**. The following information forms the solution to part (b)(i).

This section of the report uses various valuation techniques to estimate the value of the equity of V as at 30 June 2012.

Net assets basis

	SK$m
Statement of financial position value of equity	75
Adjustment for market of non-current assets (150 – 123)	27
Net asset value	**102**

With 90 million shares this is a value per share of SK$1.13 per share.

P/E basis (earnings valuation)

A summary of valuations using P/E ratios are shown below. These value have been calculated using the industry range of P/E ratios from 11 to 14 and the June 2012 earnings figure of SK$24 million. These have also been shown with a non-marketability discount of one-third, as V is not currently a listed company. Workings can be found in Appendix 1 to this report.

P/E ratio	Total equity value SK$m	Value per share SK$
11	264	2.93
7.33	176	1.96
14	336	3.73
9.33	224	2.49

Discounted free cash flow valuations

To value the equity, a cost of equity needs to be calculated using the CAPM formula. The cost of equity is calculated as 9.6% but rounded to 10% for easier working. The calculation can be found in Appendix 2.

Two discounted cash flow valuations are shown here for comparison, one assuming that expansion does not occur and growth continues at 2%. The second valuation assumes expansion occurs and builds in the growth rates expected from the expansion.

With no expansion the equity of V is valued at SK$281m with a value per share of SK$3.12.

With expansion, the equity is valued at SK$395m with a value per share of SK$4.39.

See Appendix 2 for full calculations

Dividend valuation

Using the current dividend of SK$19.2m (80% of 2012 earnings) and applying a growth rate of 2% gives a dividend valuation of 19.2m × (1.02 / 0.096 – 0.02) = SK$258 million

Summary of valuations

	Total value SK$m	Value per share SK$
Net assets basis	102	1.13
P/E ratio 11	264	2.93
P/E ratio 11 with discount	176	1.96
P/E ratio 14	336	3.73
P/E ratio 14 with discount	224	2.49
DCF no expansion	281	3.12
DCF with expansion	395	4.39
Dividend	258	2.87

> **Tutorial note.** The following information forms the solution to part (b)(ii).

Appropriateness of each of the valuation methods used

Net assets method

This method gives the price that V's shareholders would receive if the company stopped trading and the assets were sold off.

However this method is not appropriate when the business will continue as a **going concern**. It is based on market values of non-current assets whereas it is assumed that the acquiring company intends to keep these assets within the business to generate future revenue.

Another issue with this method is that it does not include the **value of intangible assets**, such as the brand name and customer goodwill associated with V. The value of the equity of V is thus underestimated.

Earnings valuation method based on P/E ratios

Historic earnings figures from a single year have been used in this valuation. This may not be a good representation of sustainable future earnings. However, growth has been steady at 2% of after-tax cash flows over the past few years, so it could be argued that this is a **sustainable figure**.

Both the upper and lower P/E ratios from the industry range have been used to obtain valuations as well as including a non-marketability discount to take into account the fact that V is unlisted at the moment. There is a danger that the non-marketability discount is just an **arbitrary figure** that does not truly reflect the differences between V and the listed companies in the travel industry.

There is no indication of whether the higher or lower P/E ratio is more likely to apply to V. To gauge this further a detailed investigation into the risk profile of similar companies and comparison to V would be required.

DCF valuation method

This method is generally considered to be the most appropriate valuation technique as it is based on actual forecast **future cash flows** of the business. These cash flows have been discounted at V's cost of equity, which depends on an estimated beta value, which may not be accurate.

The DCF valuation taking into account assumes a growth rate of 5% from year 3 in perpetuity. In reality this would be very difficult to achieve and therefore this valuation is likely to **overstate** the value of V's equity.

Dividend valuation model

This model assumes constant growth in perpetuity which is unlikely and is not as detailed as the DCF approach, which provides a more realistic valuation, and therefore the DCF valuation is the preferred approach.

Tutorial note. The following information forms the solution to part (b)(iii).

As alluded to above when discussing the net assets valuation method, V has some intangible assets that are not included in the equity valuation. One of these intangibles is the strength of the **brand**, although this only has value in the areas in which V currently operates. It is believed that customers value our friendly, direct personal service. This is also known as **customer goodwill** and means that the same customers will always use V to book their holidays. A further intangible could be in the **knowledge and expertise** of V's branch staff, particularly as staff turnover is low. Similarly the reputation of the holiday reps and other support services can enhance the value of the brand. These intangible assets are **difficult to quantify**, but it is thought they add significant value to the business.

When setting a target price, it may not be possible to factor the full perceived value of the intangible assets into the price as these intangibles are not necessarily visible to the buying public, particularly if they are institutional investors, who may not have heard of V before due to its relatively small size. It is also true that the value of a brand can be damaged quickly due to adverse publicity, which adds **risk and uncertainty** to the true value of the company.

Tutorial note. The following information forms the solution to part (b)(iv).

Looking at the range of valuations calculated in part (b)(i), only **two of the seven valuation methods** give a value per share above the target value of SK$3.40. Of these two, the discounted cash flow assumes that 5% growth can be maintained from year 3 in perpetuity. Prospective shareholders may not be convinced by this – the results of the tender offer would suggest this is the case. The other valuation of more than SK$3.40 is based on V being at the higher end of the P/E ratio range. An average of the valuation using P/E ratios of 11 and 14 suggests that around SK$3.30 may be more realistic, but this does not take into account any effect of V not being a listed company.

From the evaluation, it appears that SK$3.40 was probably **too optimistic** a target price to set for the IPO. Perhaps a figure closer to the DCF valuation with no expansion of SK$3.12 would be **more realistic**.

Tutorial note. The following information forms the solution to part (c).

Following the results of the tender process, there are two pricing strategies being considered. Selling at the original target price and leaving the offer undersubscribed or setting the price at the highest level where the shares can be sold. These are referred to as strategy A and strategy B respectively.

Strategy A

From a **personal level** this may appeal to the directors as 15m shares can be sold at this price, to anyone who requested shares at a tender price of SK$3.40 or above. The directors' shares to be sold total 13 million and as these take priority in the sale over new issues these will all be sold. The directors will have increased their personal wealth by SK$0.30 per share over strategy B (see below for calculation). In the case of the Executive Chairman this would mean SK$2.4 million from the sale of his shares, which may be important if he has plans for his retirement.

In an undersubscribed share issue, the new shareholders will find that they have a bigger percentage stake in the company than they were expecting. This may seem attractive and may mean a **greater total dividend** income than would have been the case if all the shares were subscribed.

However, as all the directors will continue to hold a significant stake in V they should look past this short-term gain and look at what is best for the business. Having such an undersubscribed IPO may **damage the reputation** of V, which could cause the share price to fall and **reduce existing shareholder wealth** too. In any case the market is likely to decide that the shares were overpriced and the share price will fall. This will also affect the new shareholders as their shares would be worth less than they paid for them. This may cause a problem for any directors who are looking to sell more shares at a later date as the share price could be significantly lower.

This strategy will mean that the company only sells 2 million shares, as the directors' sales take priority. Selling 2 million share at SK$3.40 would raise SK$6.8 million, which is significantly less than the expansion cost of SK$50 million. Although the IPO is only going to partly fund the expansion it is likely that this is well below the amount needed to be raised by the IPO. Indeed the expansion plan may be unable to proceed with this level of finance.

Strategy B

From the point of view of the directors, all except the Operations Director will have **realised some of their investment in V**, although at a lower price than under strategy A. The price will be the highest price at which the 23 million shares can be sold. This is calculated as follows

Price	No of shares (millions)	Cumulative total (millions)
3.60	4	4
3.50	5	9
3.40	6	15
3.30	3	18
3.20	3	21
3.10	2	23

This shows that the striking price is SK$3.10, as noted in the discussion of strategy A above. Although this is less than the strategy A amount the shareholders will **still be able to sell their shares**.

The market will then judge whether the shares are issued at a fair price. The results of the tender show that SK$3.10 per share is more likely to be considered fair than SK$3.40. This reduces the likelihood of the share price falling immediately after the IPO. A stable share price would indicate **market confidence** in V.

Selling 10 million new shares at SK$3.10 would raise SK$31 million, although V will receive SK$3 million less than if the target offer was fully subscribed so there may still be a funding gap, however it would be a **significantly lower gap** than under strategy A.

Under this strategy there will be more new public shareholders than under strategy A, with each receiving their expected stake in V.

If you have any questions about the contents of this report, please do not hesitate to contact me.

Appendices

(1) P/E valuations

The earnings value used is the profit after tax figure for the year ended 30 June 2012 of $24 million.

P/E		Earnings	Total equity value SK$m	Value per share SK$
11		24	264	2.93
7.33	(11 × 2/3)	24	176	1.96
14		24	336	3.73
9.33	(14 × 2/3)	24	224	2.49

Note there are 90 million shares currently in issue, which is the figure used in the value per share calculations.

(2) Discounted cash flow valuations

k_e using CAPM

k_e = 2% + 1.9(6% – 2%) = 9.6% say 10%

Assuming no expansion

The cash flow from the year ended 30 June 2012 is the profit after tax plus the depreciation less the capex

Cash flow = 24 + 3 – 5 = SK$22m

This is expected to grow at 2% in perpetuity.

Therefore the present value of the cash flows is given by

PV = $CF_1/(k_e – g)$ = (22 × 1.02)/(0.10 – 0.02) = SK$281m

281/90 = SK$3.12 per share.

With expansion

As above the base cash flow is SK$22m. This grows at 3% for two years and then 5% in perpetuity.

Time	0 SK$m	1 SK$m	2 SK$m	3+ SK$m
Operating cash flows (W1)		22.66	23.34	24.51
Initial investment	(50.00)			
Annuity factor (W2)				20
Discount factor (10%)	1.000	0.909	0.826	0.826
DCF	(50.00)	20.60	19.28	404.91

PV = SK$395m

395/90 = SK$4.39

Note: the 90 million existing shares have been used in the value per share calculation as it is not known at this stage how many shares will be in issue following the IPO.

Workings

1 Time 1 cash flows = 22m × 1.03 = 22.66m

Time 2 cash flows = 22.66m × 1.03 = 23.34m

Time 3 cash flows = 23.34m × 1.05 = 24.51m

2 Annuity factor = 1/(0.1 – 0.05) = 20

BPP
LEARNING MEDIA

Question 2

(a)   Economic variables

The main economic variable that will affect BBD is the **exchange rate**. As a Canadian company it is assumed that the majority of BBD's cash flows, and its financial reporting, are in Canadian dollars, but the wholesale price of gas is in US dollars. Therefore any change in the US dollar to Canadian dollar exchange rate will affect revenue for BBD.

If the Canadian dollar **weakens**, the Canadian dollar value of the sale of gas will be higher and therefore profits will increase, assuming all other costs remain the same.

Market prices

The market price of wholesale gas will fluctuate as a result of global **demand and supply**. Demand for gas may be seasonal in some parts of the world, so it may depend on which countries buy from BBD as to whether demand may be a factor in changing the price. If a significant new supply of gas is found, such as from increased use of fracking, this should mean that the wholesale price will fall. A significant change in market prices may affect BBD's future earnings on which the debt finance is based.

External constraints

There are a number of **environmental concerns** about the use of fracking. Public outcry over this issue may force the Government to act, so the profitability of BBD could be reduced if the Canadian Government decides to **ban** or **restrict** fracking due to these concerns.

There is also a risk of loss as a result of legal action for damage to property caused by fracking.

(b)   (i)   A credit downgrade would have a number of effects on BBD. The **creditworthiness** of BBD would be seen as being lower. Therefore any provider of new debt would seek a higher return than at present. Alternatively existing debt may not be able to be renewed on the same terms. This would increase BBD's overall cost of debt.

The change in creditworthiness may also influence suppliers to impose **shorter credit terms** on BBD.

Some customers may view the credit downgrade as a signal that BBD is performing badly and may start looking at **alternative suppliers** for their gas.

Shareholders may be similarly concerned about the credit downgrade and may start selling their shares and cause the share price of BBD to fall.

This signalling effect could even affect **employees**, who may seek alternative employment.

(ii)   Response A - Cancel the project

Advantages

This should mean than BBD **avoids the credit downgrade** and the associated implications discussed in part (b) (i).

This option means that BBD will maintain **public goodwill** and may be seen as a company that cares about the environment.

Disadvantages

The major disadvantage of this approach is that there is **no increase in shareholder wealth** that would come from the fracking project. Given that the majority of shares are owned by institutions such as pension funds they are more likely to be concerned about **financial returns** than environmental matters. In addition investors may be expecting BBD to invest in alternative extraction methods, given the limited supplies using traditional extraction methods.

Response B – Proceed with the project

Advantages

The **increase in shareholder wealth** associated with the project will be realised if the project goes ahead.

Disadvantages

If the credit downgrade occurs, the **debt finance may not be available** for the project to take place.

Any additional financing is likely to be **more expensive** than if the project did not occur.

There may be significant **adverse publicity** arising from the fracking operations.

Response C – Cancel the current year dividend to fund the project

Advantages

According to Modigliani and Miller, it is **irrelevant** whether a company retains earnings for investment or pays them out as dividends. Therefore this method of avoiding the credit downgrade is attractive. The Modigliani and Miller theory is often thought not to apply in the real world where dividends are often seen as having a **signalling effect**. However if the move is explained to the shareholders fully then they may be happy. Also shareholders may be concerned about the increased interest burden if debt is used, which may impact earnings per share and also future dividends.

Disadvantages

The majority of shareholders are **institutional investors**, who may prefer a stable dividend income to potential capital growth from the project.

(iii) It is recommended that BBD **proceeds with the project** as this will increase shareholder wealth. The preferred option to do this would be option C as it would avoid the risk associated with the credit downgrade. However, it is not known whether it would also be possible to reduce the dividend, so that there is still an amount payable to shareholders and also enough to fund the project. This would be an even better option.

> **Note:** The above answer is based on the assumption that a company specialising in extracting gas is unlikely to abandon a project on environmental grounds. It is possible to justify any of the three strategies as long as it is backed by a good supporting argument.

Question 3

Text references. Forecasting is dealt with in Chapter 3 and equity finance is covered in Chapter 5.

Top tips. In part (a) take the PBIT figure given and work through the interest and tax charges under each scenario. A layout like the answer below should help here.

In part (b)(i) don't forget to comment on what each strategy means for each individual objective.

In part (b)(ii) it is important to ensure your comments relate to the scenario.

Easy marks. The forecasts in part (a) are fairly straightforward.

(a)   Forecast income statement

	Strategy 1 £m		Strategy 2 £m	
PBIT	650.0		650.0	
Interest	(87.5)	1,250 at 7%	(87.5)	1,250 at 7%
	(75.0)	1,250 at 6%		
PBT	487.5		562.5	
Tax at 30%	(146.3)		(168.8)	
PAT	341.2		393.7	
Dividends	119.4	35% of PAT	137.8	35% of PAT
Retained earnings	221.8		255.9	

Forecast debt and equity schedule

	Strategy 1 £m		Strategy 2 £m	
Debt	2,500.0		1,250.0	
Equity	2,050.0	b/f	2,050.0	b/f
	221.8	retained	255.9	retained
			1,250.0	Rights issue
	2,271.8		3,555.9	

(b)   (i)   Gearing at 50% or less

From the calculations in part (a) gearing can be calculated as

Strategy 1:   2,500/(2,500 + 2,271.8) = 52.4%

Strategy 2:   1,250/(1,250 + 3,555.9) = 26.0%

This shows that strategy 2 would mean than XRG would be meeting its gearing objective, but strategy 1 would not. However, it should be noted that strategy 1 is closer to the objective than the predicted ratio at the end of the current year which is 54.9% (2,500/(2,500 + 2,050)). Strategy 1 may be consider too high risk, but on the other hand Strategy 2 could be considered to be too low with not enough advantage being taken of valuable tax relief.

Earnings per share of £0.30

The number of existing shares = £500m/£0.50 = 1,000m

The number of shares to be issued in the rights issue can be calculated as follows

£3.33 × 0.75 = £2.4975 say £2.50

To raise £1,250 million this will need 500 million shares (a 1 for 2 issue).

From the calculations in part (a) earnings per share can be calculated as

	Strategy 1	Strategy 2
Earnings (£m)	341.2	393.7
Number of shares (m)	1,000	1,500
EPS (£)	0.341	0.262

Strategy 1 would allow XRG to fulfil its earnings per share objective but Strategy 2 would not. This is because increased earnings need to be shared amongst more shares under Strategy 2.

Dividend per share of £0.10

From the calculations in part (a), and above, dividend per share can be calculated as

	Strategy 1	Strategy 2
Dividends (£m)	119.4	138.7
Number of shares (m)	1,000	1,500
Dividend per share (£)	0.119	0.092

Strategy 1 would allow XRG to fulfil its dividend per share objective but Strategy 2 would not. As above this is because increased earnings (and therefore higher dividends) need to be shared amongst more shares under Strategy 2.

(ii)   Debt providers

Under strategy 1 there is exactly the **same risk** to the providers of debt finance as there is currently, since the debt being renegotiated is secured on the non-current assets of XRG.

Under strategy 2 there is less debt, but it is unsecured and therefore carries greater risk than the secured debt. Therefore the providers of debt finance will have less risk, but not significantly less.

Shareholders

Shareholders may be concerned that strategy 1 is risky because the level of gearing would be significantly **above the industry average** of 40%. However, as noted above, it would be lower than the expected current gearing ratio, so it may be fair to assume that the existing shareholders are happy with this level of risk. This strategy does forecast higher earnings per share and dividend per share to compensate for this additional risk.

Although the rights issue in Strategy 2 should make no difference to shareholder wealth, it will cause the share price to fall. The TERP would be:

No of shares	Price	Total value £m
1,000m	£3.33	3,330
500m	£2.50	1,250
1,500m		4,580

TERP = 4,580/1,500 = £3.05.

However, this price is only theoretical. If the rights issue was perceived badly by the market the share-price could fall even further.

In addition the shareholders would need to be convinced to take up the rights in the first place. Shareholders who take up their rights, stand to receive higher total dividends, as these shareholders will own 50% more shares than they currently do, despite the lower dividend per share.

Strategy 2 would also reduce the gearing of XRG, which may lower the shareholders' required return (the cost of equity).

Question 4

Text references. Investment appraisal is dealt with in Chapter 11. Project specific cost of capital is covered in Chapter 9 and APV in Chapter 13.

Top tips. In (a)(ii) there is a debt beta given. This means that the parts of the ungearing and regearing formulae that are not normally used will be needed. Also note that when regearing you should use APT's funding for the specific project, not the company as a whole.

Part (b) contains a fairly straightforward APV calculation with only one financing benefit to calculate. Remember to discount at the pre-tax cost of debt though.

Part (c) is a discussion of the strengths and weaknesses of the various methods in the context of this scenario.

Easy marks. There are easy marks to be picked up in part (a)(i) as all the information used is given in the question.

(a)   (i)

Time	0	1	2	3	4	5
	EUR m	EUR m	EUR m	EUR m	EUR m	EUR m
After tax cash flows	(500.0)	70.0	100.0	115.0	115.0	115.0
Residual value of machinery						170.0
Total cash flows	(500.0)	70.0	100.0	115.0	115.0	285.0
Discount factor (11%)	1.000	0.901	0.812	0.731	0.659	0.593
DCF	(500.0)	63.1	81.2	84.1	75.8	169.0

NPV = EUR (26.8)m

The project is unacceptable at the current WACC.

(ii)   Ungearing YYY's beta

YYY's geared beta = 1.3

Using the formula

$$\beta_u = \beta_g \left[\frac{V_E}{V_E + V_D(1-t)} \right] + \beta_d \left[\frac{V_D(1-t)}{V_E + V_D(1-t)} \right]$$

β_u = 1.3[660/660 + 250(1 − 0.28)] + 0.2[250(1 − 0.28)/660 + 250(1 − 0.28)]

β_u = 1.021 + 0.043 = 1.064

Regearing for APT (project funding 50% debt and 50% equity)

Using the formula

$$\beta_g = \beta_u + (\beta_u - \beta_d)\frac{V_D(1-t)}{V_E}$$

β_g = 1.064 + (1.064 − 0.2)[250(1 − 0.28)/250] = 1.687

Cost of equity using CAPM

k_e = 4.5% + 1.687 (9.5% − 4.5%) = 12.94%

k_d = 7% on new borrowings (NB this is pre-tax)

Adjusted WACC (using project funding 50% debt and 50% equity)

WACC = 0.5 × 12.94% + 0.5 × 7% × (1 – 0.28) = 8.99% say 9%

Time	0	1	2	3	4	5
	EUR m	EUR m	EUR m	EUR m	EUR m	EUR m
After tax cash flows	(500.0)	70.0	100.0	115.0	115.0	115.0
Residual value of machinery						170.0
Total cash flows	(500.0)	70.0	100.0	115.0	115.0	285.0
Discount factor (9%)	1.000	0.917	0.842	0.772	0.708	0.650
DCF	(500.0)	64.2	84.2	88.8	81.4	185.3

NPV = EUR 3.9m

The project is acceptable at the project specific discount rate.

(b)   Base case scenario as if all equity funded

The ungeared cost of equity can be calculated using the ungeared beta calculated earlier and CAPM

k_{eu} = 4.5% + 1.064 × (9.5% – 4.5%) = 9.82% say 10%

Time	0	1	2	3	4	5
	EUR m	EUR m	EUR m	EUR m	EUR m	EUR m
After tax cash flows	(500.0)	70.0	100.0	115.0	115.0	115.0
Residual value of machinery						170.0
Total cash flows	(500.0)	70.0	100.0	115.0	115.0	285.0
Discount factor (10%)	1.000	0.909	0.826	0.751	0.683	0.621
DCF	(500.0)	63.6	82.6	86.4	78.5	177.0

NPV = EUR (11.9)m

Adjustment for tax relief on debt (using pre-tax cost of debt)

Annual interest on borrowing = 250m × 7% = 17.5m

Annual tax relief on interest = 17.5m × 0.28 = 4.9m

Present value of annuity 7% years 1 to 5 = 4.9m × 4.100 = 20.1m

APV

(11.9)m + 20.1m = EUR 8.2m

The project is acceptable.

(c)   Using existing WACC

The use of WACC as a discount rate is only suitable where, business and financial risk remain unchanged, the project is small relative to the size of the company and there are no special financing issues such as subsidised loans. The existing WACC is calculated based on APT's **existing business and financial risk**. The current level of gearing of APT is 17% (250/(250 +1,200)). This would increase significantly with the borrowing required to fund the project and therefore **financial risk** would increase. However it should be noted that the change in financial risk will only be for the length of the project, which is 5 years.

Because the project is in a different area from APT's current operations their business risk will also change. The equity betas of APT and YYY suggest that this new area is **less risky**.

Given that financial risk and business risk are different for the new project it is inappropriate to use the existing WACC as the discount rate.

Using project specific rate

A project specific rate can be calculated by using an equity beta from a proxy company to strip out the financial risk and then regearing using the capital structure of the project. A project specific rate does take into account the business risk and the financing structure of the **project**. As a result it deals with the issues arising from using WACC.

It could be argued that it may overstate financial risk in this case as it is calculated on a 50% debt and 50% equity split, but APT overall has significantly more equity and therefore financial risk for APT will be

lower. However, it could also be argued that this builds in a degree of **prudence** into the analysis. However it does not take into account the post investment gearing of the **company** This could not be done without knowing the NPV of the project, which could not be calculated without a post investment WACC. This cyclical problem can be dealt with by the use of APV.

<u>Using APV</u>

The APV method does take into account the effect of the change in capital structure by including the value of the **tax shield** in the analysis. However, the difficulties with this method are in the identification and calculation of each of the discount rates used in the analysis, particularly with the ungeared cost of equity.

APV is more useful where there is a long-term change in the capital structure, which is not the case here, therefore APV should not be used as the primary measure for this investment decision.

<u>Conclusion</u>

In conclusion it is recommended that the project-specific discount rate is the best method to use in these circumstances.

MATHEMATICAL TABLES AND EXAM FORMULAE

MATHS TABLES AND FORMULAE

Present value table

Present value of 1.00 unit of currency ie $(1+r)^{-n}$ where r = interest rate, n = number of periods until payment or receipt.

Periods (n)	1%	2%	3%	4%	5%	6%	7%	8%	9%	10%
1	0.990	0.980	0.971	0.962	0.952	0.943	0.935	0.926	0.917	0.909
2	0.980	0.961	0.943	0.925	0.907	0.890	0.873	0.857	0.842	0.826
3	0.971	0.942	0.915	0.889	0.864	0.840	0.816	0.794	0.772	0.751
4	0.961	0.924	0.888	0.855	0.823	0.792	0.763	0.735	0.708	0.683
5	0.951	0.906	0.863	0.822	0.784	0.747	0.713	0.681	0.650	0.621
6	0.942	0.888	0.837	0.790	0.746	0.705	0.666	0.630	0.596	0.564
7	0.933	0.871	0.813	0.760	0.711	0.665	0.623	0.583	0.547	0.513
8	0.923	0.853	0.789	0.731	0.677	0.627	0.582	0.540	0.502	0.467
9	0.914	0.837	0.766	0.703	0.645	0.592	0.544	0.500	0.460	0.424
10	0.905	0.820	0.744	0.676	0.614	0.558	0.508	0.463	0.422	0.386
11	0.896	0.804	0.722	0.650	0.585	0.527	0.475	0.429	0.388	0.350
12	0.887	0.788	0.701	0.625	0.557	0.497	0.444	0.397	0.356	0.319
13	0.879	0.773	0.681	0.601	0.530	0.469	0.415	0.368	0.326	0.290
14	0.870	0.758	0.661	0.577	0.505	0.442	0.388	0.340	0.299	0.263
15	0.861	0.743	0.642	0.555	0.481	0.417	0.362	0.315	0.275	0.239
16	0.853	0.728	0.623	0.534	0.458	0.394	0.339	0.292	0.252	0.218
17	0.844	0.714	0.605	0.513	0.436	0.371	0.317	0.270	0.231	0.198
18	0.836	0.700	0.587	0.494	0.416	0.350	0.296	0.250	0.212	0.180
19	0.828	0.686	0.570	0.475	0.396	0.331	0.277	0.232	0.194	0.164
20	0.820	0.673	0.554	0.456	0.377	0.312	0.258	0.215	0.178	0.149

Interest rates (r)

Periods (n)	11%	12%	13%	14%	15%	16%	17%	18%	19%	20%
1	0.901	0.893	0.885	0.877	0.870	0.862	0.855	0.847	0.840	0.833
2	0.812	0.797	0.783	0.769	0.756	0.743	0.731	0.718	0.706	0.694
3	0.731	0.712	0.693	0.675	0.658	0.641	0.624	0.609	0.593	0.579
4	0.659	0.636	0.613	0.592	0.572	0.552	0.534	0.516	0.499	0.482
5	0.593	0.567	0.543	0.519	0.497	0.476	0.456	0.437	0.419	0.402
6	0.535	0.507	0.480	0.456	0.432	0.410	0.390	0.370	0.352	0.335
7	0.482	0.452	0.425	0.400	0.376	0.354	0.333	0.314	0.296	0.279
8	0.434	0.404	0.376	0.351	0.327	0.305	0.285	0.266	0.249	0.233
9	0.391	0.361	0.333	0.308	0.284	0.263	0.243	0.225	0.209	0.194
10	0.352	0.322	0.295	0.270	0.247	0.227	0.208	0.191	0.176	0.162
11	0.317	0.287	0.261	0.237	0.215	0.195	0.178	0.162	0.148	0.135
12	0.286	0.257	0.231	0.208	0.187	0.168	0.152	0.137	0.124	0.112
13	0.258	0.229	0.204	0.182	0.163	0.145	0.130	0.116	0.104	0.093
14	0.232	0.205	0.181	0.160	0.141	0.125	0.111	0.099	0.088	0.078
15	0.209	0.183	0.160	0.140	0.123	0.108	0.095	0.084	0.074	0.065
16	0.188	0.163	0.141	0.123	0.107	0.093	0.081	0.071	0.062	0.054
17	0.170	0.146	0.125	0.108	0.093	0.080	0.069	0.060	0.052	0.045
18	0.153	0.130	0.111	0.095	0.081	0.069	0.059	0.051	0.044	0.038
19	0.138	0.116	0.098	0.083	0.070	0.060	0.051	0.043	0.037	0.031
20	0.124	0.104	0.087	0.073	0.061	0.051	0.043	0.037	0.031	0.026

Cumulative present value of 1.00 unit of currency per annum

Receivable or Payable at the end of each year for n years $\left[\dfrac{1-(1+r)^{-n}}{r}\right]$

Periods (n)	Interest rates (r)									
	1%	2%	3%	4%	5%	6%	7%	8%	9%	10%
1	0.990	0.980	0.971	0.962	0.952	0.943	0.935	0.926	0.917	0.909
2	1.970	1.942	1.913	1.886	1.859	1.833	1.808	1.783	1.759	1.736
3	2.941	2.884	2.829	2.775	2.723	2.673	2.624	2.577	2.531	2.487
4	3.902	3.808	3.717	3.630	3.546	3.465	3.387	3.312	3.240	3.170
5	4.853	4.713	4.580	4.452	4.329	4.212	4.100	3.993	3.890	3.791
6	5.795	5.601	5.417	5.242	5.076	4.917	4.767	4.623	4.486	4.355
7	6.728	6.472	6.230	6.002	5.786	5.582	5.389	5.206	5.033	4.868
8	7.652	7.325	7.020	6.733	6.463	6.210	5.971	5.747	5.535	5.335
9	8.566	8.162	7.786	7.435	7.108	6.802	6.515	6.247	5.995	5.759
10	9.471	8.983	8.530	8.111	7.722	7.360	7.024	6.710	6.418	6.145
11	10.368	9.787	9.253	8.760	8.306	7.887	7.499	7.139	6.805	6.495
12	11.255	10.575	9.954	9.385	8.863	8.384	7.943	7.536	7.161	6.814
13	12.134	11.348	10.635	9.986	9.394	8.853	8.358	7.904	7.487	7.103
14	13.004	12.106	11.296	10.563	9.899	9.295	8.745	8.244	7.786	7.367
15	13.865	12.849	11.938	11.118	10.380	9.712	9.108	8.559	8.061	7.606
16	14.718	13.578	12.561	11.652	10.838	10.106	9.447	8.851	8.313	7.824
17	15.562	14.292	13.166	12.166	11.274	10.477	9.763	9.122	8.544	8.022
18	16.398	14.992	13.754	12.659	11.690	10.828	10.059	9.372	8.756	8.201
19	17.226	15.679	14.324	13.134	12.085	11.158	10.336	9.604	8.950	8.365
20	18.046	16.351	14.878	13.590	12.462	11.470	10.594	9.818	9.129	8.514

Periods (n)	Interest rates (r)									
	11%	12%	13%	14%	15%	16%	17%	18%	19%	20%
1	0.901	0.893	0.885	0.877	0.870	0.862	0.855	0.847	0.840	0.833
2	1.713	1.690	1.668	1.647	1.626	1.605	1.585	1.566	1.547	1.528
3	2.444	2.402	2.361	2.322	2.283	2.246	2.210	2.174	2.140	2.106
4	3.102	3.037	2.974	2.914	2.855	2.798	2.743	2.690	2.639	2.589
5	3.696	3.605	3.517	3.433	3.352	3.274	3.199	3.127	3.058	2.991
6	4.231	4.111	3.998	3.889	3.784	3.685	3.589	3.498	3.410	3.326
7	4.712	4.564	4.423	4.288	4.160	4.039	3.922	3.812	3.706	3.605
8	5.146	4.968	4.799	4.639	4.487	4.344	4.207	4.078	3.954	3.837
9	5.537	5.328	5.132	4.946	4.772	4.607	4.451	4.303	4.163	4.031
10	5.889	5.650	5.426	5.216	5.019	4.833	4.659	4.494	4.339	4.192
11	6.207	5.938	5.687	5.453	5.234	5.029	4.836	4.656	4.486	4.327
12	6.492	6.194	5.918	5.660	5.421	5.197	4.988	4.793	4.611	4.439
13	6.750	6.424	6.122	5.842	5.583	5.342	5.118	4.910	4.715	4.533
14	6.982	6.628	6.302	6.002	5.724	5.468	5.229	5.008	4.802	4.611
15	7.191	6.811	6.462	6.142	5.847	5.575	5.324	5.092	4.876	4.675
16	7.379	6.974	6.604	6.265	5.954	5.668	5.405	5.162	4.938	4.730
17	7.549	7.120	6.729	6.373	6.047	5.749	5.475	5.222	4.990	4.775
18	7.702	7.250	6.840	6.467	6.128	5.818	5.534	5.273	5.033	4.812
19	7.839	7.366	6.938	6.550	6.198	5.877	5.584	5.316	5.070	4.843
20	7.963	7.469	7.025	6.623	6.259	5.929	5.628	5.353	5.101	4.870

FORMULAE

Valuation models

(i)   Irredeemable preference shares, paying a constant annual dividend, d, in perpetuity, where P_0 is the ex-div value:

$$P_0 = \frac{d}{k_{pref}}$$

(ii)   Ordinary (equity) shares, paying a constant annual dividend, d, in perpetuity, where P_0 is the ex-div value:

$$P_0 = \frac{d}{k_e}$$

(iii)   Ordinary (equity) shares, paying an annual dividend, d, growing in perpetuity at a constant rate, g, where P_0 is the ex-div value:

$$P_0 = \frac{d_1}{k_e - g} \text{ or } P_0 = \frac{d_0[1 + g]}{k_e - g}$$

(iv)   Irredeemable bonds, paying annual after-tax interest, i [1 – t], in perpetuity, where P_0 is the ex-interest value:

$$P_0 = \frac{i[1 - t]}{k_{d\,net}}$$

or, without tax:

$$P_0 = \frac{i}{k_d}$$

(v)   Total value of the geared entity, V_g (based on MM):

$$V_g = V_u + TB$$

(vi)   Future value of S, of a sum X, invested for n periods, compounded at r% interest:

$$S = X[1 + r]^n$$

(vii)   Present value of 1·00 payable or receivable in n years, discounted at r% per annum:

$$PV = \frac{1}{[1 + r]^n}$$

(viii) Present value of an annuity of 1.00 per annum, receivable or payable for n years, commencing in one year, discounted at r% per annum:

$$PV = \frac{1}{r}\left[1 - \frac{1}{[1 + r]^n}\right]$$

(ix)   Present value of 1·00 per annum, payable or receivable in perpetuity, commencing in one year, discounted at r% per annum:

$$PV = \frac{1}{r}$$

(x)   Present value of 1·00 per annum, receivable or payable, commencing in one year, growing in perpetuity at a constant rate of g% per annum, discounted at r% per annum:

$$PV = \frac{1}{r - g}$$

Cost of capital

(i)   Cost of irredeemable preference shares, paying an annual dividend, d, in perpetuity, and having a current ex-div price P_0:

$$k_{pref} = \frac{d}{P_0}$$

(ii)   Cost of irredeemable bonds, paying annual net interest, i [1 − t], and having a current ex-interest price P_0:

$$k_{d\,net} = \frac{i[1 - t]}{P_0}$$

(iii)   Cost of ordinary (equity) shares, paying an annual dividend, d, in perpetuity, and having a current ex-div price P_0:

$$k_e = \frac{d}{P_0}$$

(iv)   Cost of ordinary (equity) shares, having a current ex-div price, P_0, having just paid a dividend, d_0, with the dividend growing in perpetuity by a constant g% per annum:

$$k_e = \frac{d_1}{P_0} + g \text{ or } k_e = \frac{d_0[1 + g]}{P_0} + g$$

(v)   Cost of ordinary (equity) shares, using the CAPM:

$$k_e = R_f + [R_m - R_f]\beta$$

(vi)   Cost of ordinary (equity) share capital in a geared entity :

$$k_{eg} = k_{eu} + [k_{eu} - k_d]\frac{V_D[1 - t]}{V_E}$$

(vii)   Weighted average cost of capital, k_0 or WACC

$$WACC = k_e \left[\frac{V_E}{V_E + V_D}\right] + k_d (1 - t) \left[\frac{V_D}{V_E + V_D}\right]$$

(viii)   Adjusted cost of capital (MM formula):

$$k_{adj} = k_{eu}[1 - tL] \text{ or } r^* = r[1 - T^*L]$$

(ix)   Ungear ß:

$$\beta_u = \beta_g \left[\frac{V_E}{V_E + V_D (1-t)}\right] + \beta_D \left[\frac{V_D (1 - t)}{V_E + V_D (1-t)}\right]$$

(x)   Regear ß:

$$\beta_g = \beta_{u +} (\beta_u - \beta_d) \frac{V_D(1 - t)}{V_E}$$

(xi)   Adjusted discount rate to use in international capital budgeting (International Fisher effect)

$$\frac{1 + \text{annual discount rate B\$}}{1 + \text{annual discount rate A\$}} = \frac{\text{Future spot rate A\$/B\$ in 12months' time}}{\text{Spot rate A\$/B\$}}$$

where A\$/B\$ is the number of B\$ to each A\$

Other formulae

(i) Expectations theory:

$$\text{Future spot rate A\$/B\$} = \text{Spot rate A\$/B\$} \times \frac{1 + \text{nominal country B interest rate}}{1 + \text{nominal country A interest rate}}$$

where:

A\$/B\$ is the number of B\$ to each A\$, and

A\$ is the currency of country A and B\$ is the currency of country B

(ii) Purchasing power parity (law of one price):

$$\text{Future spot rate A\$/B\$} = \text{Spot rate A\$/B\$} \times \frac{1 + \text{country B inflation rate}}{1 + \text{country A inflation rate}}$$

(iii) Link between nominal (money) and real interest rates:

[1 + nominal (money) rate] = [1 + real interest rate][1 + inflation rate]

(iv) Equivalent annual cost:

$$\text{Equivalent annual cost} = \frac{\text{PV of costs over n years}}{\text{n year annuity factor}}$$

(v) Theoretical ex-rights price:

$$\text{TERP} = \frac{1}{N+1}[(N \times \text{Cum rights price}) + \text{Issue price}]$$

(vi) Value of a right:

$$\text{Value of right} = \frac{\text{Theoretical ex rights price} - \text{Issue price}}{N}$$

where N = number of rights required to buy one share.

Review Form – Paper F3 Financial Strategy (01/13)

Name: _____   Address: _____
_____
_____

How have you used this Kit?
(Tick one box only)

☐ Home study (book only)
☐ On a course: college _____
☐ With 'correspondence' package
☐ Other _____

Why did you decide to purchase this Kit?
(Tick one box only)

☐ Have used the complementary Study text
☐ Have used other BPP products in the past
☐ Recommendation by friend/colleague
☐ Recommendation by a lecturer at college
☐ Saw advertising
☐ Other _____

During the past six months do you recall seeing/receiving any of the following?
(Tick as many boxes as are relevant)

☐ Our advertisement in *Student Accountant*
☐ Our advertisement in *Pass*
☐ Our advertisement in *PQ*
☐ Our brochure with a letter through the post
☐ Our website www.bpp.com

Which (if any) aspects of our advertising do you find useful?
(Tick as many boxes as are relevant)

☐ Prices and publication dates of new editions
☐ Information on product content
☐ Facility to order books off-the-page
☐ None of the above

Which BPP products have you used?

Text	☐	*Success CD*	☐	*Interactive Passcards*	☐
Kit	☑	*i-Pass*	☐	*Home Study Package*	☐
Passcard	☐	*Learn Online*	☐	*Home Study PLUS*	☐

Your ratings, comments and suggestions would be appreciated on the following areas.

	Very useful	Useful	Not useful
Passing F3	☐	☐	☐
Planning your question practice	☐	☐	☐
Questions	☐	☐	☐
Top Tips etc in answers	☐	☐	☐
Content and structure of answers	☐	☐	☐
'Plan of attack' in mock exams	☐	☐	☐
Mock exam answers	☐	☐	☐

Overall opinion of this Kit	Excellent ☐	Good ☐	Adequate ☐	Poor ☐

Do you intend to continue using BPP products?   Yes ☐   No ☐

The BPP author of this edition can be e-mailed at: andrewfinch@bpp.com

Please return this form to: Stephen Osborne, CIMA Publishing Manager, BPP Learning Media, FREEPOST, London, W12 8BR

Review Form (continued)

TELL US WHAT YOU THINK

Please note any further comments and suggestions/errors below.

Ghost Boy

Martin Pistorius
and
Megan Lloyd Davies

SIMON &
SCHUSTER

London · New York · Sydney · Toronto · New Delhi

A CBS COMPANY

First published in Great Britain by Simon & Schuster UK Ltd, 2011
This edition published in Great Britain by Simon & Schuster UK Ltd, 2012
A CBS COMPANY

Copyright © 2011 by Martin Pistorius and Megan Lloyd Davies

1 3 5 7 9 10 8 6 4 2

Simon & Schuster UK Ltd
1st Floor
222 Gray's Inn Road
London WC1X 8HB

www.simonandschuster.co.uk

Simon & Schuster Australia, Sydney
Simon & Schuster India, New Delhi

A CIP catalogue record for this book
is available from the British Library.

ISBN: 978-0-85720-333-5

Typeset by M Rules
Printed and bound by CPI Group (UK) Ltd, Croydon CR0 4YY

MARTIN PISTORIUS was born in Johannesburg, South Africa, in 1975. An unknown illness at the age of twelve left him wheelchair-bound and unable to speak, and he spent fourteen years in institutions. In 2001 he learned to communicate via computer, make friends and change his life. In 2008 he met the love of his life, Joanna, and emigrated to the UK. In 2009 they married and in 2010 he started his own business. He describes himself as a geek with a wicked sense of humour and a love of technology. He loves animals, is a keen photographer, enjoys watching cricket, Formula 1 Grand Prix and films, listening to music, spending time with friends and, most of all, being with his wife.

Praise for *Ghost Boy*

'It is a deeply affecting and at times shocking book ... *The Diving-Bell and the Butterfly* but with a happy ending' *Sunday Times*

'Deeply moving' *Mail on Sunday*

'Deeply affecting memoir' *Sunday Times Best Reads*

'[Pistorius's] levels of empathy are remarkable, perhaps because he was forced for so many years into the role of watcher and listener, hearing people unburden their problems around him, abs[...] ... [his] commun[...] [...]he way he confro[...]

'Martin tells the story of his remarkable recovery-and how he eventually came to find love, a home and a job . . . Now in a deeply moving – and ultimately uplifting – new book, Martin Pistorius tells the amazing story of life as the Ghost Boy' *Irish Mail*

'Incredible memoir' *Star Magazine*

For my wife, Joanna,
who listens to the whispers of my soul
and loves me for who I am

Contents

Prologue

Barney the Dinosaur is on the TV again. I hate Barney – and his theme tune. It's sung to the notes of 'Yankee Doodle Dandy'.

I watch children hop, skip and jump into the huge purple dinosaur's open arms before looking at the room around me. The children here lie motionless on the floor or slumped in seats. A strap holds me upright in my wheelchair. My body, like theirs, is a prison that I can't escape: when I try to speak, I'm silent; when I will my arm to move, it stays still.

There is just one difference between me and these children: my mind leaps and swoops, turns cartwheels and somersaults as it tries to break free of its confines, conjuring a lightning flash of glorious colour in a world of grey. But no one knows because I can't tell them. They think I'm an empty shell, which is why I've been sitting here listening to *Barney* or *The Lion King* day in, day out, for the past nine years, and just when I thought it couldn't get any worse, *Teletubbies* came along.

I'm twenty-five years old but my memories of the past only begin from the moment I started to come back to life from wherever I'd been lost. It was like seeing flashes of light in the darkness as I heard people talking about my sixteenth birthday and wondering whether to shave the stubble on my chin. It scared me to listen to what was being said because, although I had no memories or sense of a past, I was sure I was a child and the voices were speaking about a soon-to-be man. Then I slowly realised it was me they were discussing, even as I began to understand that I had a mother and father, brother and sister I saw at the end of every day.

Have you ever seen one of those movies in which someone wakes up as a ghost but they don't know they've died? That's how it was, as I realised people were looking through and around me and I didn't understand why. However much I tried to beg and plead, shout and scream, I couldn't make them notice me. My mind was trapped inside a useless body, my arms and legs weren't mine to control and my voice was mute. I couldn't make a sign or a sound to let anyone know I'd become aware again. I was invisible – the ghost boy.

So I learned to carry my secret and became a silent witness to the world around me as my life passed by in a succession of identical days. Nine years have passed since I became aware once more and during that time I've escaped using the only thing I have – my mind – and to explore everything from the black abyss of despair to the psychedelic landscape of fantasy.

That's how things were until I met Virna, and now she alone suspects there's an active consciousness hidden inside me. Virna believes I understand more than anyone thinks possible. She wants me to prove it tomorrow when I'm tested at a clinic specialising in giving the silent a voice, helping everyone – from those with Down's syndrome and autism to brain tumours or stroke damage – to communicate.

Part of me dares not believe this meeting might unlock the person inside the shell. It took so long to accept I was trapped inside my body – to come to terms with the unimaginable – that I'm afraid to think I might be able to change my fate. But, however fearful I am, when I think about the possibility that someone might finally realise I'm here, I can feel the wings of a bird called hope beating softly inside my chest.

I

Counting Time

I spend each day in a care home in the suburbs of a large South African city. Just a few hours away are hills covered in yellow scrub where lions roam looking for a kill. In their wake come hyenas that scavenge for leftovers and finally there are vultures hoping to peck the last shreds of flesh off the bones. Nothing is wasted. The animal kingdom is a perfect cycle of life and death, as endless as time itself.

I've come to understand the infinity of time so well that I've learned to lose myself in it. Days, if not weeks, can go by as I close myself down and become entirely black within – a nothingness that is washed and fed, lifted from wheelchair to bed – or I immerse myself in the tiny specks of life I see around me. Ants crawling on the floor exist in a world of wars and skirmishes, battles being fought and lost, with me the only witness to a history as bloody and terrible as that of any people.

I've learned to master time instead of being its passive

recipient. I rarely see a clock but I've taught myself to tell the time from the way sunlight and shadows fall around me after realising I could memorise where the light fell whenever I heard someone ask the time. Then I used the fixed points that my days here give me so unrelentingly – morning drink at 10 a.m., lunch at 11.30, an afternoon drink at 3 p.m. – to perfect the technique. I've had plenty of opportunity to practise, after all.

It means that now I can face the days, look at them square on and count them down minute by minute, hour by hour, as I let the silent sounds of the numbers fill me – the soft sinuousness of sixes and sevens, the satisfying staccato of eights and ones. After losing a whole week like this, I give thanks that I live somewhere sunny. I might never have learned to conquer the clock if I'd been born in Iceland. Instead I'd have had to let time wash over me endlessly, eroding me bit by bit like a pebble on the beach.

How I know the things I do – that Iceland is a country of extreme darkness and light or that after lions come hyenas, then vultures – is a mystery to me. Apart from the information that I drink in whenever the TV or radio is switched on – the voices like a rainbow path to the pot of gold that is the world outside – I'm given no lessons nor am I read to from books. It makes me wonder if the things I know are what I learned before I fell ill. Sickness might have raddled my body but it only took temporary hostage of my mind.

It's midday now, which means there are less than five hours to go before my father comes to collect me. It's the brightest moment of any day because it means the care home can be left behind at last when Dad picks me up at 5 p.m. I can't describe how excited I feel on the days my mother arrives after she finishes work at 2.

I will start counting now – seconds, then minutes, then hours – and hopefully it will make my father arrive a little quicker.

One, two, three, four, five . . .

I hope Dad will turn on the radio in the car so that we can listen to the cricket together on the way home.

'Howzat?' he'll sometimes cry when a ball has been bowled.

It's the same if my brother David plays computer games when I'm in the room.

'I'm going up to the next level!' he'll occasionally shriek as his fingers fly across the console.

Neither of them has any idea just how much I cherish these moments. As my father cheers when a six is hit or my brother's brow knits in frustration as he tries to better his score, I silently imagine the jokes I would tell, the curses I would cry with them, if only I could, and for a few precious moments I don't feel like a bystander any more.

I wish Dad would come.

Thirty-three, thirty-four, thirty-five . . .

My body feels heavy today and the strap holding me up cuts through my clothes into my skin. My right hip aches. I wish someone would lie me down and relieve the pain. Sitting still for hours on end isn't nearly as restful as you might imagine. You know those cartoons when someone falls off a cliff, hits the ground and smashes – kerpow! – into pieces? That's how I feel – as if I've been shattered into a million pieces and each one is hurting. Gravity is painful when it's bearing down on a body that's not fit for the purpose.

Fifty-seven, fifty-eight, fifty-nine. One minute.

Four hours, fifty-nine minutes to go.

One, two, three, four, five . . .

Try as I might, my mind keeps returning to the pain in my hip. I think of the broken cartoon man. Sometimes I wish I could hit the ground as he does and be smashed into smithereens. Because maybe then, just like him, I could jump up and miraculously become whole again before starting to run.

2

The Deep

Until the age of twelve, I was a normal little boy – shyer than most maybe and not the rough-and-tumble kind but happy and healthy. What I loved most of all was electronics and I had such a natural ability with them that my mother trusted me to fix a plug socket when I was eleven because I'd been making electronic circuits for years. My flair also meant I could build a reset button into my parents' computer and rig up an alarm system to protect my bedroom from my younger brother and sister, David and Kim. Both were determined to invade my tiny Lego-filled kingdom but the only living thing allowed to enter it, apart from my parents, was our small yellow dog called Pookie, who followed me everywhere.

Over the years I've listened well during countless meetings and appointments, so I learned that in January 1988 I came home from school complaining of a sore throat and never went back to classes again. In the weeks and months that followed, I stopped eating, started sleeping for hours every day and complained of how painful it was to walk. My body began to weaken as I stopped using it and so did my mind: first I forgot facts, then familiar things like watering my bonsai tree and finally even faces.

To try and help me remember, my parents gave me a frame of family photos to carry around, and my mother, Joan, played me a video of my father, Rodney, every day when he went away on business. But while they hoped the repetition might stop the memories slipping from my mind, it didn't work. My speech deteriorated as I slowly forgot who and where I was. The last words I ever spoke were about a year after I first got ill as I lay in a hospital bed.

'When home?' I asked my mother.

But nothing could reach me as my muscles wasted, my limbs became spastic and my hands and feet curled in on themselves like claws. To make sure I didn't starve as my weight plummeted, my parents woke me up to feed me. As my father held me upright, my mother spooned food into my mouth and I swallowed instinctively. Other than that, I didn't move. I was completely unresponsive. I was in a kind of waking coma that no one understood because the doctors couldn't diagnose what had caused it.

At first, the medics thought my problems were psychological and I spent several weeks in a psychiatric unit. It was only when I was taken to casualty suffering from dehydration after the psychologists failed to persuade me to eat or drink that they finally accepted my illness was physical and not mental. So brain scans and EEGs, MRI scans and blood tests were done, and I was treated for tuberculosis and cryptococcal meningitis but no conclusive diagnosis was made. Medication after medication was tried – magnesium chloride and potassium, amphotericin and ampicillin – but to no effect. I'd travelled beyond the realms of what medicine understood. I was lost in the land where dragons lie and no one could rescue me.

All my parents could do was watch me slip away from them day by day: they tried to keep me walking but I had to be held up as my legs got weaker and weaker; they took me to hospitals all over South Africa as test after test was run but nothing was found; and they wrote desperate letters to experts in America, Canada and England, who said their South African colleagues were surely doing all that could be done.

It took about a year for the doctors to confess that they had run out of treatment options. All they could say was that I was suffering from a degenerative neurological disorder, cause and prognosis unknown, and advise my parents to put me into an institution to let my illness run its course. Politely but firmly the medical profession washed its hands of me as my mother and father effectively were told to wait until my death released us all.

So I was taken home, where I was cared for by my mother, who gave up her job as a radiographer to look after me. Meanwhile my father worked such long hours as a mechanical engineer that he often didn't get home to see David and Kim before they went to bed. The situation was untenable. After about a year at home, at the age of fourteen it was decided that I should spend my days in the care centre where I am now but I'd go home each night.

Years passed with me lost in my dark, unseeing world. My parents even tried putting mattresses on the living-room floor so that they, Kim and David could all live as I did – at floor level – in the hope of reaching me. But I lay like an empty shell, unaware of anything around me. Then, one day, I started coming back to life.

Last 'normal' family photo taken in 1987

3

Coming Up for Air

I'm a sea creature crawling along the ocean floor. It's dark here. Cold. There's nothing but blackness above, below and all around me.

But then I begin to see snatches of light glimmering overhead. I don't understand what they are.

Something tells me I must try to reach them. It drives me upwards as I kick towards the shards of light, which skitter across the surface far above me. They dance as they weave patterns of gold and shadow.

*

My eyes focus. I'm staring at a skirting board. I'm sure it looks different than it normally does but I don't know how I know this.

*

A whisper across my face – wind.

*

I can smell sunshine.

*

Music, high and tinny. Children singing. Their voices fade in and out, loud then muffled, until they fall silent.

*

A carpet swims into view. It's a swirl of black, white and brown. I stare at it, trying to make my eyes focus but the darkness comes for me again.

*

A wash cloth is pushed cold across my face and I feel my cheek flame in disapproval as a hand holds my neck steady.

'I won't take a second,' a voice says. 'We've got to make sure you're a clean boy now, haven't we?'

*

The snatches of light become brighter. I'm getting closer to the surface. I want to break through it but I can't. Everything is too fast whereas I am still.

*

I smell something.

I drag my eyeballs upwards. They feel so heavy.

A little girl is standing in front of me. She is naked from the waist down. Her hand is smeared brown. She giggles as she tries to open the door.

'Where are you going, Miss Mary?' a voice asks as a pair of legs appears at the edge of my vision.

I hear the door being closed and then a grunt of disgust.

'Not again, Mary!' the voice exclaims. 'Look at my hand!'

The little girl laughs. Her delight is like a ripple of wind carving a groove in sand running smooth across a deserted beach. I can feel it vibrating inside me.

*

A voice. Someone is speaking. Two words: sixteen and death. I don't know what they mean.

*

It's night-time. I'm in my bed. Home. I gaze around in the half-darkness. A row of teddy bears lies beside me and there's something on my feet. Pookie.

But as the familiar weight disappears, I can feel myself rising. I'm confused. I'm not in the sea. I'm in real life now. But still I feel as if I'm floating, leaving my body and moving upwards towards my bedroom ceiling.

Suddenly I know that I'm not alone. Reassuring presences are wrapping themselves around me. They comfort me. They want me to follow them. I understand now that there's no reason to stay here. I'm tired of trying to reach the surface. I want to let go, give myself up to the deep or to the presences that are with me now – whichever takes me first.

But then one thought fills me: I can't leave my family.

They are sad because of me. Their grief is like a shroud that envelops me whenever I break through the surface of the waves. They'll have nothing to grab on to if I leave. I can't go.

Breath rushes into my lungs. I open my eyes. I'm alone again. Whatever was with me is gone.

Angels.

I have decided to stay.

4

The Box

E ven as I became aware, I didn't fully understand what had happened to me. Just as a baby isn't born knowing it can't control its movements or speak, I didn't think about what I could or couldn't do. Thoughts rushed through my mind that I never considered voicing and I didn't realise the body I saw jerking or motionless around me was mine. It took time for me to understand I was completely alone in the middle of a sea of people.

But as my awareness and memories slowly started to mesh together and my mind gradually reconnected to my body, I began to understand I was different. Lying on the sofa as my father watched gymnastics on TV, I was fascinated by the bodies that moved so effortlessly, the strength and power they revealed in every twist and turn. Then I looked down at a pair of feet I often saw and realised they belonged to me. It was the same with the two hands that trembled uncontrollably whenever I saw them nearby. They were part of me too but I couldn't control them at all.

I wasn't paralysed: my body moved but it did so independently of me. My limbs had become spastic. They felt distant, as if they were encased in concrete, and I couldn't control them. People were always trying to make me use my legs – physios bent them in painful contortions as they tried to keep the muscles working – but I couldn't move unaided.

If I ever walked, it was to take just a few shuffling steps with someone holding me up because otherwise I would crumple to the floor. If I tried to feed myself, my hand would smear food across my cheek. My arms wouldn't instinctively reach out to protect me if I fell so I'd hit the ground face first. I couldn't roll myself over if I was lying in bed so I'd stay in the same position for hours on end unless someone turned me. My limbs didn't want to open up and be fluid; instead they curled into themselves like snails disappearing into shells.

Just as a photographer carefully adjusts his camera lens until the picture becomes clear, it took time for my mind to focus. But while my body and I were locked in an endless fight, my mind was slowly getting stronger as the pieces of my consciousness knitted themselves together.

Gradually I became aware of each day and every hour in it. Most were forgettable but there were times when I watched history unfold. Nelson Mandela being sworn in as president in 1994 is a hazy memory while Diana's death in 1997 is clear.

I think my mind started to awaken at about the age of sixteen and by nineteen it was fully intact once more: I knew who I was and where I was, and I understood that I'd been robbed of a real life. I was completely entombed.

That was six years ago. At first I wanted to fight my fate by leaving some tiny sign to guide people back to me, like the pieces of bread Hansel and Gretel left behind to help them find their way out of the dark woods. But gradually I came to understand that my efforts would never be enough: even as I came back to life, no one fully understood what was happening.

As I slowly regained enough control of my neck to start jerking my head down and to the right, lifting it occasionally or smiling, people didn't realise what my new movements meant. They didn't believe miracles happened twice: I'd already survived doctors' predictions that I would surely die so no one thought to look for divine intervention a second time. As I started 'replying' yes or no to simple questions with a turn of my head or a smile, they thought it showed only the most basic improvement. No one considered that my improved responses might mean my intelligence was some-how intact. They'd been told long ago that I was severely brain-damaged so when the young man with stick-like limbs, empty eyes and drool running down his chin occasionally lifted his head that's what they saw.

And so I was cared for – fed and watered, wiped and cleaned – but never really noticed. Again and again I'd ask my unruly limbs to make a sign and show someone I was still there but they would never do as I asked.

I'm sitting on my bed. My heart is beating as my father undresses me. I want him to know, to understand that I've returned to him. He must see me!

I stare at my arm, willing it to work. Every bit of me condenses into this moment. I stare at my arm – pleading, cajoling, admonishing and begging. My heart leaps as I feel it respond to my pleas. My arm is waving high above my head. At last I'm leading the way back to myself with the kind of sign I've spent so long trying to make.

But when I look at my father, neither shock nor surprise is written on his face. He simply carries on pulling off my shoes.

Dad! I'm here! Can't you see?

But my father doesn't notice me. He continues to undress me and my gaze slides unwillingly to my arm. It's only then I realise it's not moving. However powerful my hope seems, its only outward manifestation is a muscular twitch close to my elbow. The movement is so tiny I know my father will never notice it.

Rage fills me. I feel sure I'll burst. I gasp for breath.

'Are you okay, boy?' Dad asks as he hears my ragged breathing and looks up.

I can do nothing but stare at him, praying that my silent desperation will somehow communicate itself.

'Let's get you into bed, shall we?'

A pyjama top is pulled on over my head and I'm laid down. Anger bites into my stomach. I know I must switch it off: it will hurt too much if I don't. I must lose myself in nothingness or else I'll go mad.

At other times I tried to groan, hoping that if a noise escaped my chest someone would wonder what it meant, but I could never make a sound. In later years I'd sometimes try to speak but I was always silent. I couldn't pick up a pen to scrawl a message or utter a plea for help. I was marooned on the island of myself, and hope guttered inside me as I realised that I would never be rescued.

Horror came first, then bitter disappointment, and I turned in on myself to survive. Like a turtle retreating into its shell, I learned to escape reality in fantasy. I knew I was going to spend the rest of my life as powerlessly as I lived each present day and eventually I didn't try to respond or react but stared at the world with a blank expression.

To other people, I resembled a pot plant: something to be given water and left in the corner. Everyone was so used to me not being there that they didn't notice when I began to be present again.

I'd been put into a box long before, after all. Each of us has. Are you the 'difficult' child or the 'histrionic' lover, the 'argumentative' sibling or the 'long-suffering' spouse? Boxes make us easier to understand but they also imprison us because people don't see past them.

We all have fixed ideas of each other even though the truth can be far removed from what we think we see. That is why no one asked what it might mean when I started to improve enough to answer simple questions like 'Would you like tea?' with a turn of my head or a smile.

For most of the people who met me, I was just a job. To the staff at my care home, I was a familiar fixture they didn't take any notice of after so many years; to care workers at other places I was sent when my parents went away, I was just a passing patient; and for the doctors who saw me, I was 'the one who can't do too much', as one memorably told his colleague while I lay like a starfish on an X-ray table.

Meanwhile, my parents had full-time jobs and two other children to look after as well as me but they did everything from changing my nappy to cutting my toenails. Attending to

my physical needs took so much time and energy, it's no surprise my mother and father didn't stop to think about whether
I'd defied medical odds and had a recovery that was nothing
short of a miracle.

So that's why I stayed inside the box I'd been put into so
long before. It was the one marked with a single word:
'imbecile'.

Dad (Rodney) and Martin sitting on the couch at home

5

Virna

The smell of the mandarin oil is sharp but sweet as Virna massages my arm. Her hands move seamlessly as she works the leaden muscles. As I stare at her, she raises her head to smile at me and I wonder yet again why I didn't notice hope when it first arrived in my life.

To begin with, all I knew was that Virna never showed her teeth when she smiled and she twitched her leg nervously as she sat cross-legged in a chair. She'd started working at my care home as a relief carer and I noticed such details about her because that's what you learn to do when people don't talk to you. But then Virna started speaking to me and I realised she was someone I could never forget. Most people speak at, around, over or about me so anyone who treats me like a cut above the average root vegetable is unforgettable.

One afternoon Virna told me her stomach was aching. It's the kind of everyday confession I've heard for years as people have chatted unguardedly, thinking I'm not really with them. What I don't know about some of the carers' health problems is hardly worth knowing: one has a husband with Alzheimer's, another has problems with her kidneys and one woman's vaginal tumour almost left her childless.

But when Virna spoke to me it was different. She wasn't talking to herself, someone else or even the empty room like most people do. She was speaking to me, chatting as she would to anyone her own age about the thoughts that floated through her mind like dust motes in sunlight. It was a conversation any twenty-something friends might have but I'd never experienced it before. Soon Virna started telling me about everything from the sadness of her grandmother's illness to the new puppy she'd got and the boy she was excited to be going on a date with. I felt almost as if I was making my first friend.

That was the reason I started looking at Virna, which is not something I often do. My head usually feels like a breeze block when I try to lift it and I'm rarely at the same eye level as other people because I'm always sitting in a chair or lying down. It takes so much effort that a long time ago I gave up making eye contact with people who look but never see. I sit for hours each day staring blankly into space. But that changed when Virna began giving me and some of my fellow inmates aromatherapy massages to soothe our twisted limbs. Lying on my back while she kneaded my aching muscles, I was able to let my eyes follow her as she spoke to me and bit by bit I started to peep out from the shell I'd retreated into.

Virna looked at me properly, which was something no one

had done for a long time. She saw that my eyes really were the windows to my soul and became more and more convinced that I understood what she said. But how could she convince anyone else that the unresponsive ghost boy was capable of more?

Months turned into one year and then two. Then about six months ago Virna saw a TV programme about a woman who'd been helped to communicate after being rendered mute by a stroke. Soon afterwards Virna went to an open day at a nearby centre where she'd heard experts talk about what could be done to help those who can't speak and she came back excited to tell me about what she'd learned.

'They use switches and electronic devices to help people communicate,' she said. 'Do you think you could do something like that, Martin? I'm sure you could.'

Other care staff had also gone to the open day but weren't as convinced as Virna was that I might be a suitable candidate.

'Do you really think he's got it in him?' one of them asked.

The woman bent towards me with the shadow of a grin on her face and I smiled to try and show her that I understood what she was saying. But my only two gestures – jerking my head down to the right and smiling – are interpreted as the knee-jerk reactions of an undeveloped mind, the kind of responses that any six-month-old baby can make, so she didn't take any notice.

The carer looked at me and sighed as her grin faded. I wondered if she knew that her breath was bitter from the coffee she'd recently been drinking.

'Can you imagine anything so ridiculous?' she said later to

her friend after Virna had left. 'There's no way any of them could communicate.'

The two women looked around the room.

'Maybe Gertje?'

They looked at a little boy who was playing with a toy car nearby.

'He's a bit better than some, isn't he?'

The women were silent for a moment before their eyes came to rest on me. They didn't say anything as they looked at me sitting in my wheelchair. They didn't need to. I know I'm considered one of the lowest functioning subjects in a place where the only entry requirement is an IQ of 30 or less.

Despite all these doubts, Virna wouldn't be swayed. A fire of conviction had been lit within her. After telling people again and again that she thought I could understand what was being said to me, she'd spoken to my parents, who had agreed to have me tested. Tomorrow they're taking me to the place where I might finally be offered a key to my prison door.

'You're going to do your best, aren't you?' Virna says now as she looks at me.

I can see she's worried. Doubt flickers across her face like cloud shadows racing across the horizon on a sunny day. I stare back, wishing I could tell her that I'll use every fibre of my being to make the most of an opportunity I never thought would come. This is the first time I've ever been assessed like this and I'll do all I can to give some small sign that I'm worthy of the attention.

'Please do as much as you can, Martin,' Virna says. 'It's so important that you show them what you can do because I know you can.'

I look at her. Tears glimmer silver in the corners of her eyes. Her faith in me is so strong I must repay it.

6

Awakening

Two glass doors slide open in front of me with a hiss. I've never seen doors like this before. The world has surprised me again. I sometimes see it as it passes the window of a car I'm sitting in but other than that I remain separate from it. The small glimpses I have of the world always intrigue me. I once spent days thinking about a doctor's mobile phone after seeing it clipped to his belt: it was so much smaller than Dad's that I couldn't stop wondering what kind of battery was powering it. There are so many things I wish I could understand.

My father is pushing my wheelchair as we enter the Centre for Augmentative and Alternative Communication at the University of Pretoria. It is July 2001 – thirteen and a half years since I first fell ill. On the pavement outside I saw students walking along in the sunshine and jacaranda trees arching overhead but everything is quiet inside the building. Sea-green carpet tiles stretch down a corridor; the walls are covered in information posters. We are a small band of explorers entering this unknown world: my parents, my brother David and Virna, plus Marietta and Elize, a carer and physiotherapist who have known me for years.

'Mr and Mrs Pistorius?' a voice asks and I raise my eyes to see a woman. 'My name is Shakila and I'll be assessing Martin today. We're just getting the room ready but it won't be long.'

Fear washes cold over me. I can't look into the faces around me; I don't want to see the doubt or hope in their eyes as we silently wait. Soon we're ushered into a small room where Shakila is waiting with another woman called Yasmin. I hang my head as they start talking to my parents. The inside of my cheek feels sore. I accidentally bit myself as I was fed my lunch earlier today and my mouth still feels tender even though the bleeding has stopped.

As Shakila asks my parents about my medical history, I wonder what they're thinking after all this time. Do they feel as afraid as I do?

'Martin?' I hear a voice say and my wheelchair is pushed across the room.

We come to rest in front of a large sheet of perspex suspended on a metal stand directly in front of me. Red lines criss-cross the screen, dividing it into boxes with small black and white pictures stuck in some of them. These line drawings show simple things – a ball, a running tap, a dog – and Shakila stands on the other side of the screen watching me intently as I stare at them.

'I want you to look at the picture of the ball, Martin,' Shakila says.

I raise my head a little and let my eyes search the screen.

I can't control my head enough to move it properly from side to side so my eyes are the only part of my body that I'm totally the master of. They slide back and forth across the pictures until I find the ball. I fix my eyes on it and stare.

'Good, Martin, that's very good,' Shakila says softly as she looks at me.

I feel afraid suddenly. Am I looking at the right picture? Are my eyes really fixed on the ball or are they looking at another of the symbols? I can't even be sure of that.

'Now I want you to look at the dog,' Shakila says and I start to search again.

My eyes move slowly over the pictures not wanting to make a mistake or miss a thing. I search slowly until I find the cartoon dog to the left of the board and look at it.

'And now the television,' she says.

I soon find the picture of the television. But although I want to keep staring at it to show Shakila that I've found what she'd asked me to, my chin drops towards my chest. I try not to panic as I wonder if I'm failing the test.

'Shall we try something different?' Shakila asks and my wheelchair is pushed towards a table covered in cards.

Each one has a word and a picture drawn on it. Panic. I can't read the words. I don't know what they say. If I can't read them, will I fail the test? And if I fail the test, will I go back to the care home and sit there forever? My heart starts to thump painfully inside my chest.

'Can you point to the word "Mum" please, Martin?' Yasmin, the other speech therapist, asks me.

I don't know what the word 'Mum' looks like but even so I stare at my right hand, willing it to move, wanting it to make some small sign that I understand what I'm being asked. My hand trembles furiously as I try to lift it from my lap. The room is deathly silent as my arm slowly lifts into the air before jerking wildly from side to side. I hate my arm.

'Let's try again, shall we?' Shakila says.

My progress is painfully slow as I'm asked to identify symbols by pointing at them. I feel ashamed of my useless body and angry that it can't do better the first time anyone asks anything of it.

Soon Shakila goes to a large cupboard and pulls out a small rectangular dial. It has more symbols on it and a large red pointer in the middle. Shakila sets it on the table in front of me before plugging in some wires that run from a yellow plate fixed to the end of a flexible stand.

'This is a dial scan and a head switch,' Yasmin explains. 'You can use the yellow switch to control the pointer on the scan as it goes around and stop it to identify the symbol you want. Do you understand, Martin? Can you see the symbols on the scan?

'When we ask you to identify one, we want you to push your head against the switch when the pointer reaches the symbol. Do you think you can do that?'

I look at the symbols: one shows water running from a tap, another a plate of biscuits, a third a cup of tea. There are eight symbols in total.

'I want you to stop the pointer when it reaches the tap, please,' Yasmin says.

The red pointer starts to inch around the dial. It goes so slowly that I wonder if it'll ever reach the picture of the tap. Slowly it drags its way around the dial and I watch until it nears the tap. I jerk my head against the switch. The pointer stops at the right place on the dial.

'Good, Martin,' a voice tells me.

Amazement fills me. I've never controlled anything before. I've never made another object do what I wanted it to. I've fantasised about it again and again but I've never raised a fork to my mouth, drunk from a cup or changed TV channels. I can't do up my shoes, kick a ball or ride a bike. Stopping the pointer on the dial makes me feel triumphant.

For the next hour, Yasmin and Shakila give me different switches to use as they try to find out if there is any part of my body that I can control enough to use switches properly. My head, knee and rebellious limbs are all put close enough to switches for me to try to make contact with them. First there's a black rectangular box with a long white switch that sits on the side of the table in front of me. It's called a wobble switch. I pull my right arm up before jerking it down, hoping to make contact with the switch and knowing it'll be by luck rather than judgement if I do. Then there is a huge yellow switch, as big and round as a saucer, that I flail my unruly right hand near because my left is almost completely useless. Again and again Yasmin and Shakila ask me to use the switches to identify simple symbols: a knife, a bath, a sandwich – the easiest kind of pictures, which even those with the lowest intelligence can identify. Sometimes I try to use my right hand but more often I stare at the symbol I'm being asked to pick out.

After what feels like forever, Shakila finally turns to me. I'm looking intently at a symbol that shows a big yellow swirl.

'Do you like McDonald's?' she asks.

I don't know what she's talking about. I can't turn my

head or smile to answer yes or no because I don't understand the question.

'Do you like hamburgers?'

I smile at Shakila to let her know that I do and she gets up. Going back to the large cupboard, she pulls out a black box. The top is divided into small squares by an overlying plastic frame and inside each one I can see a symbol.

'This is a communication device called a Macaw,' Shakila tells me softly. 'And if you can learn to use switches, then you might be able to use one of these some day.'

I stare at the box as Shakila turns it on and a tiny red light flashes slowly in the corner of each square in turn. The symbols in the squares aren't black and white like those on the cards. These are brightly coloured and there are words written next to them. I can see a picture of a cup of tea and a drawing of a sun. I watch Shakila to see what will happen next as she hits a switch to select a symbol.

'I am tired,' a recorded voice says suddenly.

It comes from the box. It's a woman's voice. I stare at the Macaw. Could this small black box give me a voice? I can hardly believe that anyone would think me capable of using it. Do they realise I can do more than point at a child's ball drawn in thick black lines on a card?

'I'm sure that you understand us,' Shakila says as she sits in front of me. 'I can see from the way your eyes travel that you can identify the symbols we ask you to and you are trying to use your hand to do the same. I feel sure we'll be able to find a way to help you communicate, Martin.'

I stare at the floor, unable to move any more today.

'Wouldn't you like to be able to tell someone that you are

tired or thirsty?' Shakila says softly. 'That you would like to wear a blue jumper instead of a red one or that you want to go to sleep?'

I'm not sure. I've never told anyone what I want before. Would I be able to make choices if I was given them? Would I be able to tell someone that I want to leave my tea to cool instead of drinking it in hurried gulps when they lift a straw to my mouth because I know it'll be the only opportunity I'll have to drink for several hours? I know most people make thousands of decisions every day about what to eat and wear, where to go and who to see but I'm not sure I'll be able to make even one. It's like asking a child who has grown up in the desert to throw themselves into the sea.

7

My Parents

While my father's faith in me has been stretched almost to breaking point, I don't think it's ever disappeared completely. Its roots were planted deeply many years ago when Dad met a man who'd recovered from polio. It had taken him a decade to get well again but his experience convinced my father that anything was possible. Each day Dad has proved his faith in me in a string of tiny acts: washing and feeding me, dressing and lifting me, getting up every two hours throughout the night to turn my still body. A bear of a man with a huge grey beard like Father Christmas, his hands are always gentle.

It took time for me to realise that while my father looked after nearly all of my physical needs, my mother hardly came near me. Anger and resentment at what had happened poured out of her whenever she did. As time passed I saw that my family had been divided into two – my father and me on one side; my mother, David and Kim on the other – and I realised that my illness had driven a deep wedge into the heart of a family I somehow instinctively knew had once been so happy.

Guilt filled me when I heard my parents arguing. Everyone was suffering because of me. I was the cause of all the bad feeling as my parents returned to the same battleground again and again: my mother wanted to put me into full-time residential care just as the doctors had advised; my father did not. She believed my condition was permanent and I needed so much special care that having me at home would harm David and Kim. My father, on the other hand, still hoped I might get better and believed it would never happen if I was sent away to an institution. This was the fundamental disagreement that reverberated through the years, sometimes as shouts and screams, sometimes as loaded silences.

For a long time I didn't understand why my mother felt so differently to my father but eventually I pieced together enough of the facts to realise that she had almost been destroyed by my illness and she wanted to protect David and Kim from a similar fate. She had lost one child and she didn't want her healthy surviving son and daughter to be hurt in any way.

It hadn't always been this way. For the first two years of my illness, my mother searched as tirelessly as my father for a cure to save the son she thought was dying as he slipped a little more out of their reach every day. I can't imagine how my parents suffered as they watched their healthy child disappear and pleaded with doctors, watched me being given medications and agreed to have me tested for everything from tuberculosis of the brain to a host of genetic disorders only to be told that nothing could help me.

Even when traditional medicine ran out of answers, my mother wasn't prepared to give up. For a year after the doctors told my parents they didn't know how to treat me she cared for me at home and tried everything from having me prayed over by faith healers to intensive vitamin regimes in the hope of helping me. Nothing worked.

My mother was tortured by her growing guilt that she hadn't been able to save me. She was sure she had failed her child and felt increasingly desperate as her friends and family stayed away – some because they found my undiagnosed illness frightening, others because they were unsure how to comfort people who were facing any parents' worst nightmare. Whatever their reason, people kept their distance as they hugged their healthy children close to them in silent gratitude and my family became more and more isolated.

My mother's unhappiness soon spiralled so badly out of control that she tried to commit suicide one night about two years after I first fell ill. After taking handfuls of pills, she lay down to die. But as she did so, Mum remembered what her mother had once told her about her father's sudden death of a heart attack: he'd never said goodbye. Even in her fog of despair, my mother wanted to tell my father one last time how much she loved us all and this saved her. When Dad realised what she'd done, he put her into the car with David, Kim and me, and one of David's friends who was staying the night, and drove us all to the hospital.

The doctors pumped Mum's stomach but after that night my brother's friend was never allowed to stay again and the isolation that my parents felt started to infect my younger brother and sister. They, too, suffered while my mother was treated on a psychiatric ward. By the time she came home, her doctors had decided that she could no longer help care for me. According to them, she was mourning the loss of her child and should have as little as possible to do with me to avoid further upset. She – ill, grief-stricken and desperate – took the doctors at their word and concentrated on caring for her two healthy children and returning to work full-time once she was well enough. Meanwhile, my father held down a demanding job and looked after me, for the most part, single-handedly.

It was like this for many years but gradually the situation has changed as my mother has softened and become more involved in my care. Now she looks after me almost as much as my father does, makes me the spaghetti and mince with peach chutney that she knows I like and sometimes even lays my head on her lap if I'm lying on the sofa. It makes me happy to know that she can touch me now after shying away for so long, just as it makes me sad when I hear her playing music late at night because I know that sorrow is filling her as she listens to lyrics and remembers the past.

Sadness fills me too when I think of my father, who buried his ambitions, lost out on promotions and took demotions to care for me. Each person in my family – my parents, brother and sister – has paid a high price for my illness. While I can't be sure, I sometimes wonder if all these lost hopes and dreams are the reason why a man as intelligent as my father has learned to hide his emotions so deeply that I sometimes wonder if he knows where they are any more.

8

Changes

They call it the butterfly effect: the huge changes that a pair of silken wings can create with an almost imperceptible flutter. I think a butterfly is beating its wings somewhere in my life. To the outward eye, things have hardly changed since I was assessed: I still go to my care centre each morning and sigh gratefully when the afternoon comes to an end and I can go home to be fed, washed and prepared for bed. But monotony is a familiar foe and even the subtlest changes in it are noticeable.

The various care staff I see at my day centre, during appointments for physio or with doctors at the hospital, don't seem overly worried that an expert has said I might soon be able to communicate. Considering some of the things I've seen, I'm surprised some of them aren't a little more concerned. But I can certainly feel a change in the way my parents are speaking to me since I was assessed by the speech therapists. When Mum asks if I've had enough food, she waits just a little longer for my head to jerk its way down or my mouth to smile. My father talks to me more and more now as he brushes my teeth at night. The changes are so small that my parents might not even be aware of them but I can sense hope in the air for the first time in years.

I've heard enough of what they've said to know that if I'm to start communicating properly it will be at the most basic level. This will not be a Hollywood movie with a neat happy ending or a trip to Lourdes where the mute are miraculously given a voice. The speech therapists' report has recommended that my mother and father start trying to communicate with me in the tiniest of ways. Apparently my head-jerk and smile are not as reliable as I thought they were and I must learn a more consistent way to signal yes and no. Because my hands are too unruly to point properly, the best way for me to start 'speaking' is by staring at symbols.

I'll use symbols because I can't read or write. Letters hold no meaning for me now, and so pictures will rule my life from now on: I'm going to live and breathe them as I learn their language. My parents have been told to make me a folder of words and their corresponding symbols. 'Hello' is a picture of a stick man waving his hand, 'like' is his face up close with a huge grin and 'thank you' is a drawing of an egg-shaped face with two hands held flat just below the mouth.

Once Mum and Dad have made up all the pages telling people my name and where I live, that I would like my jumper put on or to be moved out of the way of the sun, they can put them in my folder. Then the person I'm speaking to can slowly turn the pages and I'll stare extra hard at the symbol I want to choose. If I need to let my parents know at mealtimes that my food is too hot, cold or bland, I can stare at one of the laminated pieces of A4 paper they've been advised to stick onto my place mat.

Of course no one has any idea how much of this I can understand because they've never tried to do anything like it with me before. During my assessment, I showed that I can obey simple commands – but so can a toddler. That's why I must start with small steps and hope the people teaching me will soon realise I'm capable of more.

It'll take time but at least there is one way I'll be able to show people I understand things they haven't considered before. Babies might eat puréed food day after day without complaint but I'll soon be able to ask someone to pass me the salt. For the first time in my life, I'll be able to season my food.

9

The Beginning and the End

The care home I've attended since I fell ill is called Alpha and Omega, the beginning and the end. But there isn't too much of either to be found here for me because I'm trapped in a purgatory of bland days, which ebb one into the other.

The centre is housed in a single-storey building with two bright and airy classrooms, a small physiotherapy room and a garden. Sometimes I'm wheeled out into the sunshine but usually I stay inside, where I'm moved from a sitting position in my chair to lying on a mat on the floor. Mostly I'm rested on my side or back but occasionally I'm put face down on a large cushioned wedge so that a care worker can encourage me to try lifting my head by tapping it with the palm of their hand. Otherwise I lie inert, looking at mint-green walls and listening to the tinny chirpiness of the television or radio that provides a constant backdrop to my days. I prefer it when the radio is on because trying to watch the television requires effort that I often can't muster. Instead I stare at the brown carpet tiles and listen to footsteps clicking on the lino floor in the corridor outside.

Classroom language is used here but I'm not sure why because none of the children are thought to be educable. Whatever the reason, my fellow inmates and I have 'teachers' and are divided into two 'classes', which are randomly changed every so often. Sometimes we are split into children-who-can-walk and children-who-can't; at other times it's a question of dividing up those who don't get on. Once we were even separated according to IQ, although when everyone's is considered to be 30 or under it seemed a bit like splitting hairs to me.

Usually about half a dozen staff, who look after us each day, do activities such as stretching our legs or covering our hands in paint before pressing them onto pieces of paper. A couple of the children can join in a little but most are like me and can't control their movements enough to do anything. I've often wondered who these activities are supposed to benefit as I've sat having my hand smeared with cold red paint before it is dragged across a sheet of paper: us or our parents? Are we being forced to collude in a necessary lie when a member of staff draws a picture using our hand? I've seen so many parents being given a drawing they must know their child couldn't have done but none of them says a word as they stare at it.

I've only ever heard one mother question whether her son actually produced the painting and the carer gave her a silent smile when she did, as if pleading with her not to crack the façade of false optimism that has been built around us. I understand why parents want a strand of hope to cling on to, however fragile, just as I understand why such activities might be enjoyable for those children who find being touched and spoken to a relief from a monotonous day, but mostly I wish I could be left alone.

I'm usually trying to listen to the radio when someone comes to disturb me with a smile. I know they mean well, of course, but I'm the oldest here and the activities are aimed at much younger children. No one seems to consider that even people who are thought to be intellectually impaired can change as they grow older.

Despite all this, I know from experience that Alpha and Omega is a far better care centre than many. Over the years I've often heard people talking in shocked whispers about what they've seen at other places. They're right to be shocked. I've seen things for myself: I was sent to other homes when my father went away on business because my mother wasn't confident about looking after me alone, and when my family had a holiday because they needed a break from caring for me.

Each time I was left, I felt terrified I would never be taken home again and my anxiety would build day by day as fear took control of me. On the day I was due to be picked up, each minute felt like a year as I waited to hear the familiar voices of my mother and father. My greatest fear is that I will be left in one of those places where children like me sit all day with no interaction or stimulation. That would be the worst kind of living death.

So I'm grateful to the staff here, who at least try to give our lives a little more texture, because working in a place like

this is not everyone's cup of tea. I've lost count of the carers
I've seen come and go over the years. Many disappear almost
as soon as they arrive and I've learned how to recognise the
look of almost revolted confusion they get before even they
realise they feel that way. I understand. Some people are
scared by what they can't comprehend. It makes them uncomfortable to see the elfin features of a child with Down's
syndrome, the twisted limbs of one with cerebral palsy or the
unseeing stare of an infant with brain damage.

But for all the people who can't bear to look after the children here, there are some for whom this work is a calling.
First among them is Rina, the principal of the home, who has
a round, smiling face and taught me one of my earliest lessons
about the people who care for me.

Years ago, when Rina was a teacher instead of being in
charge, she became very attached to a little girl called Sally
who had been born with severe cerebral palsy. Rina adored
Sally: she fed her the gem squash she loved, cradled her tightly
in her arms and played the music that always made her smile.
Rina was so close to the little girl, in fact, that she was at the
hospital on the night Sally died of pneumonia, aged six.

After that, some of the light went out of Rina's eyes and
seeing how bitterly she missed Sally taught me that children
like myself could be so much more than just a job. It has been
a comforting thought to carry with me throughout the years
and all the meetings with people who have treated me like little
more than a carcass to be handled as a chicken is manoeuvred
into the pot. Not a shred of human warmth melts their chilly
professionalism. Humping you like a sack of potatoes, they
wash you briskly with freezing water and always get soap in

your eyes, however hard you squeeze them shut, before thoughtlessly feeding you food that is either too cold or too hot. All the while they don't speak a word or smile for fear of seeing a person staring back.

Worse though are the so-called carers whose callousness becomes far more personal. I've been called 'the obstacle', 'donkey' and 'rubbish' by people who assume they're superior but in so doing show just how stupid they really are. Do they think that a limited intellect means a child can't feel viciousness in a person's touch or hear anger in the tone of their voice? I remember, in particular, the rush of cold air that always used to wake me when one woman impatiently ripped off my blanket as I slept each afternoon and the temporary worker who threw me into a chair so roughly that I fell out of it as it tipped forwards and dived head first onto the floor.

Such experiences aside, I've come to the conclusion that there are more good people than bad looking after children like me because when I look back over the years I see a stream of smiling faces. There was Unna, who always seemed to be sweating because her nose was permanently shiny, and Heila, who pulsed with such anxious energy that even her tongue couldn't stop moving as she nervously licked her lips. Today there's Marietta, who loves *Days of Our Lives* and has a fiery temper under her calm exterior; Helen, who giggles as she tickles me and has fingernails with a dark-brown stripe down the middle that I can never stop staring at; and my own personal favourite, Dora – middle-aged, plump and smiling, her calmness reassures me and kindness makes her eyes a soft, liquid brown.

However different they are, the one thing all these women have in common is a love of chatting and gossiping, exchanging news and sympathising with each other's troubles. I've heard stories of snakes that have slithered into houses at night and been beaten to death by a brave husband, tales of water leaks that made it rain inside and threatened to bring down ceilings and descriptions of grandchildren bouncing furiously up and down on beds whenever a certain song is played. I also know about the trials of coping with a parent who has Alzheimer's, the problems of caring for sick relatives and the difficulties of getting maintenance from an unwilling ex-husband.

Whatever else they talk about, though, I've come to know that there are three topics women will return to again and again in conversation: their husbands, who are often a disappointment; their children, who are usually wonderful; and their weight, which is always too high. Again and again, I hear them commiserate with each other about how difficult it is to make men more responsible and diets more effective. While I don't understand their problems with their husbands, my heart always sinks whenever I hear them talk about calorie counting. Women seem to think they go on diets in order to feel happier, but I know from experience that this isn't true. In fact, I can safely say that the less women eat, the grumpier they get.

10

Day by Day

Life is finally starting to happen to me as my parents discuss how best to help me. Their ambitions for me now extend far beyond paper symbols and they have decided to buy me an electronic communication device like the black box we saw at my assessment. It is a leap of faith that I wish I could thank them for. They still have no idea if I'll be able to use such a device but they are willing to try because the small spark of hope ignited by my assessment has lit a fire within them.

Together we are discovering a new world called Augmentative and Alternative Communication, or AAC. It's the place where the mute can find a voice through everything from the most basic forms of communication, such as pointing, blinking or staring at symbols held up by another person, to high-tech speech-generating devices and computer programmes that one person uses alone.

To operate a device independently, I must be able to use

switches, so my mother takes me back to see Shakila and a physiotherapist called Jill. After testing me again, they identify the two switches I might best be able to use: one, called a lolly switch, is a small rectangular box that sits in my palm and is operated by curling my fingers to press the button; the other is a wobble switch, which is long enough for my inaccurate right hand to connect with sometimes if I flail it in the right direction.

At first I was overwhelmed with excitement when my parents decided to buy me a device. But then frustration filled me as I realised the black box could only store about 250 words and phrases. It does not seem like much to say when the words inside me feel so limitless.

But then South African currency suddenly devalues and my parents have to cancel the order for the device after it almost doubles in price. Instead they decide to buy me a computer that can be loaded with communication software. It's a brave decision because no one else in South Africa uses one. Speech therapists won't be able to help us – no one will. If I'm to learn anything it will be entirely down to me and my parents, and they don't even know if I'm capable of using a computer.

For now, they must decide what software to buy me and whatever they choose could change things for me completely. It is nerve-racking but exhilarating. My emotions jostle for space like baby birds in a nest: excitement at the thought of learning to communicate, guilt that I'm happy I won't be getting the black box and remorse I feel this way when my parents showed such faith in me by ordering the device. Each feeling is different: excitement makes my stomach shiver, guilt brings a soft swell of nausea deep inside and remorse makes my heart feel heavy. These emotions are so different to what I've known for so long – feelings that I muted to grey to save myself from being driven mad by my powerlessness over every identical day.

'Hello, boy,' my father says when he walks into my room at 6 a.m. each morning.

Dad is always dressed by the time he gets me up. Then he washes me and puts on my clothes before wheeling me into the kitchen, where I'm fed a bowl of cereal. I'm also given a cup of coffee, which I drink through a straw. By the time it's finished I know we'll soon be leaving for the care centre. Dad drops me off on his way to work each morning and the final thing he does before leaving the house is to put a bag onto my lap containing the clean clothes, incontinence pads and bibs I'll need for the day, plus a cooler bag with all my food and drinks.

The moment the front door opens is always a tiny thrill for me. Wondering what the weather will be like is one of the few unpredictable elements of my day, after all. Will there be a snap in the air or a cloudy sky? Given that the sun shines a lot here, it isn't usually much of a surprise but I revel in those few short moments of suspense as my father opens the door.

After Dad puts me into the car and folds my wheelchair into the boot, he gets in beside me, switches on the radio and we drive without speaking. Half an hour later, we reach the care home, where he gets me out of the car again and puts me back into my wheelchair. Then Dad lays my bag on my lap and wheels me to the brown gate that secures the entrance to

Alpha and Omega. As he pushes me down the corridor to my
classroom and my wheelchair comes to a halt, I know that I'm
going to be left for another day. It's usually between 7.15 and
8.10 a.m. by the time Dad leaves, which means I'll have to wait
for anything up to eleven hours until I see him again.

'Bye, boy,' he says as he bends down to kiss me and I hear
his footsteps disappearing as he walks back up the corridor.

The days at the care home don't really start properly until
about 9.30 a.m., so I sit in my chair until then or sometimes
I'm put onto a bean-bag, which I prefer because it supports
my body so well. Then I lie or sit for the rest of the morning
and sometimes I'm lifted up to do stretching exercises or an
activity. After a mid-morning cup of tea, I'm sometimes taken
outside for fresh air, and ninety minutes later it's time for
lunch, which is the same every day – stewed fruit and yoghurt
followed by orange or guava squash. Then at midday someone lies me down to sleep with the other children and three
precious hours are lost until I'm woken up for my afternoon
drink and put into my wheelchair again to wait for Dad.

I often find this part of the day hard because, although the
centre officially closes at 5.15 p.m., Dad doesn't usually arrive
until sometime between 5.20 and 6.30 p.m. because he can't
leave work early and often gets held up in rush-hour traffic.
Some of the staff don't like it and I often overhear conversations criticising him. It upsets me each time because I know
my father is doing the best he can.

'Hello, boy,' he says with a smile when he finally walks into
my classroom and I breathe a sigh of relief because I've
finally reached the end of another day.

Then my bag is put back onto my lap, I'm wheeled to the

car, my chair is stowed in the boot once more and we drive home listening to the radio. After pulling into the driveway and going inside, we usually find Mum cooking, then we sit around the dining-room table to eat before I'm given a cup of milky coffee and laid on the sofa in the lounge in front of the TV. Most nights my father falls asleep in his armchair while he watches a programme, then he wakes up, puts me back into my chair, wheels me to the bathroom to brush my teeth and puts me into bed after undressing me.

The only change to the routine comes at weekends, when I get to stay at home and am given a lie-in until I'm lifted out of bed and taken to the lounge, where I spend the day lying or sitting. But at least my family are around me and I get to hear everyone talking. These are the days that always give me strength for another week because I love being with my parents and David – Kim too before she moved to the UK. That is why sadness always fills me when my father washes my hair as he bathes me on Sunday nights and prepares me to start another week at the care centre. Every second or third week, he cuts my nails and I hate having that done.

This is the routine of my life and has been for as long as I can remember. So is it any wonder that I hang on to every word my parents say as they discuss what to do and I begin to dream of a future I never thought I would have?

11

The Wretch

It was Virna alone who offered me safe passage from my silent self after we first met three years ago. Unlike the people who are now trying to reach me with symbols and dials, switches and screens, Virna only ever used intuition. Like a master detective following the clues I sometimes inadvertently left, she never looked for one conclusive piece of evidence. Instead she was content to piece together a string of tiny fragments to make a whole.

It took time. I wasn't willing at first to see that someone wanted to communicate with me. I was scared to believe someone might. But when I realised that Virna wasn't going to give up, I gradually opened up and over the months and years that followed we became friends.

'How are you today, Martin?' she'd ask as she walked into the tiny room at Alpha and Omega where she massaged me once a week.

Lying on my back, I'd watch as she unzipped the small bag

filled with oils that she always carried with her. As I heard the sound of a bottle being opened, I'd wait to see what smell would fill the air. Sometimes it was citrus, sometimes mint or eucalyptus, but each time the fragrance hit my nostrils I was taken from Kansas to Oz.

'I'm going to do your legs first today and then I'll do your back,' Virna tells me. 'We haven't done it for a couple of weeks and I'm sure it must be sore.'

She looks at me with her enquiring eyes. Virna is small and slight with a voice to match and I've always known she is a kind person. I could hear it the first time she spoke to me and feel it in the healing fingertips that worked muscles long knotted by disuse.

My heart swells as I look at Virna. We have forty-five minutes together now and, just as a child counts out shells collected on a day at the beach, I will go through each one again. I must take care not to rush through these moments. Instead I will slow each one down so that I can replay them because they are what sustain me now. Virna is the only one who sees me. More importantly, she believes in me. She understands my language – the smiles, gazes and nods that are all I have at my disposal.

'Is your family well?' Virna asks as she massages me.

My eyes follow her as I lie on my back. I keep my face still to let her know that someone is sick.

'Is your father ill?'

I don't respond.

'Your mother?'

Again nothing.

'Is it David?'

I give Virna a half smile to show that she is right.

'David is poorly then,' she says. 'What is it? Does he have a cold?'

I jerk my head down.

'Tonsilitis?'

I give another twitch of my feeble neck but it is enough for Virna to understand. Moving down through ear, nose and throat, she finally reaches the chest and I give her another half smile.

'He's got a chest infection?'

I knit my eyebrows to let her know that she is almost right.

'Not pneumonia?' she asks.

I push air sharply through my nose.

'What else is there?'

We stare at each other.

'Bronchitis?' Virna says at last.

Happiness surges through me as I smile. I am Muhammad Ali, John McEnroe, Fred Trueman. Crowds are roaring their approval as I take a lap of honour in the stadium. Virna smiles back at me. She understands. I will replay this moment again and again until we next meet because this one – and the others like it – puncture the shroud of invisibility that has been wrapped around me.

Virna even inspired others to talk to me more – in particular, my sister Kim. I always knew that she looked after me: feeding me gravy she'd saved from her plate because she knew I liked it, bringing Pookie to sit on my lap or pushing my wheelchair close to her while she watched TV. But after Kim realised that I was responding to Virna, she started to talk to me more – telling me about her life the way any sister might tell her older brother. She spoke to me about what was happening at university and the coursework she was worried about as she trained to become a social worker, or the friends who had made her happy and the ones who hadn't. Kim didn't know it, of course, but I understood every word and thought my heart might burst with happiness as I watched her walk up to accept her degree. Other than Virna, she was the one person who could interpret what I was trying to communicate at times, guessing what I liked and didn't like better than most.

That's why I've missed Kim so much since she moved to England a year ago but at least I still have Virna. In a life where people talk relentlessly about my physical needs – am I hot or cold, tired or hungry? – she sees me as more than an empty vessel. And now Kim is no longer here to hug me, Virna is the only person who touches me in anything but a perfunctory way. Others wash and wipe, dress and dust me down but it's always as a means to an end. Only Virna touches me for no other reason than to soothe my aching body – she comforts and heals, making me feel like something other than the repulsive creature I know I am.

I understand that people don't touch me affectionately because they are scared to. I'm a little scared of myself if truth be told. When I catch sight of my reflection in the mirror, I quickly look away because staring back at me is a man with glazed eyes, a bib to catch his drool and arms that are drawn up to his chest like a dog begging for bones. I hardly recognise this stranger so I understand if other people find him hard to stomach. Years ago I went to a family party where I heard one of my relatives talk about me as I sat in the corner.

'Look at him,' she said sadly. 'Poor thing. What kind of life is that?'

Embarrassment flooded through me as the woman looked away. She couldn't bear to look at me and I knew I was ruining whatever pleasure she might have taken from the party. It wasn't surprising. How could anyone enjoy themselves when confronted with such a wretched sight?

12

Life and Death

I'm poised to bury the first crampons in the rockface of communication. The switches I'll use to operate the computer which will speak for me have arrived and I've started practising with them, knowing they are so much more than nuts and bolts, discs of plastic or networks of electric wires. Talking, chatting, arguing, joking, gossiping, conversing, negotiating, chitchatting: these are all within my reach now thanks to the switches. Praising, questioning, thanking, requesting, complimenting, asking, complaining and discussing: they are almost at my disposal too.

First we must decide which software programme to buy so my parents order various demonstation CDs from Europe and America to test out. Weeks turn into months as my mother spends hours looking at website pages loading slowly on the Internet while my father devotes his evenings to reading information he has printed during his day at work.

As I watch and listen, I begin to understand what will help

me best express myself. Like an artist mixing paint to just the right consistency for his canvas, I must choose the right software. Now, nearly six months after I was first assessed, my parents urge me to tell them what I want. They're asking me because they've seen that I don't hang my head like a beaten dog any more now there's something interesting to look at. Hope rises off my mother and father like steam from a scalding bath as they begin to see tiny signs of what I might be capable of.

I can't stop thinking about how my life will change once we finally decide which software to buy. The thought that I might soon hear my 'voice' say 'I'm hungry' as many times as I want it to astounds me. Realising that I might be able to ask 'What's on the TV?' amazes me. These simple words are my own personal Mount Everests and to think I might soon conquer them is almost unimaginable.

I find myself drawn back to certain symbols that I look at in wonder. 'Who' is represented by a blank face with a question mark on it and 'what' is a square with a question mark inside. These are the building blocks of questions I haven't been able to ask. 'I want' is represented by a pair of hands reaching towards a red block, while two parallel thick black lines mean 'I am'. This is the symbol I return to perhaps more than any other because I am so unsure of what to say after those two small words. I am ... What? Who? I don't know. I've never been given a chance to find out.

Before I begin to answer those questions, I must master the basics of any sentence – single words and their symbols. Juice, tea, sugar, milk, hello, goodbye, I, you, we, they, no, yes, chicken, chips, meat, and, hair, mouth, bread, goodbye: only once I've learned these can I start to put them together to make sentences.

'I would like orange juice.'

'No, thank you.'

'I'm hungry.'

'I would like to go to bed.'

'I am cold.'

'I would like radishes and toast with jam.'

First, though, I must show my parents which software programme I want by nodding my head when they read out the names, but it feels impossible to decide. Again and again they've asked me but I can't bring myself to choose and we've been stuck in the doldrums of indecision for weeks now.

'Sometimes in life you just have to move forward,' my father told me a few days ago. 'You have to make a decision and stick with it. We just want you to show us which software you'd like us to buy. We're pretty sure you know which one you want, Martin.'

He looks at me as I stare mutely back at him.

'This is just the start,' Dad says softly. 'It isn't life and death.'

But it feels like it to me.

I've never made decisions before and now I must make the hardest one of all. How do you pick the bridge you will use to travel from one world into another? This software isn't just a piece of equipment: it will be my voice. What if I make the wrong choice? What if I pick something that limits me too much or is too complex for me to use? If I make a mistake, I might never get this chance again.

'We can buy something else if we don't get it right at first,' my mother tells me.

But her reassurances don't soothe away my terrors. Even as one part of me wonders how far my parents' faith will stretch – if I can't use the software, will they give up the wild dream the sceptics around us think will never come true – I find myself questioning what it will mean if all goes well and my world starts to open up. My parents might now believe I'm capable of more than anyone thought possible, as they've watched my right hand get a little steadier with the switches and seen me speed up as I practise selecting symbols, but they still don't completely understand. What will happen to us if the world we've known for so long changes to the extent that it tips off its axis? I'm so used to a cage that I don't know if I'll be able to see the open horizon even when I'm staring at it.

As doubts and anxiety fill me, I force myself to think of a telephone call my parents and David made to Kim a few weeks ago at Christmas. As they chatted, I sat nervously in front of my parents' computer and my hands shook even more than usual as I slowly clicked on symbols. Then my father held the phone close to the computer speakers and I pressed the switch for a final time.

'Hello, Kim,' my disembodied computer voice said. 'Happy Christmas.'

There was silence for a moment before my sister spoke but then I heard the joy in her voice from almost six thousand miles away. And in that moment I knew the ghost boy was finally coming back to life.

13

My Mother

Frustration flickers across my mother's face as she stares at me. I know this look well. Sometimes her features become so still that her face almost freezes. We're working at the computer together as we try to add words to my growing vocabulary. It's August 2002, a year since I was first assessed, and we've been learning to use my communication system for about six months. Kim brought the software with her on a visit from the UK after I finally decided what I wanted and I even have my own laptop now after Mum took me to buy one.

'These are all too old,' she said purposefully as she looked at the laptops lined up like gravestones in a computer shop. 'I want the newest one you have – top of the range, please. It must be quick and powerful. My son mustn't have any problems with it.'

Once again I watched her negotiate for me just as I'd seen her do so many times over the years. In her firm but polite manner, I've seen Mum insist to doctors who've said I was well that they must examine me again and argue with other medics who've wanted to put me at the back of the queue. Now she was going to make sure I got the best laptop the shop had to offer.

I hardly dared touch the laptop at first and simply stared at it whenever Dad, Mum or David switched it on. Listening in awe to the music that played like magic when the black screen burst into life, I'd wonder how I was ever going to learn to control this strange machine when I didn't even understand the keyboard. Letters might be just another kind of symbol but, unlike the pictures I'd spent so much time getting to know over the past few months, I don't know how to read them.

Just as you choose the words you speak naturally, I must pick what I want my new computer 'voice' to say by selecting words from grids – or pages – of vocabulary. My software came with very little pre-programmed so now my mother and I must input every word I want in my vocabulary and its corresponding symbol. Then I will be able to use my switches to move the words around and select what I want to say on-screen before the computer voices it.

Today my mother and I are working on words about colour because, just as she did when I was a child, she is helping me learn a new language. Mum has even given up her job as a radiographer to teach me intensively and we work together for several hours every day now when she comes to pick me up from the care centre at about 2 p.m. After going home, we work on building grids for about four hours before she leaves me to practise using them alone.

I know the speed with which I'm learning has surprised

her. At first, she had to teach herself how to use the software before showing me. But as time has gone on, she's seen that I can complete every task she gives me and trusts me to do more. So instead of sitting and reading the computer manuals alone, Mum now reads them to me and I commit everything she says to memory as we learn together. More and more, I seem to understand the instructions better than she does and there are times when I have to wait until she realises what she's doing wrong. But there is nothing I can do to tell her because, despite all my progress, I'm still communicating using only the most basic words and phrases.

Now I look at Mum as she stares at me before turning to the screen. So far today we've added the colours of the rainbow to my new grid – red, yellow, pink, green, purple and orange – as well as the other most obvious choices like blue, black and brown. But it's getting harder now that we're moving into the further reaches of the colour spectrum.

'Cerise?' Mum asks.

I keep my face still.

'Emerald?'

I know exactly what word I want. We often reach an impasse like this as we build a grid.

'Magenta?'

I don't respond in any way.

'Navy?'

For a moment, frustration builds inside me. It claws at the back of my throat as I wish my mother could guess the word I want because, if she can't, I'll never be able to say it. I'm entirely dependent on her to suggest every word I want added to my new vocabulary.

Sometimes there are ways to show the word I'm thinking of and earlier I used a switch to click on the symbol showing an ear and then the one bearing the picture of a sink.

'Sounds like sink?' Mum asked. 'Do you want pink?'

I smiled and the word was added to my grid. Now there's just one more shade I want – turquoise. As Mum runs through the spectrum, I wonder how I'll describe the colour of a summer sky if she doesn't think of it.

While it's frustrating for me, I sometimes wonder if my mother's desire to find the words I want is even more powerful than my own. She is as consumed by this process as I am and never seems to tire of sitting with me at the computer for hour after hour, day after day. When we aren't working together, my mother carries around pieces of paper on which she scribbles word lists as she thinks about the next grid we'll build and the words I might want to add to it. Because the more we work, the more she realises how extensive my vocabulary is, and I can see the shock in her eyes as she realises how much I know.

I think she's beginning to realise how underestimated I've always been but I've no idea how it makes her feel. I suspect it might horrify her to think that I've been fully aware for years but we don't talk about it and I don't think we ever will. Does she see my rehabilitation as a penance for sins of the past? I can't be sure but in her urgency and dedication to me, I wonder if she is fending off memories of those dark years after I first fell ill and the countless arguments when David, Kim and Pookie would disappear and I'd be left sitting in the corner.

'Look at us!' my mother would scream at my father.

'We're a mess. Martin needs special care that we can't give him and I don't understand why you won't let him have it.'

'Because he needs to be here with us,' my father would roar back, 'not with strangers.'

'But think of David and Kim. What about them? David used to be such an outgoing little boy but he's getting more and more withdrawn. And I know Kim seems brave but she needs more of your attention than she gets. She wants to spend time with her father but you're always so busy with Martin. Between him and work you never get a chance to be with the rest of us.'

'Well, that's how it has to be because I'm the only one looking after Martin, aren't I? I'm sorry, Joan, but we're a family and he's part of it. We can't just send him away. We've got to stay together.'

'Why, Rodney? Whose sake are you keeping him here for? Yours, Martin's or ours? Why can't you just accept that we can't look after him?'

'He would be better off somewhere being cared for properly by people who are experts. We could visit him and Kim and David would be so much happier.'

'But I want him here. I can't let him go.'

'And what about me, Kim and David? This isn't doing any of us any good. It's too much.'

On and on the fight would go, spiralling out of control as each battled with the other to win the war and I would listen to it all, knowing I was the cause, wishing I could be in some safe, dark place where I never had to listen to this argument again.

Sometimes, after a particularly bad row, Mum would storm

out of the room but one night Dad put me into the car before driving away. As I wondered if we'd ever go home again, I was filled with guilt about what I'd done to my family. It was my fault this was happening to them. If I'd died, everyone would have been better off. Eventually we went home, of course, and the familiar stony silence that always followed a row calcified around us again.

But there was one fight I'll never forget because after Dad had stormed out, Mum was left crying on the floor. She was wringing her hands, moaning, and I could feel the raw grief flowing out of her: she looked so alone, so confused and desperate. I wished I could reassure her, stand up from my wheelchair and leave behind this shell of a body that had caused so much pain.

Mum looked up at me. Her eyes were filled with tears.

'You must die,' she said slowly as she looked at me. 'You have to die.'

The rest of the world felt so far away when she said those words, and I stared blankly as she got up and left me in the silent room. I wanted to do as she bid me that day. I longed to leave my life because hearing those words was more than I could bear.

As time passed, I gradually learned to understand my mother's desperation, because as I sat in the care home and listened to other parents talk, I discovered many others felt just as tormented as she did. Little by little I learned why it was so hard for my mother to live with such a cruel parody of the once healthy child she had loved so much. Every time she looked at me she could see only the ghost boy he'd left behind.

My mother was far from alone in having these feelings of darkness and desperation. A couple of years after she spoke to me that night, a baby called Mark started coming to the care centre and his learning difficulties were so severe that he had to be tube fed, never made a sound and wasn't expected to survive for long. I never saw him because he lay in a cot all day but I could hear him. I knew what his mother sounded like too because, although I was usually lying on the floor when she came in with Mark, I became familiar with her voice. That's how I heard a conversation she had with Rina one morning.

'There's a moment every morning when I wake up and I don't remember,' Mark's mother said. 'I feel so light inside, so free. Then reality comes crashing back and I think of Mark, another day, another week, as I wonder if he's suffering and how long he might live.

'But I don't get out of bed to go to him straight away. Instead I lie there, looking at the light coming through the window, the curtains blowing in the breeze and each morning I know that I'm building up the courage to go and look in my own son's cot.'

Mark's mother wasn't fighting fate any more. She had accepted the inevitability of her son's death and now waited each morning for it to come, unsure how she'd feel when it did. Neither she nor my mother was a monster – they were just afraid. I long ago learned to forgive Mum for her mistakes. But as I look at her now, her brow knitting in concentration as she tries so hard to think of the colour I want to add to a grid, I wonder if she's forgiven herself. I hope so.

14

Other Worlds

When I needed to forget, I could always be free. However desperate I felt, there was always one place where I knew I could lose myself: my imagination. There I could be anything I wanted to be.

Once I was a pirate boy, stealing onto an enemy ship to take back the gold that had been stolen from my father. I could hear laughter as I climbed up a rope ladder onto the ship and jumped silently onto the wooden deck. A pirate was in the crow's nest far above me, looking out to sea through a telescope – he didn't know an enemy was creeping aboard right under his nose. At the other end of the deck I could see a group of pirates huddled together. They were crouching over a map, passing around a bottle of rum and laughing as they wondered which ship they'd attack next, whose gold they'd steal this time.

I licked my finger and stuck it into the air to find out which way the wind was blowing. I had to make sure the pirates didn't sniff me out because they tied up their prisoners and left them for the birds to pick out their eyes before making them walk the plank. Flinging myself onto the deck, I pulled myself along on my elbows, sliding forward silently, knowing my cutlass was by my side if I needed it. I was ready to slice off the head of any pirate who came too close but they were all too busy staring at their map to notice me. Without a sound, I climbed down the ladder into the ship. I had to find the pirate king's cabin because that was where my father's gold would be.

I came to a door and pushed it open. The pirate king was asleep in a chair but I could tell that he was so tall his head would nearly touch the ceiling if he stood up. He had a big black beard and a patch over one eye, and he was wearing a captain's hat. In front of him was a chest filled with jewels and money, precious stones and cups, and I crept towards it as I scanned the treasure. Then I saw it – the brown leather bag that held my father's gold. It was half hidden underneath a pile of coins and I pulled it carefully, inching it out bit by bit, careful not to make a sound until it was safely in my hand.

I could have left as quietly as I'd arrived, but I didn't.

I walked around the desk to where the pirate king was sitting. His nose was big and red and there was a scar running down his cheek. A parrot, blue and green and yellow, sat on a perch beside him. I fed it some bread from my pocket to keep it quiet before leaning forward and snatching the pirate king's hat as I started to laugh. He opened his good eye and saw me.

'AAAAAAAAAAAAAAARGH!' he roared and I laughed at him even harder.

He leaped up and drew his sword but I was too fast for him. I pushed his hat onto my head, ran for the door and smashed it closed behind me. I could hear the sound of wood splitting as the pirate king kicked his leg through the door and got stuck. Ha! He wouldn't be able to come after me now.

'Thief!' he screamed.

I pulled out my cutlass and pointed it in front of me. It was made of silver so shiny that the sun bounced off it as I ran onto the deck. The pirates were waiting for me but I twisted the cutlass and the light shining off my blade blinded them. They fell to their knees, screaming as they covered their eyes, and I ran to the side of the boat as one of the pirates tried to follow me. I could hear his sword swishing in the air; I could feel him close by. He wanted to catch me for the birds.

I spun around and my cutlass clashed against metal. The pirate's sword flew out of his hand and across the deck as I jumped onto the rigging, still holding my father's gold. I was the pirate boy. I could run and swim, steal and fight, face and outwit my enemies. I smiled as the pirates rushed at me.

'You'll never catch me,' I yelled as I jump off the rigging.

I fell down and down, my body diving like an arrow into the deep blue water, which closed over me. I knew the sea would safely carry me far away. I'd find my father and fight another day. I was the pirate boy and no one's prisoner.

That is where I went to escape the feelings that threatened to overwhelm me when I thought I'd be trapped forever. Now I sometimes wish I could retreat there again as I begin to experience an exquisite torture of hope, frustration, fear and joy as I reconnect with the world. Deep down I know, of course, that I no longer need to lose myself in fantasy because I'm living life at last. But I'll always be thankful for my imagination because I learned long ago that it was my greatest gift: it was the key that unlocked my prison and allowed me to escape, the door through which I entered new worlds and conquered them – the place where I was free.

15

Fried Egg

The band around my head feels tight this morning as I practise on my computer. At its centre is a small black dot, which I'm trying to use to shine an infrared beam on the computer screen with a slight turn of my head. Pressing my feeble hands into one of my switches enables me to choose the word I want to say. This gadget is supposed to help speed up the communicating process but it's taking a long time to learn how to use it.

The desire to master my communication system is all-consuming as I try to control my switches and remember where the symbols we've inputted into my computer are within the word grids. Most days I still go to the care centre for a few hours to give my mother some time to herself, but instead of losing myself in fantasies now, I flick through mental images of the grids to test myself on how to find my way from one to the other, and remember where particular words are stored. When I get home, I work for six, seven, eight hours, sometimes wasting words just to hear myself 'speak'. Like a child in a sweet shop, I gorge myself: verbs are my chocolate bon-bons, nouns are my sticky toffees, adverbs are my jelly sweets and adjectives are my liquorice allsorts. In bed at night, I see symbols running through my head and into my dreams.

Now I watch as each individual word cell on the grid in front of me is highlighted one by one. It contains words about breakfast and the other symbols I've already selected for the sentence are hovering at the top of the screen. 'I would like', 'orange juice', 'and', 'coffee', 'please' stand patiently like a queue of passengers hoping to see a bus they fear might never turn the corner because they've been waiting for so long. Each time I select a symbol, I must wait for the cursor to go back to the beginning of the grid and click slowly through each word cell again. Now I wait because I want to ask my mother for a fried egg for breakfast this morning as well as coffee and juice.

A picture of a steaming cup – 'instant coffee' – is illumi-nated. Then a picture of a carton – 'milk'.

Honey.

Toast.

Muffin.

Marmite.

Porridge.

Strawberry.

Apricot.

Marmalade.

Jam.

Butter.

Margarine.

Grapefruit.

Orange.

Banana.

Raisin Bread.

There's just one more line of words to go.

I watch as 'omelette', 'tomato' and 'sausage' are highlighted. The cursor moves to the line beginning with 'bacon' and ending with 'fried egg'. That's the symbol I want. I revel in the knowledge that I can now be so specific when I ask for food. Scrambled eggs won't do nor will poached – I want sunny side up, a disc of sunshine yellow to brighten my plate.

I curl my right hand around my lolly switch in readiness. The right one is my most useful hand, the hand I trust. I will ask it now to do as I wish.

The cursor moves on and each cell is highlighted for a few seconds before the next is lit up. 'Egg' and 'scrambled egg' are left behind as the cursor moves forwards. 'Fried egg' is coming up. It nestles between 'poached' and 'boiled'. I wait to pounce on it.

At last. The symbol is illuminated. But as I go to squeeze my fingers around my switch, I realise they won't move fast enough. I try to squeeze them closed again but they won't obey me. My hand has failed me and a wave of anger pulses through me as I watch the highlighter move on to the next symbol. I have missed fried egg. It has been and gone. I must wait for the cursor to click through the whole grid again before I'll get another chance to select it.

I take a deep breath. Communicating is a particularly arduous game of verbal snakes and ladders for me. It takes the kind of patience I'm now almost glad I had years to master.

I watch as the words light up in front of me once more. Come what may, I will get my fried egg. Then I will click on one last symbol – 'speak' – and my electronic voice will finally have its say.

16

I Tell a Secret

I can't pinpoint the exact moment when I first fell in love with Virna. Perhaps the feeling settled so slowly, layer by layer, that I didn't realise it had become part of me, or maybe I just never allowed myself to think it. But all I know in this moment, as I look at her, is that I love her.

I'm at the day centre and Virna is talking to me. I look forward to her visits now more than ever because they are a soothing antidote to the resentment that's beginning to flicker inside me. I don't understand why I'm still being sent to the care centre even though I'm getting better and better at using my communication system. It's late 2002 – more than a year since I was assessed – and even though I'm sure I've proven I shouldn't be here, no one seems to know what to do with me because there is nowhere else for me to go. If being here was hard when no one knew my intelligence was intact, then it's a thousand times more so now.

I have two lives: one in which I'm at home, working on my

computer, feeling as if I might soon become a part of the world for the first time; and the other, in which I sit in the care home with a folder of symbols lying on my lap that no one takes much notice of, feeling as dead as I ever did. It's getting harder and harder to move between the two.

Not long ago, my parents went away on a short trip and I was sent to an unfamiliar residential home. Each morning I was wheeled into a dirt yard surrounded by a high metal fence, where I would sit like an animal in a zoo. At the end of each afternoon, I was taken back inside, where there was no TV or radio, nothing to break the monotony. The only thing that ever changed was the sound of cars on a nearby road and whenever I heard one approach I dreamed it was someone coming to take me away. But I was never rescued and there was nothing I could do to stem the rage and disappointment surging through my veins. When would people start to see me for who I am instead of the broken shell that encases me? What must I do to convince them that I don't fit into these places any more and it's wrong to try and make me?

Even though some people have seen how much I'm capable of, I'm still usually treated like a child who doesn't know his own mind. It feels as if Virna is the only one who sees me as an equal and I'm more and more certain that I mean something to her. Why else would she have such faith in me? I long ago stopped listening to the staff here making jokes about how much time Virna spends with me. But now I've started to think about what they say and I know her eyes shine with pleasure when she asks how I'm getting on with my computer. I can't tell her a lot about my progress because I don't bring my laptop to the centre for fear something might happen to it.

It is far too precious to bring to this place. But Virna asks me questions that I answer more surely now that my head movements are getting better and my hands a little steadier. Like a rusty old machine that runs more smoothly with use, my body is growing stronger.

But it's not just Virna's interest in my progress that tells me she cares; she's told me in other ways too: by giving me a mobile she'd made of wire fish decorated with sea-green and blue marbles, which now hangs in my bedroom, and by visiting me on my birthday. Virna is the only person who's ever come to see me at home apart from my school friend Stephen, who came around during the years after I fell sick. Each year, he would arrive with a birthday card that he would read out to me. But I've not seen Stephen for a long time now because he moved across the country to study to be a doctor. So I was overwhelmed when Virna came to see me. It happened even before I was assessed and she gave me a box that she'd painted for my birthday. No one but Virna believed in me back then and I gazed at the box in wonder, holding it as gently as a religious relic, as she and her cousin Kim chatted to my parents.

'We'll be back,' Virna said softly as she got up to leave and smiled at me. 'This won't be the last time we visit you.'

That's why I feel so hopeful now that Virna might be able to care for me even more as I learn to communicate. Soon I'll be able to say whatever I want, talk about any subject quickly and easily, and be the kind of person that Virna might like.

I wonder why I'm surprised to realise that I've fallen in love with her. The clues to my feelings were there all along if only I'd looked back long enough to see them. Soon after Virna started working at the centre, I can remember hearing a conversation that should have told me all I needed to know. Envy filled me as I heard her talking to another carer about a cinema date she was going on with a man she'd met. How I longed to be the one to take Virna out and make her smile.

I didn't hear anything more about it until a couple of months later when I heard her talking to Marietta. But this time her eyes didn't dance when she spoke about the man.

'He's not worth getting upset over!' Marietta said to Virna. 'You've just got to forget about him. There are plenty more fish in the sea.'

Virna gave Marietta a weak smile and I could see she was upset. What a fool the man was. She'd felt something real for him and he'd hurt her. It angered me.

I smile to myself now as I think back to that day four years ago when I should have realised I felt something more than just friendship for Virna. Then I look at her as she talks softly to me and I know as certainly as I've ever known anything that I love her.

'My cousin Kim's met a new guy,' she says, her voice bright and excited. 'She really likes him. She wasn't sure what was happening for a while because they went out a few times but he didn't say anything to her about what he wanted.'

I look at Virna. The more I learn about what happens between men and women, the more I realise that what you see on TV isn't like real life: real life is never that simple. But surely this man wouldn't take Kim out if he didn't like her?

'It's all fine now, though,' Virna says with a smile. 'They had a chat last night and he told Kim that he thinks she's great. She's really happy.'

Suddenly, I'm filled with the desire to tell Virna how I feel.

She's told me about Kim and her new boyfriend. I want what they have. I must tell Virna because I'm sure she wants this too.

I lift my hand and watch it wave haphazardly in the air. It flails inconclusively between us but I smile at Virna. I've never told anyone anything like this before, never dared imagine that it might be possible for someone to love me. But surely it is now that I'm learning to communicate and showing people a little of what I'm capable of? Virna, of all people, must be able to see past my broken body?

My hand waves in the air once more before it drops to my side. Virna looks at me silently. Her face is steady and serious. What's wrong with her? She's so quiet.

'Do you think there could be something between us, Martin?' she asks eventually.

I smile, feeling nervous and excited, scared and hopeful. I'm so sure that she feels as I do. Why else would she be a friend like no other? Why else would she help me?

Then I see sadness flicker in Virna's eyes.

'I'm sorry, Martin,' she says.

All the happiness that was rippling off her a few moments ago as she talked to me about Kim has suddenly disappeared. Virna is flat, lifeless. I can feel her withdrawing from me. I want her to stay but she's disappearing.

'We can only ever be friends,' Virna says slowly. 'You must understand that. There never can be anything between us, Martin. I'm sorry.'

My smile sets in my face like concrete. I don't know how to wipe it off as I listen to her speak.

'I'm so sorry if you feel differently,' Virna tells me. 'But I have to be honest and say there will never be anything more between us.'

My smile finally shatters. I can feel a pain in my chest. I've never known anything like it before but I know what it is. I've heard it talked about in movies and listened to people describe it in songs. I understand what it is now even as it pierces me: heartbreak.

17

The Bite

I was sitting on the toilet. I'm not sure why. I must have
been a teenager and maybe Dad had just given me a bath.
Whatever the reason, I was naked and I'd had enough. It had
been a bad day – not bad because something awful had happened but because nothing ever happened.

Dad leaned over and stretched his arms around me. I felt
his fingers closing around a pimple on my back. It hurt. I
didn't want him to touch it. I wanted him to stop, to leave me
alone. I stared at my father's stomach, which was level with
my eyes. It was big, round and sturdy. It wasn't just because
of his beard that my mother often called him 'Father
Christmas'.

Rage welled up inside me as I looked at Dad's stomach. He
leaned even closer and his belly grazed my mouth as I felt his
fingers dig questioningly into my pimple. The pain was so
sharp, I wanted to roar at him to stop, shake his hands off me
and storm out of the room, just as I'd seen Kim and David do

so many times when they were annoyed. For once, I wanted to be able to decide who did what to me, when and how. I wanted my father to stop touching me and just let me be. Even a baby can scream its dissatisfaction but I couldn't even do that.

Rage burned bitter in the back of my throat as I opened my mouth as wide as I could before sinking my teeth into my father's stomach.

He gasped in shock as he stepped back and looked at me in surprise.

'That bloody hurt,' he said as he rubbed his tummy.

Guilt filled me first – and then sweet relief.

18

The Furies

If there were Three Furies in my story, their names were Frustration, Fear and Loneliness. These were the phantoms that plagued me for seven long years – nine if my awareness is dated from the time I started to dip in and out of life. But while the Furies almost beat me many times, thankfully I learned how to defeat them every now and again too.

Frustration came first. If there was an Olympic gold in outrunning her, I'm sure I would have won it. Frustration was a twisted, hissing mistress, unique because she was all-consuming. Fear might have been a sudden cold punch in my stomach and Loneliness a dead weight on my back but Frustration started in my chest, turned my guts into twisted metal and soon overwhelmed my entire body. Every molecule vibrated with anger as she infected me.

Frustration rose up inside me so often because I was constantly reminded that I couldn't determine my own fate in even the smallest of ways. If people wanted me to sit in the same position for hour after hour, there was nothing I could do about it, although pain shot through me. Words can't express how much I sometimes hated the cold custard and prunes that I ate every lunchtime for years. And other people's determination to make me walk was always sure to start Frustration wailing again.

My parents still believe that I might be able to walk again because, although they are spastic and uncontrollable, my limbs aren't paralysed. It was my mother who started taking me to physiotherapy sessions to make sure my muscles and joints didn't freeze completely through inactivity. She and my father were so committed to the belief that I would walk some day that neither would listen when a doctor suggested permanently severing some of the tendons in my feet to reduce the spasticity. He said it wouldn't matter because surely I would never use my feet again? My parents refused his advice, took me to see a new medic and two years ago I had the first of two extensive foot surgeries to flatten my curled-in feet in the hope that it might help me to walk again one day.

Not being able to walk always felt almost insignificant to me compared to my other limitations. It seemed far more problematic not to be able to use my arms to feed or wash myself, make a gesture or hug someone. Not having a voice to say I'd had enough food or the bath water was too hot or to tell someone I loved them was the thing that made me feel most inhuman. Words and speech separate us from the animal kingdom, after all. They give us free will and agency as we use them to express our desires and refuse or accept what others want us to do. Without a voice, I couldn't control even the simplest things and that's why Frustration so regularly started her violent lament inside me.

Next came her sister Fear — the fear of being powerless over what happened to me from day to day or in the future, the fear that I was growing up and would be put into permanent residential care because my parents couldn't cope with me as they got older. Every time I was sent to one particular residential home in the country, when my family went on holiday or my father was away on a business trip, terror filled me when I thought I might never leave it again. Those few hours each day with my family were what kept me alive.

I hated that care home in the country more than any other place I was sent. Years ago, after overhearing my parents talk about what time they would leave the next day to take me there, I knew I had to do something to stop them. When Fear woke me up in the middle of the night, I realised I had to rid myself of her forever. After listening to check everyone was asleep, I wriggled my head off my pillow and into the plastic pillowcase encasing it. As it crackled around my head, I pressed my face into the pillow itself as hard as I could as I told myself that I wouldn't have to go to the country the next day; I would soon be free of Fear.

Breathing faster and faster, I began to sweat as my head started to feel light. I'd found a way to escape Fear and I felt elated. But the emotion soon gave way to despair as I realised that I wasn't going to succeed. However hard I tried, I couldn't stop my pitiful body from breathing. The next day I went to the country as planned and carried on visiting the home there once or twice a year.

'They can look after you better than I can,' my mother would tell me again and again if she was the one who was driving me there.

She always said the same thing, like an incantation she hoped would ward off the guilt as it rose inside her.

'You'll be well looked after,' she'd insist, clinging on to the words as she said them.

If Mum had known what happened to me in that place, then I'm sure she never would have said this. But she didn't know and I felt torn between rage and sadness as I listened to her: rage that my parents were making me go to a place I hated so much and sadness that my mother truly seemed to believe strangers could care for me better than she could. The fire of my longing to stay with her burned white hot inside me and I wished she could see it and know how much I wanted to be with her and no one else.

Last came Loneliness and she was perhaps the most terrifying of all the Furies because she could slowly suck the life out of me even as I sat in a room surrounded by people. As they hurried to and fro, chatted, argued, made up and fell out again, I could feel the paralysing bony fingers of Loneliness clamp tightly around my heart.

However isolated she made me feel, Loneliness could always find new ways to make her presence felt. A few years ago I had an anaesthetic after going into hospital for an operation and Mum and Dad had left to go to work by the time I was wheeled into the operating theatre. A nurse held out my arm as a needle was put into a vein and an anaesthetist connected a syringe full of white liquid to it.

'Sweet dreams,' he said softly as I felt a burning sensation move up my arm towards my chest.

The next thing I knew, I was lying on my side on a cold hospital bed. It was moving and I couldn't see properly. I felt utterly disoriented as I struggled to understand where I was. But as I felt a hand take mine to adjust a needle going into a vein, I grabbed on to it as hard as I could, hopeful for a moment of connection that would defeat the feeling of being completely alone. But the hand was pulled roughly from my weak grip and I heard footsteps retreat as I lay squirming with shame, thinking how repulsive I must be.

What saved me was discovering that Loneliness had an Achilles heel, which meant the skein of isolation she wound around me could occasionally be unravelled. I just never knew when it might happen.

I once remember my father talking about a book one of his work colleagues had read. It was about a man who had been disabled as an adult and complained that one of the worst things about sitting in a wheelchair was the discomfort that came from being badly positioned in it. My ears pricked up immediately because as I'd grown older I'd become increasingly aware that I was often left sitting on my balls. The feeling was a very specific type of discomfort: pain gave way to numbness before pain put in a follow-up appearance, like a music hall actress making a bawdily triumphant encore to a delighted crowd.

After the conversation with his colleague, my father was always extra careful to position me gently and make sure I wasn't trapping my testicles beneath me when he sat me in my wheelchair. And each time he did, Loneliness went snarling back to her solitary cave, because when my father showed that he was thinking about me, we defeated Loneliness together.

19

Peacock Feathers

I will my hands not to shake as I stare at the computer. I must think methodically, reason my way step by step through the problem on the screen in front of me. I have to be calm and considered if I'm going to solve it.

'What do you want me to do next?' Virna asks as she sits next to me.

I'm not sure yet. I stare at the screen and feel my mind flipping back through all I've learned about computers, the hours spent watching software demonstrations and practising new programmes. I feel sure the answer is somewhere inside me. I just need to find it.

It's February 2003, a year after I first got my laptop and nearly two years since I was assessed. I'm sitting with Virna in front of a computer at the health centre that shares a building with my care home. She started working here a few months ago and we still see each other often because she is so close by. Virna has remained true to her word that we could be friends even after I told her how I felt, and we talk as we always have. Mostly it's everyday stuff, which is how I knew there were problems with the computers in her office.

'Apparently there are issues with the cooling fans,' she told me.

I doubted if this was the real reason for the glitches. Teaching myself to read might be taking a long time but learning the language of computers has been easy in comparison. Just as I once learned to tell time by memorising shadows, I'm trying to commit letter shapes to memory and can now understand a few written words. Maybe it's simply a question of reawakening the aptitude for electronics I had as a child but I've discovered that I understand computers almost intuitively since getting my own. In recent months I've taught myself to use a string of software programmes, including one that translates my symbols into words so that I can send emails, and another that allows me to answer the phone via my laptop.

'Hello, this is Martin Pistorius speaking,' my computer voice says. 'I am unable to talk so I speak via a computer and this takes some time, so please be patient.'

Even so, most people ring off because the blandness of my computerised voice is so hypnotic they think they're talking to an answerphone. But I have at least started to address the problem after being asked to give a talk about my experiences. The staff here at the health centre had heard my story from people at the care home and asked me to tell them more about my communication system. But after spending forty hours inputting an eight-minute speech, I realised that my voice was so monotonous even Romeo would have bored Juliet if he'd used it to declare his love.

So I started to experiment with ways to make my computer voice sound more natural. First, I inputted full stops into the middle of sentences so that my computer voice would sound as if it was pausing for 'breath'. Next I decided to modify my American 'voice' so that I say 'tomARto' instead of 'tomAYto' in an effort to sound more as I would if I could speak. I also had to choose which voice to use: just as some people pick from a list of fonts when they type, I was able to select one of a dozen voices contained in my computer software. The one I chose is called 'Perfect Paul' because he sounds like a good fit for me – not too high, not too gruff.

Tailoring my speech has certainly made me feel more confident and yet it didn't allay the fear that filled me on the day of the talk itself. I knew I would recognise many of the people in the room and the constant tremor in my hands – one of the legacies of my past – got worse and worse as I became more anxious. Virna was sitting near me while I gave my talk but even so I shook so much I could hardly hit the switches to start the computer. I forced myself to breathe deeply as I stared at the screen and heard my voice start to speak.

'Hello everybody and thank you for coming today,' it said. 'I am really nervous so I wrote a few things down.'

Line by precious line, I went on to describe what had happened to me since the day of my assessment and all that I'd learned since then – the software and symbols, the switches and headmouse – and people came up to congratulate me when I'd finished. Then they turned to discuss what I'd said with each other and it was strange to know they were talking about words I'd spoken. It was the first time that had ever happened.

The ease I have with computers is what made my father suggest I might be able to help with the problems here at the health centre. Apparently he said they should give me a chance to fix them, which is why Virna came to get me from my classroom at the care centre. I think my teacher that day must have thought the world had gone mad if anyone was entertaining the idea that someone from her end of the corridor might be able to fix a computer. But to me it felt like a sign, the chance I'd been waiting for to show what I was capable of.

My nerves twisted as Virna pushed me down the hall. I wanted to prove that I could do more than just speak words via a laptop. Sitting down in front of the computer, I stared at the screen. Virna was going to have to be my hands and use the mouse to navigate into the system so that I could fix it as she read to me what was written on the screen and I told her what to do. Repairing a computer is a bit like going into a maze, after all: you might go down dead ends but eventually you find your way through. I just had to trust my instincts as the computer prompted us with commands and we sat there for hours, fixing first one problem, then another and finally solving a third.

I was filled with exhilaration when we'd finished. I'd done it! I could hardly believe I'd managed to work out a problem that no one else had been able to. I had Virna check the computer again and again just to make sure that I'd really solved it, and each time it was clear the system was working properly again.

'Well done, Martin!' Virna kept saying, smiling at me with pleasure. 'I can't believe you did that. The technicians couldn't manage it but you did!'

She laughed to herself as she pushed me back down the corridor to the care centre. 'That will show them!' she kept saying.

Even going back to my classroom couldn't dampen my mood. I didn't notice where I was any more. I didn't care. All I could see was the computer screen and its inner workings flashing around my head as I navigated myself and Virna around the maze. I'd done it!

A few days later, there was another problem with the email system, and once again Virna told me about it. My heart began to race with excitement and I wished with all my might I'd be asked back to help out again. But it was several days before Virna finally came down the corridor to get me. Maybe her manager thought I'd just been lucky the first time and wasn't sure I'd be able to repeat my success.

But now Virna and I are sitting together in front of a computer screen once more.

'Shall I hit F1?' she asks.

I jerk my head to the side to tell her not to.

'How about F10?'

I smile.

She hits the key and we're taken into the first layer of the computer's modem settings. I know there will be many more to come before I find the problem. I must calm myself down and think clearly. I have to show for a second time what I'm capable of and prove beyond doubt that I really know what I'm doing. I'm focused as I tell Virna where to go next.

Somehow I know I'll be able to fix this problem. I can feel it. I'm sure that with Virna's help I'll be able to navigate my way inside this machine and find whatever is troubling it.

It's then that I feel it – an emotion I hadn't felt until I first fixed the computer last week. Now it's back again and the feeling is strange, like a peacock splaying its multicoloured tail feathers; it puffs me out and makes me feel vital. Then I realise what it is: pride.

20

Daring to Dream

Is there anything more powerful than a mother's love? It's a battering ram that breaks down castle doors, a tidal wave that washes away all in its wake. Mum's eyes are bright with it as she turns to me.

'I'll just run in to check where we need to go and then I'll come back and get you,' she says.

Mum gets out of the car and slams the door. I sit with the spring sunshine pouring through the windscreen, making me squint. We've come to the communication centre where I was first assessed nearly two years ago because I've been invited to attend an open day with students after my mother insisted on updating the experts about my progress.

'You've come so far, Martin!' she told me. 'I'm going to go and see them. They'll want to know. You've only been using your computer for just over a year and look at all you can do on it!'

I knew there was no point trying to stop Mum after she'd

made the decision to boast so I waited while she went off to the centre a few weeks ago and on her return listened while she excitedly told me what had happened.

'They want to see you,' she said. 'They can't believe how quickly you've progressed. They've invited you to attend a workshop with some students.'

I can understand everyone's surprise. Even I feel a little swept off my feet now that I have a job. In fact, I have to check I'm not dreaming each time I'm pushed into the office where I volunteer one day a week. I'm working at the health centre where I helped fix the computers with Virna and I can hardly believe that I'm being asked to do more than stare blankly at the walls of a care home. The work is simple – I photocopy and file because my right arm has grown strong enough to lift paper now and a wonderful colleague called Haseena helps me if there is something I can't do. I also fix the computers as and when problems arise.

The best thing about the job is that it means I've finally been able to leave the care home. It's the strangest feeling every Tuesday when I'm pushed through the doors of the building and my body imperceptibly leans right towards my old classroom, only to be turned in the opposite direction towards the health centre. Leaving the care home is a fork in the road; I'd die if I were sent back to one now. I sometimes wonder whether a shadow of the ghost boy lingers in the place where I spent so many years. But I push the thought away. I refuse to think about the past now that I have a future.

My body is getting stronger in a number of tiny ways as I start to use it more. On the days when I'm not working, I'm at home practising on the computer. I'm a little sturdier when I sit upright now. My neck muscles are strong enough for me to use my headmouse most of the time and I'm beginning to use the touchpad on my laptop a little because my right hand in particular is getting more reliable. My left is still largely uncontrollable so I might not be a butterfly quite yet but I'm slowly emerging from my chrysalis.

The only visible link with my past is the bib I still wear, a legacy of the days when I would drool so uncontrollably down my chest that a speech therapist recommended my mouth be filled with icing sugar to force me to swallow. I don't really need the bib any more and my mother doesn't want me to wear it but I can't quite bring myself to stop. Maybe I'm afraid of losing the magical powers I've gained unexpectedly if I test them too much by taking off the bib. Maybe my reluctance to give up the trappings of my baby years is the only act of rebellion I have at my disposal and I want to make the most of it as I start to realise what it means to make my own decisions. Choosing whether or not to wear my bib each day is often the only opportunity I have to make a decision so I'm determined to be the one to make it.

Now, as I sit inside the car waiting for my mother, I watch students walking up and down the road in front of me. The communication centre is part of a university and I dream of studying at a place like this because I know that one day I'd like to work full-time with computers. There are occasions when they seem like the simplest things in the world compared to everything else I'm learning.

I've even started testing software for a company in the UK. I use their communication programmes on my computer and Mum and I have been finding bugs in the software every now and again since we started using it. The makers used to email solutions to the problems to my mother, but gradually I became the one they corresponded with. When they realised how well I knew the systems, they asked me to start testing them. I've no idea how or why I understand computers so well but I've stopped asking. It's often like that these days: there are things I do without thinking that surprise people.

When my father came into the office recently, he looked at me quizzically as I put documents into alphabetical files.

'How do you know what goes where?' Dad asked in surprise.

I hadn't really thought about it. I still can't read properly but I'd matched the letter I saw on the name of the document to the one on front of the file. Letters are just symbols after all – an 'A' looks like a man clasping his hands above his head, 'M' is the top of a mountain range and 'S' is a slithering snake.

The car door opens and Mum leans down towards me.

'Are you ready?'

She sets my wheelchair beside the door and lifts my legs out of the car before taking my arm in hers. We pull against each other as I stand up before wriggling down into the chair. Mum puts my laptop on my knee and pushes me towards the building, where I watch the electric doors I'd never even seen two years ago glide open to let us in. A woman directs us to a room where coffee is being served and my eyes slide over the people who are standing together and talking. Two of them are men, neither of whom is in a wheelchair, but each carries a box that looks a little like the device Mum and Dad once almost bought me. I look at the men with interest, like an ornithologist might look at a rare bird. I've never met someone as silent as me before.

'Shall we get you ready?' I hear Mum ask.

She pushes me into a small lecture room filled with desks and chairs lined up in neat rows. A woman is unpacking papers as she stands in front of a whiteboard at the other end of the room.

'Where do you want to sit?' Mum asks and I point to the back row of chairs.

When we're settled, Mum unzips my laptop. A peal of notes bursts into life as she switches it on and the woman at the whiteboard looks up. She's middle-aged with cropped grey hair, glasses and a shawl draped around her shoulders. She smiles at me. I look down, unsure what to do. I've never been to something like this before. I haven't sat among a group of people who are learning and discussing things. I don't want them to notice me.

Mum and I wait as people slowly file into the room before sitting down. They chat with each other, say hello and smile until finally everyone is seated and the woman with glasses starts to speak.

'Good morning,' she says with a smile. 'My name is Diane Bryen and I work at Temple University in Philadelphia, where I run a programme called ACES, which aims to help adult users of communication technology determine and govern their own lives.

'I believe this is the way we will help new voices to emerge and break down stereotypes about those with disabilities.'

The woman's voice is bright and full of energy. She looks around the room encouragingly.

'There's no doubt that those with disabilities face significant barriers,' she says. 'Barriers to equal quality education, barriers to getting family support so that children can be raised with that support, barriers to affordable and accessible housing, barriers to equal access to healthcare and employment.

'These are consistent barriers that you come across with each disability group but what I am here to talk about today are not the most obvious injustices. Instead I want to talk about the whole host of other limitations imposed upon people by society because disability is as much about disabling attitudes as it is physical, cognitive or sensory limitations. If someone does not expect or is not expected to achieve, then they never will.'

I look at Dr Bryen. I've never heard someone speak with such passion and conviction about people like me before.

'I believe that if those with disabilities are to break down the barriers facing them then they must realise they have the *right* to, that they can have goals just like anyone else – and to do that they must dare to dream.'

I watch as Dr Bryen looks around the room.

'The man I'd like to meet most before I die is Nelson Mandela,' she says. 'Because despite being imprisoned for so long, he had a dream that he held on to even when he was deprived of freedom and basic nutrition. Mr Mandela was bold in his dream and followed it until he saw it realised.

'I've met other people with dreams too. One of the best bosses I ever had was a man called Bob Williams, who worked in politics and had cerebral palsy. He also had a great job, a service dog and a wife who loved him very much.

'He was living the life he dreamed of and I've met many more people like him. For instance, I know a musician who dreamed of singing and programmed his communication device to do it for him and a lecturer at the university where I work who has cerebral palsy and does a job she loves. Personally, too, I've seen someone I love dare to dream – because my brother is blind.

'Each of these people has achieved so much but what every one of them did was dare to dream. It is a powerful thing and we must all learn to do it.'

Dr Bryen looks at a man sitting near the front of the room.

'What's your dream?' she says to him.

He is able-bodied and shifts uneasily in his seat as the spotlight falls on him.

'To write a book one day,' he says quietly.

'And how are you going to achieve it?'

'I'm not sure.'

Dr Bryen smiles at him.

'That's why we need to think long and hard about our dreams, because once we dare to have them, we can start the process of trying to realise them.

'Dreams don't have to be huge though. I know of one woman who dreams of having a subscription to a soap opera magazine and another who wants to eat macaroni cheese for dinner each week.

'Dreams can be any size you want them to be. But the important thing is that you have one that is yours.'

Dr Bryen looks around the room again. Her eyes travel

over the rows of people, further and further back until they come to rest on me.

'What do you think you need to achieve a dream?' she asks.

Everyone looks at me. I don't know what to say. I want to be left alone. I've never been looked at by so many people at once. I don't know what to do.

'I think Martin would say you need to work hard,' Mum says.

She is speaking for me, trying to fill the silence I'm carving open like a gash. I wish I could disappear.

'But I want to know what *you* think,' Dr Bryen asks as she looks at me. 'It's Martin, isn't it? I want you to tell me what you believe a person needs to achieve their dream.'

There's no escape. The room feels so quiet as I point my headmouse at the laptop and start clicking on switches. After what seems like forever, I finally speak.

'You need to be given the chance to decide for yourself what your dream is,' my computer voice says.

'What do you mean, Martin?'

I click on my switches again and again.

'People must help you work out what your dream is. They must enable you to have one.'

'Oh no!' Dr Bryen exclaims. 'I don't agree with you at all. Don't you see, Martin? You can't ask other people to give you permission to dream. You just have to do it.'

I'm not sure if I understand what Dr Bryen means. I've spent my whole life being given the food others chose for me and put into bed when they decided I was tired. I've been dressed as they saw fit and spoken to as and when they wanted to speak to me. I've never been asked to think about what *I* want. I don't know what it's like to make decisions for myself, let alone dare to dream. I look at her. I know so much about other people's expectations and so little about my own.

But is what she's saying true? Might I really start to make decisions for myself now that I'm finding my voice? I'm only just beginning to realise that somewhere at the end of this journey there might be the kind of freedom I could never even have imagined once. I'll be able to be the person I want to be but do I really dare to dream who he is?

21

Secrets

The unexpected side to being a ghost boy was that people inadvertently showed me their secret worlds. I heard farts rip like bullets from a gun as people walked across a room or watched them check their reflections so often it seemed as if they were hoping to see a more beautiful version of their face magically appear. I've known people to pick their noses and eat what they found or adjust their clinging underwear before scratching their crotch. I've heard them swear and mumble to themselves as they pace around a room. I've listened to arguments unfold as lies were twisted into facts to try and win a contest.

People revealed themselves in other ways too: in a touch that was gentle and caring or rough and unthinking; in feet that shuffled with fatigue when they walked into a room. If someone was impatient, they would sigh as they washed or fed me; if they were angry, they would pull off my clothes just a little more roughly than usual. Happiness fizzed off them like a small electric pulse, while anxiety had a thousand telltale signs from the nails people bit to the hair they pushed behind their ears again and again to try to contain their worry.

Sadness, though, is probably the hardest thing of all to hide because sorrow has a way of seeping out however well people think they're containing it. You only have to look to see the signs, but most people don't, which is why so many seem to end up feeling lonely. I think that's why some of them talked to me: speaking to another living creature – however inanimate – was better than no one at all.

One of the people who confided in me was Thelma, a carer who worked at the home when I was first there and often ended up sitting with me and some of the other kids as we waited to be picked up at the end of the day. Every afternoon, I would sit listening for the white gate at the end of the corridor to squeak open as someone pushed it. Then, as footsteps started to echo down the hall, I'd try to work out who it was: the click of high heels meant that Corinne's mum had come to get her, heavy army boots told me it was Jorika's father, while the soft pad of Dad's shoes spoke of the sturdy man he still is today and my mother's shoes were almost silent except for the muffled rustle of her rapid steps. Some days I could guess who everyone was before I saw them but on others I got them all wrong.

Each afternoon the other children would leave one by one and the building would slowly fall silent: phones would stop ringing and people would stop rustling, my ears would hiss as the air conditioning was switched off and my brain would fill the silence with white noise. Soon it would be just Thelma and me waiting and I was always glad it was her because she didn't get angry if my father was late.

One afternoon we were sitting together when a song came on the radio and Thelma stared into space as she listened to it. I could feel she was sad today.

'I miss him so much,' she said suddenly. Although my head was bent to my chest, I could hear that she had started to cry.

I knew what she was talking about: her husband had died. I'd heard people speaking about it in low voices.

'He was a good man,' she whispered. 'I think of him all the time, every day.'

There was a creak as Thelma shifted her weight on the chair beside me. Her voice cracked as she spoke and her tears fell faster.

'I can't stop seeing him at the end. I keep wondering if he understood what was happening. How did he feel? Was he scared or in pain? Did I do enough? I keep going over and over it in my mind. I can't stop thinking of him.'

She sobbed even more.

'If only I'd told him more that I loved him,' she said. 'I didn't say it enough and now I won't get a chance again. I'll never be able to tell him.'

Thelma cried a little more as I sat beside her. I could feel my stomach knotting inside me. She was a kind person who didn't deserve such sadness. I wished I could tell her she'd been a good wife – I was sure she had been.

22

Out of the Cocoon

Was it inevitable that I would become terrified of solitude after spending so many years alone? After attending the workshop at the communication centre last month, I'm back attending a week-long course about augmentative and alternative communication or AAC. Everyone, from people like me who use AAC to the parents, teachers and therapists working with us, comes to this centre. But this particular course is for students studying for a degree in AAC, and I was invited to take part by the centre's director, Professor Alant. Mum has come with me each day but this morning she has had to go to a hardware shop because there's a problem with one of my switches. It means I'm all alone.

As I look around the room full of strangers, I realise that I can't remember ever being without a family member or carer close by. I spent years in enforced solitary confinement inside myself but I was never physically alone until now. I can't remember being a child who ventured further and further down the road until I found the courage to turn the corner alone for the first time. I was never a teenager who took my first steps towards adulthood and independence as I defied my parents by staying out all night.

I feel terrified. What should I say? What should I do? I sit in my chair at the back of the lecture room, hoping to be inconspicuous, and breathe a sigh of relief when the first lecture starts. Then there's the tea break. I know that if I'm going to join in someone will have to push my chair for me, put a straw into a mug and put it near enough for me to bend my head down to drink it. So when one of the students asks if I'm coming for tea, I tell her that I would prefer to stay where I am. I'm too scared to accept the offer. I don't want to be a burden or impose myself on people I don't know.

But as I sit in the room and watch people file out past me, chatting and laughing together, I know that my resistance is pointless. I will always need help to navigate through the so-called real world – to move around, negotiate doors, eat, drink and go to the toilet. I can't do any of these things alone so if a stranger wants to open a door, I must smile at them; if someone offers to push me up a step, I have to accept their help even if I don't want it. It's only when I begin to let strangers help me that I'll start moving beyond the limiting place where my parents are always with me and everyone is familiar. As the cocoon I've been hidden in for so long begins to break apart, I have to learn new ways.

'Martin?'

I look up to see Michal, a speech therapist at the communication centre I'd met at the workshop last month.

'Shall I take you to the tea room and we'll get a drink?' she asks.

Michal smiles. Relief floods into me. I click on just one symbol.

'Thank you.'

23

An Offer I Can't Refuse

Apparently I'm a rare species. Like a parrot or a monkey, I'm of interest to the experts. Partly it's because I'm both a new user of AAC and a young adult, which is somewhat unusual. Most people who learn to communicate via AAC are either children who have been born with problems like cerebral palsy, autism or a genetic disorder, or older adults who have lost their speech through illnesses such as strokes or motor neurone disease. People like me, who lose their speech in the middle of life rather than at the beginning or end through illness or accident, are rarer. But more important is the fact that I've learned so much so quickly about computer communication *and* I'm teaching myself to read and write – that's the real novelty because many AAC users never become literate. So the students have gathered to listen to me speak on the last day of the course.

'Adjusting to my new life has been challenging and frightening at times,' I tell them. 'There's so much I don't know and

I've often felt completely overwhelmed. I'm on a steep learning curve but everything is changing drastically for the better.'

As the students swarm around to congratulate me after my speech, I feel uplifted to be among them. People my own age seem so bright, as if they've been drawn in rainbow colours, with their huge smiles and loud voices. In honour of the occasion, I decided to stop wearing my bib and I look a little more like them now.

'You were great!' I hear an American voice say.

Erica is a student I met earlier this week on the morning when Mum had gone to the store and Michal took me for tea. After getting me a drink, Michal got distracted and I stared at my cup, knowing I wouldn't be able to drink what was in it because she hadn't given me a straw.

'Do you need something?' a voice asked.

I turned my head to see a woman who looked to be about my age. She had short blonde hair and energy bubbled off her. I waved my hand downwards.

'It's in your bag?'

The woman bent down, found a straw and put it into my mug.

'My name's Erica,' she said. 'Do you mind if I join you?'

I liked how direct she was. Erica told me she was on a ten-month visit from her university in America, where she had studied to be a speech and language therapist; now she was doing a postgraduate course in South Africa. I marvelled at how she talked to me about anything and everything. It wasn't often that someone spoke to me so easily.

'I don't find it cold here even though it's the middle of winter!' Erica said with a giggle. 'I'm so used to harsh winters in Wisconsin that this is nothing. I can't believe everyone looks so cold when all I want is to walk around in a T-shirt.'

We carried on chatting until the tea break was over and Erica pushed me back to the lecture room.

'It's been nice talking to you, Martin,' she said.

We've chatted on and off ever since and now Erica is smiling at me once again. She looks mischievous as she bends down towards me.

'I've decided that we should be friends,' she says.

She leans closer so that no one else can hear.

'But there's one condition: no parents.'

I smile at Erica as I give her my email address and she heads off to talk to someone else as Professor Alant comes to see me.

'I'd like to talk to you if possible, Martin?' she says. 'Alone, if that's okay?'

I'm sure that I must look almost as surprised as my mother does. I don't often talk one on one with people I don't know. But Professor Alant looks resolute as she sits down beside me and my mother leaves us.

'We've enjoyed having you with us this week,' she says. 'Have you enjoyed being here?'

I nod.

'I'm glad because your insight into being an AAC user is invaluable and we've been so impressed by all the hard work you've put in and the amazing results you've achieved,' she tells me. 'That's why I want to speak to you, because your mother has told me you're doing voluntary office work one day a week and apparently you enjoy it a lot.

'So I wanted to ask if you'd consider doing a work trial

here too? I'd like to see how it goes one morning a week for the next month and then we can discuss the possibility of something more permanent. How does that sound?'

I stare at Professor Alant in disbelief. I'm too surprised to look at my laptop, let alone programme it with a reply. My world isn't just opening up – it's exploding.

24

A Leap Forward

'What do you think, Martin?'

Juan looks at me expectantly. She works here at the communication centre and is one of my new colleagues.

I'm not sure what to say. Juan wants to know what I think would best help a child who was assessed here recently. But I'm so unused to being asked my opinion that I don't know how to give it properly yet. Working here is so different to the health centre, where many people seemed unsure at first about how to interact with someone like me.

'Can you find the January files, please?' they might ask Haseena, my colleague, when they walked into our office.

Even if she was obviously busy, there were those who didn't ask me to help them. It took time for people to trust me professionally and I enjoy the fact that they do now.

But here, at the communication centre, people have asked me what I think from the moment I arrived. I'm the one person who has put their theories into practice and they're keen to know my opinion. This unnerved me at first but I'm slowly getting used to it.

The first day I came to work here, I sat in the same room where Shakila had once assessed me and I realised I had even less of an idea about what was expected of me now. I was going to have to make my own decisions about how to start and finish the admin tasks I'd been given, such as creating a story written in symbols for the centre's newsletter.

In the second week, I was moved into an office with a woman called Maureen, whom I soon became friends with, and by the third week I'd discovered how invigorating it was to be in a place where people weren't afraid of me.

It's now the fourth week I've been at work and this morning is the end of my trial – the moment of truth. To calm my nerves about my upcoming meeting with Professor Alant, Erica pushes me through the campus to get a coffee. We've become good friends. It's a beautiful spring morning. The trees are heavy with blossom and the sky is bright blue above us.

'Do you think you'll get the job?' Erica asks.

On my lap lies a large laminated sheet covered in the letters of the alphabet. It also contains commonly used words and phrases like 'Thank you' and 'I want'. I use this alphabet board a lot now that I'm spelling better because it's not always practical to have a laptop with me. Literacy is an inexact science though. While I still find reading hard, writing is easier for some reason; I'm not sure why. Maybe it's because writing means breaking down words into their individual letter shapes rather than reading a whole string of symbols that have blurred together to make a word.

'I hope so,' I tell Erica as I point to the letters in front of me. 'I really do.'

'I think you will.'

'How come?'

'Because you're brilliant, Martin!'

I am not so sure. Being in an office has revealed to me just how huge the gaps in my knowledge are. With no memories of my formal education, my brain is a dumping ground where bits of information are thrown together and I have no idea where they come from. In many ways, I feel further behind now than I did before.

Mum and Dad are waiting as Erica and I arrive at the centre and then the three of us go in to see Professor Alant.

'I have to be honest and say that situations like this often don't work out,' she says as soon as my parents sit down.

My heart sinks.

'But even so, we would like to offer you a paid position here, Martin,' Professor Alant says with a smile. 'We feel you could provide really invaluable assistance to the work we do and we'd like you to become a salaried member of staff working one day a week. How does that sound?'

'That's great news!' my father exclaims.

He smiles broadly at me and my mother beams too.

'There are conditions to this offer, though, because if you are to become a member of staff, you will need to be as independent as possible,' Professor Alant adds. 'We'll do all we can to help you achieve this but the one thing you need that we can't provide is an electric wheelchair you can operate independently.

'At the moment, your wheelchair needs to be pushed by

someone but that won't always be possible when you're working alongside colleagues.'

I nod as Professor Alant speaks.

'The reason I'm saying this, Martin, is because your job
here won't work if you have to rely on the other staff to help
you.'

I look at my parents, praying they will agree to this.

'We understand,' my mother says. 'I'm sure Martin will be
only too pleased to do everything he can to help. This job
means a great deal to him.'

I nod.

'There's just one other thing,' Professor Alant says. 'I
think you need to consider projecting a more professional
image and I'd suggest perhaps a shirt and trousers?'

I stare down at my familiar T-shirt and jogging bottoms.
My mother opens and closes her mouth like a goldfish.

'Does that sound acceptable?' Professor Alant asks.

My finger points to one word on my alphabet board.

'Yes,' I reply.

'Then that's all agreed,' she says with a smile. 'Welcome
to the team, Martin. I'll look forward to seeing you next
week.'

My father pushes me out into the hall but no one speaks
until we're safely out of earshot.

'Your clothes?' my mother exclaims incredulously.
'What's wrong with your clothes?'

She sounds a little angry. Mum has always bought my
clothes and I've never given them any thought.

'And did you hear what she said about things like this
never working out?' Mum continues. 'What did she mean?'

'I think she was just trying to say that employing someone with a disability can be challenging,' my father says softly.

'Well then, she hasn't met anyone like Martin before, has she?' my mother roars. 'If anyone can do it, he can. You'll show them, won't you?'

My parents look down at me as we reach the front door of the centre. It is almost two years to the day since our first visit here for my assessment.

'Well, we'll leave you to get on with your day,' Dad says as he squeezes my shoulder, his grip tightening as he wordlessly expresses his excitement.

'You'll prove anyone who doubts you wrong, won't you, son?' Mum says as she smiles. 'I know you will.'

Happiness bursts inside me as I look at them. I hope I will make them proud.

25

Standing in the Sea

I had only the rarest glimpses of my father's feelings when I was the ghost boy. Once, as he came into the lounge after everyone else had gone to bed, I felt hopelessness seep from him in the darkness.

'Martin?' he said as he looked at me.

I was silent, of course, as Dad sat down in a chair and began to talk. As he sat staring out of the window at the night beyond, he told me about his childhood in the country. When he was growing up, my grandfather, GD, always wanted to be a farmer but he ended up working in the mines. Even so, he tried to provide as much as possible for his family by growing food like potatoes, peas and onions and harvesting honey from his beehives. He also had cows to provide milk, cream and butter and one of these animals had provoked my father into a childish act of vicious rebellion he'd never forgotten. Now he told me about it in the silence of the night.

'I hit one of the cows with a stick,' Dad said softly. 'I can't remember why I did it any more but I cut its eyelid. I should never have done it.'

He was silent for a moment.

'But for some reason I can't stop thinking about it now and I think it's because when I remember that day, I realise I got more reaction from a cow than I get from you, my own son.

'I just don't understand how that can be. How can you be so still and silent year after year?'

Dad's breath came out of him in jagged gulps. I longed to comfort him, but there was nothing I could do as he sat silently until his breathing evened out again. Then he stood up and bent down to kiss me on the forehead as I felt his hands close softly around my head. He held it for a few seconds just as he did every night.

'Let's get you to bed, boy,' he said.

That was the only time during all the years he cared for me alone that my father ever gave me any hint of just how desperate he felt at times. But I didn't realise how much his unwavering strength had sustained me until I went on holiday with my family for the first time when I was twenty-five.

Usually I went into residential care when they went away but this time I was taken on the trip to the sea. I was so excited. I couldn't remember seeing the sea before and the huge rolling mass took my breath away. I did not know whether to be awed or afraid. The sea repelled me as much as it fascinated me. Over the years, I'd learned to like the way water lifted and supported my body, freed me in a way that nothing else could. But I'd always found it frightening to think I had no defences against it and wouldn't be able to kick my legs or paddle my arms enough to keep above the surface if I started to sink.

I felt both excited and scared as my father pushed my wheelchair closer to the waterline and I listened to the beat of the waves. Then he helped me to my feet and started shuffling me across the sand towards the water. But the closer I got to it, the more fearful I became and my father must have felt it.

'Relax, Martin,' Dad kept saying again and again as the waves began to curl over my feet.

But I couldn't listen. Adrenalin pumped through my body and my powerlessness felt more overwhelming than ever before as I confronted the sea. I knew it could take me so easily if it wanted to.

My father guided a few more of my halting steps into the water.

'You're safe,' he kept telling me.

But I felt terrified as the sea closed around my feet and legs. I was sure I was going to be swept away and I'd have no choice but to go. Suddenly I felt Dad lean closer to me.

'Do you really think that I would let you go?' he shouted above the sound of the waves. 'Do you think that after all these years, I would let something happen to you now?

'I'm here, Martin. I've got you. I won't let anything happen. There's no need to be scared.'

And it was only in that moment, as I felt my father's arms holding me upright and his strength keeping me steady, that I knew his love was strong enough to protect me from an ocean.

26

She Returns

I open my eyes in the darkness. My heart thumps. Terror fills me. I want to scream, yell, cry out the fear that is running cold in my veins.

I turn my head to look at the clock.

It's 5 a.m., the fourth time I've woken tonight, and just 47 minutes since I last opened my eyes to try and escape my dreams. Tonight they are particularly bad. I wonder if they will ever stop. These are the moments when I feel most alone, as the world sleeps peacefully and I wake in the grey light of an empty dawn.

The nightmare that woke me this time was not so very different from the last. They never are. If my dreams weren't so terrifying, they would be almost boringly predictable.

She was standing in front of me, looking down at my face. I knew what she was going to do and I wanted to push her away, but I couldn't. My arms stayed beside me as lifeless as ever as her face came closer. I felt horror surge up my throat as I longed to plea for mercy.

Then I woke up.

It's like this most nights now. However hard I try to submerge the past, it bubbles up into the cracks I can't fill with thoughts of work and home, lists of jobs to do and things I want to experience.

What exhausts me is that I'm no longer haunted only at night. On any ordinary day a thousand tiny triggers lie in wait for me; these are things that no one else would notice but they instantly take me back to the past: a few lilting notes of classical music play in a shopping centre and I'm back at the home in the country where I was trapped like an animal and longed for escape.

'It's so peaceful here,' my mother always used to say when she dropped me off for a stay.

As we entered the building, the restful tones of Vivaldi or Mozart were usually seeping out of a stereo somewhere and I would look at my mother, pleading for her to understand what the music was hiding.

That's why hearing it sends me hurtling back to the past. Or I see a car that reminds me of the one driven by a person who used to hurt me and I'm there again: heart beating, sweat pricking cold across my skin and breath coming in gasps.

No one seems to notice when this happens. Have I really learned to disguise my feelings so well that I can hide even such raw terror from view? I don't understand how I do it but somehow I can. I'm completely alone as I try to bring myself back to the present by reminding myself that the past is behind me.

My heart begins to still as I lie in bed. I must fall asleep again, however fearful I am of being sent back to the world I try so hard to forget. I want to be bright and alert tomorrow at work. I can't let what happened once ruin this chance for me. I can't let it pull me down.

I close my eyes but still I see her face.

27

The Party

The girl sways as she stands in front of me. Her eyes look dazed and she's smiling.

'You're handsome,' she says. 'I'm going to flirt with you.'

Music pumps out of a stereo. The beat is like a hammer and the room is full of students I don't know. I'm at a party on the university campus with Erica and other friends called David and Yvette I met through her.

I can't quite believe I'm here. The theme of the party is 'jungle' and I'm dressed as the king of it with banana leaves in a crown on my head. I've even tried alcohol for the first time after so many people asked me if I wanted anything to drink that I asked Erica to get me a rum and Coke.

'What do you think?' she asked with a smile as I took a sip.

The alcohol filled my mouth before tickling my nose. It was strong and pungent. I didn't like the taste. I smiled half-heartedly at Erica, who was wearing a sarong and had her fluffy toy monkey Maurice hanging around her neck. I leaned

my head forward to finish my drink. I wanted to get the odd-
tasting concoction out of the way as soon as possible.

'Sip it!' Erica shrieked before laughing.

I took another gulp of the drink and swallowed it
quickly.

'Why don't I get you a straight Coke?' Erica asked.

I smiled at her before she disappeared into the crowd and
I wondered if she'd find her way back to me or whether
anyone else would talk to me. My alphabet board was lying on
my lap ready to chat but I wasn't sure anyone would see me
sitting down because the room was so crowded. Then the girl
who is standing over me now found me.

'What star sign are you?' she asks as she leans towards
me.

She is wearing a gold dress and butterfly wings on her
head. She has dark hair and a mouth full of huge white teeth.
She is pretty and has nice eyes.

'K-A-P-P-R-Y-K-O-R-N,' I spell out on my board.

'Crappy?'

'K-A-P-P-R-Y-K . . .'

'Oh! Do you mean Capricorn?'

I nod. My spelling is still very bad. People have to think
laterally if they want to talk to me.

'That's no good,' the girl says. 'I'm Libra.'

What does she mean? I look at the girl as I wonder what
to say. She is drunk. Why is she talking to me about astrol-
ogy? Is this just the white noise that I'm supposed to fill before
asking her out on a date? I know nothing about how men and
women behave with each other. All I've seen is what's on the
TV or in stolen moments of other people's lives. But slowly

I'm discovering that talking to women in any other way than as friends is like using a language I hardly know exists, let alone speak. Is this one in front of me now flirting, as she promised she would?

I have the words at my disposal to talk to women, of course, the lingual mechanics of sex and relationships that Mum and I inputted onto my word grids. It was inevitable we would get to a topic that is just a short step from words like hug and kiss. And even though my mother was the one who had to give the new vocabulary to me, I knew I wanted to have it because sex intrigues me as much as it does any twenty-something man. People might think someone like me has been neutered but they'd be wrong.

In the early days of my awareness, I would count down the time until a French TV drama was shown at the weekend because I knew I'd see women wearing corsets so tight their breasts spilled out of them. Seeing them made me aware of feelings I'd never had before and I enjoyed them. My sexual awareness then told me I wasn't completely dead. It's something I've thought about more since learning to communicate, as I begin to hope that one day a woman might want to be with me.

'Where shall we start?' Mum said in her most resolute voice as we sat together to build the new grid of words. 'Erection?'

At least she didn't have to explain that one. I had them like everyone else.

'Vagina.'

No need for a description of that either. I'd picked up most words on this subject along the way.

But I could have sworn Mum's voice was getting louder
and I prayed that David wouldn't hear what we were doing.

'Orgasm!' Mum exclaimed.

'Ejaculation.'

'Sperm.'

My face turned crimson as I waved my hand to plead with
my mother to stop.

'No, Martin!' she said. 'You need to know all this. It's
important.'

Time stood still as my mother carried on intoning words
from the sexual vocabulary. With each second that passed, I
wished harder than ever that she'd stop, even as I railed
against being a suddenly unwitting hostage to her desire to
ensure I was fully informed. It was only when Mum had
finally decided enough was enough that I could ask her to hide
the grid deep within the others, somewhere only I could find
it.

I'd suspected then that I might not use it that much and
now I know I won't as I look at the girl standing in front of
me. The words I have are too cold and clinical. Talking to
women seems to be more about understanding the gaps
between the words than the words themselves, interpreting
the silent nuances that mean so much. But I have no idea how
to do it. I know nothing. Does this girl expect to be kissed by
me? And if she does, what do I do? Does she want me to
reach out for her or sit waiting until she kisses me? And if she
does, then how do I kiss? I've never kissed anyone before. The
list of questions in my brain gets longer and longer until it
almost seizes up, just as a computer crashes when too much is
asked of it.

'Do you know that Capricorns and Librans are incompatible?' the girl asks suddenly.

I really don't understand what she's talking about. I decide to change the topic.

'What course are you doing?' I spell out on my alphabet board.

'Economics.'

I'm not sure what economists look like but I don't think they usually wear butterfly wings on their head. I'm silent as I wonder what to say and the girl weaves around in front of me.

'I'm going to talk to my friends,' she says suddenly. 'Bye.'

She lurches off across the room and I'm left alone again. Will I ever understand? My eyes scan the room as I look at men and women dancing and chatting, laughing at each other's jokes and leaning closer towards each other. One couple is kissing and another man has his arm around a girl's shoulders. I wonder if I'll ever learn the code that will gain me entry to their world.

'Are you okay?'

It's Erica. At least things are simple with her because we both know there's nothing more than friendship between us. Erica has a special place in my heart because over the past three months she has shown me so much of what the world has to offer.

Before we met, my parents did things with me like taking me shopping and to the cinema. I knew I would never forget the first moment in that twilight world when people stared upwards as music started to play and faces the size of skyscrapers rose on the screen above me. I could hardly believe it was real. Why then did everyone around me look almost expressionless? I could see neither fascination nor delight on their faces and I wondered if it was possible to get so used to joy that you stopped noticing it?

But with Erica I've seen how people my own age live. I've experienced the fun of eating hamburgers in McDonald's, wasting an afternoon wandering through a shopping centre and tasting biscuits that she's just baked in the oven. We've also visited botanical gardens and an orphanage, where we cuddled abandoned babies who would die without the kindness of a human touch. I understand that feeling well.

All of it amazes me and Erica seems to enjoy showing me. She's a special person – the first I've encountered, apart from my family and those paid to care for me, to accept my physical limitations without question. With Erica, I know they are only part of what defines me rather than the whole, and she treats me as she would any other friend. She's never said a word or given me a glance that has made me feel like a burden she's embarrassed to carry. Even when I've stayed over at her flat and she has had to lift me on and off the toilet or get me dressed, she's done it easily. Care that's given in spite of someone's distaste is easily recognisable but with Erica it's not an issue. Perhaps that's why I can sleep for hours on end when I stay at her flat, free of my nightmares for one precious night.

'Are you ready to go?' Erica asks.

We leave the party with David and Yvette and cross the road to Erica's. When we get to the flight of stairs leading to the flat, David and Erica stand me up out of my wheelchair and support my weight as I slowly shuffle up the stairs step by step. I smile as I listen to the others talk about who did what, where and with whom. I wish I understood what it all meant.

'I'm sorry if that wasn't the best first party,' Erica says when we get into her flat. 'The music was awful, wasn't it?'

I have no idea but the party was unforgettable.

28

Henk and Arrietta

Love between men and women has always interested me: the way it ebbs and flows like a living thing, or how it is revealed in secret smiles or anguished conversations. Perhaps I've always found it so captivating because it was the starkest reminder of how alone I was.

The first time I saw love was soon after I became aware again. At that time a woman called Arrietta was working part time at my care centre and her son, Herman, was a pupil there. Arrietta had a daughter called Anya, who must have been about three, and on this particular day she was with us at the care centre as we waited for my father to come. I knew Arrietta's husband, Henk, would soon arrive to take his family home, just as I knew my stomach would thrill when he did because I'd be able to see the gun he always carried on his hip. Henk was a policeman and however many times I saw the gun I couldn't believe I was lucky enough to see a real one up close.

Henk knew Arrietta would have to stay until I was collected when he saw me lying on a mat on the floor. I watched
him kiss Arrietta before sitting down at the table to wait and
opening his newspaper, just as he always did. Herman
and Anya were playing outside on the veranda. As Arrietta
walked out into the sunlight to check on them, I watched the
contours of her breasts appear through the thin fabric of her
blouse.

'Did you have a good day?' Henk asked Arrietta as she
walked back inside.

'Long,' she replied as she started to pack up some toys.

They were silent for a minute.

'We need to stop at the supermarket on the way home,'
Arrietta said absent-mindedly. 'What would you like to eat?'

Henk looked at Arrietta.

'You,' he replied, his voice a little deeper than usual.

How could Henk eat Arrietta? I didn't understand what he
meant. She stopped what she was doing to look at him as she
laughed softly.

'We'll have to see about that,' she said.

Suddenly it felt as if time had stopped as Henk and
Arrietta smiled at each other. I knew I was seeing something
new: the secret world of adults that I'd begun to suspect
existed as I grew older. Just as my body was changing and
chairs I'd used for years had slowly became too small for me
even as I began to be shaved regularly, I had caught glimpses
of things between adults that I'd not seen before. They
intrigued me.

Now there was something about Henk and Arrietta's
voices, the softness in them and the smile they shared. I didn't

understand what it was but the air between them hummed for those brief moments, as Henk looked at his wife and she smiled. Then they looked away from each other and the moment was gone.

'Tell me about them,' Henk said to Arrietta as he gestured at the empty room.

They were back to their ordinary selves just as quickly as they'd gone to a place I didn't recognise.

'Who?'

'The children here – I come every day and don't know anything about them.'

Arrietta sat down next to Henk as she started telling him about some of the children I knew so well: Robby, who'd been injured when his father's car crashed into the back of a coal truck and now cried for hours each day. Katie, who was born with a degenerative syndrome and loved food so much that she'd been nicknamed 'Little Fatty'; Jennifer, who'd been born with a brain the size of a chicken's egg after her mother fell ill during pregnancy and shrieked with joy every time she saw her father at the end of each day; Elmo, Jurike, Thabo and Tiaan; Doorsie, Joseph, Jackie and Nadine, who each had a story to tell. Then there were the children who came and went so quickly I never learned their names, like the little girl who was born with learning difficulties and raped by an uncle whose final act of cruelty was to set fire to her genitals.

'What about him?' Henk said finally as he gestured to me.

'Martin?'

'Yes.'

Arrietta told him my story and Henk listened silently until she'd finished.

'His is the saddest,' he said as he looked at me.

'Why?'

'Because he wasn't born like that. He was healthy and then his parents had to watch their child suffer without knowing why. I don't know if I could bear it.'

Arrietta put her arm around him as they looked at me.

'None of us knows what we can bear until we're asked,' she told him gently.

29

The Healer

After seeing Henk and Arrietta's secret world, I was on the lookout for love as I discovered that what I'd seen was rare. It was something unlike anything I'd ever known, and I hoped to get another glimpse of it. Although I had to wait, eventually I saw love again when I was about nineteen.

It happened after my father had a work meeting with a man he didn't know and the stranger turned to Dad as they ate lunch together afterwards.

'How is your son?' he asked.

'Which one?' my father replied in surprise.

'The one who's dying,' the man said.

A rush of anger filled Dad at being asked about the most private part of his family history. But something about the man piqued his interest and that night I heard him telling my mother about their conversation.

'He wants to see Martin,' Dad said as I listened. 'He's a faith healer and believes he can treat him.'

My mother had no reason not to allow it because she'd accepted long ago that the answer to the mystery of my illness would never be provided by traditional medicine. So a few weeks later Dad took me to a flat in the suburbs, where a short, grey-haired man with a beard was waiting for us.

He told me his name was Dave and I knew at once he was kind: his eyes were full of light as he looked at me. I was lifted out of my wheelchair and laid on a bed. Then Dave fell completely silent as he closed his eyes and placed his hands a few centimetres above my chest. He started moving them up and down my body, following the contours of my withered frame but never making contact with it. I felt my skin prickling with waves of heat.

'Your son's aura has been fractured,' Dave eventually said to Dad. 'It's rare but it happens when something traumatic has occurred.'

Dave fell silent again and spoke only once more during the next hour to tell my father that he thought I had problems with my stomach because he could feel pain there. I didn't understand how he knew what none of the doctors did and it scared me. But Dave didn't say any more as he fell silent again and carried on working.

'Can I pay you for your time?' my father asked when Dave had finally finished.

'No,' he replied. He never once asked my parents for a penny although he continued to see me every week for the next three years. It was as if Dave had a calling to treat me, a belief so strong that he had to act.

Each time I saw him, a look of complete concentration would come over his face as he tried to open up the deep reservoir of self-healing energy he believed my body held. Running his hands over the air just above it, he would map the aura he said he could feel had been damaged by my illness. His face still, peaceful and relaxed, his eyes always closed, he concentrated on healing me. Then, when the treatment was over, his features would become as animated as ever.

Months turned into years and as far as the people around me knew, there had been no improvement in my condition. But Dave's faith didn't waver. He still saw me week in, week out, and bent to hold his hands above me with the most intense look of peace and concentration I'd ever seen.

Gradually I began to look forward to seeing him more and more, because as time passed he started talking to me a lot, laughing and joking with me, telling stories about lions and animals that I wished he would write down in books for children one day. His words came in a soothing stream of smiles and jokes as I was laid on the bed and he worked to cure me.

It was about two years after I first met Dave that he married a fellow healer called Ingrid and the two of them started to treat me together from time to time. One morning, as I lay looking up at them, they abruptly stopped what they were doing as they gazed at each other and suddenly the world stopped just as it had when Henk and Arrietta looked at each other. There was no reason why Dave and Ingrid had stopped, no sign that it was going to happen. But just as a ball hangs in the air a moment too long before plummeting towards the ground, time slowed down. Emotion crackled between Dave and Ingrid as their eyes locked and they leaned forward to kiss each other.

'I love you,' they murmured before smiling.

I knew I'd seen that secret world again and wished I understood it. I didn't know what happened between two people. It seemed so strange and mysterious, like an alchemy that willed something into existence. But even though that was the only time I saw it happen between Dave and Ingrid; I knew afterwards it was always there.

One weekend about six months later Dad and I pulled into Dave's driveway to see an unfamiliar car parked there. A Mercedes.

'Have you got lucky, Dave?' Dad asked with a smile as he got me out of the car.

'No!' Dave replied. 'It's my boss's car. He was going away for the weekend with his wife so I drove them to the airport and I'm picking them up tomorrow.'

He and my father began to chat about events a world away as I was pushed inside.

'Have you seen the pictures on TV?' Dave asked my father. 'It's extraordinary.'

I knew what they were talking about. Princess Diana had been killed in a car crash and the outpouring of emotion that had followed her death had been all over South African television screens. I'd watched the footage of flowers piled high in an English palace garden and thought about them now — such an outpouring of love for one woman, a person who had touched so many lives.

After Dave finished treating me, he said he would see me again the next week and then said goodbye. But two days later, Kim came to pick me up from the care centre and we got home to find our parents waiting. I knew instantly that something terrible had happened.

'Dave is dead,' my father said to Kim in a rush as she helped me out of the car.

I felt a pain in my chest as I listened to my parents tell Kim what had happened. The previous night, Dave and Ingrid had got into the Mercedes to drive to the airport to pick up Dave's boss and his wife just as they'd promised. But as they'd reversed out of their gate, some men had jumped in front of them and demanded the car. In the beam of the headlights, Dave and Ingrid could see the men had guns.

The robbers also wanted their jewellery and Dave had silently handed them his watch and wedding ring, hoping it might be enough to persuade them to go. But suddenly, without warning, one of the men pulled the trigger and a single shot went through Dave's forehead. As he slumped forward, another car pulled up, which the robbers jumped into. Dave survived for just a few hours after being airlifted to hospital and the robbers were never caught.

'It's so terrible,' my mother said sadly. 'How could they do it? He was such a good man.'

I felt breathless as I heard the news, unable to believe Dave's life had been ended so brutally. I thought how unfair it was that I'd clung on to mine even when I hadn't wanted it at times and yet Dave, who had loved his so much, had lost it. Then I thought of Ingrid and the love that had been extinguished by a bullet. I still didn't fully understand what I'd seen between her and Dave so many months before but instinctively I knew her grief for its loss would be almost unbearable.

30

Escaping the Cage

Learning to communicate is like travelling along a road only to find the bridge you need to cross the river has been washed away. Even though I have thousands of words on my grids now, there are still ones I think of but don't have. And when I do have them, how do I take a thought and put it into symbols or feel an emotion and trap it on a screen? Talking is about so much more than words and I'm finding the ebb and flow, rhythm and dance of it almost impossible to master.

Just think of the man who raises his eyebrows when the waiter gives him the restaurant bill for the anniversary dinner he's just had with his wife.

'You've got to be joking!' he says as he looks at it.

As his wife listens, she'll know from his tone and look whether his words are an angry accusation about money he begrudges or an affectionate ribbing of the woman he would spend his last penny on. But I can't spit out syllables in anger or shriek them happily; my words will never quaver with emotion, rise expectantly for a laugh just before a punchline or drop dangerously in anger. Instead I deadpan each and every one electronically.

After tone, comes space. I used to spend hours day-dreaming about what I'd say or having endless conversations in my head. But now that I'm able to talk, I don't always get the chance to say what I want to. A conversation with me is slow and takes time and a patience that many people don't have. The person I talk to must sit and wait while I input symbols into my computer or point to letters on my alphabet board. People find the silence so hard, they often don't talk to me.

I've been working now for more than six months; I have friends and colleagues; I meet strangers when I go out into the world; and I'm interacting with them all. In doing so, I've learned that people's voices move in a seamless cycle, sentences running one into another while they talk. But I interrupt the rhythm and make it messy. People must make a conscious effort to look at me and listen to what I have to say. They must allow me the space to speak because I can't butt in and many don't want to listen to the silence I create as they wait for me to input words into a computer. I understand why it is hard. We live in a world in which we seldom hear nothing at all. There is usually a television or radio, telephone or car horn to fill the gaps and if not there is meaningless small talk. But a conversation with me is as much about the silences as it is about the words, and I notice if my words are listened to or not because I choose each one so carefully.

I'm not nearly as talkative as I once thought I would be.

When my family chat over dinner, I often stay silent and when colleagues talk about what they did at the weekend, I sometimes don't join in. People don't mean to be unkind; they just don't think to stop and give way to me. They assume I'm taking part in their conversation because I'm in the same room but I'm not. The best time for me to talk is with one person who knows me well enough to pre-empt whatever I'm going to say.

'You want to go to the cinema?' Erica will say as I point to 'C' and 'I'.

'You think she's cute?' she'll ask when I smile at a woman who passes.

'Water?' she'll declare when I bring my drinks grid up on my laptop.

I like it when Erica does this because I'm as keen to take shortcuts as anyone else. Just because my life is lived as slowly as a giant toddler who needs nappies, bottles, straws and a sunhat before he can set foot outside the house doesn't mean I enjoy it that way. That's why I'm glad when people who know me well help me to speed up a little. Others seem to worry that I'll be offended if they butt in while we talk. If only they knew what I would give to enjoy the rapid cut and thrust of the conversations I hear around me.

I often wonder if people think I have any sense of humour at all. Comedy is all in the timing, the rapid delivery and arched eyebrow, and I might just manage the last of that trio but the first two are a serious problem for me. People have to know me well to know that I enjoy joking around and the fact that I'm often so silent means it's easy for them to assume I'm serious. It feels at times as if I'm still someone others create their own character for, just as I was during all the years when

I couldn't communicate. I remain in so many ways a blank page onto which they write their own script.

'You're so sweet,' people will often say.

'What a gentle nature you have!' person after person tells me.

'You are such a kind man,' someone else trills.

If only they knew of the gnawing anxiety, fiery frustration and aching sexual desire that course through my veins at times. I'm not the gentle mute they often think I am; I'm just lucky that I don't unwittingly betray my feelings by snapping in anger or whining in annoyance. So often now I'm aware that I'm a cipher for what other people want to think of me.

The only time I can guarantee they will be keen to know what I'm saying is when I'm not actually talking to them. Children aren't the only ones who reveal their inbuilt voyeurism by staring – adults just hide it better. I'm often stared at as I spell out words on my alphabet board with hands that are still perhaps the most capricious part of my body. While my left hand remains largely unreliable, I can use my right to point at the letters on my alphabet board and operate my computer switches. But I can't hold firmly on to something like a mug. Even though I can lift finger food to my mouth, I can't hold an interloper like a fork for fear I might stab myself because my movement is so jerky. At least I'm getting so fast at using my board now that strangers find it harder and harder to look over my shoulder and listen in.

'He goes too quickly for me!' my mother said with a laugh to a man who'd been staring at us as we chatted in a super-market queue.

The man looked embarrassed as Mum spoke to him, obviously fearful that he was going to be chastised. But we are so used to being listened to that neither my mother nor I take much notice any more. Despite these difficulties in communicating, I still treasure the fact that I was given the chance to speak at all. I was given an opportunity that I took and without it I wouldn't be where I am now. My rehabilitation is the work of many people – Virna, my parents, the experts at the communication centre – because I would never have been able to talk without their help. Others are not so lucky.

Recently, in the same supermarket where the man tried to listen to my conversation with Mum, we saw an older woman being pushed around in a wheelchair. She looked about fifty. Soon my mother started chatting to her and her carer. Maybe the woman was using sign language or pointing at things but for some reason my mother discovered that she'd lost the power of speech after a stroke.

'Does your family know about all the things that can be done to help you communicate again?' Mum asked the woman before showing her my alphabet board. 'There's so much out there but you have to find it.'

The carer told us the woman had an adult daughter. Mum urged her to explain that she'd met someone who had told her about all the things that could be done for her mother.

'There's no reason why you shouldn't be able to communicate with your daughter again,' Mum said to the woman. 'You just have to find out what works best for you.'

But when we next met, the carer told us that the woman's daughter hadn't done anything about what she'd been told.

'Why don't you give me her phone number?' Mum said. 'I'd be happy to reassure her that she mustn't give up hope or listen to what the doctors say.'

As the carer wrote out the phone number on a piece of paper, I looked at the woman sitting opposite me in her chair.

'G-O-O-D-L-U-C-K,' I spelled out on my alphabet board and she stared at me for the longest moment.

A few days later Mum came back into the living room after calling the woman's daughter.

'I don't think she really wanted to hear from me,' she said. 'She just didn't seem interested.'

We said no more about it. We both knew that the woman would never escape the straitjacket of her own body – she wasn't going to be given the chance to. She'd be silent forever because no one was going to help set her free.

After that, I often thought about the woman and wondered how she was. But whenever I did, I remembered her eyes as she looked at me the last time I saw her in the supermarket. They'd been filled with fear. Now I understood why.

31

The Speech

I can hardly believe I'm here. It's November 2003 and I'm sitting on a low stage in a huge lecture room with my colleague Munyane, who has just addressed the audience in front of us. There must be more than 350 people waiting for me to speak. I've been working at the communication centre for four months now and have been chosen to address a conference of health professionals.

First Munyane gave an overview of AAC and now it's my turn to talk. Even though all I must do is press the button that will make Perfect Paul's voice boom out of the sound system to which my laptop is connected, I don't know if I'll be able to do it. My hands are shaking so much I'm not sure I'll be able to control them.

Somehow I've become an accidental public speaker in recent months and my story has even been featured in the newspapers. It has surprised me that a room full of people at a school or community centre want to hear about me, and I can't think why so many have come today. I wish Erica were here to give me a smile. She's gone back to the States and it's in moments like this that I miss her most. The friendship I treasured so much must now be contained in emails and the door she gave me onto the world has closed.

I should have known this was a big event when Mum and I arrived and were offered lunch from a table covered in more dishes than I'd ever seen before. The prospect of picking exactly what I wanted to eat was almost too much for me and the sticky toffee pudding I'd finished my meal with rolls uneasily in my stomach now as I stare out into the audience.

Munyane smiles.

'They're ready when you are,' she whispers.

I push the tiny lever that controls my new electric wheel-chair and glide to the centre of the stage. Just as Professor Alant predicted, it has made me far more independent. A month before my twenty-eighth birthday, I was finally able to control where I went and when for the first time. Now if I want to leave the room because the television is boring, I can go; if I decide to explore the streets around the house where my parents have lived since I was a child, then I'm able to.

I got the chair after writing an open letter on a website I belong to asking for any suggestions about how to get one because I knew my parents couldn't afford the cost. Over the past few months I've made friends in countries like England and Australia by joining Internet groups and meeting more people in the AAC community. It's a strange but reassuring feeling to know that I have friends in so many places now. Getting to know people via my computer feels liberating. I'm exploring the world and the people I meet don't see my chair: they just know *me*.

But I never expected the Internet to be as powerful as it turned out to be after my letter was seen by someone in Canada who had a relative living not far from me in South Africa. Soon he had contacted me to say that his Round Table group wanted to buy me a new chair with some of the money they'd raised for charity. Words can't express how grateful I am to have it even though I'm not sure everyone around me is quite so pleased.

Controlling my own movement for the first time is interesting, as I totter like a toddler learning to move independently. I've crashed into doors, fallen off pavements and run over the toes of unsuspecting strangers as I've revelled in my new-found liberation.

I've become more independent in other ways too. My colleague Kitty, who is an occupational therapist, has worked with me on tiny details that have made my work life easier. Now I have a new handle on my office door, which means I can open it without help. I've also started wearing weights on my wrists to try to strengthen my muscles and stabilise my hand tremors. I continue to be well acquainted with drinking yoghurt, which means no one has to feed me at lunchtime, and I'm careful never to ask for tea or coffee unless someone offers because I'm determined not to be a drain on anyone. As for my clothes, I'm wearing a shirt and tie today. Soon I'm hoping to get my first suit.

Life is changing in so many ways but perhaps none is more terrifying than this. I look out at the audience again and force myself to breathe deeply. My hands are trembling and I will them to let me control my laptop. Turning my head slowly to the left, I shine the headmouse's infrared beam onto the screen and click on one of my switches.

'I would like you all to stop for a moment and really think about not having a voice or any means to communicate,' my computer voice says. 'You could never say "Pass the salt" or tell someone the really important things like "I love you". You can't tell someone that you're uncomfortable, cold or in pain.

'For a time, when I first discovered what had happened to me, I went through a phase where I would bite myself in frustration at the life I found myself in. Then I just gave up. I became totally and completely passive.'

I hope the pauses I programmed into my speech are enough to help the audience follow what I'm saying. It's hard to listen to synthesised speech when you are used to voices that pause, rise and fall. But there's nothing more that I can do now. The room is quiet as I talk about meeting Virna and my assessment, the hunt for a communication device and the cancellation of the black box. Then I tell them about the months of research into computer software, the money my grandfather GD left to my father when he died that allowed my parents to buy me equipment and the work I've done learning to communicate.

'In 2001 I was at a day centre for the profoundly mentally and physically disabled,' I say. 'Eighteen months ago, I didn't know anything about computers, was completely illiterate and had no friends.

'Now I can operate more than a dozen software programmes, I've taught myself to read and write and I have good friends and colleagues at both of my two jobs.'

I stare out at the rows of faces in front of me. I wonder if

I'll ever be able to convey my experiences to people. Is there a limit to words? A place where they can take us after which there is a no man's land of incomprehension? I can't be sure. But I must at least hope that somehow I can help people to understand if they want to. There are so many eyes on me, hundreds of pairs, and my heart thumps as my computer carries on speaking.

'My life has changed dramatically,' I say. 'But I'm still learning to adjust to it and although people tell me that I'm intelligent, I struggle to believe it. My progress is down to a lot of hard work and the miracle that happened when people believed in me.'

As I timidly look out at the room, I realise that no one is fidgeting or yawning. Everyone is completely still as they listen.

'Communication is one of the things that makes us human,' I say. 'And I am honoured to have been given the chance to do it.'

Finally I fall silent. My speech is over. I've said all that I wanted to say to this room full of strangers. They are silent for a split second. I stare out at them, unsure what to do. But then I hear a noise – the sound of clapping. It's soft at first but the hands beat together louder and louder and I watch as one person and then another gets to their feet. One by one, the crowd rises. I stare at the faces in front of me, people smiling and laughing as they clap, while I sit in the middle of the stage. The sound swells and swells. Soon it's so big that I feel it might suck me under. I stare down at my feet, hardly daring to believe what I'm seeing and hearing. Finally I push the lever of my chair and move to the side of the stage.

'Mr Pistorius?'

The woman who interpreted my speech into sign language for deaf members of the audience is standing in front of me.

'I just wanted to say that you're an inspiration,' she says in a rush. 'You are a truly extraordinary man. To have experienced what you have and remain so positive is an example for us all.'

I can hear how emotional she is as she speaks in a rush and see the strength of her feeling etched on her face.

'Thank you for telling us your story,' she says. 'I feel proud to have been here today.'

Before I can reply another person comes up to congratulate me and then another and another – so many faces stare down at me as they laugh and smile.

'You were wonderful!'

'So inspiring!'

'Your story is just amazing.'

I don't know what to say. I feel shocked and unsure as Munyane smiles at me reassuringly. I can hardly understand why people are reacting this way but as they talk to me I think of a mother I met recently after speaking at a school for disabled children.

'My son is a pupil here and I would be proud if he grew up to be like you,' she told me afterwards.

I didn't understand what she meant at the time but now perhaps I am beginning to. As hands clap my back and congratulations are given, I sit amid the noise and movement and realise that people want to hear the story of the boy who came back from the dead. It amazes them – it amazes me too.

32

A New World

Life and I are in constant collision. At every turn my eyes open in wonder as I crash into another experience: seeing a man with a plume of brightly coloured hair like parrot feathers running down the centre of his head; tasting a cloud of melting sugar called candyfloss that melts on my tongue; feeling the warm pleasure that comes with going shopping for the first time to buy Christmas presents for my family; or the sharp surprise of seeing women dressed in short skirts with faces painted in bright red and blue cosmetics. There is so much to know and I am impatient, eager, starving for all the information I can gather.

In January 2004, a few months after I gave my speech, I started working four days a week – two at the communication centre and two at the health centre. I do everything from editing newsletters and maintaining computer networks to meeting other AAC users. I'm even learning how to build websites and have been accepted onto a university course after Professor Alant encouraged me to apply for it.

I have no memory of school and my textbooks will have to be dictated onto tapes because I can't yet read well enough to study them. The rest of my fellow students, however, will be postgraduates – many of them teachers. I won't get a full degree because I haven't graduated from high school but I'll be awarded an advanced certificate in education if I finish the course. The course is about the theory and practice of educating those with AAC needs and I'll need to study every spare minute that I'm not at work in order to keep up.

I'm finally daring to dream that independence might be within my reach. Work and study are what will help me get a better job, a higher income and maybe even a home of my own one day. These are the things I want and I must do my best to achieve them.

'Look at you,' Diane Bryen said with a smile when we saw each other at a conference. It was a gathering of AAC users from all over Africa and experts from around the world. I was one of the speakers, as was Diane.

'You were so fearful when I first met you,' she said. 'But now you're beginning to roar!'

Change is hard to see when it's your own. I'd never stopped to notice the person I was becoming until I attended Diane's workshop for the second time and she asked us to draw a picture of our dreams. Virna was assisting me at the conference. As the pencil in her hand hovered over a blank sheet of paper, I told her what I dreamed of. In strong, bright strokes, she captured my hopes on the paper: I watched as she drew a house with a picket fence around it and a dog wagging its tail. This is what I wanted and when I thought about having a life so much my own, it made me feel as if I was soaring inside.

A few days after I returned to work, I was sitting with Virna during our lunch break at the health centre when she turned towards me.

'I hardly know who you are any more,' she said.

I looked at her, unsure what she meant, and nothing more was said. But I continued to feel confused as I thought about it in the days that followed because I'd always thought Virna was the person who knew me best in the world. Although my feelings for her remain as strong as ever, I've been careful not to reveal them again. Instead I've talked to Virna as a friend about my deepest secrets and fears, and described to her all the emotions I have as I go out into the world. That's why I couldn't understand when she said she didn't recognise me.

Now I wonder if learning to communicate more will change the things I thought would always stay the same. Virna has always rejoiced in the new person I'm becoming. But does she find it hard to recognise a man who is finally beginning to see a world without her as its axis? She kept me grounded for so long. Now I'm beginning to fly – but I'm spreading my wings alone.

33

The Laptop

I stare at my laptop. The screen has gone blank. Terror fills me. I can feel it creep and crawl, scrabble and scratch over my heart. I've been having problems with my laptop for a while and out of politeness sent an email to everyone I knew earlier this evening warning them that something like this might happen. But I never thought my link to the world would actually be lost and I'd suddenly go silent.

I know enough about computers to suspect this is terminal. My laptop is completely lifeless, flatlined. I feel sick. If I don't have my computer, then I can't send text messages or emails, do college assignments or finish off the work I bring home from the office in the evenings to make sure I keep on top of everything. I can't laugh and joke with my friends online, tell them about my day and ask about theirs. I can't describe to them how I'm feeling or make plans to meet up. My physical world might still be limited to the home and office but there are parts of my life that know no boundaries as I chat to people on different continents. All I'll have to communicate with now is a battered old alphabet board that won't reach around the globe the way I need it to.

Panic turns my stomach in cartwheels. My life is ruled by the press of a single button. It stands and falls on a network of wires and I will never know when they're about to go wrong. They aren't like a body that can give me a sign, such as a spike in temperature, a rush of sickness or a sudden pain. Instead, I must spend the rest of my life relying on a hunk of metal that might give up suddenly without a hint of warning.

I can hardly breathe. My life is so fragile. I've spent all this time thinking that I'd left the ghost boy behind forever. It's only now that I realise how closely he still shadows me.

34

The Counsellor

'How are you feeling today, Martin?'

I look at the counsellor sitting opposite me. I'm not really sure what he's expecting me to say. I stare at my laptop and click on three symbols.

'I am well, thank you,' my voice intones.

'Good,' the counsellor says with a smile. 'Can you remember what we were talking about the last time you came to see me?'

I'm not sure. Do we ever actually talk during the hour I spend in this office each week? We speak, of course – the counsellor sitting behind his glass desk in a sturdy, black office chair that sways to and fro when he leans back, me on the other side in my wheelchair with a laptop in front of me. But I'm not sure if this exchange of words is really talking.

When I'm here, I often think of a film I once saw on TV called *Short Circuit*. It's about a robot that developed a human personality and an insatiable desire to understand the world around him. No one, except for the girl who rescued him after he ran away from the laboratory where he'd been created, believed he could really have feelings. He was just a machine, after all. He couldn't be something he wasn't.

As time passes, I feel more and more like that robot because the counsellor, like other people, doesn't seem to know quite what to make of me when I try to communicate. I didn't notice it when I first rejoined the world because in the rush of excitement at being able to say even a few words, I didn't see clearly how other people responded to me. But now I watch the counsellor staring at the ceiling and checking his nails as he waits for me to talk, or hear him rush on with the conversation as I'm left trailing in his wake, trying to answer a question he asked ten sentences ago, and I'm filled with frustration – just as I often am when I speak to people now.

I feel more and more bewildered by a world that I often don't understand. When I was a ghost boy, I could understand people: if they dismissed, doubted or undermined each other, I could see it; if they praised, teased or were shy, I could tell. But I'm no longer an outsider. I see things from a different perspective now. It's impossible at times to recognise how people are behaving towards me as I try to interact with them. All my reference points have changed. It's as if I can only calibrate others when they have nothing to do with me: if someone is rude, I don't realise it; if they are impatient, I can't see it.

When Mum and I went out shopping recently, we met a woman whose son had been in my class at school.

'How's Martin?' she asked my mother.

The woman didn't even glance at me.

'Why don't you ask him?' Mum replied.

But the woman couldn't bring herself to make eye contact or ask me a simple question. It seemed almost normal to me because after so many years of being invisible, it's sometimes hard even now to remember that I'm not. My mother was livid at the way the woman had treated me, and it was only her reaction that helped me to understand someone had slighted me.

It happens a lot. When a TV crew came to film at the communication centre, I knew something bad had happened after Professor Alant introduced me to the producer.

'I'm from Canada,' he said in a very loud voice, carefully enunciating each syllable. 'It's a very long way away.'

I stared at the man, unsure why he was telling me something so obvious in such a loud voice. Only my colleagues' outraged expressions told me that he had been rude.

My mother is the one who decided that I should see the counsellor after I told my parents a little about what had happened to me during all my years in institutions. She believes I'm angry about what I told her, which is why I should talk to someone. But all I want is to move forward instead of look back. Nevertheless I'm brought here each week to see the counsellor. After my mother has accompanied me into his office and checked my laptop is working properly, she leaves us alone as I try to make sense of all that has happened.

'You have to accept that you are very intelligent,' the counsellor tells me again and again.

I never know what to say when he says this. It's as if the words won't permeate my brain. The concept is too big for

me to fit into my consciousness. I spent years being treated as
an imbecile and now the man paid to be my friend tells me I'm
clever?

'Most people have ways to express their emotions,' he says.
'They can slam doors or shout and swear. But you only have
words, Martin, and that makes it hard to show your feelings.'

Then he sits back in his chair, looks at me seriously and
I'm at a loss once again about what I'm supposed to say. It
feels like I'm trying to play a game but I'm missing all the
clues. Although I send the counsellor an email each day telling
him how I feel, just as he asked me to, he rarely replies. Then,
when I see him, he talks in platitudes I don't understand. It
makes me wonder if he's really interested in what I think or
if I'm just a case study to be intrigued by. Will he help me
solve the problems that I never even considered I'd have when
I dreamed of being able to speak? Or will I end up as the subject of a scholarly study about the man without a voice?

The counsellor stares at the ceiling as he waits for me to
speak. What can I say? That I thought my life would change
completely when I started to communicate and now I know it
isn't going to? That my greatest challenge is not learning to
communicate but being listened to? That people don't hear
what they don't want to and I have no way of making them
listen?

I look at him, frozen by indecision. I know I must try to
discuss emotions that I buried deep within myself years ago,
dig up a past I'm still trying to outrun each night when I fall
asleep. Although I've talked a little about the past to my parents, I understand it is a minefield they don't want to cross
with me for fear of triggering an explosion. I, too, am scared

of destroying the fragile peace we've created together. I don't want words, even those spoken to a stranger in an anonymous room, to open up a Pandora's box I'll never be able to close again. But I know I must try to communicate some of what I've seen; I must attempt to put it into words for this man who sits so still and silent in front of me.

My pulse races at the thought of confession. What happened to me is a darkness that is always with me and I fear I will be tormented forever if I don't try to speak of it.

35

Memories

'Eat it, you fucking donkey,' the carer snaps.

I stare at the mince lying grey on the spoon in front of me. I am twenty-one years old and still the ghost boy.

'Eat it!'

I open my mouth and burning hot food is shovelled in. A rancid taste fills my mouth. Bile rises in my throat. I force myself to swallow.

'And another.'

I open my mouth obediently. I must think of something else if I'm to persuade my stomach to accept what it is being fed. I look around the room. The jarringly soft strains of classical violins play in the background as I look at the other children here. Some cry; others are silent. My throat burns as I swallow.

'Hurry up, you heap of rubbish. We'll be here for hours if you don't speed up.'

The metal spoon crashes against my teeth as she forces another mouthful into me. I wish she would leave me hungry, but I know she won't.

'Eat up!'

She pulls my hair – two short tugs that make my eyes water – before she raises another spoon of food towards my mouth. My lips close around it and my heart starts to race as I swallow. I can feel nausea rising inside me. I can't be sick. I breathe deeply.

'Come on, freak. What's wrong with you tonight?'

She lifts up another spoonful of food and a thick smell washes over me. Too late to choke it back down, I can feel the vomit surging up and there is nothing I can do to stop it, however desperately I want to.

'You piece of shit!' the woman screams as I'm sick all over myself and the plate in front of me.

She slaps me around the face. She is so close that I can feel her breath hot on my cheek.

'Do you think you're clever?' the woman screams. 'Do you think you can get out of eating just by puking up?'

I watch as she pushes the spoon towards my plate. She guides it through the vomit and fills the spoon to the brim before raising it to my mouth.

'Eat!'

I open my mouth. I have no other choice. I must force myself to swallow the food that my body has just rejected, praying that it won't do so again or worse will happen. The woman has done this before; she will do it again. I've learned that I can't cry because it only makes her angrier. As the spoon is rammed into my mouth, I hear peals of laughter. I fight down the nausea that is rising once again inside me. The woman smiles, relishing her triumph.

That is the reason why I hated the home in the country so much: one woman there tormented me while other carers laughed. Some days I was just pinched or slapped; on others I was abandoned outside in the blazing heat or left to freeze after being taken out of the bath, shivering until she finally decided to dress me.

There were times when I wondered if she scared herself with her own violence: after giving me an enema so forcefully I bled, she put me into the bath and I watched the water turn bright red. After getting me out, she dipped a toothbrush into the filthy water before cleaning my teeth with it. Later, after she'd set me on the toilet, I stared at the water turning red once more below me and thanked God that I was going to die, smiling at the irony that a bleeding arsehole would be the thing to finish me off.

If I flinched when she touched me, she'd hit me so hard the wind would be knocked out of my lungs. Or she'd smack me on the back of the head if I cried after being left sitting in my own dirt for so long that my skin turned a livid red.

Each day I'd count down the minutes until it was over and I was another twenty-four hours closer to going home. Usually I was at the care centre for only a few days but sometimes my stay was as long as six weeks, and panic filled me whenever I heard the phone ring. Was it a call to say my parents had been killed in a car accident? Would I be left here forever, a prisoner in an institution where no one would remember me? The fear would build inside me day by day until I could almost taste it. When my mother or father finally came to pick me up, I listened helplessly as they were told I'd had another good stay.

Even when I went home I found it hard not to be afraid because I would soon start to wonder when I'd have to go back again. I wasn't taken there often – maybe once or twice a year – but each time I was put into the car and driven out of the city, I'd start to cry as I realised where we were going. When we crossed over a railway line, I knew we were nearing the home and I'd listen to rocks ricocheting off the bottom of the car as we drove along a dirt road littered with them. As my heart beat and my throat tightened, I would long to scream, and wondered if I could make my parents hear my thoughts if only I tried hard enough.

But the one thing I wished for more than anything as I sat strapped in a seat, powerless to tell anyone about what I knew would soon happen to me, was for someone to look at me. Surely then they would see what was written on my face? Fear. I knew where I was. I knew where I was going. I had feelings. I wasn't just a ghost boy. But no one looked.

36

Lurking in Plain Sight

Similar things happened in other places too, where children and adults were too weak, silent or mentally defenceless to tell their secrets. I learned that the people who play out their darkest desires on us, however fleetingly, aren't always the most easily recognisable. They aren't bogey men or women; they are ordinary, forgettable people. Maybe they are even entirely blameless until the chance to use a seemingly empty vessel encourages them to cross a line they might otherwise never have dared breach.

Sometimes it was nothing more than a feeling, as if an invisible line had been overstepped, which made me feel unsafe. I couldn't explain it properly because even though I was a young man, there was so much I didn't understand.

'Kiss, kiss,' one woman whispered in a breathy voice that no one else could hear as she bent her head towards me. She sounded flirtatious, like a girl tempting an embrace from an unwilling suitor.

On another occasion, the mother of a child I knew came into a room as I was lying alone and naked from the waist down, waiting to be changed.

What's this?' she said as she scratched my penis gently.

The incident was over as soon as it began because a carer came back to the room. But it made me feel confused, unsure, and I didn't know what to make of the troubled feelings that filled me.

It wasn't always like this though. Sometimes it was only too clear what was happening and fear would wash over me as I realised I was being attacked in a way that I could never defend myself against.

'Look at you,' a carer once said as she bathed me.

The next day I watched silently as she looked around the empty room, lifted up her dress and straddled my hip before rubbing herself against me. I lay unmoving, unblinking, unseeing, until I felt her weight rise off me. I was left with the gnawing fear that she might touch me again but she didn't.

What was I to these women – a perverse fantasy long held and buried or a moment of madness? I can't be sure. But to another woman who also abused me for several years, I know I was never more than a thing, an object to be used as and when she wished before being dropped again.

Solitude was the oxygen that gave life to her behaviour: she always found a way for us to be alone. The first time she touched me, I knew with absolute clarity what she was doing as I felt her hand push questioningly at the crotch of my trousers. It was as if she was afraid, uncertain, and the incident was brief. But she was bolder the next time, as her hands lingered on my penis. Soon she had become even braver, as if realising that opening the door to this darkness wasn't as terrifying as she'd thought it might be.

Sometimes she would wrap her legs around my body and thrust against me harder and harder until I heard her gasp. Or she would stand behind me as I lay on my back and pull my arms above my head so that my hands rested against her thighs. As my fingers trembled uncontrollably, just as she knew they would, I would hear her breathing become ragged as she pushed my fingers against her sex.

She was usually silent when she took her fill of me. Sometimes it would go on for what felt like forever as she rocked and pressed herself against me, her body jerking mine in time with hers, until she was finally still. Each time, I would try to lose myself in the quiet, closing myself down inside. Yet still I could feel my soul freezing over. It was only later that feelings of shame filled me.

If she spoke to me at all, it was as a child would speak to a doll she knows isn't really there.

'Let's fidget,' she whispered once as she pulled me out of my wheelchair.

The one thing she always made sure of was that I could never see her.

'You shouldn't be looking,' she said as she turned my head to face away from her. But it wasn't me she spoke to: it was herself.

It didn't happen all the time. Sometimes weeks or months went by before she touched me again and then it would happen on several consecutive meetings. It was worse that way because I never knew what she was going to do or when.

Nothing made me feel more powerless as I waited for her to come for me again. Anxiety about what she might do when I saw her next would build up inside me as I wondered whether I would escape this time or not. Fear threw a veil across my days. I knew I couldn't stop her or speak out. I was just an unresponsive object that she used as and when she wanted, the blank canvas onto which she painted her black appetites. And so I would sit and wait, listening until I heard her voice again, knowing that the moment I did, I'd never more desperately want to run.

'Hello, Martin,' she says with a smile as she looks down at me.

I stare at her. My stomach turns with nausea. I can feel a scream unfurling inside me like a flag snapping in the wind but I can't let it out.

'Off we go,' she says and I feel my chair begin to move.

She takes me into a room where no one will see us and lies me down on a bench. Lifting one foot off the floor and resting it beside me, she keeps her other foot on the ground as she lifts her skirt. She lowers herself down, pressing herself against the big toe of my left foot as she starts to move rhythmically against me. I try to disappear.

Later I lie unmoving as she sits down beside me. She reads a magazine, flicking through the pages absent-mindedly while picking her nose. Eventually she looks at her watch and stands up. But just as she prepares to leave, she turns again. She has remembered something.

I watch as she drags her finger slowly down the arm of my T-shirt, wiping herself off on me. A trail of mucus glistens on my sleeve. Her contempt is complete now.

Sometimes she lies beside me, at others on top of me. Sometimes she touches herself, at others she touches me. But whatever happens, I'm nothing to her, forgotten until she decides to come for me, while she never leaves me. She is an ogre residing in my dreams, chasing me and screeching, tormenting and terrifying me. Night after night, I wake up sweating and terrified after she's come to me again as I've slept. She is a parasite that has wormed its way into my soul. As I lie in the dark, I wonder if I will ever be rid of her.

37

Fantasies

It was at this time more than any other that I needed to rely on my imagination. If my fantasy world had one recurring theme it was escape, because I could be anything I dared to be and more: not just a pirate but a pilot, a space raider or a Formula One driver, a merman, a secret agent or a Jedi warrior with mind-reading powers.

Sometimes I'd sit in my wheelchair in my classroom at the care centre and feel myself shrinking as I left the world behind. As the chair got bigger and bigger, I'd imagine myself to be as small as a toy soldier, so tiny I could fit into the jet plane waiting for me in the corner of the room. To everyone else it might look like a toy but I alone knew it was a fighter jet and the engines were running, ready for me.

In my dreams, my body was always strong. I'd leap up out of my wheelchair before looking around as I listened for footsteps. If someone saw me, they'd be shocked. I was ready to fight back. They might think that I was a trick of their imagination but I wasn't; I was real. Throwing myself off the edge of the chair and landing on the floor with a soft thump, I looked down to see that my T-shirt and shorts had disappeared and I was wearing a grey flying suit. It rustled as I ran over to the jet, climbed up the steps and wriggled in behind the controls as I put on my helmet. Engines growled and lights flashed in front of me but I didn't worry. I understood why they did this because I was a trained fighter pilot.

I pushed a lever forward and the plane started to move. Faster and faster, it raced across the lino floor of my classroom before lifting into the air and flying into the corridor. Marietta was walking towards me but I sped around her head. I was too fast and small for her to see as I pulled the lever again and the plane shot forward.

I was thrown back by the G-force as a trolley reared up ahead of me and, as I darted to miss it, I knew that one wrong move would clip my jet's wings and send me crashing to the ground. But my hand stayed steady. Bam! I flew out the other side of the trolley towards the doors leading outside.

They were closing as I approached them so I flipped the plane on its side. The jet rushed cleanly between the doors as they creaked closed and I was free. The sky above me was blue and the outside world smelled of dust and sun. I nosed the plane upwards, knowing that soon I would be high enough to look down at the earth below me: splots of green and splashes of brown rushing past. I pulled the lever back as far as it could go – full throttle, sonic thrusters on max – and the jet shot up into the sky in a corkscrew. It spun me round and round.

My head was dizzy but I felt light. I started laughing.

Roger and out – I was free.

Below, the highway was filled with cars and people going home from work. I knew where the roads would take me if I followed them – home.

When I lay in bed at the care home in the country I'd think of the train tracks nearby and imagine myself stealing outside, running through the long brown grass of the Highveld. In the distance, I'd see a train pulling faded brown goods carriages behind it, some covered in tarpaulins, some open and filled with glistening black coal. Running towards the train, I'd grab on to the last carriage just before it disappeared down the line. I didn't know where the train would take me. All I cared about was that I was leaving.

Water was another thing I loved to dream about, fantasising that it would rush into whatever room I was sitting in, lift me up and bear me away on the crest of a wave. In the water, I would duck and dive, my body free and strong. Or I'd imagine that my wheelchair had grown James Bond wings and I'd soar into the sky as the care staff stared up, open-mouthed, unable to prevent me from flying away.

In my fantasy world, I was still the child I'd been when I first fell asleep. The only thing that changed as I grew older was that I started to imagine myself as a world-famous cricket player because I'd cultivated an interest in the sport as I watched Dad and David enjoy it.

My brother was very good at cricket and would tell Mum, Dad and Kim about his latest match when he came home. I so wanted to share something with him. David always made me smile by telling me jokes, talking in funny voices or tickling me, so I started listening intently whenever the cricket came on the radio or TV.

Soon I could lose days and weeks in matches that I imagined going on in my head. Each one would start with me sitting in a silent changing room as I laced up my shoes before stepping outside into the sunshine. As I walked across the pitch, I'd rub the ball on the edge of my shirt before checking to see if it was shiny enough and I'd stare at the batsman as the crowd hushed. I didn't feel scared by all the people watching me. All I could think of was running down the wicket and feeling the ball, round and solid in my hand, before I flung it at the batsman.

A flash of cherry red would fly through the air as the ball shot out of my hand and I heard the soft click of bails flying off the stumps as the crowd roared. I wasn't always a sure shot, though. Sometimes I'd miss the batsman completely with a ball that went wildly off course, or I'd be bowled out for a duck, which meant I'd walk off the pitch knowing I hadn't done so well that day. But somehow it didn't matter because I was a sporting star. I lived in matches like these day after day as the South African team's most famous all-rounder, who saved the game more often than he lost it. The games became almost endless, over after over of balls were bowled and wickets were won or lost as I retreated from reality.

The one person I talked to was God but He wasn't part of my fantasy world. He was real to me, a presence inside and around that calmed and reassured me. Just as North American Indians might commune with their spirit guides or pagans look to the seasons and the sun, I spoke to God as I tried to make sense of what had happened to me and asked Him to protect me from harm. God and I didn't talk about the big things in life – we didn't engage in philosophical debates or argue about religion – but I talked to Him endlessly because I knew we shared something important. I didn't have proof that He existed but I believed in Him anyway because I knew He was real. God did the same for me. Unlike people, He didn't need proof that I existed – He knew I did.

38

A New Friend

The noise is like a train gathering speed in the distance. It gets louder and louder until suddenly it explodes into the room – a ball of yellow fur, a huge red tongue and sodden paws that leaps onto the sofa, drenching it in seconds. A huge tail wags frenziedly and big brown eyes stare around the room.

'Kojak! Down!'

The dog takes no notice as he carries on looking around before finally taking a flying leap off the sofa towards me. I could swear he's smiling.

'Kojak! No!'

The dog doesn't listen to a word his owner is saying to him. All he wants is to say hello to the strange man sitting in the strange chair.

'Get down!'

The man drags the huge yellow Labrador off me and wrestles him to a sitting position. But even pinned to his master's side with a firm hand on his collar, the dog keeps moving. He waves his head around wildly and wriggles his bottom. His tongue lolls out of his mouth because even his breath can't keep up with him.

I look at Mum and Dad. I've never seen them look scared before.

'So this is the dog that you're looking to rehome?' my father says in a neutral voice.

'Yes,' the man replies. 'We're moving to Scotland and want to find him a new family. He's such a loving dog. I'm sorry he's so wet. Kojak just loves the swimming pool!'

Horror steals its way onto my mother's face like a blind being drawn down a window. I know that she dares not let herself speak.

'He's had all his injections and we've done some obedience training with him,' the man continues. 'Obviously, he's only eight months old so he's still full of energy.'

As if on cue, Kojak wrenches against his master's grip as a volley of barks explode from him. I almost expect my mother to start screaming.

'What do you think, Martin?' Dad asks me.

I stare at the dog. He is too big and boisterous, obviously deaf to any kind of command and will wreak havoc in my parents' neat home. In four months of searching, I've never seen a dog like him but, even so, something tells me that he's the one for me.

I smile at Dad.

'Well, I think Martin has made his mind up,' he says.

'That's great news!' Kojak's owner exclaims. 'You won't regret it.'

I look at Mum. I think she's trying not to cry.

39

Will He Ever Learn?

I've never forgotten Pookie, which is why I want a dog so much. I've always remembered the bond we shared and I want a companion just like her. I want something to care for that isn't aware of all my limits and defects. Despite my enthusiasm, my mother doesn't like the idea. She doesn't want something else to look after, let alone a huge dog that will trail hair and mud in its wake.

Kim was the one who in the end came to my rescue when she was home on a visit from the UK earlier this year. She quickly saw that I was working harder than ever – literally day and night at times – and sometimes getting just four or five hours' sleep as I tried to keep up with everything.

It's now April 2005 – almost four years since I was first assessed – and in that time I've never stopped working. It's as if I can't allow myself to let go of life for a second after being given a chance at it. I don't have a social life or hobbies. All I do is work as I struggle not just to keep up but to carry on improving. Because I was static for so long, I want to keep moving forward. I still can't believe that people are giving me opportunities. I constantly feel afraid that I might be found out as inexperienced at life so I work hard to make up for what I believe I lack because I feel like a fraud.

After being put in charge of redesigning the communication centre's website, I was seconded from my job there to a scientific research institute where I helped create disability-related Internet resources. It opened up a new world of possibilities for me and I left my job at the health centre. I'm now working three days a week at the communication centre and two as a computer technologist at the scientific research institute.

Outside office hours, I continue to raise awareness about AAC and I've joined the executive committee of a national organisation for people like me with little or no functioning speech. I even took my first-ever flight in January to do a whistle-stop tour of five cities nationwide for a charity fundraising event. It made me wonder why birds ever come down to earth because my body felt so free when the plane took off.

If I'm not doing paid or voluntary work, I'm studying.

But all this activity is why Kim knew something had to change when she came to visit. She could see there was little else in my life other than work so she talked to Mum and Dad, who agreed I could get a dog.

'You'll have to take care of it, though,' Mum warned. 'Feed it and clean it. I'm already looking after four people in this house so the dog will be your responsibility.'

'I won't ask you to do a thing,' I told her, although I had

yet to understand just what taking an enthusiastic young Labrador for a walk in a wheelchair would really mean.

That was how the search for Kojak started. Although people wanted me to get something small, my heart was set on a yellow Labrador because they seemed to me to be the happiest dogs of all. I looked at some litters but saw many puppies that were too sickly while others had some physical characteristic that told me they hadn't been bred correctly. I couldn't afford a top of the range pedigree dog so I waited several months to find the one that would be the perfect fit for me. I then got a tip from a breeder about one she'd sold that now needed a new home. The moment I saw Kojak, I knew he was meant to be mine.

Taking care of a wild child like him is proving to be more difficult than I expected. From the moment he arrived, Kojak has caused controversy. Seconds after I shut the front door, he bounded off to sniff every nook and cranny of his new home and sent a cup of tea flying with his tail as he ran into the living room. As my parents got up from their armchairs to clear up the mess, Kojak leaped onto Dad's chair.

'Get down!' shrieked my mother.

Kojak did as he was told – then jumped onto Mum's chair. With just one look, he'd understood the pecking order in our house.

'Will we ever get control of this dog?' Mum asked wearily. I, too, wondered if we would later that evening, after Kojak had been locked in the kitchen while we ate supper.

'What has he done?' Mum roared when she walked into the kitchen and found the floor covered in cooking oil and vomit.

Kojak had gulped down most of a bottle of oil so

enthusiastically that it had reappeared almost immediately. Even so he still looked as if he was smiling. As my mother raged, the two of us went outside. We didn't go back in until I knew she'd gone to bed and the coast was clear.

That's the kind of dog Kojak is: intelligent but charmingly troublesome; clever enough to understand when he's being naughty and desperate to please but somehow unable to do so always. His chewing budget has threatened to rage out of control, as he has gobbled up mobile phones, disappeared with several TV remote controls and destroyed almost every established plant in my parents' garden.

'It's been Kojaked,' my mother says now with a sigh when she looks at the craters in her flower border, because for some reason he can't get enough of a clump of bright orange birds of paradise flowers that she was once proud of.

Kojak's idiosyncrasies don't stop there. If a car window is opened, he'll try to climb out of it, and he can't sit still long enough to have a pee, which means that he hops from foot to foot as he does it, like a boxer preparing for a fight. He's also knocked over my wheelchair several times after lunging at something and pulling me over. Whether it's a dog barking or a new smell, he can't resist investigating, and he wants to jump in and save me whenever I get into our swimming pool. He made a break for freedom one day during an obedience training class only to find a five-foot drop on the other side of the wall that he'd jumped over. Suspended in mid-air by his lead, Kojak stared at me as if pleading for his life with an executioner while Dad rescued him with the help of the woman who ran the training class. The other dogs just looked on in despair.

I know, however, that buried deep within Kojak is a sensible dog trying its hardest to come out. I knew even before I got him that the only hope I had of having any kind of control over a dog was by teaching him some rules so I'd signed us up for obedience training classes. Kojak is now learning to respond to non-verbal commands and each weekend my mother or father takes the two of us to dog school, where we are slowly learning to understand each other.

Raising my fist to my chest tells Kojak to sit down, while a finger pointed at the ground instructs him to lie flat. A fist held next to my body asks him to get up again and a hand held straight up tells him to wait. Happily, he has quickly learned the basics and we've moved on to the more playful stuff: if I wave at him now, he waves his paw back; if I hold up my hand, he bats it with his paw in a 'high five'; and if I hold out my hand, he raises his paw so he can shake it.

It's taking time but I'm sure Kojak is slowly calming down. He's even learned some service skills, such as opening doors and closing drawers for me. These can sometimes be haphazard because teaching him to take off my socks has given him such a taste for them that he now steals every pair he can find in the washing basket. Teaching him to do things around the house also sparked the idea of teaching him to ring the doorbell and he has taken to running off just so he can come home and let us know he's back.

But whatever his shortcomings, Kojak is what I wanted him to be: a companion who always makes me smile with his unfailing cheerfulness and loving nature. Whatever mistakes he makes, his presence has made my world a far happier place.

40

GD and Mimi

My grandparents, GD and Mimi, taught me perhaps my most important lesson about love: if it's true, it will last a lifetime and if it's strong enough, it can be passed from generation to generation.

I'd heard stories about GD and Mimi all my life: how GD won a medal for bravery at the age of sixteen after diving off rocks into the sea to save a drowning woman and how Mimi loved dances so much when she was a girl that she would travel miles to attend them. GD, who was working as a trainee miner when they met, would cycle thirty miles to see Mimi. He was so determined to provide her with a good life after she'd agreed to marry him that he took his mining exams eleven times in order to qualify as a manager. GD was the youngest of sixteen children and Mimi was the eldest of four so it was perhaps inevitable that they would want kids of their own and soon they had my father and his two sisters. While Mimi taught her children to do the Charleston as she ran their home, GD built a house for his family so they could move out of mining accommodation.

My grandparents lived together happily for almost sixty years and continued to do so even after Mimi was confined to bed when she fell and broke her hip soon after my awareness started to return. She never got up again but Mimi ran her home like a sergeant-major from the comfort of her bed. GD was told what to buy at the shops, how to cook it and when to take his heart medication. He could never see the irony when he went to visit 'the old dears' in the local home for pensioners.

I loved them both very much. Whenever we went to visit, my wheelchair would be put next to Mimi's bed so she could reach out to take my hands in hers. Staring at her paper-thin skin, which looked so delicate I thought it might tear, I wondered if I would ever grow so ancient. But then, when I was twenty-three, Mimi fell ill and this time there was nothing that could be done. Her body was simply wearing out. As she got weaker and weaker, I'd watch Mimi slip in and out of consciousness as I sat beside her.

My grandfather seemed lost. It was during one of those final visits that I heard him tell my father what he wanted more than anything in the world.

'I'd like to sleep next to my wife one last time,' GD said, because Mimi had been so ill that he hadn't been able to.

Two days later, the phone rang at home and Dad picked it up. He talked quietly for a few moments before putting it down.

'Mimi has died,' he said and I watched him walk up the passageway with his hands held behind his head, as if trying to massage the realisation that he'd lost his mother into his skull.

I was filled with sadness for my father as he put me into the car and drove us to his parents' home to see Mimi for the last time. She was lying on the bed when we got there and my father kissed her as I watched. No one knew that I completely understood what had happened, of course, and I longed to comfort GD as he cried while we all sat waiting for the undertakers to arrive.

'I feel as if my arm has been amputated,' he sobbed and I knew his heart was breaking for the woman he'd loved for so many years and now lost.

Their love had lasted a lifetime; their stories had become woven together so tightly that they'd forgotten where one ended and another began. All around us were scattered the tiny clues of their love, enmeshed in even the most mundane objects like the winter coat my father and aunts found in Mimi's wardrobe. GD had spent precious money on his wife because he was anxious to keep her warm.

A few days later Dad spoke at Mimi's funeral about the love she had passed on to her children. When he was a boy, he told the congregation, his mother had knitted his clothes in 'love stitches' and her calm, quiet presence was always with him. One day when he was a small boy helping her to bottle peaches, my father had accidentally spilled burning syrup on Mimi, which had instantly blistered her skin, but she didn't get cross or shout. Instead, she simply washed the burn in cold water, bandaged it and quietly carried on.

As I listened to my father, I realised that I was learning another lesson about the love I'd seen between men and women: sometimes it was playful like Henk and Arrietta's, sometimes peaceful like Ingrid and Dave's, but if you were lucky, it could last forever just as it had between GD and Mimi. That kind of love can be passed from one person to the next, like a life force that will comfort anyone it touches and create memories that burn strong years after the events that inspired them.

This was the kind of love my father had known and now, as he spoke, I knew he could see his mother in his mind's eye as clearly as he had when she was still alive. As he remembered that moment in his childhood, he could feel her touch and hear her voice as once more he became a boy enveloped in love on the day he bottled peaches with his mother.

41

Loving Life and Living Love

The waves roll onto the beach as the smell of fried chicken wafts on the salty wind. My mouth waters as I lift another piece of meat to my mouth. How good it tastes.

It's December 2006 and I'm sitting on the edge of a beach in Cape Town with my friend Graham. He became a fellow AAC user after suffering a bilateral brain stem stroke while he was working on an island off the coast of South Africa more than two decades ago. After Graham was airlifted to hospital, he woke up only to be told that he was paralysed from the eyes down. He was twenty-five.

Today Graham can't move or talk yet he lives life roaring like a lion at anyone who doubts him. Completely physically dependent on others, he refused to go home to be cared for by his mother as he was expected to do after he was paralysed. She lived on the other side of the country, after all, and Graham wanted to continue to live in Cape Town. So he went into a nursing home, where he still lives today, and I've never met anyone whose love of life is so infectious.

He lives every minute and loves to break rules: I'm pretty sure that he'll soon ask to be given a mouthful of fried chicken even though he isn't supposed to eat solid food. I understand the kind of longing that's too strong to deny. 'You can't do everything the doctors tell you to,' he says to anyone who might question him. He's told me that it's not just the taste but the physical act of chewing and swallowing he craves. That's why the advice of doctors gets forgotten every now and again as Graham treasures eating a small mouthful of food.

We first met at a conference about eighteen months ago, and I'm in Cape Town now because we're giving speeches at an event tomorrow. But first we have come to the beach to sit side by side like metal birds on a wire and watch the sea. As I chew my chicken, I think of a photograph Graham showed me earlier.

'She's an acquaintance,' he said as I looked at the beautiful woman smiling into the camera lens.

Graham's eyes twinkled as he used the infrared pointer that tracks the tiny movements he can make with his head to operate his communication device and talk to me. I wished I had a picture to show him too, a photo of a woman I love. But I don't and I'm beginning to fear that I never will because, lesson by painful lesson, I'm learning that few women can see past the body that encases me.

I don't know if my longing for love was always a part of me or whether its seeds were sown on a day I can still remember vividly although it was over ten years ago. It was late afternoon when a group of nursing students visited the care home and I was lying on a mattress when I felt someone kneel down beside me. As a straw was put into my mouth, I looked up to see a young woman. Long brown hair framed her face and suddenly I was filled with a longing so strong it almost made me gasp when I felt the gentleness in her hands. I wished I could stretch that tiny moment into forever as the girl who smelled of flowers and sunshine became the world to me. Was it that or all I saw between Henk and Arrietta, Dave and Ingrid, GD and Mimi that coaxed the longing for love to life inside me? Or perhaps it was because of the years of devotion my parents showed me, my brother, my sister and each other.

Whatever the reason, my yearning for love burned stronger still when I started to communicate and it's only now that I can see how naive I've been. I really did believe that I could will love into existence if I wanted it enough and I would find someone to share the kind of feelings I'd seen as a ghost boy. Then Virna taught me that it was going to be far harder than I'd thought at first and I tried to accept the lesson. But although I've run from my feelings and buried them in work, and counted my blessings one by one, there are times now when I feel as lonely as I did before I could communicate.

I realised long ago that my love for Virna was a myth I wrote for myself, a sprite of my own creation that I'd never have been able to capture for real. Whatever I thought, she only ever saw me as a friend and I can't blame her for that. But I didn't learn the lessons she inadvertently tried to teach and I've repeated the same mistake again and again. Although I'm

thirty now, there are times when I think I have as much understanding of women as I did when I was a twelve-year-old boy
submerged in darkness.

Earlier this year, I travelled with my father to a conference
in Israel and sat in a darkened auditorium listening to a professor talk about the challenges facing people like me in having
romantic relationships. However much I didn't want to
believe it, I knew he was right.

Ever since I started to communicate, my hope has been
drawn time and again towards women like a moth to a flame,
only for me to be burned by the scalding chill of their indifference. I've met women who have found me an oddity to be
inspected, and others who think I'm a challenge to be overcome. One woman I met through an Internet dating site
stared at me as if I was an exhibit at the zoo, while another,
who was a speech therapist, gave me a straw when I arrived
to see her socially before asking me to blow through it as she
would a patient doing a breathing exercise. I longed to tell
these women that I'm not a neutered dog with no bark or bite;
I have longings and feelings just like they do.

Soon after returning from Israel, I met a woman who captured my attention just as others had done and once again I
allowed hope to take root inside me. I told myself the professor was wrong. What did he know? I had confounded
expectations in other ways and would do so again. I was sure
this woman's interest in me was genuine and my heart soared
when we went out one evening to eat pizza and chat. For a few
short hours, I felt as normal as everyone else. Then the woman
emailed me to let me know that she had a new boyfriend and I
felt crushed again.

I was such a fool. How could I hope that a woman might love me? Why would she? I know I bruise too easily and am too quick to feel pain and sadness. It makes me envy people my age who had teenage years in which to be knocked by life and learn to play by its rules. However hard I try not to care, I find it almost impossible to accept that the desire for love that burns so strongly inside me will never be reciprocated.

Now I look out at the sea as I watch waves crashing onto the sand and remember a couple who came to one of the open days I host at the communication centre. I noticed them at once because the man, who arrived with his wife and two small children, was about my age and everything about the couple – from the way they looked at each other to the silences and smiles that communicated so much – told me they were very much in love.

'My husband has a terminal brain tumour and is losing the power of speech,' the woman said to me quietly as her husband looked at some of the equipment we had on show. 'But we want to carry on talking to each other for as long as we can, which is why we came here today to see if you could help.

'He wants to tape video messages for our children while he's still able to and I think he wants to leave one for me as well.'

Suddenly the woman's face froze.

'I'm not ready to let him go yet,' she whispered.

Desolation swept across the woman's face like wind across a deserted winter's beach as she thought of the uncertainty of a future without the man who had anchored her to life.

'Do you think you could help us?' she asked softly.

I nodded at her before she turned to walk back to her husband and I felt grief pierce me. How could a family that loved so much be torn apart? Then another feeling filled me, a kind of envy, because as I looked at the man and woman smile at each other, I realised they'd had the chance to love and be loved that I so fiercely wanted.

Martin giving a presentation at an international conference in Israel

42

Worlds Collide

My mother smiles at the physiotherapist who is pushing me out of her room. I'm sick of coming here week after week, being lifted up and encouraged to take faltering steps on my painful legs and feet. Nevertheless I do it because my parents have never given up the hope of seeing me walk again. I've wondered at times if my family remember the boy I used to be and miss him, which is why they've always wanted me to walk again so badly or to use a computer-generated voice to talk instead of an alphabet board.

It is hard to convince them that my body is unpredictable: just because I can stand up one day, doesn't mean I'll be able to do it the next. It sometimes feels as if I'm almost failing my parents because I don't progress physically in the way they hope I might but I know this is often the case with parents.

When a boy came to the communication centre once to be assessed, we told his mother that he would have to start learning to communicate using a head switch because his neck was the only part of his body he could stabilise. But his mother was adamant: she wanted her son to use his hand not his head. She wanted him to fit in in any way he could, to be as like everyone else as he could in whatever small way.

I understand why my parents want to see me walk and talk but it's exhausting to live in a body that feels like the property of everyone else. That's why I told my mother yesterday that I wanted to have physio only once this week and I'm hoping she'll agree to this compromise.

'Shall we make an appointment for Friday?' the physio asks as my chair comes to rest.

I stare at my mother, willing her to remember what I said.

'Yes,' she says, without looking at me.

The anger I feel burns white hot through my veins. Tomorrow I will go to see my colleague Kitty and rage to her about what has just happened.

'What's the point of communicating if no one listens?!' I'll say. 'Why is it that I talk yet people still refuse to hear what I say even after all these years?'

For now, though, I wrestle back my rage to stop it from dragging everything else down with it. Because, as powerful as it is, the fear I feel about expressing my anger is even stronger. Anger is one of the emotions I still find almost impossible to show because I had to force myself to swallow it for so long. I don't feel I can express it even now, trapped as I am by both the monotone of my computer-generated voice and the constant fear of alienating people. After spending so long as an outsider, I don't want to do anything that might make me one again.

As time passes, I realise that I feel afraid a lot now: I'm

scared of doing the wrong thing, offending someone or not doing a job well enough; I'm fearful of stepping on someone's toes, not being up to what is asked of me or expressing an opinion that will surely be ridiculed. The feeling is almost constant and it's the reason why I don't tell my mother what I really think six years after starting to communicate.

There's another world I inhabit, though. In that world I became one of the first two South Africans with non-functioning speech ever to graduate when I finished my university course and was chosen to meet President Thabo Mbeki. I've travelled, spoken in front of hundreds of people and I'm respected by my colleagues.

But in my personal life, even though my family and friends are my lifeline, I remain in many ways a passive child who is wiped and wheeled, smiled at and sidelined at times, just as I've always been. My parents continue to care for me physically, protecting me from much of the outside world and the harms it might inflict, but I wish they'd listen to me more sometimes. With my sister Kim, I sometimes feel as if I'm a rehabilitation project rather than a brother when she brings home new pieces of equipment from the UK – anti-slip mats for the bathroom or plastic borders to stop food falling off my plate. To others, I'm an occasional charity project, someone who needs to be fixed, or the silent man who sits smiling placidly in a corner. Taken together it makes me feel as if I have no right to life, as if I must always ask permission for fear of doing the wrong thing. The past continues to cast its shadow over me.

I long to rebel but I don't know how. Once I had petty, hidden ways at my disposal and can remember the grim satisfaction that filled me years ago when I watched my leg callipers gouge the paintwork on my mother's car. I was wearing them after a particularly painful operation so I was pleased by my accidental act of rebellion as Mum helped me out of the car.

Today I can't justify such bad behaviour nor can I lay all the blame for my frustration at other people's doors. Even a lion cub won't leave its mother if it's too afraid. I know independence is taken as much as it's given and I must learn to claim mine but sometimes I wonder if I will ever find the courage to do so. It's 2007 and earlier this year, I finally left my job at the communication centre and started working full time at the scientific research institute. It's an excellent promotion – the kind of professional good fortune that many people like me never get the chance to experience.

As everyone at my new workplace is encouraged to study, I applied to do a part-time degree at a university but was told that I had to graduate from high school first. No one would listen, however patiently I tried to explain, that I'd just graduated from another university course as one of the top of the class. The mountain I'd climbed to achieve my qualification meant nothing now that I was applying somewhere different with its own set of rules.

So now I'm studying each night when I get back from work for a high school diploma that sixteen year olds do, and I question if there's any point in trying to move forward in life when the weight of everything holding me back feels too heavy to bear at times. As I consider it all, I wonder if soon I'll feel too afraid, too disbelieving that I have earned a place in life to be able to fight for one any more.

43

Strangers

It was only when I finally gave up on life that I realised we don't need ropes and chains to keep us tethered to this world – even the most insignificant acts can keep us bound to it.

It was 1998 and I was twenty-two years old. I'd started to become aware six long years before and was convinced by then that no one would ever know I was whole inside. After so many years of hoping in vain that I might be rescued, the thought of never escaping the crushing monotony of my existence had made me shut down inside. I just wanted my life to end and nearly got my wish when I became seriously ill with pneumonia.

Finding out that I would have to go to the care home in the country that I hated so much was what made me finally give up. I can remember my parents taking us all to see some friends of theirs. As my mother fed me lunch, I knew there was nothing I could do to show anyone that I didn't want to be sent away again. My family had no idea how desperate I felt inside as they chatted and laughed around me.

The following week I got a runny nose that quickly got worse. People soon realised it wasn't just a cold when my temperature rose and I started vomiting. In fact, I became so ill that my parents took me to the emergency department at the local hospital, where a doctor gave me some medication before sending me home again. When I got worse again, my mother took me back to the hospital and demanded that someone take an X-ray of my chest. They then discovered that I had pneumonia.

I didn't care whether I was treated or not. All I could think about was being sent away when Dad went on his upcoming business trip. I knew I couldn't bear it again. As my kidneys and liver started to shut down, I could hear my parents talking worriedly as they sat beside me and I dipped in and out of consciousness. I knew I was in a room with other patients and sometimes I could hear nurses rushing in to see them when an alarm went off.

Sadness created a chasm inside me. I was tired of living. I didn't want to fight any more. As a mask was slipped over my face so that I could be given oxygen, I prayed for it to be taken off; when a physiotherapist came to pound my ribcage and clear my chest, I hoped she wouldn't be able to; and as she tried feeding a tube down my unwilling throat to relieve the congestion in my chest, I wished she'd leave me alone.

'I've got to get this into you,' she said to me almost angrily. 'You'll die if I don't.'

I rejoiced when I heard those words. I prayed that the infection would overwhelm me and free me from purgatory as it battled for control of my body. I could hear my parents talking about the information file beside my bed that Dad always read whenever he arrived. Kim came to see me too and the sound of the clogs she was wearing echoed through the corridor outside my room, while the brightness of her smile as she looked at me almost cut through the darkness. But nothing reached me and I listened without hearing to nurses complaining about their working conditions or the dates they'd been on with their boyfriends.

'I had a good look at him when he walked into the cinema in front of me,' one said to another as they washed me. 'He's got such a sexy bum.'

'You've got a one-track mind,' her friend admonished with a giggle.

It was as if I was being sucked deeper and deeper down a rabbit hole. I urged my body to give up. I wasn't needed in this world by anyone and no one would notice if I disappeared. I wasn't interested in the future because all I wanted was to die. So hope was like a breath of fresh air blowing through a tomb when it came.

I was lying in bed one afternoon when I heard someone talking to a nurse. Then a face appeared and I realised that it was a woman I knew a little called Myra. She worked in the office where my father got cheques signed in his role as chairman of the management committee for my care centre. But now Myra had come to see me and I didn't understand why because only my family ever visited.

'How are you, Martin?' Myra said as she bent over me. 'I wanted to come and see you because I've heard how ill you've been. You poor boy. I hope they're looking after you well here.'

Myra's face was anxious as she looked down at me. As she smiled hesitantly, I suddenly realised that another human being, unconnected to me by blood or obligation, had thought about me. However much I didn't want it to, that realisation gave me strength. Almost unconsciously after that I began to notice warmth from other people: a nursing sister I overheard telling another that she liked me because I was a good patient, a carer who soothed my aching skin by rubbing lotion into my shoulder to stop me developing a bedsore, and a man who smiled as he walked by while I was sitting in the car on the day I left hospital. All these incidents didn't come together at once but, looking back, I know these tiny gestures from strangers were what started to tether me to the world again.

I was finally roped to it by something that occurred when I got back to my care home. Despite all that had happened to convince me I had a place in the world, disappointment pervaded: I hadn't even been able to die properly. Breath filled my body, I woke up in the morning and fell asleep at night, I was fed food to build up my strength and put out to sit in the sunshine like a plant that needed tending. There was nothing I could do to stop people from keeping me alive.

But as I lay on a bean-bag one day, a carer sat down beside me. She was new so I didn't really know her but I recognised her voice as she spoke to me. Her hands took hold of one of my feet as she started to massage it and I felt her pummel my aching and ugly foot with her hands, soothing out the knots and relaxing away the tension. I couldn't believe that she wanted to touch me and the fact that she did made me realise that maybe there was some tiny reason not to give up on life completely. Perhaps I wasn't as repulsive as I believed I was.

Then I heard the familiar crunch of the zipped pencil bag the woman always carried around with her, which was full of the oils she used for aromatherapy. 'There, now,' she said softly as the smell of mint pierced the air. 'I'm sure that feels much better, doesn't it? Why don't we do your other foot and see if we can relax that a bit too?'

The woman's name, of course, was Virna and it was the first time she'd really spoken to me. But that moment was the one that drew all the other pieces together and made the jigsaw whole. I didn't know what each of those strangers had given me until one of them touched my broken, twisted, useless body and made me realise that I wasn't completely abhorrent. And it was then that I realised that families might be the ones who pick us up time and again but strangers can also rescue us – even if they don't know they're doing so.

44

Everything Changes

I know a life can be destroyed in an instant: a car spins out of control on a busy road, a doctor sits down to break bad news or a love letter is discovered hidden in a place where its owner thought it never would be found. All these things can shatter a world in just a few moments. But is it possible for the opposite to happen – for a life to be created in a moment instead of destroyed? For a man to see a face and know it belongs to the woman he will spend the rest of his life with?

She is the kind of woman who would make any man's heart sing and yet I feel sure there is something about her that speaks to me alone. I met her on New Year's Day a month ago when Kim called from England. I didn't pay much attention at first as my parents chatted to my sister via webcam and I heard her introducing them to the friends she was spending the day with. But then I turned my head, saw a woman with blue eyes, blonde hair and the warmest smile I'd ever seen and my world shifted forever.

She was sitting between Kim and a third woman with dark brown hair. They giggled together as their faces squeezed onto the screen.

'This is Danielle,' Kim said, gesturing to the dark-haired woman. 'And this is Joanna.'

'Hi Martin,' they said in unison.

I could hear immediately that they were both South African. She smiled. I smiled back.

'Ooh!' said Danielle. 'He's handsome.'

My face burned crimson as the three of them laughed together before Kim got up to go and do something and I was left alone with Joanna and Danielle.

'Show us your arms!' Danielle said. 'I'm an occupational therapist so I know guys like you usually have great arms!'

I felt my face burn even redder as I looked at them. I wasn't sure what to say.

'How are you both?' I wrote.

'Good!' Danielle said. 'What are you doing today?'

'Working, like every other day. How was your New Year's Eve?'

'Fun. We went into London. It was great.'

Joanna was quieter than Danielle but I watched her eyes slide downwards whenever I wrote something. She was listening to every word I said. I wanted to hear her speak.

'So how do you know my sister, Joanna?' I asked.

'We work together,' she said. 'I'm a social worker like Kim.'

'How long have you been in the UK?'

'Seven years.'

'And do you like it?'

'Yes. I work too hard but I enjoy it.'

She smiled and the two of us started talking. It was nothing out of the ordinary. We just chatted about our Christmases and the resolutions we were making for the New Year, music we liked and films we wanted to see. But as Danielle drifted away from the computer and we carried on talking, the words hardly seemed to matter. Joanna was beautiful, so beautiful, and easy to chat to: she laughed and made jokes, listened to what I said and asked me questions. It was unusual for me to find someone I could talk with so easily and two hours slid by in a blur.

'I have to go,' I said reluctantly when I realised that it was well past midnight.

'But why?' Joanna asked. 'Aren't you enjoying talking?'

I longed to tell her how much.

'I've got an early start tomorrow,' I said, not wanting to say that my father needed to put me to bed because it was late and he wanted to sleep.

'Okay,' Joanna replied. 'Shall we be Facebook friends so that we can talk some more?'

'Yes. Let's speak again soon.'

We said goodbye and excitement buzzed inside me as I shut down the computer and took Kojak outside for his final run of the night. Joanna was so friendly. She seemed interested in me and obviously wanted to talk more.

But then reality hit again. Just before Christmas I'd met a woman I'd liked very much and was pleased when she invited me to the theatre. Then she arrived with her boyfriend and I felt like a particularly pathetic kind of dog that was being given a treat. Why was I letting myself get excited again now?

It had been proven to me over and over again that I wasn't the kind of man women wanted to love and I'd been rejected too many times. If Joanna wanted friendship from me – just like every other woman I met – then I would have to content myself with that.

As I went inside and got into bed, I made a promise to forget what had happened. Joanna was a world away from me and it would stay that way. I was being foolish, wishing for something I'd been shown time and again was impossible for me to have.

Then an email arrived.

'Hi Martin,' Joanna wrote. 'I was waiting for a message from you but didn't get one so I thought I'd contact you instead. I enjoyed talking to you so let me know if you want to chat some more.'

What could I do? No man could resist such temptation.

45

Meeting Mickey?

'I have something to ask you,' Joanna says as I look at her face on the screen.

It is the middle of February and we've been in constant contact since we met. For the first week or so we sent polite emails, edging our way forwards together like swimmers dipping their toes into the sea before deciding to dive in. But we soon forgot our caution and started talking every evening over the Internet. Each night was as easy as the first and we once found ourselves chatting online as dawn broke before realising there was still more to say.

I've never known it could be like this with another person – so easy and simple – or that talking to a woman could feel as natural as it does with Joanna. I want to know everything about her and words tumble out of us as we tell each other about our lives and what has happened in them – from tiny, insignificant details like the songs we love to the most important events of my life as a ghost boy and the death of Joanna's father, whom she adored. It is as if there is nothing I can't say because Joanna listens in a way I've never known before: she is interested, funny and sensitive, positive, enquiring and a dreamer just like me. We talk about the tiny details of our days and our hopes for the future, we joke together and laugh, and talk more honestly about our innermost feelings than I've ever done before. There is no need to hide.

I feel I can trust her. Every time she smiles, my resolve to keep my feelings in perspective weakens a little more and reason is forgotten as I feel myself plunging ever more deeply into this new world. At thirty-three, Joanna is a year older than me. She is a social worker like my sister Kim and lives near her in Essex. But the link with Kim is just the last in a long line of almost meetings we've had over the years. Joanna and I realised that we attended the same regional sports event when we were schoolchildren and she even visited my care home when she was a student. We have come so close to meeting so many times it seems inevitable we finally did. If I believed in fate, I'd think we were destined to meet.

Joanna looks a little nervous now as she opens her mouth to speak and I smile to myself. Even after such a short time, I know her face well enough to know if she is tired or happy, annoyed or exasperated. I've spent hour after hour studying her as we talk and I've realised that her face is not a mask like some people's – instead every emotion can be found written on it if I look hard enough.

'I'm going to Disney World on holiday later this month,' she says, the words coming out in a rush. 'And I've been thinking about this all night so I'm just going to say it: will you come with me? I know it's soon but it just seems right somehow.'

I stare at the screen in disbelief. Happiness fills me with every syllable she speaks.

'I know you haven't flown long haul before but I'm sure we could find an airline that would take you,' she says. 'I've looked at tickets and there are seats available.

'I'm going for two weeks but you could stay as long as you want. I've contacted the hotel I'm booked into and the room I'll be staying in has two beds so we can share it. Please think about what I'm saying. Don't just say no.

'I want to meet you and I think you want to meet me too. Please don't let money be the issue or worry too much about work. I understand you might feel you can't just leave things but sometimes in life you have to, don't you think?'

My hand freezes above the keyboard. What almost surprises me most is that I'm not afraid or uncertain. I feel overwhelmed but I'm ecstatic, not fearful. She wants to meet me. I don't need to ask myself if I want to go. I want to meet Joanna more than I've ever wanted anything in my life. But as I wonder how I will tell her this, I realise that words will never be enough.

'I'd love to come,' I type. 'I really would.'

'Really?'

She smiles and waits for me to say something more but I can't. My mind is whirring as I look at her on the computer screen in front of me.

'I know you'll need some help and I don't mind doing

that,' she says. 'It's just that we have this chance to meet and I think we should grab it!'

She giggles. I love it when she laughs.

'Why do you want to meet me?' I say.

I have to ask. The question has been running around my head ever since she first asked me to take part in this crazy plan.

She is silent for a moment.

'Because you're the most honest man I've ever met,' she says. 'And because, although I've only known you for a few weeks, you've made me so happy. You make me laugh, you're interesting and you understand what I say in a way no one else ever has before.'

We are silent for a moment. I can see her on the webcam as she lifts her hand towards the screen and I know she is reaching out to touch me from 6,000 miles away.

'So you're definitely going to come?' she asks.

'I want to,' I say. 'I will do all that I can to meet you.'

I look at her face. I can hardly believe she is so sure of life that she believes it can be as simple as buying a plane ticket and meeting a stranger. She is so certain that we will both find love one day and tells me we can't hurry or control it, we must just let it unfold as it wants to. She doesn't feel defeated by love as I do at times and I can feel her optimism infecting me cell by cell, making me believe that anything is possible.

'Things happen at the right time,' Joanna tells me. 'There's a plan for each one of us.'

I raise my hand to cover hers on the screen in front of me. How I long to feel Joanna close to me; how my heart turns when I look at her face and realise she really means what she says. She wants to meet me. She wants to spend time getting to know me. I can't wait to know her. But first there is something I must talk to her about.

'I want to tell you about myself physically,' I write. 'I want you to understand exactly who I am.'

'Okay,' she says.

46

The Real Me

'I'm not going to sugar-coat it,' I write to her in an email. 'I'm going to tell you everything I need help with and if you change your mind after reading it, that's fine.

'I eat everything and can feed myself finger food but I need help with a knife and fork. I can't get in and out of the shower alone but I can wash and dry myself, although I might ask you to unscrew the shampoo lid.

'I also need to be shaved because I can't do it myself and I can pretty much dress myself if my clothes are laid out next to me. I can't do up buttons, zips or shoelaces though.

'I need help getting on and off the toilet and in and out of cars from my wheelchair. I can't sit up unsupported so I need to be leaned against something if I'm not in my chair.

'I can use my feet to move my wheelchair around on floorboards but not on carpeted floors and while I can move my chair by pushing off from surfaces with my arms, I'm not strong enough to push myself along a road or pavement if I'm in my manual chair.

'I think that's basically it. Oh, and I drink with a straw.'

I stare at the screen one last time. My heartbeat quickens as I hit the send button. I wonder if I'm mad to spell this out so bleakly in black and white. But I want to be completely honest with Joanna because I don't need a carer or someone who pities me. I don't want a dreamer whose fantasy will crumble when reality hits, someone who wants to rescue me or a woman who loves me in spite of my less than perfect body. If I want to be loved for who I am, then Joanna must know all of me. Even though I'm afraid of telling her this, I somehow feel sure she won't care. I can't explain exactly why. I just know she won't.

The next morning I receive a reply to my message.

'None of it matters,' Joanna writes. 'We can work it out as we go along.'

The feeling inside me is like the peace that comes when the final leaf falls from a tree in an autumn wood. Everything is quiet. I've lived my whole life as a burden. She makes me feel weightless.

47

A Lion's Heart

How did Joanna come to be so fearless? I've asked myself this again and again in the days since she left for America alone because I couldn't get a visa in time to meet her there. We were both bitterly disappointed but at least we know now that it is only a question of when, not if, we will meet.

For now, I'm learning to negotiate my way around the edges of the unexpected new shape my life is taking on. Until now my existence has been full of the straight corners and neat edges that come with order and routine. But suddenly it is full of unexpected curves and the kind of chaos that I'm learning another person can create. Joanna is uprooting everything I trained myself to expect and accept: I'd resigned myself to leading a serious life full of work and study, yet suddenly she makes me laugh until I cry; I believed I would never find a woman to love and now I'm beginning to hope that I have. I'm usually so careful and considered but Joanna is making me reckless. She doesn't see barriers but possibilities; she is utterly unafraid and I'm beginning to feel that way too.

She told me it was a childhood friend of hers who taught her to look beyond a person's body after he was paralysed from the neck down. He was only in his twenties and might have thought his life had no meaning after the night when the car he was travelling in was hit by a train. Instead, he determined to become a farmer like his father. Today he is married and runs a 1,000-acre farm.

'He might not be able to drink tea on his own but he can manage a farm because he can speak and that's all he needs,' Joanna told me. 'He's also far happier than most people I know.'

But I believe the roots of her fearlessness stretch further back to her childhood in the South African countryside when the freedom that is so much a part of the land there seeped into her. And if there is one person responsible for her courage, I think it is her father, At Van Wyk. He was also a farmer and from the moment his three daughters and son were old enough to look after themselves he let them loose on his land.

'You should always try things until you can't do them any more,' he used to tell his children, 'rather than say no and not try at all.'

So Joanna and her siblings learned to handle guns safely when they were still young and roamed free around the land their father farmed. When At had a heart attack at the age of thirty-six, one of the first things he did after coming out of hospital following a bypass operation was to throw a loop of rope over the highest tree branch he could find and hoist up a swing for his children. It hung far above a dry riverbed.

'How high can you go?' he called in delight as they soared through the air above him.

At knew he'd come close to death decades earlier than he should have but he wasn't going to be intimidated into being overly cautious about himself or his children. So when he took them to the coast to see the sea, he'd let them swim into the waves, always keeping an eye on them to make sure they were safe but letting them test the water and themselves. When they went into the bush to spot game, he'd let Joanna, her sisters and brother sit in the back of an open-top truck.

'I'll stop and pick them up when they fall out but not before then,' he told the mother of one of Joanna's friends when she objected to how the children were going to travel.

Joanna's most treasured memories are of the holidays she and her family took each year to a farm on the edge of the Kruger National Park that belonged to her father's best friend. For those precious weeks Joanna and her siblings would roam the bush, searching for lions, wildebeest, elephants and impala as they learned valuable lessons about the wildlife and themselves.

First, came the humility of understanding how little human wishes really matter: elephants treading their familiar paths to water will trample over people if their route is blocked, and a swarm of bees won't stand for a thieving finger that wants a taste of honey. However important we each think we are, we are but a footnote to the natural cycle.

Secondly, they learned to be aware every moment after discovering that lions become almost invisible when they lie down in long, arid bush grass to sleep each afternoon. The children had to be constantly vigilant, watching every step they made, to avoid inadvertently stumbling upon a sleeping pride.

And finally, they learned the art of bravery and how to apply it: faced with an angry elephant, they knew they had to run as fast as possible but if a lion charged at them, they must fool the cat into thinking they weren't prey worth having by staying rooted to the spot.

These were the lessons Joanna learned as a child and this fearlessness gave her a freedom of spirit that I'd never known existed until now. But bit by bit she is beginning to pass it on to me and I feel as if I am beginning to soar inside.

48

I Tell Her

Late last night I wrote to her: 'I can't stop thinking about you. I love you. I had to tell you.'

How do I know this? I can't say for sure but something other than logic and reason tells me it's true. I've known her for only a few weeks, yet I'm sure I will know her for a lifetime now.

'My love,' Joanna writes the next morning. 'Do you know how long I've wanted to start a letter with those words? But until now there has never been an opportunity for me to do it. How happy you make me. I love you so much it's almost painful.'

My heart turns over when I read those words.

'I know it's crazy because we haven't even met yet,' I write. 'But I'm more sure of you than I've been of anything before.'

'I understand,' she tells me. 'I have to keep reminding myself this is real because sometimes I can't quite believe I feel this way. How can I? I never knew I could have feelings like this and it makes me almost afraid. It's as if I don't have control over my emotions any more.'

'But however many times I ask myself if I'm mad, I know that I don't care,' I tell her. 'I love you. It's as simple as that.'

We talk urgently, words flying back and forth on emails, text messages and down Internet phone lines, as we try to make sense of what we are experiencing.

'But how can you be sure of how you feel when we haven't met?' Joanna asks.

'Because I can feel it physically, within every fibre,' I tell her. 'My heart contracts when I say the words to you. I know it doesn't make sense on so many levels but it's as though we're connected. I feel more accepted by you than anyone I've ever met before.'

'I feel almost mad,' she writes. 'It's as if I have to stop and pinch myself sometimes because I'm totally in love with a man I haven't even met and yet I feel as if I've known you for years.'

I understand why we must ask questions about a hurricane that has stormed into both of our lives without warning. It is disorienting when your world becomes a different place almost overnight. But love isn't about logic and our phantom doubts are easily dismissed. Over the years, I'd often heard people say that you know when you meet the right person and now I understand what they meant. The feeling is unlike anything I've ever known.

49

Sugar and Salt

I'm losing myself in Joanna as we dream together.

'I want to dance with you,' I tell her.

We paint pictures with words as we tell each other about all the things we'll do when we finally meet. We are online almost constantly now when we aren't at work. Our days have fallen into a rhythm that we share from opposite sides of the world because the time difference between South Africa and England is only a couple of hours. It means I can wake Joanna up in the morning with a text, chat to her before we go to work and email throughout the day before spending all evening online together. We don't turn our computers off even when one of us needs to eat or answer a telephone call. If Joanna calls me last thing at night, I speak to her using beeps on my phone for 'No' and 'Yes' so we can say a final few words to each other.

Our longing for each other is so strong that I recently decided to text her after waking up in the early hours of the morning, knowing that she would be on her way home from a night out with friends.

'You've just woken me up,' I joked and seconds later my phone beeped.

'You're not going to believe this,' Joanna messaged back. 'But I just dropped my keys as I was unlocking the door and thought I must have woken you up before realising that I couldn't possibly have.'

Another day my right hand started to hurt and I told Joanna I didn't understand why it was painful.

'I hurt my right hand today too!' she said as she laughed.

I can't explain these things but I don't need to question mysterious coincidences when I can concentrate on what is real. It is April 2008 and I've booked a flight to go to the UK at the beginning of June. It's just eight weeks until Joanna and I will be together and we can decide what will happen next for us. We already know that we love each other, which means we have no choice but to find a way to be together.

My parents are quietly agitated. Will the airline agree to let me fly so far alone? Who will feed me from the tiny plate of food that I will be given or hold me in my seat to make sure I don't hit my head when gravity thrusts me forward as we land because I don't have enough balance to resist it? But even as their questions buzz in the air around me, I remind myself of the promise I made to gain my independence. I am thirty-two years old. It's been almost seven years since I was first assessed and I've learned so much. It's time now. I don't have to be afraid any longer.

However sure Joanna and I are, though, we know we must learn to steer our relationship through the rocks of other people's misgivings if it is to survive. As the weeks have turned into months, it's become more and more clear that some suspect our feelings are a fiction we are writing together without the inconvenience of mundane reality to ruin our plot. They think the illusion won't be sustained by real life and I can understand their scepticism: we've never met, our lives are completely different and this doesn't make any sense. But there are also times when I wish that Joanna didn't have to experience the pain of other people's good intentions. Even though I'm well used to it, I'd do anything to protect her from its bite.

'What's happened?' I asked her one evening.

Her face was flatter than usual, the light drained out of it.

'I've had a terrible afternoon,' she said.

'Why?'

'I saw some friends and was so excited to talk to them about you. But they just didn't want to listen. All they kept asking was whether I realised how vulnerable you must be. They thought I was being cruel to make you believe we might have a future together.'

Her voice cracked with sadness.

'It was awful,' she told me. 'I couldn't say anything because I didn't trust myself to speak.'

'I'm so sorry.'

'It's not your fault. But I don't understand how my friends could even say such things to me. Don't they know me at all? It's as if I'm a child they don't trust.'

'I know the feeling well.'

Her face lightened for a moment before becoming sad again.

'It makes me wonder what other people will think when they meet us,' she says. 'It upsets me to realise that all they might see is your chair. It's so wrong. My friends didn't even mention the fact that we hadn't met yet. All they were worried about was what matters the least.'

'It often happens that way,' I wrote. 'People forget everything except the fact that I can't walk.'

'I know,' she said sadly. 'But it shouldn't be that way.'

As I watched Joanna talk, I was filled with the desire to reach out and touch her, physically reassure her that we will prove people wrong. I wished I had some way to show her how sure I am that we will. Love is another form of faith, after all. I know ours is real and I believe in it completely.

'People will have to learn to deal with us because this is how we feel and we can't change it,' I told her.

'But do you think they will?'

'Yes.'

She was silent for a moment.

'It just makes me feel sad to know that I won't be able to discuss you with my friends again. It feels as if I'll never be able to trust them with the most precious thing in my life.'

'Maybe in time you will. They might change their minds when they see that we're staying together whatever happens.'

She smiled at me.

'Maybe, my liefie,' she said softly.

That is my name now: my liefie, my love.

We face obstacles, for sure. Being on different continents and talking solely via the phone and Internet, instead of face to face, can easily give rise to misunderstandings so we've started to make rules. The first is that we must always be honest with each other; the next is that we'll solve problems together.

'You've got to eat a little salt,' South African mothers say to their children as they try to teach them that nothing is perfect when they come home crying about a playground injustice.

Joanna and I know this and the setbacks we are experiencing – whether it's other people's questions or the reluctance of the airline authorities to fly me to the UK – are bringing us closer together. To get booked on a flight to London, I've needed medical clearance and permissions, forms filled out and notes written by doctors. But Joanna has been as determined as I am that we won't be beaten. It felt like we'd taken on the world and won when she called me at work one morning.

'The airline has agreed to fly you,' I heard her say. 'You're coming to the UK.'

It was a huge victory for us but there are other smaller troubles that we are also learning to overcome together.

'I've realised that I'll never hear you say my name,' Joanna told me one night.

We'd never spoken about it before but I could hear the pain in her voice as she talked to me.

'It makes me feel so sad to know that I'll never hear the words "I love you",' she said. 'And although I have no idea why I'm thinking about this, for some reason I can't stop now. It's as if I've lost something even though I'm not sure what it is.'

I longed to comfort her but didn't know how to at first. I take my silence almost for granted after so many years and long ago stopped grieving for a voice that I don't even remember having but I understood that Joanna was mourning something precious. A few days later we were talking online as I started to hit the keys on my laptop to activate my communication system. I rarely use it to speak to Joanna because my hands are strong enough now for me to type while we talk and my laptop isn't compatible with our Internet phone line. But ever since she'd spoken about wanting to hear my voice, I'd been working on something for her.

'Listen,' I wrote. 'There is something that I want to say.'

She fell silent as I hit a final key on the laptop keyboard in front of me.

'Joanna,' a voice said.

It was Perfect Paul and he pronounced Joanna's name just as I'd taught him to after spending hours unravelling his vowel and consonant pronunciation. Instead of saying it in the English way – Jo-A-nA – Perfect Paul had pronounced it with an Afrikaans inflection, just as she is used to hearing – Jo-nAH.

'I love you,' Perfect Paul said.

Joanna smiled before laughing.

'Thank you.'

Recently I sent her an envelope containing a photocopy of my hands after she told me again and again how much she longed to touch them.

'Now I have you with me,' she said with a smile from a world away.

It's true there is salt as well as sweet in every life. I hope we'll always share both.

50

Falling

It's right to say that people fall in love. We don't glide, slip or stumble into it. Instead we tumble head first from the moment we decide to step off the edge of a cliff with someone and see whether we'll fly together. Love might be irrational but we make the choice to risk everything. I know I'm taking a gamble with Joanna because there will always be a fraction of doubt, however tiny, until we meet. The greatest lesson I'm learning with her, though, is that living life is about taking chances, even if they make you feel afraid.

It was about a week after we met that I made the choice to allow myself to fall in love with Joanna. She'd sent me an email and I was just about to reply when I suddenly stopped myself.

'Am I going to take another chance with my heart?' I thought. 'Am I going to gamble again?'

I knew the answer to my question as soon as I'd asked it because the prize at stake was the one I wanted most, after all.

I knew what I had to do. But I promised myself that if I was going to find a real love, one that could weather the inevitable storms a lifetime together would bring, I mustn't pretend to be what I wasn't. I wanted to be completely honest with Joanna about whatever we discussed – whether it was the abuse I'd suffered, my care needs or the longing I had to make love to a woman – because I couldn't let fear force me to hide myself.

Sometimes I felt brave when I told her things, at others my terror of rejection was the spectre that stalked me, but I forced myself to continue. Everything I've learned since the day I was wheeled into a room and asked to focus my eyes on a picture of a ball has made me able to now risk my heart. The lessons had been painful at times but being out in the world, making mistakes and progressing has taught me that life can't be experienced at arm's length like an academic project. It must be lived and for too long I've tried to keep it at bay by burying myself in work and study.

I understand now why it happened. For a long time I didn't know how to be in the world. I found it confusing, disorienting, and in many ways I was like a child. I believed back then that good and bad were black and white just as I'd seen on the television for so many years, and I spoke the truth exactly as I saw it. But I quickly learned that people don't always want to hear the truth. What might seem like the right thing isn't always necessarily so. It was hard, though, because most of what I had to learn was unseen and unspoken.

The most difficult thing to master was the complex web of manners and hierarchies my colleagues navigated. I knew that understanding these rules would help me in so many ways but

I was too scared even to try at first for fear of making a mistake. Instead of speaking up at meetings and using some of the words I'd spent hours inputting onto my computer just in case I needed them, I stayed silent. And rather than talk openly to colleagues I didn't know well, I was quiet. When one told me she was just 'babysitting' me, I stared at her blankly because I wasn't sure what to say.

But gradually I've learned to trust my own judgement – even if it is sometimes wrong – as I've realised that life is about shades of grey, instead of black and white. And the most important thing I've learned is how to take risks because I'd never taken them before I started to communicate. But I was forced to after I started working because I knew I'd never move up the career ladder if I didn't. So I put in hours of extra time, kept quiet when I was given tasks I didn't understand and crushed my disappointment when colleagues were praised for work I felt I'd contributed towards. On the other hand, I met so many people who helped and guided me, listened and bolstered me when I doubted myself.

It is impossible to underestimate how hard I found it at times to believe in myself. When I was sitting trying to solve a complex computer problem, ghosts from all the years of being treated as an imbecile would haunt me. It wasn't until I started work that I realised how deeply the need for familiarity and routine had been drilled into me by my years in institutions. All I wanted was to keep moving forward but I felt lost at times, mired in self-doubt, and I found it impossible to relax.

Perhaps this love of routine was why I found it hard to leave jobs behind once I had them – whether it was the health centre, where I got my first job doing filing and photocopying, or the communication centre, where I was given a chance to stretch myself. I felt safe in each place and it was difficult to relinquish that.

While moving to a full-time job at the scientific research institute where I work today was unnerving in many ways, it also forced me to get used to freedom because suddenly I was in an environment where my workload could change unpredictably or deadlines alter without warning. I found it overwhelming at first to be surrounded by people with qualifications, education and experience, when I'd taught myself to read and write at the age of twenty-eight and learned most of what I knew about computers sitting alone at my desk. I felt sure I couldn't keep up with my colleagues, let alone compete with them.

But gradually I realised that it doesn't matter how you reach a place, as long as you deserve to be there. As time has passed, my confidence has grown and I've realised that I'm trusted by my colleagues. It didn't matter that I was self-taught because living life is about checks and balances, small victories and minor failures. I'd spent years longing for things to happen to me, for events to take my life somewhere unexpected. Although I found it disorienting when it started to happen each day, week or month, I learned that this is what life is like – unpredictable, uncontrollable and exciting.

I was still removed from it in many ways because I'd never had the chance to know someone completely, to connect with them in the way that you can do only when you fall in love. Then I met Joanna and now I'm prepared to take the greatest chance with her. For the first time in my life, I don't care what others think or worry about keeping up appearances and creating a good impression. I don't care about letting someone down or not doing a good enough job. I've been trying to justify myself ever since I started to communicate through work and study, learning and achieving. But the one thing I will not justify is Joanna.

Recently I told her that I wanted her to see exactly what I looked like before I arrived in England. Sitting in front of the computer, I held a web camera in my right hand, which I guided back and forth. First I showed her my face, then my arms and the loose cotton T-shirt covering my chest before pulling the camera back so that she could see the chair I sit in each and every day. She'd seen it before, of course, but now I trained the camera on myself and showed her every detail so that nothing was hidden. Joanna laughed softly as I pointed the camera at the metal plates that supported my bare feet.

'Hobbit toes!' she said with a giggle.

But even as I searched her face on the screen in front of me for signs of fear or confusion, I knew I wouldn't find them. After a lifetime of such looks, I can recognise them in an instant but there was nothing on Joanna's face except a smile.

'You're beautiful,' she said softly.

It is her belief in me that tells me I'm right to risk everything for her.

51

Climbing

I stare at the sand dune above me. It shimmers in the heat.
'Are you ready?' my brother David asks.

I nod.

We're on holiday in Namibia. My mother was born here and we have come to see the country where she grew up after Kim arrived on a trip from the UK. I look at the dune and wonder how I'm ever going to get up it: it is more than a hundred metres high. Mum and Dad have gone off to explore and I've told David that I want to reach the top of the dune. Surprise flitted across his face before he got out of the car, unloaded my chair from the boot and helped me into it before pushing me through the sand. Now I look up at the dune rising above me. I want to get Joanna some sand from the top of it. This dune is one of the highest in the world and the desert is one of her favourite places.

'The silence is so complete that you don't realise you've never heard anything like it until you're there,' she told me.

'And the landscape is so huge that it changes with every hour of the day. Even the sand is softer than anything you've touched before.'

That's why I want to bottle some sand from the top of the dune for her and send it back to the UK with Kim as a reminder of me and the trips she once made to the desert with her family. Heat shimmers in waves as I look up at people running down the dune after reaching the top. They are laughing and shrieking as they hurtle down after the long climb.

'How are we going to do this?' my brother asks.

I'm not sure. David takes me under the right arm and helps me to stand up before I drop onto my knees in the sand. I can't crawl so my brother pulls me forward as I try to help by digging my other arm into the sand to propel myself too. Slowly we start to move up the dune as people walking back down to cool drinks and shade stare at us in surprise. It's almost midday, too late to be doing something like this. The sand is so warm and soft by now that it keeps collapsing and I must dig myself out before carrying on upwards. We should have come at dawn when the sand was cooler and firmer.

The sun beats down as David hauls me upwards. We both begin to sweat as we climb – he pulling, me digging my elbow into the sand and pushing against it to try and take some of the load of my dead weight from my brother. Higher and higher we climb, me wriggling in the sand and David pulling me upwards. The dune gets steeper the nearer to the top we get.

'Do you really want to get all the way up there?' David asks as we stop to rest.

He stares upwards and my eyes follow his. I have to get to the summit. Like a tribesman superstitiously dancing for rain,

I must convince the heavens to smile on me and prove to Joanna that there is no barrier I will not overcome for her — even my own body. This will be the final proof that she is a part of me now and I must show her that she will make me more than I ever thought I could be.

David sighs in exasperation as I smile at him and we start edging our way up again, metre by metre. There is sand in our hair, mouths and eyes, and the light bouncing off the dune is blinding.

'Don't stop!' a voice calls. 'You're so nearly there.'

I look down. Kim is walking up to join us. Far below, I can see our parents standing by the car and staring up at the three of us. They wave as I look down.

'Let's go,' David says.

We've been climbing for about forty-five minutes now and the people who started the journey with us have long since walked back down to earth. We must make one final effort to get to the top of the dune. It is so close now. I think of Joanna once more as I dig into the sand and push myself upwards. Bit by bit I scrabble towards the summit. The sky is azure blue above me and my mouth is dry. My heart beats with exertion and I can hear David panting as he gives my body one final heave. Suddenly we stop to rest.

We are at the top of the sand mountain and Kim sits down beside us. No one speaks as we struggle to get our breath back. Beneath us, the desert spreads out like an endless sea. Kim leans towards me. In her hand is a glass bottle. I watch as she opens it before handing it to me. I push it into the sand.

52

The Ticket

Is it anger or frustration that bites most bitterly at the back of my throat as I stare at the computer screen? It's ten days before I'm due to fly to the UK and I'm at work. I've just received an email from a travel agent I contacted to ask for a quote for flights to Canada. I'm attending a conference there in three months and have asked Joanna to accompany me to the event instead of my mother and father, who have always assisted me in the past. The travel agent is wondering whether I want to go to Canada with my mother or my girlfriend? Apparently Mum picked up the phone when he called to give me some information and told him she was going to book the flights. I know what she's thinking.

'Kim had a friend who met someone on the Internet and thought she was completely in love with him,' Mum said a few nights ago. 'But then she met the man and realised they had nothing in common. It happens a lot, so I hear.'

I'm unsure for a moment how to convince my mother I

know what I'm doing. It's like trying to tell someone who is colour blind that the sky is blue when they are sure it's green.

'Joanna and I know each other too well for that to happen,' I sign to her on my alphabet board. 'We are sure of how we feel. Everything will be fine when we meet.'

Mum sighs.

'I hope so for your sake, Martin,' she says. 'I really do.'

I understand her fear. Her child is spreading his wings two decades after he was supposed to. She has waited a long time for this moment and it frightens her now it has come. I've been suspended in almost childhood all my life: first as a ghost boy and then in recent years as my parents have been involved in every step of my progress. It's hard for them to think of me flying halfway across the world without them and I understand because I'm apprehensive too.

I've only been on one short domestic flight on my own; now I'll have to cross oceans alone to see Joanna and there are so many practical considerations to take into account. I know all my parents want is to keep me safe but I also know I can't spend the rest of my life easing myself away from their expectations and fears. At some point I will have to leap into the unknown without them.

'My love?'

A message from Joanna pops up on my screen. I texted her a few minutes ago to tell her that I needed to talk.

'Thank goodness you're here,' I type back. 'I have something to tell you.'

I explain to her what my mother has done and the worry I have about dissuading her from doing what she believes is for the best.

'But why is your mother involved at all?' Joanna writes when I've finished explaining.

'Because she found out that I was going to book the flights and says she is worried the prices will go up if I don't get the tickets soon,' I reply.

I don't need to say Mum is also worried Joanna and I will break up during my visit to the UK, which will leave me with a useless plane ticket.

'But can't you stop her?' Joanna types. 'Tell her that we're organising it together?'

'I'll try, but I'm not sure she'll listen.'

'She'll have to!'

My screen goes blank for a minute.

'I'm getting angry,' Joanna eventually writes. 'I don't understand why your mother is involved in this at all. Isn't it up to you? If you need help with anything, then I can do it.'

I wish I could explain it to her, make her see that it's not so simple. We have always understood each other until now but suddenly I wonder if this will be the first time we won't be able to.

'This all makes me so angry,' she types. 'Why can't you just tell her not to interfere?'

It's the closest we've ever come to an argument and I feel afraid. How can I explain myself to the girl who roamed the bush and swam in deep water? How do I make her understand when our experiences of life have been so very different?

'My parents are the ones who get me out of bed in the morning,' I write. 'And they are also the ones who help me to dress, feed me my breakfast and wash me, drive me to work and pick me up again.

'What would I do if I made them so angry that they didn't want to do all of those things? I know it wouldn't happen, of course, because they love me and would never do anything to hurt me.

'But knowing something doesn't always mean you aren't afraid of it and being in a wheelchair means that you need people in so many ways that those who aren't don't.'

My screen is blank for a moment. Then five words pop up on the screen from Joanna: 'I am sorry, my love.'

We agree to speak tonight but first I want to talk to my father, so I email him to ask if he will speak to my mother on my behalf. Nothing is said, though, until I sit down with my parents after supper.

'I need to talk to you both,' I say, using my alphabet board. 'It's important.'

My parents look at me. My heart pummels my chest. I have to be direct with them if I'm ever going to make them see how important this is to me.

'I'm going to go to Canada with Joanna,' I say. 'She is going to assist me on this trip because I want her to.'

My mother looks as if she might say something and I pray that she will be silent long enough to let me finish speaking.

'I know you don't think it's a good idea but it's time you started trusting me,' I tell them. 'I have to be able to make my own decisions and mistakes. You can't protect me forever and I'm more sure than I've been of anything before that Joanna and I will make this work.'

My mother is silent for a moment.

'We don't want to stop you from doing anything, Martin,' she says. 'All we want is your happiness.'

'I know,' I tell her. 'But if that's really what you want, then you must give me the chance to find out what my happiness is. Please let me have it. Please let me do this.'

My parents are silent for a moment before my mother gets up.

'I'm going to make more coffee,' she says quietly.

Neither my mother nor my father says anything else. There are so many things my parents leave unsaid. I can only hope that this time they will listen to me.

53

Coming Home

My heart felt as if it was going to stop beating a thousand times after the pilot announced we were flying over Paris. Now I almost wish it had, as a man pushes me through Heathrow airport. Joanna is just a few moments away on the other side of a wall somewhere in this vast building. I try to breathe smoothly but can't. Will the Technicolor world we've lived in for the past six months be dulled to shades of grey when we finally meet?

'Nearly there, sir,' I hear a voice say.

I wonder if this could be a dress rehearsal. Will a director shout 'Cut' so I can go back over my lines one final time? In fact, what are my lines? What am I going to say? My mind has gone blank.

The flight was like an assault course that I had to master stage by stage: get home from the office and pick up my bag; get to the airport and check in; get on the flight and fly for eleven hours without eating or drinking to make sure I didn't spill anything down myself and arrive looking untidy to meet Joanna. But just as I thought I'd got over all the hurdles, a stern-looking official came onto the plane after we had touched down.

'Where are you going?' he asked.

Joanna and I had talked again and again about what kind of questions I might be asked and I'd prepared a special communication board for the flight. But the answer to this question wasn't on it and the man looked annoyed as he waited for me to say something.

'Where is your connecting flight taking you?' he asked.

I stared at him.

'What is your final destination?'

He sighed in frustration at my silence before finally asking me a question I could answer.

'Is London your final stop?'

I nodded and he gestured to an older man.

'He's all yours,' he said, and I was pushed off the plane and interviewed by a poker-faced customs officer, who stamped my passport before I was taken to the baggage carousel.

Now I've travelled through miles of corridor to reach two white doors that are gliding open automatically in front of me. As I'm pushed through them, I see a long metal barrier with people standing on the other side of it. Some are holding up signs that they wave in my direction; others are gathered in small family groups with expectant faces. Dozens of eyes flick over me before people realise I'm not who they were hoping to see. Signs droop and faces look away as they prepare to carry on their wait. I look around, scanning faces and feeling nervous that there has been a mistake and Joanna won't be here to greet me. What would I do then?

'Martin?'

I turn my head. She's here. I can hardly breathe. She is more beautiful than I ever thought possible. She smiles at me as she leans down.

'My liefie,' she says in Afrikaans. 'My love.'

I feel awkward for a moment before our arms close around each other. Then, as I hold her for the first time, I realise that she smells of sweets and flowers. I know that I will never let go of her again.

I am home.

54

Together

I am drunk, intoxicated by everything that is happening to me for the first time: seeing her smile when she looks up at me sitting opposite her and losing myself in her kiss, watching her eyebrows knit together as she tries to decide what she wants to eat from a restaurant menu or sitting together underneath a hornbeam tree in the pouring rain.

'My liefie,' she says over and over, as if trying to convince herself that I'm really here. 'My love.'

We've come to Scotland after spending a few days at Joanna's flat, where we celebrated her birthday with Kim and some friends. But now we are all alone and we've hardly seen the rolling hills and sky that lowers and glimmers by turns outside our cottage. Instead we stay indoors, sitting or lying side by side, always connected by a hand within a hand, a shoulder against a shoulder or a leg carelessly thrown across a lap. After all these months of longing for each other, we can't bear to be apart even for a moment.

I've hardly used the alphabet board. Instead I draw letters on her skin with my finger, words traced on her flesh that she can read. In many ways they are almost useless. We've said enough after so many months of talking and often don't need words because Joanna understands so much just by looking at my face. An eyebrow or a glance is usually enough to answer many of her practical questions. Whatever fleeting thoughts I'd had before I arrived about whether we'd stutter politely as we wondered what to say or self-consciously try to entertain each other with jokes have come to nothing. From the moment we met at the airport, we have drunk each other in, comfortable in one other's presence.

I've never known a person who accepts me so completely and has so much peace inside them. Joanna doesn't fill the spaces between us with mindless chatter. Instead we drift on the current of simply being together and there are times when I jump almost in surprise as she touches me – my fingers flexing when she strokes my hand or my jaw twitching when she kisses my eyes. It's as if my body can't quite believe her gentleness. I've never had someone take pleasure in me before. It is the simplest but most perfect of feelings.

We are cartographers of each other's skin, following the lines of each other's cheeks, jaws and hands with our fingertips, imprinting the feel of each other onto ourselves for hour after hour. Her hands fit perfectly into mine and I stroke the scar she got when she caught her hand in the chicken coop as a child. I didn't realise that love would pierce all of my senses as it has: every part of me is attuned to her as I watch her smile, breathe in her smell, listen to her voice, taste her kisses and touch her skin.

The one thing we don't do is make love to each other. We agreed before I arrived that we would wait because we have the rest of our lives, after all. I haven't proposed but Joanna and I know we will marry. We discussed it even before I got here and know that I'm going to move to the UK in order for us to start a life together here. It amazes me how easily we can make such decisions; it's as if we are each an extension of the other. I revel in such simplicity after a life in which even the most inconsequential things can be complicated. Making love to each other will be the final piece of our jigsaw together. We will save it for our wedding night.

For now it feels as if Joanna is healing all that has been dammed inside me for so long as we learn more about each other day by day. I'm used to people trying to cajole me into doing things or wanting me to sit passively while they do everything for me. But Joanna accepts me as I am today and doesn't mourn what I once was. What surprises me most, though, is that she seems almost uninterested in my rehabilitation. She doesn't push me to do things or raise an eyelid if I can't. It doesn't matter to her that I only have my alphabet board here because it wasn't practical to bring my old laptop with me. She doesn't want to hear my 'voice'. Nor does she hover like a mother waiting to pick up a crawling child. Instead she helps me only as and when I need it. She trusts me to know my own body while accepting that there are some days when it can do less than it can on others.

'It's not you that's not working, it's your hands,' she told me one day when I got frustrated while struggling to pull on a jumper. 'Just give them a rest and try again tomorrow.'

Even the unwitting mistakes she sometimes makes don't panic or embarrass her as they would so many others.

'My liefie!' she cried as she came in one morning to find me sprawled across the bed.

She'd left me getting dressed but I'd lost my balance as I pulled on my jumper and toppled over like a fallen oak.

'Are you okay?' Joanna said with a giggle as she helped me up. 'I must make sure I prop you up better next time!'

She didn't apologise in embarrassed confusion or feel guilty that she'd done something wrong, and her simplicity made me feel at ease. Instead she just smiled before kissing me and leaving the room so I could finish dressing. If she does want to say something, then she does it matter-of-factly, as she did a few mornings ago when I bent down to drain my coffee cup as I always do.

'I don't understand why you always drink and eat so quickly,' Joanna said. 'It's like you're always in a rush.'

For a moment, I hardly knew what she meant. I've never eaten or drunk slowly. These have always been hurried activities, mere refuelling exercises to be got out of the way as soon as possible because people spend precious time helping me to do them. I've hardly even considered savouring food or drink. But that evening Joanna gave me my first-ever spoon of crème caramel and I made myself slow down long enough to taste it. First there was sweetness, then the dark richness of caramel as it flooded over my tongue, followed by the faintest hint of bitterness and finally the richness of cream with the scent of vanilla above it.

'You look so happy,' Joanna said.

She has told me that the pleasure I take in things is one of the greatest joys I give her. She says that she has never seen anyone revel in things as much as I do and it makes her happy to see that the world astounds me so often because there are almost as many new things as there are ways to experience joy.

But until now these have been mostly private thoughts and it is a pleasure to share my joy so completely with Joanna. She laughs when my eyes open wide at a crimson sunset or I smile in wonder as we drive around a bend in the road to see the beauty of an emerald green landscape stretching out ahead of us.

Her acceptance of me is the reason I've started trying to do more since I got here. She makes me want to start trusting a body that I lost confidence in so long ago. A couple of mornings ago, after a week of watching Joanna in the kitchen, I decided it was my turn to try. I'd never made so much as a cup of coffee on my own before because my shaking hands are a liability that few people will trust in a kitchen. But Joanna had cooked for me all week and didn't say a word when I told her it was my turn to make breakfast.

After fastening a foam grip on my right hand to help me pick up small objects like knives and spoons, she loosened the tops of the coffee and jam jars that she knew I would never be able to open on my own before turning to leave.

'I'm going to read my book,' she said.

I stared at the kettle in front of me. I wouldn't dare to try to pour boiling water but I could flick the switch to heat it. I turned the kettle on before looking at the jar of coffee on the counter in front of me. It was almost at eye level and I fixed it in my sights as I stretched my hand out and leaned as far forward in my chair as I possibly could. My fingers closed around the jar as I pulled it towards me and knocked off the lid. Then I picked up a spoon, my very particular kind of nemesis – a tiny object that my unfeeling hands won't close around properly.

The spoon clattered in my shaking hand as I pushed it inside the jar and dug into the coffee. Grains flew off the trembling spoon as I tried pulling it out and the last remaining few scattered across the counter when I finally did. Frustration burned. I wished I could command my unruly hands to submit to my will just once. Once, twice, three times I tried to get a spoonful of coffee into two cups before moving on to the sugar. By the time I knew I was beaten, one cup contained enough coffee to make syrupy tar and the other a watery imitation. It was a start.

Next came the toast. Joanna had left some slices of bread in the toaster and I pushed the switch down before pulling myself along the worktop to reach the butter and jam. I put them on my lap before pushing myself off from the counter towards the table, where I left them. Then I pushed off across the kitchen once again to get to the cupboard where the plates were kept. Bending down, I opened it and took out what I needed before going back to the table and laying it.

Finally I needed knives. Whoever said that breakfast is the simplest meal of the day? It didn't seem like it to me. There were so many different things to get right. The toast had popped up and was getting cold, and the water in the kettle had boiled. I needed to hurry if I wanted Joanna to have something warm.

I got two knives out of a drawer, dropped the toast into my lap and pushed off for a final time towards the table. Although

I wasn't going to fill up the coffee cups, I was determined to try spreading the toast at least. I put it and one of the knives on the table before picking up the other and trying to steady it as it waved about wildly in the air. Pushing the blade towards the butter, I watched as it crashed through the top and out again. I stared at the huge crevasse I'd carved in what had been a perfect rectangular pat of yellow before jerking the knife down towards the toast. A yellow slick of butter appeared halfway across it.

Now for the jam – my final Everest. I pulled the jar towards me and thrust my knife into it. It clattered inside the jar before skidding off in the opposite direction to the toast when I pulled it out. I forced the knife downwards, cleaving it to my will as it hit the side of the toast before skittering across the plate and leaving a glistening red slick on the table. I stared at the battered toast before looking at the floor, which was covered in coffee granules and sugar. The butter looked as if a wild animal had chewed it and jam had erupted like a volcano across the table.

Euphoria filled me. I'd made toast, coffee was waiting in the cups and the water had boiled – Joanna was going to have breakfast. I banged a spoon on the table to let her know I was ready and a smile spread across her face as she walked in.

'How nice to have breakfast made for me!' she said.

As she sat down, I vowed that I would learn to do more for her, teach my body to listen to my commands more closely so that I could look after her better in the future.

'My liefie,' Joanna said as she studied the table before looking at me. 'You don't have to use a knife, you know.'

I raised my eyebrows in disbelief.

'Why not just use your hand next time?' she said. 'It would be far easier for you that way. It doesn't matter how you do something, does it, as long as you find a way?'

Without another word, we ate our toast together. Later I raised my hand to stroke her cheek. At last I understood what love was. I knew I'd never feel about another woman the way I did about Joanna. She was everything I would ever need.

55

I Can't Choose

'Martin?'

I hold on to the box I'm carrying like a shield I'm trusting to protect me from attack.

'Martin? Are you okay?'

I can't look at her. I'm frozen. Lights glare above me and music pumps out from stereo speakers. Teenagers shriek as they walk around my chair and a wall of trainers rises up in front of me. I'm supposed to pick one from pair after pair stacked one above the other but I can't do it. I don't know how.

'Do you want white or a colour?'

'Nike or Adidas?'

'Classics, hi-tops or skate shoes?'

'Below £50 or above £100?'

At first, I enjoyed the fact that shop assistants spoke to me here in England. But now all I can think about is the pair of brown leather shoes in the box on my lap that Joanna has just bought for me. She has already spent so much money; I don't deserve more.

'Would you like to try something on?' the assistant asks. 'Or shall I measure your feet?'

I stare at my black, sturdy shoes. I've had them for about eight years and they are built up at the ankles to support my feet. I'd never thought about owning another pair. These are my shoes. I wear them every day. When I'm not wearing them, I have slippers. But when Joanna suggested that I might want something new, I agreed because I didn't know what else to say. But what will I do with three pairs of shoes?

I know that I must make a decision and show that I know my own mind. If not, Joanna will see the truth that I've been trying to hide from her for so long. It's a secret I've kept for all the months that we've known each other. I've hidden it so well that I've prevented it from being brought out into the open. But now there is nothing else I can do to conceal it: I'm not worthy of her. How will I ever be a good husband if I can't even pick a pair of shoes? I'm lost in Joanna's world, where there are constant decisions to be made – what to eat, where to go and when to do things. As soon as one decision is made, it feels as if another is snapping at its heels and I feel overwhelmed by choices I'm not used to making.

'What cereal would you like?' Joanna asked me on our first trip to the supermarket.

I gazed at the tapestry of primary-coloured cardboard boxes on the shelves in front of me and realised I had no idea how to start making a decision. How did people ever get anything done with their days when just choosing what to eat at the start of them could take hours? It was the same with everything in the supermarket: there wasn't one kind of soup but thirty, not one loaf of bread but a hundred.

Seeing that I couldn't decide, Joanna asked me to tell her what I wanted to eat but I couldn't even do that. I forgot long ago what it was to be hungry or to yearn for a particular food after teaching myself to ignore the sensation of a gnawing stomach or a craving I knew I could never satisfy. Now I can occasionally decide on something I want to eat but I can't choose enough to fill a whole shopping trolley the way other people do.

I stare up at the trainers again. I've been waiting for this moment to come. I knew I would be forced to make a decision for myself sometime, but Joanna refused to listen. Instead she tried to reassure me that I could cope in her world so I've tried to make her see the error of her ways by asking her again and again exactly why she loves me.

'Because you are a good, kind man who is unlike anyone I've ever known,' she says. 'Because you're intelligent and thoughtful, warm and wise. Because you love so completely and have taught me to slow down and take notice of a world that I've spent so long rushing past.

'There are so many reasons, Martin: your smile, the way you look at me. I can't tell you them all.'

Her reassurances mean little now though. I can't even decide what shoes I want. She's going to realise that deep down I still don't understand adult life. My fear of the world feels like a boulder that weighs heavy inside me, a shadow that is threatening to blot out all of her light. I'm not what she thinks I am. I'm a fraud.

'What a beautiful man,' she said a few days ago when she was shaving me.

As Joanna smiled at me in the mirror, I couldn't smile back. In fact, I felt almost frozen because I'd never heard a woman call me a man before. I'd longed to hear those words from a woman for so long but I also felt afraid when I did because it had taken me years to accept that I was an adult. When Joanna looked at me in the mirror, I couldn't bring myself to stare back at my own reflection because I couldn't believe what she was saying.

'Look at yourself, Martin,' she told me gently. 'Please just look at yourself.'

She wouldn't have told me I was a man if she knew the truth: that when we met Kim and Joanna's friends to celebrate her birthday, I felt overwhelmed being among so many people I didn't know; that when I look at restaurant menus, I don't know what many of the foods are, let alone if I want to eat them; that apologies for something I'm sure I've done wrong bubble up inside me almost every minute.

It's not that I don't want to be what Joanna thinks I am. All I want is to protect her and keep her safe. But as she looks at me now, I realise it doesn't matter what I want; I'm not the kind of man Joanna needs. She will never be able to depend on me. I'm so overwhelmed by the world now that I'm trying to step out of the tiny strip of it I've come to know and understand.

'Martin, my love,' Joanna says. 'Are you okay?'

My heart thuds in panic as I raise my head. Her face

shimmers in front of me as my eyes fill with tears. There is nothing I can do to stop them as they start to fall. Sitting in the middle of the shop, I begin to weep as I feel her arms close around me.

56

Fred and Ginger

There are so many moments with her that I will never forget and this is one of them. It is about 11 p.m. and we are in Trafalgar Square in central London. After spending the day visiting sights and going to the theatre, we are now in the middle of this vast square. Above us, Nelson stands on his column keeping watch over London. He is guarded by four huge lions and there is a fountain illuminated by lights. It is dark at last. The light doesn't fade in England until late in the evening but now the sky above us is black. Soon we must leave but first there is something we must do.

My head is full of pictures from the last two weeks, snapshots that I will take back with me when I leave: lifting Joanna in my arms for the first time when we went swimming and the water supported me enough to hold her; entering York Minster and feeling overwhelmed by the beauty of the cathedral – the stone and light, peace and tranquillity – as I felt her hand in mine; sitting in a rose garden together and eating lunch in the sun; inhaling the smell of fresh coffee as she sat opposite me and I realised with wonder that we were together at last. There were so many memories to keep safe: falling asleep beside her even as characters roared on the cinema screen in front of us, smiling at her face as she tried to swallow bitter Scottish whisky and watching her smile at me as we sat together in Sherwood Forest.

Now we are silent as we look at each other. There were so many things that we dreamed of doing before we met and this is one of them. I take her hand as I push against the concrete with my feet. I move gently forwards in my chair as I guide Joanna around me in a circle. I look at her and know she can hear the music that I hear too. It is a happy tune – not too fast, not too slow. She laughs as she spins around and her hair is lifted a little by the breeze. Joy rushes through me. We are dancing.

Joanna (Joan) and Martin – June 2008

57

Leaving

If I ever felt that Joanna was a dream, then this is the moment I know for sure she's real. Pain pierces me as I watch her cry. I'm leaving the UK today and it will be two months before we meet again in Canada. As I look at her, I tell myself that we must look forward to the end of the year, when she will fly to South Africa for Christmas before we return to England to start a life together. That is what we've decided we're going to do but for now we won't tell anyone until we've made our final plans. It all feels so far away though, as I kiss Joanna's cheek. She's quiet as she sits up and wipes away her tears.

'What will I do without you, my liefie?' she asks as she leans forward to kiss me.

I look at her and know she understands all that I want to say. She pulls away and stands up with a sigh.

'I'll put the bags in the car,' she says. 'We'll need to leave soon.'

Her fingers trail slowly out of my hand, as if she wants to

stay connected to me for as long as she can. But we both know that we must give in to the inevitable as she leaves the room. My heart feels like a stone in my chest as I look at the open doorway but I must be strong for Joanna after all the reassurance she has given me.

'I understand things won't always be this way,' she told me after I explained my fears that she'd unwisely chosen a man so disoriented by her world. 'This was just the first visit and you were bound to feel overwhelmed. I know it won't last forever because you'll get used to life here.

'I know what a strong, capable man you are, Martin. Look at all you've achieved. Please don't let this trip make you doubt yourself.'

As she smiled at me, I knew I would never tire of sitting at a table and talking with her. It's one of the greatest pleasures we share and we are often the last to leave restaurants.

'Good on you, son,' an old man said to me one day as he walked past our table and saw Joanna and I talking.

We both looked at him, unsure what he meant.

'For learning your alphabet!' he said, as he pointed to my board.

But our laughter seems so far away now as I turn my head to look around the empty room. I can already feel the pain of missing Joanna. I try to push it down. I mustn't give in to it. I have to be strong for her. But the pain keeps rising higher. Everything has changed in just two weeks. I've got used to seeing her first thing in the morning and last thing at night, and feeling her touch again and again during the day. Now I must go back to my old life. But how can I when I'd waited so long to find her?

My chest tightens and the pain sharpens. I gulp in air as I hear a muffled half noise, a rasping gasp of pain. It comes from nowhere. I look around. The room is empty. I made the noise. It is the first sound I've ever heard myself make. It is the low yelp of a wounded animal.

58

A Fork in the Road

This conversation has been hanging in the air like a bird waiting to swoop ever since I got home.

'You disappeared,' my father says as he sits down opposite me. 'You should have let us know where you were and what you were doing. Your mother was frantic when we didn't hear from you.'

I don't think his heart is really in this conversation but I've been expecting it ever since Kim took me to one side just before I left the UK.

'Mum and Dad have been really worried,' she said. 'And Dad was very upset that you didn't get in touch on Father's Day.'

I wasn't sure this was completely true. Both my parents are used to knowing everything I do, when and how, but I think my mother would have struggled most when I forgot my family for the first time. My head is so full of the future, though, that I can hardly think about the present as my father chastises me.

Joanna and I have only the Internet and the phone once again and I wonder how we ever survived for the first six months of knowing each other. It is far harder to be apart from her now than it was before we met.

But instead of driving myself mad by counting down every hour of each day until I get on the plane to Canada, I'm trying to keep myself busy with other things. My biggest distraction at the moment is a ring I'm having made for Joanna. It's a copy of one she bought cheaply but loves and I've asked a jeweller to make it using real gold overlaid with a pattern of intertwined leaves encrusted with tiny emeralds. I'm going to give it to Joanna on the day that I ask her to be my wife.

'Martin?'

My father looks at me.

'Are you listening?'

Sometimes I'm glad that I don't have to say anything.

'Well, then do you agree that you have a responsibility to let people know how you are?' he asks me. 'I know you were busy with more important things when you were away but you should have kept in touch.'

I nod.

My father's face relaxes a little as he stands up to leave. For the moment he is reassured. His world is back in place because I'm home again. As he walks out of the room, I realise for the first time how hard it will be for my parents when I tell them that I'm moving to the UK to be with Joanna. I'm not just leaving home, I'm moving across the world. While teenagers might fight thoughtlessly against their parents when they are trying to break free, it is impossible for me not to know that altering the course of my life will change my parents' lives forever too.

59

Confessions

I didn't realise that dreams are in constant motion until I looked back at mine and saw how much they'd changed. I made this discovery when Joanna and I were in Canada. At the conference we attended Diane Bryen's dream workshop, as I'd done several times since that first one at the communication centre.

'What would you like me to draw?' Joanna asked as we sat together.

I remembered all the times I'd asked myself what I dared to dream since meeting Diane. All I wanted when I first asked myself the question was to be able to communicate more and go out into the world. Once I'd achieved that and started working, I dreamed of living a more independent life and finding someone to share it with. Now I've met Joanna and her dream is mine too – a wedding and a house together.

These things are almost within our reach now because ever

since I returned from the UK, I've been applying for a visa to move to England. My parents know I'm going through the process, just as my brother David is, but we haven't spoken about it in any detail because I've been reluctant to discuss my plans until they are fully in place. But I knew as I sat in the dream workshop that I had to start trying to tell people what I wanted from my life, so I told them that Joanna and I were planning to marry.

Word soon spread because I'm well known in the AAC community to academics and experts, fellow users and their families. Although I'd feared some people might resent me for leaving my life in South Africa and all the work I've done here, my friends and colleagues were more positive than I'd dared hope. All of them celebrated with us and I've been counting down the weeks until I leave for England ever since.

Leaving my parents will be hard, of course, and knowing that I must soon part from Kojak is almost impossible – we've been constant companions. Although Joanna has looked into the possibility of taking him to England, we both know it wouldn't work because he wouldn't be able to bear spending six months in quarantine. I'm sure that Mum and Dad will agree to keep him because they're almost fond of him now, but even so I dread the moment when it comes to saying goodbye.

I've put off telling my parents about our plans because I want them to be concrete first. Now they are. In just a few weeks, Joanna arrives in South Africa for Christmas, after which I will fly back to the UK with her. That's why I can't put off the inevitable any longer and tonight I want to tell my parents that I'm planning to propose to Joanna while she's here.

'I'd like to speak to you,' I tell them as the three of us sit working at our desks in the study.

As they look at me, I think of all the hours we've spent together in this room. First we researched communication devices and then tested them out. Next the study was filled with cardboard boxes full of equipment and I watched as my parents patiently loaded software onto my computer. I remember the wonder I felt as I realised that soon I would have so many words to say, all the months my mother sat with me for hour after hour, week after week, helping me to learn to communicate and the excitement that energised Mum and Dad on the day they watched me slowly clicking on enough symbols to say a sentence for the first time.

They were equally proud when I was offered a job at the health centre and when they found out that I'd been accepted on a university course. They've been with me for every step of my journey into the wider world: accompanying me to conferences and meetings; filling out forms and helping me to travel; sitting through lectures and standing by my side as I've been introduced to people; encouraging and cajoling me when I'm down and celebrating my successes. They've also looked after every one of my daily practical needs whether we were at home or away. Instead of slipping into comfort-able middle age, they've devoted themselves to looking after me and all I can hope now is that they understand why I'm leaving.

Since returning from my trip to England, I've seen their ini-tial worries about Joanna slowly fade. They understand now that our relationship is real and they're pleased that I have someone in my life to care about. My mother has told me that she's never seen me so happy. My parents ask about Joanna, chat with her over the Internet sometimes and are looking forward to having her here with us for Christmas. Now I hope they'll be happy to welcome her into our family permanently and understand why I must leave them to make a new life.

'What is it?' Mum asks as she and Dad sit down beside me. 'Has something happened?'

I've prepared something to say and they watch as I press a button and bring up the message on the screen.

'There's something I want to tell you and I hope you will be happy,' they read.

Neither of them says a word as they read what I want to tell them.

'As you know, Joanna and I are very much in love but there is something else you need to know.

'When she arrives here in December, I'm going to ask Joanna to marry me and after Christmas we are planning to go back to the UK together.

'We have been talking about it for months and I know this is the right thing for me to do. I hope you will be happy for me.'

I put my hand into my pocket and pull out the ring I've had made for Joanna. My parents stare at it and neither of them speaks for a moment.

'It's beautiful,' Mum says eventually. 'Oh, Martin! It's beautiful.'

She starts to laugh and my father does too. Relief floods over me.

'Congratulations, boy!' Dad says as he puts his arm around me. 'It's wonderful news.'

He leans towards me.

'We're so proud of you,' he says.

My parents are happy. They understand the time has come to let me go.

60

Up, Up and Away

It's dark outside as I wait for Joanna to get dressed but it
will soon be sunrise. I've told her we are doing something
special but she doesn't know what it is. All I've said is that she
must wear light cotton clothes because it'll soon be hot. It's
December and the days can be scorching. Joanna has just
arrived for Christmas and we're spending a couple of nights
together at a farm in the bush. It's been four months since we
last saw each other and I know she's as thankful as I am that
we'll never have to say goodbye again. On Boxing Day – six
days short of a year since we were first introduced – we'll fly
back to the UK to start our new life.

The ring I've had made for Joanna is hidden in my pocket,
secured to my waistband by cotton thread so that it will be safe
even if my shaking hands drop it when I ask her to marry me.
I can hardly believe I'm sitting here about to propose to her.
Is it possible? Could my life really have changed so much or
is this a dream like the ones I used to lose myself in for weeks

at a time when I was a ghost boy? I dare not pinch myself because I might wake up and I never want that to happen.

Joanna arrived three days ago and, after meeting my parents, she took me to see her mother on the farm where she lives. I'd been writing to Joanna's mother for several months, knowing that I would one day ask her for her daughter's hand and now I handed her a final letter.

'I would like to ask Joanna to marry me,' it said. 'But first I would like to ask you for your blessing.'

For the longest moment, her mother said nothing before she smiled at me. She is a generous woman who can recognise love when she sees it – even if it comes in a form that some people can't appreciate.

I look up and smile as Joanna walks into the room.

'I'm ready,' she says as she walks towards me.

She is silhouetted against a white wall in the half-light. My heart skips a beat. She is so beautiful.

We go outside into the cool morning air and get into the car we've hired. I tell Joanna which way to go, but as we drive further into the bush, she doesn't ask where we are going any more. Does she know what I'm planning or does she think this is just another of the everyday surprises that I often give her?

As we drive up a dusty dirt road towards a clearing in the savannah, I see the carcass of a hot air balloon lying on the ground ahead of us. Joanna has always wanted to see the earth from the sky and she laughs as she realises what is waiting for her.

'I can't believe you've done this!' she says as she turns and kisses me.

The two of us get out of the car. The balloonist in charge

of our trip is waiting in the grey morning light and soon the orange fires of the balloon's burner start to illuminate the darkness as slivers of light appear on the horizon. The sun is rising and soon we'll see it from the clouds. Joanna and I watch as the balloon slowly ascends from where it has been lying before getting into the basket when it's ready. I sit on a high stool so that I'm level with Joanna and hold on to the edge of the basket as she climbs in after me.

The balloon pilot smiles to let us know that we are about to take off and the basket lifts silently off the ground. I watch Joanna's face as we begin to float upwards. She is smiling as she stares at the bush disappearing below us. We rise up higher and I look out at the horizon. It's getting lighter now. The sky is pink and the muted colours of the bush below us are slowly being illuminated green and brown. The earth rushes away as I listen to the silence. It's so quiet up here that all we can hear is the rush of the balloon's burner and the occasional birdcall.

Joanna and I put our arms around each other as the sun rises higher in the sky – bright white behind grey clouds, then pink lightening the darkness with flashes of orange. The horizon that was black in front of us is gradually turning golden in the sun and we can see the earth beneath us: a river, trees and a waterfall falling into a valley; zebra galloping, wildebeest and warthog drinking at a waterhole, giraffe feeding from tree branches.

'It's so beautiful,' Joanna tells me.

It's time now. I put my hand into my pocket and pull out my mobile phone. I've recorded a message on it, words that I want Joanna to hear. She looks at me as I hand her some tiny earphones and she puts them into her ears before I press a button.

'There are no words in any language that will ever truly capture what I feel for you,' I tell her. 'You came into my life and gave meaning to it. You flooded my otherwise grey world with vivid colour and I feel like I've known you forever.

'It's like time stops when we are together. You give my heart not just a reason to beat but to sing and rejoice.'

She smiles as she looks at me and I squeeze her hand.

'With every passing day my love for you gets stronger and deeper, richer and more profound because you are beautiful inside and out,' I say. 'And while life is not all milk and roses – and sometimes we eat a little salt too – what I do know is that I don't work without you and I don't want to spend a moment of my life without you.

'You are my soulmate, my best friend, my companion, my lover, my rock and strength, my soft place to fall in this crazy world.

'And that is why I want to hold you, cherish you, take care of you, protect you and love you with everything I have.

'So will you do me the honour, the enormous privilege, of sharing the rest of my life with me and becoming my wife?'

I push my hand into my pocket and pull out the ring. There are tears in Joanna's eyes as I hold it up to her – a pool of gold hanging by a thread that glints in the early morning light. She bends towards me.

'Yes, my liefie,' she says. 'I will be proud to be your wife.'

She kisses me for the longest moment before pulling away. I wrap my arms around her as we look out to the horizon. It stretches out endlessly in front of us.

Newly engaged couple

61

Saying Goodbye

The cardboard box sits on the other side of the room but I'm not sure I want to see what's inside it. The box is full of the Lego that I have been told I loved so much as a child. But do I have the strength to invoke the phantom of the ghost boy again and see his withered limbs and empty eyes rise up in front of me? I've seen him so many times over recent days, I'm not sure I can confront him again.

Joanna and I are packing up as I prepare to leave for England. As well as everyday belongings, we've been sorting through the boxes my parents have kept over the years and I've learned that much of what happened to me has been captured in dispiriting mementoes of my past: old X-rays and medical records packed side by side with the hand splints that once kept my fingers from curling into claws; an old cushion for my wheelchair stacked on top of the bibs that once caught my drool. While for me each object makes a memory resurface, it's vividly brought my story to life for Joanna for the first time.

She's only known me since I've grown so much stronger but now she can see all that I once was and the extent of my parents' vain hopes captured forever in spoons with oversized handles that they once thought I would learn to grip again.

At times I've felt shocked by what I've seen because as I rushed forward into life I'd almost forgotten how sick I was. Although I've sensed how hard it's been for Joanna, I also know there is no one else on earth I could have done this with. I would have felt ashamed for anyone else to see this and uncomfortable to have had so many bad memories dragged up again in front of them. But with Joanna here, the only feeling that's filled me as I've watched the ghost boy come back to life is sadness that his existence was so wretched.

Yesterday my mother told me there was another stash of boxes in the garage but both she and my father seemed reluctant to get them for me. I realised why when Joanna and I found them. While Kim and David's boxes were stuffed with the belongings of a teenager's life – music tapes and study files, old posters and clothes – mine, piled in a corner of the garage, yellowed with age and covered with dust, contained only a child's toys. It was as if a boy had died and his life had been hurriedly packed away – then I remembered he had.

'Look at this!' Joanna said, after dragging some of the boxes inside and opening one.

In her hand was a multicoloured cuddly toy.

'His name was Popple,' my mother said quietly.

I looked up to see her standing in the doorway, as if afraid to step into the room and see the rest of what we were unpacking.

'He was Martin's favourite,' she said.

I looked at the toy, trying to remember a time when an orange cuddly dog with lime-green hair, red ears, a purple nose and blue paws was my favourite thing in the world. I wanted to remember so much. I long to have the kind of memories other people do and know what it feels like to be a child who loves a toy so much that he can't let it go. But however hard I've searched, I've never been able to find even a glimmer of a memory inside me. There is nothing there – not even a shred of an image that I can cling on to.

But it was comforting for me to see a link to a past I'd sometimes wondered existed at all, even though I knew that it was a painful reminder of all they'd lost for my parents. As Mum stood by me while Joanna unpacked more boxes – a wooden horse GD had made for me, the telegram announcing my birth and schoolbooks – I could feel her distress. Mum said nothing when Joanna found a single piece of ruled notepaper in the bottom of one box. On it was written a letter I'd sent to Father Christmas when I was eight years old, the words almost painfully neat on the page. I read it slowly, trying to hear myself in the words I'd written so long before.

Dear Father Christmas,
Thank you for our presents last year. They were just the presents I wanted. Here are some of the things I would like for this Christmas: a speedometer, a skateboard, Meccano, space Lego, water bottle for my bike, a solar cell, a radio-controlled car.
    Father Christmas, I'll ask my father to leave the Christmas tree lights on. Father Christmas, in my list I

mention Meccano. If you decide to give me Meccano could you give me electronic Meccano?

Your loyal present receiver,
Martin Pistorius

PS I will leave a glass with some things to drink in it if I can and some things to eat. I will ask my father if we can leave the Christmas tree lights on. We will leave our stockings where the tree is.
PPS Also a walkie-talkie set.

I felt both sadness and joy when I looked at that letter – sadness that I couldn't remember being that happy little boy and joy that I was once him. Then I looked at my mother and saw that her face had frozen as she'd listened to his words. None of us spoke as Joanna put the note carefully back into the box and closed the lid.

'Shall we stop for today?' she said.

Now we are back in the room with the boxes once again and I'm looking at the one that contains my Lego. When Joanna opens it, I see a mass of pieces: some tiny, some large, some broken and others covered in dirt. There are so many of them that the box is almost full to the brim and I know there are at least another two like this.

'It was always your favourite,' Mum says. 'You so loved playing with it. You would spend hours in here building it. That Lego was your favourite thing in the world. You were such a bright little boy.'

Her voice is full of sadness. Tears are barely contained within it.

'I should never have let David have it,' she says. 'He asked me again and again and I always said no until one day I finally agreed. He was never as careful as you with his toys.'

As she stares at the box, I know she is seeing a happy, healthy little boy who once smiled in delight as he pieced together brightly coloured plastic blocks.

'I gave it to your brother because I thought you weren't going to want it again,' Mum says quietly. 'I didn't think you would ever come back to me.'

As my mother looks at me and admits that she stopped believing in hope, I know the wounds of the past are in some ways still as fresh for her today as they ever were. While the child who loved Lego is just a stranger to me, he is all too real for my parents. He is the child they loved and lost.

62

Letting Go

I'm sitting on a bed at the farm where Joanna's mother lives. In a few days we will return to England. Joanna has just packed up the last of my Lego after washing it. Although I'll be taking it to the UK with me, I don't feel content that my past has been neatly sorted through and repacked. Instead I've felt a sadness lying in the pit of my stomach ever since I left my parents' house, and it's getting heavier and heavier as the days pass.

I keep remembering my mother's face as she looked at my Lego. She seemed so lost, so wounded, and I'm sure my father is suffering as well even though he hides his feelings better. I can't stop thinking about them, about me and the happy child I found hidden in those boxes. I'd never truly understood what he was like until I opened them up and found a boy who loved electronics and Meccano, who wrote politely to Father Christmas and adored his parents. I can't stop thinking of him now.

My tears come slowly at first, running silently down my cheeks as Joanna looks up.

'Martin?' she exclaims.

She gets up from the floor and puts her arms around me. My breath comes in heavy gasps and my shoulders heave as I think about all that my parents, brother, sister and I have lost. Guilt fills me as I think about the pain I've caused and wish I could take it back. If only I could give my family the simple, happy life they deserved. Then confusion swells up as I wonder why my parents took so long to rescue me. Why didn't they see that I'd come back to them and protect me from harm? Finally I cry for all the love they gave to a child who slowly sickened, for the devotion they've shown me ever since and for the little boy I've only just met but will never truly know however much I might wish to. All I have of him are scraps of paper and old toys and I know he will never seem real to me. He'll be a sprite, a memory captured in fading photographs of someone I'll never know.

Joanna hugs me even tighter as tears flood out of me. I cry and cry, unable to stop myself from grieving for all that has been lost for so many people. But as she holds me, I know that Joanna will never have to comfort me like this again. A dam has been broken inside as I've confronted the past. Now I'm mourning it. One day soon I hope to say a final goodbye.

63

A New Life

Our flat in the UK is so small that my electric wheelchair is too big to fit into it, I can only move freely up and down one small strip of corridor in my manual chair and I've burned myself repeatedly trying to master the kettle and the toaster. I've set a dishcloth on fire and used furniture polish to clean the kitchen tiles. But for me the two-metre sweep of floor that I can negotiate is my very own Hollywood Boulevard, the garden I see outside the window is the Alhambra and the tiny kitchen where I try to cook is the finest Parisian restaurant. I was wrong to think for so long that the only worthwhile challenges were to be found at work or in my studies when there are so many in everyday life.

I've become stronger in the months since arriving in England and I can now move around quite easily in the small part of the flat that is accessible to my chair by pushing off the floorboards with my feet. My arms aren't yet strong enough to control my chair but I can sit up well all day now. My left hand is still unreliable but my right is getting steadier all the time. I hardly ever try to use both. Instead I do everything with my right arm and my body seems to like being pushed in new directions because my failures are matched by successes: I'm not so good at opening bottles but I can now get coffee into cups; I can't yet tie my shoelaces but I'm able to push the vacuum cleaner around the wooden floor.

So much of everyday life, though, is literally above me. I feel useless as I watch Joanna hanging curtains or I stare at things in cupboards soaring overhead. After deciding to cook supper one night, I tried to dislodge a bag of flour from a shelf using a broom and watched it hurtle down towards me, knowing there was nothing I could do to stop it. Joanna found me – and the rest of the flat – covered in flour when she got home that night.

My worst mistake came when I tried to garden. Joanna had looked for a flat with a garden for so long that I was anxious to keep it perfect. So when dandelions started bursting bright yellow through the grass, I decided that something had to be done. But after I'd carefully sprayed the dandelions – and the rest of the lawn – with weedkiller, we woke up the next day to find that the grass had turned yellow. All we could do was watch its final death throes as we realised what I'd done wrong. Joanna and I have scattered the ground with seeds now and we hope that the rain that falls so steadily in England will encourage a new lawn to grow.

I'm working freelance as a web designer but the rest of my time is devoted to being a house husband in training. I enjoy learning how to look after a home and Joanna chastises me so little for my mistakes that I wonder if she realises quite how inept I am.

'What shall we do?' she wailed when we found a nail sticking out of one of our car tyres.

I had no idea.

'Shall I pull it out?' Joanna asked me.

It is becoming more and more clear to me that she assumes there is a long list of internal practical data hidden inside me simply because I'm a man. But after realising that I had no advice to give, Joanna bent down and pulled the nail out. As air hissed out of the tyre and we watched it slowly flatten, we looked at each other and laughed.

'We'll know what not to do next time,' she said.

But there have also been times when her patience has worn a little thinner and recently she turned to me as we were getting ready to go out one weekend morning.

'Shall we go to the supermarket first or the chemist?' she asked.

I wasn't sure. I still find planning my days so hard that I'm happy to follow the pattern Joanna wants them to follow.

'I don't mind,' I typed.

But instead of getting up from her chair and chattering to me as she usually does, Joanna didn't move.

'What's wrong?' I typed on the small portable keyboard she's given me to use instead of my alphabet board.

'Nothing,' she said.

But still she didn't move.

'Are you sure?'

'Completely.'

We sit together silently.

'I'm just waiting,' Joanna said eventually.

'For what?'

'For you to decide what we're going to do this morning. I'm tired and I want you to make a decision.

'I know you can do it because I've seen you at work. You were the centre of attention at the conference in Canada and you're completely in control in that world – you guide people and reassure them, advise and lead them.

'So now I want you to do the same at home. I know you're not used to it but I'm tired of making all the decisions, my liefie. So that's why I'm going to sit here until you decide what you want us to do today.'

I wasn't sure what to say. But as I looked at Joanna, I knew that she would wait all day if she had to.

'How about the supermarket first?' I said eventually.

Without a word, she got up and we left. Slowly I'm learning to choose what to do or eat and decide if I'm hungry or thirsty. But there's no escape from decision-making when it comes to our wedding in June, which is only a couple of months away.

Joanna is so busy at work that I'm doing a lot of the organising. She dreamed of this day for so long that she collected more than a hundred gold plates that she wanted to use for our guests. But when we realised that so many people would have to come from far away we decided to do something very different and we're going to have a simple service in a church attended by just eight people – my parents, David and Kim, Joanna's mother and three of her friends who live in England. However small our wedding is going to be, food, flowers, outfits, transportation, venues and menus must still be arranged. There are so many details, in fact, that I've built a file full of information that

Joanna and I read through together before deciding what we want.

The only aspect that I'm completely certain of is the ring I had made for Joanna before I left South Africa. It is a wide band made of yellow gold, which is dotted with diamonds and filigree work bearing the symbol of two mussel shells nestling together. They represent our love because nothing can prize mussels apart once they fuse together as one on a beach – even the might of the sea.

64

Waiting

The church is cool and quiet. At the end of long aisle stretching ahead of me, my mother, brother and sister sit in a pew; friends are in another. I'm waiting just inside the door of the church and gaze up at the huge stained-glass window behind the altar ahead of me. I'm glad that its colours are beginning to brighten. It rained a little earlier this morning and I don't want anything to ruin this day. But now I can see bright sunshine as I turn my head to look out of the door. It's the kind of glorious June day that seems to exist only in England with hedgerows thick with flowers, roses in bloom and an azure sky that appears endless overhead.

I think of Joanna. I've not seen her since early this morning before she left to get ready at the country house where we'll all go later to celebrate. It's a Georgian manor with lawns stretching green in front of it and lavender in beds around which bees fly lazily – picture perfect. None of us will forget this day. My mother smiles as I look down the aisle. She has been glowing with happiness ever since she arrived from South Africa. My brother and sister sit quietly beside her. How good it is to see them here. My father is standing with me because he is going to be my best man.

'She'll be here soon,' he says with a chuckle as he looks at me. 'Don't get too worried.'

I won't. All I feel is a happy impatience to see Joanna. I'm so anxious to marry her that I arrived nearly two hours ago. I'm glad Dad is beside me as I wait. As he helped me get dressed earlier – buttoning up my white shirt and tying my red cravat, helping me into my charcoal-grey pin-striped suit and lacing up my black shoes – I realised that his quiet and steady presence was what I needed most today of all days. It gives me such a familiar feeling of reassurance; it's one of the earliest memories I have, after all.

I wonder now if Dad is thinking about his own wedding day as quiet contentment radiates from him. My parents' married life has been far from easy and I suspect that neither of them can believe this day has arrived. They remind me of children who dare not think a fairy tale is coming true at last. Their eyes have been a little brighter, their smiles wider as Joanna and I have shown them our flat and all the other details of our life here. They have celebrated each one with us.

It is 1.25 p.m. Joanna will now be in the horse-drawn carriage that is bringing her to the church. She will look like a fairy-tale princess and I am her less than traditional prince. I think of her. Is she happy? Nervous? Only a few more minutes until I see her. I look down at the speech box that is sitting on my knee. It's an old device I've had for a few years now, a more sophisticated version of the black box my parents once so nearly bought me. I don't often use it but I have it with me today because I must say my wedding vows to make them legal. Apparently, a person has to speak their promises for them to be binding and a witness must watch over me to vouch that I press the 'I will' button without being coerced into doing it.

Now I think of the words that I will soon say. Each was seared onto my memory one by one as I inputted them on my communication device.

> For better, for worse,
> For richer, for poorer,
> In sickness and in health,
> Til death do us part.

I'll never say words that mean more. Each syllable, each line, will reverberate inside me as I think of the vows I'm sealing with them. Is it possible that one month shy of the eight years since I was first assessed, I am sitting here about to commit my life to Joanna?

It is she who has taught me to understand the true meaning of the Bible passage we are having read during the service: 'There are three things that will endure – faith, hope and love – and the greatest of these is love.' My life has encompassed all three and I know the greatest of all is indeed love – in all its forms. I've experienced it as a boy and man, as a son, brother, grandson and friend, I've seen it between others and I know it can sustain us through the darkest of times. Now it's lifting me closer to the sun than I ever thought I would fly.

I hear a flurry of steps.

'She's here!' a voice cries. 'Close the doors!'

My father leans towards me as the organist starts to play.

'Are you ready, boy?' he asks.

I nod and he starts pushing me down the aisle as memories flash through my mind. I've seen so much. I've come so far. As I stop in front of the altar, there is a rustle of excitement and I turn my head to see Joanna. She is wearing a long white dress encrusted with crystals and a veil covers her face. She is holding a bouquet of red roses and she smiles. My heart stills.

I will not look back today. It is time to forget the past.

All I can think of is the future.

She is here.

She is walking towards me.

Joanna (Joan) and Martin just married – June 2009
© JeffTurnbull.com

Acknowledgements

I would like to thank my family, who have in no small way helped me to become the person I am today. Mum, Dad, Kim and David taught me many lessons – not least to laugh, the importance of family and sticking by each other through good times and bad. I love you all dearly.

Thank you to Pookie and Kojak for their unconditional love, which proved that dogs truly are man's best friend.

I would also like to thank Virna van der Walt, Erica Mbangamoh, Karin Faurie, Dr Kitty Uys, Professor Juan Bornman, Maureen Casey, Kerstin Tonsing, Dr Michal Harty, Simon Sikhosana, Dr Shakila Dada, Jéanette Loots, Corneli Strydom, Alecia Samuels, Professor Diane Nelson Bryen, Elaine Olivier, Sue Swenson, Cornè Kruger, Jackie Barker, Riëtte Pretorius, Ronell Alberts, Tricia Horne and Sandra Hartley for all their support and the lessons they taught me about the value of friendship.

There are so many others I would like to mention. Suffice to say I am indebted to friends, colleagues and complete strangers who have all in some way made a difference to my life and helped me on my journey through it.

To all my friends and colleagues at the Centre for Augmentative and Alternative Communication, thanks for your help, support and the years we spent together. I would also like to thank God, without whom I wouldn't be here today and for all the blessings I have and continue to receive.

Thank you also to Cilliers du Preez, who was always willing to help me with computer problems, to Albie Bester at Microsoft South Africa and Paul and Barney Hawes and the rest of the folk at Sensory Software, who were always there to lend a hand when it was needed.

Finally, thank you to Ivan Mulcahy, who was never more than an email away, Kerri Sharp at Simon & Schuster, who believed in my story, and last but not least Megan Lloyd Davies for the hours of hard work and the journey that was the writing of this book.

You can find out more about Martin and augmentative and alternative communication (AAC) on his personal website www.martinpistorius.com.